# Dana Carpender's Every-Calorie-Counts Cookbook

# Dana Carpender's Every-Calorie-Counts Cookbook

500 Great-Tasting, Sugar-Free,
Low-Calorie Recipes
That the Whole Family Will Love

**Dana Carpender**

GLOUCESTER, MASSACHUSETTS

First published in the USA in 2006 by
Fair Winds Press, a member of
Quayside Publishing Group
33 Commercial Street
Gloucester, MA 01930



10 09 08 07 06 1 2 3 4 5

ISBN 1-59233-197-1

Library of Congress Cataloging-in-Publication Data

Carpender, Dana.
The every calorie counts cookbook : 500 great-tasting, sugar-free, low-calorie recipes that the whole family will love / Dana Carpender.
p. cm.
Includes index.
ISBN 1-59233-197-1
1. Low-calorie diet--Recipes. 2. Sugar-free diet--Recipes. 3. Quick and easy cookery. I. Title.
RM222.2.C3243 2006
641.5'635--dc22

2005036739

Cover design by Mary Ann Smith
Book design by Leslie Haimes
Printed and bound in Canada

The information in this book is for educational purposes only. It is not intended to replace the advice of a physician or medical practitioner. Please see your health care provider before beginning any new health program.

*For John, Liz, Henry, and Halliday.*
*But especially for Liz,*
*who shares my interest in all things health-oriented.*

# Contents

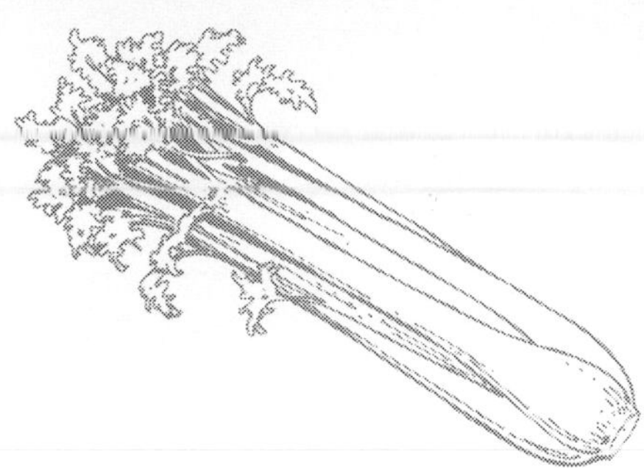

# Introduction

## What Is the "Every-Calorie-Counts" Philosophy?

It's not a big secret that I'm a low-carber. I've written six low-carb cookbooks. I started my writing career with *How I Gave Up My Low-Fat Diet* and Lost 40 Pounds, about my shift from a low-fat diet, high in whole grains and beans—which made me fat, tired, and miserable—to a low-carb diet, on which I thrived and continue to thrive.

So why the cookbook with a focus on calories? Have I changed my mind? Sold out?

Neither.

I still eat low-carb, and indeed, I expect to eat low-carb for the rest of my life. And if you are doing well and are happy with a low-carb diet, I would urge you to continue eating that way for the rest of your life, too. Why mess with success? You'll find plenty of recipes in this book that will support you in your low-carb lifestyle.

As the fact that the quantity and quality of carbohydrates we eat (or don't eat) has a vast impact on health, energy, and weight has sunk into the public consciousness, a vast array of permutations has arisen. It's not a case anymore of "I'm on Atkins," or "I'm on South Beach"—there are nearly as many variations of carb control as there are people who are paying attention to their carb intake. Some people continue to strictly keep their carb grams under a particular number every day. Others, especially those who don't have serious symptoms of genetic carbohydrate intolerance, are simply increasing their protein and avoiding the worst of the sugary and starchy junk. There are unlimited gradations in between.

Also, many people who have found that they feel better on a low-carbohydrate diet find that they also need to keep an eye on calories to lose weight. My email tells me that this is particularly true for women approaching menopause.

With this book, I hope to serve the larger community of people who limit carbohydrates while also keeping an eye on calories.

But there's one other purpose: To assure that everything you eat serves your health. Too often we get focused simply on carbohydrates or calories, and we forget that the most important function of food is to nourish our bodies—to supply not only protein, fats, and carbohydrates, but also vitamins, minerals, and other micronutrients that are essential for both physical and mental health.

I have often seen dieticians make excuses for including empty, valueless foods in our diets. "You need a little junk food to be happy!" they'll say. "So long as 80 percent of what you eat is good for you, it's okay if the other 20 percent is cookies and chips."

I couldn't disagree more. I wouldn't fill 20 percent of my car's gas tank with water. I wouldn't be happy if 20 percent of my investments showed no return. I wouldn't buy a ten-room house and simply close off two rooms. I wouldn't hire eight great employees and two good-looking and charming incompetents.

I want everything I put in my mouth, and everything you put in your mouth, to be as nourishing and hunger-satisfying as it is delicious, so that Every Calorie Counts. How's that for a great way to live?

## A Tale of Two Diet Myths

Let's talk a little more about carbs versus calories.

Surely you know that there are two main schools of thought regarding weight loss and maintenance: Calorie theory and carbohydrate theory. Calorie theory says it all boils down to calories in versus calories out, and you just have to eat fewer calories than you burn to lose weight. Carbohydrate theory says that limiting carbs alone will result in weight loss. Both of these theories have merit, but both also come with common misconceptions. It is the aim of this cookbook to take what is useful from both of these theories while debunking the useless myths built up around them. So let's look at them one at a time.

### Calorie Theory

What is a calorie, anyway? A "calorie" is a measurement of fuel, of food energy. Just as we buy energy for our cars by the gallon, we buy energy for our bodies by the calorie. (By the way, this means that when ads says a food is "full of energy" they really mean it's full of calories.) The most prevalent theory of weight gain and loss has long been that if you eat more calories than you burn, you'll gain weight, and if you eat fewer calories than you burn, you'll lose it. Since there are 3,500 calories in a pound of fat, we've been told that for every pound of fat we want to lose, we need to eat 3,500 fewer calories than we burn.

This appears to be roughly true. If people restrict their calorie intake sufficiently and exercise more, thus burning more calories, many of them will indeed lose weight. But there are problems with calorie theory.

The worst problem with reducing calories is that it usually makes people hungry. Since *whatever you do to lose weight is what you must do for the rest of your life to keep it off*—you know, that whole "lifestyle change" thing—this is a huge stumbling block. I know very few people who are willing to feel hungry for the rest of their lives. This simple fact alone is responsible for the failure of millions of low-calorie dieters.

Also, it has been assumed for a long time that "a calorie is a calorie is a calorie"—that for weight-loss purposes (but not health purposes, of course) 500 calories of cake and 500 calories of steak are equal. But is this true?

Calorie counts are largely determined by the "4-9-4 rule." This food industry formula is based on the idea that proteins have 4 calories per gram, fats have 9 calories per gram, and carbohydrates have 4 calories per gram. The protein, fat, water, and ash (mineral) content of a food is determined by testing; the rest is assumed to be carbohydrates. Then they multiply the grams of protein by 4, the grams of fat by 9, the grams of carbohydrate by 4, and add 'em up.

Turns out that this is simplistic. The biggest problem is that those figures (4-9-4) were originally determined by burning samples of foods in a *calorimeter*, a closed chamber that measures how much heat a sample of food gives off when burning. I'm sure you can see that the biochemical processes by which we burn calories in our bodies are quite different than burning something in a chamber in a lab.

Not all calories are digested and absorbed equally. Eggs are easily digested and absorbed, and they really do contribute about 4 calories per gram of protein and 9 calories per gram of fat. Fiber is a carbohydrate, and therefore it's counted as 4 calories per gram. But fiber is not digestible in the human gut, which is why you can't live on grass the way a cow does. So if you eat wheat bran, which is very rich in fiber, only a little over half of it is digested and absorbed, and you only get about 2.4 calories per gram. This skews calorie counts; 10 grams of carbohydrates in the form of squishy white bread will actually contribute more calories than 10 grams of carbohydrates in the form of fiber-enriched whole-grain bread, because of the indigestibility of fiber.

More importantly, evidence is accumulating that different kinds of foods affect calorie burning differently. The medical and nutritional establishments hate this idea, claiming it violates the laws of physics—which it would, if your body were a machine. But your body is not a machine; it's a living, changing, adapting organism, and I, for one, don't find it surprising that what kind of fuel you feed your body affects how that fuel is burned.

## Carbohydrate Theory

This is where carbohydrate theory comes in. Starting as far back as the 1950s, there have been repeated clinical studies that demonstrate that cutting carbohydrates increases the number of calories you burn. It started with two British doctors named Kekwick and Pawan, who discovered that obese people who had trouble losing weight on 1,000 calories per day of carbohydrate lost weight easily on 1,000 calories per day of protein and fat. Thus began the raging controversy that continues to this day—the question of whether what we eat influences our metabolism.

I'm convinced it does.

One very dramatic demonstration of diet influencing metabolism is a study that was done in 2000 at Schneider's Children's Hospital in New Hyde Park, New York, comparing a low-fat/high-carb diet and a low-carb/high-fat diet for weight loss in obese adolescents. In 12 weeks, the low-carb group lost twice as much weight as the low-fat group—while eating, on average, 66 percent more calories every day! More recent, if less dramatic, is a 2003 study done at the Harvard School of Public Health in which adult low-carbohydrate dieters were fed 300 more calories per day than low-fat dieters, yet lost just as much weight.

Apparently a calorie is not a calorie is not a calorie.

Add to this the demonstrated fact that low-carbohydrate diets reduce appetite. A 2005 study published in *Annals of Internal Medicine* showed that obese diabetics put on the very low-carbohydrate "induction" phase of the Atkins diet spontaneously ate about 1,000 fewer calories per day than they had on their regular diets, despite being told that they could eat as much as they liked of the permitted foods, and despite their self-declared enjoyment of the foods they could eat. A 1999 study published in Pediatrics compared the effects of low-carbohydrate and high-carbohydrate breakfasts on appetite. The kids who ate the high-carb breakfast of instant oatmeal, skim milk, and fruit were so much hungrier that they ate 81 percent more calories during the day than the kids who ate a cheese omelet, *even though the breakfasts contained the same number of calories*. That's a heck of a difference in appetite.

These two things combined—increased calorie burn and reduced appetite—

mean that cutting carbohydrates will let you eat enough calories to be comfortable, and still lose weight. For those of us who have happily eaten low-carb for years (I'm one of them), this is perhaps the most important reason for our success: We never have to feel hungry.

Unfortunately, Americans have been trained by junk food advertising and humongous restaurant portions to eat for entertainment rather than for the satisfaction of genuine hunger. Too many people seized on the instructions to eat as much low-carbohydrate food as they needed to feel satisfied as meaning they could eat unlimited calories and still lose weight. One outrageous news story reported a couple on the Atkins diet who were thrown out of a buffet restaurant when they demanded their money back after being denied a twelfth serving each of roast beef! They seemed to think that so long as they ate very low-carb, they could eat over 7,000 calories per meal and still lose weight.

But I know of no study that shows that this is so. For example, in the Schneider's Children's Hospital Study mentioned above, the kids on the low-carb diet ate an average of 1,860 calories per day. In the study with obese diabetics, their low-carbohydrate diets ended up having an average of 2,164 calories a day. That's enough to be comfortable, but it's hardly unlimited.

## Tunnel Vision

Both sides tend to get tunnel vision—to take nothing into account but calories or carb grams, depending on what program they're following.

For the past few years, as the low-fat fad crumbled beneath the low-carb successes of millions, I heard naysayers cry over and over, "But low-carb is bad! You cut out whole categories of food!" Where were these people when low-fat dieters were omitting such incredibly beneficial foods as nuts, seeds, cheese, olives, and avocados because they were high in the dreaded fat and calories? (For that matter, where are they when it comes to vegetarianism, or more extreme, veganism? Talk about cutting out whole categories of food!)

Low-carbers, on the other hand, sometimes decide that if low-carb is good, no-carb is better—to the point where they'll eat nothing but meat, eggs, and cheese, figuring they'll lose their weight fast-fast-fast this way. A no-carb diet is a bad idea. Foods like vegetables, fruits, and nuts and seeds are loaded with vitamins, minerals, and beneficial antioxidants. Just as important, these foods add flavor, texture, and variety to your diet—and anything that makes your food more interesting bodes well for your long-term success. Remember: *Anything you do to lose weight is what you must do for the rest of your life to keep it off.* I don't know anyone who can face a lifetime of nothing but meat.

And while I remain unconvinced that grains and beans are in any way essential to human nutrition, it is the rare person who doesn't miss them occasionally. Better to learn how to add them back in a controlled fashion than to suddenly freak out and devour a whole loaf of French bread or four bagels.

While overzealous low-carbers are shunning carrots, low-calorie dieters search for the lowest calorie or fat count, regardless of nutritional value. How many times have you seen women's magazines make recommendations like, "Instead of snacking on 1 ounce of peanuts, have 1 ounce of pretzels instead—you'll save more than 40 calories!" This is true, but utterly beside the point. Those pretzels consist of little but refined white flour and have almost no nutritional value. Worse, from the dieter's perspective, their blood-sugar destabilizing high-impact carbs will leave you hungry again an hour later. The peanuts, on the other hand, have vitamins, minerals, protein, and good fats, and they will satisfy your hunger for a few hours—a better bargain all the way around.

Tunnel vision works in another, far more insidious way: It makes us prey to processed junk.

Americans started getting heavy-duty low-fat propaganda in the mid-to-late 1980s, and we took it to heart. We cut fat as a percentage of our calories by about 25 percent—but at the same time, we started eating more calories. This was due, in a large part, to the fact that a low-fat/high-carb diet makes you hungry. But it was also due to what I call the Snackwells Phenomenon—the flooding of the marketplace with low-fat versions of all the same nutrition-free processed garbage we'd been eating all along. Further, junk foods that had always been low in fat—because they were mostly sugar and refined starch—sprouted "low-fat" labels and started advertising campaigns crowing about their lack of fat. ("Hershey's Syrup: Now, as always, a fat-free food.") Being low-fat didn't make this stuff any less junky, but since this junk had the magic words "low-fat!" on the label, we didn't stop with a couple of sandwich cookies, a handful of chips, or a scoop of ice cream. Oh, no. We sat down and ate half a package.

When I went low-carb in 1995 (yes, I've been eating this way for over a decade!), there were no low-carb specialty foods. As a result, going low-carb forced me and other early converts to eat real food—meat, poultry, fish, eggs, cheese, vegetables, low-sugar fruits, nuts, and seeds. I suspected at the time that some of the health benefit of a low-carb diet was due to eating real, unprocessed food.

Well, by 2002 the whole country was joining us, and by 2003 the food processors were flooding the market with low-carb, sugar-free junk food—cookies, jelly beans, quick-bread mixes, chips, cold "cereal," and macaroni-and-cheese mix. I'm pleased to say that much of this stuff tanked in the marketplace. In part this was due to many of these products being wretchedly bad. (Did you try soy pasta? Yuck.) But I also like to think that we'd learned from the Snackwellification of the low-fat diet and were wary.

Still, I have heard from low-carbers who just don't know what they're going to do without the low-carb junk food. The answer is, was, and will remain, "Eat real food." This goes for everyone—low-carb dieters, low-calorie dieters, and folks who aren't worried about their weight but just want to be well and feel well. Stop eating processed, packaged junk. Eat real food.

In this book you will find a wider range of carbohydrate counts than in my previous cookbooks—though as I mentioned, you'll also find plenty of recipes that are suitable for a true low-carbohydrate diet. What carbohydrates you find will be of the "good carbs" kind. Further, nothing will be empty junk; everything will contribute vitamins, minerals, and antioxidants. To demonstrate this, along with the calorie, carbohydrate, protein, and fat counts, you'll find a listing of the vitamins and minerals for each recipe. You'll be able to see at a glance just what each meal is contributing to your health.

## How Much Do I Need of What?

Here are the Daily Reference Intakes (the new term for what used to be called the RDAs, Recommended Daily Allowances), the government recommendations for how much you need each day of the vitamins and minerals you'll find listed with each recipe. These actually vary a bit with age and sex. I went with what a woman between about 30 and 60 needs; it's the median. Men need a little more, and of course children need less, but will eat smaller portions.

**Potassium:** 4.7 g (4700 mg)

**Calcium:** 1–2.5 g (1000–2500 mg)

**Iron:** 18–45 mg

**Zinc:** 8–40 mg

**Vitamin A:** 700–3000 IU (International Units) from animal sources; up to six times that if from fruits and vegetables because your body has to convert the beta carotene in fruits and vegetables into vitamin A, and not all of it converts.

**Thiamin (B1):** 1.1–1.2 mg

**Riboflavin (B2):** 1.1–1.3 mg

**Niacin (B3):** 14–35 mg

**B6:** 1.3 mg–100 mg (Yes, that's a huge variation, but it's what the chart says!)

**B12:** 2.4

**Vitamin C:** 75–2000 mg

**Folate:** 400–1000 mg

## What's a "Serving"?

I've gotten a couple of queries from folks who bought *500 Low-Carb Recipes* and want to know how big a serving size is, so I thought I'd better address the matter.

To be quite honest, folks, there's no great technical determination going on here. For the most part, a "serving" is based on what I think would make a reasonable portion, depending on the carbohydrate count, how rich the dish is, and, for main dishes, on the protein count. You just divide the dish up into however many portions the recipe says, and you can figure the carb counts on the recipes are accurate. In some cases I've given you a range—"3 to 4 servings" or whatever. In those cases, I've told you how many servings the carb counts are based on, and you can do a little quick mental estimating if, say, you're serving 4 people when I've given the count for 3.

Of course, this "serving" thing is flukey. People are different sizes, with different appetites. For all I know, you have three children under 5 who might reasonably split one adult-size portion. On the other hand, you might have one 17-year-old boy who's shot up from 5'5" to 6'3" in the past year, and what looks like 4 servings to me will be a quick snack for him. You'll just have to eyeball what fraction of the whole dish you're eating, and go from there.

I've had a few people tell me they'd rather have specific serving sizes, such as "1 cup" or the like. I see a few problems with this. First of all, it sure won't work with things like steak or chops—I'd have to use weights instead, and then all my readers would have to run out and buy scales. Second, my recipes generally call for things like "1/2 head cauliflower" or "2 stalks celery." These things vary in size a bit, and as a result yield will fluctuate a bit, too. Also, if one of my recipes calls for "1½ pounds boneless, skinless chicken breasts" and your package is labeled "1.65 pounds," I don't expect you to whack off that final 0.15 of a pound to get the portions exact.

In short, I hate to have to weigh and measure everything, and I'm betting that a majority of my readers feel the same way, even if some do not.

So I apologize to those who like exact measures, but this is how it's gonna be for now, at any rate.

## What's a "Usable Carb"?

Each of these recipes has a "usable carb count" alongside the calories, protein, fat, fiber, and carbohydrate counts. What does it mean?

"Usable carbs" (also called "net carbs," "effective carbs," and "impact carbs") refers to the number of grams of carbohydrates that you can digest. Since fiber is a carbohydrate, it is included in the total carbohydrate count. But since you can't digest or absorb fiber, it doesn't count, both literally and figuratively. So the "usable carb count" refers to the grams of carbohydrates that are actually available to raise your blood sugar and release insulin.

There's one glitch, and that's polyols, aka sugar alcohols. As you'll read in the section on polyols (see page 46), because different polyols are absorbed at different rates, there's very little way for me to calculate how much of the carbohydrate in them you'll absorb, though we know you'll absorb far less than all of them. As an admittedly poor compromise, I've left polyols out of the usable carb counts.

## What Are "Glycemic Index" and "Glycemic Load"?

We're going to talk in a minute about which carbs are "good carbs," but before we do, you need to understand a little about "glycemic index" and "glycemic load." You're going to hear these terms more and more, especially if you pay attention to medical research on the effects of carbohydrates. It's emerging that a diet with a high glycemic load is associated with everything from cancer to diabetes to heart disease—all the things that were recently blamed on high-fat diets—so we'd better get clear on what a high glycemic load is.

Put very simply, glycemic load is a way of measuring the impact any carb food has on your blood sugar. To understand glycemic load, you first need to understand the glycemic index.

### What's the Glycemic Index?

Often abbreviated as "GI" or just "G" (as in, "potatoes are really high-G"), the glycemic index is a measure of how quickly a particular carbohydrate food is absorbed and therefore how fast and high it will spike your blood sugar. This, in turn, is largely predictive of how much insulin you will release in response and how fast and hard your blood sugar will crash, causing irritability, fatigue, and gnawing rebound hunger. That insulin surge also causes a cascade of hormonal imbalances in your body, influencing everything from sex hormones to inflammation levels to your body's production and use of cholesterol. This is important stuff.

Glycemic index is determined by feeding a group of subjects a carefully measured portion of the food being tested. That portion of food must contain 50 grams of carbohydrate. The subjects' fasting blood sugar is taken before they eat the food and then at regular intervals over a few hours. The results are averaged out and then ranked in comparison to a "reference food"—usually glucose, the simplest sugar, which is absorbed very rapidly and spikes blood sugar very high. Glucose is rated 100, and other foods are ranked by comparison. This ranking becomes the food's GI number.

I've looked over some fairly extensive tables of these results, and I find them fascinating! There are some real surprises.

For instance, for the past 20 years or so, we've had "complex carbohydrates"—grains, beans, potatoes, and other starches—pushed at us. We've been told that they're not as hard on the body as sugar, because they break down more slowly and give us "sustained energy."

Piffle! Table sugar, poisonous as it is (and I'm convinced it's as deadly and addictive a drug as heroin or cocaine), has a much lower glycemic index than does the low-fat dieter's darling, the baked potato. In fact, potatoes come in at a whopping 98, just 2 points lower than glucose! Rice cakes—you know, those nasty, flavorless Styrofoam things you ate all those years because you thought they were good for you—are a 77. No wonder they never filled you up! And almost all cold cereals have a high GI, even whole-grain cereals that don't have a ton of sugar added. Cheerios, for example, have a glycemic index of 74.

So complex carbohydrates are not necessarily easier on your blood sugar than sugar is, though they often have more vitamins and minerals.

Science has not yet determined all the factors that affect the impact of carbohydrates, but we do know a few things. Carbohydrates that contain a lot of fiber have a lower impact than those that have the fiber removed. Apparently the fiber acts a little like a sponge, slowing the absorption of the carbohydrates a bit. Whole kernel grains or very coarsely ground grains have a milder impact than those that are ground into fine flour; in fact, the less processed the grain, the better. We also know that you can lessen the impact of a high-impact food by combining it in a meal with a lot of low-impact foods, especially protein and fat.

But there are some things we can't explain. For instance, whole-wheat pita bread has a lower impact on blood sugar than whole-wheat loaf bread. Why? You got me! It just does, that's all. Barley and rye have a far lower impact than rice or wheat; again, why that should be so is anybody's guess. But the nice thing is that we don't have to totally understand this principle to put it to work!

## So What's Glycemic Load?

Remember the point I made several paragraphs back, that it was important to understand that the glycemic index tests involved eating whatever size portion of the test food was needed to make up 50 grams of carbohydrate? *This* is the weakness of the whole concept of the glycemic index. Because of this particular point, some foods appeared taboo for the carbohydrate intolerant, when in reality, they could be tolerated *in the sort of quantity that people actually eat them.*

Carrots are a case in point. Many low-carbers have avoided carrots because they have a high glycemic index. It is true that eating enough carrots to consume 50 grams of carbohydrate will jack your blood sugar around pretty good, but do you know how many carrots that is? More than 50 of those little baby carrots, that's how many. I don't know about you, but I don't like carrots that much!

Enter the concept of the *glycemic load.*

"Glycemic load" is a new way of using those glycemic index tables to make them apply to food *as people actually eat it.* To calculate the glycemic load of a given food, you simply multiply the glycemic index of the food by the number of grams of carbohydrate that you are actually eating. If the result is a number less than 10, the food is considered to have a low glycemic load; 10 to 19 is a medium glycemic load, and anything over 20 is high.

For example: The glycemic index of soft drinks is 97. There are 42 grams of carbohydrates in a 12-ounce can of soda, and .97 x 42 = 40.74, or something you *really* don't want to touch! Pumpernickel bread has a glycemic index of 71. There are about 16 grams of carbohydrates per slice, and .71 x 16 = 11.36, giving it a medium glycemic load. But while cooked carrots have a glycemic index of 56, a half-cup serving has only about 8.2 grams of carbohydrates, and .56 x 8.2 = 4.592, putting carrots in the "low glycemic load" category.

(Why those decimal points? Because technically, that 100 at the top of the scale is really 1.00. So soda is really a 0.97, while pumpernickel is a 0.71.)

You can see the usefulness of this concept. The glycemic load gives us a real-world idea of what various foods are likely to do to our blood sugar and our bodies.

Please keep in mind that none of this can tell you how much carbohydrate is appropriate for *your own personal body*. I know that I gain weight if I eat too much carbohydrate, *regardless of the source*. However, I know many people who do well eating 100, 150, even 200 grams of carbohydrate per day, so long as it comes from sources with a low G, because it moderates their glycemic load.

## So Do These Recipes List Their Glycemic Loads?

No, they don't, for the simple reason that recipes combine a lot of different ingredients, each one with its own glycemic index. While it's pretty easy to come up with a carb count, working out the glycemic indices of those combinations is impossible. I'd have to pay for vast, expensive clinical trials to test the glycemic index of each recipe. We're talking research that would cost many millions of dollars and take years. I'm a cookbook author, not a research lab!

So how can I know that these recipes have a low glycemic load? We'll be using mostly carbohydrates that have very low glycemic loads to begin with, such as vegetables and fruits. When we use ingredients that have higher glycemic loads, such as whole grains or potatoes, we'll dilute their impact by combining them with plenty of ingredients that have lower glycemic loads, either because they have less total carbohydrate per serving, because they have a low glycemic index, or both. For instance, you'll find many recipes where I've mixed grains with shredded cauliflower "rice." In the recipes for baked goods, I've combined whole grains with ground nuts and other low-carbohydrate, high-protein ingredients.

It's important to remember, too, that eating carbohydrates with proteins and fats will buffer their absorption, lessening their blood sugar impact.

Since glycemic load equals glycemic index times grams of carbohydrate, watching that bottom line carbohydrate gram number will help you keep your glycemic load low, as well. In other words, don't eat all the highest-carb recipes from this book in the same day, or even the same week! Even diets that advocated "good carbs," like South Beach, recommend one slice of whole grain bread in a day, not three or four.

## Which Are the Good Carbs?

The media has gone from trumpeting the merits of low carb diets to insisting we should all eat "good carbs." But what are "good carbs"? What makes a particular carb food "good"? There are a number of factors I've taken into account when deciding whether to include a particular carbohydrate-containing food in this book.

- **Glycemic index/glycemic load.** How drastic an impact will a given carbohydrate have on blood sugar level and insulin release?
- **Fiber content.** This is closely tied to glycemic index, since fiber buffers the absorption of digestible carbohydrates, blunting the blood sugar curve.
- **Nutrient density.** How many vitamins, minerals, antioxidants, and other beneficial substances does the food contain, compared to its carbs and calories?
- **Processing.** The less processed the food, the better. Processing reduces nutrient density and increases blood sugar impact, especially with grains. Whole-grain cold cereals tend to have a very high glycemic index, while coarsely ground whole-grain bread or steel cut oats will have a gentler effect. Processing is also when hydrogenated oil, high fructose corn syrup, and other noxious substances creep in.
- **History.** I'm convinced that we do better eating foods that have been in the human diet since time immemorial than we do eating foods that have only become part of our diet since the Agricultural Revolution 10,000 years ago. Ten thousand years sounds like a long time, but it's only a tiny fraction of our history as a species. Grains and beans were virtually nonexistent in the human diet before we learned to farm and cook them.

Taking these criteria into account, it becomes a little easier to "rate the good carbs." From the best to the worst, they are:

- **Vegetables.** Loaded with fiber, vitamins, minerals, and beneficial photochemicals, pretty much unprocessed, mostly low glycemic index, and a huge part of the human diet since the hunter-gatherer days, vegetables are the best possible carb foods. Green and leafy vegetables are the best of all, but it's hard to think of a really bad vegetable. On our Every Calorie Counts plan, we'll eat vegetables in abundance.
- **Nuts and seeds.** A staple food of our ancestors, with plenty of good fats, protein, and vital minerals, nuts and seeds are just as valuable today. Sunflower

and pumpkin seeds are higher in carbohydrates than almonds, walnuts, pecans, and the other tree nuts, but they're also higher in minerals. Sadly, these wonderful foods were often cut out of low-fat diets because they are, indeed, high in fat calories. This is a mistake; they satisfy hunger for a long time. We'll use nuts and seeds often in our Every Calorie Counts cuisine, we'll just keep an eye on portions.

- **Fruits.** Fruits vary a lot in carb content, and all cultivated fruit is higher in sugar than its wild ancestors. However, most of it has a modest glycemic index, and it all contributes vitamins, minerals, fiber, and phytochemicals. In particular, many of our Every Calorie Counts desserts will be based on fruits.
- **Milk.** There are pluses and minuses here. Milk has protein and calcium, of course, which are great. Milk also has 12 grams of carbs per cup, in the form of lactose. Many people are lactose intolerant, but milk has a modest blood sugar impact, making it a good choice if you can tolerate it. Dairy agriculture is believed to have predated grain agriculture, making milk an "older" food than grains and beans, but commercial pasteurized and homogenized milk is a far cry from the food our ancestors ate. You'll find milk in quite a few Every Calorie Counts recipes. If you're lactose intolerant or you limit carbohydrates very strictly, you can use Carb Countdown Dairy Beverage, which has the lactose removed, or half water, half heavy cream. You could also use Lactaid-treated milk, but since the lactase enzyme breaks lactose down into simpler sugars, this has a higher glycemic load than regular milk.
- **Legumes.** A relatively new addition to the human diet, legumes do have a low glycemic index, lots of fiber, and a fair amount of protein. However, they're a very concentrated carbohydrate and thus still have a high glycemic load. We'll use them occasionally, combined with lots of lower glycemic load foods.
- **Whole grains.** The least desirable of the "good" carbs. Very carb-dense and fairly calorie-dense, with less fiber and nutritional value per carb gram than any of the other foods listed here. Grains are also very common allergens, and the gluten in some grains causes bad reactions for many people. Since all whole grains, even those with the lowest glycemic indexes, have a considerable glycemic load, we'll mix them with lots of other foods to get their flavor and texture without their blood sugar impact. But if you have intestinal problems, in particular, you should consider dropping grains entirely.

A personal note: While writing this book, I ate more grains than I normally do because I was testing recipes. I came up with both the bran muffin recipe and the pizza crust recipe in the same day, and I ate them both. By bedtime I had a flock of teeny red bumps all over my inner arms and a few on my chin, and it took them four days to vanish completely. I will be going back to largely shunning grains when this book is done. However, throughout recipe development my husband ate the grain foods I cooked liberally. He had no bad reaction at all.

We all have to figure out through trial and error what works for us. Which leads to the question:

## How Do I Know How Many Carbs I Should Eat?

Perhaps the question I get most frequently from readers is, "How many grams of carbohydrates should I eat per day?" I'm afraid the answer is, "I haven't the foggiest notion." This is one of those things that is utterly individual and has to be worked out by paying attention to your own body.

There are some glaring signs of carbohydrate intolerance. They are:

- If you eat carbs for breakfast—cold cereal, oatmeal, a muffin, a bagel, toast and juice, whatever—and you're hungrier 90 minutes later than you would have been had you eaten nothing at all.
- You gain weight mostly on your abdomen, rather than your butt and thighs (the "apple" pattern).
- You've had a weight problem most of your life.
- You have a history of binging on carbohydrate foods—sweets, chips, bread, crackers, or the like.
- You have one or more of the carbohydrate intolerance diseases—high triglycerides, high blood pressure, high cholesterol with a bad LDL/HDL ratio, female cancers, alcoholism—and most especially if you're a type II diabetic or prediabetic.
- If you don't have these problems yet but they run in your family, and you're still young.

If any or all of this describes you, you need to be very careful with carbs. On the other hand, if you've just put on a few pounds since you turned 40, or since you took a desk job, you're likely to do well just by increasing protein, cutting carbs a bit, and ditching the really bad stuff.

Two more guidelines:

- The more you are willing to cut carbs, the less you will need to cut calories.

The more you are willing to cut calories, the less you will need to cut carbs. (Personally, I'd rather eat more calories and fewer carbs and never feel hungry, but that's your decision to make.)

- The number of carbs you can eat and maintain your weight is going to be slightly higher than the number of carbs you need to cut back to in order to actively lose weight.

Me, I'm badly carb intolerant. I need to stay under 50 grams of nonfiber carbohydrate per day. And indeed, I put on a few pounds while writing this book because I was eating a bit too much carb for my own personal body while testing recipes for those who can tolerate a few more carbs. As I write this, it's two weeks till the deadline for this book, and I have every intention of cutting back to no more than 30 grams per day for a couple of weeks as soon as I turn in the manuscript, to shake that extra weight.

But I know many people who do very well eating as much as 100 to 150 grams per day of carbohydrates, so long as they eat no junk carbs. My husband is one of them.

There's just no substitute for paying attention to your own body, I'm afraid.

## What About Fat?

No piece of advice has been repeated more often in the past couple of decades than "limit fats to 30 percent of calories or less." In particular, we were told that this would help us stay slim, but we were also told that limiting fats would prevent heart disease, cancer, and a host of other ills. So it may shock you to know that there simply was never much in the way of scientific data to back up that 30 percent figure.

To be fair, the idea that limiting fat intake would cause weight loss made sense on the surface. As you'll recall, fats generally have 9 calories per gram, while carbs and proteins run about 4 calories per gram. If a calorie is a calorie is a calorie, and fats have more than twice the calories of carbs and proteins, then cutting fats should cause weight loss, right?

Except, of course, as we have seen, a calorie isn't a calorie isn't a calorie. What we eat changes how many calories we burn. And a diet where fats are replaced with carbohydrates, even complex carbohydrates, doesn't satisfy hunger the way a diet high in proteins and fats does—leading us to eat more calories, not fewer.

Furthermore, telling people to limit fats to 30 percent of calories or less discourages people from eating some excellent foods, such as nuts and seeds, avocados, olives and olive oil, and fatty fish like salmon, sardines, and mackerel, all of which have been shown to reduce your risk of disease. It also fails to distinguish between truly horrible fats, such as the overprocessed, overheated, hydrogenated oils used to make cheap restaurant fried foods, and the truly excellent fats, such as fresh butter, coconut oil, and extra virgin olive oil.

So am I advocating a high-fat diet? Sort of.

For a long time, the government and other authorities have been advocating getting no more than 30 percent of your calories from fat, no more than 15 percent of your calories from protein, and between 55 and 65 percent from carbohydrates. If you are eating 2,500 calories per day and following these guidelines, you'll get no more than 750 calories from fat. This means you'll be getting about 83 grams of fat per day.

But say that by eating 50 percent of your calories from fat, 30 percent from protein, and 20 percent from carbohydrates (making sure they're good carbs,) you are so much less hungry that you spontaneously eat 700 fewer calories per day, for a total of 1,800 calories? You'll be eating 90 grams of fat per day, or just 7 more grams than you did on your "low-fat" diet. That's a difference of just a half a tablespoon of olive oil per day.

(This, by the way, would not be a particularly low-carbohydrate diet; it allows for 90 grams of carbohydrates per day. That's enough for piles and piles of vegetables, a couple of pieces of fruit, and even a slice of whole-grain bread.)

In this example, the diet would be fairly high in fat as a percentage, but not particularly high in total fat intake.

Your protein intake is essential—you need to get about half a gram of protein for each pound of body weight, minimum, every day, and more protein (up to about twice that) seems to limit hunger and improve metabolism. So if you weigh 150 pounds, you need a minimum of 75 grams of protein per day, and 100 to 125 grams per day is quite reasonable. At 4 calories per gram, that will account for 400 to 500 calories per day.

The rest of your calories will be distributed between fats and carbohydrates. These two foods are what your body uses for energy. Remember that "energy" and "calories" are the same thing. So if you're going to modestly limit your calories, you're going to have to limit carbs, fats, or both.

Even the lowest carbohydrate diets, like the two-week Atkins Induction, contain at least 20 grams of nonfiber carb per day, and most of us will eat a few more—I find that 50 grams a day is about right for my body. Those carb grams are where your fruits and vegetables come in, so you don't want to cut them out completely. Remember, no-carb is a bad idea.

So if your protein and carbohydrate intake are both fixed, it's the fat fraction of your diet that can be expanded and contracted to adjust your calorie intake. If you get less of your fuel from carbohydrates, you'll need to get more of your fuel from fats. If you eat less fat, you'll need more carbohydrates.

(And no, you shouldn't just eat lean protein, with no fat and no carbohydrates. As pioneers who sometimes had nothing to eat but very lean game (such as rabbit) found out, an all-protein diet will make you sick.)

## Which Are the Good Fats?

You think there's been misinformation going around about carbs? Multiply that by about ten, and that's how much bad information has gotten around about fats.

The problem is that people like simple advice. So various authorities come out with pronouncements like, "Saturated fats are bad, unsaturated fats are good," or "Animal fats are bad, vegetable oils are good." But fats are quite complicated, and simplistic advice like this is often more harmful than helpful.

Let's start with this simple piece of information: Fats are essential to the human diet. Carbohydrates are not.

Surprised?

I should explain that "essential" has a very specific meaning in nutrition: It means that your body needs it and *can't make it*. It's true that glucose—the simplest sugar—is needed by some of the cells in your body (though others, especially your muscles, will run quite happily on fat), but so long as you eat plenty of protein, your body can make all the glucose it needs. Carbohydrates are not essential.

On the other hand, there are fats that our bodies must have that they simply cannot make—they must be consumed. So some fats are essential, but carbohydrates are not. (This doesn't mean that carbohydrates don't carry some essential things along with them. The carbs in an orange or a pepper bring vitamin C along with them; the vitamin C is essential, the carbohydrates are not.)

Also, your body has more uses for fats than for carbohydrates. Your body can only use carbohydrates for one thing: fuel. Fats, on the other hand, are used in repairing cell walls, creating nerve tissue, producing hormones—many essential processes in the body—along with being useful for fuel. This makes giving your body the right fats one of the most important things you can do for your health.

But which fats are the right fats?

Up until about a century ago, most of the fat in the human diet was animal fat: butter, lard, tallow, suet, chicken fat, and the fats in the meats and dairy products we ate. Yet before the 1920s, heart disease was rare. The rate of coronary artery disease has actually *accelerated dramatically* as our consumption of animal fats has dropped and our intake of vegetable oils has increased. We have greatly increased our consumption of vegetable oils, and particularly of hydrogenated vegetable oils, with their deadly trans fats. Because of this fear of more traditional, naturally saturated fats, most of the baked goods in your grocery store use hydrogenated oils instead of lard, butter, or coconut oil. Of course, it doesn't help our health that our consumption of sugar and corn syrup has skyrocketed at the same time!

Starting in the 1970s, we were told that "all vegetable" margarine was a healthier choice than that "highly saturated" butter—you know, that delicious stuff that had been in the human diet for longer than the bread we spread it on has been. Margarine, invented as a cheap substitute for butter, was suddenly marketed as being "heart healthy"; after all, it was made from unsaturated vegetable oils, and it had no cholesterol.

The problem turned out to be that those unsaturated oils (which, as we'll see in a minute, weren't so great to begin with) had been partially hydrogenated, which is a way of artificially saturating fats to make liquid oils solid at room temperature. This process creates trans fats, which are clearly far worse for us than any naturally saturated fat. Trans fats raise total cholesterol while lowering HDL ("good") cholesterol, increasing our risk of heart disease. They also incorporate themselves into our cell walls, making it hard for nutrients to enter our cells. Many researchers feel that there is no safe level of trans fat intake.

The same thing happened in the fast food industry—animal fats, used for deep-frying for untold centuries, were replaced with highly processed, hydrogenated vegetable oils. This was not a nutritional improvement.

It turns out fats are pretty complicated. It may shock you to know that lard, which many people would consider one of the worst possible fats, actually has more monounsaturated fat (the same heart-healthy fat we find in olive oil and nuts) than saturated fat, which is why bacon grease is soft at room temperature. (This applies only to unprocessed lard and bacon fat. The lard you can buy in blocks or buckets in the grocery store has been hydrogenated to make it solid at room temperature.)

Beef fat, which was widely used for frying at one time, also has more monounsaturated fat than saturated fat. Furthermore, much of the saturated fat in beef is in the form of stearic acid, which acts like a monounsaturate in the body, lowering bad cholesterol and raising good cholesterol. (Oddly enough, the other big source of stearic acid is cocoa butter. Yay, chocolate!)

On the other hand, many of the fats that we've been told are healthy turn out to be dreadful. Polyunsaturated oils—safflower, corn, sunflower, soy, and the like—are among the least healthy fats you can eat. Why?

Well, first of all, they require extensive processing (very high heat and solvents) to extract. Think about it: If you squeezed an ear of corn or a soybean, would you expect oil to come out? You can imagine what it takes. That processing forms dangerous trans fats (soy oil can be made of as much as 50 percent trans fats) and destroys any nutrients that were originally there. That's pretty darned bad right there.

Also, because of their chemical structure, polyunsaturated oils become dangerously rancid very easily. They form oxidized molecules called "free radicals," which damage cell walls and DNA, and accelerate aging.

The other problem is that our bodies simply aren't made for large quantities of these kinds of fats. They've never existed in the human diet in any quantity before the twentieth century, and our bodies don't know what to do with the overload. It's very much analogous to what happened when we learned how to concentrate sugar from sugar cane and beets and increased our intake twentyfold.

Remember what I said about some fats being essential, meaning that your body needs them and can't make them? There are two basic groups of these essential fats, and they're both polyunsaturated. One group has gotten a lot of press in the last decade or so—the omega-3 fatty acids. These are the fats we find in fish oils and flax seeds, the ones that are being shown to reduce heart disease, lessen inflammation, and do all sorts of other healthy things.

The other group is the omega-6 fatty acids, and these are the ones found in those highly polyunsaturated vegetable oils. So if they're essential, why are they bad?

Both kinds of fats are involved in creating hormones, called eicosanoids, that control much of what happens in our bodies. Eicosanoids come in "series one" and "series two," and they do opposite things: Dilating or constricting blood vessels, increasing or decreasing inflammation and pain, thinning blood or making it more likely to clot, increasing or decreasing susceptibility to cancer, strengthening or weakening the immune system, dilating or constricting airways.

Now, both series one and series two eicosanoids are needed—you don't want your blood to clot in your veins and cause a stroke, but on the other hand, you don't want to bleed to death from a scratch, either. We need a balance.

Because the two kinds of eicosanoids need to be balanced, the two types of fats, omega-3s and omega-6s, need to be balanced for us to be healthy; the ideal ratio is 1:1. By dramatically increasing our intake of omega-6 fatty acids, we have thrown ourselves desperately out of balance; many Americans get as much as 20 times the amount of omega-6 fatty acids as they do omega-3 fatty acids. When we decided to substitute vegetable oils for the traditional fats in the human diet, we flooded our bodies with omega-6 oils, and we dramatically increased our bodies production of the series two eicosanoids—and in doing so opened ourselves up to high blood pressure, arthritis, heart disease, and even cancer.

(This, incidentally, is why you hear so many good reports about the effects of omega-3-rich fish oils: They help correct the balance and therefore bring many of the illnesses caused by rampant series two eicosanoid formation under control.)

So, for the above reasons, we will not be using polyunsaturated oils in this book.

We will also not be using canola oil. Canola is widely touted as a "heart-healthy monounsaturated fat," and I have used it in previous books. I've changed my mind. Canola is a newcomer to the human diet. There's actually no such thing as a "canola"—it's a trade name for a particular hybrid of the unfortunately named rapeseed oil. Rapeseed oil, used in paints and varnishes, is high in a toxic chemical called erucic acid; "canola" has been bred for much lower levels. Still, it does contain some erucic acid, and I'm not sure I want any.

Also, canola oil is generally extracted with those same damaging high-heat-and-solvent processes that the polyunsaturates are. These processes can create trans fats, which explains why some studies have shown canola oil to have levels of trans fat as high as 4 percent. And while canola has a lot of monounsaturates, it also has considerable amounts of those omega-6 polyunsaturates we're trying to get away from.

This brings us back to the traditional fats in the human diet, and these are what we'll be using. In particular, we will choose:

- **Butter.** You know, that stuff you stopped eating because you thought it was bad for you. Hah. Because it's saturated, it's very stable, meaning that it doesn't form free radicals easily. It doesn't have the trans fats of margarine. It has vitamin A—and did you know that when the push to get Americans to stop eating saturated fats started, many doctors objected on the grounds that omitting butter and cream would result in vitamin A deficiencies? Butter also contains vitamins D, E, K, and the minerals zinc, chromium (important for stable blood sugar!), selenium, and iodine.

  But it gets even better! Butter is also a source of CLA, a fat shown to reduce the tendency to store fat, and of lauric acid, a fat that is also found in mother's milk and which helps your immune system to function.

Please, please, do not use margarine. Use butter. It's good for you.

- **Coconut oil.** One of the big crusades of the 1980s was the movement to get tropical oils such as coconut oil out of our foods. Boy, was that a mistake! First of all, they were replaced by trans fat–laden hydrogenated vegetable oils. That's bad enough. But it turns out that coconut oil is so remarkably good for you, many researchers are recommending you take it as a supplement!

It's true coconut oil is highly saturated. This is a good thing. It means the stuff simply doesn't go rancid, forming damaging free radicals. Coconut oil will keep for a couple of years without refrigeration! The stuff has a strong antioxidant effect. Worried about heart disease? Don't be. Studies done in India, where coconut oil is part of the traditional diet, expected to find that those who used the traditional fat had a higher rate of heart disease. They didn't—and indeed one study stated that polyunsaturated oils were making matters worse and people would do better to return to coconut oil and ghee (clarified butter).

It gets better. Coconut oil is a "low-fat fat"—it actually has fewer calories per gram than most fats. Furthermore, it stimulates metabolism, apparently by improving thyroid health. Farmers who tried to fatten pigs by feeding them coconut oil actually ended up with skinnier hogs!

Coconut oil is rich in what are called "medium-chain triglycerides." These are fats that can be used directly by the muscles for fuel, giving a quick energy boost similar to that of sugar—but without the subsequent crash.

Even better, half of coconut oil is immune-system boosting lauric acid. Lauric acid is converted in the body to a substance called monolaurin, which is antiviral, antibacterial, and antifungal.

You might expect coconut oil to have a strong coconut flavor, but it doesn't; it's pretty bland. Fry your eggs in it, and they'll taste like fried eggs, not a macaroon. Coconut oil also makes an excellent substitute for "vegetable shortening" (you know, those nasty hydrogenated oils like Crisco) in baking. However, coconut oil is solid at room temperature, so it isn't suited to salad dressings.

Look for coconut oil in the Asian section of any big grocery store, or, for that matter, in Asian or international markets. Hip health food stores carry it, though some are still on the "saturated is bad" bandwagon. Some of those stores will have it in the cosmetic section because coconut oil is also great for your skin and hair.

- **Olive oil.** This is a monounsaturate and a gourmet's dream. Surely you've read of the Mediterranean diet, full of olive oil, and how it's good for your heart? Extra virgin is best (recent studies even suggest that it has anti-inflammatory compounds in it) but if you don't like the full-bodied, fruity taste of extra virgin olive oil, you can pick a lighter variety.
- **Nut oils.** I especially like macadamia. Nut oils are largely monounsaturated, and they're wonderful for you. Macadamia nut oil is particularly high in monounsaturates, and what polyunsaturates are in it are in a 1:1 balance—half omega-6, half omega-3, which is ideal. It also has a high smoke point, making it good for high-temperature frying. I use Mac Nut Oil brand, and I like it very much. Almond oil and walnut oil are also fine choices.
- **Peanut oil.** This oil is also largely monounsaturated, but read the label to make sure it's not hydrogenated. Peanut oil is a good choice when you want a bland oil that's liquid at room temperature, and it's less expensive than oils from the tree nuts.

## What About Cholesterol?

You may notice that the nutritional information in this book leaves out cholesterol. This was deliberate.

Cholesterol is not, is not, is not the dietary poison it has been made out to be. It is actually essential to health—our cell walls are largely made of cholesterol, our brains and nerves contain a great deal of cholesterol, and many of our hormones are made of cholesterol. Cholesterol is so vital that our bodies *make it for us*. Indeed, roughly 75 percent of the cholesterol in your body at any given time has been made by your liver, with only about 25 percent coming from food. If you eat more, your liver will make less. If you eat less, your liver will make more.

Which explains why studies show that raising or lowering dietary cholesterol levels makes only a minimal impact on blood cholesterol. To quote the Harvard School of Public Health:

"While it is well known that high blood cholesterol levels are associated with an increased risk for heart disease, scientific studies have shown that there is only a weak relationship between the amount of cholesterol a person consumes and their blood cholesterol levels or risk for heart disease. For some people with high cholesterol, reducing the amount of cholesterol in the diet has a small but helpful impact on blood cholesterol levels. For others, the amount of cholesterol eaten has little impact on the amount of cholesterol circulating in the blood.

In a study of over 80,000 female nurses, Harvard researchers actually found that increasing cholesterol intake by 200 mg for every 1,000 calories in the diet (about an egg a day) did not appreciably increase the risk for heart disease."

Indeed, it is emerging that high blood cholesterol is largely driven by trans fats. Ironic but true, the hydrogenated vegetable oils with which we replaced animal fats have turned out to be one of the greatest causes of high cholesterol. Another is high blood insulin levels, driven by a high glycemic load. Those high insulin levels trigger your liver to make too much cholesterol.

This explains why, despite dire pronouncements that all that meat and all those eggs would cause high cholesterol, clinical studies have shown that low-carbohydrate diets improve cholesterol levels more than low-fat diets do, despite putting no limits on eggs, meat, or high-cholesterol shellfish.

In short, I didn't want you to spend your time worrying about dietary cholesterol. It's not bad for you.

chapter one

# Some Ingredients You'll Need To Know About

We've talked about fats, so now let's discuss some other ingredients. This is by no means an exhaustive rundown of every single ingredient used in this book; it's just the ones I thought you might have questions about. I've grouped them by use; within those groupings, they're in alphabetical order.

## Baked Goods

### Breads

There are not a lot of breads that I consider worth buying. Please, please, please read the ingredients lists, and if a bread contains more than the tiniest trace of sugar or corn syrup, or any hydrogenated vegetable oil at all, don't buy it!

Be aware that most "wheat" breads are not 100 percent whole wheat, or even close to it. If the ingredient label says "enriched flour," "unbleached flour" or "wheat flour," it's made with white flour. If it's whole wheat flour, it will say "whole wheat flour."

Even 100 percent whole wheat bread has a high glycemic load. Whole wheat pita bread has a somewhat lower glycemic index than whole wheat loaf bread. If you can find whole grain rye bread (check a health food store), this should have an even lower glycemic index. Even so, these are all too high-carb for me; judge by your own body.

There are some good low-carb breads out there. My favorites come from Natural Ovens of Manitowoc; they're whole grain, with a great texture and flavor, no bad fats, and no corn syrup. Sadly, these breads are not available everywhere—they're mostly available in the Midwest. Happily, Natural Ovens will ship to you. Take a look at their website: www.naturalovens.com. If you have a freezer, it is absolutely worth it to order several loaves and stock up.

More widely available is Pepperidge Farm Carb Style Bread. I don't buy the white stuff, but the whole wheat and the 7 grain are good, with no hydrogenated shortening. They do have a little corn syrup, which is unfortunate, but the overall carb count is still quite low.

## Crackers

Most crackers are nutritionally dreadful, containing refined flours, sugar, and hydrogenated oils—the Bad-Nutrition Trifecta. A few have recently gotten rid of the hydrogenated shortening and now say "no trans fats" on the label, but many of these are made with soy oil, which is also not great.

The only crackers I can really recommend are fiber crackers, which consist mostly of bran stuck together, and Scandinavian-style rye crackers. In particular, I like Fiber Rich and Bran-a-Crisp, which, as far as I can tell, are exactly the same fiber crackers in different packages. I also like Finn Crisp, which, along with having a pretty good fiber content, are made of low-GI whole grain rye, have no added fat (and therefore no bad fat), and are so thin that the per-cracker carb level is quite low. Oh, and did I mention that they taste really good, too?

Some of the Wasa crackers, especially the fiber rye, are also good.

## Tortillas

You'll find several recipes in this book that give you a choice between whole wheat tortillas and low-carb tortillas. I use the low-carb tortillas; indeed, they've become a staple in my house, and at least here in Bloomington, Indiana, every grocery store carries them. They're low-carb mostly because the fiber count has been greatly ramped up. La Tortilla Factory brand has 8 grams of fiber in a 6-inch (15-cm) tortilla! This makes them very useful if you feel you're not getting enough fiber.

Whole wheat tortillas are also widely available. While they have more carbohydrates than low-carb tortillas, they have less than a slice of bread and are more nutritious than white flour tortillas. Many tortillas have hydrogenated shortening, so read the label!

If you've been more concerned with calories than carbs, you might note that low-carb tortillas are much lower in calories than whole wheat tortillas are.

## Eggs

The greatest nutritional slander of our time is the idea that eggs are bad for you. Nothing could be further from the truth—eggs are a superb food. They're the gold standard for protein, full of vitamins and minerals, and a good source of both DHA and choline, essential for proper brain function.

What about cholesterol? There's little evidence that eating cholesterol increases coronary risk. A 1994 study in the *Journal of Internal Medicine* looked at 12 men and 12 women, each eating 2 eggs per day for 6 weeks. Their total cholesterol did rise by 4 percent—but their HDL (good) cholesterol rose by 10 percent, meaning that their coronary risk had decreased. In an article in the American *Journal of Clinical Nutrition*, researchers looked at the Framingham study—the biggest, longest-lasting study of heart disease to date. They found no relationship between egg consumption and coronary disease. And *The Journal of Nutrition* ran an article last year showing that even men who had an abnormally strong response to dietary cholesterol stayed within National Cholesterol Education Program Guidelines when adding 640 mgs of egg cholesterol per day to their diets.

We need cholesterol. It's essential for every cell in our bodies. Cholesterol insulates nerve fibers, maintains cell walls, and produces vitamin D, various hormones, and digestive juices. If we eat less cholesterol, we make it in our liver. If we eat more, we make less. It's a clever natural balance. For most of us, it's high insulin levels caused by eating tons of carbs that throw that balance off, creating high blood cholesterol, with high LDL and low HDL. This is why all the studies of the very low-carb Atkins Induction diet have demonstrated that cholesterol levels improve, rather than worsen.

So eat some eggs!

There are a few recipes in this book that call for raw eggs, an ingredient that is currently frowned upon by officialdom because of the risk of salmonella. However, I have it on pretty good authority that only one out of every 16,000 uncracked, properly refrigerated eggs is actually contaminated. As one woman with degrees in public health and food science put it, "The risk is less than the risk of breaking your leg on any given trip down the stairs." So I use raw eggs now and again, and I don't worry about it, and we've never had a problem around here.

*However*, this does not mean that there is no risk. You'll have to decide for yourself if this is a worry for you. Among other things, I generally take the safest route by using very, very fresh eggs from local small farmers, which may well be safer than eggs that have gone longer distances, with greater risk of cracking or refrigeration problems.

One useful thing to know about eggs: While you'll want very fresh eggs for frying and poaching, eggs that are at least several days old are better for hard boiling. They're less likely to stick to their shells in that maddening way we've all encountered. So if you like hard-boiled eggs—they're certainly one of the most convenient low-carb foods—buy a couple of extra cartons of eggs and let them sit in the refrigerator for at least three or four days before you hard boil them.

## Flours, Grains, and the Like

### Barley

If you can afford to eat some grains, it's good to know that barley has the lowest glycemic index of any grain, considerably lower than rice. Look in health food stores for whole grain barley.

### Brown Rice and Wild Rice

There are a number of recipes in this book that call for wild rice and a few that call for brown rice. Wild rice is available in most grocery stores; don't mistake "wild rice blends" for plain wild rice. Plain wild rice is just long, skinny kernels that are a very deep brown. It has far more fiber than white rice, or even brown rice. It also has a deep, rich, nutty flavor, which makes it great for recipes where we'll dilute its carbohydrate content with other ingredients.

Brown rice—simply unrefined rice—is getting harder and harder to find in grocery stores, at least here in Bloomington, Indiana. They have "instant brown rice," but this is a highly processed product with a nasty blood sugar impact. Some have brown and white rice blends, but again, this isn't what we're looking for. You want just plain brown rice. You may need to go to a health food store to find it—at which point, you may find more of a selection than you bargained on! Many health food stores carry a wide variety of rice in the bulk bins. Again, my recipes call for just plain brown rice—short, medium, or long grain, it doesn't matter which.

### Cornmeal

There are a few recipes in this book that call for whole grain cornmeal—including a terrific recipe for Skillet Buttermilk Cornbread (see page 118). Please do not use standard grocery store "enriched" cornmeal—the vitamins and fiber have largely been removed from that stuff. (See "Whole Wheat Flour" on page 38 for an explanation of the refining and enriching process.) Whole grain cornmeal can be found at health food stores, and it is nutritionally far superior.

If you can't find whole grain cornmeal, you can, in a pinch, grind whole corn kernels in your blender! Unless you use it up quickly, store whole grain cornmeal in your refrigerator.

## Ground Almonds and Almond Meal

Finely ground almonds or almond meal are wonderful for replacing some or all of the flour in many recipes, especially cakes and cookies. Packaged almond meal is becoming easier to find; the widely distributed Bob's Red Mill brand makes one. It's convenient stuff, and you certainly may use it in any of the recipes that call for almond meal.

However, I have gone back to making my own almond meal by grinding shelled almonds in my food processor, using the S-blade. It takes only a minute or so to reduce them to the texture of corn meal, after which I store the meal in a tightly lidded container. Why do I bother?

Because I grind my almonds with the brown skins still on them, my almond meal has a higher fiber and mineral content than commercial almond meal, which is made from almonds that are "blanched" (have the skins removed). The carb and fiber counts in this book reflect my homemade, high-fiber almond meal.

It's good to know that almonds actually expand a little during grinding; this was something that surprised me because I thought they'd compress a bit. Figure that between 2/3 and 3/4 cup of whole almond kernels will become 1 cup of meal when ground.

## Guar and Xanthan Gums

These sound just dreadful, don't they? But they're in lots of your favorite processed foods, so how bad can they be? What the heck are they? They're forms of water-soluble fiber, extracted and purified. Guar and xanthan are both flavorless white powders; their value to us is as thickeners. Unlike refined white flour, cornstarch, or arrowroot, all of which are nutritionless, high-impact bad carbs, these consist of nothing but fiber. They swell up when they hit liquids, which is how they thicken things.

You'll find guar or xanthan used in tiny little quantities in a lot of these recipes. Don't go dramatically increasing the quantity of guar or xanthan to get a thicker product. Why not? Because in large quantities they make things gummy, and the texture is not terribly pleasant. But in these tiny quantities they let you add "oomph" to sauces and soups without using flour.

Get yourself an extra salt shaker, fill it with guar or xanthan, and put it by the stove. When you want to thicken something, simply sprinkle a little of the thickener over the surface while stirring with a whisk. Stop when your sauce, soup, or gravy is a little less thick than you want it to be; it'll thicken a little more on standing.

Your health food store may well be able to order guar or xanthan for you if they don't have them on hand. (I slightly prefer xanthan, myself.) You can also find suppliers online. Keep either one in a jar with a tight lid, and it will never go bad—I bought a pound of guar over 15 years ago, and it's still going strong.

### Oat Flour

One or two recipes in this book call for oat flour, which has a higher fiber content than most whole grain flours. Oat flour is available at health food stores. In a pinch, you can grind up oatmeal in your blender or food processor.

### Rolled Oats

Also known as old fashioned oatmeal—you know, oat grains that have been squashed flat. Available in every grocery store in the western hemisphere. Do not substitute instant or quick-cooking oatmeal.

### Whole Wheat Flour

Years ago a friend, having been told to eat only whole wheat bread, asked me plaintively, "What's whole wheat? All the bread I see is made of wheat that's been ground up." So perhaps I'd better explain.

A wheat kernel has three parts: The bran, which is the outer protective coating; the germ, which is the little nub inside that will become a new plant if the seed grows; and the endosperm, in between, which is the little bit of fuel the germ needs to send down roots and start getting nourishment from the soil. The bran is mostly fiber and is a good source of several minerals, including potassium, magnesium, and iron, plus some B vitamins. The germ is an even better source of B vitamins and minerals, has about half as much protein as it does carbohydrates, and contains a pretty good whack of fiber. It also contains a little fat. The endosperm is mostly carbohydrates—starch—with a little protein, and it has far fewer vitamins and minerals than the bran or germ. It contains no fiber.

Whole wheat flour is made by grinding all three of these parts of the wheat kernel together, with nothing removed. It has the carbohydrates of the endosperm, but it also has the vitamins and minerals of the bran and the vitamins, minerals, and protein of the germ. The fiber is also retained. However, because whole wheat flour contains the fat from the wheat germ, it can eventually go rancid. Because it's highly nutritious, mold likes to grow on whole grain bread. And because of the fiber content, it doesn't make baked goods that are "light and fluffy."

So some genius got the idea to refine flour. Millers started removing the bran and the germ from the endosperm and making flour only from that starchy bit—and white flour was born. It made nice fluffy bread that didn't go moldy nearly as easily as whole wheat bread.

(For years, this simple fact has struck me as a telling sign that refining was a bad idea. I mean, if a "food" won't support life on a primitive level, what's it going to do for me?)

Refining turned out to be a very bad idea, causing nutritional deficiencies. Diseases like pellagra (niacin deficiency) become so common that "enriched" bread and flour were eventually created. "Enriched" means that after they take out all of the vitamins and minerals and fiber in the bran and germ, they put back four vitamins and some iron. It's very much as if a robber held you up, took everything you had, including the clothes off your back, then gave you back your shoes and a quarter for the bus and told you you'd been "enriched."

Of course, removing the fiber from the bran and the germ and milling white flour very finely also drastically increased the blood sugar impact of the bread made from it, and thus its glycemic load.

Us long-time "health food freaks" have refused to eat "enriched" bread and flour for decades. And for a long time, registered dieticians and the medical establishment derided this as "food faddism." Sample menus for a "healthy diet" would specify "whole grain or enriched bread," as if they were nutritionally equivalent—which they insisted they were.

Then came the disastrous Food Pyramid years, when Americans, told they needed 6 to 11 servings of grains per day, started eating even more white flour than they had before. Obesity and diabetes became epidemics. And eventually, millions of us figured out that eating all of those carbohydrates just wasn't doing us the good that the government claimed it would—and we dropped grains out of our diets almost completely.

Faced with a huge population of folks who had discovered that they became healthier by dropping the bread and pasta, all of a sudden the USDA has discovered whole grains. They're telling us we need to eat lots of whole grains. I don't buy it. We all come from hunter-gatherer ancestors who ate virtually no grains at all, and I know I feel best (and stay slimmest) if I keep my grain intake to a rock-bottom minimum.

But there is absolutely no question that whole grains are far, far better for you than refined and "enriched" grains.

In this book, you'll find recipes that call for whole wheat flour. I've combined that flour with lower-carbohydrate ingredients to create baked goods that have a modest blood sugar impact.

There are three kinds of whole wheat flour—bread flour, pastry flour, and just plain old "whole wheat flour." The first two are found largely at health food stores. The difference between them is the protein content and how finely the flour is ground; whole wheat bread flour is from high-protein wheat and is more coarsely ground, while whole wheat pastry flour is from lower-protein wheat and is more finely ground. Just plain "whole wheat flour" is between the two in protein content. For most of the recipes in this book, whole wheat pastry flour is preferable, but just plain whole wheat flour should do fine.

Unless you're going to use it up quite quickly, keep whole wheat flour in your refrigerator.

### Whey Protein Powder

Whey is the liquid part of milk—if you've ever seen yogurt that has separated, the clearish liquid is the whey. Whey protein is of extremely good quality, and the protein powder made from it is tops in both flavor and nutritional value. For use in any sweet recipe, the vanilla flavored whey protein powder, readily available in health food stores, is best. Yes, this is the kind generally sold for making shakes with. Protein powders vary some in their carbohydrate counts, so find the one with the least carbohydrate, and beware of sugar-sweetened protein powders. I use Designer Whey French Vanilla, which is stevia-sweetened. It's available at GNC stores.

Natural whey protein powder is just like vanilla whey protein powder, except that it has not been flavored or sweetened. It has a bland flavor and is used in recipes where a sweet flavor is not desirable.

## Liquids

### Bottled "Light" Salad Dressings

Quite a few recipes in this book call for bottled reduced calorie salad dressing—mostly Italian, red wine and vinegar, balsamic vinaigrette, or Caesar dressings. Be very careful when purchasing these, and carefully read the labels—many reduced-fat salad dressings are full of sugar, and almost all fat-free dressings are. I use Paul

Newman's (Newman's Own) salad dressings because they taste good, don't have a lot of chemicals, and the "light" versions generally don't have any more carbs than the full-fat versions. That they give all their profits to charity is a nice bonus, but primarily I'm interested in the quality of the products.

## Broths

Canned or boxed chicken broth and beef broth are very handy items to keep around, and using them is certainly quicker than making your own. However, the quality of most of the canned broth you'll find at your local grocery store is appallingly bad. The chicken broth has all sorts of chemicals in it, and often sugar as well. The "beef" broth is worse—it frequently has no beef in it whatsoever. I refuse to use these products, and you should, too.

However, there are a few canned or boxed broths on the market worth buying. Many grocery stores now carry a brand called Kitchen Basics, which contains no chemicals. It is packaged in boxes, much like soy milk. Kitchen Basics comes in both chicken and beef. Health food stores also have good-quality canned and boxed broths—Shelton, Health Valley, and Pacific brands are widely distributed in the United States. Read the labels on the broths sold at your grocery store, and buy the ones that are all-natural, with no added sugar. Low-sodium broths are a good choice, as you have better control over the saltiness of your finished dish.

For some odd reason, boxed broth comes in 1 cup and 1 quart containers, while canned broth comes in 14-ounce cans—just under 2 cups. I use 1-quart boxes, so I measure broth in quarts, but you can substitute two 14-ounce cans, and your results will be fine. You could add a little water to make up the difference, if you like, but it hardly seems essential.

Decent packaged broth will cost you a little more than the stuff that is made of salt and chemicals, but it won't cost you a whole lot more. If you watch for sales, you can often get it as cheaply as the bad stuff, and stock up then.

## Carb Countdown Dairy Beverage

I've used milk in several recipes in this book, and as carbohydrate foods go, I think it's a pretty good one. But if you need to keep your carb intake very low, you can substitute Carb Countdown in any recipe that calls for milk.

Carb Countdown is nationally distributed, so you should be able to find it near you. However, if you cannot, try substituting half-and-half, or equal parts of heavy cream and water.

### Vinegar

Various recipes in this book call for wine vinegar, cider vinegar, rice vinegar, tarragon vinegar, white vinegar, and balsamic vinegar. If you've always thought that vinegar was just vinegar, think again. Each of these vinegars has a distinct flavor all its own, and if you substitute one for the other, you'll change the whole character of the recipe—one splash of cider vinegar in your Asian Chicken Salad, and you've traded your Chinese accent for an American twang. Vinegar is such a great way to give bright flavors to foods while adding few carbs or calories that I keep all of these varieties on hand; it's not like they go bad or anything.

As with everything else, read the labels on your vinegars. Beware of apple cider flavored vinegar—this is white vinegar with artificial flavors added. I bought this once by mistake, so I thought I'd give you the heads-up.

## Nuts, Seeds, and Nut Butters

### Nuts and Seeds

Low in carbohydrates and high in healthy fats, protein, and minerals, nuts and seeds are great foods for us. Not only are they delicious for snacking or for adding crunch to salads and stir-fries, but when ground, they can replace some of the flour in low-carb baked goods—in particular, you'll find quite a few recipes in this book calling for ground almonds. Since these ingredients can be pricey, you'll want to shop around. In particular, health food stores often carry nuts and seeds in bulk at better prices than you'll find at the grocery store. I have also found that specialty ethnic groceries often have good prices on nuts; I get my best deal on almonds at my wonderful Middle Eastern grocery, Sahara Mart.

By the way, along with pumpkin and sunflower seeds, you can buy sesame seeds in bulk at health food stores for a fraction of what they'll cost you in a little shaker jar at the grocery store. Buy them "unhulled" and you'll get both more fiber and more calcium. You can also get unsweetened shredded coconut at health food stores.

### Flax Seed Meal

Flax seed comes from the same plant that gives us the fabric linen, and it is turning out to be one of the most nutritious seeds there is. Along with good-quality protein, flax seeds have tons of soluble, cholesterol-reducing fiber, and they're a good source of omega-3s.

The recipes in this book that use flax seed call for it in meal form—that is, ground up. You can buy preground flax seed meal—Bob's Red Mill puts it out, among others. Once I've opened this, I keep it in a zipper-lock bag in the freezer because flax oil is perishable.

If you'd like to grind your own, an electric coffee grinder works well. You'll want to keep a separate grinder for this purpose, though!

### Peanut Butter

The only peanut butter called for in this cookbook is "natural" peanut butter, the kind made from ground up roasted peanuts, peanut oil, salt, and nothing else. Most big grocery stores now carry natural peanut butter; it's the stuff with the layer of oil on top. The oil in standard peanut butter has been hydrogenated to keep it from separating out (that's what gives Skippy and Jif that extremely smooth, plastic consistency), and it's hard to think of anything worse for you than hydrogenated vegetable oil. Except for sugar, of course, which is also added to standard peanut butter. Stick to the natural stuff.

Smuckers now has a "natural peanut butter with honey." Do I have to explain that honey is a sugar? Buy the plain natural peanut butter.

Keep all natural nut butters in the refrigerator unless you're going to eat them up within a week or two.

## Seasonings

### Bouillon or Broth Concentrate

Bouillon, or broth concentrate, comes in cubes, crystals, pastes, or liquids. It is generally full of salt and chemicals, and it doesn't taste notably like the animal it supposedly came from. It definitely does not make a suitable substitute for good-quality broth if you're making a pot of soup. However, these products can be useful for adding a little kick of flavor here and there—more as seasonings than as soups—and for this use, I keep them on hand. I use a paste bouillon concentrate product called "Better Than Bouillon" that comes in both chicken and beef flavors; I do find it preferable to the other kinds, because it actually contains chicken or beef! But, hey, use what you have on hand; it should be okay.

### Chili Garlic Paste

This is a traditional Asian ingredient, consisting mostly, as the name strongly implies, of hot chiles and garlic. If, like me, you're a chili-head, you'll find endless ways to used the stuff once you have it on hand. Chili garlic paste comes in jars and keeps for months in the refrigerator. It's worth seeking out at Asian markets or in the international foods aisle of big grocery stores. By the way, my tester Julie says I should tell you, "You're looking for the jar with a rooster on the front!" (At least, that's what my chili garlic paste comes in, and halfway across the country, Julie's did, too.)

### Fish Sauce or Nuoc Mam or Nam Pla

This is a salty, fermented seasoning widely used in Southeast Asian cooking. It's available in Asian grocery stores and in the Asian food sections of big grocery stores. Grab it when you find it; it keeps nicely without refrigeration. Fish sauce is used in a few (really great) recipes in this book, and it adds an authentic flavor. In a pinch, you can substitute soy sauce, although you'll lose some of your Southeast Asian accent.

### Garlic

Garlic is an essential flavoring ingredient in many recipes. If you've only used powdered garlic before, be aware that a "clove" is one of those little individual bits you get in a whole garlic bulb. If you read "clove" and use a whole bulb (aka a "head") of garlic, you'll get a lot stronger garlic flavor than you bargained for.

I only use fresh garlic, except for occasional recipes for sprinkle-on seasoning blends. Nothing tastes like the real thing. To my taste buds, even the jarred, chopped garlic in oil doesn't taste like fresh garlic. You may use jarred garlic if you like—half a teaspoon should equal about 1 clove of fresh garlic. If you choose to use powdered garlic, well, I can't stop you, but I'm afraid I can't promise that the recipes will taste the same, either. One-quarter teaspoon of garlic powder is the rough equivalent of 1 clove of fresh garlic.

By the way, the easiest way to crush a clove or two of garlic is to put the flat side of a big knife on top of it and smash it with your fist. Pick out the papery skin, which will now be easy to do, finely chop your garlic, and toss it into your dish. Oh, and keep in mind that the distinctive garlic aroma and flavor only develops after the cell walls are broken (that's why a pile of fresh garlic bulbs in the grocery store doesn't reek), so the more finely you crush or mince your garlic, the more flavor it will release.

## Gingerroot

Many recipes in this book call for fresh ginger, sometimes called gingerroot. Fresh ginger is an essential ingredient in Asian cooking, and dried, powdered ginger is not a substitute. Fortunately, fresh ginger freezes beautifully. Just drop your whole gingerroot (called a "hand" of ginger) into a zipper-lock freezer bag, and toss it in the freezer. When the time comes to use it, pull it out, peel enough of the end for your immediate purposes, and grate it. (It will grate just fine while still frozen.) Throw the remaining root back in the baggie, and toss it back in the freezer.

Jarred grated gingerroot is available at some very comprehensive grocery stores and in Asian markets. I find this very handy.

## Low-Sugar Preserves

In particular, I find low-sugar apricot preserves to be a wonderfully versatile ingredient. I buy Smucker's brand, and I like it very much. This is lower in sugar by far than the "all fruit" preserves, which replace sugar with concentrated fruit juice. Folks, sugar from fruit juice is still sugar. I also use low-sugar orange marmalade.

## Vege-Sal

If you've read my newsletter, Lowcarbezine, or my previous cookbooks, you know that I'm a big fan of Vege-Sal. What is Vege-Sal? It's a salt that's been seasoned, but don't think "seasoned salt." Vege-Sal is much milder than traditional seasoned salt. It's simply salt that's been blended with some dried, powdered vegetables; the flavor is quite subtle, but I think it improves all sorts of things. I've given you the choice between using regular salt or Vege-Sal in a wide variety of recipes. Don't worry, they'll come out fine with plain old salt, but I do think Vege-Sal adds a little something extra. Vege-Sal is also excellent sprinkled over chops and steaks in place of regular salt. Vege-Sal is made by Modern Products and is widely available in health food stores.

## Wasabi Paste

If you haven't had sushi, you might not be familiar with wasabi. Some people call it "Japanese horseradish"—it's a root that, when grated, yields an extremely pungent condiment. Generally it's available either as a powder, which is then mixed with water, or as a paste, in a tube. I've used the paste form of wasabi in several recipes here. Look for it in the international aisle of big grocery stores, or at Asian markets.

## Sweeteners

### Blackstrap Molasses

I've found that combining Splenda with a very small amount of molasses gives a good, brown sugar flavor to all sorts of recipes. Always use the darkest molasses you can find—the darker it is, the stronger the flavor, and the less sugar it contains. That's why I specify blackstrap, the darkest, strongest molasses there is. It's nice to know that blackstrap is also where all the minerals they take out of sugar end up—it may be sugary, but at least it's not a nutritional wasteland. Still, I only use small amounts.

If you can't get blackstrap molasses (health food stores carry it), buy the darkest molasses you can find. Most "grocery store" brands come in both light and dark varieties.

Why not just use some of the artificial brown sugar–flavored sweeteners out there? Because I've tried them, and I haven't tasted a one I would be willing to buy again. Ick.

### Polyols

Polyols, also known as sugar alcohols, are widely used in sugar-free candies and cookies. There are a variety of polyols, and their names all end with *tol*: sorbitol, maltitol, mannitol, lactitol, xylitol, and the like. (Okay, there's one exception: isomalt. I don't know what happened there.) Polyols are carbohydrates, but they are carbohydrates that are made up of molecules that are too big for the human gut to digest or absorb easily. As a result, polyols don't create much rise in blood sugar, nor much of an insulin release.

This does not, however, mean that polyols are completely unabsorbed. I have seen charts of the relative absorption rates of the various polyols, and I am here to tell you that in varying degrees, you do, indeed, absorb carbohydrates and calories from these sweeteners. Sadly, the highest absorption rate seems to be for maltitol, which is the most widely used of the polyols. You absorb about 2.5 calories for every gram of maltitol you eat. Since you would absorb 4 calories for a gram of sugar, simple arithmetic tells us that you're absorbing more than half of the carbohydrate in the maltitol you eat. For that matter, the most extensive chart of glycemic indexes I've seen rated maltitol no lower than a 30, and quite a lot higher in some tests, and some tests rated it higher than table sugar!

Why do manufacturers use polyols instead of sucralose (Splenda)? Polyols are used in commercial sugar-free sweets because unlike Splenda and other artificial sweeteners, they will give all of the textures that can be achieved with sugar.

Polyols can be used to make crunchy toffee, chewy jelly beans, slick hard candies, chewy moist brownies, and creamy chocolate, just as sugar can.

However, there are one or two problems with polyols. First of all, there is some feeling that different people have differing abilities to digest and absorb these very long chain carbohydrates, which means that for some people, they may cause more of a derangement of blood sugar than for others. Once again, my only advice is to pay attention to your body.

The other problem with polyols is one that is inherent in all indigestible, unabsorbable carbohydrates: They can cause gas and diarrhea. Unabsorbed carbs ferment in your gut, and intestinal gas is the result; it's the exact same thing that happens when people eat beans. I find that even half of a low-carb chocolate bar is enough to cause me social embarrassment several hours later. And I know of a case where eating a dozen and a half sugar-free taffies before bed caused the hapless consumer 45 minutes of serious gut-cramping intestinal distress at four in the morning.

Don't think, by the way, that you can get around these effects of polyol consumption by taking Beano. It will work, but it will work by making the carbohydrates digestible and absorbable—meaning that any low-carb advantage is gone. I've known folks who have gained weight this way.

What we have here, then, is a sweetener that *enforces* moderation. Personally, I think this is a wonderful thing

Polyols have become available for the home cook. I have started to use them in my recipes, because they do, indeed, offer a textural advantage. In particular, I got a fair number of complaints about the cookie recipes in *500 Low-Carb Recipes*. People liked the flavor of the cookies but found them too crumbly, and sometimes too dry. Polyols solve this problem.

I use erythritol whenever possible, in preference to maltitol, isomalt, or any of the other granular polyols. Why? Because erythritol has the lowest digestion and absorption rate of all the polyols. You get only 0.3 calories per gram of erythritol, which tells us that we're absorbing very little indeed. Erythritol also seems to be easier on the gut than the other polyols. (*See* Resources on page 541 for mail-order sources of erythritol.) Xylitol is another preferred choice; it has a glycemic index of 7, which is very low, and it seems to actually have a protective effect on teeth!

I confess, I am at a loss as to how to count the carbohydrate grams that polyols add to my recipes, since I can't know which of the polyol sweeteners you'll be using and they do, indeed, have differing absorption rates. Therefore, I have left them out of the nutritional analyses in this cookbook, which puts me on the same footing as the food processors, I guess. I have mentioned this in the recipe analyses. Be aware that you're probably getting at least a few grams of extra carbohydrate per serving in these recipes.

## Splenda

This is the one big exception to "eat real food." Yes, Splenda is an artificial sweetener. I have had readers write to me, alarmed about reports that sucralose—the sweetener in Splenda—caused thymus shrinkage and kidney swelling in lab rats. This is true, but the doses used were extremely high—the equivalent of a 150-pound person eating more than 10,000 teaspoons per day of Splenda. At doses that equaled a few thousand teaspoons per day—still a massive dose—the problems didn't occur. Since it's a very rare day when I consume more than eight or ten teaspoons of Splenda, I remain unconcerned. Artificial sweeteners are not 100 percent safe (I know of nothing that is), but I am convinced that Splenda is far, far safer than sugar or corn syrup. (And why do they never feed the rats that much sugar or corn syrup to see what happens?)

It is true that sugar is "natural," and if you chewed fresh sugar cane, little harm would come to you. But there is nothing natural about the extreme concentration of refined sugar, nor about its complete lack of vitamins and minerals. To claim that sugar is okay because it's natural is like claiming that cocaine is okay because it's natural. (And there's nothing natural at all about corn syrup. It's a man-made product, and it's even more destructive than sugar.)

The truth is, the best thing would be for us all to stop eating sweet stuff, and truth to tell, I eat desserts very infrequently. But most people are unwilling to give up sweet stuff entirely. Splenda is a compromise, but I believe it is a better choice by far than sugar. (Are you thinking, How about honey? Honey has a pretty good name in some nutritional circles, but honey is a highly concentrated sugar, too, with an even higher glycemic index than table sugar.)

Splenda tastes very good. Feed nondieting friends and family Splenda-sweetened desserts, and they will never know that you didn't use sugar.

Splenda has some other advantages. The table sweetener has been bulked so that it measures spoon-for-spoon, cup-for-cup, like sugar. This makes adapting recipes much easier. Also, Splenda stands up to heat, unlike aspartame, which means you can use it for baked goods and other things that are heated for a while.

Be aware that Splenda granular (the stuff that comes in bulk, in a box, or the baker's bag) is different than the stuff that comes in the little packets. The stuff in the packets is considerably sweeter, apparently. All my Splenda measurements are for granular Splenda. I'm afraid I don't have the packets on hand (I've never purchased them), so I can't work a conversion for you. Take a look at the box and see how many teaspoons of sugar each packet equals, and work from there, remembering that there are 48 teaspoons in a cup.

(Also be aware that there's a "Splenda Sugar Blend" on the market. Steer clear.)

Splenda is not carb-free. Because of the malto-dextrin used to bulk it, granular Splenda has about one-half gram of carbohydrates per teaspoon, or about one-eighth of the carbs of sugar. So count 1/2 gram per teaspoon, 1 1/2 grams per tablespoon, and 24 grams per cup. The stuff in the packets, since it's bulked less, has fewer carbs, so if you want to do the conversion, you can save a few grams. Me, I'd go buggy tearing open all those little packets.

## Stevia/FOS Blend

Stevia is short for Stevia rebaudiana, a South American shrub with very sweet leaves. Stevia extract, a white powder from stevia leaves, is growing in popularity with people who don't care to eat sugar but who are nervous about artificial sweeteners.

However, stevia extract has a couple of faults: first, it's so extremely sweet that it's hard to know just how much to use in any given recipe, and second, it often has a bitter taste, as well as a sweet one. This is why some smart food packagers have started blending stevia with fructooligosaccharide, also known as FOS. FOS is a sugar, but it's a sugar with a molecule so large that the human gut can neither digest nor absorb it, so it doesn't raise blood sugar or cause an insulin release. FOS has a nice, mild sweetness to it; indeed, it's only half as sweet as table sugar. This makes it the perfect partner for the too-sweet stevia.

I have been experimenting more and more with stevia/FOS because I know that many of my readers are uncomfortable with using artificial sweeteners. My experiments have been somewhat hit-or-miss. For instance, stevia/FOS works very well in my ketchup recipe, but made truly vile teriyaki sauce. The stevia bitterness comes through in some recipes and not in others. If you would like to try experimenting, the conversion factors are:

1/4 teaspoon Stevia/FOS = 1 teaspoon sugar or Splenda
3/4 teaspoon stevia/FOS = 1 tablespoon sugar or Splenda
1 tablespoon stevia/FOS = 1/2 cup sugar or Splenda
2 tablespoons stevia/FOS = 1 cup sugar or Splenda

Stevia/FOS is available in health food stores, both in packets and in shaker jars. The brand I use is called SteviaPlus, and it's from a company called Sweet Leaf, but any stevia/FOS blend should do for the recipes that call for it. If you can't find it locally, search online and you'll find several Web sites happy to ship it to you.

My favorite use for this stevia/FOS blend, by the way, is to sweeten my yogurt. I think it tastes quite good in yogurt, and FOS actually helps the good bacteria take hold in your gut, improving your health.

### Sucanat

Sucanat is to sugar what whole wheat flour is to white flour—the unrefined version, with all the original nutrients in it. Sugar cane juice is simply evaporated until it's dry, then ground up into a granular form. Sucanat tastes a lot like brown sugar, though it doesn't have the moist, sticky quality brown sugar does.

Sucanat is actually a product I do not use. It may be unrefined and contain some vitamins and minerals, but it's still a concentrated, high-impact carb, and it's not kind to either my blood sugar or my waistline. I do not recommend it for any of you who are seriously restricting your carb intake, and certainly not for any of you who are diabetic.

So why do I mention it? Because some folks have serious gastrointestinal trouble with polyols. If you cannot tolerate polyols and can tolerate somewhat higher levels of carbohydrate, you can substitute Sucanat for polyols in the recipes that call for them. It will give a similar textural effect, and it is, at least, superior to sugar or honey nutritionally. Sucanat is available in health food stores.

### Sugar-Free Pancake Syrup

This is actually easy to find. All my local grocery stores carry it, and indeed, have more than one brand. It's usually with the regular pancake syrup, but it may be lurking with the diabetic or diet foods. It's just like regular pancake syrup, only it's made from polyols instead of sugar. I use it in small quantities in a few recipes to get a maple flavor.

### Genuine Maple Syrup

If you insist, you may use genuine maple syrup in the recipes that call for sugar-free pancake syrup, though I don't recommend this—the stuff has 13 grams of sugar per tablespoon! However, it does contain some trace minerals, which makes it marginally better than sugar, and the flavor is strong enough that not a lot is needed to make a big impact.

Don't even think about using regular cheap "pancake syrup." It's just plain evil.

### Canned Tuna

You'll find several tuna recipes in this book. As a long-time fan of tuna salad, I am sorry to have to inform you that tuna is now considered a risk for mercury contamination. It's important to know that "light" tuna generally has about 75 percent less mercury than the more expensive "white" or "albacore" tuna. Save your health and your budget at the same time—buy light tuna. Still, I'm learning to limit myself to one can each week.

## Vegetables and the Like

### Currants

You'll find several recipes in this book that call for dried currants. If you haven't tried them, dried currants are very much like raisins, only smaller. Why did I choose them instead of the more familiar raisins? Because both raisins and currants are high enough in natural sugars that I needed to limit quantity, and the smaller currants distribute more evenly in a dish. If you can't get them (though all my local grocery stores carry them), you can use raisins instead, but I'd suggest snipping each one into two or three pieces—a tedious task, I'll admit. If you do this, spray your knife or kitchen shears with nonstick cooking spray first!

Sometimes dried currants are too dry—maybe even downright crusty. (No doubt you've seen raisins that were this way, too.) Covering them with boiling water and letting them sit while you prepare the rest of your dish lets them "puff" back to their chewy, yummy selves.

### Frozen Vegetables

You'll notice that many of these recipes call for frozen vegetables. I use these because I find them very convenient, I think that the quality is quite good, and most plain frozen vegetables don't have any additives. If you like, you may certainly substitute fresh vegetables in any recipe. You will need to adjust the cooking time, and if the recipe calls for the vegetable to be used thawed but not cooked, you'll need to "blanch" your vegetables—boil them for just 3 to 5 minutes.

It's important to know that frozen vegetables are not immortal, no matter how good your freezer is. Don't buy more than you can use up in 4 to 6 weeks, even if they're on sale. You'll end up throwing them away.

### Onions

If you're not an accomplished cook, you need to know that different types of onions are good for different things. There are mild onions, which are best used raw, and there are stronger onions, which are what you want if you're going to be cooking them. My favorite mild onions are sweet red onions; these are widely available, and you'll see I've used them quite a lot in the recipes. However, if you prefer, you can substitute Vidalia or Bermuda onions anywhere I've specified sweet red onions. Scallions, also known as green onions, are also mild, and they're best eaten raw or quickly cooked in stir-fries. To me, scallions have their own flavor, and I generally don't substitute for them, but your kitchen won't blow up or anything if you use another sort of sweet onion in their place.

When a recipe simply says "onion," what I'm talking about is good old yellow globe onions, the ones you can buy 3 or 5 pounds at a time in net sacks.

### Tomatoes and Tomato Products

You'll notice that I call for canned tomatoes in a fair number of recipes—even some recipes where fresh tomatoes might do. This is because fresh tomatoes aren't very good for much of the year, while canned tomatoes are all canned at the height of ripeness. I'd rather have a good canned tomato in my sauce or soup than a mediocre fresh one. Since canned tomatoes are generally used with all the liquid that's in the can, the nutritional content doesn't suffer the way it does with most canned vegetables.

I also use plain canned tomato sauce, jarred pizza sauce, and jarred salsa. When choosing these products, you need to be aware that tomatoes, for some reason, inspire food packers to flights of sugar-fancy. They add sugar, corn syrup, and other bad carbs to all sorts of tomato products. So it is even more important that you read the labels on all tomato-based products to find the ones with no added sugar. And keep on reading them. The good, cheap brand of salsa I used for quite a while showed up one day with "New, Improved " on the label. Guess how they'd improved it? Right. They'd added sugar. I found a new brand.

## Dairy

### Reduced-Fat Dairy Products

You'll find that I've called for some reduced-fat cheeses and light sour cream in this book. Note that these, unlike many reduced-fat products, do not have a pile of carbohydrates added to them to replace the fat. You may use full-fat products if you prefer; your calorie counts will be higher, of course. Do not use fat-free products. Not only do they generally have a lot of junk added, they're icky.

### Yogurt and Buttermilk

Yogurt and buttermilk both fall into the category of "cultured milks"—milk that has deliberately had a particular bacteria added to it and then been kept warm until the bacteria grows. It is these bacteria that give yogurt and buttermilk their characteristic thick textures and tangy flavors.

If you look at the labels of either of these cultured milk products, you'll see that the nutrition label claims 12 grams of carbohydrate per cup (and, by the way, 8 grams of protein), which is the same carbohydrate count as the milk they're made from. For this reason, many low-carbers avoid yogurt and buttermilk.

However, in *The GO-Diet*, Drs. Goldberg and O'Mara explain that in actuality, most of the lactose (milk sugar) in the milk is converted into lactic acid by the bacteria. This is what gives these foods their sour taste. The labels say "12 grams carbohydrate" largely, they say, because carbohydrate count is determined by "difference." What this means is that the calorie count is first determined. Then the protein and fat fractions are measured, and the number of calories they contribute is calculated. Any calories left over are assumed to come from carbohydrates.

However, Goldberg and O'Mara say, this is inaccurate in the cases of yogurt and buttermilk. They say we should count just 4 grams of carbohydrates per cup for these cultured milks. Accordingly, I have added them back into my diet, and I have had no trouble—no weight gain and no triggering of "blood sugar hunger." I really enjoy yogurt as a snack.

Keep in mind that these numbers *only* apply to plain yogurt. The sweetened kind is always higher in carbohydrates.

The carb counts in this book for recipes using plain yogurt or buttermilk are calculated using that 4 grams of carbohydrate per cup figure.

## Soy

You may be surprised to find very little in the way of soy foods used in these recipes. There is a reason for this: I do not consider soy safe. This will come as a shock to many of you. I know that soy has a reputation for being the Wonder Health Food of All Existence, but there are reasons to be cautious.

Soy has been known to be hard on the thyroid for decades now, and if you're trying to lose weight and improve your health, a slow thyroid is the last thing you need. More alarmingly, there was a study done in Hawaii in 2000 that showed a correlation between the amount of tofu subjects ate in middle age and their rate and severity of cognitive problems in old age. Since scientists suspect the problem lies with the soy estrogens that have been so highly touted, any unfermented soy product, including canned soy beans, is suspect.

Soy also interferes with mineral absorption, and fed to young lab rats, it slowed growth. Please, don't assume soy formula and soy milk are better for your children than dairy products. (It's estimated that babies fed on soy formula get the estrogen equivalent of 5 birth control pills a day.) Another concern for woman and children is a drastically increased rate of penile birth defects in boy babies born to vegetarian mothers. No one knows for sure what causes it, but soy estrogens are high on the list of suspects.

While soy has been pushed at women as preventing breast cancer, the evidence is equivocal, at best. A 1996 study showed that women who ate soy had a higher rate of early malignancies, while a 1997 study suggested that soy may increase the risk that already-established breast cancers will spread. And you need to balance those reports of "heart healthy" soy with the knowledge that soy contains a substance called *hemagglutinin* that makes platelets stickier and more likely to clot.

This doesn't mean we must completely shun soy beans and soy products, but it does mean we need to approach them with caution and eat them in serious moderation. I use very few soy-containing products and no soy milk, soy cheese, soy protein powder, or other highly processed, unfermented soy foods. There is nothing traditional about these "foods" and I do not consider them fit for human consumption.

I do use low-carbohydrate tortillas, which have a small amount of soy in them, and I very occasionally use black soy beans in a soup or chili recipe. That's about it for my soy consumption—and the soy you'll find in this book.

chapter two

# Starters, Snacks, and Party Foods

In this chapter, you will find an assortment of what I would call "pick up food"—stuff that people can simply pick up and eat with their hands. Great for parties or to stash in the fridge against a sudden attack of the munchies, these recipes also make terrific light meals. In particular, I like the idea of putting out an assortment of these foods on family movie night or on busy, happy occasions, like the night you trim your Christmas tree.

You'll also find some great first courses for those occasions when you want to really knock their socks off with a great "starter." Some of these would also make terrific light meals.

## Popcorn

Why a recipe for popcorn? Because popcorn, though carb-y, is a lot more healthful than chips, if—and this is a big "if"—it isn't made with bad fats. Sadly, most people use microwave popcorn these days, and that stuff is usually loaded with hydrogenated oils, turning a reasonably okay snack into a terrible one. Yet since the advent of microwave popcorn, most households don't even have a popcorn popper. You can still get them, though, and if you and your family are popcorn fiends, it would be an excellent investment —especially since bulk popcorn is a whole heckuva lot cheaper than microwave popcorn! (Either an air or oil popper is fine by me. Personally, I think oil-popped corn tastes better, but if people want to use an air-popper I don't have any objections—except that the salt doesn't stick. Unless you butter the popcorn, that is, which kind of does away with the point of using an air popper.)
If you eat popcorn only occasionally and don't want to give up cabinet space to another appliance, you can just pop it the way your ancestors did: in a soup kettle on the stove.

1 tablespoon (5 ml) oil (I'd use coconut, but peanut oil would be fine.)

1/2 cup (4 g) popcorn

Put the oil in the bottom of a fairly deep, heavy soup kettle, and dump in the popcorn. Cover the kettle, put it over high heat, and shake that sucker back and forth till the popping stops. That's it! You can butter it if you like, and salt is *de rigueur*. I find that just this little bit of oil is enough to get the salt to stick to the popped corn, and I'm happy.

**Yield:** About 4 cups (4 g), or 4 servings

**Nutritional Analysis:** Each will have: 85 calories; 6 g fat; 1 g protein; 6 g carbohydrates; 1 g fiber; 5 g usable carbs.

| | | | | | |
|---|---|---|---|---|---|
| Potassium (mg): | 25 mg | Vitamin C (mg): | trace | Thiamin/B1 (mg): | trace |
| Calcium (mg): | 1 mg | Vitamin A (i.u.): | 17 i.u. | Riboflavin/B2 (mg): | trace |
| Iron (mg): | trace | Vitamin B6 (mg): | trace | Folacin (mcg): | 2 |
| Zinc (mg): | trace | Vitamin B12 (mcg): | 0 mcg | Niacin/B3 (mg): | trace |

## Celery Chips

These are a lot of work, and furthermore, they leave you with that fryer oil to dispose of. So I wouldn't have included them if both my husband and I didn't think they were great. If you haven't tried celeriac (also called celery root,) it's a big, knobby, ugly-looking root with bumpy skin. When you peel it, you'll discover that it smells just like celery! (And indeed, it's a relative of celery that is bred for the root, rather than the stalks.) In this recipe, though, the celery flavor vanishes, leaving just brown and crispy chips that are far lower in carbs and calories than potato chips.

1 large celeriac

Peanut oil for frying

Seasoned salt

Peel your celeriac, whack it into chunks, and use a very sharp knife to slice it as paper-thin as you possibly can. (No, you can't use your food processor's slicing blade; the slices will come out too thick. Yes, this is tedious. This is why some of us have a kitchen television.)

Meanwhile, have your oil heating for deep frying. I wouldn't try this without a deep-fat fryer, but if you're brave, you can do it in a big, heavy soup kettle. You'll need a frying thermometer, though. Either way, you want your oil at 375°F (190°C). Get it all the way up to temperature before you start frying!

Add the celeriac in modest batches, and fry for about 7 minutes, or until golden brown. Drain the chips on paper towels, sprinkle with seasoned salt, and stuff in your face. You may just forget about potato chips!

**Yield:** 4 servings

**Nutritional Analysis:** Each will have: 16 calories (of celeriac); fat calories unknown; 1 g protein; 4 g carbohydrates; 1 g fiber; 3 g usable carbs.

| | | | | | |
|---|---|---|---|---|---|
| Potassium (mg): | 117 mg | Vitamin C (mg): | 3 mg | Thiamin/B1 (mg): | trace |
| Calcium (mg): | 17 mg | Vitamin A (i.u.): | 0 | Riboflavin/B2 (mg): | trace |
| Iron (mg): | trace | Vitamin B6 (mg): | 0.1 mg | Folacin (mcg): | 3 mcg |
| Zinc (mg): | trace | Vitamin B12 (mcg): | 0 | Niacin/B3 (mg): | trace |

**Note:** It's impossible to give an accurate calorie count on these, since it's hard to know exactly how much oil they absorb. My fryer didn't lose more than a few tablespoons while making the whole batch, though. But here's the reason these are worth making: 8 ounces of celeriac have 95 calories, 21 grams of carbohydrates, and 4 grams of fiber. In contrast, 8 ounces of potato have 179 calories, 41 grams of very high-impact carbs, and 4 grams of fiber. So you'll save roughly half the calories and the carbs of potato chips, and use healthy oil, to boot.

## Tuna Tapenade

This dip tastes quite sophisticated and is a great source of healthy fats—both fish oils and olive oil. It's filling, too; this would make a good lunch. Just put the dip in one snap-top container, and put cut-up veggies in another.

6 ounces (170 g) chunk light tuna canned in water, drained

1/4 cup (25 g) pitted black olives

1/4 cup (25 g) pitted green olives

2 anchovy fillets

2 tablespoons (18 g) rinsed and drained capers

1 tablespoon (14 ml) lemon juice

1 teaspoon (5 g) Dijon mustard

1/2 teaspoon dried basil

1 pinch pepper

1 clove garlic, peeled and chopped

2 tablespoons (28 ml) olive oil

2 tablespoons (28 g) light mayonnaise

2 tablespoons (20 g) diced red onion

Just assemble everything in your food processor and pulse until the olives are chopped, but not pureed. You want a slightly rough texture.

Serve as a dip with vegetables, fiber crackers, or rye crackers, or stuff into celery or cherry tomatoes for a killer appetizer.

**Yield:** 6 servings

**Nutritional Analysis:** Each will have: 104 calories; 7 g fat; 8 g protein; 2 g carbohydrates; 1 g fiber; 1 g usable carbs.

| | | | | | |
|---|---|---|---|---|---|
| Potassium (mg): | 93 mg | Vitamin C (mg): | 2 mg | Thiamin/B1 (mg): | trace |
| Calcium (mg): | 21 mg | Vitamin A (i.u.): | 75 i.u. | Riboflavin/B2 (mg): | trace |
| Iron (mg): | 1 mg | Vitamin B6 (mg): | 0.1 mg | Folacin (mcg): | 3 mcg |
| Zinc (mg): | trace | Vitamin B12 (mcg): | 0.9 mcg | Niacin/B3 (mg): | 4 mg |

## Ray's No-Mayo Blue Cheese Dip

This is great to serve with crudités at a party.

1/4 cup (60 g) cottage cheese

6 tablespoons (90 g) plain yogurt

1/4 teaspoon Worcestershire sauce

1 clove garlic, peeled and crushed

1/8 teaspoon peanut oil

1/2 teaspoon vinegar

1/2 teaspoon lemon juice

1 teaspoon guar or xanthan

1/4 cup (30 g) blue cheese, crumbled

Put the cottage cheese, yogurt, Worcestershire sauce, garlic, peanut oil, vinegar, lemon juice, and guar or xanthan in your food processor with the S-blade in place, and spin it for about 3 minutes. (Be sure to have the plunger in place, too, or you'll spray it all over the kitchen!)

Add the blue cheese, and spin it again until it's creamy.

Add more xanthan, if the mixture is not thick enough.

**Yield:** 7 fluid ounces (200 ml), or 3 servings

**Nutritional Analysis:** Each will have: 73 calories; 4 g fat; 6 g protein; 2 g carbohydrates; trace fiber; 2 g usable carbs.

| | | | | | |
|---|---|---|---|---|---|
| Potassium (mg): | 99 mg | Vitamin C (mg): | 2 mg | Thiamin/B1 (mg): | trace |
| Calcium (mg): | 102 mg | Vitamin A (i.u.): | 120 i.u. | Riboflavin/B2 (mg): | 0.1 mg |
| Iron (mg): | trace | Vitamin B6 (mg): | trace | Folacin (mcg): | 8 mcg |
| Zinc (mg): | 1 mg | Vitamin B12 (mcg): | 0.4 mcg | Niacin/B3 (mg): | trace |

## Artichoke Crab Dip

If you have the dressing on hand, this is a snap.

1 cup (245 g) plain yogurt

1 cup (240 ml) More-than-Ranch Dressing (see page 221)

14 ounces (390 g) canned artichoke hearts, drained and chopped fairly fine

1/4 green bell pepper, minced

6 ounces (170 g) canned crabmeat, drained and flaked

Just mix everything together, and serve with cut-up vegetables.

**Yield:** 4 cups (905 g), or 12 servings

**Nutritional Analysis:** Each will have: 63 calories; 3 g fat; 6 g protein; 4 g carbohydrates; trace fiber; 4 g usable carbs.

| | | | | | |
|---|---|---|---|---|---|
| Potassium (mg): | 113 mg | Vitamin C (mg): | 4 mg | Thiamin/B1 (mg): | trace |
| Calcium (mg): | 61 mg | Vitamin A (i.u.): | 92 i.u. | Riboflavin/B2 (mg): | 0.1 mg |
| Iron (mg): | trace | Vitamin B6 (mg): | trace | Folacin (mcg): | 10 mcg |
| Zinc (mg): | 1 mg | Vitamin B12 (mcg): | 0.2 mcg | Niacin/B3 (mg): | trace |

## Chili Dip

This easy dip is good to put out with vegetables before dinner. It's not terribly hot, so the kids should like it, too.

1/2 cup (125 g) plain yogurt

1/2 cup (115 g) light sour cream

2 teaspoons (2.5 g) dried basil

1 teaspoon paprika

1 teaspoon chili powder

4 teaspoons (20 g) no-sugar-added ketchup

1/2 teaspoon salt

2 cloves garlic, peeled and crushed

Just mix everything together well, and chill. Serve with cut-up vegetables.

**Yield:** 1 cup (225 g), or 8 servings

**Nutritional Analysis:** Each will have: 19 calories; 1 g fat; 1 g protein; 2 g carbohydrates; trace fiber; 2 g usable carbs.

| | | | | | |
|---|---|---|---|---|---|
| Potassium (mg): | 52 mg | Vitamin C (mg): | 1 mg | Thiamin/B1 (mg): | trace |
| Calcium (mg): | 36 mg | Vitamin A (i.u.): | 381 i.u. | Riboflavin/B2 (mg): | trace |
| Iron (mg): | trace | Vitamin B6 (mg): | trace | Folacin (mcg): | 3 mcg |
| Zinc (mg): | trace | Vitamin B12 (mcg): | 0.1 mcg | Niacin/B3 (mg): | trace |

## Spinach Dip

This perennial favorite is highly nutritious—look at those numbers!

10 ounces (280 g) frozen chopped spinach, thawed and drained

1 cup (225 g) creamed cottage cheese

1/4 cup (15 g) chopped parsley

1/3 cup (80 g) light mayonnaise

1 tablespoon (15 g) prepared horseradish

2 tablespoons (20 g) diced red onion

2 tablespoons (28 ml) lemon juice

Salt and pepper

Easy! Just put everything in your food processor with the S-blade in place, and run until the lumps are gone from the cottage cheese. Serve with cut-up vegetables for dipping.

**Yield:** 2 cups (455 g), or 8 servings

**Nutritional Analysis:** Each will have: 62 calories; 3 g fat; 4 g protein; 5 g carbohydrates; 1 g fiber; 4 g usable carbs.

| | | | | | |
|---|---|---|---|---|---|
| Potassium (mg): | 189 mg | Vitamin C (mg): | 13 mg | Thiamin/B1 (mg): | trace |
| Calcium (mg): | 59 mg | Vitamin A (i.u.): | 2890 i.u. | Riboflavin/B2 (mg): | 0.1 mg |
| Iron (mg): | 1 mg | Vitamin B6 (mg): | 0.1 mg | Folacin (mcg): | 50 mcg |
| Zinc (mg): | trace | Vitamin B12 (mcg): | 0.2 mcg | Niacin/B3 (mg): | trace |

## Smoked Salmon Spread

Put this on a cracker, and you'll forget about the cracker.

5 ounces (140 g) light cream cheese

1/2 cup (220 g) Fromage Blanc (see page 494)

1 tablespoon (15 g) prepared horseradish

2 tablespoons (30 g) light sour cream

1 tablespoon (14 ml) lemon juice

5 ounces (140 g) smoked salmon, finely chopped

Salt and pepper

1 tablespoon (4 g) minced fresh parsley

This is easiest to do in your food processor. With the S-blade in place, put the cream cheese, Fromage Blanc, horseradish, sour cream, and lemon juice in the bowl. Run till everything's well combined. Spoon out into a bowl.

Add the smoked salmon, and use a fork to mash it into the cheese mixture until it's flaked, but still has a bit of texture. Stir in salt and pepper to taste. Smooth the top, and sprinkle the parsley over it. Serve with rye crackers, fiber crackers, celery sticks, or all of the above.

**Yield:** 3 servings

**Nutritional Analysis:** Each will have: 227 calories; 13 g fat; 19 g protein; 7 g carbohydrates; trace fiber; 7 g usable carbs.

| Potassium (mg): | 234 mg | Vitamin C (mg): | 3 mg | Thiamin/B1 (mg): | trace |
|---|---|---|---|---|---|
| Calcium (mg): | 302 mg | Vitamin A (i.u.): | 637 i.u. | Riboflavin/B2 (mg): | 0.3 mg |
| Iron (mg): | 1 mg | Vitamin B6 (mg): | 0.1 mg | Folacin (mcg): | 21 mcg |
| Zinc (mg): | 2 mg | Vitamin B12 (mcg): | 1.4 mcg | Niacin/B3 (mg): | 1 mg |

## Basil Boursin

Easy, delicious, and pretty. This is a party food that makes great leftovers, either as lunch with a bag of celery or as the filling for an omelet at breakfast.

4 ounces (115 g) light cream cheese

15 ounces (420 g) part-skim ricotta cheese

3 cloves garlic, peeled

2/3 cup (40 g) chopped fresh basil

1/3 cup (20 g) chopped fresh parsley

2 scallions, root and the limp part of the green removed, cut into 1/2-inch (1.25-cm) sections

12 kalamata olives, pitted

Salt

Put the cream and ricotta cheeses in your food processor, with the S-blade in place. Throw the garlic in, too. Run the processor until the whole thing is very, very smooth.

Turn off the processor, and add the basil, parsley, and scallions. Run again until the herbs are so finely chopped that the whole thing takes on a delicate pale green color. Turn the processor off.

Add the olives, and pulse only as many times as is needed to chop the olives fairly fine but leave bits of olive intact. Add salt to taste, pulsing briefly to mix, and serve with fiber crackers or vegetables.

**Yield:** 10 servings

**Nutritional Analysis:** Each will have: 101 calories; 7 g fat; 6 g protein; 4 g carbohydrates; trace fiber; 4 g usable carbs.

| Potassium (mg): | 103 mg | Vitamin C (mg): | 4 mg | Thiamin/B1 (mg): | trace |
|---|---|---|---|---|---|
| Calcium (mg): | 142 mg | Vitamin A (i.u.): | 490 i.u. | Riboflavin/B2 (mg): | 0.1 mg |
| Iron (mg): | 1 mg | Vitamin B6 (mg): | trace | Folacin (mcg): | 14 mcg |
| Zinc (mg): | 1 mg | Vitamin B12 (mcg): | 0.2 mcg | Niacin/B3 (mg): | trace |

## Pesto Dip

Practically instant to make, and easy to clean up!

$^1/_2$ cup (115 g) cottage cheese

$^1/_2$ cup (115 g) light sour cream

$^1/_4$ cup (60 ml) jarred pesto sauce

Put the cottage cheese and sour cream in your food processor with the S-blade in place, and run till the mixture's very smooth. Transfer to a bowl, swirl in the pesto, and serve with cut-up vegetables.

**Yield:** 5 servings

**Nutritional Analysis:** Each will have: 89 calories; 7 g fat; 6 g protein; 3 g carbohydrates; trace fiber; 3 g usable carbs.

| | | | | | |
|---|---|---|---|---|---|
| Potassium (mg): | 62 mg | Vitamin C (mg): | 1 mg | Thiamin/B1 (mg): | trace |
| Calcium (mg): | 106 mg | Vitamin A (i.u.): | 140 i.u. | Riboflavin/B2 (mg): | 0.1 mg |
| Iron (mg): | 1 mg | Vitamin B6 (mg): | trace | Folacin (mcg): | 6 mcg |
| Zinc (mg): | trace | Vitamin B12 (mcg): | 0.2 mcg | Niacin/B3 (mg): | trace |

## Green Bean Parmesan Dip

This is a surprisingly good flavor combination, and it's very quick and easy to make.

28 ounces (785 g) canned green beans, drained

$^1/_4$ cup (55 g) light mayonnaise

$^1/_3$ cup (35 g) grated Parmesan cheese

2 teaspoons (2 g) dried basil

Salt and pepper

Drain the green beans very well, and dump 'em in your food processor with the S-blade in place. Add the mayonnaise, cheese, and basil, and pulse until the beans are pureed. Taste it, and decide whether you want to add some salt and pepper. If so, add them, and pulse again to mix.

Chill for several hours to let the flavors blend, then bring the dip back to room temperature and serve with vegetables, fiber crackers, rye crackers, or whole wheat pita chips.

**Yield:** 8 servings

**Nutritional Analysis:** Each will have: 53 calories; 3 g fat; 3 g protein; 6 g carbohydrates; 2 g fiber; 4 g usable carbs.

| | | | | | |
|---|---|---|---|---|---|
| Potassium (mg): | 125 mg | Vitamin C (mg): | 5 mg | Thiamin/B1 (mg): | trace |
| Calcium (mg): | 80 mg | Vitamin A (i.u.): | 405 i.u. | Riboflavin/B2 (mg): | 0.1 mg |
| Iron (mg): | 1 mg | Vitamin B6 (mg): | trace | Folacin (mcg): | 33 mcg |
| Zinc (mg): | trace | Vitamin B12 (mcg): | trace | Niacin/B3 (mg): | trace |

# Molded Crab Spread

A molded spread always adds panache to the appetizer table, and this one tastes as good as it looks.

- 4 teaspoons (9 g) unflavored gelatin
- 1/4 cup (60 ml) cold water
- 8 ounces (225 g) Neufchâtel cheese or light cream cheese, softened
- 8 ounces (225 g) creamed cottage cheese
- 2 tablespoons (28 ml) dry sherry
- 1/2 teaspoon seasoned salt
- 12 ounces (340 g) canned crabmeat, well-drained and flaked
- 1 jar (2 ounces, or 55 g) pimientos, drained
- 1/4 cup (25 g) scallions, finely minced
- 1/3 cup (40 g) celery, finely minced
- 1/4 cup (15 g) chopped fresh parsley

Sprinkle the gelatin over the water in a small saucepan, and let it sit and soften for 5 minutes. Move the gelatin and water to a burner set on low until the gelatin is completely dissolved. Remove from the heat.

Put the softened Neufchâtel or light cream cheese and cottage cheese in your blender, or in your food processor with the S-blade in place. Add the sherry and the seasoned salt. Turn on the blender or food processor and combine, stopping to scrape down the sides of the container as needed, until the mixture is very smooth. Pour in the gelatin, and process for another minute or so, again scraping down the sides to make sure everything is evenly combined. Pour into a mixing bowl.

Now stir in the crab, pimientos, scallion, celery, and half of the parsley. Combine everything well.

Spray a 4-cup (945-ml) mold really well with nonstick cooking spray. Pour in the crab-and-cheese mixture, and refrigerate for at least 5 hours or until firmly set.

To unmold, dip the mold briefly into tepid water and run the tip of a knife around the edge. Put a plate over it, invert, and lift off the mold. Sprinkle with the remaining parsley, and serve with whole grain crackers, celery, or cut-up peppers. Or you could cut the spread into slices and serve it on a bed of lettuce.

**Yield:** 24 servings

**Nutritional Analysis:** Each will have: 54 calories; 3 g fat; 5 g protein; 2 g carbohydrates; trace fiber; 2 g usable carbs.

| | | | | | |
|---|---|---|---|---|---|
| Potassium (mg): | 87 mg | Vitamin C (mg): | 4 mg | Thiamin/B1 (mg): | trace |
| Calcium (mg): | 30 mg | Vitamin A (i.u.): | 225 i.u. | Riboflavin/B2 (mg): | trace |
| Iron (mg): | trace | Vitamin B6 (mg): | trace | Folacin (mcg): | 10 mcg |
| Zinc (mg): | 1 mg | Vitamin B12 (mcg): | 0.1 mcg | Niacin/B3 (mg): | trace |

## Mexican Crab Dip

Feel free to kick the hotness of this dish up or down a notch by using more or less hot sauce—or hotter or milder hot sauce, for that matter. Julie, who tested this recipe, says the crab claw meat has more flavor than other canned crab.

8 ounces (225 g) Neufchâtel cheese or light cream cheese, softened

8 ounces (225 g) creamed cottage cheese

6 ounces (170 g) canned crab claw meat, well drained and flaked

1/2 cup (115 g) chunky salsa

2 tablespoons (5 g) minced fresh cilantro

1 teaspoon (3 g) cumin powder

1/4 teaspoon salt

1 tablespoon (14 ml) hot sauce

Combine the Neufchâtel and cottage cheeses in your food processor with the S-blade in place, and process till smooth. Scrape into a mixing bowl.

Add the crab, salsa, cilantro, cumin, and salt to the bowl. Mix until well blended. Add the hot sauce to taste, and serve with vegetables for dipping.

**Yield:** 12 servings

**Nutritional Analysis:** Each will have: 84 calories; 5 g fat; 7 g protein; 2 g carbohydrates; trace fiber; 2 g usable carbs.

| | | | | | |
|---|---|---|---|---|---|
| Potassium (mg): | 393 mg | Vitamin C (mg): | 3 mg | Thiamin/B1 (mg): | trace |
| Calcium (mg): | 95 mg | Vitamin A (i.u.): | 330 i.u. | Riboflavin/B2 (mg): | 0.1 mg |
| Iron (mg): | trace | Vitamin B6 (mg): | 0.1 mg | Folacin (mcg): | 13 mcg |
| Zinc (mg): | 1 mg | Vitamin B12 (mcg): | 1.4 mcg | Niacin/B3 (mg): | 1 mg |

## Herbed Shrimp Dip

1 pound cooked shrimp, peeled and deveined, with tails removed

2 scallions

2 tablespoons (20 g) chopped onion

1/2 clove garlic, peeled and crushed

2 tablespoons (8 g) chopped fresh basil

2/3 cup (150 g) light mayonnaise

2/3 cup (155 g) light sour cream

2/3 cup (165 g) plain yogurt, with any whey poured off

1/2 teaspoon Worcestershire sauce

1/2 teaspoon Tabasco sauce or Louisiana Hot Sauce

Drain any excess water from the shrimp, then put them in your food processor with the S-blade in place.

Cut the roots and the soft part of the green shoot off the scallions; you want to keep the crisp part! Whack each trimmed scallion into 2 or 3 pieces, and throw them into the food processor, too. Add the onion, garlic, basil, mayo, sour cream, yogurt, Worcestershire sauce, and hot sauce.

Pulse the processor until the shrimp are finely chopped. Transfer to a pretty serving bowl, cover with plastic wrap, and chill for at least 3 hours before serving. Serve with cut-up vegetables.

**Yield:** 12 servings

**Nutritional Analysis:** Each will have: 83 calories; 4 g fat; 9 g protein; 3 g carbohydrates; trace fiber; 3 g usable carbs.

1/4 teaspoon pepper

1/4 teaspoon nutmeg

1/2 cup (40 g) shredded Parmesan cheese

Preheat the oven to 325°F (170°C, or gas mark 3). Spray a 5-cup (1175-ml) casserole with nonstick cooking spray.

Cut the potato into small chunks, and put 'em in a microwaveable casserole with a lid. Add a couple of tablespoons (30 ml or so) of water, cover, and nuke on high for 2 minutes.

While that's happening, trim the bottom of the stem and leaves off the cauliflower. Whack the cauliflower into small chunks, too, including the stem.

When the microwave beeps, add the cauliflower to the potato in the casserole, re-cover, and nuke for another 8 minutes, or until the cauliflower is tender.

While that's cooking, dump your thawed spinach into a strainer. Press it with the back of a spoon or pick it up with clean hands and squeeze it; either way, get as much water out of it as you can.

When the cauliflower and potatoes are done, pull 'em out of the microwave, drain 'em, and use your blender, food processor, or a hand blender to puree them together. Dump the puree into the prepared casserole.

Add the butter, milk, and cream, and stir them in thoroughly. Now stir in the drained spinach, along with the salt, pepper, and nutmeg. Smooth the top, and sprinkle with the Parmesan.

Bake for 25 to 30 minutes.

**Yield:** 5 servings

**Nutritional Analysis:** Each will have: 139 calories; 8 g fat; 7 g protein; 12 g carbohydrates; 4 g fiber; 8 g usable carbs.

| | | | | | |
|---|---|---|---|---|---|
| Potassium (mg): | 561 mg | Vitamin C (mg): | 47 mg | Thiamin/B1 (mg): | 0.1 mg |
| Calcium (mg): | 187 mg | Vitamin A (i.u.): | 4667 i.u. | Riboflavin/B2 (mg): | 0.2 mg |
| Iron (mg): | 2 mg | Vitamin B6 (mg): | 0.3 mg | Folacin (mcg): | 106 mcg |
| Zinc (mg): | 1 mg | Vitamin B12 (mcg): | 0.1 mcg | Niacin/B3 (mg): | 1 mg |

## Garlic Lemon "Rice"

This is especially good with poultry.

- 1/2 head cauliflower
- 1 1/2 teaspoons (7 g) butter
- 6 cloves garlic, peeled and minced
- 1/2 cup (120 ml) dry white wine
- 1 tablespoon (14 ml) lemon juice
- 1 teaspoon chicken bouillon concentrate
- 2/3 cup (110 g) cooked wild rice
- 1/4 teaspoon pepper
- 1/2 cup (30 g) chopped fresh parsley

Trim the bottom of the cauliflower stem, and cut off the leaves. Run the cauliflower through the shredding blade of your food processor. Put the resulting "cauli-rice" in a microwaveable casserole with a lid, add a few tablespoons (30 ml or so) of water, and cover. Nuke on high for 6 minutes.

Give a big, heavy skillet a shot of nonstick cooking spray, and put it over low heat. Add the butter, let it melt, then throw in the garlic. Let the garlic cook very slowly in the butter for 5 minutes.

Somewhere in here, the microwave will beep. Uncover the cauliflower right away, to prevent overcooking.

When you've stewed the garlic in the butter for 5 minutes, add the wine and lemon juice. Turn the burner up to medium and let the whole thing simmer for 10 minutes or so, till the liquid is reduced to about one-third of its original volume. Stir in the bouillon concentrate.

Now add the cauli-rice and wild rice, and stir everything together to combine very well. Stir in the pepper and parsley, and serve.

**Yield:** 5 servings

**Nutritional Analysis:** Each will have: 72 calories; 1 g fat; 3 g protein; 10 g carbohydrates; 2 g fiber; 8 g usable carbs.

| | | | | | |
|---|---|---|---|---|---|
| Potassium (mg): | 270 mg | Vitamin C (mg): | 37 mg | Thiamin/B1 (mg): | trace |
| Calcium (mg): | 32 mg | Vitamin A (i.u.): | 369 i.u. | Riboflavin/B2 (mg): | 0.1 mg |
| Iron (mg): | 1 mg | Vitamin B6 (mg): | 0.2 mg | Folacin (mcg): | 48 mcg |
| Zinc (mg): | 1 mg | Vitamin B12 (mcg): | trace | Niacin/B3 (mg): | 1 mg |

# Pecan Rice

This beautiful dish is fabulous with a simple broiled steak.

- 1/4 cup (25 g) chopped pecans
- 1/2 head cauliflower
- 1/4 cup (60 ml) dry white wine
- 1 teaspoon beef bouillon concentrate
- 2/3 cup (110 g) wild rice, cooked
- 1/2 cup (65 g) frozen peas, thawed
- 1/4 cup (15 g) chopped fresh parsley
- 6 scallions, thinly sliced
- 1/4 teaspoon pepper

Preheat your oven to 350°F (180°C, or gas mark 4) while you chop your pecans. Spread them in a shallow baking tin, put them in the oven, and set a timer for 10 minutes. (If you have a toaster oven, it's ideal for this.)

Meanwhile, run the cauliflower through the shredding blade of your food processor. Put the resulting "cauli-rice" in a microwaveable casserole with a lid, add a couple of tablespoons (30 ml or so) of water, cover, and nuke on high for 6 minutes.

Put the wine in a big saucepan or a skillet over medium heat; you want to cook it down by about half.

As soon as the microwave beeps, uncover your cauliflower so it doesn't turn to mush. When the wine is cooked down to about half its volume, stir in the bouillon concentrate. When that's dissolved, drain the cauliflower and throw it in with the wine. Add the wild rice and peas, and stir everything together to combine well.

Stir in the parsley, scallions, toasted pecans, and pepper, and serve.

**Yield:** 6 servings

**Nutritional Analysis:** Each will have: 86 calories; 4 g fat; 3 g protein; 10 g carbohydrates; 3 g fiber; 7 g usable carbs.

| | | | | | |
|---|---|---|---|---|---|
| Potassium (mg): | 267 mg | Vitamin C (mg): | 31 mg | Thiamin/B1 (mg): | 0.1 mg |
| Calcium (mg): | 31 mg | Vitamin A (i.u.): | 291 i.u. | Riboflavin/B2 (mg): | 0.1 mg |
| Iron (mg): | 1 mg | Vitamin B6 (mg): | 0.2 mg | Folacin (mcg): | 54 mcg |
| Zinc (mg): | 1 mg | Vitamin B12 (mcg): | trace | Niacin/B3 (mg): | 1 mg |

# Curried Currant "Rice"

Bright yellow, with the dark currants. Pretty!

- 1/2 head cauliflower
- 3 tablespoons (20 g) dried currants
- 1 tablespoon (14 ml) boiling water
- 2 teaspoons (10 g) butter
- 1 small onion, chopped
- 1 teaspoon curry powder
- 1/2 teaspoon turmeric
- 1/2 teaspoon finely minced garlic
- Salt and pepper

Trim the leaves and the bottom of the cauliflower stem, and run the rest through the shredding blade of your food processor. Put the "cauli-rice" in a microwaveable casserole with a lid, add a couple of tablespoons (30 ml or so) of water, cover, and nuke it on high for 6 minutes.

While that's nuking, take a look at your currants. If they're soft and pliable, they're ready to use. If they're dried out and hard, put them in a little dish and pour the boiling water over them. Let them sit and "puff" for a few minutes.

Spray a big, heavy skillet with nonstick cooking spray, and put it over medium heat. Add the butter, let it melt, and start sautéing the onion.

When the onion's translucent, add the curry powder, turmeric, and garlic. Turn the burner down to medium-low, stir the seasonings into the onion, and let the whole thing cook for another minute or two.

By now the cauliflower should be done. Drain it, and add it to the skillet. Stir the onions and seasonings into the cauliflower till it's all well combined. Now stir in the currants, add salt and pepper to taste, and serve.

**Yield:** 3 servings

**Nutritional Analysis:** Each will have: 90 calories; 3 g fat; 3 g protein; 16 g carbohydrates; 4 g fiber; 12 g usable carbs.

| | | | | | |
|---|---|---|---|---|---|
| Potassium (mg): | 451 mg | Vitamin C (mg): | 48 mg | Thiamin/B1 (mg): | 0.1 mg |
| Calcium (mg): | 42 mg | Vitamin A (i.u.): | 128 i.u. | Riboflavin/B2 (mg): | 0.1 mg |
| Iron (mg): | 1 mg | Vitamin B6 (mg): | 0.3 mg | Folacin (mcg): | 64 mcg |
| Zinc (mg): | trace | Vitamin B12 (mcg): | trace | Niacin/B3 (mg): | 1 mg |

## Spicy Lime-Cilantro "Rice"

I made this up when I found hot Hungarian wax peppers at my local farmer's market, but any hot-but-not-too-hot pepper will do. (Anaheims are widely available, and they're probably closest to Hungarian wax peppers for heat.) This would be good with any Mexican or Tex-Mex main dish.

1 head cauliflower

3 Hungarian wax peppers (or Anaheims)

1 tablespoon (14 ml) olive oil

2 teaspoons (5 g) chicken bouillon concentrate

1 tablespoon (14 ml) lime juice

1/2 cup (30 g) chopped fresh cilantro

5 scallions, sliced, including the crisp part of the green

Trim the leaves and the bottom of the cauliflower stem. Run the cauliflower through the shredding blade of your food processor. Put the resulting "cauli-rice" in a big microwaveable casserole with a lid, add a couple of tablespoons (30 ml or so) of water, cover, and nuke on high for 8 minutes.

Meanwhile, slice the peppers in half lengthwise, remove the cores and seeds, and slice 'em thin, crosswise.

Spray your biggest skillet with nonstick cooking spray, and put it over medium-high heat. Add the olive oil, then throw in the peppers, and sauté them till they're just starting to soften.

By now the microwave has beeped! Uncover the cauliflower, drain, and add to the sautéed peppers. Stir them together.

Add the bouillon concentrate and lime juice, and stir till the bouillon has dissolved and everything is evenly flavored. Stir in the cilantro and scallions, cook for just another minute, and serve.

**Yield:** 8 servings

**Nutritional Analysis:** Each will have: 41 calories; 2 g fat; 2 g protein; 5 g carbohydrates; 2 g fiber; 3 g usable carbs.

| | | | | | |
|---|---|---|---|---|---|
| Potassium (mg): | 273 mg | Vitamin C (mg): | 45 mg | Thiamin/B1 (mg): | trace |
| Calcium (mg): | 26 mg | Vitamin A (i.u.): | 132 i.u. | Riboflavin/B2 (mg): | 0.1 mg |
| Iron (mg): | 1 mg | Vitamin B6 (mg): | 0.2 mg | Folacin (mcg): | 53 mcg |
| Zinc (mg): | trace | Vitamin B12 (mcg): | 0 mcg | Niacin/B3 (mg): | 1 mg |

# Currant-Pine Nut "Pilaff"

If you cook the wild rice ahead and keep it ready in the fridge, this elegant side dish takes a big 15 minutes to throw together.

1/2 head cauliflower
1 small onion, chopped
1/2 tablespoon (7 ml) olive oil
1/2 tablespoon (7 g) butter
3 tablespoons (20 g) dried currants
2 cloves garlic, peeled and minced
3/4 cup (125 g) cooked wild rice
2 1/2 teaspoons (6 g) chicken bouillon concentrate
1/4 teaspoon pepper
1/4 cup (35 g) toasted pine nuts (pignolia)
1/4 cup (15 g) minced fresh parsley

Trim the leaves and the bottom of the cauliflower stem. Run the cauliflower through the shredding blade of your food processor. Put the shredded cauliflower in a microwaveable casserole with a lid, add a couple of tablespoons (30 ml or so) of water, cover, and nuke on high for 7 minutes.

While that's happening, put a big skillet over medium-low heat and start sautéing the chopped onion in the oil and butter. If the currants are dried out and hard, put 'em in a dish, add just enough boiling water to cover, and let them sit while you're sautéing the onion.

When the onion's limp and translucent and the cauliflower's done, add the cauliflower to the skillet. (Don't drain it first; that water's going to dissolve your chicken bouillon concentrate.) Add the garlic, wild rice, bouillon concentrate, and pepper, and stir everything well until the bouillon is dissolved. Drain the currants and stir them in, too, along with the pine nuts and parsley, and serve.

**Yield:** 4 servings

**Nutritional Analysis:** Each will have: 162 calories; 8 g fat; 6 g protein; 20 g carbohydrates; 4 g fiber; 16 g usable carbs.

| | | | | | |
|---|---|---|---|---|---|
| Potassium (mg): | 436 mg | Vitamin C (mg): | 41 mg | Thiamin/B1 (mg): | 0.1 mg |
| Calcium (mg): | 41 mg | Vitamin A (i.u.): | 277 i.u. | Riboflavin/B2 (mg): | 0.1 mg |
| Iron (mg): | 2 mg | Vitamin B6 (mg): | 0.3 mg | Folacin (mcg): | 66 mcg |
| Zinc (mg): | 1 mg | Vitamin B12 (mcg): | trace | Niacin/B3 (mg): | 1 mg |

## Wild Rice Vegetable Medley

This is colorful, what with the white cauliflower, the dark brown wild rice, and the carrot and pepper. It really dresses up a simple chop or steak.

1 cup (165 g) cooked wild rice
1/2 head cauliflower
1 medium carrot
1 medium onion
1 medium green bell pepper
2 tablespoons (28 ml) olive oil
8 ounces (225 g) sliced portobello mushrooms
2 teaspoons (5 g) beef bouillon concentrate
1/4 teaspoon pepper

If your wild rice isn't already cooked, you'll need to do that first, and it'll take about an hour. Since it's fairly time-consuming, you may as well make up a whole bunch and refrigerate the leftovers for another day. My brown rice comes in 4-ounce packages; I combine the whole thing in a heavy saucepan with 2 1/2 cups (570 ml) of water. Cover and set over a low burner until all the water is absorbed—this will take 60 to 90 minutes.

Trim the leaves and the bottom of the cauliflower stem, and run it through the shredding blade of your food processor. Put the resulting "cauli-rice" in a microwaveable casserole with a lid, add a couple of tablespoons (30 ml or so) of water, cover, and nuke on high for 7 minutes. Keep in mind that you'll want to uncover it right away when the microwave beeps, even if you're not ready to add it to everything else yet, or it'll get mushy on you.

Run the carrot through the shredding blade, while it's handy. Now swap it out for your S-blade, and chop the onion and the pepper together till they're a medium consistency.

Heat the olive oil in your big, heavy skillet over medium-high heat, and add the carrot, onion, and pepper. Dump in the sliced mushrooms, too. Sauté everything together until the mushrooms have changed color and softened and the onion's soft, too. Now drain the cauli-rice and add it to the skillet, along with the wild rice. Finally, stir in the beef bouillon concentrate, and keep stirring till it's dissolved and evenly distributed. Add pepper to taste, then serve.

**Yield:** 4 servings

**Nutritional Analysis:** Each will have: 162 calories; 7 g fat; 5 g protein; 21 g carbohydrates; 5 g fiber; 16 g usable carbs.

| | | | | | |
|---|---|---|---|---|---|
| Potassium (mg): | 627 mg | Vitamin C (mg): | 65 mg | Thiamin/B1 (mg): | 0.2 mg |
| Calcium (mg): | 34 mg | Vitamin A (i.u.): | 5265 i.u. | Riboflavin/B2 (mg): | 0.4 mg |
| Iron (mg): | 2 mg | Vitamin B6 (mg): | 0.4 mg | Folacin (mcg): | 78 mcg |
| Zinc (mg): | 1 mg | Vitamin B12 (mcg): | trace | Niacin/B3 (mg): | 4 mg |

**Note:** My grocery store carries little portobellos—the size of the familiar button mushrooms—both whole and sliced. If yours does, too, buy 'em already sliced! If all you can get are the big portobellos, 3 to 4 inches (7.5 to 10 cm) across, just slice 'em into strips, then cut the strips into shorter pieces.

## Mushroom Herb "Rice"

This is a bit like Rice-a-Roni, only tastier, lower-carb, lower-calorie, more nutritious, and faster to make!

1/2 head cauliflower
1 1/2 tablespoons (21 g) butter
1 1/2 tablespoons (21 ml) olive oil
4 ounces (115 g) sliced mushrooms, chopped into small pieces
1/2 small onion, chopped
1/2 cup (120 ml) chicken broth
1 1/2 teaspoons poultry seasoning
1/4 cup (15 g) minced parsley
Salt and pepper

Trim the leaves and the bottom of the cauliflower stem. Run the cauliflower through the shredding blade of your food processor. Put it in a microwaveable casserole with a lid, add a couple of tablespoons (30 ml or so) of water, and cover. Microwave on high for 7 minutes.

While that's cooking, heat the butter and olive oil together in a big heavy skillet over medium-high heat. Add the mushrooms and onion. Sauté until the onion is translucent and the mushrooms soften and change color. Stir in the chicken broth and poultry seasoning. Turn the burner up to boil the broth hard.

Somewhere in here your microwave is going to beep—make sure you uncover the cauliflower right away, or it'll turn into mush!

When the liquid in the skillet is getting syrupy, stir in the cauliflower and the parsley, combining everything well. Add salt and pepper to taste, and serve.

**Yield:** 4 servings

**Nutritional Analysis:** Each will have: 121 calories; 10 g fat; 3 g protein; 7 g carbohydrates; 3 g fiber; 4 g usable carbs.

| | | | | | |
|---|---|---|---|---|---|
| Potassium (mg): | 395 mg | Vitamin C (mg): | 40 mg | Thiamin/B1 (mg): | 0.1 mg |
| Calcium (mg): | 32 mg | Vitamin A (i.u.): | 383 i.u. | Riboflavin/B2 (mg): | 0.2 mg |
| Iron (mg): | 1 mg | Vitamin B6 (mg): | 0.2 mg | Folacin (mcg): | 57 mcg |
| Zinc (mg): | 1 mg | Vitamin B12 (mcg): | trace | Niacin/B3 (mg) | 2 mg |

# Cauliflower with Anchovy Butter

This is easy, and my anchovy-loving husband gave it top honors. I liked it quite well myself, despite being less of a fan of the little salty fishies.

1 head cauliflower

4 tablespoons (60 g) butter

5 anchovy fillets

Salt and pepper

Trim the leaves and the bottom of the cauliflower stem. Chop the cauliflower into biggish chunks. Put 'em in a microwaveable casserole with a lid, add a couple of tablespoons (30 ml or so) of water, cover, and nuke on high for 8 minutes.

While the cauliflower cooks, melt the butter in a small skillet over lowish heat. Chop the anchovy fillets, then stir 'em into the butter, and sauté until they've pretty much dissolved.

When the cauliflower is done, drain it and put it in a bowl. Pour on the anchovy butter. Toss to coat, salt and pepper to taste, and serve.

**Yield:** 6 servings

**Nutritional Analysis:** Each will have: 99 calories; 8 g fat; 3 g protein; 5 g carbohydrates; 2 g fiber; 3 g usable carbs.

| | | | | | |
|---|---|---|---|---|---|
| Potassium (mg): | 311 mg | Vitamin C (mg): | 44 mg | Thiamin/B1 (mg): | 0.1 mg |
| Calcium (mg): | 31 mg | Vitamin A (i.u.): | 310 i.u. | Riboflavin/B2 (mg): | 0.1 mg |
| Iron (mg): | 1 mg | Vitamin B6 (mg): | 0.2 mg | Folacin (mcg): | 55 mcg |
| Zinc (mg): | trace | Vitamin B12 (mcg): | trace | Niacin/B3 (mg): | 1 mg |

# Asian "Noodles"

Not only is spaghetti squash lower in carbs and lower in calories than real noodles, it has more vitamins, too. But if you can afford the carbs and calories, you could use this same seasoning mixture with cooked soba (Japanese buckwheat noodles).

1 medium spaghetti squash, cooked

2 tablespoons (28 ml) soy sauce

1 1/2 tablespoons (21 ml) dark sesame oil

1 tablespoon (14 ml) rice vinegar

1 1/2 teaspoons (.75 g) Splenda

1/2 teaspoon chili garlic paste

1/4 cup (25 g) sliced green onions

2 tablespoons (15 g) toasted sesame seeds

1 teaspoon grated gingerroot

The easiest way to cook the spaghetti squash is to stab it all over with a fork, then throw it in the microwave on high for 12 minutes. When it's done, let it cool till you can handle it without burning your fingers. Whack it in half the long way, and scoop out and discard the seeds. Then take a fork and scrape the flesh; it will separate into strands that look like spaghetti. Scrape all of the flesh out of your squash, and put it in a bowl.

Add the soy sauce, oil, vinegar, Splenda, garlic paste, onions, sesame seeds, and gingerroot to the bowl. Toss till everything's well combined. You can serve this hot or chilled.

**Yield:** 4 servings

**Nutritional Analysis:** Each will have: 84 calories; 7 g fat; 1 g protein; 5 g carbohydrates; 1 g fiber; 4 g usable carbs.

| | | | | | |
|---|---|---|---|---|---|
| Potassium (mg): | 82 mg | Vitamin C (mg): | 2 mg | Thiamin/B1 (mg): | trace |
| Calcium (mg): | 17 mg | Vitamin A (i.u.): | 38 i.u. | Riboflavin/B2 (mg): | trace |
| Iron (mg): | 1 mg | Vitamin B6 (mg): | 0.1 mg | Folacin (mcg): | 12 mcg |
| Zinc (mg): | 1 mg | Vitamin B12 (mcg): | 0 mcg | Niacin/B3 (mg): | 1 mg |

## Kim's Stuffing

This is my sister's recipe, and she says it's just exactly enough stuffing for a 13-pound turkey, which happened to be the size she was cooking the day she wrote down all the ingredient amounts. You can easily double it for a monster-size bird. Kim also says to feel free to play with this recipe—she usually just "plays it by ear," and it comes out fine.

- 8 slices whole grain low-carb bread (or 100% whole grain, if you can afford the carbs)
- 3 1/2 tablespoons (50 g) butter
- 3 big celery ribs, diced
- 1 medium onion, diced
- 8 ounces (225 g) sliced mushrooms
- 1/4 to 3/4 cup (60 to 175 ml) chicken broth (you'll need less if you cook it inside your turkey, more if you like it very damp or plan to cook it in a casserole)
- 1 pound (455 g) turkey sausage
- 1 1/2 tablespoons (13.5 g) poultry seasoning

If you're cooking your stuffing outside of your turkey, preheat the oven to 350°F (180°C, or gas mark 4).

Tear the bread into little pieces, and put it in a big mixing bowl.

Spray your big, heavy skillet with nonstick cooking spray, and put it over medium heat. Add 1 1/2 tablespoons (21 g) of the butter, and start sautéing the onion and celery. When they're soft, add them to the bowl with the bread.

Put your skillet back over medium heat, and melt the remaining butter. Dump in the mushrooms, and sauté them for 5 minutes or so. They'll soak up all the butter, and you'll think you should add more. Don't! Add the chicken broth, instead. Cover the skillet and let the mushrooms simmer in the broth for another 5 minutes, then add them to the other stuff in the mixing bowl.

Put that skillet back over the heat and brown and crumble your turkey sausage. When it's all browned, drain any fat that's accumulated in the pan and add the sausage to the mixing bowl, too.

Sprinkle about half the poultry seasoning over the stuff in the bowl, and use clean hands to mix it all together. Sprinkle on the rest of the poultry seasoning, and mix again.

If you like your stuffing quite damp or if you'll be cooking it outside of your turkey (such as in a casserole), add another 1/4 to 1/2 cup (60 to 120 ml) of broth. Now either stuff your turkey, or put your stuffing in a casserole.

Obviously, if you're cooking the stuffing inside the turkey, it'll cook for however long your turkey cooks. If you're cooking it in a casserole, bake it for 20 to 25 minutes. Kim just slides it into the oven for however long it takes her to make her gravy.

**Yield:** 12 servings

**Nutritional Analysis:** Each will have: 141 calories; 8 g fat; 11 g protein; 8 g carbohydrates; 3 g fiber; 5 g usable carbs.

| | | | | | |
|---|---|---|---|---|---|
| Potassium (mg): | 122 mg | Vitamin C (mg): | 2 mg | Thiamin/B1 (mg): | trace |
| Calcium (mg): | 90 mg | Vitamin A (i.u.): | 152 i.u. | Riboflavin/B2 (mg): | 0.1 mg |
| Iron (mg): | 2 mg | Vitamin B6 (mg): | trace | Folacin (mcg): | 15 mcg |
| Zinc (mg): | trace | Vitamin B12 (mcg): | trace | Niacin/B3 (mg): | 1 mg |

## Asparagus with Browned Butter and Parmesan

The quality of your Parmesan will make a big difference here. If you get yourself a microplane grater, you'll find yourself grating fresh Parmesan easily!

- 1 1/2 pounds (670 g) asparagus
- 3 tablespoons (45 g) butter
- 1/4 cup (25 g) freshly grated Parmesan cheese

Snap the ends off of the asparagus where they want to break naturally. Discard the ends and put the spears in a microwaveable casserole with a lid, or in a glass pie plate—anything microwaveable that's big enough to let your asparagus lie down. Add a couple of tablespoons (30 ml or so) of water, cover (use a plate or plastic wrap, if you're cooking in a pie plate), and nuke it on high for about 6 minutes. You want it just tender, but still brilliant green.

Meanwhile, melt the butter in a small pan, and heat it until it turns a rich brown—but don't go too far and burn it!

Drain the asparagus, and arrange it on a serving platter. Drizzle the butter over it, taking care to leave the blackened solid bits in the bottom of the pan.

Sprinkle the Parmesan over the top, and serve.

**Yield:** 6 servings

**Nutritional Analysis:** Each will have: 80 calories; 7 g fat; 3 g protein; 3 g carbohydrates; 1 g fiber; 2 g usable carbs.

| | | | | | |
|---|---|---|---|---|---|
| Potassium (mg): | 170 mg | Vitamin C (mg): | 8 mg | Thiamin/B1 (mg): | 0.1 mg |
| Calcium (mg): | 60 mg | Vitamin A (i.u.): | 591 i.u. | Riboflavin/B2 (mg): | 0.1 mg |
| Iron (mg): | 1 mg | Vitamin B6 (mg): | 0.1 mg | Folacin (mcg): | 77 mcg |
| Zinc (mg): | trace | Vitamin B12 (mcg): | 0.1 mcg | Niacin/B3 (mg): | 1 mg |

# Asparagus with Apricot Vinaigrette

Tender-crisp asparagus with a nice sweet-and-sour zing!

1 pound (455 g) asparagus

2 tablespoons (40 g) low-sugar apricot preserves

2 tablespoons (28 ml) rice vinegar

1/4 teaspoon minced garlic

1/4 teaspoon grated gingerroot

Break the ends off of the asparagus where they want to break naturally. Discard the spears and put the spears in a microwavable casserole with a lid, or in a glass pie plate. Either way, add just a tablespoon (14 ml) or so of water, cover (use plastic wrap for a pie plate), and microwave on high for 5 minutes. Be sure to uncover your asparagus the moment it's done cooking—it will just as soon overcook as look at you.

While the asparagus cooks, measure the preserves, vinegar, garlic, and ginger into a small, nonreactive saucepan. Put it over medium heat, and stir until the preserves melt into the rest. Simmer for just a minute or two.

Now toss your beautifully tender-crisp asparagus with the vinaigrette, and serve.

**Yield:** 4 servings

**Nutritional Analysis:** Each will have: 26 calories; trace fat; 1 g protein; 6 g carbohydrates; 1 g fiber; 5 g usable carbs.

| | | | | | |
|---|---|---|---|---|---|
| Potassium (mg): | 173 mg | Vitamin C (mg): | 8 mg | Thiamin/B1 (mg): | 0.1 mg |
| Calcium (mg): | 13 mg | Vitamin A (i.u.): | 351 i.u. | Riboflavin/B2 (mg): | 0.1 mg |
| Iron (mg): | 1 mg | Vitamin B6 (mg): | 0.1 mg | Folacin (mcg): | 77 mcg |
| Zinc (mg): | trace | Vitamin B12 (mcg): | 0 mcg | Niacin/B3 (mg): | 1 mg |

## Lemon Grilled Asparagus

Easy and good. Asparagus takes beautifully to grilling.

1 pound (455 g) asparagus

1 tablespoon (14 ml) lemon juice

1 tablespoon (14 ml) olive oil

1 clove garlic, peeled and minced

Snap the ends off of the asparagus where they want to break naturally. Discard the ends and place the spears in a plate with a rim—a glass pie plate will do nicely.

Mix together the lemon juice, oil, and garlic, and pour the mixture over the asparagus. Turn the asparagus this way and that, to coat. Let it sit.

Heat your electric tabletop grill. When it's good and hot, lay the asparagus in a single layer. Grill for 10 minutes, and serve.

**Yield:** 3 servings

**Nutritional Analysis:** Each will have: 61 calories; 5 g fat; 2 g protein; 4 g carbohydrates; 2 g fiber; 2 g usable carbs.

| | | | | | |
|---|---|---|---|---|---|
| Potassium (mg): | 229 mg | Vitamin C (mg): | 13 mg | Thiamin/B1 (mg): | 0.1 mg |
| Calcium (mg): | 19 mg | Vitamin A (i.u.): | 469 i.u. | Riboflavin/B2 (mg): | 0.1 mg |
| Iron (mg): | 1 mg | Vitamin B6 (mg): | 0.1 mg | Folacin (mcg): | 103 mcg |
| Zinc (mg): | trace | Vitamin B12 (mcg): | 0 mcg | Niacin/B3 (mg): | 1 mg |

## Grilled Asparagus with Wasabi Mayonnaise

Actually, the Wasabi Mayonnaise is so good you could eat it with shoelaces, but it's especially good on asparagus—and asparagus is especially good grilled.

1 pound (455 g) asparagus

4 tablespoons (55 g) Wasabi Mayonnaise (see page 490)

Snap the ends off of your asparagus where they want to break naturally. Discard the ends.

If you're grilling this on your outdoor grill, a small-holed grill rack will prevent the tragedy of losing asparagus through your grill. If you don't have a grill rack, just lay your asparagus across the grill and be careful when turning it. You'll want coals that are burned down to a glowing bed, for gentle heat, or to set your gas grill on medium-low.

Alternately, you can just grill this in your electric tabletop grill; just preheat the grill, then lay the asparagus in a single layer. I can fit a whole pound of asparagus in mine, but if you have a smallish electric grill, you may have to do it in batches.

Either way, grill your asparagus until it's got some brown spots—about 5 to 7 minutes. Pull it off the heat, divide it between 4 plates, and give everybody 1 tablespoon (14 g) of Wasabi Mayonnaise for dipping. Unbelievably delicious.

**Yield:** 4 servings

**Nutritional Analysis:** Each will have: 50 calories; 3 g fat; 1 g protein; 5 g carbohydrates; 1 g fiber; 4 g usable carbs.

| | | | | | |
|---|---|---|---|---|---|
| Potassium (mg): | 169 mg | Vitamin C (mg): | 8 mg | Thiamin/B1 (mg): | 0.1 mg |
| Calcium (mg): | 13 mg | Vitamin A (i.u.): | 351 i.u. | Riboflavin/B2 (mg): | 0.1 mg |
| Iron (mg): | 1 mg | Vitamin B6 (mg): | 0.1 mg | Folacin (mcg): | 77 mcg |
| Zinc (mg): | trace | Vitamin B12 (mcg): | 0 mcg | Niacin/B3 (mg): | 1 mg |

## Green Beans with Orange Essence and Maple-Glazed Pecans

Very, very special. This would be a terrific side dish for a holiday meal.

2 tablespoons (28 g) butter

1/2 cup (50 g) chopped pecans

2 tablespoons (28 ml) sugar-free pancake syrup or real or genuine maple syrup

2 pounds (905 g) frozen or fresh green beans, trimmed and cut into 1-inch (2.5-cm) pieces

1/2 medium onion, minced

1 clove garlic, peeled and minced

Juice and zest of 1 navel orange

2 teaspoons (5 g) chicken bouillon concentrate

Put a medium skillet over medium heat, and add 1 tablespoon (14 g) of the butter. When it's melted, add the chopped pecans. Sauté them until they smell toasty—3 to 4 minutes. Now add the syrup and continue sautéing and stirring until the syrup dries onto the pecans. Remove from the heat, and set aside.

Put the green beans in a microwaveable casserole with a lid, add a couple of tablespoons (30 ml or so) of water, cover, and microwave on high for 7 minutes. Check to see if they're cooked through; they probably won't be. Stir, re-cover, and give 'em another 3 to 4 minutes.

While the beans are cooking, spray a big, heavy skillet with nonstick cooking spray, and put it over medium-low heat. Add the remaining tablespoon (14 g) of the butter, and start sautéing the onion and garlic. When they're softened, stir in the orange juice and zest and the bouillon concentrate. Keep stirring till the bouillon is dissolved.

By this time, your beans should be just tender. Add them to the skillet, tossing everything together till the beans are coated with the sauce. Stir in the pecans, and serve.

**Yield:** 6 servings

**Nutritional Analysis:** Each will have: 156 calories; 11 g fat; 4 g protein; 14 g carbohydrates; 5 g fiber; 9 g usable carbs.

| | | | | | |
|---|---|---|---|---|---|
| Potassium (mg): | 340 mg | Vitamin C (mg): | 20 mg | Thiamin/B1 (mg): | 0.2 mg |
| Calcium (mg): | 72 mg | Vitamin A (i.u.): | 887 i.u. | Riboflavin/B2 (mg): | 0.1 mg |
| Iron (mg): | 2 mg | Vitamin B6 (mg): | 0.1 mg | Folacin (mcg): | 28 mcg |
| Zinc (mg): | 1 mg | Vitamin B12 (mcg): | trace | Niacin/B3 (mg): | 1 mg |

# Green Bean Casserole

2 pounds (905 g) frozen green beans, cross-cut, or fresh, trimmed and cut into 1-inch (2.5-cm) pieces

2 medium onions

1 tablespoon (14 ml) olive oil

2 tablespoons (8 g) chopped fresh parsley

2 cloves garlic, peeled and finely minced

1 1/2 cups (340 g) 2% cottage cheese

1/2 cup (55 g) shredded, reduced-fat Cheddar cheese

4 eggs, beaten slightly

1 teaspoon salt or Vege-Sal

1/4 teaspoon pepper

Preheat the oven to 325°F (170°C, or gas mark 3).

Microwave or steam the green beans until they're tender-crisp. (I'd use frozen and not bother to thaw them first.) Just put them in a microwaveable casserole with a lid, add a couple of tablespoons (30 ml or so) of water, cover, and nuke them on high for 10 minutes. Give them a stir, and zap them for another 5 minutes or so.

Meanwhile, chop up the onions. Now give your big, heavy skillet a shot of nonstick cooking spray, and put it over medium heat. Add the olive oil and sauté the onions until they're translucent. Turn off the burner and add the parsley, garlic, cottage cheese, 1/4 cup (28 g) of the cheddar, eggs, salt, and pepper to the skillet. Stir all of this together well.

Spray a 2-quart (1.9 l) casserole with nonstick cooking spray. Drain your green beans very well. Now layer the green beans with the cheese mixture, ending with a layer of the cheese mixture on top. Scatter the remaining cheddar over the top to make it look pretty.

Bake, uncovered, for 20 to 25 minutes.

**Yield:** 8 servings

**Nutritional Analysis:** Each will have: 147 calories; 5 g fat; 13 g protein; 13 g carbohydrates; 4 g fiber; 9 g usable carbs.

| | | | | | |
|---|---|---|---|---|---|
| Potassium (mg): | 335 mg | Vitamin C (mg): | 18 mg | Thiamin/B1 (mg): | 0.1 mg |
| Calcium (mg): | 125 mg | Vitamin A (i.u.): | 779 i.u. | Riboflavin/B2 (mg): | 0.3 mg |
| Iron (mg): | 2 mg | Vitamin B6 (mg): | 0.1 mg | Folacin (mcg): | 40 mcg |
| Zinc (mg): | 1 mg | Vitamin B12 (mcg): | 0.6 mcg | Niacin/B3 (mg): | 1 mg |

## Green Beans with Ham and Mushrooms

1 pound (455 g) frozen cross-cut green beans or fresh beans cut into 1-inch (2.5-cm) pieces

2 teaspoons (28 g) butter

4 ounces (115 g) sliced mushrooms

2 ounces (55 g) turkey ham

1 tablespoon (14 ml) lemon juice

Put the green beans in a microwaveable casserole with a lid (don't bother to thaw them first), add a couple of tablespoons (30 ml or so) of water, cover, and nuke 'em on high for 7 minutes.

While that's happening, give your big, heavy skillet a shot of nonstick cooking spray. Put it over medium heat, melt the butter, and start sautéing the mushrooms.

Cut the turkey ham into a few cubes, and throw it into your food processor with the S-blade in place. Pulse until it's ground up.

When the mushrooms are starting to look limp, throw the ground turkey ham in with them, and stir the two together. Sauté for a few more minutes.

Somewhere in here your microwave is going to beep. Go stir the green beans, and give 'em another 5 minutes on high.

When the beans are done, drain 'em and dump 'em into the skillet with the mushrooms and ham. Add the lemon juice, toss everything together, and serve.

**Yield:** 3 servings

**Nutritional Analysis:** Each will have: 64 calories; 2 g fat; 4 g protein; 8 g carbohydrates; 3 g fiber; 5 g usable carbs.

| | | | | | |
|---|---|---|---|---|---|
| Potassium (mg): | 294 mg | Vitamin C (mg): | 14 mg | Thiamin/B1 (mg): | 0.1 mg |
| Calcium (mg): | 41 mg | Vitamin A (i.u.): | 494 i.u. | Riboflavin/B2 (mg): | 0.2 mg |
| Iron (mg): | 1 mg | Vitamin B6 (mg): | 0.1 mg | Folacin (mcg): | 19 mcg |
| Zinc (mg): | 1 mg | Vitamin B12 (mcg): | trace | Niacin/B3 (mg): | 2 mg |

## Balsamic Green Beans with Bacon and Pine Nuts

Make this with fresh green beans, if you prefer. I just like the simplicity of frozen beans.

- 2 slices bacon
- 1 pound (455 g) frozen green beans
- 1 tablespoon (14 ml) olive oil
- 1 teaspoon (5 g) butter
- 1/4 medium onion, finely minced
- 1 teaspoon dried marjoram
- 1/4 cup (35 g) toasted pine nuts (pignolia)
- 3 tablespoons (45 ml) balsamic vinegar

Lay the bacon on a microwave bacon rack or in a glass pie plate. Nuke it on high for 2 minutes, or until it's crisp. Remove from the microwave, drain, and set it aside.

While the bacon's cooking, put the green beans, still frozen, in a microwaveable casserole with a lid. Add a couple of tablespoons (30 ml or so) of water, cover, and put 'em in the microwave for 7 minutes on high.

Now spray a big skillet with nonstick cooking spray, put it over medium heat, and add the oil and butter. When the butter's melted, swirl it into the oil, then add the onion. Sauté for just a few minutes, till the onion's translucent. Stir in the marjoram. Turn off the heat if the beans aren't done yet—you don't want to burn the onion!

When the microwave beeps, stir the green beans and give 'em 3 more minutes. You want them tender, but not overcooked.

Okay, the beans are done. Drain 'em, and throw 'em in the skillet with the onion. If you've turned off the heat, turn it back on to medium-high. Stir it up. Now crumble the bacon into the skillet, sprinkle the pine nuts over everything, and stir it up again. Add the balsamic vinegar, stir one more time, and serve.

**Yield:** 6 servings

**Nutritional Analysis:** Each will have: 98 calories; 7 g fat; 3 g protein; 7 g carbohydrates; 2 g fiber; 5 g usable carbs.

| | | | | | |
|---|---|---|---|---|---|
| Potassium (mg): | 202 mg | Vitamin C (mg): | 11 mg | Thiamin/B1 (mg): | 0.1 mg |
| Calcium (mg): | 37 mg | Vitamin A (i.u.): | 397 i.u. | Riboflavin/B2 (mg): | 0.1 mg |
| Iron (mg): | 1 mg | Vitamin B6 (mg): | trace | Folacin (mcg): | 16 mcg |
| Zinc (mg): | trace | Vitamin B12 (mcg): | trace | Niacin/B3 (mg): | 1 mg |

**Note:** If you can't find toasted pine nuts, you can toast them easily yourself. Just spread them on a shallow pan and give them 7 or 8 minutes at 325°F (170°C, or gas mark 3). You want them just turning golden. (A toaster oven is perfect for this. Who wants to heat up the oven for a little job like this?) Or you can stir them in a dry skillet over medium heat till they're golden. But many stores carry pretoasted pine nuts!

## Green Beans with Ham and Tomatoes

Julie says her green-bean–hating kid ate this "without grabbing his throat and pretending to be poisoned." We call that a very good sign!

1 pound (455 g) frozen cross-cut green beans, or fresh beans cut into 1-inch (2.5-cm) pieces

1 tablespoon (14 ml) olive oil

2 cloves garlic, peeled and minced

$^1/_3$ cup (55 g) finely diced red onion

1 ounce (15 g) turkey ham, finely chopped

1 medium tomato, diced, or $^1/_2$ cup (20 ml) diced canned tomatoes

$^1/_2$ teaspoon dried oregano

2 teaspoons (10 ml) lemon juice

Salt and pepper

Put the green beans in a microwaveable casserole with a lid (don't bother thawing them), add a couple of tablespoons (30 ml or so) of water, and cover. Nuke on high for 7 minutes. Stir, and nuke for another 3 to 4 minutes.

While the beans cook, heat the oil in a big, heavy skillet over a medium-low burner, and start sautéing the garlic and onion. When the onions are soft, add the ham, tomato, and oregano.

Drain the beans, throw 'em in the skillet, and stir everything up. Stir in the lemon juice, add salt and pepper to taste, and serve.

**Yield:** 4 servings

**Nutritional Analysis:** Each will have: 91 calories; 4 g fat; 4 g protein; 12 g carbohydrates; 4 g fiber; 8 g usable carbs.

| | | | | | |
|---|---|---|---|---|---|
| Potassium (mg): | 336 mg | Vitamin C (mg): | 23 mg | Thiamin/B1 (mg): | 0.1 mg |
| Calcium (mg): | 58 mg | Vitamin A (i.u.): | 750 i.u. | Riboflavin/B2 (mg): | 0.1 mg |
| Iron (mg): | 1 mg | Vitamin B6 (mg): | 0.1 mg | Folacin (mcg): | 25 mcg |
| Zinc (mg): | 1 mg | Vitamin B12 (mcg): | trace | Niacin/B3 (mg): | 1 mg |

## Creamed Spinach

An old favorite! Good as a side dish, and if you make a double batch, you'll have leftovers to use in omelets and other dishes.

10 ounces (280 g) frozen chopped spinach

1 teaspoon (14 g) butter

2 tablespoons (20 g) minced onion

1 clove garlic, peeled and minced

$^1/_2$ cup (120 ml) milk

2 tablespoons (28 g) Neufchâtel cheese or light cream cheese

Guar or xanthan gum

Put the frozen brick of spinach in a microwaveable casserole with a lid. Add a couple of tablespoons (30 ml or so) of water, cover, and microwave on high for 7 minutes.

Meanwhile, melt the butter in a small skillet or saucepan over medium-low heat, and start sautéing the onion and garlic. When the onion is translucent (but not browned—no browning!), add the milk. Bring it to just below a simmer, and whisk in the Neufchâtel until it's melted. Thicken a tad with the guar or xanthan, if you think it needs it.

Check the spinach; if it still has a cold spot in the center, stir it up and give it another 1 to 2 minutes. You want it just barely done, not cooked to death.

When the spinach is done, put a strainer in the sink, dump the spinach into it, and press it with the back of a spoon to remove all the excess water. Now stir it into the cream sauce, and serve.

**Yield:** 3 servings

**Nutritional Analysis:** Each will have: 75 calories; 4 g fat; 5 g protein; 7 g carbohydrates; 3 g fiber; 4 g usable carbs.

| | | | | | |
|---|---|---|---|---|---|
| Potassium (mg): | 387 mg | Vitamin C (mg): | 24 mg | Thiamin/B1 (mg): | 0.1 mg |
| Calcium (mg): | 161 mg | Vitamin A (i.u.): | 7484 i.u. | Riboflavin/B2 (mg): | 0.2 mg |
| Iron (mg): | 2 mg | Vitamin B6 (mg): | 0.2 mg | Folacin (mcg): | 117 mcg |
| Zinc (mg): | 1 mg | Vitamin B12 (mcg): | 0.2 mcg | Niacin/B3 (mg): | trace |

## Pepperoncini Spinach

Pepperoncini peppers are those little hot salad peppers you sometimes get in a Greek salad. Look for 'em in the pickle section of your grocery store. If you're nervous about hot food, be aware that these are a lot milder than jalapeños.

10 ounces (280 g) frozen chopped spinach, thawed and drained

$1\frac{1}{2}$ teaspoons (7.5 ml) olive oil

1 clove garlic, peeled

2 pepperoncini peppers, drained and minced

1 tablespoon (14 ml) lemon juice

Thaw the spinach, put it in a strainer, and either press it with the back of a spoon or actually pick it up with clean hands and squeeze it. You want all the excess water out of it.

Give a medium-size skillet a shot of nonstick cooking spray, put it over medium-high heat, and add the olive oil. When it's hot, add the spinach, garlic, and peppers. Sauté, stirring often, for about 5 minutes. Stir in the lemon juice, let it cook for another minute, and serve.

**Yield:** 3 servings

**Nutritional Analysis:** Each will have: 47 calories; 3 g fat; 3 g protein; 5 g carbohydrates; 3 g fiber; 2 g usable carbs.

| | | | | | |
|---|---|---|---|---|---|
| Potassium (mg): | 316 mg | Vitamin C (mg): | 26 mg | Thiamin/B1 (mg): | 0.1 mg |
| Calcium (mg): | 107 mg | Vitamin A (i.u.): | 7332 i.u. | Riboflavin/B2 (mg): | 0.1 mg |
| Iron (mg): | 2 mg | Vitamin B6 (mg): | 0.1 mg | Folacin (mcg): | 114 mcg |
| Zinc (mg): | trace | Vitamin B12 (mcg): | 0 mcg | Niacin/B3 (mg): | trace |

## Spinach with Sour Cream and Pine Nuts

My spinach-loving husband ate the whole batch!

1 tablespoon (14 ml) olive oil

3 tablespoons (30 g) minced onion

10 ounces (280 g) frozen chopped spinach, thawed and drained

1 tablespoon (15 g) light sour cream

1 tablespoon (9 g) toasted pine nuts

Put the olive oil in a big, heavy skillet over medium-low heat. When the oil is hot, add the onion and sauté it. After a couple of minutes, add the spinach, and stir the onion into it. Sauté the spinach for 3 to 4 minutes. Stir in the sour cream, sprinkle with the pine nuts, and serve.

**Yield:** 2 servings

**Nutritional Analysis:** Each will have: 126 calories; 10 g fat; 5 g protein; 8 g carbohydrates; 5 g fiber; 3 g usable carbs.

| | | | | | |
|---|---|---|---|---|---|
| Potassium (mg): | 507 mg | Vitamin C (mg): | 35 mg | Thiamin/B1 (mg): | 0.1 mg |
| Calcium (mg): | 164 mg | Vitamin A (i.u.): | 10998 i.u. | Riboflavin/B2 (mg): | 0.2 mg |
| Iron (mg): | 3 mg | Vitamin B6 (mg): | 0.2 mg | Folacin (mcg): | 175 mcg |
| Zinc (mg): | 1 mg | Vitamin B12 (mcg): | 0 mcg | Niacin/B3 (mg): | 1 mg |

**Note:** If you have fresh baby spinach on hand, you can certainly upgrade this dish by using it instead of frozen! I'm just more likely to have frozen spinach on hand. Two 5-ounce bags of baby spinach are perfect. Just add them to the skillet after sautéing the onion. They'll overwhelm your skillet at first, but will wilt down very quickly. Sauté for just a few minutes; you want the spinach just wilted and hot through. Then add the sour cream and pine nuts, and serve.

## Spinach with Sour Cream and Mint

This would be good with fresh oregano, too.

- 2 teaspoons (10 ml) olive oil
- 1 small onion, chopped
- 1 clove garlic, peeled and minced
- 8 ounces (225 g) fresh baby spinach
- 1 1/2 teaspoons finely chopped fresh mint
- 3/4 cup (175 g) light sour cream
- Salt and pepper

Spray a big, heavy skillet with nonstick cooking spray, and place it over medium-high heat. Add the oil. When the oil is hot, add the chopped onion and sauté for just a few minutes.

Now add the garlic, stir for a minute, and then add the spinach. Sauté until the spinach is just wilted. Stir in the mint and light sour cream, add salt and pepper to taste, and serve immediately.

**Yield:** 3 servings

**Nutritional Analysis:** Each will have: 79 calories; 4 g fat; 4 g protein; 9 g carbohydrates; 3 g fiber; 6 g usable carbs.

| | | | | | |
|---|---|---|---|---|---|
| Potassium (mg): | 488 mg | Vitamin C (mg): | 24 mg | Thiamin/B1 (mg): | 0.1 mg |
| Calcium (mg): | 109 mg | Vitamin A (i.u.): | 5115 i.u. | Riboflavin/B2 (mg): | 0.1 mg |
| Iron (mg): | 2 mg | Vitamin B6 (mg): | 0.2 mg | Folacin (mcg): | 155 mcg |
| Zinc (mg): | trace | Vitamin B12 (mcg): | 0 mcg | Niacin/B3 (mg): | 1 mg |

## Cheesy Creamed Spinach

2 packages (10 ounces, or 280 g each) frozen chopped spinach, thawed and drained

1 1/3 cups (305 g) light sour cream

2/3 cup (160 ml) whole milk

1/3 cup (55 g) minced onion

1 pinch ground nutmeg

1 large egg, beaten

Salt and pepper

1 cup (115 g) shredded, reduced-fat Cheddar cheese

Spray a 2-quart (1.9-l) casserole with nonstick cooking spray. Preheat the oven to 350°F (180°C, or gas mark 4).

Combine the spinach, light sour cream, milk, onion, nutmeg, egg, salt and pepper to taste, and half the cheese in a big mixing bowl. Spoon into the prepared casserole.

Smooth the top, spread the rest of the cheese over the top, and bake for about 30 minutes, or until set.

**Yield:** 6 servings

**Nutritional Analysis:** Each will have: 104 calories; 4 g fat; 10 g protein; 8 g carbohydrates; 3 g fiber; 5 g usable carbs.

| | | | | | |
|---|---|---|---|---|---|
| Potassium (mg): | 382 mg | Vitamin C (mg): | 24 mg | Thiamin/B1 (mg): | 0.1 mg |
| Calcium (mg): | 241 mg | Vitamin A (i.u.): | 7456 i.u. | Riboflavin/B2 (mg): | 0.3 mg |
| Iron (mg): | 2 mg | Vitamin B6 (mg): | 0.2 mg | Folacin (mcg): | 122 mcg |
| Zinc (mg): | 1 mg | Vitamin B12 (mcg): | 0.3 mcg | Niacin/B3 (mg): | trace |

## Spinach with Olive Oil and Lemon

3 pounds (1.4 kg) fresh spinach (buy the "triple-washed" stuff in a bag)

Salt

3 tablespoons (45 ml) extra virgin olive oil

1 lemon, quartered

Rinse the spinach one more time, just to be safe. (Or, if you've been so unlucky as not to be able to buy prewashed spinach, wash each leaf carefully under running water. Spinach can hold a lot of grit.)

Put the spinach in a big pot with just the water that's still on the leaves from rinsing it. Salt it lightly, and toss it to distribute the salt. Cover the pot, set the burner to medium, and cook for 6 to 8 minutes, or until the spinach is wilted.

Drain the spinach very well in a colander. The put it on a serving platter, drizzle with the oil, and serve with wedges of lemon to squeeze over it.

**Yield:** 4 servings

**Nutritional Analysis:** Each will have: 167 calories; 11 g fat; 10 g protein; 13 g carbohydrates; 9 g fiber; 4 g usable carbs.

| | | | | | |
|---|---|---|---|---|---|
| Potassium (mg): | 1921 mg | Vitamin C (mg): | 103 mg | Thiamin/B1 (mg): | 0.2 mg |
| Calcium (mg): | 341 mg | Vitamin A (i.u.): | 22869 i.u. | Riboflavin/B2 (mg): | 0.6 mg |
| Iron (mg): | 9 mg | Vitamin B6 (mg): | 0.6 mg | Folacin (mcg): | 664 mcg |
| Zinc (mg): | 2 mg | Vitamin B12 (mcg): | 0 mcg | Niacin/B3 (mg): | 2 mg |

## Sautéed Sesame Spinach

This is an easy dish that goes well as a side with a simple entrée.

1 tablespoon (7.5 g) sesame seeds

1 tablespoon (14 ml) coconut oil or peanut oil

1 pound (455 g) fresh triple washed, bagged spinach

2 tablespoons (28 ml) soy sauce

Put the sesame seeds in a small, heavy skillet over medium-high heat, and stir or shake them until they're golden brown and toasty. Remove from the heat and set them aside.

If you have a wok, use it. If not, spray a big, heavy skillet with nonstick cooking spray. Either way, put the pan over high heat and add the oil. When the oil is hot, add the spinach and stir-fry till it's just barely wilted. Stir in the soy sauce, and transfer to serving plates.

Sprinkle sesame seeds on each serving, and serve.

**Yield:** 4 servings

**Nutritional Analysis:** Each will have: 72 calories; 5 g fat; 4 g protein; 5 g carbohydrates; 3 g fiber; 2 g usable carbs.

| Potassium (mg): | 660 mg | Vitamin C (mg): | 32 mg | Thiamin/B1 (mg): | 0.1 mg |
|---|---|---|---|---|---|
| Calcium (mg): | 136 mg | Vitamin A (i.u.): | 7622 i.u. | Riboflavin/B2 (mg): | 0.2 mg |
| Iron (mg): | 4 mg | Vitamin B6 (mg): | 0.2 mg | Folacin (mcg): | 224 mcg |
| Zinc (mg): | 1 mg | Vitamin B12 (mcg): | 0 mcg | Niacin/B3 (mg): | 1 mg |

## Spinach and Tomatoes

Very pretty, and very yummy! The spinach is even good enough to stand on its own.

2 packages (10 ounces, or 280 g each) frozen chopped spinach

4 large tomatoes

2 tablespoons (28 g) butter

1 small onion, minced

1/4 teaspoon salt or Vege-Sal

1/2 cup (50 g) grated Parmesan cheese

1 clove garlic, peeled and very finely minced

1/2 teaspoon dried thyme

2 eggs, beaten slightly

Preheat the oven to 350°F (180°C, or gas mark 4).

Put the spinach, still frozen, in a microwaveable casserole with a lid. Add a couple of tablespoons (30 ml or so) of water, cover, and microwave it on high for 10 minutes.

Cut the cores out of the tomatoes, then whack each one in half through the "equator." Spray a flat baking dish with nonstick cooking spray and arrange the tomatoes in it, cut sides up.

Spray a big, heavy skillet with nonstick cooking spray, and put it over medium heat. Add the butter, and sauté the onion in it.

When the microwave beeps, stir the spinach and give it another 3 to 5 minutes. When it's good and hot clear through, but not overcooked, dump it into a strainer and press it hard with the back of a spoon to remove the excess liquid. Dump the strained spinach into a mixing bowl.

When the onion is translucent, add the spinach, salt, 1/3 cup (80 ml) of the Parmesan, garlic, and thyme to the skillet. Stir this all together well. Now stir in the beaten eggs.

Spoon the spinach mixture onto the tomato halves, shaping it into neat little mounds. Sprinkle the rest of the Parmesan on top, and bake the whole thing, uncovered, for 15 to 20 minutes.

**Yield:** 8 servings

**Nutritional Analysis:** Each will have: 101 calories; 6 g fat; 6 g protein; 7 g carbohydrates; 3 g fiber; 4 g usable carbs.

| | | | | | |
|---|---|---|---|---|---|
| Potassium (mg): | 409 mg | Vitamin C (mg): | 30 mg | Thiamin/B1 (mg): | 0.1 mg |
| Calcium (mg): | 162 mg | Vitamin A (i.u.): | 6098 i.u. | Riboflavin/B2 (mg): | 0.2 mg |
| Iron (mg): | 2 mg | Vitamin B6 (mg): | 0.2 mg | Folacin (mcg): | 103 mcg |
| Zinc (mg): | 1 mg | Vitamin B12 (mcg): | 0.2 mcg | Niacin/B3 (mg): | 1 mg |

## Sautéed Mushrooms and Spinach with Pepperoni

Julie says, "I wish more restaurants would have interesting side dishes like this."

1 ounce (28 g) sliced pepperoni

2 tablespoons (28 ml) olive oil

1 pound (455 g) sliced mushrooms

1 bunch scallions, sliced

2 cloves garlic, peeled and minced

5 ounces (140 g) bagged baby spinach

Salt and pepper

Slice the pepperoni into very thin strips. Heat 1 tablespoon (14 ml) of the oil in a big, heavy skillet, add the pepperoni, and sauté it until it's crisp. Lift it out with a slotted spoon, and drain it on paper towels.

Add the remaining tablespoon (14 ml) of oil to the skillet, and let it heat over a medium-high burner. Add the mushrooms, and sauté them until they're softened and starting to brown. Add the sliced scallions and sauté for another few minutes, until they're starting to brown, too. Stir in the garlic, then add the spinach. Turn the whole thing over and over, just until the spinach wilts. Stir in the pepperoni bits, season with salt and pepper, and serve.

**Yield:** 4 servings

**Nutritional Analysis:** Each will have: 134 calories; 10 g fat; 5 g protein; 7 g carbohydrates; 2 g fiber; 5 g usable carbs.

| Potassium (mg): | 659 mg | Vitamin C (mg): | 15 mg | Thiamin/B1 (mg): | 0.2 mg |
|---|---|---|---|---|---|
| Calcium (mg): | 47 mg | Vitamin A (i.u.): | 2394 i.u. | Riboflavin/B2 (mg): | 0.6 mg |
| Iron (mg): | 3 mg | Vitamin B6 (mg): | 0.2 mg | Folacin (mcg): | 96 mcg |
| Zinc (mg): | 1 mg | Vitamin B12 (mcg): | 0.2 mcg | Niacin/B3 (mg): | 5 mg |

## Roasted Artichokes with Roasted Garlic-Lemon Mayonnaise

Double this for a dinner party—it's no more work, and you'll impress your friends!

2 medium artichokes

Juice and zest of 1 lemon

3 tablespoons (45 ml) olive oil

Salt

8 cloves garlic, unpeeled

1/3 cup (75 g) light mayonnaise

Lemon juice

Preheat the oven to 400°F (200°C, or gas mark 6).

Grate the zest of the lemon into a small bowl. Whack the lemon in half, flick out the pits with the tip of the knife, and squeeze the juice into another small bowl. If you missed any pits, fish 'em out. Set both bowls aside.

Fill a big bowl with water and add a couple of tablespoons (30 ml or so) of the lemon juice. Trim the bottoms of the stems of the artichokes. Now quarter them, and use the tip of a spoon to scrape out the fuzzy choke. As you finish doing this to each quarter, drop it into the bowl of water.

Drain the artichokes well, and put them in a roasting pan (a metal one is better than glass). Drizzle them with the oil, getting down between the leaves, then stir to coat them even more. Sprinkle the artichokes with a bit of salt. Add the garlic cloves to the pan without peeling them, and slide the pan into the oven. Roast for 40 minutes, turning 2 or 3 times during roasting.

When time's up, pull the pan out of the oven, and remove the garlic cloves. Turn off the oven, and put the pan of artichokes back in to stay warm while you make the sauce.

Press each garlic clove with the back of a fork to squeeze the roasted pulp out. Put the pulp in a bowl, and mash it up as much as you can with the fork.

Add the lemon zest and juice to the garlic pulp. Now add the mayo, and whisk the whole thing together until well blended.

Remove the artichokes from the oven again. Arrange 2 artichoke quarters on each of 4 plates, add a puddle of sauce for dipping, and serve.

**Yield:** 4 servings

**Nutritional Analysis:** Each will have: 178 calories; 14 g fat; 3 g protein; 13 g carbohydrates; 4 g fiber; 9 g usable carbs.

| | | | | | |
|---|---|---|---|---|---|
| Potassium (mg): | 284 mg | Vitamin C (mg): | 17 mg | Thiamin/B1 (mg): | 0.1 mg |
| Calcium (mg): | 43 mg | Vitamin A (i.u.): | 123 i.u. | Riboflavin/B2 (mg): | trace |
| Iron (mg): | 1 mg | Vitamin B6 (mg): | 0.1 mg | Folacin (mcg): | 45 mcg |
| Zinc (mg): | trace | Vitamin B12 (mcg): | 0 mcg | Niacin/B3 (mg): | 1 mg |

# Artichoke Hearts with Basil and Garlic

The best thing about this is that it looks like it's some trouble, when it's actually easier and faster to make than mac and cheese is. This would be great for when you get 30 minutes notice that someone is coming for dinner.

1 tablespoon (14 ml) olive oil

1 clove garlic, peeled and minced

1/2 teaspoon dried basil

14 ounces (390 g) canned quartered artichoke hearts, drained

Salt and pepper

This is just a simple way to dress up canned artichoke hearts. In your big, heavy skillet, heat the oil over medium heat. Sauté the garlic and basil for a minute or two. Add the drained artichoke hearts, and stir everything up. Let the artichoke hearts heat through, add salt and pepper to taste, and serve.

**Yield:** 3 servings

**Nutritional Analysis:** Each will have: 92 calories; 5 g fat; 3 g protein; 9 g carbohydrates; trace fiber; 9 g usable carbs.

| | | | | | |
|---|---|---|---|---|---|
| Potassium (mg): | 13 mg | Vitamin C (mg): | trace | Thiamin/B1 (mg): | 0 mg |
| Calcium (mg): | 7 mg | Vitamin A (i.u.): | 23 i.u. | Riboflavin/B2 (mg): | trace |
| Iron (mg): | trace | Vitamin B6 (mg): | trace | Folacin (mcg): | 1 mcg |
| Zinc (mg): | trace | Vitamin B12 (mcg): | 0 mcg | Niacin/B3 (mg): | trace |

## Sautéed Radicchio

This method of cooking mellows the bitter edge of radicchio.

- 1 head radicchio
- 1 tablespoon (14 ml) olive oil
- 1 clove garlic, peeled and finely minced
- 1 tablespoon (14 ml) balsamic vinegar

Whack the head of radicchio in half, cut out the core, and chop it quite coarsely.

Give a big, heavy skillet a shot of nonstick cooking spray, and put it over medium-high heat. Add the oil, get it good and hot, and then throw in the radicchio. Sauté, stirring fairly often, until the radicchio is wilted and has quite a few brown spots. Add the garlic, and sauté for another minute or two.

Stir in the balsamic vinegar, add salt and pepper to taste, and serve.

**Yield:** 4 servings

**Nutritional Analysis:** Each will have: 34 calories; 3 g fat; trace protein; 1 g carbohydrates; trace fiber; 1 g usable carbs.

| | | | | | |
|---|---|---|---|---|---|
| Potassium (mg): | 37 mg | Vitamin C (mg): | 1 mg | Thiamin/B1 (mg): | 0 mg |
| Calcium (mg): | 4 mg | Vitamin A (i.u.): | 3 i.u. | Riboflavin/B2 (mg): | trace |
| Iron (mg): | trace | Vitamin B6 (mg): | trace | Folacin (mcg): | 6 mcg |
| Zinc (mg): | trace | Vitamin B12 (mcg): | 0 mcg | Niacin/B3 (mg): | trace |

## Stilton Mushrooms

The blue cheese makes this seem decadent, but it's really not that high in calories, and the full flavor makes it very satisfying. Stilton is a very strong blue cheese imported from England, but if you really don't care for very sharp cheeses, use something milder—Gorgonzola would be good. Still, I think Stilton is best!

- 1 1/2 tablespoons (21 ml) olive oil
- 1/4 medium onion, finely diced
- 1 clove garlic, peeled and minced
- 8 ounces (225 g) sliced mushrooms
- 1 tablespoon (14 ml) dry sherry
- 1/4 teaspoon dried thyme
- 1/4 cup (30 g) crumbled Stilton
- Salt and pepper

Spray a big, heavy skillet with nonstick cooking spray, and put it over medium heat. Add the oil, onion, and garlic. Sauté, stirring often, until the onion is translucent (just a minute or two).

Add the mushrooms, and sauté until they have softened and changed color. Be aware that most of the oil will be absorbed by the mushrooms; this is where that nonstick cooking spray comes in handy. Just keep sautéing and stirring from time to time, and the mushrooms will start to exude a little liquid to moisten the pan.

When the mushrooms are soft and have gone brown all over, add the sherry and the thyme. Stir them in, and keep cooking until most of the sherry has evaporated.

Add the Stilton, stir till it melts, add salt and pepper to taste, and serve.

**Yield:** 3 servings

**Nutritional Analysis:** Each will have: 129 calories; 10 g fat; 4 g protein; 5 g carbohydrates; 1 g fiber; 4 g usable carbs.

| | | | | | |
|---|---|---|---|---|---|
| Potassium (mg): | 331 mg | Vitamin C (mg): | 4 mg | Thiamin/B1 (mg): | 0.1 mg |
| Calcium (mg): | 69 mg | Vitamin A (i.u.): | 86 i.u. | Riboflavin/B2 (mg): | 0.4 mg |
| Iron (mg): | 1 mg | Vitamin B6 (mg): | 0.1 mg | Folacin (mcg): | 22 mcg |
| Zinc (mg): | 1 mg | Vitamin B12 (mcg): | 0.1 mcg | Niacin/B3 (mg): | 3 mg |

## Teriyaki Mushrooms

This is great as a side dish, but would also be nice over a grilled chicken breast.

1 tablespoon (14 ml) coconut oil

8 ounces (225 g) sliced mushrooms

2 tablespoons (10 ml) soy sauce

2 tablespoons (3 g) Splenda

1 tablespoon (14 ml) rice vinegar

1/4 teaspoon chili garlic paste

1 clove garlic, peeled and minced

2 scallions, sliced

Give a big, heavy skillet a squirt of nonstick cooking spray, and put it over medium-high heat. Add the oil, and when it's hot, start sautéing the mushrooms. The mushrooms will absorb all the oil pretty quickly, but keep sautéing till they're softened and they change color.

Stir in the soy sauce, Splenda, rice vinegar, chili garlic paste, and garlic. Let the whole thing continue to cook until the liquid has cooked down to less than half its original volume. Stir in the scallions, cook for just another minute, and serve.

**Yield:** 3 servings

**Nutritional Analysis:** Each will have: 74 calories; 5 g fat; 2 g protein; 7 g carbohydrates; 1 g fiber; 6 g usable carbs.

| | | | | | |
|---|---|---|---|---|---|
| Potassium (mg): | 338 mg | Vitamin C (mg): | 5 mg | Thiamin/B1 (mg): | 0.1 mg |
| Calcium (mg): | 15 mg | Vitamin A (i.u.): | 39 i.u. | Riboflavin/B2 (mg): | 0.4 mg |
| Iron (mg): | 1 mg | Vitamin B6 (mg): | 0.1 mg | Folacin (mcg): | 24 mcg |
| Zinc (mg): | 1 mg | Vitamin B12 (mcg): | 0 mcg | Niacin/B3 (mg): | 4 mg |

## Sautéed Mushrooms with Wine

- 2 teaspoons (10 ml) olive oil
- 2 teaspoons (10 g) butter
- 1 pound (455 g) sliced mushrooms
- 2 cloves garlic, peeled and finely minced
- 1 teaspoon fresh thyme leaves or 1/2 teaspoon dried thyme
- 4 teaspoons (20 ml) lemon juice
- 1/4 cup (60 ml) dry white wine
- 2 tablespoons (15 g) minced parsley

Spray a big, heavy skillet with nonstick cooking spray, and put it over medium-low heat. Add the oil and butter, swirling the two together as the butter melts. Add the mushrooms and garlic and sauté them, stirring frequently.

When the mushrooms are softened a bit, stir in the thyme, lemon juice, and wine. Let everything simmer together, uncovered, for 5 minutes.

Stir in the chopped parsley, and serve.

**Yield:** 6 servings

**Nutritional Analysis:** Each will have: 53 calories; 3 g fat; 2 g protein; 4 g carbohydrates; 1 g fiber; 3 g usable carbs.

| | | | | | |
|---|---|---|---|---|---|
| Potassium (mg): | 304 mg | Vitamin C (mg): | 6 mg | Thiamin/B1 (mg): | 0.1 mg |
| Calcium (mg): | 9 mg | Vitamin A (i.u.): | 120 i.u. | Riboflavin/B2 (mg): | 0.3 mg |
| Iron (mg): | 1 mg | Vitamin B6 (mg): | 0.1 mg | Folacin (mcg): | 18 mcg |
| Zinc (mg): | 1 mg | Vitamin B12 (mcg): | trace | Niacin/B3 (mg): | 3 mg |

## Cumin Mushrooms

This will make any simple main dish special. Use chicken or beef broth, according to what you're planning to serve it with—not to mention what you have on hand! You could even use a couple of tablespoons (30 ml or so) of water and a scant 1/4 teaspoon of chicken or beef bouillon concentrate, if you wanted.

2 teaspoons (28 g) butter

2 teaspoons (10 ml) olive oil

8 ounces (225 g) sliced mushrooms

2 tablespoons (28 ml) chicken broth or beef broth

1 teaspoon ground cumin

1/4 teaspoon pepper

2 tablespoons (28 g) light sour cream

Spray a big, heavy skillet with nonstick cooking spray, and put it over medium-high heat. Add the butter and oil, and swirl them together as the butter melts. Now add the mushrooms and sauté them, stirring often, for 5 minutes. They will suck up all the butter and oil. That's okay. Just keep stirring them from time to time.

Add the broth, cumin, and pepper, cover the skillet, and turn the heat down to low. Let the mushrooms cook for another 5 minutes.

Stir in the sour cream just before serving.

**Yield:** 3 servings

**Nutritional Analysis:** Each will have: 76 calories; 6 g fat; 2 g protein; 4 g carbohydrates; 1 g fiber; 3 g usable carbs.

| | | | | | |
|---|---|---|---|---|---|
| Potassium (mg): | 303 mg | Vitamin C (mg): | 3 mg | Thiamin/B1 (mg): | 0.1 mg |
| Calcium (mg): | 16 mg | Vitamin A (i.u.): | 105 i.u. | Riboflavin/B2 (mg): | 0.3 mg |
| Iron (mg): | 1 mg | Vitamin B6 (mg): | 0.1 mg | Folacin (mcg): | 16 mcg |
| Zinc (mg): | 1 mg | Vitamin B12 (mcg): | trace | Niacin/B3 (mg): | 3 mg |

## Feta-Lime Mushrooms and Onions

Unusual!

- 1 1/2 tablespoon (7 g) butter
- 1 1/2 tablespoon (7 ml) olive oil
- 1 medium onion, sliced
- 8 ounces (225 g) sliced mushrooms
- 2 tablespoons (28 ml) lime juice
- 1/4 cup (30 g) crumbled feta cheese

Spray a big, heavy skillet with nonstick cooking spray, and put it over medium-high heat. Add the butter and oil, and swirl them together as the butter melts. Add the onion and mushrooms and sauté, stirring frequently, until the onions are translucent and the mushrooms have softened and changed color.

Stir in the lime juice and let the whole thing cook for another minute or two. Crumble in the feta, stir, and serve.

**Yield:** 4 servings

**Nutritional Analysis:** Each will have: 79 calories; 5 g fat; 3 g protein; 6 g carbohydrates; 1 g fiber; 5 g usable carbs.

| | | | | | |
|---|---|---|---|---|---|
| Potassium (mg): | 261 mg | Vitamin C (mg): | 6 mg | Thiamin/B1 (mg): | 0.1 mg |
| Calcium (mg): | 56 mg | Vitamin A (i.u.): | 97 i.u. | Riboflavin/B2 (mg): | 0.3 mg |
| Iron (mg): | 1 mg | Vitamin B6 (mg): | 0.1 mg | Folacin (mcg): | 20 mcg |
| Zinc (mg): | 1 mg | Vitamin B12 (mcg): | 0.2 mcg | Niacin/B3 (mg): | 2 mg |

## Spiced Coconut Mushrooms

Exotic!

- 1 tablespoon (14 ml) coconut oil
- 8 ounces (225 g) sliced mushrooms
- 1/2 cup (65 g) chopped onion
- 2 cloves garlic, peeled and minced
- 2 teaspoons (10 g) chili garlic paste
- 1/2 cup (120 ml) coconut milk
- Salt and pepper
- 2 tablespoons (7.5 g) minced cilantro

Give a big, heavy skillet a shot of nonstick cooking spray, and put it over medium heat. Add the oil, and when that's melted, add the mushrooms and onion. Sauté until the onion is translucent and the mushrooms have softened and changed color.

Stir in the garlic, chili garlic paste, and coconut milk. Let the whole thing simmer for 4 or 5 minutes. Add salt and pepper to taste, stir in the cilantro, and serve.

**Yield:** 4 servings

**Nutritional Analysis:** Each will have: 124 calories; 11 g fat; 2 g protein; 7 g carbohydrates; 2 g fiber; 5 g usable carbs.

| | | | | | |
|---|---|---|---|---|---|
| Potassium (mg): | 329 mg | Vitamin C (mg): | 5 mg | Thiamin/B1 (mg): | 0.1 mg |
| Calcium (mg): | 15 mg | Vitamin A (i.u.): | 15 i.u. | Riboflavin/B2 (mg): | 0.3 mg |
| Iron (mg): | 1 mg | Vitamin B6 (mg): | 0.1 mg | Folacin (mcg): | 21 mcg |
| Zinc (mg): | 1 mg | Vitamin B12 (mcg): | 0 mcg | Niacin/B3 (mg): | 3 mg |

## Sautéed Portobellos and Artichoke Hearts

14 ounces (390 g) canned artichoke hearts, drained

2 teaspoons (10 ml) olive oil

2 teaspoons (10 g) butter

2 tablespoons (20 g) minced onion

1 clove garlic, peeled and finely minced

3 large portobello mushroom caps, sliced 1/4 inch (6 mm) thick

1/4 teaspoon salt

1/4 teaspoon pepper

Slice the artichoke hearts lengthwise into 1/4-inch (6-mm) slices.

Spray a big, heavy skillet with nonstick cooking spray, and put it over medium-high heat. Add the oil and butter, and swirl the two together as the butter melts. Add the onion, garlic, mushrooms, salt, and pepper. Sauté, stirring, for 2 to 3 minutes or until the onion and mushrooms both start to soften.

Add the sliced artichoke hearts, and stir them in. Sauté everything together for another minute or two, and serve.

**Yield:** 6 servings

**Nutritional Analysis:** Each will have: 67 calories; 3 g fat; 3 g protein; 8 g carbohydrates; 1 g fiber; 7 g usable carbs.

| | | | | | |
|---|---|---|---|---|---|
| Potassium (mg): | 240 mg | Vitamin C (mg): | 3 mg | Thiamin/B1 (mg): | 0.1 mg |
| Calcium (mg): | 6 mg | Vitamin A (i.u.): | 48 i.u. | Riboflavin/B2 (mg): | 0.3 mg |
| Iron (mg): | 1 mg | Vitamin B6 (mg): | 0.1 mg | Folacin (mcg): | 14 mcg |
| Zinc (mg): | trace | Vitamin B12 (mcg): | trace | Niacin/B3 (mg): | 3 mg |

# Portobellos with Garlic and Parsley

This is great by itself, and it makes an excellent base for any number of other recipes.

- 2 tablespoons (28 g) butter
- 4 cloves garlic, peeled and minced
- 2 tablespoons (28 ml) olive oil
- 1 pound (455 g) small portobello mushrooms, sliced (I can buy these already sliced in my grocery store)
- 1 cup (60 g) minced fresh parsley
- 1/4 teaspoon cayenne pepper
- Salt

In a big, heavy skillet, melt 1 tablespoon (14 g) of the butter over medium heat. Add the garlic, and stir it in. Add the remaining tablespoon (14 g) of butter and the olive oil, then add the portobellos. Sauté, stirring frequently, until they're softened and changing color. Stir in the parsley, then sprinkle the cayenne evenly over the mushrooms and stir that in, too. Sauté for just another minute or two, add salt to taste, and serve.

**Yield:** 4 servings

**Nutritional Analysis:** Each will have: 148 calories; 13 g fat; 3 g protein; 7 g carbohydrates; 2 g fiber; 5 g usable carbs.

| | | | | | |
|---|---|---|---|---|---|
| Potassium (mg): | 507 mg | Vitamin C (mg): | 25 mg | Thiamin/B1 (mg): | 0.1 mg |
| Calcium (mg): | 34 mg | Vitamin A (i.u.): | 1043 i.u. | Riboflavin/B2 (mg): | 0.5 mg |
| Iron (mg): | 2 mg | Vitamin B6 (mg): | 0.1 mg | Folacin (mcg): | 46 mcg |
| Zinc (mg): | 1 mg | Vitamin B12 (mcg): | trace | Niacin/B3 (mg): | 5 mg |

## Lemon-Mustard Brussels Sprouts

If you've only had brussels sprouts boiled and buttered and you don't think you like them, try this. You just might change your mind. Sliced and sautéed, they're a whole different vegetable!

1 pound (455 g) brussels sprouts

1 tablespoon (14 ml) brown mustard

4 teaspoons (20 ml) lemon juice

1/2 teaspoon Splenda

3 tablespoons (40 g) butter

Trim the stems of the brussels sprouts, and remove any bruised or wilted leaves. Run the sprouts through the slicing blade of your food processor.

In a small dish, mix together the mustard, lemon juice, and Splenda. Reserve.

Spray a big, heavy skillet with nonstick cooking spray, and put it over medium heat. Melt the butter, then add the shredded sprouts. Sauté them, stirring often, until they're softening a little and have a few brown spots.

Stir in the mustard and lemon juice mixture, cook for another minute or so, stirring constantly, and serve.

**Yield:** 6 servings

**Nutritional Analysis:** Each will have: 83 calories; 6 g fat; 3 g protein; 7 g carbohydrates; 3 g fiber; 4 g usable carbs.

| | | | | | |
|---|---|---|---|---|---|
| Potassium (mg): | 274 mg | Vitamin C (mg): | 59 mg | Thiamin/B1 (mg): | 0.1 mg |
| Calcium (mg): | 34 mg | Vitamin A (i.u.): | 819 i.u. | Riboflavin/B2 (mg): | trace |
| Iron (mg): | 1 mg | Vitamin B6 (mg): | 0.1 mg | Folacin (mcg): | 42 mcg |
| Zinc (mg): | trace | Vitamin B12 (mcg): | trace | Niacin/B3 (mg): | 1 mg |

## Brussels Sprouts with Orange Beurre Noisette

Easy, yet elegant.

1 pound (455 g) brussels sprouts

2 tablespoons (28 g) butter

1 orange

Trim the bottoms of the stems of the brussels sprouts, and remove any bruised or wilted leaves. Put the sprouts in a microwaveable casserole with a lid, add a couple of tablespoons (30 ml or so) of water, cover, and put 'em in the microwave on high for 8 minutes.

Meanwhile, put the butter in a small, heavy skillet over medium heat. Heat it until the butter browns, but don't let it burn!

When the brussels sprouts are done nuking, remove them from the microwave, drain them, and put them in a serving bowl. Pour the browned butter over them, and toss.

Grate 1 teaspoon of the orange's rind into the brussels sprouts, then whack the orange in half and squeeze the juice over the sprouts, too. Toss again, to let everything get acquainted, and serve.

**Yield:** 4 servings

**Nutritional Analysis:** Each will have: 110 calories; 6 g fat; 4 g protein; 13 g carbohydrates; 5 g fiber; 8 g usable carbs.

| | | | | | |
|---|---|---|---|---|---|
| Potassium (mg): | 458 mg | Vitamin C (mg): | 104 mg | Thiamin/B1 (mg): | 0.1 mg |
| Calcium (mg): | 58 mg | Vitamin A (i.u.): | 1186 i.u. | Riboflavin/B2 (mg): | 0.1 mg |
| Iron (mg): | 1 mg | Vitamin B6 (mg): | 0.2 mg | Folacin (mcg): | 72 mcg |
| Zinc (mg): | trace | Vitamin B12 (mcg): | trace | Niacin/B3 (mg): | 1 mg |

## Fennel with Parmesan

My sister Kim, who tested this recipe, rated it a 12—on a 1-to-10 scale!

- 3 large or 4 medium fennel bulbs
- 2 tablespoons (28 g) butter
- 1 shallot, minced
- 2 cloves garlic, peeled and minced
- 1 teaspoon dried thyme
- 1/2 teaspoon salt
- 1/4 cup (60 ml) chicken broth
- 3 tablespoons (15 g) grated Parmesan cheese

Trim the stalks off the fennel and discard. (Or save those tasty leaves for another recipe!) Trim the very base of the bulbs, too. Now halve 'em lengthwise, and slice 'em lengthwise about 1/2 inch (1.25 cm) thick.

Spray a big, heavy skillet with nonstick cooking spray, and put it over medium heat. Melt the butter, then add the shallot and garlic. Sauté for a minute or two. Add the thyme and fennel, and mix everything up well.

Sprinkle with the salt, and add the broth. Cover the pan, turn the burner to medium-low, and cook for 30 minutes, uncovering every 5 minutes or so for a good stir.

When the 30 minutes are up, uncover the skillet, turn the burner back up to medium, and let it cook for 5 minutes or so to evaporate off some of the liquid.

Transfer to a serving dish, sprinkle with the Parmesan, and serve.

**Yield:** 4 servings

**Nutritional Analysis:** Each will have: 130 calories; 7 g fat; 4 g protein; 14 g carbohydrates; 6 g fiber; 8 g usable carbs.

| | | | | | |
|---|---|---|---|---|---|
| Potassium (mg): | 763 mg | Vitamin C (mg): | 22 mg | Thiamin/B1 (mg): | trace |
| Calcium (mg): | 152 mg | Vitamin A (i.u.): | 804 i.u. | Riboflavin/B2 (mg): | 0.1 mg |
| Iron (mg): | 2 mg | Vitamin B6 (mg): | 0.1 mg | Folacin (mcg): | 50 mcg |
| Zinc (mg): | 1 mg | Vitamin B12 (mcg): | 0.1 mcg | Niacin/B3 (mg): | 1 mg |

## Fennel-Leek Casserole

If you have leftovers, it's not a problem. They're delicious, too!

2 fennel bulbs

2 leeks

1/2 teaspoon salt

1/2 teaspoon pepper

3 tablespoons (45 ml) half-and-half

8 ounces (225 g) Gruyère cheese, shredded

1 tablespoon (14 g) butter

Preheat the oven to 425°F (220°C, or gas mark 7). Trim the stems off the fennel bulbs. Keep a few of the feathery leaves for garnish. Slice the bulbs vertically into fairly thin slices.

Trim the roots off of the leeks, and slice the white part fairly thin, too. The base can be tough.

Toss the sliced fennel with 1/4 teaspoon each of the salt and pepper. Toss the leeks with the remaining 1/4 teaspoon each of the salt and pepper.

Spray an 8 x 8-inch (20 x 20-cm) baking dish with nonstick cooking spray. Layer half of the sliced fennel in the bottom, and top with half the sliced leeks. Sprinkle with 1 1/2 tablespoons (21 ml) of half-and-half. Cover with 4 ounces (115 g) of the shredded cheese. Cut 1 1/2 teaspoons of butter into little bits, and dot them around the top layer. Now repeat the whole process—layer of fennel, layer of leeks, and the remaining half-and-half, cheese, and butter.

Bake for 30 to 40 minutes, until the cheese on top is golden.

**Yield:** 6 servings

**Nutritional Analysis:** Each will have: 226 calories; 15 g fat; 13 g protein; 10 g carbohydrates; 3 g fiber; 7 g usable carbs.

| | | | | | |
|---|---|---|---|---|---|
| Potassium (mg): | 420 mg | Vitamin C (mg): | 13 mg | Thiamin/B1 (mg): | trace |
| Calcium (mg): | 448 mg | Vitamin A (i.u.): | 699 i.u. | Riboflavin/B2 (mg): | 0.1 mg |
| Iron (mg): | 1 mg | Vitamin B6 (mg): | 0.1 mg | Folacin (mcg): | 44 mcg |
| Zinc (mg): | 2 mg | Vitamin B12 (mcg): | 0.6 mcg | Niacin/B3 (mg): | 1 mg |

## Roasted Root Vegetables

Root vegetables are higher in calories and carbs than things like leafy greens, but they're especially satisfying with winter meals. I think this would make a great side dish for Thanksgiving or Christmas, especially since this is another recipe that's easy to double.

1/2 celeriac

1/2 large turnip

1 parsnip

1 large carrot

1 medium sweet potato

1 large onion

1 1/2 tablespoons (21 g) butter

1 1/2 tablespoons (21 ml) olive oil

1/2 teaspoon salt or Vege-Sal

Preheat the oven to 400°F (200°C, or gas mark 6). Peel the celeriac, turnip, parsnip, carrot, sweet potato, and onion, and cut them into similar-size chunks. Try to get them about 1/2-inch (1.25-cm) square by 2-inches (5-cm) long.

In a big roasting pan, melt the butter and mix it with the oil. Now put the vegetables in the pan, and toss vigorously until they're evenly coated with a fine film of butter and oil. Sprinkle on the salt, and toss again.

Put the vegetables in the oven, and set the timer for 20 minutes. When it beeps, use a pancake turner to turn all the vegetables and mix them up again. Roast for another 20 minutes, and repeat the turning. Roast for another 20 minutes, then see if the vegetables are tender and browned. If so, they're done—if not, give them a final 20 minutes. Serve hot with a roast!

**Yield:** 6 servings

**Nutritional Analysis:** Each will have: 127 calories; 7 g fat; 1 g protein; 17 g carbohydrates; 4 g fiber; 13 g usable carbs.

| | | | | | |
|---|---|---|---|---|---|
| Potassium (mg): | 313 mg | Vitamin C (mg): | 17 mg | Thiamin/B1 (mg): | 0.1 mg |
| Calcium (mg): | 36 mg | Vitamin A (i.u.): | 7831 i.u. | Riboflavin/B2 (mg): | 0.1 mg |
| Iron (mg): | 1 mg | Vitamin B6 (mg): | 0.2 mg | Folacin (mcg): | 36 mcg |
| Zinc (mg): | trace | Vitamin B12 (mcg): | trace | Niacin/B3 (mg): | 1 mg |

## The Fastest, Easiest Sweet Potatoes

Sweet potatoes have a somewhat lower glycemic index than regular potatoes and a lot more vitamins, to boot. Most sweet potato recipes call for a lot of added sugar, but this one doesn't, and it's quick and easy enough to make anytime. If you can get genuine yams (no, yams and sweet potatoes aren't the same thing—they're actually different species), they have an even lower glycemic index and can be prepared the same way.

1 large sweet potato

1 tablespoon (14 g) butter, melted

Preheat your electric tabletop grill.

Scrub the sweet potato, and whack it into slices about 1/2 inch (1.25 cm) thick. Brush the slices lightly with the melted butter. Sprinkle them with a little seasoning if you like—Creole seasoning is good, as are "soul" seasoning or seasoned salt. Lay 'em in the grill, close it, and let 'em cook for about 15 minutes. That's it!

**Yield:** 3 servings

**Nutritional Analysis:** Each will have: 79 calories; 4 g fat; 1 g protein; 11 g carbohydrates; 1 g fiber; 10 g usable carbs.

| | | | | | |
|---|---|---|---|---|---|
| Potassium (mg): | 90 mg | Vitamin C (mg): | 10 mg | Thiamin/B1 (mg): | trace |
| Calcium (mg): | 11 mg | Vitamin A (i.u.): | 8838 i.u. | Riboflavin/B2 (mg): | 0.1 mg |
| Iron (mg): | trace | Vitamin B6 (mg): | 0.1 mg | Folacin (mcg): | 6 mcg |
| Zinc (mg): | trace | Vitamin B12 (mcg): | trace | Niacin/B3 (mg): | trace |

# Roasted Turnips

The roasted garlic adds a mellow twang to the turnips.

- 2 pounds (905 g) turnips, peeled and cubed
- 8 cloves garlic, whole, peeled
- 1 1/2 tablespoons (2.2 g) Splenda
- 1/2 teaspoon blackstrap molasses
- 3 tablespoons (45 ml) olive oil
- 3/4 teaspoon ground cumin

Preheat the oven to 400°F (200°C, or gas mark 6).

Put the turnips and garlic in a big bowl. In a separate bowl, mix together the Splenda, molasses, oil, and cumin. Pour the mixture over the turnips and garlic, and toss until everything's well combined.

Put everything in a baking dish, and bake, uncovered, for 15 minutes. Stir, and bake for another 15 to 25 minutes, or until the turnips are tender and the whole thing's lightly browned. While you eat, mash the garlic into the turnip.

**Yield:** 4 servings

**Nutritional Analysis:** Each will have: 154 calories; 10 g fat; 2 g protein; 15 g carbohydrates; 3 g fiber; 12 g usable carbs.

| | | | | | |
|---|---|---|---|---|---|
| Potassium (mg): | 403 mg | Vitamin C (mg): | 41 mg | Thiamin/B1 (mg): | 0.1 mg |
| Calcium (mg): | 77 mg | Vitamin A (i.u.): | 5 i.u. | Riboflavin/B2 (mg): | trace |
| Iron (mg): | 1 mg | Vitamin B6 (mg): | 0.2 mg | Folacin (mcg): | 27 mcg |
| Zinc (mg): | 1 mg | Vitamin B12 (mcg): | 0 mcg | Niacin/B3 (mg): | 1 mg |

## Rutabaga-Turnip Puree

This goes quite nicely with a ham steak.

2 pounds (905 g) rutabaga
1 pound (455 g) turnip
2 tablespoons (28 g) butter
Salt and pepper

Peel the rutabaga and turnip, and cut them into 1-inch (2.5-cm) cubes. Put 'em in a big, heavy saucepan and cover with water. Add a teaspoon of salt, and simmer until they're very tender—about 45 minutes should do it.

Drain the 'baga and turnip well, and transfer them to your food processor, with the S-blade in place. Puree till smooth.

Okay, throw the puree back into the saucepan and simmer it over medium heat, stirring often, until any excess moisture evaporates.

Stir in the butter, add salt and pepper to taste, and serve.

**Yield:** 6 servings

**Nutritional Analysis:** Each will have: 105 calories; 4 g fat; 2 g protein; 16 g carbohydrates; 5 g fiber; 11 g usable carbs.

| | | | | | |
|---|---|---|---|---|---|
| Potassium (mg): | 628 mg | Vitamin C (mg): | 51 mg | Thiamin/B1 (mg): | 0.1 mg |
| Calcium (mg): | 91 mg | Vitamin A (i.u.): | 1022 i.u. | Riboflavin/B2 (mg): | 0.1 mg |
| Iron (mg): | 1 mg | Vitamin B6 (mg): | 0.2 mg | Folacin (mcg): | 41 mcg |
| Zinc (mg): | 1 mg | Vitamin B12 (mcg): | trace | Niacin/B3 (mg): | 1 mg |

## Harvard Beets

My sister Kim, who tested this sugar-free version of the old-time favorite, pronounced it "delicious." But that's no big deal—Kim likes beets. More importantly, her husband, Jay—who does not like beets—liked this! And it's beautiful on the plate, of course.

2 cans (15 ounces, or 420 g each) sliced beets
1/3 cup (8 g) Splenda
1/4 cup (60 ml) cider vinegar

1/4 teaspoon salt

1 tablespoon (14 g) butter

Guar or xanthan gum

Open the beets, and measure 1 cup (235 ml) of their juice into a saucepan. Drain the rest of the juice, and set the beets aside.

Stir the Splenda, vinegar, and salt into the beet juice. Thicken to a slightly syrupy consistency with your guar or xanthan shaker. Put the mixture over medium heat, add the beets, and bring to a simmer. Stir in the butter, and serve.

**Yield:** 6 servings

**Nutritional Analysis:** Each will have: 71 calories; 2 g fat; 1 g protein; 13 g carbohydrates; 3 g fiber; 10 g usable carbs.

| | | | | | |
|---|---|---|---|---|---|
| Potassium (mg): | 352 mg | Vitamin C (mg): | 6 mg | Thiamin/B1 (mg): | 0 mg |
| Calcium (mg): | 24 mg | Vitamin A (i.u.): | 89 i.u. | Riboflavin/B2 (mg): | trace |
| Iron (mg): | 3 mg | Vitamin B6 (mg): | 0.1 mg | Folacin (mcg): | 46 mcg |
| Zinc (mg): | trace | Vitamin B12 (mcg): | trace | Niacin/B3 (mg): | trace |

## Sautéed Peppers and Tomatoes

Bright and colorful, and great with a grilled steak!

3 tablespoons (45 ml) olive oil

8 ounces (225 g) red bell peppers, cut into 1/2-inch (1.25-cm) slices

8 ounces (225 g) yellow bell peppers, cut into 1/2-inch (1.25-cm) slices

1 clove garlic, peeled and minced

12 ounces (350 g) plum tomatoes, sliced into wedges

1 tablespoon (9 g) capers

4 anchovy fillets, chopped

2 teaspoons chopped fresh oregano, or 1 teaspoon dried

1/4 teaspoon salt

Make sure you have all your ingredients together before starting.

Put the oil in a big, heavy skillet and place it over medium heat. Sauté the peppers in the oil, stirring frequently.

After 5 to 7 minutes, stir in the garlic, tomato wedges, capers, anchovies, oregano, and salt. Turn the heat up to medium-high. Keep sautéing, stirring occasionally, till the peppers are tender, and serve.

**Yield:** 4 servings

**Nutritional Analysis:** Each will have: 141 calories; 11 g fat; 3 g protein; 10 g carbohydrates; 2 g fiber; 8 g usable carbs.

| | | | | | |
|---|---|---|---|---|---|
| Potassium (mg): | 380 mg | Vitamin C (mg): | 189 mg | Thiamin/B1 (mg): | 0.1 mg |
| Calcium (mg): | 26 mg | Vitamin A (i.u.): | 3255 i.u. | Riboflavin/B2 (mg): | 0.1 mg |
| Iron (mg): | 1 mg | Vitamin B6 (mg): | 0.2 mg | Folacin (mcg): | 34 mcg |
| Zinc (mg): | trace | Vitamin B12 (mcg): | trace | Niacin/B3 (mg): | 2 mg |

## Zucchini with Mint

Feel free to make this with fresh oregano, instead!

1½ pounds (670 g) zucchini
2 teaspoons (12 g) salt
5 tablespoons (75 ml) olive oil
2 tablespoons (8 g) chopped fresh mint
1 clove garlic, peeled and minced
3 tablespoons (45 ml) wine vinegar
Salt and pepper

Scrub the zukes and slice them into ½-inch (1.25-cm) rounds. Put them in a colander, and toss them with the salt. Let them sit for an hour. Now rinse them, drain them, and pat them dry with paper towels. Pat them good and hard to get all the excess water.

In a big, heavy skillet, heat 4 tablespoons (60 ml) of the oil over medium-high heat. Get it good and hot, then fry the zukes in batches, getting them golden on both sides. Drain the zucchini slices on paper towels.

In a small bowl, mix the mint, garlic, vinegar, and the remaining tablespoon (15 ml) of olive oil together. Toss with the zucchini slices. Add salt and pepper to taste. Let the whole thing sit for at least an hour or two for the flavors to meld before serving.

**Yield:** 4 servings

**Nutritional Analysis:** Each will have: 176 calories; 17 g fat; 2 g protein; 6 g carbohydrates; 2 g fiber; 4 g usable carbs.

| | | | | | |
|---|---|---|---|---|---|
| Potassium (mg): | 428 mg | Vitamin C (mg): | 15 mg | Thiamin/B1 (mg): | 0.1 mg |
| Calcium (mg): | 39 mg | Vitamin A (i.u.): | 665 i.u. | Riboflavin/B2 (mg): | trace |
| Iron (mg): | 1 mg | Vitamin B6 (mg): | 0.1 mg | Folacin (mcg): | 39 mcg |
| Zinc (mg): | trace | Vitamin B12 (mcg): | 0 mcg | Niacin/B3 (mg): | 1 mg |

## Lemon-Herb Zucchini

Do you have any idea how low in calories and carbs zucchini is?

2 medium zucchini
2 tablespoons (28 ml) olive oil
2 tablespoons (28 ml) lemon juice
1/4 teaspoon dried thyme
1/2 teaspoon ground coriander
1 clove garlic, peeled and minced
2 tablespoons (8 g) chopped fresh parsley

Cut the zukes in half lengthwise, then slice them 1/4-inch (6-mm) thick.

Spray a big, heavy skillet with nonstick cooking spray, and put it over medium-high heat. Add the oil. When it's hot, add the sliced zucchini and sauté, stirring frequently, till it's just softening.

Add the lemon juice, thyme, coriander, and garlic. Stir everything together, drop the heat, and let it simmer for another few minutes.

Stir in the parsley, and serve.

**Yield:** 4 servings

**Nutritional Analysis:** Each will have: 78 calories; 7 g fat; 1 g protein; 4 g carbohydrates; 1 g fiber; 3 g usable carbs.

| | | | | | |
|---|---|---|---|---|---|
| Potassium (mg): | 269 mg | Vitamin C (mg): | 15 mg | Thiamin/B1 (mg): | 0.1 mg |
| Calcium (mg): | 22 mg | Vitamin A (i.u.): | 436 i.u. | Riboflavin/B2 (mg): | trace |
| Iron (mg): | 1 mg | Vitamin B6 (mg): | 0.1 mg | Folacin (mcg): | 26 mcg |
| Zinc (mg): | trace | Vitamin B12 (mcg): | 0 mcg | Niacin/B3 (mg): | trace |

## Sautéed Zucchini and Vidalia Onions with Balsamic Vinegar and Mint

Summertime goodness!

1 pound (455 g) zucchini (little ones are best)

1 pound (455 g) Vidalia onions or other sweet onions (Bermuda would do fine)

2 tablespoons (28 ml) extra virgin olive oil

1 tablespoon (4 g) chopped fresh mint

2 teaspoons (10 ml) balsamic vinegar

Salt and pepper

Cut the stems off the zucchini, halve them lengthwise, and cut them into 1-inch (2.5-cm) chunks.

Peel the onions, and cut them vertically into 1-inch (2.5-cm) wedges.

Spray a big, heavy skillet with nonstick cooking spray, and put it over medium heat. Add the olive oil, then the zucchini and onions. Sauté, stirring occasionally, until the vegetables are cooked through, but not mushy.

Stir in the mint, then sprinkle the balsamic vinegar over all. Cook for another minute or two, add salt and pepper to taste, and serve.

**Yield:** 4 servings

**Nutritional Analysis:** Each will have: 119 calories; 7 g fat; 3 g protein; 13 g carbohydrates; 3 g fiber; 10 g usable carbs.

| | | | | | |
|---|---|---|---|---|---|
| Potassium (mg): | 455 mg | Vitamin C (mg): | 17 mg | Thiamin/B1 (mg): | 0.1 mg |
| Calcium (mg): | 42 mg | Vitamin A (i.u.): | 424 i.u. | Riboflavin/B2 (mg): | trace |
| Iron (mg): | 1 mg | Vitamin B6 (mg): | 0.2 mg | Folacin (mcg): | 47 mcg |
| Zinc (mg): | trace | Vitamin B12 (mcg): | 0 mcg | Niacin/B3 (mg): | 1 mg |

chapter six

# Side Salads

We here in America have heard so much about our bad nutritional choices and our malign influence on world eating habits—fast food, soda pop, all that—that I thought it would be nice to let you know of one great American food innovation that can do wonders for your health: serving salad at the beginning of the meal. In the old European tradition, salad was served after the main course. But over a century ago, Californians started serving salad as the first course. The restaurant industry picked up on it as a way to get something in front of hungry diners fast, while their main dishes were cooking. And now salad first just seems right to us.

What a wonderful innovation! Serving salad first, when appetites are high, is a great way to assure that everyone does justice to the greenery. So please, serve your family salad first, whether it's one of these many and varied types, or just bagged greens tossed with your favorite dressing. Try new salads often, to keep interest high. This chapter will certainly give you plenty of ideas!

The dressings are at the end of this chapter; here we start right in with the tossed salads.

# Mixed Greens with Goat Cheese and Olives

This is the sort of salad for which I have been known to pay big bucks in a fancy restaurant. This has enough protein to make a nice light meal, if you like.

2 tablespoons (28 ml) olive oil

1 tablespoon (1.5 g) Splenda

1 tablespoon (14 ml) balsamic vinegar

1 large clove garlic, peeled and minced

4 ounces (115 g) goat cheese

1/3 cup (50 g) walnuts chopped medium-fine

1 1/2 quarts (120 g) mixed greens

1 red bell pepper

1 navel orange

1/2 cup (50 g) kalamata olives, pitted and chopped

Whisk together the olive oil, Splenda, balsamic vinegar, and garlic. Let it sit while you assemble the rest of the salad.

Cut the goat cheese into 4 slices. Press the walnuts into the goat cheese slices, and refrigerate.

Put the mixed greens in a salad bowl. Slice the pepper into short, thin strips, and add them to the bowl. Peel the orange, separate it into sections, and slice each section into 3 or 4 pieces. Add the pieces to the salad. Pit the olives (the easiest way is to press down on each one with your thumb), and chop them up. Add them to the salad, too.

Give the dressing one final whisking, pour it over the salad, and toss like crazy, until every leaf gleams. Pile salad on 4 serving plates, top each with a round of goat cheese, and serve.

**Yield:** 4 servings

**Nutritional Analysis:** Each will have: 363 calories; 31 g fat; 14 g protein; 11 g carbohydrates; 4 g fiber; 7 g usable carbs.

| | | | | | |
|---|---|---|---|---|---|
| Potassium (mg): | 425 mg | Vitamin C (mg): | 116 mg | Thiamin/B1 (mg): | 0.1 mg |
| Calcium (mg): | 351 mg | Vitamin A (i.u.): | 6335 i.u. | Riboflavin/B2 (mg): | 0.4 mg |
| Iron (mg): | 2 mg | Vitamin B6 (mg): | 0.3 mg | Folacin (mcg): | 172 mcg |
| Zinc (mg): | 1 mg | Vitamin B12 (mcg): | trace | Niacin/B3 (mg): | 2 mg |

## Mixed Greens with Walnuts, Goat Cheese, and Raspberry Dressing

The slightly bitter greens, the sweet dressing, the creamy goat cheese, and the crispy nuts make a heckuva combination!

1 quart (80 g) romaine lettuce, torn

1 quart (80 g) leaf lettuce, torn

2 cups (40 g) arugula, torn

2 cups (40 g) radicchio, torn

2 ounces (55 g) goat cheese

3 tablespoons (24 g) chopped walnuts

1/2 cup (120 ml) Easy Light Raspberry Dressing (see page 225)

Assemble the romaine and leaf lettuces, arugula, and radicchio in the salad bowl. Cut the goat cheese into little chunks. Have the chopped walnuts standing by.

Pour the dressing over the greens, and toss. Pile the salad on 5 salad plates, top each with a little goat cheese and some walnuts, and serve.

**Yield:** 5 servings

**Nutritional Analysis:** Each will have: 114 calories; 8 g fat; 6 g protein; 5 g carbohydrates; 2 g fiber; 3 g usable carbs.

| | | | | | |
|---|---|---|---|---|---|
| Potassium (mg): | 319 mg | Vitamin C (mg): | 17 mg | Thiamin/B1 (mg): | 0.1 mg |
| Calcium (mg): | 147 mg | Vitamin A (i.u.): | 1589 i.u. | Riboflavin/B2 (mg): | 0.2 mg |
| Iron (mg): | 1 mg | Vitamin B6 (mg): | 0.1 mg | Folacin (mcg): | 108 mcg |
| Zinc (mg): | 1 mg | Vitamin B12 (mcg): | trace | Niacin/B3 (mg): | 1 mg |

## Mixed Salad with Blue Cheese and Pecans

This is a wonderful autumn salad.

3 cups (60 g) romaine lettuce

3 cups (60 g) leaf lettuce

2 cups (40 g) arugula

1/4 cup (60 ml) reduced-calorie balsamic vinaigrette dressing

1/2 apple, diced

1/4 cup (30 g) chopped pecans, toasted (or just buy a can of roasted salted pecans!)

1/4 cup (30 g) crumbled blue cheese

Assemble the romaine and leaf lettuces and the arugula in a big salad bowl. Pour on the vinaigrette, and toss well. Pile the dressed greens on 4 plates. Top each salad with equal amounts of apple, pecans, and crumbled cheese, and serve.

**Yield:** 4 servings

**Nutritional Analysis:** Each will have: 119 calories; 9 g fat; 4 g protein; 7 g carbohydrates; 2 g fiber; 5 g usable carbs.

| | | | | | |
|---|---|---|---|---|---|
| Potassium (mg): | 297 mg | Vitamin C (mg): | 14 mg | Thiamin/B1 (mg): | 0.1 mg |
| Calcium (mg): | 88 mg | Vitamin A (i.u.): | 1545 i.u. | Riboflavin/B2 (mg): | 0.1 mg |
| Iron (mg): | 1 mg | Vitamin B6 (mg): | 0.1 mg | Folacin (mcg): | 96 mcg |
| Zinc (mg): | 1 mg | Vitamin B12 (mcg): | 0.1 mcg | Niacin/B3 (mg): | trace |

## Arugula Salad with Fennel, Olives, and Oranges

The arugula, fennel, orange, and olive make this salad inarguably Mediterranean.

4 cups (80 g) butter lettuce leaves, torn

4 cups (80 g) arugula leaves

1 fennel bulb

1 orange

2 tablespoons (28 ml) extra virgin olive oil

1 clove garlic, peeled and very finely minced

1 tablespoon (14 ml) balsamic vinegar

2 ounces (55 g) sliced black olives, drained

Salt and pepper

Combine the lettuce and arugula in a salad bowl.

Halve the fennel bulb vertically, then slice as thinly as possible.

Use a paring knife to peel the orange, removing all of the white pith and the outer membrane. Cut it into very thin slices, then cut across each orange "wheel," making two semi-circles of each. Remove any seeds.

Combine the oil, garlic, and vinegar, whisking them together well. Pour them over the lettuce and arugula, and toss very well. Salt and pepper lightly, and toss again.

Add the fennel and orange slices, and toss again. Sprinkle the olives over the salad, and serve.

**Yield:** 4 servings

**Nutritional Analysis:** Each will have: 123 calories; 9 g fat; 2 g protein; 11 g carbohydrates; 4 g fiber; 7 g usable carbs.

| | | | | | |
|---|---|---|---|---|---|
| Potassium (mg): | 525 mg | Vitamin C (mg): | 32 mg | Thiamin/B1 (mg): | 0.1 mg |
| Calcium (mg): | 105 mg | Vitamin A (i.u.): | 1211 i.u. | Riboflavin/B2 (mg): | 0.1 mg |
| Iron (mg): | 1 mg | Vitamin B6 (mg): | 0.1 mg | Folacin (mcg): | 86 mcg |
| Zinc (mg): | trace | Vitamin B12 (mcg): | 0 mcg | Niacin/B3 (mg): | 1 mg |

## Arugula, Fennel, Apple, and Tangerine Salad

This is best to make in the winter, when tangerines and apples are both in season. But if you want to make it out of season, you could substitute a navel orange for the tangerines.

- 1/3 cup (80 ml) extra virgin olive oil
- 1/4 cup (60 ml) fresh lemon juice
- 2 tablespoons (20 g) minced onion
- 1 clove garlic, peeled and crushed
- 1/2 teaspoon lemon zest
- 1 large fennel bulb
- 1 large gala apple
- 6 cups (120 g) arugula
- 2 tangerines, peeled, separated, and with each section cut into 3 pieces

Whisk together the oil, lemon juice, onion, garlic, and lemon peel. Let the dressing sit while you assemble the salad.

Slice the fennel bulb seriously thin, down to the stem. This is easiest with a mandolin slicer. If you have a thin-slicing blade on your food processor, that would work, too. If you're using a knife, you can use the fennel stem as a kind of handle. Toss the stems. Core the apple, and cut it into matchstick strips. Put the fennel and apple in a bowl, add 2 tablespoons (28 ml) of the dressing, and toss to coat.

Put the arugula in a large salad bowl, pour on the rest of the dressing, and toss. Pile the arugula on 6 salad plates and top with the fennel-apple mixture and bits of tangerine.

**Yield:** 6 servings

**Nutritional Analysis:** Each will have: 154 calories; 12 g fat; 1 g protein; 12 g carbohydrates; 3 g fiber; 9 g usable carbs.

| | | | | | |
|---|---|---|---|---|---|
| Potassium (mg): | 326 mg | Vitamin C (mg): | 23 mg | Thiamin/B1 (mg): | trace |
| Calcium (mg): | 59 mg | Vitamin A (i.u.): | 799 i.u. | Riboflavin/B2 (mg): | trace |
| Iron (mg): | 1 mg | Vitamin B6 (mg): | 0.1 mg | Folacin (mcg): | 38 mcg |
| Zinc (mg): | trace | Vitamin B12 (mcg): | 0 mcg | Niacin/B3 (mg): | trace |

# Tossed Salad with Arugula, Corn, and Tomatoes

The corn and tomatoes mark this as a summer salad. It would be beautiful next to some grilled chicken!

3 cups (60 g) torn leaf lettuce leaves
3 cups (60 g) torn arugula leaves
1 cup (60 g) chopped fresh basil
1 cup (225 g) corn kernels (preferably fresh, but thawed frozen will do)
1 cup (150 g) cherry tomatoes, halved
2 tablespoons (28 ml) olive oil
2 tablespoons (28 ml) lemon juice
2 ounces (55 g) Parmesan cheese
Salt and pepper

Put the lettuce, arugula, basil, corn, and tomatoes in a big bowl. Pour on the oil, and toss till every leaf is coated and gleaming. Now add the lemon juice, and toss again. Add salt and pepper to taste.

Pile the salad on 4 serving plates. Use a vegetable peeler to shave the Parmesan on top of each plate, then serve.

**Yield:** 4 servings

**Nutritional Analysis:** Each will have: 178 calories; 11 g fat; 8 g protein; 13 g carbohydrates; 3 g fiber; 10 g usable carbs.

| | | | | | |
|---|---|---|---|---|---|
| Potassium (mg): | 336 mg | Vitamin C (mg): | 18 mg | Thiamin/B1 (mg): | 0.1 mg |
| Calcium (mg): | 247 mg | Vitamin A (i.u.): | 1234 i.u. | Riboflavin/B2 (mg): | 0.1 mg |
| Iron (mg): | 1 mg | Vitamin B6 (mg): | 0.1 mg | Folacin (mcg): | 64 mcg |
| Zinc (mg): | 1 mg | Vitamin B12 (mcg): | 0.2 mcg | Niacin/B3 (mg): | 1 mg |

## Butter Lettuce Salad with Peaches, Blackberries, and Parmesan Crisps

It is essential for this recipe that the shredded Parmesan have no additives. Read the label! If you can't get preshredded Parmesan with nothing added, you'll just have to buy a chunk of Parmesan and shred your own.

- 1/2 cup (40 g) shredded Parmesan cheese
- 1 quart (80 g) butter lettuce
- 2 tablespoons (28 ml) olive oil
- 1/4 teaspoon Splenda
- 1 tablespoon (14 ml) balsamic vinegar
- 1 pinch salt
- 1/2 cup (120 ml) peeled, diced peaches (if you can't get good fresh peaches, thawed unsweetened frozen peach slices work okay)
- 1/2 cup (55 g) blackberries

Spray a large microwaveable plate or glass pie plate with nonstick cooking spray, and spread the shredded Parmesan in an even layer on it. Microwave on high for 1 minute. When this cools, you should have a sheet of crisp Parmesan! If it's not crisp when cooled, give maybe 10 to 20 more seconds, but go easy—it's easy to overcook cheese in the microwave.

Tear up the lettuce in a big salad bowl. Drizzle the oil over the lettuce, and toss until every leaf is lightly coated with oil. Dissolve the Splenda in the vinegar, pour it over the lettuce, and toss well again. Sprinkle a little salt over the salad, and toss again. Add the peaches and blackberries, then crumble the sheet of crispy cheese into bite-size bits, and add them, too. Serve!

**Yield:** 4 servings

**Nutritional Analysis:** Each will have: 127 calories; 10 g fat; 5 g protein; 7 g carbohydrates; 2 g fiber; 5 g usable carbs.

| | | | | | |
|---|---|---|---|---|---|
| Potassium (mg): | 232 mg | Vitamin C (mg): | 10 mg | Thiamin/B1 (mg): | trace |
| Calcium (mg): | 150 mg | Vitamin A (i.u.): | 741 i.u. | Riboflavin/B2 (mg): | 0.1 mg |
| Iron (mg): | trace | Vitamin B6 (mg): | trace | Folacin (mcg): | 48 mcg |
| Zinc (mg): | trace | Vitamin B12 (mcg): | 0.1 mcg | Niacin/B3 (mg):: | trace |

## Artichoke, Butter Lettuce, and Tarragon Salad

Simple and classic.

2 heads butter lettuce, broken up

1 can (14 ounces, or 390 g) artichoke hearts, drained and coarsely chopped

3 tablespoons (45 ml) extra-virgin olive oil

$1\frac{1}{2}$ tablespoons (21 ml) lemon juice

1 large shallot, minced, or 2 tablespoons (20 g) minced onion plus 1 clove garlic

1 tablespoon (15 g) Dijon mustard

2 teaspoons (4 g) fresh tarragon, minced

Salt and pepper

Combine the lettuce and artichoke hearts in a big salad bowl. Pour on the oil, and toss madly until every millimeter of lettuce is coated.

In a small bowl, whisk together the lemon juice, shallot, mustard, tarragon, and salt and pepper to taste. Pour the mixture over the salad, and toss madly again. Serve immediately.

**Yield:** 4 servings

**Nutritional Analysis:** Each will have: 144 calories; 10 g fat; 4 g protein; 9 g carbohydrates; 1 g fiber; 8 g usable carbs.

| | | | | | |
|---|---|---|---|---|---|
| Potassium (mg): | 232 mg | Vitamin C (mg): | 9 mg | Thiamin/B1 (mg): | trace |
| Calcium (mg): | 31 mg | Vitamin A (i.u.): | 1107 i.u. | Riboflavin/B2 (mg): | trace |
| Iron (mg): | trace | Vitamin B6 (mg): | 0.1 mg | Folacin (mcg): | 62 mcg |
| Zinc (mg): | trace | Vitamin B12 (mcg): | 0 mcg | Niacin/B3 (mg):: | trace |

## Spinach Salad with Mushrooms and Almonds

A unique blend of tastes that just works!

$\frac{1}{2}$ teaspoon butter

2 tablespoons (16 g) sliced almonds

8 ounces (225 g) fresh baby spinach

4 ounces (115 g) sliced fresh mushrooms (buy 'em that way,

if you can!)

2 tablespoons (28 ml) olive oil

1 pinch ground nutmeg

2 tablespoons (28 ml) tarragon vinegar

Salt and pepper

Melt the butter over medium heat in a small skillet, add the almonds, and stir until they're just turning golden. Remove from the heat, and set aside.

Put the baby spinach and sliced mushrooms into a salad bowl. Add the oil, and toss until every leaf and mushroom is coated with oil. Stir the nutmeg into the tarragon vinegar, pour it over the salad, and toss again. Sprinkle on a little salt and pepper and toss again—taste a leaf to get it right.

Scatter the toasted almonds over the top, and serve.

**Yield:** 4 servings

**Nutritional Analysis:** Each will have: 111 calories; 10 g fat; 3 g protein; 5 g carbohydrates; 2 g fiber; 3 g usable carbs.

| | | | | | |
|---|---|---|---|---|---|
| Potassium (mg): | 463 mg | Vitamin C (mg): | 17 mg | Thiamin/B1 (mg): | 0.1 mg |
| Calcium (mg): | 69 mg | Vitamin A (i.u.): | 3826 i.u. | Riboflavin/B2 (mg): | 0.3 mg |
| Iron (mg): | 2 mg | Vitamin B6 (mg): | 0.1 mg | Folacin (mcg): | 118 mcg |
| Zinc (mg): | 1 mg | Vitamin B12 (mcg): | trace | Niacin/B3 (mg):: | 2 mg |

## Spinach Salad with Orange, Egg, and Avocado

This is a fresh take on the standard spinach salad with bacon and hard-boiled egg.

4 slices bacon

1/2 navel orange

1 California avocado

6 hard-boiled eggs

10 ounces (280 g) baby spinach

1/4 cup (60 ml) light balsamic vinaigrette

Place the bacon on a microwave bacon rack or in a glass pie plate, and microwave it on high for 4 minutes, or until crisp. Drain, crumble, and reserve.

Peel the half-orange, separate the sections, and cut each one into small chunks.

Whack the avocado in half, remove the stone, peel it, and cut it into cubes. Peel the eggs, and slice them into pretty circles.

Now dump the spinach into a big salad bowl. Pour on the dressing and toss well. Arrange everything else nicely on top and serve.

**Yield:** 4 servings

**Nutritional Analysis:** Each will have: 245 calories; 19 g fat; 14 g protein; 6 g carbohydrates; 4 g fiber; 2 g usable carbs.

| | | | | | |
|---|---|---|---|---|---|
| Potassium (mg): | 795 mg | Vitamin C (mg): | 25 mg | Thiamin/B1 (mg): | 0.2 mg |
| Calcium (mg): | 113 mg | Vitamin A (i.u.): | 5444 i.u. | Riboflavin/B2 (mg): | 0.6 mg |
| Iron (mg): | 3 mg | Vitamin B6 (mg): | 0.3 mg | Folacin (mcg): | 199 mcg |
| Zinc (mg): | 2 mg | Vitamin B12 (mcg): | 0.9 mcg | Niacin/B3 (mg):: | 2 mg |

## Spinach-Plum Salad

The light Asian-style dressing with the sweet plums is quite extraordinary.

3 quarts (240 g) baby spinach
2 red plums
2 scallions
2 tablespoons (28 ml) peanut oil
2 tablespoons (28 ml) rice vinegar
1 teaspoon (5 ml) soy sauce
1/2 teaspoon Splenda
1/2 teaspoon grated gingerroot

Dump the baby spinach into a big salad bowl.

Whack the plums in half, remove the pits, and cut the fruit into 1/2-inch (1.25-cm) cubes. Slice the scallions, including the crisp part of the green shoot.

In a small bowl, whisk together the oil, rice vinegar, soy sauce, Splenda, and ginger. Pour this over the spinach and toss till it's coated with the dressing. Pile the spinach on 6 salad plates, top each serving with plum cubes and scallions, and serve.

**Yield:** 6 servings

**Nutritional Analysis:** Each will have: 68 calories; 5 g fat; 2 g protein; 6 g carbohydrates; 2 g fiber; 4 g usable carbs.

| | | | | | |
|---|---|---|---|---|---|
| Potassium (mg): | 394 mg | Vitamin C (mg): | 20 mg | Thiamin/B1 (mg): | trace |
| Calcium (mg): | 64 mg | Vitamin A (i.u.): | 4119 i.u. | Riboflavin/B2 (mg): | 0.1 mg |
| Iron (mg): | 2 mg | Vitamin B6 (mg): | 0.1 mg | Folacin (mcg): | 120 mcg |
| Zinc (mg): | trace | Vitamin B12 (mcg): | 0 mcg | Niacin/B3 (mg):: | 1 mg |

## Coleslaw

This is great, traditional, creamy coleslaw—but without all the sugar and calories.

1 head cabbage

1/4 red onion, very finely minced

Coleslaw Dressing (see page 222)

Use the slicing blade of your food processor or a sharp knife to reduce the cabbage to little bitty shreds. Throw the shreds in a big darned mixing bowl.

Add the onion to the bowl, too.

Pour on the dressing, and toss.

**Yield:** 12 servings

**Nutritional Analysis:** Each will have: 32 calories; 2 g fat; trace protein; 3 g carbohydrates; trace fiber; 3 g usable carbs.

| | | | | | |
|---|---|---|---|---|---|
| Potassium (mg): | 35 mg | Vitamin C (mg): | 3 mg | Thiamin/B1 (mg): | trace |
| Calcium (mg): | 14 mg | Vitamin A (i.u.): | 16 i.u. | Riboflavin/B2 (mg): | trace |
| Iron (mg): | trace | Vitamin B6 (mg): | trace | Folacin (mcg): | 4 mcg |
| Zinc (mg): | trace | Vitamin B12 (mcg): | trace | Niacin/B3 (mg):: | trace |

## Celery Seed Slaw

Like vinegar slaw? Try this!

1/2 head cabbage

1 medium carrot

1/2 cup (120 ml) cider vinegar

1/2 cup (12 g) Splenda

1 teaspoon celery seed

½ teaspoon salt

This is easy! Shred the cabbage and carrot into a great big bowl. Stir together the vinegar, Splenda, celery seed, and salt.

Pour the mixture over the slaw, toss, and chill before serving. That's it!

**Yield:** 6 servings

**Nutritional Analysis:** Each will have: 19 calories; trace fat; trace protein; 5 g carbohydrates; 1 g fiber; 4 g usable carbs.

| | | | | | |
|---|---|---|---|---|---|
| Potassium (mg): | 82 mg | Vitamin C (mg): | 4 mg | Thiamin/B1 (mg): | trace |
| Calcium (mg): | 15 mg | Vitamin A (i.u.): | 3386 i.u. | Riboflavin/B2 (mg): | trace |
| Iron (mg): | trace | Vitamin B6 (mg): | trace | Folacin (mcg): | 5 mcg |
| Zinc (mg): | trace | Vitamin B12 (mcg): | 0 mcg | Niacin/B3 (mg):: | trace |

# Ginger-Lime Slaw

Sorta Asian, sorta Californian . . .

3 cups (210 g) shredded cabbage

¼ cup (30 g) shredded carrot

2 scallions, minced

3 tablespoons (45 ml) Ginger-Lime Vinaigrette (see page 226)

1 tablespoon (8 g) sesame seeds

Combine the cabbage, carrot, and scallions a big bowl. Drizzle on the dressing and toss.

Put the sesame seeds in a dry skillet, and stir or shake them over medium-high heat until they're toasted a light golden color. Add them to the slaw, and toss again.

**Yield:** 3 servings

**Nutritional Analysis:** Each will have: 82 calories; 5 g fat; 2 g protein; 8 g carbohydrates; 3 g fiber; 5 g usable carbs.

| | | | | | |
|---|---|---|---|---|---|
| Potassium (mg): | 267 mg | Vitamin C (mg): | 28 mg | Thiamin/B1 (mg): | 0.1 mg |
| Calcium (mg): | 49 mg | Vitamin A (i.u.): | 3013 i.u. | Riboflavin/B2 (mg): | trace |
| Iron (mg): | 1 mg | Vitamin B6 (mg): | 0.1 mg | Folacin (mcg): | 42 mcg |
| Zinc (mg): | trace | Vitamin B12 (mcg): | 0 mcg | Niacin/B3 (mg):: | 1 mg |

## Sweet Asian Slaw

I hadn't had apple in slaw before. Turns out it's quite good!

1 head Chinese cabbage

1 apple (preferably gala)

1/2 red bell pepper

5 scallions, thinly sliced, including the crisp part of the green

1 large carrot, shredded

2 tablespoons (8 g) minced cilantro

2/3 cup (160 ml) rice vinegar

3 tablespoons (4.5 g) Splenda

2 teaspoons (10 ml) soy sauce

1 tablespoon (7.5 g) sesame seeds

Shred the cabbage by taking thin slices across the whole head. Plunk the shreds into a big ol' mixing bowl.

Dice the apple into 1/4-inch (6-mm) cubes, slice the pepper into thin strips about 1 inch (2.5 cm) long, thinly slice the scallions, shred the carrot, and chop the cilantro. Add all of this to the bowl with the cabbage.

Mix together the vinegar, Splenda, and soy sauce. Pour over the vegetables, and toss to combine everything evenly.

Put the sesame seeds in a dry skillet, and stir or shake them over medium-high heat until they're toasted a light golden color. Add to the slaw and toss again. Chill for a few hours, then toss again right before serving.

**Yield:** 8 servings

**Nutritional Analysis:** Each will have: 33 calories; 1 g fat; 1 g protein; 7 g carbohydrates; 1 g fiber; 6 g usable carbs.

| | | | | | |
|---|---|---|---|---|---|
| Potassium (mg): | 139 mg | Vitamin C (mg): | 22 mg | Thiamin/B1 (mg): | trace |
| Calcium (mg): | 33 mg | Vitamin A (i.u.): | 3271 i.u. | Riboflavin/B2 (mg): | trace |
| Iron (mg): | 1 mg | Vitamin B6 (mg): | 0.1 mg | Folacin (mcg): | 16 mcg |
| Zinc (mg): | trace | Vitamin B12 (mcg): | 0 mcg | Niacin/B3 (mg):: | trace |

# Pineapple-Sesame Slaw

Welcome to the luau!

1/2 head cabbage, shredded

6 scallions, sliced, including the crisp part of the green

1 small red bell pepper, diced small

1/2 cup (120 g) pineapple chunks in juice, cut into smaller chunks

1/2 cup (100 g) canned water chestnuts, drained and chopped

1/2 cup (30 g) chopped cilantro

2 tablespoons (28 ml) pineapple juice

2 tablespoons (28 ml) soy sauce

2 tablespoons (28 ml) rice vinegar

1 tablespoon (14 ml) brown mustard

1 tablespoon (14 ml) peanut oil

1/4 teaspoon chili garlic paste

2 tablespoons (15 g) sesame seeds

Combine the cabbage, scallions, pepper, pineapple chunks, water chestnuts, and cilantro in a really big mixing bowl.

In a small bowl, whisk together the pineapple juice, soy sauce, vinegar, mustard, oil, and chili garlic paste. Pour over the vegetables, and toss well.

In a small, dry skillet, stir the sesame seeds over medium heat until they're a light golden color. Scatter over the slaw, toss again, and serve.

**Yield:** 6 servings

**Nutritional Analysis:** Each will have: 77 calories; 4 g fat; 2 g protein; 10 g carbohydrates; 2 g fiber; 8 g usable carbs.

| | | | | | |
|---|---|---|---|---|---|
| Potassium (mg): | 182 mg | Vitamin C (mg): | 46 mg | Thiamin/B1 (mg): | 0.1 mg |
| Calcium (mg): | 55 mg | Vitamin A (i.u.): | 1294 i.u. | Riboflavin/B2 (mg): | trace |
| Iron (mg): | 1 mg | Vitamin B6 (mg): | 0.1 mg | Folacin (mcg): | 25 mcg |
| Zinc (mg): | trace | Vitamin B12 (mcg): | 0 mcg | Niacin/B3 (mg):: | 1 mg |

## Saigon Slaw

The combination of cilantro and mint is characteristic of Vietnamese cooking. I've really gotten hooked on it.

4 cups (280 g) shredded Chinese cabbage

4 cups (280 g) shredded cabbage

4 scallions, sliced

1/2 cup (30 g) chopped fresh cilantro

1/2 cup (30 g) chopped fresh mint

1 small carrot, grated

1/4 cup (60 ml) fish sauce

1/2 cup (120 ml) lime juice

1/2 teaspoon chili garlic paste

Throw the Chinese and regular cabbage, scallions, cilantro, mint, and carrot into a big mixing bowl.

In a bowl or cup, mix together the fish sauce, lime juice, and chili garlic paste. Pour over the slaw, and toss everything together very well. Chill the slaw, if you're making it ahead—and if you do, toss it again before serving.

**Yield:** 12 servings

**Nutritional Analysis:** Each will have: 29 calories; 1 g fat; 1 g protein; 5 g carbohydrates; 1 g fiber; 4 g usable carbs.

| | | | | | |
|---|---|---|---|---|---|
| Potassium (mg): | 188 mg | Vitamin C (mg): | 24 mg | Thiamin/B1 (mg): | trace |
| Calcium (mg): | 50 mg | Vitamin A (i.u.): | 2639 i.u. | Riboflavin/B2 (mg): | trace |
| Iron (mg): | 1 mg | Vitamin B6 (mg): | 0.1 mg | Folacin (mcg): | 36 mcg |
| Zinc (mg): | trace | Vitamin B12 (mcg): | 0 mcg | Niacin/B3 (mg):: | trace |

## Summer Garden Slaw

This simple salad is quite different from the usual slaw—many slaw haters may well love it.

1/2 head cabbage, chopped

1 medium tomato, diced

2 cups (200 g) diced cucumber

1 cup (100 g) sliced green onions

Creamy Balsamic Dressing (see page 227)

Combine the cabbage, tomato, cucumber, and green onions in a big mixing bowl, pour on the dressing, toss, and serve.

**Yield:** 12 servings

**Nutritional Analysis:** Each will have: 36 calories; 2 g fat; 1 g protein; 4 g carbohydrates; 1 g fiber; 3 g usable carbs.

| | | | | | |
|---|---|---|---|---|---|
| Potassium (mg): | 89 mg | Vitamin C (mg): | 6 mg | Thiamin/B1 (mg): | trace |
| Calcium (mg): | 19 mg | Vitamin A (i.u.): | 143 i.u. | Riboflavin/B2 (mg): | trace |
| Iron (mg): | trace | Vitamin B6 (mg): | trace | Folacin (mcg): | 11 mcg |
| Zinc (mg): | trace | Vitamin B12 (mcg): | trace | Niacin/B3 (mg):: | trace |

## Thai Cabbage Salad

The browned garlic and onions lend a very unusual touch to this already exotic salad.

1/2 head cabbage, shredded

1/2 tablespoon (2.5 ml) coconut or peanut oil

1/4 medium onion, thinly sliced

3 cloves garlic, peeled and thinly sliced

1 tablespoon (14 ml) fish sauce

1 tablespoon (14 ml) lime juice

1 teaspoon chili garlic paste

1/4 cup (60 ml) coconut milk

2 tablespoons (16 g) chopped dry-roasted peanuts

Put the cabbage in a microwaveable casserole with a lid. Add a couple of tablespoons (30 ml or so) of water, cover, and nuke on high for 3 minutes.

While that cooks, spray a small skillet with nonstick cooking spray, add the oil, and put it over medium-high heat. Sauté the onion and garlic in the oil until they're well browned. Remove from the heat.

When the microwave beeps, put the cabbage in a large mixing bowl. Add the onions and garlic.

In a separate bowl, mix together the fish sauce, lime juice, chili paste, and coconut milk. Pour over the cabbage, and toss well. Add the peanuts, and toss again. Serve warm or at room temperature.

**Yield:** 6 servings

**Nutritional Analysis:** Each will have: 63 calories; 5 g fat; 1 g protein; 3 g carbohydrates; 1 g fiber; 2 g usable carbs.

| | | | | | |
|---|---|---|---|---|---|
| Potassium (mg): | 85 mg | Vitamin C (mg): | 5 mg | Thiamin/B1 (mg): | trace |
| Calcium (mg): | 12 mg | Vitamin A (i.u.): | 11 i.u. | Riboflavin/B2 (mg): | trace |
| Iron (mg): | trace | Vitamin B6 (mg): | trace | Folacin (mcg): | 14 mcg |
| Zinc (mg): | trace | Vitamin B12 (mcg): | 0 mcg | Niacin/B3 (mg):: | trace |

# Hot and Sweet Cucumber Salad

Oh, man. Hot and sweet, with peanuts. Too great.

3 medium cucumbers

5 scallions

1 tablespoon (14 ml) lime juice

1/2 cup (120 ml) rice vinegar

2 tablespoons (30 g) chili garlic paste

1 tablespoon (14 ml) fish sauce

1 clove garlic, peeled and minced

1 1/2 teaspoons Splenda

1/3 cup (40 g) chopped dry-roasted peanuts

Slice the cucumbers in quarters lengthwise, then slice about 1/4 inch (6 mm) thick. Put 'em in a big, nonreactive bowl. Slice the scallions, and throw them in, too.

In a separate bowl, mix together the lime juice, vinegar, chili garlic paste, fish sauce, garlic, and Splenda. Pour it over the vegetables, and toss everything together well. Stash the whole thing in the fridge for a few hours, at least, and overnight won't hurt.

Just before serving, toss in the peanuts. Stir and serve.

**Yield:** 6 servings

**Nutritional Analysis:** Each will have: 84 calories; 5 g fat; 4 g protein; 9 g carbohydrates; 2 g fiber; 7 g usable carbs.

| | | | | | |
|---|---|---|---|---|---|
| Potassium (mg): | 336 mg | Vitamin C (mg): | 12 mg | Thiamin/B1 (mg): | 0.1 mg |
| Calcium (mg): | 40 mg | Vitamin A (i.u.): | 373 i.u. | Riboflavin/B2 (mg): | trace |
| Iron (mg): | 1 mg | Vitamin B6 (mg): | 0.1 mg | Folacin (mcg): | 48 mcg |
| Zinc (mg): | 1 mg | Vitamin B12 (mcg): | 0 mcg | Niacin/B3 (mg):: | 1 mg |

## Cucumber Salad Vinaigrette

Need to take something to a friend's cookout? This is one of those convenient dishes everyone can eat—it's low-carb, low-cal, and even vegetarian. It looks nice, too. And oh yeah, I forgot—it tastes good!

- 2 large cucumbers, scrubbed, but not peeled
- 2 small tomatoes
- 1/4 small red onion
- 1/2 cup (120 ml) light balsamic vinaigrette
- 1 teaspoon dried dill weed

Slice the cucumbers in half the long way, and use the tip of a spoon to scrape out the seeds. Then slice them the long way again, making four long quarters. Slice the quarters crosswise, between 1/4 and 1/2 inch (6 mm and 1.25 cm) thick. Put the cukes in a big mixing bowl.

Dice the tomatoes and the onion fairly small, and add to the cucumbers.

Now pour on the dressing, add the dill, and stir everything together, blending well. Put in a snap-top container and stash in the fridge for a minimum of a few hours before serving.

**Yield:** 6 servings

**Nutritional Analysis:** Each will have: 25 calories; trace fat; 1 g protein; 5 g carbohydrates; 1 g fiber; 4 g usable carbs.

| | | | | | |
|---|---|---|---|---|---|
| Potassium (mg): | 252 mg | Vitamin C (mg): | 14 mg | Thiamin/B1 (mg): | trace |
| Calcium (mg): | 21 mg | Vitamin A (i.u.): | 481 i.u. | Riboflavin/B2 (mg): | trace |
| Iron (mg): | 1 mg | Vitamin B6 (mg): | 0.1 mg | Folacin (mcg): | 20 mcg |
| Zinc (mg): | trace | Vitamin B12 (mcg): | 0 mcg | Niacin/B3 (mg):: | trace |

## Apple and Wild Rice Salad

Man, I love this. The apples, the currants, the hint of orange, the crunch of the sunflower seeds—just fabulous.

1/2 head cauliflower
1/4 cup (35 g) dried currants
2 tablespoons (28 ml) balsamic vinegar
1 tablespoon (14 ml) olive oil
2 teaspoons orange zest
1 1/2 teaspoons Splenda
1 1/2 teaspoons brown mustard
1 clove garlic, peeled and minced
2 cups (250 g) chopped apple
1 cup (120 g) diced celery
1 cup (165 g) cooked wild rice
1/4 cup (55 g) toasted sunflower seeds
Salt

Run the cauliflower through the shredding blade of your food processor. Put the resulting "cauli-rice" in a microwaveable casserole with a lid. Add a couple of tablespoons (30 ml or so) of water, cover, and microwave on high for 6 minutes.

If the currants are a bit dry, put them in a small dish and add a couple of tablespoons (30 ml or so) of boiling water. Let them sit while you assemble the rest of the salad.

Whisk together the vinegar, oil, orange zest, Splenda, mustard, and garlic, or put them in your blender and run it for a few seconds.

Okay, by now the microwave has beeped! Uncover the cauliflower immediately, to stop the cooking. Let it cool for 10 minutes, stirring it once or twice during that time to let out steam. (This would be a good time to chop the apple and dice the celery, if you haven't done so already.)

Put the apple and celery in a big mixing bowl, along with the cooked wild rice.

When the cauliflower has cooled a bit, add it to the salad. Add the currants to the salad, draining them first if you've been "refreshing" them. Toss everything together.

Give the dressing one final stir, and pour it on. Toss it to coat everything.

Toss in the sunflower seeds, add salt to taste, and serve.

**Yield:** 5 servings

**Nutritional Analysis:** Each will have: 128 calories; 7 g fat; 3 g protein; 16 g carbohydrates; 3 g fiber; 13 g usable carbs.

| | | | | | |
|---|---|---|---|---|---|
| Potassium (mg): | 275 mg | Vitamin C (mg): | 17 mg | Thiamin/B1 (mg): | 0.1 mg |
| Calcium (mg): | 30 mg | Vitamin A (i.u.): | 58 i.u. | Riboflavin/B2 (mg): | 0.1 mg |
| Iron (mg): | 1 mg | Vitamin B6 (mg): | 0.2 mg | Folacin (mcg): | 45 mcg |
| Zinc (mg): | 1 mg | Vitamin B12 (mcg): | 0 mcg | Niacin/B3 (mg): | 1 mg |

## Avocado "Rice" Salad

If you want to make this ahead, do everything but peeling, seeding, and dicing the avocados. Then do that part at the last minute. You know how avocados are about browning!

1/2 head cauliflower

2 teaspoons (5 g) chicken bouillon granules

1 1/2 teaspoons dried marjoram

1 California avocado

2 scallions

1/4 cup (15 g) parsley

2 tablespoons (28 ml) lemon juice

1 tablespoon (14 ml) olive oil

Run the cauliflower through the shredding blade of your food processor. Put the resulting "cauli-rice" in a microwaveable casserole with a lid. Add a couple of tablespoons (30 ml or so) of water, cover, and nuke on high for 6 minutes.

When the cauli-rice is done, drain it and put it in a big mixing bowl. Add the bouillon, and toss till it's dissolved and evenly distributed. Toss in the marjoram, then set it all aside to cool.

When the cauliflower's cool and you're ready to serve the salad, peel and seed the avocado, and cut it into 1/2-inch (1.25-cm) cubes. Slice up the scallions and chop the parsley. Add the avocado, scallions, and parsley to the cauliflower. Add the lemon juice and oil, toss well, and serve immediately.

**Yield:** 4 servings

**Nutritional Analysis:** Each will have: 118 calories; 11 g fat; 2 g protein; 5 g carbohydrates; 3 g fiber; 2 g usable carbs.

| | | | | | |
|---|---|---|---|---|---|
| Potassium (mg): | 369 mg | Vitamin C (mg): | 19 mg | Thiamin/B1 (mg): | 0.1 mg |
| Calcium (mg): | 25 mg | Vitamin A (i.u.): | 515 i.u. | Riboflavin/B2 (mg): | 0.1 mg |
| Iron (mg): | 1 mg | Vitamin B6 (mg): | 0.2 mg | Folacin (mcg): | 48 mcg |
| Zinc (mg): | trace | Vitamin B12 (mcg): | 0 mcg | Niacin/B3 (mg): | 1 mg |

## Cauliflower and Snow Pea Salad with Mint and Lime

The mint and lime give this a lively taste.

1/2 head cauliflower

2 cups (125 g) snow pea pods, fresh

1/2 cup (50 g) sliced scallions

1/2 cup (30 g) chopped fresh mint

2 tablespoons (28 ml) olive oil

2 tablespoons (28 ml) lime juice

1 1/2 tablespoons (12 g) grated gingerroot

1 teaspoon Splenda

Salt and pepper

Run the cauliflower through the shredding blade of your food processor. Put the resulting "cauli-rice" in a microwaveable casserole with a lid, add a couple of tablespoons (30 ml or so) of water, cover, and nuke on high for 7 minutes.

When the microwave beeps, uncover the cauliflower immediately, drain it, and transfer it to the bowl you plan to serve the salad from. Stir the cauliflower every few minutes to let some of the heat escape.

While the cauliflower cools, pinch the ends off of the snow peas, pull off the strings along the sides of the pods, and cut each pod in half. Put them in a microwaveable casserole, add a couple of tablespoons (30 ml or so) of water, cover, and nuke on high for just 2 minutes. Uncover immediately when done, drain, and add to the cauli-rice.

When the veggies have cooled a bit, add the scallions and mint. Then mix together the oil, lime juice, ginger, and Splenda. Pour over the salad, and toss to combine and coat. Salt and pepper to taste. Serve warm or chilled.

**Yield:** 6 servings

**Nutritional Analysis:** Each will have: 64 calories; 5 g fat; 2 g protein; 5 g carbohydrates; 2 g fiber; 3 g usable carbs.

| | | | | | |
|---|---|---|---|---|---|
| Potassium (mg): | 159 mg | Vitamin C (mg): | 27 mg | Thiamin/B1 (mg): | 0.1 mg |
| Calcium (mg): | 37 mg | Vitamin A (i.u.): | 388 i.u. | Riboflavin/B2 (mg): | trace |
| Iron (mg): | 2 mg | Vitamin B6 (mg): | 0.1 mg | Folacin (mcg): | 32 mcg |
| Zinc (mg): | trace | Vitamin B12 (mcg): | 0 mcg | Niacin/B3 (mg): | trace |

## Cauliflower, Wild Rice, and Pea Salad

Confession: I was so taken with this recipe that I almost put it in my newspaper column twice!

1/2 head cauliflower

1/2 cup (65 g) frozen peas, thawed

1/2 cup (80 g) cooked wild rice

2 scallions, sliced

3 tablespoons (45 ml) olive oil

3 tablespoons (45 ml) lemon juice

1/2 cup (30 g) chopped fresh parsley

Salt and pepper

Run the cauliflower through the shredding blade of your food processor. Put the resulting "cauli-rice" in a microwaveable casserole with a lid. Add a couple of table-spoons (30 ml or so) of water, cover, and nuke on high for 6 minutes. Uncover as soon as it's done, to stop the cooking. Drain, and transfer to a large bowl.

Add the peas, and toss them with the cauliflower. Toss in the wild rice. Let the whole thing sit until it's cooled.

Add the scallions, then pour on the oil and lemon juice. Toss to coat everything. Toss in the parsley, and add salt and pepper to taste. You can serve this at room temperature or chill it, if you prefer. It's good either way!

**Yield:** 6 servings

**Nutritional Analysis:** Each will have: 90 calories; 7 g fat; 2 g protein; 6 g carbohydrates; 1 g fiber; 5 g usable carbs.

| | | | | | |
|---|---|---|---|---|---|
| Potassium (mg): | 108 mg | Vitamin C (mg): | 17 mg | Thiamin/B1 (mg): | trace |
| Calcium (mg): | 16 mg | Vitamin A (i.u.): | 370 i.u. | Riboflavin/B2 (mg): | trace |
| Iron (mg): | 1 mg | Vitamin B6 (mg): | 0.1 mg | Folacin (mcg): | 26 mcg |
| Zinc (mg): | trace | Vitamin B12 (mcg): | 0 mcg | Niacin/B3 (mg): | 1 mg |

## Confetti Salad

This is actually a reworking of a recipe I found in a cookbook from the 1960s. It's worth bringing into this century!

1/2 head cauliflower
1/2 cup (60 g) diced celery
1/2 cup (60 g) diced green bell pepper
1/4 cup (25 g) chopped dill pickles
2 tablespoons (17 g) capers
2 tablespoons (17 g) diced pimiento
1/2 cup (110 g) light mayonnaise
1/4 cup (60 ml) light Italian salad dressing
Salt and pepper

Run the cauliflower through the shredding blade of your processor. Put the resulting "cauli-rice" in a microwaveable casserole with a lid, add a couple of tablespoons (30 ml or so) of water, cover, and nuke on high for 6 minutes. Uncover as soon as it's done, to stop the cooking, and let it cool for at least 5 minutes, stirring now and then to let the steam out.

Put the celery, pepper, pickles, capers, and pimientos into a big mixing bowl. Add the cauli-rice when it's cool.

In a small bowl, stir together the mayo and salad dressing. Pour over the salad, toss, add salt and pepper to taste, and chill well before serving.

**Yield:** 6 servings

**Nutritional Analysis:** Each will have: 65 calories; 5 g fat; trace protein; 6 g carbohydrates; 1 g fiber; 5 g usable carbs.

| | | | | | |
|---|---|---|---|---|---|
| Potassium (mg): | 89 mg | Vitamin C (mg): | 17 mg | Thiamin/B1 (mg): | trace |
| Calcium (mg): | 8 mg | Vitamin A (i.u.): | 241 i.u. | Riboflavin/B2 (mg): | trace |
| Iron (mg): | trace | Vitamin B6 (mg): | 0.1 mg | Folacin (mcg): | 10 mcg |
| Zinc (mg): | trace | Vitamin B12 (mcg): | 0 mcg | Niacin/B3 (mg): | trace |

# Cauli-Bouli

A cyberpal posted his family's recipe for tabouli, a popular Middle Eastern salad, usually made with couscous or bulgur wheat. It looked so good, I decided to try it with cauliflower, and it was absolutely marvelous! This simple swap knocked over 100 calories and 26 grams of carbohydrates off of each serving.

- 1/2 head cauliflower
- 1 medium tomato, diced small
- 1/2 medium cucumber, diced small
- 1/4 small red onion, diced small
- 1/2 green bell pepper, diced small
- 1 cup (60 g) fresh mint leaves, minced
- 1/4 cup (60 ml) extra virgin olive oil
- 1/4 cup lemon juice
- 1 clove garlic, peeled and minced very fine
- Salt and pepper

Run the cauliflower through the shredding blade of your food processor. Put it in a microwaveable casserole with a lid, add a couple of tablespoons (30 ml) of water, and cover. Nuke it on high for 6 minutes. Uncover the cauliflower as soon as it's done, drain it, and let it cool a bit before continuing. Stir it from time to time to help release the steam and cool it faster.

Once the cauliflower's cool, put it into a big darned mixing bowl. Throw in the tomato, cuke, onion, pepper, and mint. Stir it all up.

In a separate bowl, mix the oil, lemon juice, and garlic together. Pour over the salad, and toss very well to coat everything. Add salt and pepper to taste, and chill before serving.

**Yield:** 5 servings

**Nutritional Analysis:** Each will have: 125 calories; 11 g fat; 1 g protein; 7 g carbohydrates; 2 g fiber; 5 g usable carbs.

| | | | | | |
|---|---|---|---|---|---|
| Potassium (mg): | 262 mg | Vitamin C (mg): | 30 mg | Thiamin/B1 (mg): | trace |
| Calcium (mg): | 48 mg | Vitamin A (i.u.): | 1032 i.u. | Riboflavin/B2 (mg): | trace |
| Iron (mg): | 2 mg | Vitamin B6 (mg): | 0.1 mg | Folacin (mcg): | 38 mcg |
| Zinc (mg): | trace | Vitamin B12 (mcg): | 0 mcg | Niacin/B3 (mg): | trace |

## UnPotato Salad

This is a reworking of my original UnPotato Salad in 500 Low-Carb Recipes, which in turn was based on the classic potato salad recipe that Hellmann's Mayonnaise published. If you've never tried substituting cauliflower for potatoes in potato salad, you are going to be so surprised! And this one simple swap cuts 573 calories and 133 grams of carbohydrates out of the recipe.

1 head cauliflower

1 cup (225 g) light mayonnaise

3 tablespoons (45 ml) cider vinegar

1 teaspoon salt

1 teaspoon Splenda

1/2 teaspoon pepper

2 cups (240 g) diced celery

1 cup (130 g) diced red onion

4 hard-boiled eggs

Trim the very bottom of the cauliflower stem, and cut off the leaves. Whack the rest into 1/2-inch (1.25-cm) chunks, and put them in a microwaveable casserole with a lid. Add a few tablespoons (30 ml or so) of water, cover, and microwave on high for 10 to 12 minutes. You want the cauliflower tender, but not mushy, so uncover it when it gets to that texture, or it'll continue to steam.

Put the mayo, vinegar, salt, Splenda, and pepper in a small bowl, and stir them together.

When the cauliflower is done and has cooled slightly, drain it well and combine it with the celery and onion in a really big mixing bowl. Pour the dressing over the whole thing, and stir till everything is coated.

Peel and chop the hard-boiled eggs, and add them to the salad. Fold them in gently, to preserve some hunks of yolk. Chill the salad till serving time.

**Yield:** 12 servings

**Nutritional Analysis:** Each will have: 83 calories; 6 g fat; 3 g protein; 6 g carbohydrates; 1 g fiber; 5 g usable carbs.

| | | | | | |
|---|---|---|---|---|---|
| Potassium (mg): | 131 mg | Vitamin C (mg): | 6 mg | Thiamin/B1 (mg): | trace |
| Calcium (mg): | 23 mg | Vitamin A (i.u.): | 122 i.u. | Riboflavin/B2 (mg): | 0.1 mg |
| Iron (mg): | trace | Vitamin B6 (mg): | 0.1 mg | Folacin (mcg): | 20 mcg |
| Zinc (mg): | trace | Vitamin B12 (mcg): | 0.2 mcg | Niacin/B3 (mg): | trace |

## Creamy UnPotato Salad

2 pounds (905 g) cauliflower (about 1 big head)

1/2 cup (110 g) light mayonnaise

1/4 cup (60 g) plain yogurt

1/4 cup (55 g) light sour cream

1 tablespoon (1.5 g) Splenda

2 tablespoons (28 ml) Dijon mustard

1 tablespoon (14 ml) white wine vinegar

1/2 teaspoon salt or Vege-Sal

1/2 teaspoon celery seeds

1/4 teaspoon pepper

1/8 teaspoon garlic powder

1/4 cup (30 g) sliced green onions

2 ounces (55 g) diced pimientos, drained

Trim the bottom of the cauliflower stem, and cut off the leaves. Chop the whole thing, stem and all, into 1/2-inch (1.25-cm) chunks. Put the chunks in a microwaveable casserole with a lid, add a couple of tablespoons (30 ml or so) of water, cover, and nuke on high for 8 to 10 minutes. You want it tender, but not mushy. Uncover it immediately.

Now make the dressing! Combine the mayo, yogurt, sour cream, Splenda, mustard, vinegar, salt, celery seeds, pepper, and garlic powder. Mix thoroughly.

When the cauliflower is done, drain it well and put it in a great big mixing bowl. Add the scallions, pimientos, and dressing, and toss till everything is well coated. Cover and chill for at least several hours; overnight won't hurt.

**Yield:** 8 servings

**Nutritional Analysis:** Each will have: 78 calories; 4 g fat; 3 g protein; 10 g carbohydrates; 3 g fiber; 7 g usable carbs.

| | | | | | |
|---|---|---|---|---|---|
| Potassium (mg): | 387 mg | Vitamin C (mg): | 59 mg | Thiamin/B1 (mg): | 0.1 mg |
| Calcium (mg): | 46 mg | Vitamin A (i.u.): | 231 i.u. | Riboflavin/B2 (mg): | 0.1 mg |
| Iron (mg): | 1 mg | Vitamin B6 (mg): | 0.3 mg | Folacin (mcg): | 68 mcg |
| Zinc (mg): | trace | Vitamin B12 (mcg): | trace | Niacin/B3 (mg): | 1 mg |

# Blue Cheese and Green Bean UnPotato Salad

10 ounces (280 g) frozen cross-cut green beans

1 head cauliflower

1/3 cup (80 ml) wine vinegar

1 tablespoon (14 ml) olive oil

2 teaspoons (1 g) Splenda

1/4 teaspoon salt or Vege-Sal

1/8 teaspoon pepper

1/4 cup (30 g) crumbled blue cheese

2 slices bacon, cooked crisp and drained

Put the green beans in a microwaveable casserole with a lid. Add a couple of tablespoons (30 ml or so) of water, cover, and nuke on high for 5 minutes. Stir, and give 'em another 2 to 3 minutes—you want the beans just tender. Drain them and put them in a mixing bowl.

While the beans are cooking, trim the cauliflower and whack it into 1/2-inch (1.25-cm) chunks. Put 'em in the same microwaveable casserole. Add a couple of tablespoons (30 ml or so) of water, cover, and nuke on high for 8 minutes. Drain the cauliflower and add it to the beans. Let the veggies cool enough so that they won't melt the blue cheese.

Whisk together the oil, Splenda, salt, and pepper. Pour over the veggies, and stir it up. Now crumble in the blue cheese and the bacon, stir again, and serve.

**Yield:** 8 servings

**Nutritional Analysis:** Each will have: 56 calories; 4 g fat; 2 g protein; 4 g carbohydrates; 1 g fiber; 3 g usable carbs.

| | | | | | |
|---|---|---|---|---|---|
| Potassium (mg): | 133 mg | Vitamin C (mg): | 11 mg | Thiamin/B1 (mg): | 0.1 mg |
| Calcium (mg): | 41 mg | Vitamin A (i.u.): | 203 i.u. | Riboflavin/B2 (mg): | 0.1 mg |
| Iron (mg): | trace | Vitamin B6 (mg): | 0.1 mg | Folacin (mcg): | 14 mcg |
| Zinc (mg): | trace | Vitamin B12 (mcg): | 0.1 mcg | Niacin/B3 (mg): | trace |

# Deviled UnPotato Salad

The combination of yellow mustard and paprika make this UnPotato Salad a brilliant orange—and so tasty that I scarfed down the whole batch in one day!

1 head cauliflower

1/4 red onion

1 large celery rib

1/2 cup (110 g) light mayonnaise

3 tablespoons (45 ml) yellow mustard

1 teaspoon paprika

1 teaspoon hot sauce

Salt and pepper

Trim the leaves and the bottom of the cauliflower stem, and whack the remainder into 1/2-inch (1.25-cm) chunks. Throw 'em into a microwaveable casserole with a lid. Add a couple of tablespoons (30 ml or so) of water, cover, and microwave on high for 12 minutes. You want the cauliflower tender, but not downright mushy.

Meanwhile, dice the onion and celery, and put 'em in a big mixing bowl. In another bowl, mix together the mayonnaise, mustard, paprika, and hot sauce.

When the cauliflower is done, uncover it and let it cool for a few minutes. Then drain it well, and add it to the mixing bowl. Pour on the dressing, toss to coat, add salt and pepper to taste, and chill the whole thing for several hours. That's it!

**Yield:** 8 servings

**Nutritional Analysis:** Each will have: 46 calories; 3 g fat; 1 g protein; 4 g carbohydrates; 1 g fiber; 3 g usable carbs.

| | | | | | |
|---|---|---|---|---|---|
| Potassium (mg): | 76 mg | Vitamin C (mg): | 7 mg | Thiamin/B1 (mg): | trace |
| Calcium (mg): | 11 mg | Vitamin A (i.u.): | 185 i.u. | Riboflavin/B2 (mg): | trace |
| Iron (mg): | trace | Vitamin B6 (mg): | trace | Folacin (mcg): | 10 mcg |
| Zinc (mg): | trace | Vitamin B12 (mcg): | 0 mcg | Niacin/B3 (mg): | trace |

## Cauliflower-Green Bean Salad with Pesto

Very simple.

4 cups (500 g) cauliflower

4 cups (600 g) frozen cross-cut green beans

6 tablespoons (90 ml) jarred pesto sauce

Salt

Trim the leaves and the bottom of the cauliflower stem, and whack it into medium-size chunks. Put 'em in a microwaveable casserole with a lid, add a couple of tablespoons (30 ml or so) of water, cover, and nuke on high for 8 minutes. Drain, and put in a bowl.

Put the green beans in the same casserole. Again, add a couple of tablespoons (30 ml or so) of water, and cover. Assuming the beans aren't thawed, give them 7 minutes on high in the microwave. Uncover, stir, and cook for another 3 minutes. You want the beans to be tender-crisp. Drain, and add them to the cauliflower.

Add the pesto, and toss to coat. Add salt to taste. I like to serve this at room temperature.

**Yield:** 8 servings

**Nutritional Analysis:** Each will have: 90 calories; 6 g fat; 4 g protein; 8 g carbohydrates; 3 g fiber; 5 g usable carbs.

| | | | | | |
|---|---|---|---|---|---|
| Potassium (mg): | 305 mg | Vitamin C (mg): | 32 mg | Thiamin/B1 (mg): | 0.1 mg |
| Calcium (mg): | 114 mg | Vitamin A (i.u.): | 423 i.u. | Riboflavin/B2 (mg): | 0.1 mg |
| Iron (mg): | 1 mg | Vitamin B6 (mg): | 0.2 mg | Folacin (mcg): | 41 mcg |
| Zinc (mg): | trace | Vitamin B12 (mcg): | 0.1 mcg | Niacin/B3 (mg): | 1 mg |

## Snow Pea, Cauliflower, and Water Chestnut Salad

8 ounces (225 g) fresh snow pea pods

1/2 head cauliflower

8 ounces (225 g) canned sliced water chestnuts, drained

1/2 red bell pepper, diced small

3 tablespoons (45 ml) oil

- 1 tablespoon (14 ml) soy sauce
- 1 teaspoon (1 g) Splenda
- 2 teaspoons (10 ml) rice vinegar
- 2 tablespoons (15 g) sesame seeds

Pinch the ends off of the snow peas, and pull off any strings. Cut each pod into 2 or 3 pieces. Put 'em in a microwaveable dish, add a teaspoon or two (5 to 10 ml) of water, cover (I just lay a plate on top) and microwave for just 2 minutes on high. Uncover immediately!

Trim the leaves and the bottom of the cauliflower stem, and chop it into 1/2-inch (1.25-cm) chunks. Put it in a microwaveable casserole with a lid. Add a few tablespoons (30 ml or so) of water, cover, and nuke on high for 7 to 8 minutes. Uncover immediately.

Combine the snow peas and cauliflower in a mixing bowl. Add the water chestnuts and red pepper.

In a small bowl, mix together the oil, soy sauce, Splenda, and rice vinegar. Pour over the salad, and mix everything up.

Put the sesame seeds in a dry skillet, and stir them over medium-high heat until they start to turn golden and smell toasty. Add to the salad, stir them in, and then chill the whole thing for a few hours before serving.

**Yield:** 6 servings

**Nutritional Analysis:** Each will have: 119 calories; 8 g fat; 2 g protein; 10 g carbohydrates; 3 g fiber; 7 g usable carbs.

| | | | | | |
|---|---|---|---|---|---|
| Potassium (mg): | 184 mg | Vitamin C (mg): | 46 mg | Thiamin/B1 (mg): | 0.1 mg |
| Calcium (mg): | 50 mg | Vitamin A (i.u.): | 623 i.u. | Riboflavin/B2 (mg): | trace |
| Iron (mg): | 2 mg | Vitamin B6 (mg): | 0.2 mg | Folacin (mcg): | 28 mcg |
| Zinc (mg): | 1 mg | Vitamin B12 (mcg): | 0 mcg | Niacin/B3 (mg): | 1 mg |

## Black and White Bean and Tomato Salad

Bean salads are a perennial favorite, and this one is quite unusual and colorful.

- 1 can (15 ounces, or 420 g) cannellini or Great Northern Beans
- 1 can (15 ounces, or 420 g) black soy beans (or white ones—less contrast, but no big deal)
- 1 1/2 cups (225 g) chopped tomatoes

$1/3$ cup (20 g) chopped fresh basil

$1/2$ cup (30 g) chopped fresh parsley

$1/3$ cup (40 g) crumbled feta cheese

$1/4$ cup (60 ml) balsamic vinegar

2 tablespoons (28 ml) extra virgin olive oil

$1/2$ teaspoon Splenda

$1/4$ teaspoon salt

$1/4$ teaspoon pepper

Lettuce leaves, to line plates

Drain the cannellini and soy beans, rinse them, and dump them into a bowl. Add the tomatoes, basil, parsley, and feta, and stir the whole thing up.

Whisk together the vinegar, oil, Splenda, salt, and pepper. Pour over the bean mixture, and stir again. Chill for several hours.

Stir before serving. Line 6 plates with lettuce leaves, if desired, before serving.

**Yield:** 6 servings

**Nutritional Analysis:** Each will have: 195 calories; 10 g fat; 10 g protein; 18 g carbohydrates; 7 g fiber; 11 g usable carbs.

| | | | | | |
|---|---|---|---|---|---|
| Potassium (mg): | 156 mg | Vitamin C (mg): | 16 mg | Thiamin/B1 (mg): | 0.1 mg |
| Calcium (mg): | 99 mg | Vitamin A (i.u.): | 943 i.u. | Riboflavin/B2 (mg): | 0.2 mg |
| Iron (mg): | 2 mg | Vitamin B6 (mg): | 0.1 mg | Folacin (mcg): | 32 mcg |
| Zinc (mg): | 2 mg | Vitamin B12 (mcg): | 0.1 mcg | Niacin/B3 (mg): | 1 mg |

# Bean Salad

The old potluck standby!

1 can (15 ounces, or 420 g) wax beans, drained

1 can (15 ounces, or 420 g) green beans, drained

1 can (15 ounces, or 420 g) kidney beans, drained

1 cup (130 g) chopped onion

1 cup (120 g) chopped celery

1 cup (110 g) chopped green bell pepper

$1/4$ cup (60 ml) olive oil

2/3 cup (160 ml) cider vinegar

2 teaspoons (5 g) stevia/FOS blend

1 tablespoon (1.5 g) Splenda

In a big bowl, combine the wax, green, and kidney beans with the onion, celery, and pepper. In a separate bowl, mix together the oil, vinegar, stevia, and Splenda. Stir the mixture into the veggies. Chill the whole thing for several hours, stirring occasionally, before serving.

**Yield:** 12 servings

**Nutritional Analysis:** Each will have: 103 calories; 5 g fat; 4 g protein; 12 g carbohydrates; 4 g fiber; 8 g usable carbs.

| | | | | | |
|---|---|---|---|---|---|
| Potassium (mg): | 302 mg | Vitamin C (mg): | 13 mg | Thiamin/B1 (mg): | 0.1 mg |
| Calcium (mg): | 31 mg | Vitamin A (i.u.): | 99 i.u. | Riboflavin/B2 (mg): | trace |
| Iron (mg): | 1 mg | Vitamin B6 (mg): | 0.1 mg | Folacin (mcg): | 69 mcg |
| Zinc (mg): | trace | Vitamin B12 (mcg): | 0 mcg | Niacin/B3 (mg): | trace |

**Note:** If the beans you've bought come in 15 1/2 ounce cans, don't worry about it! Half an ounce of beans, more or less, won't make a difference in how your salad comes out.

## Colorful Summer Salad

Make this one with frozen veggies and it is beyond easy.

1 pound (455 g) green beans, frozen or fresh

1 cup (165 g) corn kernels, frozen or cut off the cob

1/4 small sweet red onion, sliced paper thin

1 cup (150 g) cherry tomatoes, halved (or a medium tomato sliced into thin vertical wedges)

3 tablespoons (45 ml) olive oil

3 tablespoons (45 ml) red wine vinegar

1 1/2 teaspoons dried basil

1/4 teaspoon salt

1/4 teaspoon pepper

I confess: I use frozen cross-cut green beans and frozen corn for this salad. However, you may certainly use fresh, if you prefer. If you do, trim the beans and cut them into pieces about $1^1/2$ inches (3.75 cm) long. Either way, cook the beans until they're just done but not gray and mushy. With my frozen beans, I start with them frozen, put them in a microwaveable casserole with a lid, add a few tablespoons (30 ml or so) of water, cover, and nuke 'em on high for 5 minutes. Then I stir them, re-cover them, and give them another 3 to 4 minutes. With fresh ones, I'd nuke them for maybe 4 minutes, then check to see if they need another minute or so. Either way, drain the cooked beans and put 'em in a mixing bowl.

Put the corn kernels in the same microwavable casserole, add another couple of tablespoons (30 ml or so) of water, cover, and nuke for 3 to 4 minutes, or until just done through. Drain, and add to the beans. Let these veggies cool a bit before adding the onion and cherry tomatoes to the bowl.

In a small bowl, stir together the oil, vinegar, basil, salt, and pepper. Stir the mixture into the salad, and serve.

**Yield:** 6 servings

**Nutritional Analysis:** Each will have: 111 calories; 7 g fat; 2 g protein; 12 g carbohydrates; 3 g fiber; 9 g usable carbs.

| | | | | | |
|---|---|---|---|---|---|
| Potassium (mg): | 264 mg | Vitamin C (mg): | 17 mg | Thiamin/B1 (mg): | 0.1 mg |
| Calcium (mg): | 37 mg | Vitamin A (i.u.): | 637 i.u. | Riboflavin/B2 (mg): | 0.1 mg |
| Iron (mg): | 1 mg | Vitamin B6 (mg): | 0.1 mg | Folacin (mcg): | 38 mcg |
| Zinc (mg): | trace | Vitamin B12 (mcg): | 0 mcg | Niacin/B3 (mg): | 1 mg |

## Asparagus Salad with Lemon-Basil Mayonnaise

This trick of piping a very simple sauce in Jackson Pollock–like patterns over food is one of the tricks of the restaurant trade. It makes a simple dish look elegant, and this one is no exception.

2 pounds (905 g) asparagus

Lemon-Basil Mayonnaise (see page 490)

Snap the ends off the asparagus spears where they want to break naturally. Discard the ends and put the spears in a microwaveable casserole long enough to hold it flat, or arrange it spoke-fashion in a glass pie plate, with the tips in the center. Add a tablespoon or two (15 to 30 ml) of water, cover (use plastic wrap to cover a pie plate), and microwave for 4 to 5 minutes on high. Uncover immediately, drain, and chill.

When dinner rolls around, make the Lemon-Basil Mayonnaise, which is very easy.

Pull out the chilled asparagus, and divide it between 8 serving plates. Now spoon the Lemon-Basil Mayonnaise into a baggie. Snip a tiny bit off one corner, and squeeze cool abstract patterns of Lemon-Basil Mayonnaise over the asparagus. Garnish each plate with a basil leaf, if you have some left over, and serve right away.

**Yield:** 8 servings

**Nutritional Analysis:** Each will have: 50 calories; 3 g fat; 1 g protein; 6 g carbohydrates; 1 g fiber; 5 g usable carbs.

| | | | | | |
|---|---|---|---|---|---|
| Potassium (mg): | 175 mg | Vitamin C (mg): | 10 mg | Thiamin/B1 (mg): | 0.1 mg |
| Calcium (mg): | 15 mg | Vitamin A (i.u.): | 377 i.u. | Riboflavin/B2 (mg): | 0.1 mg |
| Iron (mg): | 1 mg | Vitamin B6 (mg): | 0.1 mg | Folacin (mcg): | 78 mcg |
| Zinc (mg): | trace | Vitamin B12 (mcg): | 0 mcg | Niacin/B3 (mg): | 1 mg |

**Note:** You could, of course, just serve a little puddle of mayonnaise on each plate for dipping—it's easier, but not quite so cool-looking.

## Radish Salad

6 ounces (170 g) radishes
2 scallions
1 teaspoon (5 ml) brown mustard
2 tablespoons (28 ml) low-calorie balsamic vinaigrette (I like Newman's Own)
1/4 teaspoon dried basil
3 tablespoons (15 g) shredded Parmesan cheese
Pepper

Slice the radishes thin—run 'em through the slicing blade of your food processor, if you like. Slice the scallions, too, including the crisp part of the green. Put 'em both in a mixing bowl.

In a small bowl, whisk together the mustard, salad dressing, and basil. Pour over the radishes and scallions, and stir it up. Now stir in the Parmesan, and add pepper to taste.

**Yield:** 3 servings

**Nutritional Analysis:** Each will have: 47 calories; 3 g fat; 2 g protein; 3 g carbohydrates; 1 g fiber; 2 g usable carbs.

| | | | | | |
|---|---|---|---|---|---|
| Potassium (mg): | 159 mg | Vitamin C (mg): | 14 mg | Thiamin/B1 (mg): | trace |
| Calcium (mg): | 86 mg | Vitamin A (i.u.): | 86 i.u. | Riboflavin/B2 (mg): | trace |
| Iron (mg): | trace | Vitamin B6 (mg): | trace | Folacin (mcg): | 21 mcg |
| Zinc (mg): | trace | Vitamin B12 (mcg): | 0.1 mcg | Niacin/B3 (mg): | trace |

## Shredded Root-Vegetable Salad

This is a great salad for the dead of winter, when the price of lettuce is sky-high.

3 medium carrots

1/2 medium celeriac

1/2 medium jicama

3 tablespoons (45 ml) lemon juice

3/4 teaspoon Splenda

1/2 teaspoon salt

1/4 teaspoon pepper

1/4 teaspoon hot sauce (optional)

1 tablespoon (14 ml) olive oil

Run the carrots, celeriac, and jicama through the shredding blade of your food processor (I like to lay the carrots down in the feed tube, to get long shreds.) Combine all the shredded vegetables in a big bowl.

In a small bowl, mix together the lemon juice, Splenda, salt, pepper, hot sauce, and oil. Pour it over the salad, and toss to coat. Chill until serving time.

**Yield:** 8 servings

**Nutritional Analysis:** Each will have: 48 calories; 2 g fat; 1 g protein; 8 g carbohydrates; 3 g fiber; 5 g usable carbs.

| | | | | | |
|---|---|---|---|---|---|
| Potassium (mg): | 186 mg | Vitamin C (mg): | 6 mg | Thiamin/B1 (mg): | trace |
| Calcium (mg): | 18 mg | Vitamin A (i.u.): | 7605 i.u. | Riboflavin/B2 (mg): | trace |
| Iron (mg): | trace | Vitamin B6 (mg): | 0.1 mg | Folacin (mcg): | 6 mcg |
| Zinc (mg): | trace | Vitamin B12 (mcg): | 0 mcg | Niacin/B3 (mg): | trace |

## Waldorf Salad

This is what Waldorf Salad was before people tarted it up with stuff like Cool Whip and marshmallows. And a beautiful thing it is, too.

- 1 granny Smith apple, cored and diced
- 3 celery ribs, diced
- 1/2 cup (60 g) chopped walnuts
- 1/4 cup (55 g) light mayonnaise

Put the apple, celery, and walnuts into a mixing bowl. Add the mayonnaise, and mix till everything's coated. Serve on a lettuce leaf.

**Yield:** 4 servings

**Nutritional Analysis:** Each will have: 150 calories; 12 g fat; 4 g protein; 9 g carbohydrates; 2 g fiber; 7 g usable carbs.

| | | | | | |
|---|---|---|---|---|---|
| Potassium (mg): | 211 mg | Vitamin C (mg): | 4 mg | Thiamin/B1 (mg): | 0.1 mg |
| Calcium (mg): | 22 mg | Vitamin A (i.u.): | 102 i.u. | Riboflavin/B2 (mg): | trace |
| Iron (mg): | 1 mg | Vitamin B6 (mg): | 0.1 mg | Folacin (mcg): | 19 mcg |
| Zinc (mg): | 1 mg | Vitamin B12 (mcg): | 0 mcg | Niacin/B3 (mg): | trace |

## Melon and Strawberry Salad

Perfect for a summer picnic potluck. This would also make a nice dessert.

- 1 medium cantaloupe
- 1 medium honeydew melon
- 2 pounds (905 g) watermelon
- 1 pound (455 g) strawberries
- 1/4 cup (15 g) chopped fresh mint
- 1/3 cup (80 ml) lime juice
- 1 tablespoon (1.5 g) Splenda

Halve the cantaloupe, honeydew, and watermelon, and remove the seeds from each. If you want to be really spiffy, use a melon baller and make pretty balls; if you want to take it easy, just peel the melons and cut them into chunks. Put the chunks in a big glass bowl (the better to see the pretty colors!).

Hull the strawberries, and cut them into quarters vertically, to make four wedges. (You could slice them instead, but I think the wedges look cool.)

Sprinkle the mint on top. Now mix together the lime juice and Splenda, pour over the salad, and stir to coat. Chill and serve.

**Yield:** 12 servings

**Nutritional Analysis:** Each will have: 80 calories; 1 g fat; 1 g protein; 20 g carbohydrates; 2 g fiber; 18 g usable carbs.

| | | | | | |
|---|---|---|---|---|---|
| Potassium (mg): | 552 mg | Vitamin C (mg): | 72 mg | Thiamin/B1 (mg): | 0.1 mg |
| Calcium (mg): | 24 mg | Vitamin A (i.u.): | 1757 i.u. | Riboflavin/B2 (mg): | trace |
| Iron (mg): | 1 mg | Vitamin B6 (mg): | 0.2 mg | Folacin (mcg): | 24 mcg |
| Zinc (mg): | trace | Vitamin B12 (mcg): | 0 mcg | Niacin/B3 (mg): | 1 mg |

## Summer Fruit Salad

Great on a nice, hot, summer day with friends.

- 1 cup (245 g) plain yogurt
- 1 teaspoon (5 ml) vanilla extract
- 1½ tablespoons (2.2 g) Splenda
- 1 tablespoon (13 g) light mayonnaise
- ¼ teaspoon orange zest
- 2 tablespoons (28 ml) orange juice
- 2 cups (330 g) sliced strawberries
- 1 kiwi fruit, peeled and diced
- 1 cup (90 g) seedless grapes, halved
- 1 navel orange, peeled, separated, and with each section cut into 3 pieces

In a large bowl, combine the yogurt, vanilla, Splenda, mayo, orange zest, and orange juice. Stir together well.

Now stir in the strawberries, kiwi, grapes, and orange, and chill for a few hours before serving.

**Yield:** 8 servings

**Nutritional Analysis:** Each will have: 58 calories; 2 g fat; 2 g protein; 9 g carbohydrates; 2 g fiber; 7 g usable carbs.

| | | | | | |
|---|---|---|---|---|---|
| Potassium (mg): | 189 mg | Vitamin C (mg): | 35 mg | Thiamin/B1 (mg): | trace |
| Calcium (mg): | 49 mg | Vitamin A (i.u.): | 94 i.u. | Riboflavin/B2 (mg): | 0.1 mg |
| Iron (mg): | 1 mg | Vitamin B6 (mg): | 0.1 mg | Folacin (mcg): | 13 mcg |
| Zinc (mg): | trace | Vitamin B12 (mcg): | 0.1 mcg | Niacin/B3 (mg): | trace |

**Note:** You could combine the fruits, spoon them into pretty serving dishes, and top with the dressing, for a fancier presentation.

# Zucchini Salad with Capers and Anchovies

Very Italian!

1 pound (455 g) zucchini

1 small red onion

1 tablespoon (9 g) capers, rinsed and drained

4 anchovy fillets, chopped a bit

2 tablespoons (28 ml) extra virgin olive oil

2 tablespoons (28 ml) tarragon vinegar

3 tablespoons (45 ml) lemon juice

1 tablespoon (14 ml) water

Salt and pepper

Slice the zucchini and onion as thin as you can. Put 'em in a salad bowl with the capers.

Combine the anchovies, oil, vinegar, lemon juice, and water in your blender or food processor with the S-blade in place, and run till smooth. Pour the dressing over the salad, and stir to coat. Chill for about 30 minutes. Add salt and pepper to taste, and serve.

**Yield:** 4 servings

**Nutritional Analysis:** Each will have: 103 calories; 7 g fat; 3 g protein; 8 g carbohydrates; 2 g fiber; 6 g usable carbs.

| | | | | | |
|---|---|---|---|---|---|
| Potassium (mg): | 374 mg | Vitamin C (mg): | 18 mg | Thiamin/B1 (mg): | 0.1 mg |
| Calcium (mg): | 35 mg | Vitamin A (i.u.): | 372 i.u. | Riboflavin/B2 (mg): | trace |
| Iron (mg): | 1 mg | Vitamin B6 (mg): | 0.1 mg | Folacin (mcg): | 33 mcg |
| Zinc (mg): | trace | Vitamin B12 (mcg): | trace | Niacin/B3 (mg): | 1 mg |

# Cherry Tomato and Mozzarella Salad

This Italian salad is so, so good. Since it has some protein from the cheese, you might want to pair this with a light main dish.

1 pound (455 g) cherry tomatoes

6 scallions

1/4 cup (60 ml) extra virgin olive oil

2 tablespoons (28 ml) balsamic vinegar

Salt and pepper

6 ounces (170 g) mozzarella cheese (Use the good stuff; you'll find it in little tubs of water in the good cheese case, not shredded in little packets in the dairy case.)

1/2 cup (30 g) chopped fresh parsley (flat-leaf is best)

1 cup (60 g) fresh basil leaves, coarsely chopped

Halve the cherry tomatoes and put them in a salad bowl. Trim the root and the limp green ends off the scallions, and finely chop the rest. Add to the tomatoes. Cut the mozzarella into 1/2-inch (1.25-cm) cubes and have it standing by.

Pour the oil and vinegar over the salad, and use clean hands to toss it well. Add salt and pepper to taste. Add the mozzarella and toss again. Cover the bowl with plastic wrap, and stash it in the refrigerator for a few hours.

Remove the salad from the fridge about 15 minutes before you want to serve it. Sprinkle the chopped parsley and basil over the top, toss once more, and serve.

**Yield:** 6 servings

**Nutritional Analysis:** Each will have: 192 calories; 16 g fat; 7 g protein; 6 g carbohydrates; 1 g fiber; 5 g usable carbs.

| | | | | | |
|---|---|---|---|---|---|
| Potassium (mg): | 262 mg | Vitamin C (mg): | 23 mg | Thiamin/B1 (mg): | trace |
| Calcium (mg): | 189 mg | Vitamin A (i.u.): | 1113 i.u. | Riboflavin/B2 (mg): | 0.1 mg |
| Iron (mg): | 1 mg | Vitamin B6 (mg): | 0.1 mg | Folacin (mcg): | 32 mcg |
| Zinc (mg): | 1 mg | Vitamin B12 (mcg): | 0.2 mcg | Niacin/B3 (mg): | 1 mg |

## Asparagus-Walnut Salad

It's interesting how well the walnuts work with the Asian dressing; it's an East-meets-West kind of thing.

2 pounds (905 g) asparagus
2 teaspoons (10 ml) oil
1/2 cup (60 g) finely chopped walnuts
1/4 cup (60 ml) soy sauce
2 tablespoons (28 ml) rice vinegar
2 tablespoons (3 g) Splenda
2 teaspoons (10 ml) dark sesame oil

Snap the ends off of the asparagus where they want to break naturally. Discard the ends, and cut the asparagus on the diagonal into 1/2-inch (1.25-cm) pieces. Put the pieces into a microwaveable casserole with a lid, add a couple of tablespoons (30 ml or so) of water, cover, and nuke on high for 3 minutes. Uncover immediately when the microwave beeps!

Put the oil into a small, heavy skillet and place it over medium heat. Sauté the chopped walnuts in the oil until they smell fragrant. Set aside.

In the bowl you intend to serve the salad in, combine the soy sauce, vinegar, Splenda, and sesame oil. Stir to combine. Now add the asparagus and walnuts, and toss until everything is well coated. Stick it in the fridge and let it chill for at least an hour; more won't hurt. If you think of it, give it a stir once or twice while it chills, and stir it before you serve.

**Yield:** 6 servings

**Nutritional Analysis:** Each will have: 118 calories; 9 g fat; 5 g protein; 7 g carbohydrates; 2 g fiber; 5 g usable carbs.

| | | | | | |
|---|---|---|---|---|---|
| Potassium (mg): | 300 mg | Vitamin C (mg): | 11 mg | Thiamin/B1 (mg): | 0.1 mg |
| Calcium (mg): | 25 mg | Vitamin A (i.u.): | 498 i.u. | Riboflavin/B2 (mg): | 0.1 mg |
| Iron (mg): | 1 mg | Vitamin B6 (mg): | 0.2 mg | Folacin (mcg): | 111 mcg |
| Zinc (mg): | 1 mg | Vitamin B12 (mcg): | 0 mcg | Niacin/B3 (mg): | 1 mg |

## Ranch Dressing

Commercial low-fat ranch dressing is usually chock-full of sugar. My version keeps the calorie count low without spiking the carb count.

1 tablespoon (4 g) dried parsley

1/4 teaspoon pepper

1/2 teaspoon onion salt

1 cup (225 g) light mayonnaise

1/2 cup (120 g) plain yogurt

1/4 teaspoon garlic salt

1/2 cup (120 ml) buttermilk

1/2 teaspoon guar or xanthan gum

Put it all in your blender, run it until it's smooth, and enjoy!

**Yield:** 2 cups (475 ml), or 16 servings

**Nutritional Analysis:** Each will have: 43 calories; 3 g fat; 1 g protein; 3 g carbohydrates; trace fiber; 3 g usable carbs.

| | | | | | |
|---|---|---|---|---|---|
| Potassium (mg): | 28 mg | Vitamin C (mg): | trace | Thiamin/B1 (mg): | trace |
| Calcium (mg): | 19 mg | Vitamin A (i.u.): | 31 i.u. | Riboflavin/B2 (mg): | trace |
| Iron (mg): | trace | Vitamin B6 (mg): | trace | Folacin (mcg): | 1 mcg |
| Zinc (mg): | trace | Vitamin B12 (mcg): | trace | Niacin/B3 (mg): | trace |

## More-than-Ranch Dressing

As the name implies, this is a kicked-up version of the classic Ranch.

3/4 cup (175 ml) buttermilk

1/2 cup (110 g) light mayonnaise

1/4 cup (15 g) minced fresh parsley

2 tablespoons (20 g) minced onion

1 clove garlic, peeled and minced

1/4 teaspoon salt or Vege-Sal

1/4 teaspoon pepper

2 tablespoons (10 g) Parmesan cheese

1/4 teaspoon guar or xanthan gum (optional)

Just assemble everything in your blender, and run it for 30 seconds to a minute. That's it! If you want to make it the consistency of a dip, just add a little extra guar or xanthan.

**Yield:** 1 1/2 cups (355 ml), or 12 servings

**Nutritional Analysis:** Each will have: 35 calories; 2 g fat; 1 g protein; 2 g carbohydrates; trace fiber; 2 g usable carbs.

| | | | | | |
|---|---|---|---|---|---|
| Potassium (mg): | 36 mg | Vitamin C (mg): | 2 mg | Thiamin/B1 (mg): | trace |
| Calcium (mg): | 32 mg | Vitamin A (i.u.): | 76 i.u. | Riboflavin/B2 (mg): | trace |
| Iron (mg): | trace | Vitamin B6 (mg): | trace | Folacin (mcg): | 3 mcg |
| Zinc (mg): | trace | Vitamin B12 (mcg): | trace | Niacin/B3 (mg): | trace |

## Coleslaw Dressing

If you read the labels on most commercial coleslaw dressings, you'll be appalled at the amount of sugar and calories in them. This tastes just as good, but look at those numbers!

1/2 cup (110 g) light mayonnaise
1/4 cup (60 g) light sour cream
1/4 cup (60 g) plain yogurt
1 1/2 tablespoons (21 ml) cider vinegar
1 1/2 teaspoons (8 g) brown or yellow mustard
1/2 teaspoon salt or Vege-Sal, or to taste
1/4 teaspoon stevia/FOS blend, or 1 teaspoon Splenda

Just stir everything together well, and toss with coleslaw.

**Yield:** 1 cup (235 ml), or 12 servings

**Nutritional Analysis:** Each will have: 29 calories; 2 g fat; trace protein; 2 g carbohydrates; trace fiber; 2 g usable carbs.

| | | | | | |
|---|---|---|---|---|---|
| Potassium (mg): | 12 mg | Vitamin C (mg): | trace | Thiamin/B1 (mg): | trace |
| Calcium (mg): | 10 mg | Vitamin A (i.u.): | 6 i.u. | Riboflavin/B2 (mg): | trace |
| Iron (mg): | trace | Vitamin B6 (mg): | trace | Folacin (mcg): | trace |
| Zinc (mg): | trace | Vitamin B12 (mcg): | trace | Niacin/B3 (mg): | trace |

## Green Goddess Dressing

This is a throwback to the 1960s. It was good then, and it's good now.

1/2 cup (115 g) light sour cream
1 cup (225 g) light mayonnaise
3 tablespoons (45 ml) cider vinegar
1 clove garlic, peeled and finely minced
1 tablespoon (15 g) anchovy paste
1/4 cup (15 g) minced fresh parsley
3 tablespoons (30 g) minced onion
1 tablespoon (14 ml) lemon juice

Toss it all in the blender, whir until smooth, and serve.

**Yield:** 2 cups (475 ml), or 16 servings

**Nutritional Analysis:** Each will have: 42 calories; 3 g fat; 1 g protein; 3 g carbohydrates; trace fiber; 3 g usable carbs.

| | | | | | |
|---|---|---|---|---|---|
| Potassium (mg): | 14 mg | Vitamin C (mg): | 2 mg | Thiamin/B1 (mg): | trace |
| Calcium (mg): | 5 mg | Vitamin A (i.u.): | 49 i.u. | Riboflavin/B2 (mg): | trace |
| Iron (mg): | trace | Vitamin B6 (mg): | trace | Folacin (mcg): | 2 mcg |
| Zinc (mg): | trace | Vitamin B12 (mcg): | 0 mcg | Niacin/B3 (mg): | trace |

## Peppercorn Parmesan Dressing

This is Ray's all-time favorite dressing.

1 cup (225 g) light mayonnaise
1/2 cup (120 g) plain yogurt
1/4 teaspoon garlic powder
1/2 cup (120 ml) buttermilk
2 teaspoons coarsely ground pepper
3/4 cup (75 g) grated Parmesan cheese
1 teaspoon guar or xanthan gum

Combine the mayo, yogurt, garlic powder, buttermilk, pepper, and cheese in your blender. Run it until the cheese disappears—it can take a good 10 minutes blending on low to get the cheese really worked in. Add the guar or xanthan and run the blender for another minute to work it in. Let it sit to thicken.

**Yield:** About 2½ cups (570 ml), or 20 servings

**Nutritional Analysis:** Each will have: 48 calories; 3 g fat; 2 g protein; 2 g carbohydrates; trace fiber; 2 g usable carbs.

| | | | | | |
|---|---|---|---|---|---|
| Potassium (mg): | 26 mg | Vitamin C (mg): | trace | Thiamin/B1 (mg): | trace |
| Calcium (mg): | 57 mg | Vitamin A (i.u.): | 31 i.u. | Riboflavin/B2 (mg): | trace |
| Iron (mg): | trace | Vitamin B6 (mg): | trace | Folacin (mcg): | 1 mcg |
| Zinc (mg): | trace | Vitamin B12 (mcg): | 0.1 mcg | Niacin/B3 (mg): | trace |

## Southwestern Dressing

Great served over crisp mixed greens, with anything grilled or barbecued.

¼ cup (60 ml) olive oil

2 tablespoons (28 ml) water

2 tablespoons (28 g) mayonnaise

2 tablespoons (28 ml) red wine vinegar

2 tablespoons (28 ml) lemon juice

½ teaspoon ground cumin

¼ teaspoon paprika

¼ teaspoon dried oregano

1 dash Tabasco sauce

Put everything in your blender and run it till it's smooth. That's all!

**Yield:** ⅔ cup (160 ml), or 6 servings

**Nutritional Analysis:** Each will have: 115 calories; 13 g fat; trace protein; 1 g carbohydrates; trace fiber; 1 g usable carbs.

| | | | | | |
|---|---|---|---|---|---|
| Potassium (mg): | 19 mg | Vitamin C (mg): | 3 mg | Thiamin/B1 (mg): | trace |
| Calcium (mg): | 4 mg | Vitamin A (i.u.): | 79 i.u. | Riboflavin/B2 (mg): | trace |
| Iron (mg): | trace | Vitamin B6 (mg): | trace | Folacin (mcg): | 1 mcg |
| Zinc (mg): | trace | Vitamin B12 (mcg): | trace | Niacin/B3 (mg): | trace |

## Easy Light Raspberry Dressing

Raspberry dressing is a favorite, but it's often high in both carbs and calories. This easy dressing is low in both and has a true raspberry flavor.

1/2 cup (120 ml) reduced-calorie Italian salad dressing with balsamic
1/2 cup (110 g) unsweetened raspberries, fresh or frozen
2 tablespoons (3 g) Splenda
1 teaspoon (5 g) Dijon mustard

Just throw everything in your blender and run it until it's smooth.

**Yield:** 1 cup (235 ml), or 8 servings

**Nutritional Analysis:** Each will have: 22 calories; 2 g fat; trace protein; 2 g carbohydrates; 1 g fiber; 1 g usable carbs.

| | | | | | |
|---|---|---|---|---|---|
| Potassium (mg): | 15 mg | Vitamin C (mg): | 2 mg | Thiamin/B1 (mg): | trace |
| Calcium (mg): | 3 mg | Vitamin A (i.u.): | 10 i.u. | Riboflavin/B2 (mg): | trace |
| Iron (mg): | trace | Vitamin B6 (mg): | trace | Folacin (mcg): | 2 mcg |
| Zinc (mg): | trace | Vitamin B12 (mcg): | 0 mcg | Niacin/B3 (mg): | trace |

## Ginger-Lime Dressing

Great not only as a salad dressing, but as a marinade, too.

2 tablespoons (28 ml) lime juice
1 tablespoon (8 g) grated gingerroot
2 teaspoons (10 g) Dijon mustard
1 pinch cayenne pepper
1/3 cup (80 ml) peanut or macadamia oil

Just whisk everything together or run it through your blender, then toss with your salad.

**Yield:** About 1/2 cup (120 ml), or 8 servings

**Nutritional Analysis:** Each will have: 83 calories; 9 g fat; trace protein; 1 g carbohydrates; trace fiber; 1 g usable carbs.

| | | | | | |
|---|---|---|---|---|---|
| Potassium (mg): | 9 mg | Vitamin C (mg): | 1 mg | Thiamin/B1 (mg): | trace |
| Calcium (mg): | 2 mg | Vitamin A (i.u.): | 6 i.u. | Riboflavin/B2 (mg): | trace |
| Iron (mg): | trace | Vitamin B6 (mg): | trace | Folacin (mcg): | 1 mcg |
| Zinc (mg): | trace | Vitamin B12 (mcg): | 0 mcg | Niacin/B3 (mg): | trace |

## Ginger-Lime Vinaigrette

This has a much more complex flavor than the previous dressing. Use this one when you want a strong Southeast Asian influence.

- 3 tablespoons (24 g) grated gingerroot
- 4 cloves garlic, peeled
- 1/4 cup (7.5 g) minced fresh cilantro
- 3 tablespoons (45 ml) dry sherry
- 4 tablespoons (60 ml) rice vinegar
- 6 tablespoons (90 ml) fish sauce
- 2 tablespoons (28 ml) lime juice
- 1 teaspoon stevia/FOS blend
- 1 tablespoon (14 ml) dark sesame oil
- 2 tablespoons (28 ml) peanut oil
- 2 tablespoons (28 ml) water

Combine everything in your food processor with the S-blade in place. Pulse until the garlic is finely minced and everything's an even consistency. Store in a tightly lidded container in the fridge.

**Yield:** 1 cup (235 ml), or 8 servings

**Nutritional Analysis:** Each will have: 83 calories; 7 g fat; trace protein; 4 g carbohydrates; trace fiber; 4 g usable carbs.

| | | | | | |
|---|---|---|---|---|---|
| Potassium (mg): | 47 mg | Vitamin C (mg): | 5 mg | Thiamin/B1 (mg): | trace |
| Calcium (mg): | 5 mg | Vitamin A (i.u.): | 39 i.u. | Riboflavin/B2 (mg): | trace |
| Iron (mg): | trace | Vitamin B6 (mg): | trace | Folacin (mcg): | 4 mcg |
| Zinc (mg): | trace | Vitamin B12 (mcg): | 0 mcg | Niacin/B3 (mg): | trace |

## Creamy Balsamic Dressing

Mmmmm...this is good as a dip, too.

- 1/4 cup (60 g) plain yogurt
- 1/4 cup (55 g) light sour cream
- 1/2 cup (110 g) light mayonnaise
- 1/4 cup (60 ml) light balsamic vinaigrette
- 2 teaspoons (10 g) yellow mustard

Whisk everything together till smooth, pour over the salad, and toss.

**Yield:** 1 1/4 cups (285 ml), or 12 servings

**Nutritional Analysis:** Each will have: 29 calories; 2 g fat; trace protein; 2 g carbohydrates; trace fiber; 2 g usable carbs.

| | | | | | |
|---|---|---|---|---|---|
| Potassium (mg): | 10 mg | Vitamin C (mg): | trace | Thiamin/B1 (mg): | trace |
| Calcium (mg): | 9 mg | Vitamin A (i.u.): | 6 i.u. | Riboflavin/B2 (mg): | trace |
| Iron (mg): | trace | Vitamin B6 (mg): | trace | Folacin (mcg): | trace |
| Zinc (mg): | trace | Vitamin B12 (mcg): | trace | Niacin/B3 (mg): | trace |

## Barbecue Vinaigrette

This really does have a strong barbecue flavor.

- 1 tablespoon (14 g) low-carb barbecue sauce
- 2 tablespoons (30 g) light mayonnaise
- 1 teaspoon (5 ml) red wine vinegar
- 1/2 teaspoon brown mustard
- 1 1/2 teaspoons (8 ml) water

Whisk everything together till smooth, pour over the salad, and toss.

**Yield:** About 1/4 cup (60 ml), or 3 servings

**Nutritional Analysis:** Each will have: 26 calories; 2 g fat; trace protein; 2 g carbohydrates; trace fiber; 2 g usable carbs.

| | | | | | |
|---|---|---|---|---|---|
| Potassium (mg): | 4 mg | Vitamin C (mg): | trace | Thiamin/B1 (mg): | trace |
| Calcium (mg): | 1 mg | Vitamin A (i.u.): | 0 i.u. | Riboflavin/B2 (mg): | trace |
| Iron (mg): | trace | Vitamin B6 (mg): | trace | Folacin (mcg): | trace |
| Zinc (mg): | trace | Vitamin B12 (mcg): | 0 mcg | Niacin/B3 (mg): | trace |

## Creamy Barbecue Dressing

This also makes a good spread for wrap sandwiches.

6 tablespoons (90 g) no-sugar-added ketchup

1 tablespoon (14 ml) Worcestershire sauce

1½ teaspoons chili powder

1 tablespoon (14 ml) cider vinegar

1 tablespoon (1.5 g) Splenda

⅓ cup (75 g) light mayonnaise

1 small clove garlic, peeled and minced

Just throw everything in the blender and run it till it's smooth.

**Yield:** ⅞ cup (200 ml), or 6 servings

**Nutritional Analysis:** Each will have: 45 calories; 3 g fat; trace protein; 5 g carbohydrates; trace fiber; 5 g usable carbs.

| | | | | | |
|---|---|---|---|---|---|
| Potassium (mg): | 38 mg | Vitamin C (mg): | 5 mg | Thiamin/B1 (mg): | trace |
| Calcium (mg): | 5 mg | Vitamin A (i.u.): | 482 i.u. | Riboflavin/B2 (mg): | trace |
| Iron (mg): | trace | Vitamin B6 (mg): | trace | Folacin (mcg): | 1 mcg |
| Zinc (mg): | trace | Vitamin B12 (mcg): | 0 mcg | Niacin/B3 (mg): | trace |

## Creamy Chipotle Dressing

Smokey-hot, and great with Tex-Mex food.

½ cup (110 g) light mayonnaise

½ cup (120 g) plain yogurt

1 chipotle chile canned in adobo

1 clove garlic, peeled and minced

2 teaspoons (10 ml) lime juice

Just throw everything in your blender and run it for a minute or so. That's it!

**Yield:** 1 cup (235 ml), or 8 servings

**Nutritional Analysis:** Each will have: 45 calories; 3 g fat; 1 g protein; 3 g carbohydrates; trace fiber; 3 g usable carbs.

| Potassium (mg): | 28 mg | Vitamin C (mg): | 1 mg | Thiamin/B1 (mg): | trace |
|---|---|---|---|---|---|
| Calcium (mg): | 19 mg | Vitamin A (i.u.): | 19 i.u. | Riboflavin/B2 (mg): | trace |
| Iron (mg): | trace | Vitamin B6 (mg): | trace | Folacin (mcg): | 1 mcg |
| Zinc (mg): | trace | Vitamin B12 (mcg): | 0.1 mcg | Niacin/B3 (mg): | trace |

## Avocado-Yogurt Dressing

You'll need to use all of this pretty pale-green dressing up right away because the avocado makes it quite perishable.

1 California avocado, peeled and seeded

1/2 cup (120 g) plain yogurt

2 tablespoons (28 ml) lemon juice

1 clove garlic, peeled and minced

Just throw everything in your blender and run it till it's smooth.

**Yield:** 1 1/2 to 2 cups (355 to 475 ml), or 8 servings

**Nutritional Analysis:** Each will have: 49 calories; 4 g fat; 1 g protein; 3 g carbohydrates; 1 g fiber; 2 g usable carbs.

| Potassium (mg): | 167 mg | Vitamin C (mg): | 4 mg | Thiamin/B1 (mg): | trace |
|---|---|---|---|---|---|
| Calcium (mg): | 22 mg | Vitamin A (i.u.): | 152 i.u. | Riboflavin/B2 (mg): | trace |
| Iron (mg): | trace | Vitamin B6 (mg): | 0.1 mg | Folacin (mcg): | 16 mcg |
| Zinc (mg): | trace | Vitamin B12 (mcg): | 0.1 mcg | Niacin/B3 (mg): | trace |

## Lemon-Mustard Vinaigrette

This is a great dressing with a Creole flair.

2 tablespoons (28 ml) red wine vinegar

1 tablespoon (10 g) minced red onion

1 tablespoon (9 g) capers, drained

1 tablespoon (14 ml) lemon juice

1/2 teaspoon salt

1/2 teaspoon stevia/FOS blend, or 2 teaspoons (1 g) Splenda

$1\frac{1}{2}$ teaspoons (8 g) brown or Dijon mustard

$\frac{1}{4}$ teaspoon pepper

$\frac{1}{4}$ teaspoon Tabasco sauce or Louisiana Hot Sauce

1 clove garlic, peeled

2 tablespoons (28 ml) olive oil

3 tablespoons (45 ml) boiling water

Just throw everything but the water in your blender, and run it until the capers and garlic are chopped up. Leave the blender running, slowly pour in the water, and you're done!

**Yield:** 5 ounces (150 ml), or 10 servings

**Nutritional Analysis:** Each will have: 26 calories; 3 g fat; trace protein; 1 g carbohydrates; trace fiber; 1 g usable carbs.

| | | | | | |
|---|---|---|---|---|---|
| Potassium (mg): | 10 mg | Vitamin C (mg): | 1 mg | Thiamin/B1 (mg): | trace |
| Calcium (mg): | 3 mg | Vitamin A (i.u.): | 1 i.u. | Riboflavin/B2 (mg): | trace |
| Iron (mg): | trace | Vitamin B6 (mg): | trace | Folacin (mcg): | trace |
| Zinc (mg): | trace | Vitamin B12 (mcg): | 0 mcg | Niacin/B3 (mg): | trace |

## Creamy Basil Dressing

If you have it on hand, you could use 1 tablespoon (4 g) of minced fresh basil in this dressing instead of the dried basil.

$\frac{1}{3}$ cup (80 ml) extra virgin olive oil

$\frac{1}{3}$ cup (75 g) light mayonnaise

$\frac{1}{3}$ cup (80 ml) water

$\frac{1}{3}$ cup (80 ml) lemon juice

$\frac{1}{3}$ cup (80 ml) red wine vinegar

1 teaspoon (.5 g) Splenda

1 teaspoon dried basil

Just put everything in your blender, and run it till it's smooth.

**Yield:** $1\frac{2}{3}$ cups (385 ml), or 15 servings

**Nutritional Analysis:** Each will have: 57 calories; 6 g fat; trace protein; 2 g carbohydrates; trace fiber; 2 g usable carbs.

| | | | | | |
|---|---|---|---|---|---|
| Potassium (mg): | 16 mg | Vitamin C (mg): | 3 mg | Thiamin/B1 (mg): | trace |
| Calcium (mg): | 3 mg | Vitamin A (i.u.): | 10 i.u. | Riboflavin/B2 (mg): | trace |
| Iron (mg): | trace | Vitamin B6 (mg): | trace | Folacin (mcg): | 1 mcg |
| Zinc (mg): | trace | Vitamin B12 (mcg): | 0 mcg | Niacin/B3 (mg): | trace |

## Creamy Southwestern Dressing

Too easy.

- 1/4 cup (55 g) light mayonnaise
- 1/4 cup (60 g) plain yogurt
- 1/4 cup (55 g) salsa
- 1/4 cup (60 g) no-sugar-added ketchup
- 1 teaspoon chili powder

Just stir everything together! Makes a good dip or sauce, too.

**Yield:** 1 cup (235 ml), or 4 servings

**Nutritional Analysis:** Each will have: 55 calories; 4 g fat; 1 g protein; 5 g carbohydrates; trace fiber; 5 g usable carbs.

| | | | | | |
|---|---|---|---|---|---|
| Potassium (mg): | 72 mg | Vitamin C (mg): | 3 mg | Thiamin/B1 (mg): | trace |
| Calcium (mg): | 25 mg | Vitamin A (i.u.): | 596 i.u. | Riboflavin/B2 (mg): | trace |
| Iron (mg): | trace | Vitamin B6 (mg): | trace | Folacin (mcg): | 4 mcg |
| Zinc (mg): | trace | Vitamin B12 (mcg): | 0.1 mcg | Niacin/B3 (mg): | trace |

## Sweet 'n' Spicy Dressing

You'll probably like this if you like Catalina or red "French" dressing—and you may like it even if you don't. I'm not crazy about those dressings, but I do like this one. I find it has a little more kick—and, of course, a whole lot less sugar.

1 tablespoon (1.5 g) Splenda

1/4 cup (60 ml) olive oil

1 clove garlic, finely minced

1/4 teaspoon celery seed

1/4 cup (60 ml) cider vinegar

1/4 cup (60 g) no-sugar-added ketchup

1 scallion, finely minced

1/4 teaspoon chili-garlic paste

Just whisk everything together, or run it through the blender.

**Yield:** 12 servings

**Nutritional Analysis:** Each will have: 43 calories; 5 g fat; trace protein; 1 g carbohydrates; trace fiber; 1 g usable carbs.

| | | | | | |
|---|---|---|---|---|---|
| Potassium (mg): | 121 mg | Vitamin C (mg): | 4 mg | Thiamin/B1 (mg): | 0 mg |
| Calcium (mg): | 29 mg | Vitamin A (iu): | 1102 i.u. | Riboflavin/B2 (mg): | trace |
| Iron (mg): | 1 mg | Vitamin B6 (mg:) | trace | Folacin (mcg): | 10 mcg |
| Zinc (mg): | trace | Vitamin B12 (mcg): | 0 mcg | Niacin/B3 (mg): | trace |

chapter seven

# Main Dish Salads

I cannot think of a better way to eat—for your palate, your waistline, or your general health—than main dish salads. Here we have protein of every sort combined with a garden full of vegetables to make an array of one-dish meals that are delicious and highly nutritious, every one. When you're just not sure what to have, have a main dish salad. It will improve your life in every way!

I learned while writing this chapter that my idea of a serving of salad and my testers' ideas of a serving of salad aren't always the same—I believe in vast, huge piles of greens! If you love big portions, indulge yourself here.

This chapter begins, as did we all, with the egg. I'm exceedingly fond of egg salad, and I make it often, as you can see. Keep hard-boiled eggs in the fridge, and you're never more than a few minutes from a good meal. (And after Easter you can make Technicolor Egg Salad with the ones where the dye seeped through the shell!)

## Chunky Egg Salad Wraps

Okay, so I like egg salad wrapped in lettuce. This is a fairly classic egg salad recipe.

4 hard-boiled eggs

2 ribs celery, diced

1/4 green bell pepper, diced

3 scallions, sliced, including the crisp part of the green

3 tablespoons (40 g) light mayonnaise

1 teaspoon (5 g) brown mustard

Salt and pepper

8 butter lettuce leaves

Peel your eggs and chop them coarsely. Throw 'em into a mixing bowl. Throw in the celery, pepper, and scallions, too. Now add the mayo and mustard, and mix. Add salt and pepper to taste.

Arrange 4 lettuce leaves on each plate, and pile the egg salad next to them. Spoon the egg salad into the leaves and roll them up to eat.

**Yield:** 2 servings

**Nutritional Analysis:** Each will have: 231 calories; 15 g fat; 14 g protein; 10 g carbohydrates; 2 g fiber; 8 g usable carbs.

| | | | | | |
|---|---|---|---|---|---|
| Potassium (mg): | 412 mg | Vitamin C (mg): | 23 mg | Thiamin/B1 (mg): | 0.1 mg |
| Calcium (mg): | 96 mg | Vitamin A (i.u.): | 1085 i.u. | Riboflavin/B2 (mg): | 0.5 mg |
| Iron (mg): | 2 mg | Vitamin B6 (mg): | 0.2 mg | Folacin (mcg): | 95 mcg |
| Zinc (mg): | 1 mg | Vitamin B12 (mcg): | 1.1 mcg | Niacin/B3 (mg): | trace |

## Deviled Egg Salad Lettuce Wraps

Spicy egg salad wrapped in fresh lettuce—yum!

4 hard-boiled eggs

1 celery rib, diced

2 scallions, sliced, including the crisp part of the green

2 tablespoons (30 g) drained and diced roasted red peppers, jarred in water (pimientos will do, if you don't have roasted red peppers)

1 teaspoon (9 g) capers, drained and chopped

2 tablespoons (20 g) light mayonnaise

$1^1/_2$ teaspoons (8 g) horseradish mustard

1 teaspoon (5 ml) lemon juice

$^1/_2$ teaspoon Creole seasoning (find this in the spice aisle of your grocery store—I use Tony Chachere's)

12 big red-leaf lettuce leaves

Peel and coarsely chop your hard-boiled eggs. Put 'em in a mixing bowl. Add the celery, scallions, peppers, and capers to the bowl.

Add the mayonnaise, mustard, lemon juice, and Creole seasoning, and stir everything up.

Arrange 6 big lettuce leaves on each of 2 plates, and divide the salad between them. Spoon the salad into the leaves and roll them up to eat.

**Yield:** 2 servings

**Nutritional Analysis:** Each will have: 212 calories; 14 g fat; 14 g protein; 8 g carbohydrates; 2 g fiber; 6 g usable carbs.

| | | | | | |
|---|---|---|---|---|---|
| Potassium (mg): | 323 mg | Vitamin C (mg): | 19 mg | Thiamin/B1 (mg): | 0.1 mg |
| Calcium (mg): | 82 mg | Vitamin A (i.u.): | 1160 i.u. | Riboflavin/B2 (mg): | 0.5 mg |
| Iron (mg): | 2 mg | Vitamin B6 (mg): | 0.2 mg | Folacin (mcg): | 88 mcg |
| Zinc (mg): | 1 mg | Vitamin B12 (mcg): | 1.1 mcg | Niacin/B3 (mg): | trace |

## Dilled Egg Salad Wraps

6 hard-boiled eggs

$^1/_4$ cup (55 g) light sour cream

2 tablespoons (20 g) light mayonnaise

4 scallions, finely chopped

1 tablespoon (3 g) dried dill weed, or 2 tablespoons (2 g) fresh, snipped fine

12 Boston lettuce leaves

Peel your eggs and chop them coarsely. Plunk 'em into a mixing bowl. Add the sour cream, mayonnaise, scallions, and dill, and stir 'er up.

Arrange 4 big lettuce leaves on each of 3 plates, and divide the salad among the plates. Wrap the salad in the lettuce burrito-style to eat.

**Yield:** 3 servings

**Nutritional Analysis:** Each will have: 198 calories; 13 g fat; 14 g protein; 6 g carbohydrates; 1 g fiber; 5 g usable carbs.

| | | | | | |
|---|---|---|---|---|---|
| Potassium (mg): | 267 mg | Vitamin C (mg): | 6 mg | Thiamin/B1 (mg): | 0.1 mg |
| Calcium (mg): | 97 mg | Vitamin A (i.u.): | 803 i.u. | Riboflavin/B2 (mg): | 0.5 mg |
| Iron (mg): | 2 mg | Vitamin B6 (mg): | 0.1 mg | Folacin (mcg): | 75 mcg |
| Zinc (mg): | 1 mg | Vitamin B12 (mcg): | 1.1 mcg | Niacin/B3 (mg): | trace |

# Egg Parmesan Salad

The Parmesan not only gives this a new flavor and an appealing texture, but it also adds calcium.

4 hard-boiled eggs

1/4 medium red onion, diced

1/2 medium green bell pepper, diced

2 tablespoons (20 g) light mayonnaise

1/4 teaspoon Tabasco sauce

1 teaspoon (5 g) brown or Dijon mustard

1/3 cup (25 g) shredded Parmesan cheese (not grated!)

Salt and pepper

Peel your eggs, and chop them coarsely. Put them in a mixing bowl with the onion and pepper.

In a small bowl, mix together the mayonnaise, Tabasco, and mustard. Pour the mixture over the salad, and mix to coat. Now stir in the Parmesan. Add salt and pepper to taste, and serve.

**Yield:** 2 servings

**Nutritional Analysis:** Each will have: 263 calories; 17 g fat; 18 g protein; 8 g carbohydrates; 1 g fiber; 7 g usable carbs.

| | | | | | |
|---|---|---|---|---|---|
| Potassium (mg): | 228 mg | Vitamin C (mg): | 28 mg | Thiamin/B1 (mg): | 0.1 mg |
| Calcium (mg): | 227 mg | Vitamin A (i.u.): | 837 i.u. | Riboflavin/B2 (mg): | 0.5 mg |
| Iron (mg): | 2 mg | Vitamin B6 (mg): | 0.2 mg | Folacin (mcg): | 56 mcg |
| Zinc (mg): | 2 mg | Vitamin B12 (mcg): | 1.3 mcg | Niacin/B3 (mg): | trace |

Next, a sizable flock of recipes using chicken. So I guess we know which came first!

## Ginger-Lime Slaw with Teriyaki Chicken

Make this with bagged coleslaw mix to save time, if you like.

- 8 ounces (225 g) boneless, skinless chicken breasts
- 3 tablespoons (45 ml) Teriyaki Sauce (see page 502)
- 3 cups (210 g) shredded cabbage
- 1/4 cup (30 g) shredded carrot
- 2 scallions, minced
- 3 tablespoons (45 ml) Ginger-Lime Vinaigrette (see page 226)
- 1 tablespoon (8 g) toasted sesame seeds

Put your chicken in a zipper-lock bag and add the teriyaki sauce. Seal the bag, squeezing out the air as you go. Turn the bag to coat the chicken. Now let it marinate for at least 20 minutes—longer would be great.

Meanwhile, make your slaw: Combine the cabbage, carrot, and scallions in a big bowl. Drizzle on the dressing and toss. Sprinkle on the sesame seeds, and toss again.

When your chicken has marinated, preheat your electric tabletop grill. Pull out the chicken, drain off the marinade into a little bowl, and throw the chicken on the grill. Set a timer for 2 minutes. When it beeps, baste the chicken with the reserved marinade, then close the grill again. Give the chicken another 3 minutes, or until done through. Pull it out of the grill, throw it on your cutting board, and slice or dice it up.

Pile the slaw on 2 plates, divide the chicken between them, and serve.

**Yield:** 2 servings

**Nutritional Analysis:** Each will have: 257 calories; 10 g fat; 28 g protein; 13 g carbohydrates; 4 g fiber; 9 g usable carbs.

| | | | | | |
|---|---|---|---|---|---|
| Potassium (mg): | 608 mg | Vitamin C (mg): | 42 mg | Thiamin/B1 (mg): | 0.1 mg |
| Calcium (mg): | 86 mg | Vitamin A (i.u.): | 4535 i.u. | Riboflavin/B2 (mg): | 0.1 mg |
| Iron (mg): | 2 mg | Vitamin B6 (mg): | 0.6 mg | Folacin (mcg): | 67 mcg |
| Zinc (mg): | 2 mg | Vitamin B12 (mcg): | 0.3 mcg | Niacin/B3 (mg): | 12 mg |

**Note:** If you could only find untoasted sesame seeds, don't worry, it's easy to toast them. Just stir them in a small, dry skillet over medium-high heat for a few minutes.

## Greek Salad with Grilled Chicken

I'm crazy about Greek Salad; this turns it into a substantial meal. This is a great supper for a hot summer night.

6 ounces (170 g) boneless, skinless chicken breast

1/4 cup (60 ml) reduced-calorie red wine and vinegar dressing

1 1/2 tablespoons (21 ml) lemon juice

2 quarts (160 g) romaine lettuce, broken up

1/2 cup (30 g) chopped fresh parsley

1 teaspoon dried oregano

1/2 green bell pepper, cut into thin strips

1/2 cup (50 g) sliced cucumber

1/2 medium tomato, sliced

1/8 small red onion, sliced paper-thin

10 kalamata olives

1/4 cup (30 g) crumbled feta cheese

Place your chicken breast in a zipper-lock bag, and add 1 tablespoon (14 ml) of the salad dressing and 1 teaspoon (5 ml) of the lemon juice. Seal the bag, pressing out the air as you go. Turn to coat, and let the chicken marinate for at least 15 minutes; an hour is better.

When you're ready to cook, preheat your electric tabletop grill, throw in your chicken, and set a timer for 5 minutes.

Make sure all of your vegetables are prepped before you begin assembling the salad. Put the romaine and parsley in a big darned salad bowl. Add the remaining salad dressing, the remaining lemon juice, and the oregano, and toss until every leaf is coated with dressing. Pile the salad on 2 big plates.

Arrange the pepper, cucumber, tomato, onion, and olives on each salad. Crumble the feta on top.

Your chicken should be done by now. Pull it out of the grill, put it on your cutting board, and cut it into thin slices across the grain. Divide the chickens between the two salads, and serve.

**Yield:** 2 servings

**Nutritional Analysis:** Each will have: 295 calories; 15 g fat; 27 g protein; 16 g carbohydrates; 6 g fiber; 10 g usable carbs.

| | | | | | |
|---|---|---|---|---|---|
| Potassium (mg): | 1111 mg | Vitamin C (mg): | 114 mg | Thiamin/B1 (mg): | 0.4 mg |
| Calcium (mg): | 227 mg | Vitamin A (i.u.): | 7199 i.u. | Riboflavin/B2 (mg): | 0.5 mg |
| Iron (mg): | 5 mg | Vitamin B6 (mg): | 0.7 mg | Folacin (mcg): | 355 mcg |
| Zinc (mg): | 2 mg | Vitamin B12 (mcg): | 0.5 mcg | Niacin/B3 (mg): | 10 mg |

# Thai Chicken and Nectarine Salad

Our tester, Barbara, proclaimed this to be "really, really good."

- 1/4 cup (60 ml) chicken broth
- 1 1/2 tablespoons (21 ml) soy sauce
- 1 1/2 tablespoons (21 ml) fish sauce
- 2 tablespoons (28 ml) Hoisin Sauce (see page 502)
- 1 tablespoon (1.5 g) Splenda
- 1 tablespoon (14 ml) peanut oil
- 2 teaspoons (10 ml) dark sesame oil
- 3 cloves garlic, peeled and minced
- 1 teaspoon chili garlic paste or red pepper flakes
- 1 pinch pepper
- 1 pound (455 g) boneless skinless chicken breasts
- 2 quarts (160 g) mixed greens
- 1 quart (120 g) fresh baby spinach, bagged
- 2 nectarines, pitted and sliced
- 4 scallions, thinly sliced, including the crisp part of the green

Put the chicken broth, soy sauce, fish sauce, hoisin sauce, Splenda, peanut oil, sesame oil, garlic, chili garlic paste, and pepper in your blender, and run it for 10 seconds, to combine well.

Preheat your electric tabletop grill. While it's heating, brush the chicken with 2 tablespoons (28 ml) of the dressing. Throw the chicken on the grill, and set the timer for 5 minutes.

Put the mixed greens and spinach in a big salad bowl, and add half the remaining dressing. Toss to coat well, then pile on 4 plates.

Top with the chicken, nectarines, and scallions, then drizzle with the rest of the dressing, and serve.

**Yield:** 4 servings

**Nutritional Analysis:** Each will have: 310 calories; 12 g fat; 32 g protein; 20 g carbohydrates; 6 g fiber; 14 g usable carbs.

| | | | | | |
|---|---|---|---|---|---|
| Potassium (mg): | 988 mg | Vitamin C (mg): | 94 mg | Thiamin/B1 (mg): | 0.2 mg |
| Calcium (mg): | 175 mg | Vitamin A (i.u.): | 8500 i.u. | Riboflavin/B2 (mg): | 0.3 mg |
| Iron (mg): | 4 mg | Vitamin B6 (mg): | 0.8 mg | Folacin (mcg): | 283 mcg |
| Zinc (mg): | 1 mg | Vitamin B12 (mcg): | 0.3 mcg | Niacin/B3 (mg): | 13 mg |

## Chicken and Cabbage Salad with Pineapple-Yogurt Dressing

I read about this combination in a Gayelord Hauser book from the 1950s, and I had to try it. It's good!

- 1/4 head cabbage, coarsely chopped
- 3/4 cup (85 g) diced cooked chicken (I like dark meat, but use breast if you prefer it)
- 2 scallions, sliced, including the crisp part of the green
- 1/4 cup (40 g) diced pineapple, in 1/4-inch (6-mm) chunks
- 1/3 cup (85 g) plain nonfat yogurt
- 3 tablespoons (40 g) crushed pineapple in juice
- Salt

Plunk the cabbage into a big bowl. Add the chicken and scallions to the bowl, along with the diced pineapple.

Mix together your yogurt and crushed pineapple, and pour it over the salad. Toss to coat, add salt to taste, and serve!

**Yield:** 1 serving

**Nutritional Analysis:** Each will have: 286 calories; 5 g fat; 38 g protein; 17 g carbohydrates; 2 g fiber; 15 g usable carbs.

| | | | | | |
|---|---|---|---|---|---|
| Potassium (mg): | 691 mg | Vitamin C (mg): | 24 mg | Thiamin/B1 (mg): | 0.2 mg |
| Calcium (mg): | 208 mg | Vitamin A (i.u.): | 208 i.u. | Riboflavin/B2 (mg): | 0.3 mg |
| Iron (mg): | 2 mg | Vitamin B6 (mg): | 0.8 mg | Folacin (mcg): | 49 mcg |
| Zinc (mg): | 2 mg | Vitamin B12 (mcg): | 0.8 mcg | Niacin/B3 (mg): | 14 mg |

# Cauliflower-Artichoke Chicken Salad with Dill

This would be a great choice for a summer luncheon or potluck—it makes a lot!

- 1 large head cauliflower
- 1 cup (225 g) light mayonnaise
- 1/2 cup (80 g) diced red onion
- 2 tablespoons (13 g) finely chopped dill pickle
- 2 tablespoons (28 ml) red wine vinegar
- 2 tablespoons (30 g) brown mustard
- 1 tablespoon (2 g) finely snipped fresh dill weed, or 1 1/2 teaspoons dried dill weed
- 1 1/2 teaspoons lemon pepper
- 1 pound (455 g) cooked boneless, skinless chicken breasts, cubed
- 12 ounces (340 g) marinated artichoke hearts, drained and chopped
- 4 hard-boiled eggs, peeled and chopped

Trim the leaves and the very bottom of the cauliflower stem, then whack it into 1/2-inch (1.25-cm) chunks, stem and all. Pile it all into a microwaveable casserole with a lid, add a few tablespoons (45 ml or so) of water, cover, and microwave on high for 10 to 12 minutes, or until the cauliflower is tender but not mushy.

While that cooks, mix together the mayo, onion, pickle, vinegar, mustard, dill, and lemon pepper in a huge bowl.

When the microwave beeps, drain your cauliflower and add it to the dressing, along with the chicken, artichoke hearts, and eggs. Fold the whole thing together gently, just until everything's coated with the dressing. Cover and chill for at least 4 or 5 hours before serving, and there's really no reason not to make this a whole day in advance.

**Yield:** 8 servings

**Nutritional Analysis:** Each will have: 264 calories; 15 g fat; 20 g protein; 14 g carbohydrates; 4 g fiber; 10 g usable carbs.

| | | | | | |
|---|---|---|---|---|---|
| Potassium (mg): | 392 mg | Vitamin C (mg): | 34 mg | Thiamin/B1 (mg): | 0.1 mg |
| Calcium (mg): | 42 mg | Vitamin A (i.u.): | 248 i.u. | Riboflavin/B2 (mg): | 0.2 mg |
| Iron (mg): | 1 mg | Vitamin B6 (mg): | 0.5 mg | Folacin (mcg): | 56 mcg |
| Zinc (mg): | 1 mg | Vitamin B12 (mcg): | 0.4 mcg | Niacin/B3 (mg): | 6 mg |

## Chicken Waldorf Salad

I've always loved Waldorf Salad—apples, celery, and walnuts tossed with mayonnaise. This makes Waldorf Salad into a meal.

1 cup (120 g) diced celery

1 cup (150 g) diced apple (leave the skin on)

1/3 cup (40 g) chopped walnuts

2 cups (220 g) diced cooked chicken

4 scallions, thinly sliced

1/3 cup (75 g) light mayonnaise

Put the celery, apple, walnuts, chicken, and scallions into a bowl. Add the mayo, toss, and serve.

**Yield:** 4 servings

**Nutritional Analysis:** Each will have: 259 calories; 13 g fat; 25 g protein; 11 g carbohydrates; 2 g fiber; 9 g usable carbs.

| | | | | | |
|---|---|---|---|---|---|
| Potassium (mg): | 393 mg | Vitamin C (mg): | 7 mg | Thiamin/B1 (mg): | 0.1 mg |
| Calcium (mg): | 42 mg | Vitamin A (i.u.): | 166 i.u. | Riboflavin/B2 (mg): | 0.1 mg |
| Iron (mg): | 1 mg | Vitamin B6 (mg): | 0.5 mg | Folacin (mcg): | 28 mcg |
| Zinc (mg): | 1 mg | Vitamin B12 (mcg): | 0.2 mcg | Niacin/B3 (mg): | 9 mg |

## Curried Chicken Waldorf

I'll curry anything that stands still long enough!

2 cups (220 g) diced cooked chicken

1 1/3 cups (160 g) diced celery

1/2 apple, diced (leave the skin on)

6 tablespoons (50 g) chopped peanuts

1 teaspoon curry powder

1/2 teaspoon salt

1 teaspoon (5 ml) cider vinegar

2 pinches cayenne pepper

6 tablespoons (85 g) light mayonnaise

Assemble the chicken, celery, apple, and peanuts in a mixing bowl. In a small dish, mix the curry, salt, vinegar, cayenne, and mayo together. Pour the dressing over the chicken mixture, mix, and serve!

**Yield:** 3 servings

**Nutritional Analysis:** Each will have: 359 calories; 19 g fat; 34 g protein; 14 g carbohydrates; 3 g fiber; 11 g usable carbs.

| | | | | | |
|---|---|---|---|---|---|
| Potassium (mg): | 556 mg | Vitamin C (mg): | 5 mg | Thiamin/B1 (mg): | 0.2 mg |
| Calcium (mg): | 60 mg | Vitamin A (i.u.): | 148 i.u. | Riboflavin/B2 (mg): | 0.2 mg |
| Iron (mg): | 2 mg | Vitamin B6 (mg): | 0.7 mg | Folacin (mcg): | 64 mcg |
| Zinc (mg): | 2 mg | Vitamin B12 (mcg): | 0.3 mcg | Niacin/B3 (mg): | 14 mg |

## Chicken Spiral Salad

Nice presentation!

1 pound (455 g) boneless, skinless chicken breasts (4 smallish breasts, or bigger ones cut into 4 portions)

4 tablespoons (60 g) no-sugar-added pizza sauce (Ragu makes one)

4 ounces (115 g) boiled ham

4 ounces (115 g) provolone cheese, sliced

1 cup (60 g) fresh basil leaves

Salt and pepper

2 tablespoons (28 ml) olive oil

2 quarts (160 g) Italian blend bagged salad

1/4 cup (60 ml) reduced-calorie Italian salad dressing

Take a chicken breast and put it in a heavy zipper-lock bag, seal the bag, and beat it to an even thickness of between 1/2 and 1/4 inch (1.25 and .6 cm). Repeat with the remaining breasts.

When all your chicken has been pounded flat, lay 1 piece on a plate. Spread 1 tablespoon (14 g) of pizza sauce on it. Top with a slice of ham and a slice of provolone. Lay basil leaves over that. Sprinkle with salt and pepper. Now roll it up tightly and repeat to make 3 more rolls.

When all the chicken is rolled up, slice each roll into 3 or 4 thick slices. Thread them onto skewers, taking care that the skewers hold the layers together.

Brush all the skewered chicken spirals with olive oil. Broil or grill them for about 5 minutes per side.

While they're cooking, toss the greens with the dressing, and pile them on 4 plates. Serve the skewers next to or on top of the salad.

**Yield:** 4 servings

**Nutritional Analysis:** Each will have: 212 calories; 16 g fat; 11 g protein; 8 g carbohydrates; 4 g fiber; 4 g usable carbs.

| | | | | | |
|---|---|---|---|---|---|
| Potassium (mg): | 458 mg | Vitamin C (mg): | 79 mg | Thiamin/B1 (mg): | 0.1 mg |
| Calcium (mg): | 337 mg | Vitamin A (i.u.): | 6402 i.u. | Riboflavin/B2 (mg): | 0.2 mg |
| Iron (mg): | 2 mg | Vitamin B6 (mg): | 0.2 mg | Folacin (mcg): | 216 mcg |
| Zinc (mg): | 1 mg | Vitamin B12 (mcg): | 0.4 mcg | Niacin/B3 (mg): | 1 mg |

## Warm Chicken Salad with Barbecue Vinaigrette

Like a barbecue in a salad!

1/4 teaspoon dried thyme

1/4 teaspoon dry mustard

1/4 teaspoon paprika

1/4 teaspoon pepper

1/2 teaspoon salt or Vege-Sal

12 ounces (340 g) boneless, skinless chicken breasts (or thighs, if you prefer)

2 teaspoons (10 ml) oil

2 quarts (160 g) romaine lettuce, torn

2 quarts (160 g) leaf lettuce, torn

Barbecue Vinaigrette (see page 227)

1 medium tomato, cut into wedges

1/4 small red onion, sliced paper-thin

Mix together the thyme, mustard, paprika, pepper, and salt. Set aside.

Cut the chicken into bite-size chunks. Give a big, heavy skillet a shot of nonstick cooking spray, and put it over medium-high heat. Add the oil, and when the pan's hot, throw in the chicken. Sauté, stirring frequently. While the chicken's sautéing, sprinkle the seasoning mixture over it, so it's coated.

Put the romaine and leaf lettuce into a big salad bowl. Pour on the dressing, and toss till it's all coated. Pile the salad on 3 plates. Top each with one-third of the sautéed chicken, one-third of the tomato wedges, and one-third of the sliced onion, and serve.

**Yield:** 3 servings

**Nutritional Analysis:** Each will have: 240 calories; 9 g fat; 30 g protein; 12 g carbohydrates; 5 g fiber; 7 g usable carbs.

| | | | | | |
|---|---|---|---|---|---|
| Potassium (mg): | 997 mg | Vitamin C (mg): | 51 mg | Thiamin/B1 (mg): | 0.3 mg |
| Calcium (mg): | 106 mg | Vitamin A (i.u.): | 4760 i.u. | Riboflavin/B2 (mg): | 0.3 mg |
| Iron (mg): | 4 mg | Vitamin B6 (mg): | 0.7 mg | Folacin (mcg): | 297 mcg |
| Zinc (mg): | 2 mg | Vitamin B12 (mcg): | 0.3 mcg | Niacin/B3 (mg): | 12 mg |

## Barbecue Chicken Coleslaw

With bagged coleslaw mix, this is quick and easy.

4 cups (280 g) shredded cabbage or bagged coleslaw mix

1 cup (110 g) diced cooked chicken

4 tablespoons (40 g) diced red onion

5 tablespoons (75 ml) Creamy Barbecue Dressing (see page 228)

1/2 teaspoon Tabasco sauce

Salt

Combine the cabbage, chicken, and onion in a mixing bowl. Whisk together the dressing and Tabasco, pour it over the salad, and toss to coat. Salt to taste, and serve.

**Yield:** 2 servings

**Nutritional Analysis:** Each will have: 209 calories; 7 g fat; 24 g protein; 14 g carbohydrates; 4 g fiber; 10 g usable carbs.

| | | | | | |
|---|---|---|---|---|---|
| Potassium (mg): | 587 mg | Vitamin C (mg): | 52 mg | Thiamin/B1 (mg): | 0.1 mg |
| Calcium (mg): | 85 mg | Vitamin A (i.u.): | 696 i.u. | Riboflavin/B2 (mg): | 0.1 mg |
| Iron (mg): | 2 mg | Vitamin B6 (mg): | 0.6 mg | Folacin (mcg): | 68 mcg |
| Zinc (mg): | 1 mg | Vitamin B12 (mcg): | 0.2 mcg | Niacin/B3 (mg): | 9 mg |

## Saigon Slaw Chicken Salad

The minute I tried the Saigon Slaw, I knew I had to turn it into a main dish salad! This would also be good with some precooked and peeled shrimp that you simply thawed.

1 batch Saigon Slaw (see page 195)
1 pound (455 g) boneless, skinless chicken breasts
1 teaspoon (5 ml) coconut oil
3 tablespoons (24 g) chopped walnuts

Preheat your electric tabletop grill. While it's heating, start making the Saigon Slaw. When the grill is hot, throw the chicken in and set a timer for 5 minutes.

Melt the coconut oil in a small skillet over medium heat, and stir the walnuts in it until they smell toasty. Remove from the heat.

Okay, assemble your salads! Pile the slaw on 3 big plates. Throw the chicken on your cutting board, and slice it into thin strips. Divide it between the 3 salads. Scatter 1 tablespoon (8 g) of walnuts over each salad, and serve.

**Yield:** 3 servings

**Nutritional Analysis:** Each will have: 312 calories; 12 g fat; 41 g protein; 22 g carbohydrates; 6 g fiber; 16 g usable carbs.

| | | | | | |
|---|---|---|---|---|---|
| Potassium (mg): | 1001 mg | Vitamin C (mg): | 98 mg | Thiamin/B1 (mg): | 0.2 mg |
| Calcium (mg): | 217 mg | Vitamin A (i.u.): | 10595 i.u. | Riboflavin/B2 (mg): | 0.2 mg |
| Iron (mg): | 5 mg | Vitamin B6 (mg): | 0.8 mg | Folacin (mcg): | 152 mcg |
| Zinc (mg): | 2 mg | Vitamin B12 (mcg): | 0.3 mcg | Niacin/B3 (mg): | 12 mg |

**Note:** It's a great idea to make the slaw in advance—then you can get supper on the table in 10 minutes' time.

## Slightly Asian Chicken Salad

A little curry and soy sauce give this salad a slightly Asian flair. Cutting up the pineapple chunks still further lets you distribute them more evenly throughout the salad.

1 tablespoon (14 ml) lemon juice

3 tablespoons (40 g) light mayonnaise

1/4 teaspoon dry mustard

1/4 teaspoon curry powder

1/4 teaspoon soy sauce

1 cup (110 g) cooked chicken, diced

1/4 cup (40 g) canned pineapple chunks in juice, each chunk quartered

3 scallions, sliced, including the crisp part of the green

1/4 cup (30 g) diced celery

Lettuce leaves, to line plates with

2 tablespoons (16 g) slivered almonds, toasted

Stir together the lemon juice, mayo, mustard, curry powder, and soy sauce. Set it aside.

In a mixing bowl, combine the chicken, pineapple, scallions, and celery. Pour on the dressing, and toss to coat. Spoon the salad onto 2 lettuce-lined plates, sprinkle 1 tablespoon (8 g) of toasted almonds over each portion, and serve.

**Yield:** 2 servings

**Nutritional Analysis:** Each will have: 259 calories; 12 g fat; 24 g protein; 13 g carbohydrates; 2 g fiber; 11 g usable carbs.

| | | | | | |
|---|---|---|---|---|---|
| Potassium (mg): | 403 mg | Vitamin C (mg): | 12 mg | Thiamin/B1 (mg): | 0.1 mg |
| Calcium (mg): | 62 mg | Vitamin A (i.u.): | 144 i.u. | Riboflavin/B2 (mg): | 0.2 mg |
| Iron (mg): | 2 mg | Vitamin B6 (mg): | 0.5 mg | Folacin (mcg): | 28 mcg |
| Zinc (mg): | 1 mg | Vitamin B12 (mcg): | 0.2 mcg | Niacin/B3 (mg): | 9 mg |

## Italian Sautéed Chicken Liver Salad with Warm Dressing

This fabulous gourmet salad is quite possibly the most nutritious dish on the planet!

- 3 cups (90 g) bagged baby spinach
- 1 1/2 cups (30 g) radicchio, torn
- 3 cups (60 g) romaine lettuce, torn
- 1 tablespoon (14 ml) olive oil
- 1 tablespoon (14 g) butter
- 8 ounces (225 g) chicken livers, cut into bite-size pieces
- 1/2 teaspoon ground sage
- 3 tablespoons (45 ml) balsamic vinegar
- Salt and pepper
- 4 tablespoons (20 g) shredded Parmesan cheese

Assemble the baby spinach, radicchio, and romaine lettuce in a big salad bowl.

Give a big, heavy skillet a shot of nonstick cooking spray, and put it over medium-high heat. When the pan is good and hot, add the olive oil and butter, and swirl them together as the butter melts.

Dust the chicken liver pieces with the sage. Toss the chicken livers into the skillet, and sauté them till they've just turned color on the surface. Do not overcook! You want them to be sealed on the outside, but still pink in the middle. When the livers are done, move them from the pan to a plate, and keep them warm.

Add the balsamic vinegar to the pan and stir it around, scraping up all the yummy brown bits. Pour this over the greens, and toss well. Add salt and pepper to taste, and toss again. Pile the salad on 2 plates.

Top each serving with the livers, scatter the Parmesan over that, then serve.

**Yield:** 2 servings

**Nutritional Analysis:** Each will have: 326 calories; 20 g fat; 27 g protein; 11 g carbohydrates; 3 g fiber; 8 g usable carbs.

| | | | | | |
|---|---|---|---|---|---|
| Potassium (mg): | 882 mg | Vitamin C (mg): | 74 mg | Thiamin/B1 (mg): | 0.3 mg |
| Calcium (mg): | 224 mg | Vitamin A (i.u.): | 28807 i.u. | Riboflavin/B2 (mg): | 2.4 mg |
| Iron (mg): | 12 mg | Vitamin B6 (mg): | 1.0 mg | Folacin (mcg): | 1058 mcg |
| Zinc (mg): | 4 mg | Vitamin B12 (mcg): | 26.2 mcg | Niacin/B3 (mg): | 11 mg |

# Chicken-Artichoke Salad

Make this with leftover chicken, if you like; I just enjoy it with the warm, freshly grilled chicken.

2 tablespoons (28 ml) olive oil

2 cloves garlic, peeled and minced

2 tablespoons (28 g) light mayonnaise

2 teaspoons (10 ml) lemon juice

12 ounces (340 g) boneless, skinless chicken breasts

1 cup (300 g) canned artichoke hearts, chopped

1 head butter lettuce

1/4 cup (20 g) shredded Parmesan cheese

Mix together the oil, garlic, mayonnaise, and lemon juice. Set the mixture aside to let the garlic infuse the dressing.

Heat your electric tabletop grill, and cook the chicken breasts for 5 minutes or until they're just done through.

While the chicken is cooking, put the artichoke hearts in a mixing bowl. Divide the lettuce between 3 serving plates.

When the chicken is done, transfer it to a cutting board and cut it into cubes. Add it to the bowl with the chopped artichoke hearts. Pour on the dressing and combine everything well. Add 3 tablespoons (15 g) of the Parmesan, and stir again. Spoon this mixture onto the beds of lettuce, top with the remaining Parmesan, and serve.

**Yield:** 3 servings

**Nutritional Analysis:** Each will have: 305 calories; 16 g fat; 31 g protein; 9 g carbohydrates; 1 g fiber; 8 g usable carbs.

| | | | | | |
|---|---|---|---|---|---|
| Potassium (mg): | 367 mg | Vitamin C (mg): | 7 mg | Thiamin/B1 (mg): | 0.1 mg |
| Calcium (mg): | 117 mg | Vitamin A (i.u.): | 586 i.u. | Riboflavin/B2 (mg): | 0.1 mg |
| Iron (mg): | 1 mg | Vitamin B6 (mg): | 0.5 mg | Folacin (mcg): | 44 mcg |
| Zinc (mg): | 1 mg | Vitamin B12 (mcg): | 0.4 mcg | Niacin/B3 (mg): | 11 mg |

# Chicken-Melon Salad

You can substitute similar sorts of melon, depending on what is in season and available. You might even try it with a tiny touch of ginger.

1 cup (180 g) cantaloupe balls or chunks

1 cup (180 g) honeydew melon balls or chunks

1 cup (30 g) seeded, 1/4-inch (6-mm) cubes cucumber

1 cup (125 g) 1/4-inch (6-mm) cubes zucchini

4 scallions, thinly sliced, including the crisp part of the green

1/3 cup (80 ml) lime juice

2 tablespoons (28 ml) peanut oil

2 tablespoons (28 ml) water

1 tablespoon (1.5 g) Splenda

1 pinch pepper

4 cups (80 g) leaf lettuce

1 pound (455 g) cubed cooked chicken

Put the cantaloupe, honeydew, cucumber, zucchini, and scallions in a big mixing bowl.

Whisk together the lime juice, oil, water, Splenda, and pepper, or just put them in the blender and zap them for a moment or two. Pour half of this over the melon mixture, and toss to coat.

Line 4 plates with the lettuce. Pile the melon mixture on top of that, and top with the chicken. Drizzle the rest of the dressing over the chicken, and serve.

**Yield:** 4 servings

**Nutritional Analysis:** Each will have: 314 calories; 12 g fat; 37 g protein; 14 g carbohydrates; 2 g fiber; 12 g usable carbs.

| | | | | | |
|---|---|---|---|---|---|
| Potassium (mg): | 803 mg | Vitamin C (mg): | 44 mg | Thiamin/B1 (mg): | 0.2 mg |
| Calcium (mg): | 56 mg | Vitamin A (i.u.): | 1727 i.u. | Riboflavin/B2 (mg): | 0.2 mg |
| Iron (mg): | 2 mg | Vitamin B6 (mg): | 0.8 mg | Folacin (mcg): | 67 mcg |
| Zinc (mg): | 2 mg | Vitamin B12 (mcg): | 0.4 mcg | Niacin/B3 (mg): | 15 mg |

## Southwestern Chicken Caesar

For a while there, we were so awash in Chicken Caesar Salads I was referring to them as "the ubiquitous Chicken Caesar Salad." This makes them new again!

- 1 pound (455 g) boneless, skinless chicken breasts
- 1/2 cup (65 g) frozen corn
- 1/2 cup (120 ml) light Caesar salad dressing (Newman's Own is good)
- 2 teaspoons chili powder
- 1/2 teaspoon cumin
- 2 tablespoons (8 g) chopped cilantro
- 3 quarts (240 g) romaine lettuce, broken up
- 1 cup (240 g) canned black beans, drained and rinsed
- 3 medium tomatoes, sliced

Preheat your electric tabletop grill. Throw in the chicken breasts, and give 'em 5 to 6 minutes, or until they're done through.

Meanwhile, put the corn in a microwaveable bowl, add 1 tablespoon (14 ml) of water, cover, and microwave it for 2 to 3 minutes on high.

Mix together the Caesar dressing, chili powder, cumin, and cilantro. Set aside.

Put the lettuce into a huge salad bowl. Pour on the dressing, and toss.

Add the beans to the salad. Drain the corn and add it, too, and toss again.

By now the chicken must be done. Put it on your cutting board, and slice it up.

Pile the salad on 4 serving plates. Top each serving with one-quarter of the chicken, decorate nicely with tomato slices, then serve.

**Yield:** 4 servings

**Nutritional Analysis:** Each will have: 324 calories; 10 g fat; 34 g protein; 25 g carbohydrates; 8 g fiber; 17 g usable carbs.

| | | | | | |
|---|---|---|---|---|---|
| Potassium (mg): | 974 mg | Vitamin C (mg): | 60 mg | Thiamin/B1 (mg): | 0.3 mg |
| Calcium (mg): | 124 mg | Vitamin A (i.u.): | 5458 i.u. | Riboflavin/B2 (mg): | 0.3 mg |
| Iron (mg): | 4 mg | Vitamin B6 (mg): | 0.7 mg | Folacin (mcg): | 254 mcg |
| Zinc (mg): | 1 mg | Vitamin B12 (mcg): | 0.3 mcg | Niacin/B3 (mg): | 13 mg |

# Easy Southwestern Grilled Chicken Salad

This is the sort of thing you'd pay a lot for at a restaurant, and it's a snap.

Salt and pepper
1 pound (455 g) boneless, skinless chicken breasts
3 quarts (240 g) romaine lettuce
2 medium tomatoes, cut into wedges
1 small red onion, sliced paper-thin
1 California avocado, pitted, peeled, and sliced
1/4 cup (60 g) light sour cream
1/4 cup (55 g) light mayonnaise
1/4 cup (50 g) salsa
Hot sauce (optional)
1/2 cup (30 g) chopped fresh cilantro

Preheat your electric tabletop grill. Salt and pepper the chicken, and throw it on the grill. Set a timer for 6 minutes.

Tear up the lettuce, and arrange it on 4 plates. Arrange the tomatoes, onion, and avocado slices artfully around the lettuce.

Mix together the sour cream, mayo, and salsa, plus a shot of hot sauce (if you like it spicy). Set this aside.

Once the chicken's done, throw it on your cutting board, slice it up, and divide it between the 4 salads. Spoon the dressing over the top. Scatter 2 tablespoons of cilantro over each serving, and you're done!

**Yield:** 4 servings

**Nutritional Analysis:** Each will have: 307 calories; 14 g fat; 30 g protein; 17 g carbohydrates; 7 g fiber; 10 g usable carbs.

| | | | | | |
|---|---|---|---|---|---|
| Potassium (mg): | 1215 mg | Vitamin C (mg): | 61 mg | Thiamin/B1 (mg): | 0.3 mg |
| Calcium (mg): | 101 mg | Vitamin A (i.u.): | 526 i.u. | Riboflavin/B2 (mg): | 0.3 mg |
| Iron (mg): | 4 mg | Vitamin B6 (mg): | 0.8 mg | Folacin (mcg): | 280 mcg |
| Zinc (mg): | 2 mg | Vitamin B12 (mcg): | 0.3 mcg | Niacin/B3 (mg): | 13 mg |

## Southwestern Grilled Chicken Salad

This is a bit more complex than the previous salad, but it's awfully good. If you've got the time, go for it!

- 3 tablespoons (45 ml) lime juice
- 1 clove garlic, peeled and minced
- 1/4 teaspoon cumin
- 1 pound (455 g) boneless, skinless chicken breasts
- 1 head romaine lettuce, broken up
- Creamy Southwestern Dressing (see page 231)
- Salt and pepper
- 1/4 cup (15 g) chopped fresh cilantro
- 1/4 red onion, sliced paper-thin
- 1/2 medium cucumber, sliced
- 1/2 California avocado, peeled and cubed
- 1 medium tomato
- 2 ounces (55 g) sliced black olives, drained
- 1/2 cup (55 g) shredded cheddar cheese

Combine the lime juice, garlic, and cumin, and put the mixture in a glass pie plate. Lay the chicken breasts in it, turning to coat both sides, and let it marinate for a few minutes while you break up the lettuce and make the Creamy Southwestern Dressing (see page 231).

Preheat your electric tabletop grill. Take the chicken out of the marinade, salt and pepper it lightly, and throw it in the grill for 5 to 6 minutes.

Add the cilantro to the lettuce, pour on the dressing, and toss until the lettuce is evenly coated with dressing. Pile it onto 4 dinner plates.

Top each salad with the onion, cucumber, avocado, tomato, and olives, artfully arranged.

When the chicken is done, pull it out of the grill, throw it onto your cutting board, and cut it into strips or cubes. Divide it into 4 equal portions, and top each salad with chicken. Sprinkle the cheese festively over all, and serve.

**Yield:** 4 servings

**Nutritional Analysis:** Each will have: 348 calories; 17 g fat; 34 g protein; 17 g carbohydrates; 6 g fiber; 11 g usable carbs.

| Potassium (mg): | 1169 mg | Vitamin C (mg): | 65 mg | Thiamin/B1 (mg): | 0.3 mg |
|---|---|---|---|---|---|
| Calcium (mg): | 239 mg | Vitamin A (i.u.): | 6453 i.u. | Riboflavin/B2 (mg): | 0.4 mg |
| Iron (mg): | 4 mg | Vitamin B6 (mg): | 0.7 mg | Folacin (mcg): | 306 mcg |
| Zinc (mg): | 2 mg | Vitamin B12 (mcg): | 0.4 mcg | Niacin/B3 (mg): | 13 mg |

# Spicy Lemon, Olive, and Green Bean Chicken Salad

Unusual!

1 cup (150 g) frozen cross-cut green beans
2 cups (220 g) diced cooked chicken
2/3 cup (80 g) diced celery
1/4 cup (40 g) diced red onion
8 green pimiento-stuffed olives, chopped
2 tablespoons (8 g) chopped fresh cilantro
3 tablespoons (40 g) light mayonnaise
1/2 teaspoon ground cumin
1/8 teaspoon paprika
1/4 teaspoon ground ginger
1/8 teaspoon turmeric
3 drops Tabasco sauce, or to taste
1 clove garlic, peeled and minced
1 tablespoon (14 ml) lemon juice

Put the frozen green beans in a microwaveable bowl. Add just 1 tablespoon (14 ml) of water, cover, and nuke on high for 4 minutes.

Meanwhile, put the chicken, celery, onion, olives, and cilantro into a mixing bowl.

In a separate bowl, stir together the mayonnaise, cumin, paprika, ginger, turmeric, Tabasco (if using), garlic, and lemon juice.

Check to see if the beans are done. You want them tender-crisp—give them another minute or two if they need it. Drain them, and add them to the stuff in the mixing bowl.

Pour the dressing over the salad, and mix well. Chill before serving.

**Yield:** 2 servings

**Nutritional Analysis:** Each will have: 357 calories; 13 g fat; 45 g protein; 14 g carbohydrates; 4 g fiber; 10 g usable carbs.

| | | | | | |
|---|---|---|---|---|---|
| Potassium (mg): | 651 mg | Vitamin C (mg): | 17 mg | Thiamin/B1 (mg): | 0.2 mg |
| Calcium (mg): | 92 mg | Vitamin A (i.u.): | 624 i.u. | Riboflavin/B2 (mg): | 0.2 mg |
| Iron (mg): | 3 mg | Vitamin B6 (mg): | 0.9 mg | Folacin (mcg): | 32 mcg |
| Zinc (mg): | 2 mg | Vitamin B12 (mcg): | 0.5 mcg | Niacin/B3 (mg): | 18 mg |

## Fiesta Chicken Salad

If you miss corn, there's enough of what Julie calls the "luscious sunshine-yellow kernels of starchy goodness" in here to make you happy!

1 pound (455 g) boneless, skinless chicken breast

1/2 cup (65 g) frozen corn

1/2 cup (115 g) light sour cream

1/3 cup (75 g) salsa

2 tablespoons (8 g) chopped cilantro

1 tablespoon (14 ml) lime juice

1 cup (240 g) canned black beans, drained and rinsed

3 medium plum tomatoes, diced

1 cup (125 g) chopped zucchini

1/2 cup (55 g) shredded cheddar cheese or "Mexican blend"

Lettuce leaves, to line plates

Preheat your electric tabletop grill.

When the grill is hot, throw in your chicken breasts and give 'em 5 to 6 minutes, or until they're done through.

While the chicken cooks, put the corn in a microwaveable bowl, add 1 tablespoon (14 ml) of water, cover, and give it 2 to 3 minutes on high. After the corn cooks, uncover it and let it cool for a few minutes.

Mix together the sour cream, salsa, cilantro, and lime juice, and set aside.

Put the beans, tomatoes, and zucchini in a mixing bowl. Drain the corn, add it to the other veggies, and toss.

By now the chicken must be done! Put it on your cutting board and cut it into 1/2-inch (1.25-cm) cubes. Let it cool for a few minutes before you add it to the rest.

Once the chicken has cooled enough so it won't cook your veggies on contact, add it to the mixing bowl. Pour on the dressing and toss to coat. Chill the salad till mealtime.

When mealtime rolls around, line 4 plates with pretty lettuce leaves and scoop the salad on top. Top each serving with the cheddar, and serve.

**Yield:** 4 servings

**Nutritional Analysis:** Each will have: 295 calories; 9 g fat; 35 g protein; 19 g carbohydrates; 5 g fiber; 14 g usable carbs.

| | | | | | |
|---|---|---|---|---|---|
| Potassium (mg): | 498 mg | Vitamin C (mg): | 17 mg | Thiamin/B1 (mg): | 0.1 mg |
| Calcium (mg): | 141 mg | Vitamin A (i.u.): | 750 i.u. | Riboflavin/B2 (mg): | 0.2 mg |
| Iron (mg): | 2 mg | Vitamin B6 (mg): | 0.6 mg | Folacin (mcg): | 31 mcg |
| Zinc (mg): | 1 mg | Vitamin B12 (mcg): | 0.4 mcg | Niacin/B3 (mg): | 12 mg |

## Turkey Salad with Strawberry Vinaigrette

If you can't get the carambola, go ahead and make the salad without it—but it sure looks pretty with it!

- 2 quarts (160 g) bagged Italian blend greens
- 1 pound (455 g) cooked turkey, cut into 1/2-inch (1.25-g) cubes (you could also use chicken, if it's what you have on hand)
- 1 kiwi fruit, peeled and sliced
- 1 carambola (star fruit), sliced into stars
- 1 cup (100 g) sliced mushrooms
- 1 cup (125 g) halved cherry tomatoes (try to use half-red, half-yellow)
- Strawberry Vinaigrette (see page 257)

This is easy. Pile the greens on 4 plates and arrange the turkey, kiwi, carambola, mushrooms, and tomatoes on top. Drizzle with the dressing, and serve.

**Yield:** 4 servings

**Nutritional Analysis:** Each will have: 267 calories; 6 g fat; 38 g protein; 16 g carbohydrates; 6 g fiber; 10 g usable carbs.

| | | | | | |
|---|---|---|---|---|---|
| Potassium (mg): | 1059 mg | Vitamin C (mg): | 131 mg | Thiamin/B1 (mg): | 0.2 mg |
| Calcium (mg): | 159 mg | Vitamin A (i.u.): | 6327 i.u. | Riboflavin/B2 (mg): | 0.4 mg |
| Iron (mg): | 4 mg | Vitamin B6 (mg): | 0.8 mg | Folacin (mcg): | 237 mcg |
| Zinc (mg): | 4 mg | Vitamin B12 (mcg): | 0.4 mcg | Niacin/B3 (mg): | 8 mg |

## Strawberry Vinaigrette

This couldn't be easier!

1 cup (110 g) fresh strawberries, or unsweetened frozen, thawed

3 tablespoons (45 ml) balsamic vinegar

1/4 teaspoon pepper

Just throw everything in your food processor with the S-blade in place, or put it all in your blender, and run till it's smooth.

**Yield:** Per batch: 53 calories; 1 g fat; 1 g protein; 14 g carbohydrates; 3 g fiber; 11 g usable carbs.

| | | | | | |
|---|---|---|---|---|---|
| Potassium (mg): | 302 mg | Vitamin C (mg): | 84 mg | Thiamin/B1 (mg): | 0 mg |
| Calcium (mg): | 26 mg | Vitamin A (i.u.): | 41 i.u. | Riboflavin/B2 (mg): | trace |
| Iron (mg): | 1 mg | Vitamin B6 (mg): | 0 mg | Folacin (mcg): | 26 mcg |
| Zinc (mg): | trace | Vitamin B12 (mcg): | 0 mcg | Niacin/B3 (mg): | trace |

## Turkey Salad with Roasted Corn and Peppers

This brightly colored salad is a great way to use up leftover turkey, should you have any on hand. If you like, you can knock off 20 calories by using reduced-fat cheese.

1/4 cup (30 g) frozen corn kernels, thawed

1 cup (110 g) diced cooked turkey

1/4 cup (50 g) jarred roasted red peppers, drained and diced

3 tablespoons (30 g) finely diced red onion

2 tablespoons (7.5 g) minced fresh cilantro

1/4 cup (60 ml) Creamy Chipotle Dressing (see page 228)

6 cups (120 g) shredded romaine lettuce

1 medium tomato, diced

1/4 cup (30 g) shredded Monterey Jack cheese

I like to roast my corn in a toaster oven. I mean, why heat up the kitchen for this? Toaster oven or regular oven, you'll want it at 350°F (180°C, or gas mark 4). Spread the corn in a single layer on a baking sheet, and roast it for 10 to 12 minutes.

If you haven't done it yet, now's a good time to dice up your turkey, roasted red peppers, and red onion. Throw 'em all in a mixing bowl together, along with the cilantro. When the corn has finished roasting, add it, pour on the dressing, and toss the whole thing to coat.

Make 2 nice big beds of romaine. Put a scoop of the turkey salad on each bed of romaine, surround it with diced tomato, and top with shredded cheese. You can sprinkle a little more cilantro on top to make it look pretty, if you like.

**Yield:** 2 servings

**Nutritional Analysis:** Each will have: 250 calories; 10 g fat; 24 g protein; 18 g carbohydrates; 5 g fiber; 13 g usable carbs.

| | | | | | |
|---|---|---|---|---|---|
| Potassium (mg): | 865 mg | Vitamin C (mg): | 70 mg | Thiamin/B1 (mg): | 0.1 mg |
| Calcium (mg): | 209 mg | Vitamin A (i.u.): | 4404 i.u. | Riboflavin/B2 (mg): | 0.3 mg |
| Iron (mg): | 4 mg | Vitamin B6 (mg): | 0.5 mg | Folacin (mcg): | 113 mcg |
| Zinc (mg): | 3 mg | Vitamin B12 (mcg): | 0.3 mcg | Niacin/B3 (mg): | 6 mg |

## Turkey Raspberry Salad

Turns precooked smoked turkey into a great summer supper.

- 1/4 cup (30 g) chopped walnuts, toasted
- 3 tablespoons (45 ml) peanut oil
- 1/4 cup (60 ml) raspberry vinegar
- 1 tablespoon (1.5 g) Splenda
- 1 teaspoon poppy seeds
- 1/2 teaspoon dry mustard
- 1/2 clove garlic, peeled and crushed
- 5 ounces (150 g) fresh spinach
- 1 quart (80 g) Boston lettuce
- 1 pound (455 g) smoked turkey breast, cubed
- 1/4 medium red onion, sliced paper-thin
- 8 ounces (225 g) fresh raspberries

Spread the walnuts on a cookie sheet or in a shallow pan, and slide them into a 325°F (170°C, or gas mark 3) oven for 7 to 10 minutes to toast.

In a small bowl, combine the oil, vinegar, Splenda, poppy seeds, mustard, and garlic. Whisk them together well, and set the bowl in the refrigerator if you aren't making the salad right away.

Assemble the spinach and lettuce in a big salad bowl. Pour the dressing over the greens, and toss well. Top with the turkey, onion, raspberries, and walnuts, and serve.

**Yield:** 4 servings

**Nutritional Analysis:** Each will have: 389 calories; 23 g fat; 34 g protein; 12 g carbohydrates; 6 g fiber; 6 g usable carbs.

| | | | | | |
|---|---|---|---|---|---|
| Potassium (mg): | 803 mg | Vitamin C (mg): | 29 mg | Thiamin/B1 (mg): | 0.1 mg |
| Calcium (mg): | 106 mg | Vitamin A (i.u.): | 3008 i.u. | Riboflavin/B2 (mg): | 0.3 mg |
| Iron (mg): | 3 mg | Vitamin B6 (mg): | 0.7 mg | Folacin (mcg): | 137 mcg |
| Zinc (mg): | 3 mg | Vitamin B12 (mcg): | 0.4 mcg | Niacin/B3 (mg): | 8 mg |

## My Favorite Lunch

Since I work at home, I have the luxury of making lunch. More often than not, this is what I make!

1 quart lettuce (romaine, leaf lettuce, whatever you've got on hand)

1/8 red onion, sliced paper-thin

1/2 small tomato, sliced vertically

1/3 cup (35 g) sliced cucumber

1/3 cup (40 g) chopped green bell pepper

1/4 cup (15 g) minced fresh parsley

2 tablespoons (28 ml) reduced-calorie salad dressing

1 hard-boiled egg, peeled and chopped

3 ounces (85 g) canned tuna in water

Tear up the lettuce, put it in a big bowl, and add the tomato, cucumber, pepper, and parsley. Toss with the dressing—I use Newman's Own Light Balsamic Vinaigrette. Then top with the egg and the tuna. Give it one more toss, and eat it out of the salad bowl!

**Yield:** 1 serving

**Nutritional Analysis:** Each will have: 293 calories; 10 g fat; 33 g protein; 20 g carbohydrates; 7 g fiber; 13 g usable carbs.

| | | | | | |
|---|---|---|---|---|---|
| Potassium (mg): | 1229 mg | Vitamin C (mg): | 120 mg | Thiamin/B1 (mg): | 0.2 mg |
| Calcium (mg): | 226 mg | Vitamin A (i.u.): | 6164 i.u. | Riboflavin/B2 (mg): | 0.6 mg |
| Iron (mg): | 6 mg | Vitamin B6 (mg): | 0.5 mg | Folacin (mcg): | 190 mcg |
| Zinc (mg): | 2 mg | Vitamin B12 (mcg): | 2.4 mcg | Niacin/B3 (mg): | 12 mg |

## Tomatoes Stuffed with Lemony Tuna Salad

You can knock some more calories off of this if you use water-pack tuna, but I really like it with good, imported olive oil–pack tuna, and the calorie count is still quite low.

1 rib celery

3 tablespoons (30 g) minced red onion

1 can (6 ounces, or 170 g) tuna in olive oil, drained

3 tablespoons (40 g) light mayonnaise

1 teaspoon (5 ml) lemon juice

2 medium tomatoes

Finely dice the celery, and include any leaves at the end of the rib—they're delicious! Throw the celery, onion, and tuna into a mixing bowl. Add the mayonnaise and lemon juice, and mix everything up.

Leaving the skin at the bottom intact, cut the stems out of your tomatoes and cut the tomatoes into eighths. Spread them open like flowers. Divide the tuna salad between the 2 tomatoes, and serve.

**Yield:** 2 servings

**Nutritional Analysis:** Each will have: 256 calories; 12 g fat; 26 g protein; 12 g carbohydrates; 2 g fiber; 10 g usable carbs.

| | | | | | |
|---|---|---|---|---|---|
| Potassium (mg): | 535 mg | Vitamin C (mg): | 27 mg | Thiamin/B1 (mg): | 0.1 mg |
| Calcium (mg): | 28 mg | Vitamin A (i.u.): | 860 i.u. | Riboflavin/B2 (mg): | 0.2 mg |
| Iron (mg): | 2 mg | Vitamin B6 (mg): | 0.2 mg | Folacin (mcg): | 32 mcg |
| Zinc (mg): | 1 mg | Vitamin B12 (mcg): | 1.9 mcg | Niacin/B3 (mg): | 11 mg |

## Tuna with Artichoke, Avocado, and Spinach Salad

Each serving of this tasty and beautiful salad has more potassium than two bananas!

6 cups (180 g) bagged baby spinach

1/4 cup (60 ml) reduced-calorie red wine and vinegar dressing

1/4 small red onion, finely diced

1/2 California avocado, peeled, seeded, and diced

1 cup (300 g) canned artichoke hearts, drained and chopped

1 can (6 ounces, or 170 g) tuna in water, drained

2 slices bacon, cooked crisp and drained

2 hard-boiled eggs

Put the spinach in a big salad bowl, add the dressing, and toss well. Pile it on 2 plates.

Top with the onion, avocado, artichoke hearts, tuna, bacon, and eggs. Serve!

**Yield:** 2 servings

**Nutritional Analysis:** Each will have: 393 calories; 20 g fat; 37 g protein; 17 g carbohydrates; 5 g fiber; 12 g usable carbs.

| | | | | | |
|---|---|---|---|---|---|
| Potassium (mg): | 1108 mg | Vitamin C (mg): | 32 mg | Thiamin/B1 (mg): | 0.2 mg |
| Calcium (mg): | 134 mg | Vitamin A (i.u.): | 6636 i.u. | Riboflavin/B2 (mg): | 0.5 mg |
| Iron (mg): | 5 mg | Vitamin B6 (mg): | 0.7 mg | Folacin (mcg): | 233 mcg |
| Zinc (mg): | 2 mg | Vitamin B12 (mcg): | 3.2 mcg | Niacin/B3 (mg): | 13 mg |

## Egg Salad with Tuna and Cottage Cheese

This packs a triple protein punch!

2 stalks celery, diced

1/2 green bell pepper, diced

1/4 cup (40 g) diced red onion

2 hard-boiled eggs, peeled and coarsely chopped

3 ounces (85 g) canned tuna in olive oil, drained

1/2 cup (110 g) 2% cottage cheese

2 tablespoons (28 g) light mayonnaise

Salt and pepper

3 medium tomatoes

This is simple: Put the celery, pepper, onion, eggs, tuna, and cottage cheese in a bowl. Stir everything up, mix in the mayo, and add salt and pepper to taste.

Leaving the skin intact at the bottom, cut the cores out of the tomatoes, then cut each one into 8 wedges. Open each tomato up like a flower. Put each one on a plate, divide the salad between the 3 tomatoes, and serve.

**Yield:** 3 servings

**Nutritional Analysis:** Each will have: 205 calories; 9 g fat; 19 g protein; 12 g carbohydrates; 2 g fiber; 10 g usable carbs.

| | | | | | |
|---|---|---|---|---|---|
| Potassium (mg): | 543 mg | Vitamin C (mg): | 44 mg | Thiamin/B1 (mg): | 0.1 mg |
| Calcium (mg): | 67 mg | Vitamin A (i.u.): | 1163 i.u. | Riboflavin/B2 (mg): | 0.3 mg |
| Iron (mg): | 2 mg | Vitamin B6 (mg): | 0.3 mg | Folacin (mcg): | 54 mcg |
| Zinc (mg): | 1 mg | Vitamin B12 (mcg): | 1.3 mcg | Niacin/B3 (mg): | 5 mg |

## My New Favorite Tuna Salad

I'm a tuna fiend. I'd made my tuna salad pretty much the same way for years, but not anymore! This fresh take on good old tuna salad brings new life to an old favorite.

1 can (6 ounces, or 170 g) tuna in water, drained

1/2 cup (60 g) diced celery

1/4 cup (40 g) diced red onion

2 tablespoons (8 g) minced cilantro

3 tablespoons (40 g) light mayonnaise

1 tablespoon (15 g) yellow mustard

1 hard-boiled egg, peeled and coarsely chopped

Easy but great—just dump everything into a mixing bowl, mix it up well, and devour. If you're feeling spiffy, spoon it out onto a lettuce-lined plate and add a sprig of cilantro for garnish.

**Yield:** 2 servings

**Nutritional Analysis:** Each will have: 208 calories; 8 g fat; 26 g protein; 7 g carbohydrates; 1 g fiber; 6 g usable carbs.

| | | | | | |
|---|---|---|---|---|---|
| Potassium (mg): | 368 mg | Vitamin C (mg): | 3 mg | Thiamin/B1 (mg): | 0.1 mg |
| Calcium (mg): | 45 mg | Vitamin A (i.u.): | 257 i.u. | Riboflavin/B2 (mg): | 0.2 mg |
| Iron (mg): | 2 mg | Vitamin B6 (mg): | 0.4 mg | Folacin (mcg): | 27 mcg |
| Zinc (mg): | 1 mg | Vitamin B12 (mcg): | 2.8 mcg | Niacin/B3 (mg): | 11 mg |

# Tuna-"Rice" Salad

I saw a recipe for a rice salad with tuna in it and immediately thought, "I know that would work with cauli-rice!"

- 1/2 head cauliflower
- 2 large celery ribs
- 1 medium apple
- 1/4 large red onion
- 2 hard-boiled eggs
- 6 tablespoons (80 g) light mayonnaise
- 1 can (6 ounces, or 170 g) tuna in water, drained

Trim the very bottom of the cauliflower stem, and cut off the leaves. Now run the cauliflower through the shredding blade of your food processor. Put the resulting "cauli-rice" in a microwaveable casserole with a lid, add a couple of tablespoons (30 ml or so) of water, cover, and microwave on high for 6 minutes.

Meanwhile, dice the celery. Core and dice the apple (but leave the skin on; it adds color and texture) and onion. Peel the hard-boiled eggs, too, and coarsely chop them. As everything is cut up, put it in a mixing bowl.

By now, the cauliflower is done. Drain it, and let it cool for at least 5 minutes, stirring once or twice to let the steam out. Add it to the stuff in the mixing bowl.

Now add the mayonnaise and tuna to the mixing bowl, and toss to combine. When everything's well coated with mayonnaise, pile the salad on lettuce-lined plates, and serve.

**Yield:** 3 servings

**Nutritional Analysis:** Each will have: 247 calories; 10 g fat; 21 g protein; 19 g carbohydrates; 4 g fiber; 15 g usable carbs.

| | | | | | |
|---|---|---|---|---|---|
| Potassium (mg): | 620 mg | Vitamin C (mg): | 50 mg | Thiamin/B1 (mg): | 0.1 mg |
| Calcium (mg): | 61 mg | Vitamin A (i.u.): | 297 i.u. | Riboflavin/B2 (mg): | 0.3 mg |
| Iron (mg): | 2 mg | Vitamin B6 (mg): | 0.5 mg | Folacin (mcg): | 83 mcg |
| Zinc (mg): | 1 mg | Vitamin B12 (mcg): | 2.1 mcg | Niacin/B3 (mg): | 8 mg |

## Tuna-Artichoke Salad with Lemon, Capers, and Parsley

This has a nice Mediterranean feel.

- 1 can (6 ounces, or 170 g) tuna in water, drained
- 4 canned artichoke hearts, drained and chopped
- 1/4 cup (40 g) diced red onion
- 1/4 cup (15 g) chopped fresh parsley
- 1 tablespoon (9 g) capers, drained and chopped
- 2 tablespoons (28 g) light mayonnaise
- 1 tablespoon (14 ml) lemon juice
- 2 medium tomatoes
- 1 tablespoon (5 g) grated Parmesan cheese

In a mixing bowl, combine the tuna, artichoke hearts, onion, parsley, and capers.

In a small bowl, whisk together the mayonnaise and lemon juice. Pour over the tuna mixture, and toss to coat.

Leaving the skin at the very bottom intact, cut the cores out of the tomatoes and cut each one into 8 equal wedges. Open up into a tomato "flower," and place each one on a serving plate. (Lining the plate with lettuce first looks nice, too.)

Pile the tuna salad high in the middles of the tomato "flowers," sprinkle each one with half the Parmesan, and serve.

**Yield:** 2 servings

**Nutritional Analysis:** Each will have: 203 calories; 5 g fat; 26 g protein; 14 g carbohydrates; 2 g fiber; 12 g usable carbs.

| | | | | | |
|---|---|---|---|---|---|
| Potassium (mg): | 562 mg | Vitamin C (mg): | 38 mg | Thiamin/B1 (mg): | 0.1 mg |
| Calcium (mg): | 65 mg | Vitamin A (i.u.): | 1223 i.u. | Riboflavin/B2 (mg): | 0.1 mg |
| Iron (mg): | 2 mg | Vitamin B6 (mg): | 0.4 mg | Folacin (mcg): | 38 mcg |
| Zinc (mg): | 1 mg | Vitamin B12 (mcg): | 2.6 mcg | Niacin/B3 (mg): | 12 mg |

## Lobster Salad

Only for luncheon with people you really like, or really want to impress!

1 pound (455 g) lobster meat, cooked

1/4 cup (55 g) dry-pack sun-dried tomatoes, chopped

1/4 cup (50 g) jarred roasted red peppers, drained and chopped

1 medium celery rib, diced

2 scallions, thinly sliced, including the crisp part of the green

3 tablespoons (40 g) light mayonnaise

Salt and pepper

4 lettuce leaves

1/4 cup (35 g) toasted pine nuts (pignolia)

This is just like making tuna salad, only more luxurious. Simply combine the lobster, tomatoes, peppers, celery, scallions, and mayo, and stir till moistened. Add salt and pepper to taste.

Line 4 plates with 1 lettuce leaf each. Scoop the salad onto the lettuce leaves, and top each serving with a tablespoon of pine nuts.

**Yield:** 4 servings

**Nutritional Analysis:** Each will have: 200 calories; 7 g fat; 26 g protein; 8 g carbohydrates; 1 g fiber; 7 g usable carbs.

| | | | | | |
|---|---|---|---|---|---|
| Potassium (mg): | 632 mg | Vitamin C (mg): | 16 mg | Thiamin/B1 (mg): | 0.1 mg |
| Calcium (mg): | 86 mg | Vitamin A (i.u.): | 553 i.u. | Riboflavin/B2 (mg): | 0.1 mg |
| Iron (mg): | 2 mg | Vitamin B6 (mg): | 0.1 mg | Folacin (mcg): | 33 mcg |
| Zinc (mg): | 4 mg | Vitamin B12 (mcg): | 3.5 mcg | Niacin/B3 (mg): | 2 mg |

**Note:** If you can't find toasted pine nuts, buy 'em untoasted and just stir them in a dry skillet over medium heat until they're golden.

# Lobster Salad with Ginger-Lime Dressing

If lobster doesn't fit into your budget, you can use monkfish or another firm-fleshed fish.

- 1/4 head cauliflower
- 1 1/2 pounds (670 g) lobster tails
- Ginger-Lime Dressing (see page 225)
- 1 head romaine lettuce
- 1/2 cup (60 g) diced celery
- 2 tablespoons (8 g) fresh basil, minced
- 1 tablespoon (4 g) fresh tarragon, minced
- 1 California avocado
- 1/2 cup (95 g) canned beets, julienned
- 2 hard-boiled eggs, peeled and quartered

Cut the cauliflower, stem and all, into 1/2-inch (1.25-cm) chunks. Put it in a microwaveable casserole with a lid, add a couple of tablespoons (30 ml or so) of water, cover, and nuke on high for 8 minutes. Uncover as soon as it's done!

While the cauliflower's cooking, put a biggish saucepan of water on the stove, and start it boiling. Throw in 1 teaspoon of salt, add the lobster tails, turn it down to a simmer, and set a timer for about 12 minutes. When the timer goes off, drain, and let the lobster cool a bit so you don't burn your fingers! Then use kitchen shears to cut down the middle of the back of each shell, pull out the meat, and dice it into 1-inch (2.5-cm) cubes.

If you haven't made the Ginger-Lime Dressing (see page 225), make that up next!

Break up the lettuce in a big salad bowl. Add the celery, basil, tarragon, cauliflower, and avocado. Now pour on the Ginger-Lime dressing, reserving a couple of tablespoons (30 ml or so), and toss to coat. Pile the salad on 4 serving plates.

Okay, we're in the home stretch. Top each serving of salad artistically with one-quarter of the lobster meat, one-quarter of the beets, and 2 egg quarters, all artistically arranged. Drizzle with the reserved salad dressing, and serve.

**Yield:** 4 servings

**Nutritional Analysis:** Each will have: 480 calories; 31 g fat; 41 g protein; 14 g carbohydrates; 7 g fiber; 7 g usable carbs.

| | | | | | |
|---|---|---|---|---|---|
| Potassium (mg): | 1559 mg | Vitamin C (mg): | 72 mg | Thiamin/B1 (mg): | 0.3 mg |
| Calcium (mg): | 194 mg | Vitamin A (i.u.): | 5785 i.u. | Riboflavin/B2 (mg): | 0.5 mg |
| Iron (mg): | 4 mg | Vitamin B6 (mg): | 0.5 mg | Folacin (mcg): | 357 mcg |
| Zinc (mg): | 6 mg | Vitamin B12 (mcg): | 1.8 mcg | Niacin/B3 (mg): | 5 mg |

## Curried Crab Salad

Nice for a summer event. Made in quantity, I could see this as the main dish at a bridal shower!

- 2/3 cup (100 g) diced pineapple
- 2/3 cup (120 g) cantaloupe
- 2/3 cup (120 g) honeydew melon
- 12 ounces (340 g) cooked lump crabmeat, picked over for shells
- 3/4 cup (90 g) diced celery
- 1/4 cup (55 g) light mayonnaise
- 1/3 cup (165 g) plain yogurt
- 1/2 teaspoon curry powder
- 1/2 clove garlic, peeled and crushed
- 6 cups (120 g) Boston lettuce, torn
- 3 tablespoons (24 g) chopped dry-roasted peanuts

In a big mixing bowl combine the pineapple, cantaloupe, honeydew, crabmeat, and celery.

In a smaller bowl, whisk together the mayo, yogurt, curry, and garlic. Pour it over the fruit-and-crab mixture, and toss to coat well.

Line 3 plates with the lettuce, and pile the crab mixture on top. Sprinkle 1 tablespoon (8 g) of chopped peanuts over each salad, and serve.

**Yield:** 3 servings

**Nutritional Analysis:** Each will have: 277 calories; 11 g fat; 26 g protein; 21 g carbohydrates; 3 g fiber; 18 g usable carbs.

| | | | | | |
|---|---|---|---|---|---|
| Potassium (mg): | 1108 mg | Vitamin C (mg): | 44 mg | Thiamin/B1 (mg): | 0.3 mg |
| Calcium (mg): | 201 mg | Vitamin A (i.u.): | 2320 i.u. | Riboflavin/B2 (mg): | 0.2 mg |
| Iron (mg): | 2 mg | Vitamin B6 (mg): | 0.4 mg | Folacin (mcg): | 175 mcg |
| Zinc (mg): | 5 mg | Vitamin B12 (mcg): | 10.3 mcg | Niacin/B3 (mg): | 5 mg |

# Asian Shrimp Salad with Peanut Sauce

Vegetables tossed with peanut sauce and topped with shrimp.
Mmmm…peanut sauce.

3 cups (210 g) Chinese cabbage, shredded

2 cups (140 g) red cabbage, shredded

3 cups (150 g) bean sprouts

1/2 pound (225 g) fresh snow pea pods

1 medium red bell pepper

5 scallions

3/4 cup (175 ml) Peanut Sauce (see page 504)

2 pounds (905 g) salad shrimp, cooked (or bigger shrimp, peeled, cooked, and chopped)

2/3 cup (40 g) chopped cilantro

Combine the Chinese cabbage, red cabbage, and bean sprouts in a big bowl.

Pinch the ends off of the snow peas, and pull off any strings. Cut them into 1/2-inch (1.25-cm) pieces. Put them in a microwaveable bowl, add a tablespoon (14 ml) of water, cover, and microwave on high for 2 minutes. Uncover immediately! Let them cool a bit, while you slice the pepper into matchstick strips and slice the scallions, including the crisp part of the green.

Drain the snow peas and add them, the pepper strips, and the scallions to the salad. Pour on the Peanut Sauce, and toss well. Divide the mixture between 6 plates, top each with one-sixth of the shrimp and a couple of tablespoons of cilantro, and serve.

**Yield:** 6 servings

**Nutritional Analysis:** Each will have: 253 calories; 5 g fat; 38 g protein; 13 g carbohydrates; 4 g fiber; 9 g usable carbs.

| | | | | | |
|---|---|---|---|---|---|
| Potassium (mg): | 693 mg | Vitamin C (mg): | 107 mg | Thiamin/B1 (mg): | 0.2 mg |
| Calcium (mg): | 154 mg | Vitamin A (i.u.): | 2762 i.u. | Riboflavin/B2 (mg): | 0.2 mg |
| Iron (mg): | 7 mg | Vitamin B6 (mg): | 0.5 mg | Folacin (mcg): | 97 mcg |
| Zinc (mg): | 3 mg | Vitamin B12 (mcg): | 2.3 mcg | Niacin/B3 (mg): | 5 mg |

## Shrimp, Coconut, and Mint Salad

This has a distinctly Southeast-Asian flavor to it.

- 1 tablespoon (14 g) butter
- 1 1/2 pounds (670 g) shrimp, peeled and deveined
- 1 1/2 tablespoons (21 ml) lime juice
- 1/2 cup (120 ml) coconut milk
- 2 tablespoons (28 ml) fish sauce
- 2 cloves garlic, peeled and crushed
- 2 teaspoons (5 g) grated gingerroot
- 2 teaspoons (30 g) chili paste
- 1/2 teaspoon Splenda
- 3 quarts (240 g) leaf lettuce
- 1/4 cup (15 g) fresh mint, minced
- 1/4 cup (18 g) coconut shreds

Give a big, heavy skillet a shot of nonstick cooking spray and set it over medium-high heat. Melt the butter, then throw in the shrimp. Sauté till they're turning pink.

Add the lime juice, coconut milk, fish sauce, garlic, ginger, chili paste, and Splenda. Stir it all up, turn the burner to the lowest possible heat, and let the shrimp simmer in this sauce while you arrange the lettuce on 4 plates.

Top each plate of lettuce with one-quarter of the shrimp. Spoon the sauce over all, to act as a warm dressing. Scatter one-quarter of the mint and one-quarter of the coconut over each salad, and serve.

**Yield:** 4 servings

**Nutritional Analysis:** Each will have: 350 calories; 16 g fat; 37 g protein; 13 g carbohydrates; 4 g fiber; 9 g usable carbs.

| | | | | | |
|---|---|---|---|---|---|
| Potassium (mg): | 727 mg | Vitamin C (mg): | 16 mg | Thiamin/B1 (mg): | 0.1 mg |
| Calcium (mg): | 142 mg | Vitamin A (i.u.): | 1195 i.u. | Riboflavin/B2 (mg): | 0.1 mg |
| Iron (mg): | 6 mg | Vitamin B6 (mg): | 0.1 mg | Folacin (mcg): | 112 mcg |
| Zinc (mg): | 2 mg | Vitamin B12 (mcg): | 1.7 mcg | Niacin/B3 (mg): | 5 mg |

# Sautéed Scallops with Asparagus and Greens

This makes an elegant first course for a date you really want to dazzle, and it's easy to double or triple for a bigger dinner party or main dish servings.

3 tablespoons (45 ml) rice vinegar

1 tablespoon (14 ml) lemon juice

1/2 teaspoon (2 ml) dark sesame oil

2 tablespoons (28 ml) peanut or macadamia oil

10 asparagus spears

2 cups (40 g) mixed greens

6 sea scallops

Salt and pepper

Whisk together 1 tablespoon (14 ml) of the vinegar with 1 1/2 teaspoons (7 ml) of the lemon juice, the sesame oil, and 1 tablespoon (14 ml) of the peanut oil. Set aside.

Snap the ends off of the asparagus spears where they want to break naturally. Discard the ends and put the asparagus spears in a microwaveable casserole with a lid, add a couple of tablespoons (30 ml or so) of water, cover, and microwave on high for 3 to 4 minutes. Uncover immediately. Divide the asparagus spears between 2 salad plates, fanning them out artistically. Top with the greens.

Sprinkle the scallops with a little salt and pepper.

Spray a big, heavy skillet with nonstick cooking spray, and put it over medium-high heat. Add the remaining tablespoon (14 ml) of peanut oil, and let it get good and hot. Add the scallops, and cook for 2 to 3 minutes per side, or until they're opaque in the center. Remove to a bowl. Put the remaining vinegar and lemon juice in the skillet and boil till it's reduced to just a couple of teaspoons. Drizzle over the scallops.

Now drizzle the dressing you made first thing over the salad greens, top each serving with 3 scallops, and serve.

**Yield:** 2 servings

**Nutritional Analysis:** Each will have: 194 calories; 15 g fat; 8 g protein; 9 g carbohydrates; 4 g fiber; 5 g usable carbs.

| | | | | | |
|---|---|---|---|---|---|
| Potassium (mg): | 545 mg | Vitamin C (mg): | 54 mg | Thiamin/B1 (mg): | 0.1 mg |
| Calcium (mg): | 84 mg | Vitamin A (i.u.): | 3451 i.u. | Riboflavin/B2 (mg): | 0.2 mg |
| Iron (mg): | 2 mg | Vitamin B6 (mg): | 0.2 mg | Folacin (mcg): | 213 mcg |
| Zinc (mg): | 1 mg | Vitamin B12 (mcg): | 0.5 mcg | Niacin/B3 (mg): | 2 mg |

## Seafood Artichoke Salad

Seafood cocktail turned into a salad!

- 1/3 cup (75 g) light mayonnaise
- 1/3 cup (80 g) no-sugar-added ketchup
- 1 1/2 tablespoons (23 g) chili garlic paste
- 2 teaspoons (10 ml) Worcestershire sauce
- 2 teaspoons (10 g) prepared horseradish
- 2 teaspoons (10 ml) lemon juice
- 3/4 pound (340 g) salad shrimp, or larger shrimp, chopped
- 3/4 cup (150 g) lump crabmeat, cooked and diced
- 3/4 cup (150 g) cooked lobster meat, diced
- 2 cans (14 ounces, or 390 g each) artichoke hearts
- 4 lettuce leaves
- 1 lemon, cut into 4 wedges

Mix together the mayo, ketchup, garlic paste, Worcestershire sauce, horseradish, and lemon juice. Refrigerate while you assemble everything else.

Throw the teeny-weeny shrimp into a big bowl with the crab and lobster. Drain the artichoke hearts, chop them coarsely, and add them to the seafood.

Pour in the dressing, and toss.

Line 4 plates with the lettuce leaves, top with the seafood salad, add lemon wedges, and serve.

**Yield:** 4 servings

**Nutritional Analysis:** Each will have: 267 calories; 5 g fat; 33 g protein; 19 g carbohydrates; trace fiber; 19 g usable carbs.

| | | | | | |
|---|---|---|---|---|---|
| Potassium (mg): | 365 mg | Vitamin C (mg): | 9 mg | Thiamin/B1 (mg): | trace |
| Calcium (mg): | 77 mg | Vitamin A (i.u.): | 562 i.u. | Riboflavin/B2 (mg): | 0.1 mg |
| Iron (mg): | 3 mg | Vitamin B6 (mg): | 0.2 mg | Folacin (mcg): | 19 mcg |
| Zinc (mg): | 3 mg | Vitamin B12 (mcg): | 4.4 mcg | Niacin/B3 (mg): | 3 mg |

## Spinach Salad with Apricot Dressing, Shrimp, and Goat Cheese

This is impressive-looking and quite tasty ... and the dressing is to die for! Our tester suggests that a few toasted slivered almonds would be nice on this, too.

4 strips bacon

8 jumbo shrimp, peeled and deveined

2 quarts (240 g) baby spinach

Apricot Dressing (see below)

5 ounces (140 g) goat cheese, crumbled

Lay the bacon strips on a microwave bacon rack or in a glass pie plate. Nuke 'em on high for 4 minutes, or until crisp but not overdone. Drain and set aside.

Fill a small saucepan with water and add a little salt. Bring it to a simmer. Throw in the shrimp and cook 'em until just done—maybe 5 minutes.

Pile your spinach in a big bowl. Pour on the dressing, and toss till it's well coated. Crumble in the crisp bacon, and toss again. Pile on 4 salad plates. Top each serving with 2 shrimp and one-quarter of the goat cheese, and serve.

**Yield:** 4 servings

**Nutritional Analysis:** Each will have: 339 calories; 27 g fat; 18 g protein; 7 g carbohydrates; 2 g fiber; 5 g usable carbs.

| | | | | | |
|---|---|---|---|---|---|
| Potassium (mg): | 491 mg | Vitamin C (mg): | 23 mg | Thiamin/B1 (mg): | 0.1 mg |
| Calcium (mg): | 390 mg | Vitamin A (i.u.): | 4935 i.u. | Riboflavin/B2 (mg): | 0.5 mg |
| Iron (mg): | 3 mg | Vitamin B6 (mg): | 0.1 mg | Folacin (mcg): | 121 mcg |
| Zinc (mg): | 1 mg | Vitamin B12 (mcg): | 0.3 mcg | Niacin/B3 (mg): | 2 mg |

## Apricot Dressing

3 apricots, peeled and seeded

3 tablespoons (45 ml) peanut or macadamia oil

1 tablespoon (1.5 g) Splenda

2 teaspoons (10 ml) lemon juice

1 teaspoon (5 g) Dijon mustard

1 tablespoon (14 g) light mayonnaise

Just put everything in your food processor with the S-blade in place, and run until it's smooth.

**Yield:** 6 servings

**Nutritional Analysis:** Each will have: 76 calories; 7 g fat; trace protein; 3 g carbohydrates; trace fiber; 3 g usable carbs.

| | | | | | |
|---|---|---|---|---|---|
| Potassium (mg): | 55 mg | Vitamin C (mg): | 3 mg | Thiamin/B1 (mg): | trace |
| Calcium (mg): | 3 mg | Vitamin A (i.u.): | 457 i.u. | Riboflavin/B2 (mg): | trace |
| Iron (mg): | trace | Vitamin B6 (mg): | trace | Folacin (mcg): | 2 mcg |
| Zinc (mg): | trace | Vitamin B12 (mcg): | 0 mcg | Niacin/B3 (mg): | trace |

## Flank Steak Salad Vinaigrette

Think only girls eat salad for dinner? Hah! Steak and blue cheese, boys. Walk away if you can.

1/2 cup (120 ml) reduced-calorie balsamic vinaigrette salad dressing

1 tablespoon (4 g) chopped fresh tarragon

1/2 teaspoon pepper

2 heads Boston lettuce, torn

1/2 head radicchio, torn

1 cup (125 g) cherry tomatoes, halved (it's especially pretty if you use half red and half yellow tomatoes)

1 cup (70 g) broccoli florets

1/2 small red onion, sliced paper-thin

12 ounces (340 g) cooked flank steak, thinly sliced (see page 398 for instructions for cooking a flank steak)

6 tablespoons (45 g) crumbled blue cheese

Combine the salad dressing, tarragon, and pepper. Set aside.

Break up the lettuce and radicchio in a big salad bowl. Pour on the dressing, and toss till the lettuce is coated. Pile on 4 serving plates.

Arrange the tomatoes, broccoli, onion, and steak on each salad, scatter 1 1/2 tablespoons (11 g) of blue cheese over each, and serve.

**Yield:** 4 servings

**Nutritional Analysis:** Each will have: 260 calories; 16 g fat; 21 g protein; 8 g carbohydrates; 2 g fiber; 6 g usable carbs.

| | | | | | |
|---|---|---|---|---|---|
| Potassium (mg): | 734 mg | Vitamin C (mg): | 33 mg | Thiamin/B1 (mg): | 0.2 mg |
| Calcium (mg): | 115 mg | Vitamin A (i.u.): | 1673 i.u. | Riboflavin/B2 (mg): | 0.2 mg |
| Iron (mg): | 2 mg | Vitamin B6 (mg): | 0.5 mg | Folacin (mcg): | 96 mcg |
| Zinc (mg): | 4 mg | Vitamin B12 (mcg): | 2.6 mcg | Niacin/B3 (mg): | 5 mg |

## Steak, Sun-Dried Tomato, and Mozzarella Salad with Bulgur

This is very, very special. The directions for cooking a perfect flank steak are on page 398. Cook a bigger steak than you need for one meal, and serve this later in the week!

1/2 head cauliflower

2/3 cup (120 g) bulgur, cooked

1/2 cup (25 g) dry-pack sun-dried tomatoes, chopped

8 ounces (225 g) cooked flank steak, diced

1/2 cup (55 g) mozzarella cheese, shredded or cubed (preshredded mozzarella works fine here)

1/2 cup (70 g) roasted red peppers jarred in water, drained and diced

1/4 cup (8 g) chopped fresh basil

2 tablespoons (28 ml) red wine vinegar

2 tablespoons (28 ml) olive oil

1 clove garlic, peeled and crushed

1/4 teaspoon salt or Vege-Sal

1/4 teaspoon pepper

1/4 cup (40 g) finely diced red onion

Lettuce leaves, to line plates

Trim the very bottom of the cauliflower stem, and cut off the leaves. Now run the cauliflower through the shredding blade of your food processor. Put the resulting "cauli-rice" into a microwaveable casserole with a lid, add a couple of tablespoons (30 ml or so) of water, cover, and nuke on high for 6 minutes.

If you don't have cooked bulgur on hand, it's very quick and easy to make: Combine 1/2 cup (90 g) bulgur with 1/2 cup (120 ml) water in a small pan. Bring to a simmer, cover, turn the burner to the lowest possible heat, and let it cook for just a few minutes. You may get a little more than 2/3 cup of cooked bulgur this recipe calls for, depending on how much yours expands.

While the cauliflower and bulgur are cooking, throw the sun-dried tomatoes, steak, cheese, roasted red peppers, fresh basil, and red onion into a big salad bowl.

When the microwave beeps, uncover the cauliflower right away. Let it cool for a minimum of 10 minutes, stirring occasionally to let out the steam (15 minutes might be better). Uncover the bulgur and let it cool, too. The point here is that you don't want the hot cauliflower and bulgur to cook the vegetables and melt the cheese.

While things are cooling off, make the dressing by whisking together the vinegar, oil, garlic, salt, and pepper.

Okay, when the cauliflower and bulgur are cool enough that they won't melt the mozzarella, add them to the big salad bowl. Toss everything together until it's all very well mixed. Give the dressing one more quick whisk, pour it on, toss to coat everything, and pile the salad on 4 lettuce-lined plates.

**Yield:** 4 servings

**Nutritional Analysis:** Each will have: 274 calories; 17 g fat; 18 g protein; 16 g carbohydrates; 4 g fiber; 12 g usable carbs.

| | | | | | |
|---|---|---|---|---|---|
| Potassium (mg): | 720 mg | Vitamin C (mg): | 61 mg | Thiamin/B1 (mg): | 0.2 mg |
| Calcium (mg): | 120 mg | Vitamin A (i.u.): | 1012 i.u. | Riboflavin/B2 (mg): | 0.2 mg |
| Iron (mg): | 3 mg | Vitamin B6 (mg): | 0.5 mg | Folacin (mcg): | 62 mcg |
| Zinc (mg): | 3 mg | Vitamin B12 (mcg): | 1.8 mcg | Niacin/B3 (mg): | 4 mg |

# Easy and Elegant Beef and Asparagus Salad

This turns simple deli roast beef into a dish you'd be proud to serve to company.

1/2 cup (110 g) light mayonnaise
1/3 cup (40 g) minced green bell pepper
1/3 cup (40 g) minced red bell pepper
1/3 cup (40 g) minced yellow bell pepper
1/2 teaspoon Splenda
2 tablespoons (28 ml) milk
2 tablespoons (8 g) chopped fresh basil, or 2 teaspoons (3 g) dried basil
3 scallions, finely minced
1/4 teaspoon salt
1/4 teaspoon pepper
1 pound (455 g) asparagus
Lettuce leaves, to line plates
3 medium tomatoes, sliced
1 medium cucumber, sliced
1 pound (455 g) deli roast beef, sliced fairly thick

Combine the mayo; red, green, and yellow bell peppers; Splenda; milk; basil; scallions; salt; and pepper. Mix well and refrigerate.

Snap the ends off of the asparagus spears where they want to break naturally. Discard the ends and arrange the asparagus in a microwaveable casserole with a lid, or in a glass pie plate. Add a couple of tablespoons (30 ml or so) of water, cover (use plastic wrap to cover a pie plate), and microwave on high for 5 minutes, or until the asparagus is just barely tender. Uncover immediately, to stop cooking. Drain and chill.

When dinner rolls around, arrange a lettuce leaf or two (red leaf looks nice) on each plate. Artfully arrange the asparagus, tomatoes, and cucumber on top of the lettuce. Fold or roll the deli roast beef prettily, and arrange that on top. Top with the refrigerated dressing, and serve.

**Yield:** 4 servings

**Nutritional Analysis:** Each will have: 329 calories; 11 g fat; 35 g protein; 23 g carbohydrates; 4 g fiber; 19 g usable carbs.

| | | | | | |
|---|---|---|---|---|---|
| Potassium (mg): | 1062 mg | Vitamin C (mg): | 96 mg | Thiamin/B1 (mg): | 0.2 mg |
| Calcium (mg): | 63 mg | Vitamin A (i.u.): | 2617 i.u. | Riboflavin/B2 (mg): | 0.2 mg |
| Iron (mg): | 4 mg | Vitamin B6 (mg): | 0.5 mg | Folacin (mcg): | 127 mcg |
| Zinc (mg): | 5 mg | Vitamin B12 (mcg): | 2.7 mcg | Niacin/B3 (mg): | 8 mg |

# Sukiyaki Salad

The nice presentation of this recipe impressed even our pickiest tester! Yet it's easy enough to be a good basic family meal.

- 1 pound (455 g) thickly cut beef round steak
- 1 tablespoon (1.5 g) Splenda
- 6 tablespoons (90 ml) rice wine or dry sherry
- 3 tablespoons (45 g) soy sauce
- 1 tablespoon (8 g) sesame seeds
- 5 ounces (140 g) bagged baby spinach
- 1 tablespoon (14 ml) peanut oil
- 7 ounces (195 g) firm tofu, cut into 1/2-inch (1.25-cm) cubes
- 8 ounces (225 g) sliced mushrooms
- 2 medium leeks, sliced 1/2 inch (1.25 cm) thick

Slice the beef quite thin—this is easiest if it's half-frozen. Mix together the Splenda, rice wine, and soy sauce, and have them sitting by the stove.

Stir the sesame seeds in a dry skillet over medium heat until they're lightly toasted. Set aside.

Divide the spinach leaves between 4 serving plates, and have them ready.

Okay! Put the oil in a big, heavy skillet or a wok, if you have one, and place it over high heat. You want the oil good and hot. Add the beef, and stir-fry until it's mostly done but still has a touch of pink.

Add the wine and soy sauce mixture, tofu, mushrooms, and leeks. Cook until the leeks are just tender. Serve on the beds of lettuce, and top with sesame seeds.

**Yield:** 4 servings

**Nutritional Analysis:** Each will have: 345 calories; 15 g fat; 34 g protein; 15 g carbohydrates; 3 g fiber; 12 g usable carbs.

| | | | | | |
|---|---|---|---|---|---|
| Potassium (mg): | 975 mg | Vitamin C (mg): | 17 mg | Thiamin/B1 (mg): | 0.3 mg |
| Calcium (mg): | 175 mg | Vitamin A (i.u.): | 2426 i.u. | Riboflavin/B2 (mg): | 1.1 mg |
| Iron (mg): | 6 mg | Vitamin B6 (mg): | 0.7 mg | Folacin (mcg): | 140 mcg |
| Zinc (mg): | 6 mg | Vitamin B12 (mcg): | 2.1 mcg | Niacin/B3 (mg): | 8 mg |

## Balsamic Glazed Lamb Salad

This is pretty fancy, and you'll love it if you love lamb. I'm crazy about lamb! By the way, this trick of boiling down balsamic vinegar can be used to turn fairly inexpensive balsamic into something passably like the expensive aged stuff.

1/4 cup (30 g) chopped hazelnuts (aka "filberts")
1 cup (235 ml) balsamic vinegar
1 tablespoon (14 ml) olive oil
1 clove garlic, peeled and minced
12 ounces (340 g) leg of lamb, cut into steaks 1/2 inch (1.25 cm) thick (the meat guys at your grocery store will gladly cut up a leg of lamb into steaks for you!)
3 cups (65 g) fresh snow pea pods, ends trimmed and any strings pulled off
6 cups (120 g) mixed greens (an Italian mix is good)

Spread the chopped hazelnuts in a shallow pan and put them in the oven at 350°F (180°C, or gas mark 4) for 8 to 10 minutes, to toast.

Put the balsamic vinegar in a small saucepan over medium-high heat. Bring it to a boil, turn it down to a simmer, and let it cook for 10 to 15 minutes, or until it's reduced to about 1/3 cup (80 ml). Stir regularly so that it doesn't burn.

Combine the oil and garlic in a small dish, and let them sit while the broiler preheats, so the garlic has time to infuse the oil. When the broiler's hot, brush the lamb steaks with the garlic-flavored olive oil. Broil 3 to 4 inches (7.5 to 10 cm) from the heat for 4 to 5 minutes per side, or until it's done to your liking. Brush both sides with the oil when you turn the steak.

While the lamb steaks are broiling, put the snow peas in a microwaveable casserole with a lid. Add a couple of tablespoons (30 ml or so) of water, cover, and nuke on high for 3 minutes. Uncover immediately!

Pile the greens on 4 serving plates. Pull the lamb steaks out of the broiler, throw them onto your cutting board, and slice them into thin strips, discarding the bone (though I like to eat the marrow first!). Top each salad with sliced lamb and one-quarter of the snow peas. Drizzle each salad with the reduced balsamic vinegar, sprinkle with nuts, and serve.

**Yield:** 4 servings

**Nutritional Analysis:** Each will have: 293 calories; 20 g fat; 17 g protein; 15 g carbohydrates; 5 g fiber; 10 g usable carbs.

| | | | | | |
|---|---|---|---|---|---|
| Potassium (mg): | 712 mg | Vitamin C (mg): | 103 mg | Thiamin/B1 (mg): | 0.3 mg |
| Calcium (mg): | 143 mg | Vitamin A (i.u.): | 4562 i.u. | Riboflavin/B2 (mg): | 0.3 mg |
| Iron (mg): | 4 mg | Vitamin B6 (mg): | 0.4 mg | Folacin (mcg): | 206 mcg |
| Zinc (mg): | 3 mg | Vitamin B12 (mcg): | 1.7 mcg | Niacin/B3 (mg): | 5 mg |

# Farmer's Chop Suey

This is a Jewish deli classic.

4 ounces (115 g) radishes, thinly sliced

4 medium cucumbers, quartered and sliced

6 scallions, sliced

3 medium tomatoes, chopped

3 cups (675 g) 2% cottage cheese

Salt and pepper

12 lettuce leaves

Just put the radishes, cukes, scallions, and tomatoes in a big bowl. Add the cottage cheese, and toss the whole thing together. Add salt and pepper to taste, and serve on lettuce leaves.

**Yield:** 6 servings

**Nutritional Analysis:** Each will have: 150 calories; 3 g fat; 18 g protein; 15 g carbohydrates; 3 g fiber; 12 g usable carbs.

| | | | | | |
|---|---|---|---|---|---|
| Potassium (mg): | 640 mg | Vitamin C (mg): | 30 mg | Thiamin/B1 (mg): | 0.1 mg |
| Calcium (mg): | 126 mg | Vitamin A (i.u.): | 1006 i.u. | Riboflavin/B2 (mg): | 0.3 mg |
| Iron (mg): | 1 mg | Vitamin B6 (mg): | 0.2 mg | Folacin (mcg): | 73 mcg |
| Zinc (mg): | 1 mg | Vitamin B12 (mcg): | 0.8 mcg | Niacin/B3 (mg): | 1 mg |

## Cottage-Apple Salad

Turns plain cottage cheese into a meal!

1 apple

2 teaspoons (10 ml) lemon juice

4 cups (900 g) cottage cheese

1/2 cup (60 g) chopped walnuts

16 scallions, thinly sliced, including the crisp part of the green

1/2 cup (30 g) minced parsley

Salt and pepper

4 large lettuce leaves

Quarter the apple, cut out the core, then cut it into small dice, leaving the skin on. Put it in a mixing bowl and toss with the lemon juice to prevent browning.

Add the cottage cheese, walnuts, scallions, and parsley. Mix everything together. Add salt and pepper to taste, and serve on lettuce leaves.

**Yield:** 4 servings

**Nutritional Analysis:** Each will have: 341 calories; 13 g fat; 36 g protein; 21 g carbohydrates; 4 g fiber; 17 g usable carbs.

| | | | | | |
|---|---|---|---|---|---|
| Potassium (mg): | 562 mg | Vitamin C (mg): | 25 mg | Thiamin/B1 (mg): | 0.1 mg |
| Calcium (mg): | 222 mg | Vitamin A (i.u.): | 871 i.u. | Riboflavin/B2 (mg): | 0.5 mg |
| Iron (mg): | 2 mg | Vitamin B6 (mg): | 0.3 mg | Folacin (mcg): | 95 mcg |
| Zinc (mg): | 2 mg | Vitamin B12 (mcg): | 1.6 mcg | Niacin/B3 (mg): | 1 mg |

## Mediterranean Cottage Cheese Salad

Low-carb, low-cal cottage cheese has always been the dieter's pal, but it can be pretty boring. But not here!

8 cups (160 g) romaine lettuce, torn

1/2 green bell pepper, diced

1/2 red bell pepper, diced

1/4 small red onion, sliced paper-thin

16 kalamata olives, pitted and chopped

1/4 cup (60 ml) reduced-calorie balsamic vinaigrette salad dressing

1 cup (225 g) cottage cheese

Put the romaine in a salad bowl with the green and red peppers, onion, and olives. Pour on the dressing, and toss well. Add the cottage cheese, toss again, and serve.

**Yield:** 2 servings

**Nutritional Analysis:** Each will have: 267 calories; 14 g fat; 20 g protein; 18 g carbohydrates; 5 g fiber; 13 g usable carbs.

| | | | | | |
|---|---|---|---|---|---|
| Potassium (mg): | 900 mg | Vitamin C (mg): | 138 mg | Thiamin/B1 (mg): | 0.3 mg |
| Calcium (mg): | 168 mg | Vitamin A (i.u.): | 7788 i.u. | Riboflavin/B2 (mg): | 0.4 mg |
| Iron (mg): | 3 mg | Vitamin B6 (mg): | 0.4 mg | Folacin (mcg): | 336 mcg |
| Zinc (mg): | 1 mg | Vitamin B12 (mcg): | 0.8 mcg | Niacin/B3 (mg): | 2 mg |

## Ham, Cheese, and Pear Salad

This is a very hearty main dish salad.

1 clove garlic, peeled

3 tablespoons (45 ml) olive oil

1 ripe and juicy pear

1 tablespoon (14 ml) lemon juice

6 ounces (170 g) mozzarella cheese

6 ounces (170 g) turkey ham

2 tablespoons (28 ml) red wine vinegar

1 teaspoon (5 g) Dijon mustard

1/4 teaspoon pepper

1 quart (80 g) romaine lettuce, torn

1 quart (80 g) leaf lettuce, torn

1 quart (80 g) butter lettuce, torn

Crush the garlic, finely mince it, and pour the oil over it. Let this sit while you assemble your salad.

Core the pear and cut it into thin slices. Toss them with the lemon juice to prevent browning.

Cut the mozzarella and ham into 1/2-inch (1.25-cm) cubes.

Whisk together the vinegar, mustard, and pepper.

Tear up the romaine, leaf, and butter lettuces, and combine 'em in a big darned salad bowl. Pour on the garlic-infused oil, and toss with barely controlled abandon until every square millimeter of lettuce is coated with the oil. Sprinkle the vinegar mixture over the lettuce, and toss again. Pile the salad on 4 plates.

Now arrange one-quarter of your pear slices, ham cubes, and cheese cubes attractively on top of each salad, and serve.

**Yield:** 4 servings

**Nutritional Analysis:** Each will have: 330 calories; 23 g fat; 20 g protein; 12 g carbohydrates; 3 g fiber; 9 g usable carbs.

| | | | | | |
|---|---|---|---|---|---|
| Potassium (mg): | 631 mg | Vitamin C (mg): | 24 mg | Thiamin/B1 (mg): | 0.1 mg |
| Calcium (mg): | 305 mg | Vitamin A (i.u.): | 2566 i.u. | Riboflavin/B2 (mg): | 0.3 mg |
| Iron (mg): | 3 mg | Vitamin B6 (mg): | 0.2 mg | Folacin (mcg): | 157 mcg |
| Zinc (mg): | 3 mg | Vitamin B12 (mcg): | 0.4 mcg | Niacin/B3 (mg): | 2 mg |

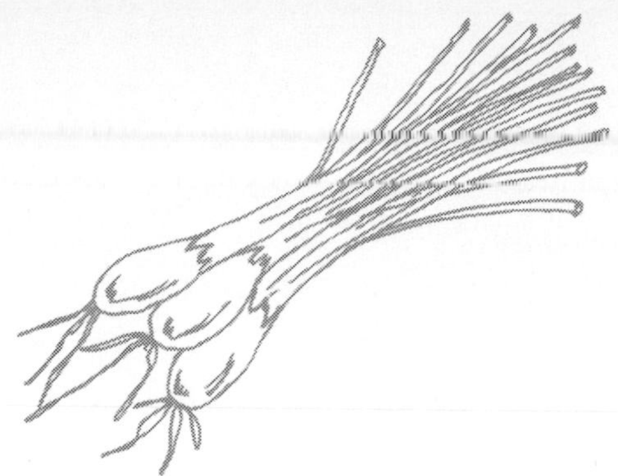

chapter eight

# Stir-Fries and Skillet Suppers

Sometimes—like, oh, about 5 nights a week—you don't want to heat up the kitchen, or cook side dishes, or really do anything but throw some stuff in your skillet and have a good, satisfying one-dish meal in almost no time. It's that sort of night these dishes are for.

Nutritionally, these dishes have a lot in common with the main dish salads in the previous chapter—they combine your protein with piles and piles of vegetables, resulting in great flavor, brilliant colors, wonderful textures—and, oh yeah, terrific nutrition. It's just that these dishes are hot.

We start with some stir-fries. You may eat your stir-fries plain (I often do), but if you want a bed of rice to put them on, you can use brown rice or cauli-rice. There's a big, big difference between the two in calorie and carb counts, however: 1 cup (165 g) of cooked brown rice has 218 calories, 46 grams of carbs, and 3 grams of fiber. 1 cup (150 g) of cauliflower has 25 calories, 5 grams of carbs, and 3 grams of fiber. Consult your own body as to which suits you best.

# Orange Chicken Stir-Fry

Bright and lively flavor.

1 pound (455 g) boneless, skinless chicken thighs
1 onion, sliced
1 red bell pepper, seeded and cut into thin strips
1 cup (65 g) snow pea pods, fresh, with the ends pinched off and any strings removed
1 clove garlic, peeled and very finely minced
1/4 cup (60 ml) soy sauce
1/4 cup (60 ml) dry sherry
1 tablespoon (16 g) tomato paste
2 oranges
2 tablespoons (28 ml) peanut oil
2 cups (100 g) bean sprouts

Cut the chicken thighs into thin strips or small cubes. Have the onion, pepper, snow peas, and garlic prepped before you start cooking. This is an absolute must when making stir-fries!

In a small bowl, whisk together the soy sauce, sherry, and tomato paste. Grate the rind of one orange, and put that in, too. Cut that orange in half and squeeze all of its juice into the sauce, as well.

Using a sharp knife, peel and segment the other orange, holding it over the bowl of sauce as you do so, to catch any dripping juice. Cut each segment into 2 or 3 chunks.

Okay, you're ready to start cooking! Hit a big, heavy skillet or a wok with some non-stick spray and place it over high heat. When it's hot, add the oil, then the chicken. Stir-fry until most of the pink is gone from the chicken.

Add the onion, pepper, snow peas, and garlic. Continue stir-frying for another 5 to 8 minutes, until the vegetables are tender-crisp.

Pour the orange sauce over the stir-fry, and stir to coat everything. Let it cook, stirring frequently, for another minute or two.

Add the orange chunks and bean sprouts, stir-fry for another 2 minutes, and serve.

**Yield:** 4 servings

**Nutritional Analysis:** Each will have: 286 calories; 13 g fat; 21 g protein; 20 g carbohydrates; 5 g fiber; 15 g usable carbs.

| | | | | | |
|---|---|---|---|---|---|
| Potassium (mg): | 563 mg | Vitamin C (mg): | 117 mg | Thiamin/B1 (mg): | 0.2 mg |
| Calcium (mg): | 67 mg | Vitamin A (i.u.): | 2019 i.u. | Riboflavin/B2 (mg): | 0.3 mg |
| Iron (mg): | 3 mg | Vitamin B6 (mg): | 0.5 mg | Folacin (mcg): | 82 mcg |
| Zinc (mg): | 2 mg | Vitamin B12 (mcg): | 0.2 mcg | Niacin/B3 (mg): | 5 mg |

## Five-Spice Beef Stir-Fry

A good basic family meal, especially if the kids like stir-fry.

1 pound (455 g) boneless beef round steak

1½ teaspoons Splenda

1 teaspoon five-spice powder

3 tablespoons (45 ml) soy sauce

2 cloves garlic, peeled and minced

1 teaspoon tenderizer

2 tablespoons (28 ml) peanut oil or coconut oil

1 cup (120 g) thinly sliced celery

1 medium carrot, thinly sliced

1 medium onion, sliced

½ cup (120 ml) beef broth

1 cup (100 g) cucumber, peeled and julienned (cut into strips)

1 medium tomato, cut into thin wedges

Guar or xanthan gum

Slice your round steak as thinly as you can (it's easier if it's half-frozen). Mix together the Splenda, five-spice powder, soy sauce, garlic, and tenderizer in a medium-size bowl. Add the beef strips, and toss to coat. Let them marinate for 30 minutes or so, stirring once or twice in that time.

If you have a wok, use it! If not, spray a big, heavy skillet with nonstick cooking spray and put it over the highest heat. Add 1 tablespoon (14 ml) of the oil, let it get good and hot, and then add the beef. Stir-fry for 4 to 7 minutes, or until it is firm and the pink is gone. Remove from the wok or skillet.

Add the second tablespoon of oil, get it good and hot, and throw in the celery, carrot, and onion. Stir-fry for 6 to 7 minutes, or until the veggies are tender-crisp.

Add the broth and cucumber strips to the pan. Let that cook for 1 minute, then add the beef back in, along with the tomato. Heat through, thicken with the guar or xanthan, and serve.

You can serve this over brown rice or cauli-rice, or just by itself in a bowl!

**Yield:** 4 servings

**Nutritional Analysis:** Each will have: 286 calories; 14 g fat; 29 g protein; 10 g carbohydrates; 2 g fiber; 8 g usable carbs.

| | | | | | |
|---|---|---|---|---|---|
| Potassium (mg): | 722 mg | Vitamin C (mg): | 13 mg | Thiamin/B1 (mg): | 0.2 mg |
| Calcium (mg): | 40 mg | Vitamin A (i.u.): | 5351 i.u. | Riboflavin/B2 (mg): | 0.3 mg |
| Iron (mg): | 3 mg | Vitamin B6 (mg): | 0.6 mg | Folacin (mcg): | 37 mcg |
| Zinc (mg): | 5 mg | Vitamin B12 (mcg): | 2.1 mcg | Niacin/B3 (mg): | 6 mg |

**Note:** Use the marinating time to prep all your other ingredients, and cook some brown rice or cauli-rice to serve your stir-fry on, if you want it.

## Beef with Broccoli

A Chinese restaurant favorite.

8 ounces (225 g) round steak
2 tablespoons (28 ml) soy sauce
1/4 cup (60 ml) dry sherry
1 teaspoon grated gingerroot
4 cloves garlic, peeled and crushed
1/2 teaspoon meat tenderizer
1 pound (455 g) frozen broccoli "cuts," thawed
1 medium onion, quartered and sliced
3 tablespoons (45 ml) peanut oil or coconut oil
Guar or xanthan gum (optional)

Slice the round steak as thin as possible across the grain. (This is easiest if the meat is partially frozen.) Put the slices in a nonreactive bowl or a zipper-lock bag.

Mix together the soy sauce, sherry, ginger, garlic, and meat tenderizer. Pour this mixture over the meat, and toss or turn to coat. If you're using a bag, seal it, pressing out the air as you go. Let this sit for at least 20 minutes, and an hour won't hurt.

Drain the marinade off the beef and reserve it. Set the beef, broccoli, onion, and reserved marinade by the stove—this goes fast!

Use a wok if you have one. If not, spray a big, heavy skillet with nonstick spray and put it over the highest heat. Add 1½ tablespoons (21 ml) of the oil. Give it a few seconds to get hot, then throw in the beef. Stir-fry until the pink is gone—3 to 4 minutes. Remove it from the pan and keep it nearby.

Add the remaining oil to the pan, and let it get hot. Throw in the broccoli and onion, and stir-fry until they're tender-crisp—5 minutes or so. Put the beef back in the skillet, along with the reserved marinade. Stir it all up. Thicken with a light sprinkle of guar or xanthan, if you like, but it's hardly essential. Cook everything together for another minute, then serve as-is, over brown rice, or over cauli-rice, depending on your nutritional goals.

**Yield:** 3 servings

**Nutritional Analysis:** Each will have: 352 calories; 23 g fat; 20 g protein; 13 g carbohydrates; 5 g fiber; 8 g usable carbs.

| | | | | | |
|---|---|---|---|---|---|
| Potassium (mg): | 670 mg | Vitamin C (mg): | 89 mg | Thiamin/B1 (mg): | 0.2 mg |
| Calcium (mg): | 106 mg | Vitamin A (i.u.): | 3127 i.u. | Riboflavin/B2 (mg): | 0.3 mg |
| Iron (mg): | 3 mg | Vitamin B6 (mg): | 0.6 mg | Folacin (mcg): | 116 mcg |
| Zinc (mg): | 3 mg | Vitamin B12 (mcg): | 2 mcg | Niacin/B3 (mg): | 4 mg |

## Chicken Almond Ding

Here's the Cantonese classic for you to cook at home.

- 12 ounces (340 g) boneless, skinless chicken breasts, cut into cubes
- 1 green bell pepper, diced
- 1 medium carrot, sliced paper-thin on the diagonal
- 3 scallions, sliced ½ inch (1.25 cm) thick on the diagonal, including the crisp part of the green
- 2 tablespoons (28 ml) soy sauce
- 2 tablespoons (28 ml) dry sherry
- 2 tablespoons (16 g) grated gingerroot
- 2 cloves garlic, peeled and crushed
- 2 tablespoons (28 ml) coconut oil or peanut oil
- ⅓ cup (40 g) sliced almonds

First things first: Cut everything up. Make sure the chicken, pepper, carrot and scallions are ready to go before you start making your stir-fry.

In a small dish, mix together the soy sauce, sherry, ginger, and garlic. Put this by the stove.

If you have a wok, use it! Otherwise, spray a big, heavy skillet with nonstick cooking spray. Put the pan over the highest heat. Add 2 teaspoons (10 ml) of the oil and the almonds. Stir-fry the almonds until they're golden, then remove them from the pan and set them aside.

Add another 2 teaspoons (10 ml) of oil to the pan, and throw in the chicken. Stir-fry it until all of the pink is gone. Remove the chicken from the pan to a plate.

Put the last 2 teaspoons of oil in the pan, and throw in the pepper, carrot, and scallions. Stir-fry them until they're just getting to the tender-crisp stage. Add the chicken back to the pan, and pour in the sauce. Stir everything together and continue to cook for just another couple of minutes. Stir in the almonds, and serve.

**Yield:** 3 servings

**Nutritional Analysis:** Each will have: 356 calories; 21 g fat; 30 g protein; 11 g carbohydrates; 3 g fiber; 8 g usable carbs.

| | | | | | |
|---|---|---|---|---|---|
| Potassium (mg): | 569 mg | Vitamin C (mg): | 41 mg | Thiamin/B1 (mg): | 0.1 mg |
| Calcium (mg): | 80 mg | Vitamin A (i.u.): | 7075 i.u. | Riboflavin/B2 (mg): | 0.2 mg |
| Iron (mg): | 2 mg | Vitamin B6 (mg): | 0.7 mg | Folacin (mcg): | 33 mcg |
| Zinc (mg): | 2 mg | Vitamin B12 (mcg): | 0.3 mcg | Niacin/B3 (mg): | 13 mg |

# Gado Gado

This vegetarian stir-fry supper is an Indonesian classic. Our tester, Kelly, loved it. Add another hard-boiled egg to each serving if you want more protein.

2 medium carrots

1/2 head cabbage

2 tablespoons (28 ml) soy sauce

1 tablespoon (15 g) no-sugar-added ketchup

1 tablespoon (16 g) natural peanut butter

1/2 clove garlic, peeled and finely minced

1/2 teaspoon grated gingerroot

2 tablespoons (28 ml) peanut oil

1 red bell pepper, seeded and cut into thin strips

1½ cups (75 g) bean sprouts

½ cup (60 g) chopped dry-roasted peanuts, salted

4 hard-boiled eggs, peeled and cut into quarters

Peel or scrub the carrots, whack off the tops, and run them through the shredding blade of your food processor. Scoop the shredded carrot out and keep it standing by. Swap the shredding blade for the slicing blade, and run the cabbage through it.

In a small saucepan over low heat, whisk together the soy sauce, ketchup, peanut butter, garlic, and ginger. Stir until the peanut butter melts into everything else and the sauce is smooth.

Put a big, heavy skillet or a wok over high head. When it's hot, add the oil, then the carrots, cabbage, and the pepper. Stir-fry them for 3 to 4 minutes, then add the bean sprouts. Stir-fry for another 2 minutes. Now add the sauce and stir to coat all the vegetables. Stir in the chopped peanuts.

Pile the stir-fry on 4 plates. Top each serving of stir-fry one-quarter of the egg, and serve immediately.

**Yield:** 4 servings

**Nutritional Analysis:** Each will have: 308 calories; 23 g fat; 14 g protein; 14 g carbohydrates; 4 g fiber; 10 g usable carbs.

| | | | | | |
|---|---|---|---|---|---|
| Potassium (mg): | 465 mg | Vitamin C (mg): | 69 mg | Thiamin/B1 (mg): | 0.2 mg |
| Calcium (mg): | 67 mg | Vitamin A (i.u.): | 12190 i.u. | Riboflavin/B2 (mg): | 0.4 mg |
| Iron (mg): | 2 mg | Vitamin B6 (mg): | 0.3 mg | Folacin (mcg): | 107 mcg |
| Zinc (mg): | 1 mg | Vitamin B12 (mcg): | 0.6 mcg | Niacin/B3 (mg): | 3 mg |

## Creamy Basil, Lemon, and Gorgonzola Chicken and Portobellos

I'm drooling just thinking of this . . .

½ head cauliflower

1 tablespoon (14 ml) olive oil

½ small onion, diced

¾ pound (340 g) boneless, skinless chicken breasts, cut into ½-inch (1.25-cm) cubes

4 ounces (115 g) portobello mushrooms, coarsely chopped

2 cloves garlic, peeled and finely minced

2 tablespoons (28 ml) dry vermouth

1 teaspoon chicken bouillon concentrate

4 ounces (115 g) Gorgonzola cheese, crumbled

1/4 cup (15 g) minced fresh basil

1/4 cup (55 g) light mayonnaise

2 tablespoons (28 ml) milk

1 tablespoon (14 ml) lemon juice

Run the cauliflower through the shredding blade of your food processor. Put the resulting cauli-rice in a microwaveable casserole with a lid, add a couple of tablespoons (30 ml or so) of water, cover, and nuke on high for 6 minutes.

Meanwhile, spray a big, heavy skillet with nonstick cooking spray, put it over medium-high heat, and add the oil. Start sautéing the onion, chicken breast, and portobellos. Somewhere in here the microwave will beep—uncover your cauliflower right away, to prevent mushiness!

When the onion is translucent and the chicken has lost all its pinkness, stir in the garlic and vermouth. A fair amount of liquid will have accumulated from the chicken and veggies, too. Let the whole thing simmer until the liquid in the skillet is reduced by about half. Add the chicken bouillon concentrate, and stir till it's dissolved.

Drain the cauli-rice and dump it into the skillet, stirring it into the veggies and chicken. Add the Gorgonzola, and stir until it melts into the cauliflower.

Add the basil, mayonnaise, milk, and lemon juice, and stir just until everything's evenly coated. Serve!

**Yield:** 4 servings

**Nutritional Analysis:** Each will have: 315 calories; 18 g fat; 28 g protein; 11 g carbohydrates; 3 g fiber; 8 g usable carbs.

| | | | | | |
|---|---|---|---|---|---|
| Potassium (mg): | 537 mg | Vitamin C (mg): | 38 mg | Thiamin/B1 (mg): | 0.1 mg |
| Calcium (mg): | 47 mg | Vitamin A (i.u.): | 141 i.u. | Riboflavin/B2 (mg): | 0.3 mg |
| Iron (mg): | 1 mg | Vitamin B6 (mg): | 0.6 mg | Folacin (mcg): | 54 mcg |
| Zinc (mg): | 1 mg | Vitamin B12 (mcg): | 0.2 mcg | Niacin/B3 (mg): | 10 mg |

## Chicken Skillet Alfredo

This is a revamped version of a skillet supper in 15-Minute Low-Carb Recipes. When I figured out reduced-calorie Alfredo Sauce, I knew I had to include this recipe, too! This is a great reason to make a double batch of Alfredo and stash the leftovers in the fridge—it means you have this practically instant supper available, your ace in the hole.

1 1/2 tablespoons (21 ml) olive oil

1 1/2 pounds (670 g) boneless, skinless chicken breasts, cut into 1-inch (2.5-cm) cubes

1/2 medium onion, halved and sliced

1/2 pound (225 g) frozen broccoli florets

1/2 pound (225 g) frozen cauliflower

1 cup (235 ml) Alfredo Sauce (see page 499)

Spray a big, heavy skillet with nonstick cooking spray and put it over medium heat. Add the oil and start sautéing the chicken and onion.

While that's happening, put the broccoli and cauliflower in a microwaveable casserole with a lid, add a couple of tablespoons (30 ml or so) of water, cover, and microwave on high for 7 minutes.

Go back and stir the chicken and onion! When the microwave beeps, check the broccoli and cauliflower. They will probably still be cold in the middle. Stir them, and give them another 4 to 5 minutes—you want them tender, but not mushy.

When the broccoli and cauliflower are done, drain them well and add them to the skillet. Now add the Alfredo Sauce, and stir to coat. Heat through, and serve.

**Yield:** 5 servings

**Nutritional Analysis:** Each will have: 288 calories; 12 g fat; 37 g protein; 8 g carbohydrates; 3 g fiber; 5 g usable carbs.

| | | | | | |
|---|---|---|---|---|---|
| Potassium (mg): | 536 mg | Vitamin C (mg): | 54 mg | Thiamin/B1 (mg): | 0.1 mg |
| Calcium (mg): | 199 mg | Vitamin A (i.u.): | 866 i.u. | Riboflavin/B2 (mg): | 0.3 mg |
| Iron (mg): | 2 mg | Vitamin B6 (mg): | 0.7 mg | Folacin (mcg): | 80 mcg |
| Zinc (mg): | 2 mg | Vitamin B12 (mcg): | 0.6 mcg | Niacin/B3 (mg): | 14 mg |

## Burger Skillet Supper

This reminds me of the meals my mom used to put together from some hamburger and whatever else came to hand; we kids always loved that stuff. This is just a tasty family supper.

1 1/2 pounds (670 g) ground round

1/2 head cauliflower

1 medium onion

3 cups (450 g) frozen green beans

1 can (14 1/2 ounces, or 405 g) tomatoes with green chiles

1 tablespoon (15 g) brown mustard

1 tablespoon (16 g) tomato paste

1 teaspoon chili powder

1 clove garlic

Salt and pepper

Set a big, heavy skillet over medium-high heat and start browning the ground beef.

While that's happening, run the cauliflower through the shredding blade of your food processor. Put it in a microwaveable casserole with a lid, add a couple of tablespoons (30 ml or so) of water, cover, and microwave on high for 7 minutes.

Go back and stir the beef. Swap the shredding blade for the S-blade in your food processor, and chop the onion. Dump it in with the ground beef, and continue to cook and crumble the beef until all the pink is gone. Take a moment to put the green beans in another microwaveable bowl (a big cereal bowl works well), and cover. (With my bowls, a butter plate is just the right size to cover!)

When the microwave beeps, pull out the cauliflower and uncover it, to stop the cooking. Put the beans in the microwave for 6 minutes on high.

Okay, back to the skillet! The beef should be cooked through by now. Add the tomatoes, mustard, tomato paste, chili powder, and garlic. Stir everything together, and let it all simmer.

When the microwave beeps again, pull out the beans. Dump them and the cauliflower in with the beef, stir everything together, add salt and pepper to taste, and serve.

**Yield:** 6 servings

**Nutritional Analysis:** Each will have: 322 calories; 20 g fat; 24 g protein; 12 g carbohydrates; 4 g fiber; 8 g usable carbs.

| | | | | | |
|---|---|---|---|---|---|
| Potassium (mg): | 724 mg | Vitamin C (mg): | 37 mg | Thiamin/B1 (mg): | 0.2 mg |
| Calcium (mg): | 68 mg | Vitamin A (i.u.): | 786 i.u. | Riboflavin/B2 (mg): | 0.1 mg |
| Iron (mg): | 3 mg | Vitamin B6 (mg): | 0.5 mg | Folacin (mcg): | 56 mcg |
| Zinc (mg): | 5 mg | Vitamin B12 (mcg): | 2.3 mcg | Niacin/B3 (mg): | 6 mg |

## Pecan Rice Steak Skillet

I invented this to use up leftover steak. It's good enough that you should deliberately broil a bigger steak than you need to, so you can have this later in the week!

Pecan Rice (see page 136)

10 ounces (280 g) flank steak, cooked, thinly sliced, and cut into bite-size pieces (see page 398)

This is an ideal supper when you've got leftover steak or roast beef—just make your Pecan Rice, cut up your leftover steak, stir it into the Pecan Rice, and cook for another minute or two to heat the bits of beef. Then serve.

**Yield:** 4 servings

**Nutritional Analysis:** Each will have: 254 calories; 13 g fat; 18 g protein; 16 g carbohydrates; 4 g fiber; 12 g usable carbs.

| | | | | | |
|---|---|---|---|---|---|
| Potassium (mg): | 643 mg | Vitamin C (mg): | 46 mg | Thiamin/B1 (mg): | 0.2 mg |
| Calcium (mg): | 50 mg | Vitamin A (i.u.): | 436 i.u. | Riboflavin/B2 (mg): | 0.2 mg |
| Iron (mg): | 3 mg | Vitamin B6 (mg): | 0.5 mg | Folacin (mcg): | 86 mcg |
| Zinc (mg): | 4 mg | Vitamin B12 (mcg): | 2.1 mcg | Niacin/B3 (mg): | 4 mg |

## Picadillo

This is my version of a dish that's popular all over Latin America—think of it as South American Sloppy Joes.

1½ pounds (670 g) ground round

1 large onion

4 cloves garlic, peeled

⅓ cup (35 g) green pimiento-stuffed olives

2 teaspoons (18 g) capers, drained

1 can (14$^1/_2$ ounces, or 405 g) tomatoes with green chiles

3 tablespoons (21 g) dried currants

2 tablespoons (28 ml) wine vinegar

$^1/_2$ teaspoon dried oregano

$^1/_2$ cup (30 g) chopped cilantro

Set a big skillet over medium-high heat and start browning the ground round in it. While that cooks, dice up the onion, crush the garlic, and slice the olives, if you didn't buy them presliced.

When a little fat has cooked out of the meat, throw in the onion and garlic. Keep frying and crumbling the meat until it's done through and the onions are translucent. Now stir in the olives, capers, tomatoes, currants, vinegar, and oregano. Turn the burner to low, and let the whole thing simmer for 5 to 10 minutes. Stir in the cilantro, and serve.

**Yield:** 5 servings

**Nutritional Analysis:** Each will have: 370 calories; 24 g fat; 27 g protein; 11 g carbohydrates; 1 g fiber; 10 g usable carbs.

| | | | | | |
|---|---|---|---|---|---|
| Potassium (mg): | 582 mg | Vitamin C (mg): | 8 mg | Thiamin/B1 (mg): | 0.1 mg |
| Calcium (mg): | 51 mg | Vitamin A (i.u.): | 464 i.u. | Riboflavin/B2 (mg): | 0.4 mg |
| Iron (mg): | 4 mg | Vitamin B6 (mg): | 0.5 mg | Folacin (mcg): | 24 mcg |
| Zinc (mg): | 6 mg | Vitamin B12 (mcg): | 2.8 mcg | Niacin/B3 (mg): | 7 mg |

**Note:** If your dried currants are somewhat soft and pliable, just throw them in. If they're overly dry and hardened, you may need to soak them in.

# Sloppy Ioseph

Like Sloppy Joes with a Greek accent. If you can't afford the carbohydrates in the whole wheat pitas, you could wrap this in a low-carb tortilla, instead.

- 1½ pounds (670 g) ground round
- 1 medium onion, chopped
- 2 cloves garlic, peeled and crushed
- 1 can (14½ ounces, or 415 g) diced tomatoes
- 8 ounces (225 g) tomato sauce
- ½ teaspoon ground cinnamon
- ¼ teaspoon ground allspice
- 3 whole wheat pita breads
- 3 tablespoons (27 g) pine nuts (pignolia), toasted
- 6 scallions, sliced
- 6 tablespoons (90 g) plain nonfat yogurt, with any whey drained off

Coat a big, heavy skillet with nonstick cooking spray, and put it over medium-high heat. Add the ground round and start browning and crumbling it. When a little fat cooks out of the meat, add the onion, and start sautéing it with the meat.

When all the pink is gone from the beef, add the garlic, tomatoes, tomato sauce, cinnamon, and allspice. Turn the burner down to low, and let the whole thing simmer for 15 minutes.

Okay, simmering time is up! Cut your pitas in half. Stuff each with the beef mixture, then sprinkle pine nuts and scallions on top of that. Serve each with a dollop of drained yogurt.

**Yield:** 6 servings

**Nutritional Analysis:** Each will have: 426 calories; 23 g fat; 28 g protein; 29 g carbohydrates; 4 g fiber; 25 g usable carbs.

| | | | | | |
|---|---|---|---|---|---|
| Potassium (mg): | 826 mg | Vitamin C (mg): | 17 mg | Thiamin/B1 (mg): | 0.3 mg |
| Calcium (mg): | 84 mg | Vitamin A (i.u.): | 827 i.u. | Riboflavin/B2 (mg): | 0.4 mg |
| Iron (mg): | 5 mg | Vitamin B6 (mg): | 0.5 mg | Folacin (mcg): | 53 mcg |
| Zinc (mg): | 6 mg | Vitamin B12 (mcg): | 2.4 mcg | Niacin/B3 (mg): | 7 mg |

**Note:** If you couldn't buy them already toasted, toast the pine nuts by stirring them in a dry skillet over medium heat until they're lightly golden.

## Sloppy Aristotle

Another Greek-inspired skillet supper, but quite different from the previous recipe.

1 pound (455 g) ground round
1 medium onion
1/2 head cauliflower
1/4 cup (15 g) chopped fresh mint
1 teaspoon minced garlic
8 ounces (225 g) tomato sauce
1/2 cup (120 ml) beef broth
1 bay leaf
Salt and pepper
3 ounces (85 g) feta cheese, crumbled

Give a big, heavy skillet a shot of nonstick cooking spray, and put it over medium-high heat. When it's hot, start browning and crumbling the ground round.

Leave the meat unattended long enough to chop up the onion and run the cauliflower through the shredding disc of your food processor. Set the onion aside for the moment. Put the cauliflower into a microwaveable casserole with a lid, add a couple of tablespoons (30 ml or so) of water, cover, and microwave it on high for 6 minutes. When your microwave beeps, uncover the cauliflower right away, so it doesn't overcook and turn to nasty mush.

Okay, back to your skillet! Some fat should have cooked out of the meat by now. Add the onion, and let it sauté with the beef.

When all the pink is gone from the ground beef, stir in the mint, garlic, tomato sauce, beef broth, and bay leaf. Add a little salt and pepper, if you want. Turn the burner down and let the whole thing simmer, uncovered, for 10 to 15 minutes.

When it's time to serve, make a heap of "cauli-rice" in 3 bowls or on 3 plates. Top each with one-third of the ground beef mixture, then top that with 1 ounce (28 g) of crumbled feta, and serve.

**Yield:** 3 servings

**Nutritional Analysis:** Each will have: 431 calories; 26 g fat; 33 g protein; 17 g carbohydrates; 5 g fiber; 12 g usable carbs.

| | | | | | |
|---|---|---|---|---|---|
| Potassium (mg): | 1128 mg | Vitamin C (mg): | 57 mg | Thiamin/B1 (mg): | 0.3 mg |
| Calcium (mg): | 207 mg | Vitamin A (i.u.): | 5310 i.u. | Riboflavin/B2 (mg): | 1.0 mg |
| Iron (mg): | 6 mg | Vitamin B6 (mg): | 1.0 mg | Folacin (mcg): | 123 mcg |
| Zinc (mg): | 6 mg | Vitamin B12 (mcg): | 14.1 mcg | Niacin/B3 (mg): | 8 mg |

# Lemon-Mint Bulgur and Cauliflower Skillet with Garlic Shrimp

Not only is this incredibly delicious, interestingly exotic, and beautiful to look at, but have you looked at the vitamins in this thing?

1/3 cup (60 g) bulgur wheat (find this at the health food store)

2/3 cup (160 ml) boiling water

1/2 head cauliflower

1 lemon

2 tablespoons (28 ml) olive oil

1 bunch scallions, sliced, including the crisp part of the green

4 cloves garlic, peeled and minced

1 pound (455 g) shrimp, peeled and deveined

1/2 teaspoon salt

1/4 teaspoon pepper

4 cups (120 g) fresh spinach, coarsely chopped (or use bagged baby spinach)

1/3 cup (20 g) fresh mint, finely chopped

First, put the bulgur in a heat-proof bowl, pour the boiling water over it, cover, and let it sit for 30 to 40 minutes while you assemble the rest.

Run the cauliflower through the shredding disc of your food processor. Put the resulting "cauli-rice" in a microwaveable casserole with a lid, add a couple of tablespoons (30 ml or so) of water, cover, and nuke on high for 6 minutes. Uncover as soon as it's done, to stop the cooking!

While that's happening, prep the rest of your ingredients as noted. Plus, grate the zest of your lemon, and set it aside. Cut the lemon in half and have it standing by, ready to squeeze!

When your bulgur is done soaking and your cauli-rice is cooked, it's time to assemble the dish! Place a big, heavy skillet over medium heat and start heating the oil. Add the scallions, and sauté for 1 minute. Then add the garlic and shrimp. Sauté, stirring constantly, until the shrimp are pink all over. Stir in the salt and pepper.

Add the spinach, mint, and lemon zest, and sauté until the spinach is just barely wilted. Stir in the bulgur and cauli-rice, combining everything well. Squeeze both halves of the lemon over everything, stir it one more time to distribute the juice, and serve.

**Yield:** 4 servings

**Nutritional Analysis:** Each will have: 257 calories; 9 g fat; 27 g protein; 18 g carbohydrates; 6 g fiber; 12 g usable carbs.

| | | | | | |
|---|---|---|---|---|---|
| Potassium (mg): | 723 mg | Vitamin C (mg): | 54 mg | Thiamin/B1 (mg): | 0.1 mg |
| Calcium (mg): | 139 mg | Vitamin A (i.u.): | 2560 i.u. | Riboflavin/B2 (mg): | 0.1 mg |
| Iron (mg): | 5 mg | Vitamin B6 (mg): | 0.3 mg | Folacin (mcg): | 118 mcg |
| Zinc (mg): | 2 mg | Vitamin B12 (mcg): | 1.1 mcg | Niacin/B3 (mg):: | 4 mg |

## Garlic Lemon Shrimp Skillet

A whole meal in a bowl, and fit for a king. And it'll take all of 15 minutes!

1/2 head cauliflower

1 1/2 teaspoons butter

6 cloves garlic, peeled and minced

1/2 cup (120 ml) dry white wine

1 tablespoon (14 ml) lemon juice

1 pound (455 g) salad shrimp (or bigger shrimp, chopped up a bit)

1 teaspoon chicken bouillon concentrate

2/3 cup (110 g) cooked wild rice

1/4 teaspoon pepper

1/2 cup (30 g) chopped fresh parsley

Run the cauliflower through the shredding blade of your food processor. Put the resulting "cauli-rice" in a microwaveable casserole with a lid, add a few tablespoons (30 ml or so) of water, and cover. Nuke on high for 6 minutes.

Give a big, heavy skillet a shot of nonstick cooking spray, and put it over low heat. Add the butter and let it melt, then throw in the garlic. Let the garlic cook very slowly in the butter for 5 minutes.

Somewhere in here, the microwave will beep. Uncover the cauliflower right away, to prevent overcooking.

When you've stewed the garlic in the butter for 5 minutes, add the wine and lemon juice. Turn the burner up to medium and let the whole thing simmer for 10 minutes or so, till the liquid is reduced to about one-third of its original volume. Add the shrimp, and let the whole thing cook for another minute or two, till they're cooked through. Stir in the chicken bouillon concentrate.

Now add the cauli rice and wild rice, and stir everything together to combine very well. Stir in the pepper and parsley, and serve.

**Yield:** 4 servings

**Nutritional Analysis:** Each will have: 270 calories; 3 g fat; 30 g protein; 26 g carbohydrates; 4 g fiber; 22 g usable carbs.

| Potassium (mg): | 630 mg | Vitamin C (mg): | 49 mg | Thiamin/B1 (mg): | 0.1 mg |
|---|---|---|---|---|---|
| Calcium (mg): | 89 mg | Vitamin A (i.u.): | 715 i.u. | Riboflavin/B2 (mg): | 0.2 mg |
| Iron (mg): | 5 mg | Vitamin B6 (mg): | 0.5 mg | Folacin (mcg): | 83 mcg |
| Zinc (mg): | 4 mg | Vitamin B12 (mcg): | 1.7 mcg | Niacin/B3 (mg): | 5 mg |

## Tequila-Lime Seafood Soft Tacos

Julie says the presentation is gorgeous. Good restaurants would like to know about this one!

1 pound (455 g) shrimp, peeled and deveined

8 ounces (225 g) bay scallops

1/4 cup (15 g) chopped cilantro

1/4 cup (60 ml) lime juice

2 tablespoons (28 ml) tequila

1 teaspoon hot sauce, or more to taste

2 cloves garlic, peeled and minced

1/2 teaspoon dried oregano, crushed

1/2 teaspoon ground cumin

1/2 teaspoon pepper

2 tablespoons (14 ml) peanut oil or macadamia oil

1 green bell pepper, cut into thin strips

1 red bell pepper, cut into thin strips

1 large onion, halved and thinly sliced

1 1/2 cups (150 g) sliced mushrooms

6 low-carb or whole wheat 10-inch (25-cm) tortillas

1 1/2 cups (175 g) shredded Monterey Jack cheese

In a nonreactive bowl, combine the shrimp and scallops with the cilantro, lime juice, tequila, hot sauce, garlic, oregano, cumin, pepper, and 1 tablespoon (14 ml) of the oil. Toss to coat. Stash the bowl in the fridge for at least a few hours, and all day is fine.

When it's time to cook, put a big, heavy skillet over medium-high heat. When it's hot, add the remaining oil and sauté the green and red peppers and onions for a couple of minutes, till they're just starting to soften. Add the mushrooms, and cook for a couple more minutes. Now add the seafood, complete with its marinade, and let the whole thing simmer, stirring constantly, until the shrimps are pink, the scallops are opaque, and the marinade has cooked down a bit.

Use a slotted spoon to scoop the mixture evenly into the tortillas, top with the cheese, roll up, and serve.

**Yield:** 6 servings

**Nutritional Analysis:** (Analysis accounts for low-carb tortillas) Each will have: 347 calories; 17 g fat; 35 g protein; 19 g carbohydrates; 9 g fiber; 10 g usable carbs.

| | | | | | |
|---|---|---|---|---|---|
| Potassium (mg): | 476 mg | Vitamin C (mg): | 64 mg | Thiamin/B1 (mg): | 0.1 mg |
| Calcium (mg): | 335 mg | Vitamin A (i.u.): | 1737 i.u. | Riboflavin/B2 (mg): | 0.2 mg |
| Iron (mg): | 3 mg | Vitamin B6 (mg): | 0.2 mg | Folacin (mcg): | 31 mcg |
| Zinc (mg): | 2 mg | Vitamin B12 (mcg): | 1.5 mcg | Niacin/B3 (mg): | 3 mg |

## Ham Fried "Rice"

Good stuff. Feel free to make this with leftover chicken or turkey, or even with a handful of salad shrimp, instead of the turkey ham.

3 eggs

2 teaspoons (10 ml) dark sesame oil

2 teaspoons (10 ml) water

1½ tablespoons (21 ml) coconut oil

6 scallions, sliced

3 cloves garlic, peeled and minced

5 ounces (140 g) turkey ham, cut into ½-inch (1.25-cm) cubes

3 cups (675 g) cauli-rice, cooked (see page 128)

1 cup (165 g) cooked wild rice

1 cup (130 g) frozen peas, thawed

2 tablespoons (28 ml) rice vinegar

2 tablespoons (28 ml) soy sauce

Scramble the eggs with the sesame oil and water. Spray a big skillet with nonstick cooking spray, and set it over medium-high heat. Let it get good and hot.

Add half the coconut oil to the skillet, let it melt, and tilt the pan to coat the bottom. Pour in the eggs, and let them cook into a flat sheet—lift the edges with a spatula, if need be, to let the uncooked egg run underneath. When the eggs are set in a solid sheet, remove to a plate. When it's cool, cut the egg sheet into strips about 1/4 inch (6 mm) wide and 1 inch (2.5 cm) long.

Have all of the remaining ingredients standing by, ready to cook.

Melt the remaining oil in the skillet over medium-high heat. Add the scallions and garlic, and stir them for 30 seconds or so. Add the ham, and stir-fry that for about a minute. Add the cauli-rice and wild rice. Stir the whole thing for a minute or two. Finally, add the peas, egg strips, vinegar, and soy sauce, and stir it all up. Cook just until everything is hot through, and serve.

**Yield:** 3 servings

**Nutritional Analysis:** Each will have: 351 calories; 17 g fat; 22 g protein; 29 g carbohydrates; 7 g fiber; 22 g usable carbs.

| | | | | | |
|---|---|---|---|---|---|
| Potassium (mg): | 763 mg | Vitamin C (mg): | 62 mg | Thiamin/B1 (mg): | 0.2 mg |
| Calcium (mg): | 90 mg | Vitamin A (i.u.): | 763 i.u. | Riboflavin/B2 (mg): | 0.5 mg |
| Iron (mg): | 4 mg | Vitamin B6 (mg): | 0.6 mg | Folacin (mcg): | 141 mcg |
| Zinc (mg): | 3 mg | Vitamin B12 (mcg): | 0.5 mcg | Niacin/B3 (mg): | 4 mg |

# Lemon-Thyme Pork Skillet Supper

Light and flavorful.

1/2 head cauliflower

1 pound (455 g) pork top loin

1 tablespoon (14 ml) olive oil

1/4 cup (60 ml) dry white wine

1 tablespoon (14 ml) lemon juice

1 teaspoon dried thyme

1 clove garlic

$\frac{1}{2}$ cup (65 g) frozen peas, thawed

1 bunch (about 8) scallions, sliced

1 teaspoon chicken bouillon concentrate

$\frac{1}{2}$ cup (85 g) cooked wild rice

$\frac{1}{2}$ teaspoon pepper

Salt

Run the cauliflower through the shredding blade of your food processor. Put the resulting "cauli-rice" in a microwaveable casserole with a lid, add a couple of tablespoons (30 ml or so) of water, cover, and nuke on high for 6 minutes. When it's done, uncover it right away to keep it from overcooking.

Meanwhile, slice the pork into thin strips across the grain, and cut any longer strips into 1-inch (2.5-cm) pieces. (This is easier if the pork is half-frozen.)

Spray a big, heavy skillet with nonstick cooking spray. Put it over medium-high heat, add the oil, and slosh it around to cover the bottom of the pan. When the pan is hot, throw in the pork strips. Stir-fry them until most of the pink is gone. Now add the wine, lemon juice, thyme, and garlic. Turn the burner down to low, throw in the peas, and let the whole thing simmer for 5 minutes or so.

When the liquid in the skillet is reduced to about one-half of its original volume, stir in the bouillon. When that has dissolved, drain the cauli-rice and add it and the wild rice to the skillet. Stir everything up, stir in the pepper, add a little salt if you think it needs it, and serve.

**Yield:** 3 servings

**Nutritional Analysis:** Each will have: 384 calories; 20 g fat; 32 g protein; 16 g carbohydrates; 4 g fiber; 12 g usable carbs.

| | | | | | |
|---|---|---|---|---|---|
| Potassium (mg): | 941 mg | Vitamin C (mg): | 53 mg | Thiamin/B1 (mg): | 1.2 mg |
| Calcium (mg): | 74 mg | Vitamin A (i.u.): | 243 i.u. | Riboflavin/B2 (mg): | 0.4 mg |
| Iron (mg): | 3 mg | Vitamin B6 (mg): | 0.9 mg | Folacin (mcg): | 90 mcg |
| Zinc (mg): | 3 mg | Vitamin B12 (mcg): | 0.7 mcg | Niacin/B3 (mg): | 8 mg |

## Balsamic Glazed Chicken and Peppers

Think of this as an Italian stir-fry!

1 pound (455 g) boneless, skinless chicken breasts

1/2 green bell pepper

1/2 red bell pepper

1 small onion, peeled and sliced

2 cloves garlic, peeled and minced

2 tablespoons (28 ml) olive oil

1 teaspoon Italian seasoning

3 tablespoons (45 ml) balsamic vinegar

Cut the chicken into 1/2-inch (1.25-cm) cubes. Cut the peppers into strips—I cut them into thin strips, lengthwise, then once crosswise. Slice the onion into vertical strips. Have the garlic standing ready, too.

Put a big, heavy skillet over medium-high heat. Add the oil, and let it get hot. Now throw in the chicken, peppers, and onions, and stir-fry them until all the pink is gone from the chicken and the vegetables are starting to soften a bit.

Add the garlic, seasoning, and vinegar, and stir everything up. Let the whole thing cook, stirring often, until the vinegar has reduced and become a bit syrupy, then serve.

**Yield:** 4 servings

**Nutritional Analysis:** Each will have: 217 calories; 10 g fat; 26 g protein; 6 g carbohydrates; 1 g fiber; 5 g usable carbs.

| | | | | | |
|---|---|---|---|---|---|
| Potassium (mg): | 322 mg | Vitamin C (mg): | 44 mg | Thiamin/B1 (mg): | 0.1 mg |
| Calcium (mg): | 24 mg | Vitamin A (i.u.): | 958 i.u. | Riboflavin/B2 (mg): | 0.1 mg |
| Iron (mg): | 1 mg | Vitamin B6 (mg): | 0.6 mg | Folacin (mcg): | 15 mcg |
| Zinc (mg): | 1 mg | Vitamin B12 (mcg): | 0.3 mcg | Niacin/B3 (mg): | 11 mg |

# Greek "Spaghetti" with Tomatoes, Feta, and Chicken

This is a huge, glorious skillet meal. If you like, you could make it with whole wheat spaghetti instead of spaghetti squash, but it would be higher in carbs and calories, and have fewer vitamins.

4 cups (900 g) cooked spaghetti squash
6 ounces (170 g) boneless, skinless chicken breasts
2 teaspoons (28 ml) olive oil
2 cloves garlic, peeled and minced
1 teaspoon dried oregano
2 medium tomatoes, diced
1/2 cup (50 g) sliced scallions
1/3 cup (20 g) chopped parsley
2 tablespoons (28 ml) lemon juice
1 cup (150 g) crumbled feta cheese
Pepper

If you haven't cooked the spaghetti squash and scraped it into strands, do that first, and have it standing by. The easiest way is to stab it all over with a fork, then throw it in the microwave for 12 to 15 minutes on high. Let it cool a bit to avoid burning your fingers, then whack it in half, scrape out the seeds, and discard. Scrape the flesh with a fork to fluff the strands.

Dice the chicken breast into 1/2-inch (1.25-cm) cubes.

In a big, heavy skillet, heat the oil over medium-high heat. Add the chicken, and stir-fry until it's lost most of its pink color. Add the garlic and oregano. Keep stir-frying till all the pink is gone from the chicken.

Add the spaghetti squash, tomatoes, scallions, parsley, and lemon juice, and toss well to combine everything. Let it cook for a few more minutes to blend the flavors. Then toss in the feta, add pepper to taste, and serve before the feta has time to melt.

**Yield:** 4 servings

**Nutritional Analysis:** Each will have: 224 calories; 12 g fat; 16 g protein; 14 g carbohydrates; 1 g fiber; 13 g usable carbs.

| | | | | | |
|---|---|---|---|---|---|
| Potassium (mg): | 429 mg | Vitamin C (mg): | 27 mg | Thiamin/B1 (mg): | 0.1 mg |
| Calcium (mg): | 240 mg | Vitamin A (i.u.): | 941 i.u. | Riboflavin/B2 (mg): | 0.4 mg |
| Iron (mg): | 2 mg | Vitamin B6 (mg): | 0.5 mg | Folacin (mcg): | 52 mcg |
| Zinc (mg): | 2 mg | Vitamin B12 (mcg): | 0.7 mcg | Niacin/B3 (mg): | 6 mg |

## Ham and Pea Skillet Supper in Cheese Sauce

Down-home comfort food. If you can afford quite a lot more calories and carbs, you can substitute 4 cups (560 g) of whole wheat spaghetti for the spaghetti squash.

- 1 cup (235 ml) 2% milk
- 1/2 cup (110 g) 2% cottage cheese
- 1/2 cup (40 g) shredded Parmesan cheese
- 1/4 teaspoon salt
- 1/8 teaspoon pepper
- 1/8 teaspoon nutmeg
- 6 ounces (170 g) turkey ham, diced
- 1 clove garlic, peeled and crushed
- 1/2 cup (65 g) frozen peas, thawed
- 4 cups (900 g) cooked spaghetti squash (See Greek "Spaghetti" with Tomatoes, Feta, and Chicken on page 304 for instructions on cooking spaghetti squash)

Combine the milk and cottage cheese in your blender, and run until smooth. Pour into a big skillet—nonstick is best, but if your skillet isn't nonstick, give it a good shot of nonstick cooking spray first. Place the milk mixture over medium heat, and add 1/4 cup (20 g) of the cheese, plus the salt, pepper, and nutmeg. Stir until the whole thing is slightly thickened and bubbly.

Stir in the ham, garlic, and peas, and let them simmer in the sauce for a minute or two. Now add the spaghetti squash, and stir everything until it's well combined. Dish it onto 4 serving plates, top with the remaining 1/4 cup (20 g) cheese, and serve.

**Yield:** 3 servings

**Nutritional Analysis:** Each will have: 265 calories; 10 g fat; 26 g protein; 19 g carbohydrates; 1 g fiber; 18 g usable carbs.

| | | | | | |
|---|---|---|---|---|---|
| Potassium (mg): | 546 mg | Vitamin C (mg): | 8 mg | Thiamin/B1 (mg): | 0.2 mg |
| Calcium (mg): | 337 mg | Vitamin A (i.u.): | 520 i.u. | Riboflavin/B2 (mg): | 0.4 mg |
| Iron (mg): | 3 mg | Vitamin B6 (mg): | 0.4 mg | Folacin (mcg): | 43 mcg |
| Zinc (mg): | 3 mg | Vitamin B12 (mcg): | 0.9 mcg | Niacin/B3 (mg): | 4 mg |

# The Doc's Skillet Supper

1 pound (455 g) bulk turkey sausage (not links)

1/2 green bell pepper

1 banana pepper

2 medium celery ribs

1/2 medium onion

1 cup (235 ml) chicken broth

1/2 large head cauliflower

2/3 cup (110 g) cooked wild rice

1 teaspoon chicken bouillon concentrate

1 1/2 tablespoons (21 ml) Worcestershire sauce

Place a big, heavy skillet over medium-high heat and start browning and crumbling the sausage while you dice the green and banana peppers, celery, and onion.

When the sausage is about halfway browned, throw in the diced veggies. Sauté, stirring frequently, till the pink is gone from the sausage.

Pour in the chicken broth, and stir it into the meat and vegetables. Leave the heat at medium-high, and leave the skillet uncovered. You're going to cook down that broth until there's just a film of liquid left on the bottom of the pan; it'll take 20 to 30 minutes.

Toward the end of that simmering time, run the cauliflower through the shredding blade of your food processor. Put the "cauli-rice" in a microwaveable casserole with a lid, add a couple of tablespoons (30 ml or so) of water, cover, and nuke the sucker on high for 6 minutes.

When the cauli-rice is cooked and most of the liquid has cooked off your sausage-vegetable combo, drain the cauli-rice and dump it into the skillet. Add the cooked wild rice and stir to combine with the meat and vegetables. Stir in the bouillon and Worcestershire, and serve.

**Yield:** 4 servings

**Nutritional Analysis:** Each will have: 255 calories; 11 g fat; 24 g protein; 16 g carbohydrates; 4 g fiber; 12 g usable carbs.

| | | | | | |
|---|---|---|---|---|---|
| Potassium (mg): | 478 mg | Vitamin C (mg): | 69 mg | Thiamin/B1 (mg): | 0.1 mg |
| Calcium (mg): | 72 mg | Vitamin A (i.u.): | 182 i.u. | Riboflavin/B2 (mg): | 0.1 mg |
| Iron (mg): | 3 mg | Vitamin B6 (mg): | 0.3 mg | Folacin (mcg): | 64 mcg |
| Zinc (mg): | 1 mg | Vitamin B12 (mcg): | 0.1 mcg | Niacin/B3 (mg): | 2 mg |

## Tequila-Lime Chicken Skillet

I came up with this recipe when I bought some terrific tequila-lime flavored chicken sausage at Sahara Mart, the local health/gourmet/international food store. It was so good, I had to come up with this version using ground chicken (for all of you who may not be lucky enough to have access to specialty sausages).

1 medium onion

1 tablespoon (14 ml) oil

1 pound (455 g) ground chicken

1/2 head cauliflower

3 tablespoons (45 ml) tequila

3 tablespoons (45 ml) lime juice

1 1/2 teaspoons ground cumin

1 teaspoon hot sauce

1 teaspoon minced garlic

1 cup (235 g) canned tomatoes with green chiles, drained

1/2 cup (110 g) canned black soy beans, drained, or 1/2 cup (120 g) canned black beans, drained

Salt and pepper

1/2 cup (30 g) chopped fresh cilantro

1 California avocado, peeled, seeded, and diced

Whack the onion into a few big chunks, peel 'em, and throw 'em in your food processor with the S-blade in place. Pulse until the onion is chopped to a medium consistency. Place a big, heavy skillet over medium-high heat, add the oil, then throw in the chicken and onion. Break up the chicken a little, then leave it to sauté while you swap the S-blade for the shredding blade in your food processor.

Run the cauliflower through, and put the resulting "cauli-rice" in a microwaveable casserole with a lid. Add a couple of tablespoons (30 ml or so) of water, cover, put in the microwave, and cook it on high for 7 minutes.

Okay, now go stir your chicken and onions, breaking up the chicken some more. When most of the pink is gone from your chicken, stir in the tequila, lime juice, cumin, hot sauce, and garlic. Keep stirring until all the pink is gone from the chicken. Stir in the tomatoes and beans.

By now your cauli-rice is done. Grab it out of the microwave and drain it. Dump it in the skillet with everything else, and stir it all together really well. Add salt and pepper to taste, and stir in the cilantro.

Divide the mixture between 5 bowls or plates, divide the avocado among them, and serve.

**Yield:** 5 servings

**Nutritional Analysis:** With black soy beans, each will have: 361 calories; 18 g fat; 32 g protein; 13 g carbohydrates; 5 g fiber; 8 g usable carbs.

| | | | | | |
|---|---|---|---|---|---|
| Potassium (mg): | 746 mg | Vitamin C (mg): | 38 mg | Thiamin/B1 (mg): | 0.2 mg |
| Calcium (mg): | 69 mg | Vitamin A (i.u.): | 671 i.u. | Riboflavin/B2 (mg): | 0.3 mg |
| Iron (mg): | 3 mg | Vitamin B6 (mg): | 0.7 mg | Folacin (mcg): | 77 mcg |
| Zinc (mg): | 3 mg | Vitamin B12 (mcg): | 0.3 mcg | Niacin/B3 (mg): | 10 mg |

**Nutritional Analysis:** With regular black beans, each will have: 350 calories; 17 g fat; 31 g protein; 13 g carbohydrates; 4 g fiber; 9 g usable carbs.

| | | | | | |
|---|---|---|---|---|---|
| Potassium (mg): | 602 mg | Vitamin C (mg): | 16 mg | Thiamin/B1 (mg): | 0.1 mg |
| Calcium (mg): | 44 mg | Vitamin A (i.u.): | 571 i.u. | Riboflavin/B2 (mg): | 0.2 mg |
| Iron (mg): | 2 mg | Vitamin B6 (mg): | 0.6 mg | Folacin (mcg): | 45 mcg |
| Zinc (mg): | 2 mg | Vitamin B12 (mcg): | 0.3 mcg | Niacin/B3 (mg): | 10 mg |

chapter nine

# Burgers and Other Ground Meat Stuff

I started out putting these recipes into the chapters for the various kinds of meat, but too many of them involve a mixture of meats. It just got too confusing. So I gave the ground meat recipes their very own chapter, and here it is.

## Heat-Wave Burgers

But a fairly mild heat wave, you know? These have just a nice bite, they're not mouth-scorching, mopping-your-forehead hot.

- 1 pound (455 g) ground round
- 1 tablespoon (10 g) minced garlic
- 1 1/2 tablespoons (21 ml) Worcestershire sauce
- 1 teaspoon pepper
- 3 tablespoons (30 g) minced onion
- 1 teaspoon chili garlic paste
- 1/4 teaspoon salt or Vege-Sal

Plunk everything into a mixing bowl and smoosh it together with clean hands until it's well mixed. Form into 3 burgers.

I like to cook these in my big, heavy skillet; if I cook them in my electric tabletop grill, they tend to come out dry, because the grill squeezes the juice out of them. So squirt a big, heavy skillet with nonstick cooking spray and put it over medium-high heat. Once it's hot, give the burgers about 5 minutes per side, or to your liking.

I don't think these need a darned thing but no-sugar-added ketchup!

**Yield:** 3 servings

**Nutritional Analysis:** Each will have: 371 calories; 26 g fat; 29 g protein; 4 g carbohydrates; trace fiber; 4 g usable carbs.

| | | | | | |
|---|---|---|---|---|---|
| Potassium (mg): | 526 mg | Vitamin C (mg): | 15 mg | Thiamin/B1 (mg): | 0.1 mg |
| Calcium (mg): | 30 mg | Vitamin A (i.u.): | 9 i.u. | Riboflavin/B2 (mg): | 0.4 mg |
| Iron (mg): | 4 mg | Vitamin B6 (mg): | 0.4 mg | Folacin (mcg): | 14 mcg |
| Zinc (mg): | 6 mg | Vitamin B12 (mcg): | 3.1 mcg | Niacin/B3 (mg): | 7 mg |

## Worcestershire Burgers

Simple and tasty.

- 1/2 pound (225 g) ground round
- 1/2 pound (225 g) ground turkey
- 1/3 cup (50 g) minced onion
- 1/3 cup (20 g) chopped fresh parsley
- 2 tablespoons (28 ml) Worcestershire sauce
- 1 tablespoon (16 g) tomato paste

Just plunk everything into a big mixing bowl, and use clean hands to mix well. Form into 3 burgers. Put 'em on a plate, and chill them for 30 minutes or so.

Pan-broil the burgers for 5 minutes per side, or put 'em in your electric tabletop grill for 5 minutes or so.

**Yield:** 3 servings

**Nutritional Analysis:** Each will have: 311 calories; 19 g fat; 28 g protein; 5 g carbohydrates; 1 g fiber; 4 g usable carbs.

| | | | | | |
|---|---|---|---|---|---|
| Potassium (mg): | 587 mg | Vitamin C (mg): | 30 mg | Thiamin/B1 (mg): | 0.1 mg |
| Calcium (mg): | 40 mg | Vitamin A (i.u.): | 495 i.u. | Riboflavin/B2 (mg): | 0.3 mg |
| Iron (mg): | 4 mg | Vitamin B6 (mg): | 0.5 mg | Folacin (mcg): | 26 mcg |
| Zinc (mg): | 5 mg | Vitamin B12 (mcg): | 1.8 mcg | Niacin/B3 (mg): | 6 mg |

**Note:** I like to serve this with a little no-sugar-added ketchup and Worcestershire mixed together, but you should use your own favorite.

## Lamb, Feta, and Spinach Burgers

10 ounces (280 g) frozen chopped spinach, thawed and drained

1 tablespoon (14 ml) lemon juice

1 teaspoon basil

1/4 cup (40 g) minced onion

1 clove garlic, peeled and finely minced

1 egg

1/4 teaspoon salt or Vege-Sal

1/4 teaspoon pepper

1 1/4 pounds (560 g) ground lamb

1/2 cup (75 g) crumbled feta cheese

1/4 cup (13 g) sun-dried tomatoes, chopped

12 kalamata olives, pitted and chopped

Make sure the spinach is well drained—I put mine in a strainer and then squeeze it with clean hands. Transfer it to a big bowl and add the lemon juice, basil, onion, garlic, egg, salt, and pepper. Stir it all up until it's well blended.

Now add the lamb, feta, tomatoes, and olives. Use clean hands to smoosh everything until it's really well combined. Make 6 burgers, keeping them at least 1 inch (2.5 cm) thick. I like to refrigerate them for at least 20 to 30 minutes before cooking.

Preheat your electric tabletop grill. Slap the burgers on the grill and give 'em 6 to 8 minutes, depending on how well-done you want them.

**Yield:** 6 servings

**Nutritional Analysis:** Each will have: 352 calories; 28 g fat; 20 g protein; 5 g carbohydrates; 2 g fiber; 3 g usable carbs.

| | | | | | |
|---|---|---|---|---|---|
| Potassium (mg): | 476 mg | Vitamin C (mg): | 14 mg | Thiamin/B1 (mg): | 0.2 mg |
| Calcium (mg): | 144 mg | Vitamin A (i.u.): | 3810 i.u. | Riboflavin/B2 (mg): | 0.4 mg |
| Iron (mg): | 3 mg | Vitamin B6 (mg): | 0.3 mg | Folacin (mcg): | 85 mcg |
| Zinc (mg): | 4 mg | Vitamin B12 (mcg): | 2.5 mcg | Niacin/B3 (mg): | 6 mg |

**Note:** I find that the burgers at the back of the grill brown sooner than the burgers at the front; don't be afraid to remove the ones that are done and continue cooking the others to taste.

## Chicken Burgers with Basil and Sun-Dried Tomatoes

This has a sunny, bright flavor. It's truly wonderful when made with fresh herbs.

- 1 pound (455 g) ground chicken
- 2 tablespoons (7 g) finely chopped dry-pack sun-dried tomatoes
- 1 tablespoon (4 g) minced fresh basil, or 1 teaspoon dried basil
- 1 teaspoon minced fresh oregano, or 1/4 teaspoon dried oregano
- 1/2 teaspoon salt or Vege-Sal
- 1/4 teaspoon pepper
- 2 tablespoons (20 g) minced onion
- 1 clove garlic, peeled and minced
- 1 teaspoon paprika
- 1/4 teaspoon cayenne pepper

Just plop everything into a mixing bowl and use clean hands to smoosh it all together until it's well-blended. Form into 3 patties. If you've got a little time, put the patties on a plate and chill them for 30 minutes before cooking.

I pan-broil these in my big, heavy skillet for 5 to 6 minutes per side.

**Yield:** 3 servings

**Nutritional Analysis:** Each will have: 345 calories; 14 g fat; 47 g protein; 5 g carbohydrates; 1 g fiber; 4 g usable carbs.

| | | | | | |
|---|---|---|---|---|---|
| Potassium (mg): | 509 mg | Vitamin C (mg): | 3 mg | Thiamin/B1 (mg): | 0.1 mg |
| Calcium (mg): | 38 mg | Vitamin A (i.u.): | 673 i.u. | Riboflavin/B2 (mg): | 0.3 mg |
| Iron (mg): | 3 mg | Vitamin B6 (mg): | 0.8 mg | Folacin (mcg): | 15 mcg |
| Zinc (mg): | 4 mg | Vitamin B12 (mcg): | 0.5 mcg | Niacin/B3 (mg): | 15 mg |

**Note:** You can top these with one of the flavored mayonnaises, if you like—Lemon Basil Mayonnaise comes to mind—but they're quite flavorful all on their own.

## Orange Burgers with Soy-Glazed Onions

This was the first recipe I came up with using the ground beef and turkey blend. The flavor is somewhere between Asian and barbecue, with a citrus twist. Good stuff.

1 pound (455 g) ground beef
1 pound (455 g) ground turkey
1 orange
2 tablespoons (10 ml) cider vinegar
1/2 teaspoon blackstrap molasses
1 teaspoon pepper
1/2 teaspoon chili powder
2 cloves garlic, peeled and minced
1 teaspoon grated gingerroot
6 tablespoons (40 g) oat bran
3 tablespoons (45 ml) soy sauce
1 tablespoon (1.5 g) Splenda
1 large onion
1 tablespoon (14 ml) olive oil

In a big mixing bowl, combine the beef and turkey. Grate the orange rind into the meats, then whack the orange in half and squeeze in the juice. Add the vinegar, molasses, pepper, chili powder, garlic, ginger, oat bran, 1 tablespoon (14 ml) of the soy sauce, and 2 teaspoons (10 g) of the Splenda. Use clean hands to smoosh everything together very well.

Form 8 burgers, lay them on a platter, and chill for a good 20 to 30 minutes.

While the burgers are chilling, slice the onion fairly thinly. Spray a big, heavy skillet with nonstick cooking spray, and put it over medium-high heat. Add the oil and onion, and sauté until the onion is quite limp. Mix the remaining 2 tablespoons (28 ml) of soy sauce with the last 1 teaspoon (.5 g) of Splenda, and stir this mixture into the onions. Keep sautéing till most of the moisture has evaporated. Remove from the heat and set aside, covering to keep warm.

Preheat your electric tabletop grill and put the burgers in for 5 minutes, or pan-broil them for 5 to 6 minutes per side. Serve with the onions on top.

**Yield:** 8 servings

**Nutritional Analysis:** Each will have: 307 calories; 22 g fat; 21 g protein; 8 g carbohydrates; 2 g fiber; 6 g usable carbs.

| | | | | | |
|---|---|---|---|---|---|
| Potassium (mg): | 375 mg | Vitamin C (mg): | 10 mg | Thiamin/B1 (mg): | 0.1 mg |
| Calcium (mg): | 32 mg | Vitamin A (i.u.): | 91 i.u. | Riboflavin/B2 (mg): | 0.2 mg |
| Iron (mg): | 2 mg | Vitamin B6 (mg): | 0.4 mg | Folacin (mcg): | 19 mcg |
| Zinc (mg): | 3 mg | Vitamin B12 (mcg): | 1.7 mcg | Niacin/B3 (mg): | 5 mg |

## Zesty Burgers

These are burgers with the ketchup and mustard already in them! You can top 'em with ketchup, mustard, or what-have-you, but these are pretty darned flavorful on their own.

- 1/2 pound (225 g) ground round
- 1/2 pound (225 g) ground turkey
- 1/4 cup (40 g) minced onion
- 1/4 cup (30 g) minced green bell pepper
- 3 tablespoons (45 g) no-sugar-added ketchup
- 1 tablespoon (15 g) prepared horseradish
- 2 teaspoons (10 g) brown mustard
- 1/2 teaspoon salt or Vege-Sal
- 1/4 teaspoon pepper

Pretty darned easy—just throw everything in a bowl, and use clean hands to smoosh it all together well. Form into 4 patties, and, if you have time, chill them for 30 minutes or so before cooking.

Pan-broil for about 5 minutes per side, or cook for 5 minutes in your electric tabletop grill.

**Yield:** 4 servings

**Nutritional Analysis:** Each will have: 231 calories; 15 g fat; 21 g protein; 3 g carbohydrates; trace fiber; 3 g usable carbs.

| | | | | | |
|---|---|---|---|---|---|
| Potassium (mg): | 334 mg | Vitamin C (mg): | 13 mg | Thiamin/B1 (mg): | 0.1 mg |
| Calcium (mg): | 22 mg | Vitamin A (i.u.): | 555 i.u. | Riboflavin/B2 (mg): | 0.2 mg |
| Iron (mg): | 2 mg | Vitamin B6 (mg): | 0.4 mg | Folacin (mcg): | 14 mcg |
| Zinc (mg): | 4 mg | Vitamin B12 (mcg): | 1.4 mcg | Niacin/B3 (mg): | 5 mg |

# Chile Verde Cheese Burgers

I made this up one night when I had both salsa verde and Monterey Jack cheese on hand, and my husband loved it.

1 pound (455 g) ground round

1/2 teaspoon salt or Vege-Sal

1/8 teaspoon pepper

1 clove garlic, peeled and finely minced

1 teaspoon chili powder

1/2 cup (60 g) shredded Monterey Jack cheese

1/4 cup (40 g) diced red onion

4 slices ripe tomato

1/4 cup (55 g) bottled salsa verde

Plunk the ground round into a mixing bowl and sprinkle the salt, pepper, garlic, and chili powder on top. Use clean hands to smoosh everything together until it's very well blended.

Form into 4 patties, put 'em on a plate, and chill 'em for a while. (Unless you're in a big hurry—then you can just cook them right away, but chilling is a good idea.)

Preheat your electric tabletop grill. When it's hot, pull the burgers out of the fridge and throw 'em in the grill for 4 to 5 minutes. Then pull them out, put 'em on a plate, top each with 2 tablespoons (15 g) of cheese, and cover them with any stray pot lid, to hold in the heat. Let them sit for a couple of minutes while the cheese melts.

Now top each with a 1 tablespoon (10 g) of onion, a slice of tomato, and 1 tablespoon (14 g) of salsa verde, and serve.

**Yield:** 4 servings

**Nutritional Analysis:** Each will have: 356 calories; 24 g fat; 26 g protein; 8 g carbohydrates; 2 g fiber; 6 g usable carbs.

| | | | | | |
|---|---|---|---|---|---|
| Potassium (mg): | 638 mg | Vitamin C (mg): | 25 mg | Thiamin/B1 (mg): | 0.1 mg |
| Calcium (mg): | 127 mg | Vitamin A (i.u.): | 1119 i.u. | Riboflavin/B2 (mg): | 0.4 mg |
| Iron (mg): | 3 mg | Vitamin B6 (mg): | 0.4 mg | Folacin (mcg): | 33 mcg |
| Zinc (mg): | 5 mg | Vitamin B12 (mcg): | 2.5 mcg | Niacin/B3 (mg): | 6 mg |

**Note:** You can, if you like, put these on whole wheat buns, but they're darned good the way they are.

# Burgers with Portobello Mushrooms

Here's another recipe from Ray.

- $1^1/_2$ pounds (670 g) ground round
- 1 tablespoon (15 g) butter or olive oil
- 4 cloves garlic, peeled and crushed
- 8 ounces (225 g) small portobello mushrooms, sliced (buy them already sliced, if you can)
- 2 tablespoons (28 ml) dark rum
- 1 medium Roma tomato, chopped
- $^1/_4$ cup (15 g) chopped fresh parsley

Form the ground round into 5 burgers, and pan-broil them in a heavy skillet. If your stove has a separate griddle, this can be done while you prepare the rest of the recipe. If not, cook them, and set them somewhere warm while you make the sauce.

Put the butter in a clean skillet over medium-low heat, and sauté the garlic in it. Add the mushrooms and rum. Sauté until the mushrooms soften and change color. Stir in the chopped tomato and parsley. Sauté for 2 more minutes.

Put your burgers on a plate, top them with the mushroom mixture, and serve.

**Yield:** 5 servings

**Nutritional Analysis:** Each will have: 373 calories; 26 g fat; 27 g protein; 4 g carbohydrates; 1 g fiber; 3 g usable carbs.

| | | | | | |
|---|---|---|---|---|---|
| Potassium (mg): | 631 mg | Vitamin C (mg): | 11 mg | Thiamin/B1 (mg): | 0.1 mg |
| Calcium (mg): | 22 mg | Vitamin A (i.u.): | 396 mg | Riboflavin/B2 (mg): | 0.5 mg |
| Iron (mg): | 4 mg | Vitamin B6 (mg): | 0.4 mg | Folacin (mcg): | 29 mg |
| Zinc (mg): | 6 mg | Vitamin B12 (mcg): | 2.8 mg | Niacin/B3 (mg): | 8 mg |

## Albondigas

These are Mexican meatballs, and they're very tasty. Often Mexican recipes call for a blend of ground beef and ground pork. I've substituted the leaner ground turkey for the pork, here.

1/2 pound (225 g) ground turkey
1/2 pound (225 g) ground round
2 medium onions
1/4 cup (25 g) oat bran
1 teaspoon dried oregano
1/2 teaspoon ground cumin
1/2 teaspoon salt
1/2 teaspoon pepper
1 egg
2 cloves garlic, peeled and minced
1 chipotle chile, canned in adobo
3/4 cup (175 ml) beef broth
1 can (14 1/2 ounces, or 415 g) diced tomatoes
1/3 cup (85 g) tomato paste
2 tablespoons (28 ml) oil

Plunk the ground turkey and round into a big mixing bowl. Finely dice 1 onion and put it and the oat bran, oregano, cumin, salt, pepper, and egg into the bowl. Use clean hands to squish everything together really well; when you're done, the 2 meats should be completely blended.

Form the mixture into 1 1/2-inch (3.25-cm) balls, put the balls on a plate, and chill 'em while you make the sauce.

Put the oil in a medium-size saucepan over medium-low heat. Finely dice the second onion and sauté it and the garlic for 3 to 4 minutes, to soften.

While that's happening, chop your chipotle. Add it to the onion and garlic, and stir it up. Stir in the beef broth, tomatoes, and tomato paste. Bring everything to a boil, then reduce to a simmer.

Preheat your oven to 325°F (170°C, or gas mark 3). Give a big, heavy skillet a squirt of nonstick cooking spray, and put it over medium-high heat. Add the oil. When the oil is hot, fry the meatballs in batches for about 5 minutes per batch, browning them all over. Use a slotted spoon to transfer the finished batches to a shallow casserole.

When all the meatballs are in the casserole, pour the sauce over the top. Bake, uncovered, for 20 minutes or so.

You can serve this with brown rice (if you can afford the calories and carbs), with cauli-rice, or just on a plate!

**Yield:** 4 servings

**Nutritional Analysis:** Each will have: 389 calories; 23 g fat; 28 g protein; 21 g carbohydrates; 3 g fiber; 18 g usable carbs.

| | | | | | |
|---|---|---|---|---|---|
| Potassium (mg): | 958 mg | Vitamin C (mg): | 29 mg | Thiamin/B1 (mg): | 0.3 mg |
| Calcium (mg): | 82 mg | Vitamin A (i.u.): | 1210 i.u. | Riboflavin/B2 (mg): | 0.4 mg |
| Iron (mg): | 4 mg | Vitamin B6 (mg): | 0.7 mg | Folacin (mcg): | 44 mcg |
| Zinc (mg): | 4 mg | Vitamin B12 (mcg): | 1.5 mcg | Niacin/B3 (mg): | 6 mg |

## Sloppy Joes

Do you have any idea how much sugar is in that canned Sloppy Joe mix? Don't do it! Make these instead.

- 1 1/2 pounds (670 g) ground round
- Salt and pepper
- 1 large onion, chopped
- 2 cloves garlic, peeled and minced
- 1 medium bell pepper, diced small
- 16 ounces (455 g) tomato sauce
- 2 tablespoons (3 g) Splenda
- 1/2 teaspoon blackstrap molasses
- 1 tablespoon (14 ml) cider vinegar
- 1 teaspoon (5 ml) Worcestershire sauce

Spray a big, heavy skillet with nonstick cooking spray and put it over medium heat. When it's hot, throw in the ground round and start browning and crumbling it.

When the meat is browned, salt and pepper it a bit. Add the onion and garlic, and sauté them with the meat for 5 minutes.

Add the pepper, sauce, Splenda, molasses, vinegar, and Worcestershire, and stir 'er up. Turn the burner to low, and let the whole thing simmer for 20 minutes, until it has thickened a bit.

Serve on whole wheat buns, stuffed into whole wheat pitas, or, to really save carbs and calories, over cauli-rice.

**Yield:** 6 servings

**Nutritional Analysis:** Without buns, pita, or cauli-rice, each will have: 306 calories; 20 g fat; 23 g protein; 10 g carbohydrates; 2 g fiber; 8 g usable carbs.

| | | | | | |
|---|---|---|---|---|---|
| Potassium (mg): | 694 mg | Vitamin C (mg): | 25 mg | Thiamin/B1 (mg): | 0.1 mg |
| Calcium (mg): | 32 mg | Vitamin A (i.u.): | 866 i.u. | Riboflavin/B2 (mg): | 0.3 mg |
| Iron (mg): | 3 mg | Vitamin B6 (mg): | 0.5 mg | Folacin (mcg): | 24 mcg |
| Zinc (mg): | 5 mg | Vitamin B12 (mcg): | 2.3 mcg | Niacin/B3 (mg): | 6 mg |

## Gyros without the Big Rotating Machine

Everyone loves gyros, but who has that big old machine they make them on? These burgers achieve a similar flavor and can be used as a home substitute for gyro meat, though their texture won't be as firm.

- 1/2 pound (225 g) ground lamb
- 1/2 pound (225 g) ground round
- 2 cloves garlic, peeled and crushed
- 2 tablespoons (8 g) chopped fresh parsley
- 1 teaspoon salt or Vege-Sal
- 1/4 teaspoon pepper
- 1/4 teaspoon ground fenugreek seed
- 1/4 teaspoon cumin
- 1 egg
- 1/4 cup (25 g) oat bran

Preheat your electric tabletop grill.

Dump everything into a bowl and use clean hands to squish it all together really, really well.

Form the whole thing into a couple of big patties. Slap them on the grill for 7 to 8 minutes. Leave them on longer if needed—you want them pretty well done.

Slice the patties into strips. Serve on a Greek salad or stuffed into a whole wheat pita with lettuce, tomato, thinly sliced red onion, and Tzatziki (see page 491).

**Yield:** 4 servings

**Nutritional Analysis:** Without additional garnish and sauce, each will have: 328 calories; 25 g fat; 23 g protein; 5 g carbohydrates; 1 g fiber; 4 g usable carbs.

| | | | | | |
|---|---|---|---|---|---|
| Potassium (mg): | 356 mg | Vitamin C (mg): | 3 mg | Thiamin/B1 (mg): | 0.2 mg |
| Calcium (mg): | 33 mg | Vitamin A (i.u.): | 169 i.u. | Riboflavin/B2 (mg): | 0.3 mg |
| Iron (mg): | 3 mg | Vitamin B6 (mg): | 0.3 mg | Folacin (mcg): | 26 mcg |
| Zinc (mg): | 5 mg | Vitamin B12 (mcg): | 2.6 mcg | Niacin/B3 (mg): | 6 mg |

## Highly Vegetableiferous Meat Loaf

Okay, it's a silly name—but it's a good meat loaf!

1 tablespoon (14 ml) olive oil

2 cups (260 g) finely chopped onion

2 cloves garlic, peeled and crushed

1 carrot, shredded

1 pound (455 g) ground round

1 pound (455 g) ground turkey

1/4 cup (25 g) oat bran

2 eggs

3 tablespoons (15 g) grated Parmesan cheese

1 teaspoon paprika

1/4 teaspoon cayenne pepper

1 teaspoon salt or Vege-Sal

1/2 teaspoon ground dried rosemary

10 ounces (280 g) frozen chopped spinach, thawed

2 ounces (55 g) shredded mozzarella cheese

Give a big, heavy skillet a squirt of nonstick cooking spray, add the oil, and put it over medium-low heat. Add the onion and garlic, and sauté without browning until the onions are soft. Transfer to a mixing bowl.

Add the carrot, ground round, ground turkey, oat bran, eggs, cheese, paprika, cayenne, salt, and rosemary to the mixing bowl. Use clean hands to squish everything together very well.

Dump the spinach into a strainer, and press it with the back of a spoon to squeeze out the water. Mix it with the mozzarella.

Preheat the oven to 350°F (180°C, or gas mark 4). Spray a roasting pan with nonstick cooking spray.

Put half the meat mixture into the prepared pan, and form it into a rectangle about 4 x 9 inches (10 x 22.5 cm).

Put a "tunnel" of the spinach mixture down the middle of the meat mixture. Top with the remaining meat, and form into a loaf. Place on your broiler rack, and bake for 1 hour. Serve with tomato sauce, if you like.

**Yield:** 8 servings

**Nutritional Analysis:** Each will have: 317 calories; 20 g fat; 26 g protein; 9 g carbohydrates; 3 g fiber; 6 g usable carbs.

| | | | | | |
|---|---|---|---|---|---|
| Potassium (mg): | 548 mg | Vitamin C (mg): | 13 mg | Thiamin/B1 (mg): | 0.2 mg |
| Calcium (mg): | 139 mg | Vitamin A (i.u.): | 5630 i.u. | Riboflavin/B2 (mg): | 0.4 mg |
| Iron (mg): | 3 mg | Vitamin B6 (mg): | 0.5 mg | Folacin (mcg): | 68 mcg |
| Zinc (mg): | 4 mg | Vitamin B12 (mcg): | 1.5 mcg | Niacin/B3 (mg): | 5 mg |

## Corn Pone

This is serious down-home comfort food. My husband adored it, giving it a perfect "10." You'll need a skillet with an oven-safe handle—a cast iron skillet is ideal.

- 1 pound (455 g) ground round
- 1 pound (455 g) ground turkey
- 1 medium onion, chopped
- 2 teaspoons chili powder
- 8 ounces (225 g) tomato sauce
- 1 can (14½ ounces, or 405 g) tomatoes with green chiles
- 1 tablespoon (14 ml) Worcestershire sauce
- ½ cup (70 g) whole grain cornmeal
- ½ cup (70 g) homemade almond meal
- 3 tablespoons (26 g) flax seed meal

3 tablespoons (24 g) vanilla whey protein powder

1/4 teaspoon baking soda

1 teaspoon baking powder

1 teaspoon salt

1 egg, beaten

1 cup (235 ml) buttermilk

Spray a big, heavy skillet with nonstick cooking spray and put it over medium-high heat. Throw in the ground round and turkey, and start browning and crumbling them together. When they're about half-cooked, pour off the grease that has accumulated, to help the browning continue.

When a little more fat has accumulated in the skillet, add the onion. Keep cooking and crumbling the meat until all the pink is gone. Drain off the grease.

Stir in the chili powder, tomato sauce, tomatoes, and Worcestershire sauce. Turn the burner down to medium-low, and let the whole thing simmer for 15 minutes or so.

Preheat the oven to 425°F (220°C, or gas mark 7).

In a mixing bowl, combine the cornmeal, almond meal, flax seed meal, protein powder, baking soda, baking powder, and salt. Stir them together so all the ingredients are evenly distributed. Measure the buttermilk in a glass measuring cup with a pouring lip, and add the egg. Stir them together, and set them aside.

When the meat mixture is done simmering and your oven is all the way up to temperature, smooth the meat mixture into an even layer in the skillet. Pour the buttermilk and egg into the dry ingredients, and stir with a few swift strokes of your whisk. Stir just till you're certain that everything is evenly wet.

Now pour this batter over the meat mixture in the skillet, and place the skillet in your oven. Bake for 25 to 30 minutes, or until the cornbread is golden and done through. Cut into wedges to serve.

**Yield:** 8 servings

**Nutritional Analysis:** Each will have: 260 calories; 14 g fat; 20 g protein; 13 g carbohydrates; 3 g fiber; 10 g usable carbs.

| | | | | | |
|---|---|---|---|---|---|
| Potassium (mg): | 413 mg | Vitamin C (mg): | 5 mg | Thiamin/B1 (mg): | 0.3 mg |
| Calcium (mg): | 105 mg | Vitamin A (i.u.): | 492 i.u. | Riboflavin/B2 (mg): | 0.4 mg |
| Iron (mg): | 2 mg | Vitamin B6 (mg): | 0.6 mg | Folacin (mcg): | 25 mcg |
| Zinc (mg): | 4 mg | Vitamin B12 (mcg): | 1.7 mcg | Niacin/B3 (mg): | 4 mg |

## Turkey Chili

1 tablespoon (14 ml) olive oil

1 pound (455 g) ground turkey

1 small onion, chopped

10 ounces (280 g) canned tomatoes with green chiles

8 ounces (225 g) tomato sauce

1½ tablespoons (14 g) chili powder

1 tablespoon oregano

1 teaspoon minced garlic

⅓ ounce (9 g) unsweetened chocolate, grated

1 cup (240 g) canned black soy beans, drained and rinsed, or 1 cup (225 g) canned pinto beans, drained and rinsed

½ teaspoon salt

Put the oil in a big, heavy skillet and set it over medium heat. When the oil's hot, start browning and crumbling the ground turkey. As a little more fat collects in the pan, add the onion, and sauté it with the turkey.

When all the pink is gone from the turkey, add the tomatoes, tomato sauce, chili powder, oregano, and garlic. Bring to a simmer.

Make sure your chocolate is finely grated—a microplane grater is perfect for this. Stir in the chocolate, a little at a time, till it's all melted in. Stir in the soy beans and salt. Turn the burner to low, cover, and let the whole thing simmer for at least one-half hour; an hour will help blend the flavors even better.

Serve with shredded cheese, chopped onion, light sour cream—all the usual accoutrements.

**Yield:** 4 servings

**Nutritional Analysis:** With black soy beans, each will have: 317 calories; 18 g fat; 27 g protein; 16 g carbohydrates; 7 g fiber; 9 g usable carbs.

| | | | | | |
|---|---|---|---|---|---|
| Potassium (mg): | 689 mg | Vitamin C (mg): | 12 mg | Thiamin/B1 (mg): | 0.2 mg |
| Calcium (mg): | 109 mg | Vitamin A (i.u.): | 2127 i.u. | Riboflavin/B2 (mg): | 0.3 mg |
| Iron (mg): | 4 mg | Vitamin B6 (mg): | 0.7 mg | Folacin (mcg): | 42 mcg |
| Zinc (mg): | 4 mg | Vitamin B12 (mcg): | 0.4 mcg | Niacin/B3 (mg): | 6 mg |

**Nutritional Analysis:** With pinto beans, each will have: 309 calories; 15 g fat; 25 g protein; 21 g carbohydrates; 5 g fiber; 16 g usable carbs.

| | | | | | |
|---|---|---|---|---|---|
| Potassium (mg): | 870 mg | Vitamin C (mg): | 13 mg | Thiamin/B1 (mg): | 0.2 mg |
| Calcium (mg): | 95 mg | Vitamin A (i.u.): | 1900 i.u. | Riboflavin/B2 (mg): | 0.3 mg |
| Iron (mg): | 4 mg | Vitamin B6 (mg): | 0.7 mg | Folacin (mcg): | 67 mcg |
| Zinc (mg): | 3 mg | Vitamin B12 (mcg): | 0.4 mcg | Niacin/B3 (mg): | 6 mg |

## Ray's Slow-Cooker Chili

This is our tester Ray's chili, and as you can see, the trick here is cooking it for a long, long time.

1/2 pound (225 g) ground round

1/2 pound (225 g) ground turkey

4 cups (940 g) water

1 medium onion

3 teaspoons (27 g) chili powder

1 can (15 ounces, or 420 g) black soy beans

1/2 teaspoon cumin

1/2 teaspoon red pepper flakes

1/4 teaspoon ground cloves

1 can (14 ounces, or 390 g) diced tomatoes

In a heavy skillet over medium heat, brown and crumble the ground round and ground turkey, drain it, and transfer it to your slow cooker.

Add the water, onion, chili powder, soy beans, cumin, pepper flakes, cloves, and tomatoes, and stir it up. Cover the slow cooker, and set it to high. Cook for 3 to 4 hours, then turn it down and cook for another 20 hours, at least! Stir every few hours, if possible.

**Yield:** 4 servings

**Nutritional Analysis:** Each will have: 353 calories; 20 g fat; 31 g protein; 15 g carbohydrates; 8 g fiber; 7 g usable carbs.

| | | | | | |
|---|---|---|---|---|---|
| Potassium (mg): | 1916 mg | Vitamin C (mg): | 48 mg | Thiamin/B1 (mg): | 0.4 mg |
| Calcium (mg): | 130 mg | Vitamin A (i.u.): | 3824 i.u. | Riboflavin/B2 (mg): | 1.0 mg |
| Iron (mg): | 10 mg | Vitamin B6 (mg): | 1.8 mg | Folacin (mcg): | 90 mg |
| Zinc (mg): | 15 mg | Vitamin B12 (mcg): | 5.4 mcg | Niacin/B3 (mg): | 20 mg |

# Hamburger Plus

This is more an idea than a recipe. Organ meats are wildly nutritious, but most people aren't in the habit of eating them—indeed, many are squicked out by them. This is an easy, painless way to get organ meats into your diet. Eaten by itself—just in a plain grilled or broiled burger—this tastes a little different than regular ground beef. It's not bad, just a little richer-tasting. The mixture is also somewhat softer than regular ground beef. But in a highly seasoned dish—a chili, for example—you'd be hard-pressed to tell the difference between this and your standard ground beef. Only your body will know, because this is an amazing source of Vitamin A, all the Bs, and zinc, as well as a good source of potassium and iron.

10 pounds (4.5 kg) beef chuck

2 pounds (905 g) beef heart

1 pound (455 g) beef liver

Ask your butcher or the nice meat guys at the grocery store to grind these things together for you. Take it home, make it into patties, and freeze it. Use it in place of ground beef in chili and such, for a big nutritional boost.

**Yield:** 39 servings

**Nutritional Analysis:** Assuming 1/3 pound (155 g) per serving, each will have: 281 calories; 19 g fat; 24 g protein; 1 g carbohydrates; 0 g fiber; 1 g usable carbs.

| | | | | | |
|---|---|---|---|---|---|
| Potassium (mg): | 392 mg | Vitamin C (mg): | 4 mg | Thiamin/B1 (mg): | 0.2 mg |
| Calcium (mg): | 8 mg | Vitamin A (i.u.): | 4115 i.u. | Riboflavin/B2 (mg): | 0.7 mg |
| Iron (mg): | 4 mg | Vitamin B6 (mg): | 0.5 mg | Folacin (mcg): | 36 mcg |
| Zinc (mg): | 5 mg | Vitamin B12 (mcg): | 13.6 mcg | Niacin/B3 (mg): | 6 mg |

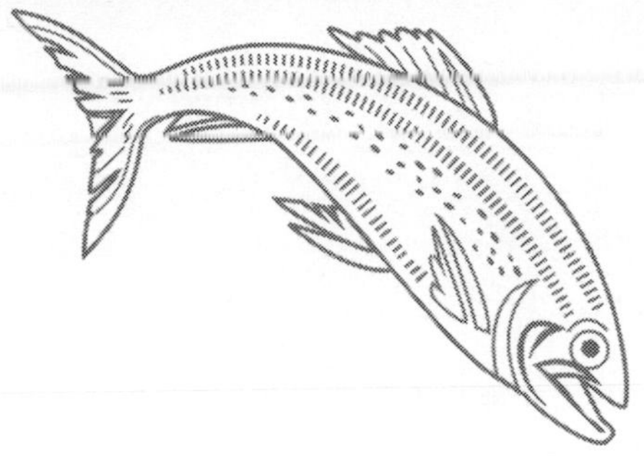

chapter ten

# Fish

In the great Nutrition Wars, when no one seems to be able to agree on a thing, fish live in the nutritional equivalent of Switzerland: blessed neutral ground. Everyone agrees that fish is good food. They're low in calories and carbs. Many of them are also good sources of valuable omega-3 fatty acids. They're even incredibly quick to cook!

We start out this chapter with a school of shrimp recipes. Shrimp are quick and easy to prepare, delicious, low-carb, low-calorie, and exceedingly popular. Here are 7 new ways to serve them!

## Ginger-Lime Poached Shrimp

Please use this recipe for inspiration, and try poaching shrimp in any tasty liquid you can think of!

1/2 cup (120 ml) Ginger-Lime Vinaigrette (see page 226)

1 pound (455 g) fairly big shrimp, peeled and deveined

This is easy: Put the Ginger-Lime Vinaigrette in a nonreactive pan big enough that your shrimp can lie in a single layer. Put it over medium-low heat, and bring to a simmer. Throw in the shrimp, and poach for 3 to 4 minutes per side, or until they're pink clear through. Serve with the dressing from the pan drizzled over them.

You can also chill these and serve them cold.

**Yield:** 3 servings

**Nutritional Analysis:** Each will have: 271 calories; 12 g fat; 31 g protein; 7 g carbohydrates; trace fiber; 7 g usable carbs.

| | | | | | |
|---|---|---|---|---|---|
| Potassium (mg): | 343 mg | Vitamin C (mg): | 9 mg | Thiamin/B1 (mg): | trace |
| Calcium (mg): | 86 mg | Vitamin A (i.u.): | 324 i.u. | Riboflavin/B2 (mg): | trace |
| Iron (mg): | 4 mg | Vitamin B6 (mg): | trace | Folacin (mcg): | 10 mcg |
| Zinc (mg): | 2 mg | Vitamin B12 (mcg): | 1.5 mcg | Niacin/B3 (mg) | 4 mg |

## Buffalo Shrimp

Want something quick and easy that your friends will devour? Here's your dish.

1 1/2 tablespoons (21 ml) olive oil

2 cloves garlic, peeled and crushed

18 ounces (505 g) shrimp, peeled and deveined

6 tablespoons (90 ml) Louisiana-style hot sauce (or more to taste)

Quick and Easy Blue Cheese Dip (see page 487)

Put the oil in a big, heavy skillet, and place it over medium heat. Add the garlic, stir it around, then throw in the shrimp. Sauté, stirring frequently. When the shrimp are about half pink, stir in the hot sauce. Keep sautéing until the shrimp are pink and done clear through. Serve with Quick and Easy Blue Cheese Dip.

**Yield:** 3 servings

**Nutritional Analysis:** Each will have: 353 calories, 18 g fat; 38 g protein; 8 g carbohydrates; trace fiber; 8 g usable carbs.

| | | | | | |
|---|---|---|---|---|---|
| Potassium (mg): | 449 mg | Vitamin C (mg): | 26 mg | Thiamin/B1 (mg): | trace |
| Calcium (mg): | 193 mg | Vitamin A (i.u.): | 511 i.u. | Riboflavin/B2 (mg): | 0.1 mg |
| Iron (mg): | 4 mg | Vitamin B6 (mg): | 0.1 mg | Folacin (mcg): | 13 mcg |
| Zinc (mg): | 2 mg | Vitamin B12 (mcg): | 2 mcg | Niacin/B3 (mg) | 4 mg |

## Lemon-Mustard Grilled Shrimp

You could also do this as an appetizer at your next barbecue—just use twice as many skewers, to make the portions smaller, or even spear each shrimp on its own cocktail pick.

1 pound (455 g) large shrimp, peeled and deveined

Lemon-Mustard Vinaigrette (see page 229)

4 lemon wedges

Put the shrimp in a zipper-lock bag, and pour the Lemon-Mustard Vinaigrette over them. Seal the bag, pressing out the air as you go. Turn to coat. Let your shrimp marinate for at least 15 minutes, and up to an hour is fine. At the same time, put 4 bamboo skewers into water to soak.

You can grill your marinated shrimp on your outdoor grill or in your electric table-top grill. Either way, get the grill hot—preheat an electric grill, let a gas grill preheat for 5 minutes or so at medium flame, or build a charcoal fire and let it burn down to well-ashed coals.

When the grill is ready, pull out the shrimp and pour off the marinade into a bowl. Thread the shrimp onto skewers, going through both the head and tail ends, so they end up looking a little like a "cents" sign.

Now put 'em on the grill and let 'em cook. They won't take long—5 to 6 minutes on an outdoor grill, and just 2 to 3 minutes in an electric grill. During the grilling, baste once or twice with the reserved marinade, stopping at least 1 minute before cooking time is up. (When I do these in my electric grill, I set the timer for 1 minute, baste, then set it for 2 more minutes.)

Serve each skewer with a lemon wedge to squeeze over it.

**Yield:** 4 servings

**Nutritional Analysis:** Each will have: 188 calories; 9 g fat; 23 g protein; 3 g carbohydrates; trace fiber; 3 g usable carbs.

| | | | | | |
|---|---|---|---|---|---|
| Potassium (mg): | 244 mg | Vitamin C (mg): | 8 mg | Thiamin/B1 (mg): | trace |
| Calcium (mg): | 68 mg | Vitamin A (i.u.): | 209 i.u. | Riboflavin/B2 (mg): | trace |
| Iron (mg): | 3 mg | Vitamin B6 (mg): | trace | Folacin (mcg): | 5 mcg |
| Zinc (mg): | 1 mg | Vitamin B12 (mcg): | 1.1 mcg | Niacin/B3 (mg): | 3 mg |

# Pesto Shrimp

Another quickie dish using jarred pesto sauce to advantage.

1½ tablespoons (21 ml) olive oil

3 tablespoons (45 g) jarred pesto sauce

18 ounces (505 g) shrimp, peeled and deveined

How easy can it get? Combine the olive oil and pesto in a big, heavy skillet over medium-high heat. When the mixture's hot, throw in the shrimp and sauté them until they're pink clear through. Serve with all the pesto scraped over them.

**Yield:** 4 servings

**Nutritional Analysis:** Each will have: 237 calories; 12 g fat; 28 g protein; 2 g carbohydrates; trace fiber; 2 g usable carbs.

| | | | | | |
|---|---|---|---|---|---|
| Potassium (mg): | 274 mg | Vitamin C (mg): | 4 mg | Thiamin/B1 (mg): | trace |
| Calcium (mg): | 143 mg | Vitamin A (i.u.): | 346 i.u. | Riboflavin/B2 (mg): | trace |
| Iron (mg): | 3 mg | Vitamin B6 (mg): | trace | Folacin (mcg): | 7 mcg |
| Zinc (mg): | 1 mg | Vitamin B12 (mcg): | 1.3 mcg | Niacin/B3 (mg): | 3 mg |

## Shrimp in Tomato Sauce

This is a very simple, quick sauce, using pantry ingredients. But feel free to poach shrimp in your favorite tomato-based pasta sauce—so long as it has no added sugar or corn syrup!

12 ounces (340 g) shrimp, peeled and deveined

8 ounces (225 g) tomato sauce

1 clove garlic

1 1/2 teaspoons dried oregano

1/2 teaspoon dried basil

1/4 cup (20 g) shredded Parmesan cheese

In a large, nonreactive saucepan, combine the tomato sauce, garlic, oregano, and basil over medium-high heat. Bring to a simmer, turn the burner down, and let everything simmer together for 5 minutes or so.

Add the shrimp, and poach 'em until they're pink clear through. Spoon the shrimp and sauce onto serving plates.

Sprinkle each serving with 2 tablespoons (10 g) Parmesan, and serve.

**Yield:** 2 servings

**Nutritional Analysis:** Each will have: 262 calories; 6 g fat; 40 g protein; 11 g carbohydrates; 2 g fiber; 9 g usable carbs.

| | | | | | |
|---|---|---|---|---|---|
| Potassium (mg): | 783 mg | Vitamin C (mg): | 11 mg | Thiamin/B1 (mg): | 0.1 mg |
| Calcium (mg): | 258 mg | Vitamin A (i.u.): | 1593 i.u. | Riboflavin/B2 (mg): | 0.1 mg |
| Iron (mg): | 6 mg | Vitamin B6 (mg): | 0.2 mg | Folacin (mcg): | 21 mcg |
| Zinc (mg): | 2 mg | Vitamin B12 (mcg): | 1.8 mcg | Niacin/B3 (mg): | 6 mg |

## Shrimp with Wine and Dill

This is very Continental. Add a green salad and a loaf of crusty whole grain bread, pour some white wine, and feel sophisticated.

1 tablespoon (14 g) butter

1/4 cup (40 g) minced onion

1 cup (235 ml) dry white wine

2 tablespoons (8 g) minced fresh dill weed, or 1 1/2 teaspoons dried dill weed

2 1/2 tablespoons (35 ml) lemon juice

1/8 teaspoon ground cloves

24 ounces (670 g) shrimp, peeled and deveined

Guar or xanthan gum

Melt the butter in a big, nonreactive saucepan over medium-low heat. Start sautéing the onion. When it's translucent, add the wine, dill, lemon juice, and cloves. Bring this mixture to a bare simmer. Add the shrimp, and let them poach until they're pink clear through. Use a slotted spoon to remove the shrimp, and put them on 4 serving plates.

Thicken the poaching liquid with just a tiny bit of guar or xanthan. You want it maybe the thickness of half-and-half, but no thicker. Pour it over the shrimp, and serve.

**Yield:** 4 servings

**Nutritional Analysis:** Each will have: 252 calories; 6 g fat; 35 g protein; 4 g carbohydrates; trace fiber; 4 g usable carbs.

| | | | | | |
|---|---|---|---|---|---|
| Potassium (mg): | 393 mg | Vitamin C (mg): | 9 mg | Thiamin/B1 (mg): | trace |
| Calcium (mg): | 98 mg | Vitamin A (i.u.): | 438 i.u. | Riboflavin/B2 (mg): | trace |
| Iron (mg): | 4 mg | Vitamin B6 (mg): | trace | Folacin (mcg): | 9 mcg |
| Zinc (mg): | 2 mg | Vitamin B12 (mcg): | 1.7 mcg | Niacin/B3 (mg): | 4 mg |

# Sizzling Moroccan Shrimp

This combination of spices is wonderful and exotic. This would be a great recipe to double for an impressive company dinner.

1 tablespoon (14 ml) olive oil

1 pound (455 g) shrimp, peeled and deveined

2 cloves garlic, peeled and minced

1 teaspoon ground cumin

1/2 teaspoon ground gingerroot

2 teaspoons (4 g) paprika

1/8 teaspoon cayenne pepper, or to taste

2 teaspoons (10 ml) lemon juice

Spray a big, heavy skillet with nonstick cooking spray, and put it over high heat. When it's hot, add the oil and shrimp. Sauté, turning often, until they're just barely pink all over. Stir in the garlic, cumin, ginger, paprika, cayenne, and lemon juice. Sauté for another minute or so, till the shrimp are pink through, and serve.

**Yield:** 3 servings

**Nutritional Analysis:** Each will have: 212 calories; 7 g fat; 31 g protein; 4 g carbohydrates; 1 g fiber; 3 g usable carbs.

| | | | | | |
|---|---|---|---|---|---|
| Potassium (mg): | 346 mg | Vitamin C (mg): | 6 mg | Thiamin/B1 (mg): | trace |
| Calcium (mg): | 92 mg | Vitamin A (i.u.): | 1242 i.u. | Riboflavin/B2 (mg): | trace |
| Iron (mg): | 4 mg | Vitamin B6 (mg): | 0.1 mg | Folacin (mcg): | 7 mcg |
| Zinc (mg): | 2 mg | Vitamin B12 (mcg): | 1.5 mcg | Niacin/B3 (mg): | 4 mg |

## Asian Shark Steaks

Don't overcook this—it's a quick jump from done to dry.

- 1 pound (455 g) shark steaks, in 4 portions
- 1/2 cup (120 ml) soy sauce
- 2 tablespoons (28 ml) dark sesame oil
- 2 tablespoons (28 ml) lemon juice
- 2 tablespoons (28 ml) dry sherry
- 2 teaspoons (2 g) dry mustard
- 2 teaspoons (10 ml) honey or 2 teaspoons (1 g) Splenda
- 2 teaspoons (5 g) grated gingerroot
- 4 teaspoons (10 g) sesame seeds
- 3 tablespoons (11 g) minced cilantro

Put the steaks in a zipper-lock bag. In a small bowl, combine the soy sauce, oil, lemon juice, sherry, mustard, honey, and ginger, and pour over the steak. Seal the bag, pressing out the air as you go, and turn it a few times to coat the steak. Let it marinate for 10 minutes.

While that's happening, put the sesame seeds in a dry skillet and stir them over medium-high heat until they're lightly golden. Set aside.

Start warming your electric tabletop grill 5 or 6 minutes into the marinating time. When the grill's hot and the fish is done marinating, open the baggie. Pour off the marinade into a small saucepan, and throw the fish in the grill. Set a timer for 5 minutes.

While the fish is grilling, put the marinade over high heat and boil it hard for 2 to 3 minutes, to kill any raw fish germs. When the timer goes off, place the fish on a serving plate and spoon a little marinade over it. Sprinkle with sesame seeds and cilantro, and serve.

**Yield:** 4 servings

**Nutritional Analysis:** With honey, each will have: 269 calories; 14 g fat; 26 g protein; 8 g carbohydrates; 1 g fiber; 7 g usable carbs.

| | | | | | |
|---|---|---|---|---|---|
| Potassium (mg): | 291 mg | Vitamin C (mg): | 4 mg | Thiamin/B1 (mg): | 0.1 mg |
| Calcium (mg): | 79 mg | Vitamin A (i.u.): | 291 i.u. | Riboflavin/B2 (mg): | 0.1 mg |
| Iron (mg): | 2 mg | Vitamin B6 (mg): | 0.5 mg | Folacin (mcg): | 13 mcg |
| Zinc (mg): | 1 mg | Vitamin B12 (mcg): | 1.7 mcg | Niacin/B3 (mg): | 5 mg |

**Nutritional Analysis:** With Splenda, each will have: 260 calories; 14 g fat; 26 g protein; 5 g carbohydrates; 1 g fiber; 4 g usable carbs.

| | | | | | |
|---|---|---|---|---|---|
| Potassium (mg): | 289 mg | Vitamin C (mg): | 4 mg | Thiamin/B1 (mg): | 0.1 mg |
| Calcium (mg): | 78 mg | Vitamin A (i.u.): | 291 i.u. | Riboflavin/B2 (mg): | 0.1 mg |
| Iron (mg): | 2 mg | Vitamin B6 (mg): | 0.5 mg | Folacin (mcg): | 13 mcg |
| Zinc (mg): | 1 mg | Vitamin B12 (mcg): | 1.7 mcg | Niacin/B3 (mg): | 5 mg |

**Note:** I like to use kitchen shears to snip up my fresh cilantro.

# Mustard Vinaigrette Shark Steak

If you like, you could streamline this by using bottled Dijon vinaigrette dressing—but this is better!

- 1 pound (455 g) shark steaks
- 1/2 cup (120 ml) olive oil
- 1/4 cup (60 ml) wine vinegar
- 4 teaspoons (20 g) brown mustard
- 1 teaspoon salt
- 1 teaspoon pepper
- 8 teaspoons (10 g) minced parsley
- 4 teaspoons (13 g) minced red onion

Put your shark steaks in a zipper-lock bag, or lay them in a glass pie plate. Whisk together the olive oil, vinegar, mustard, salt, and pepper, and pour it over the fish, turning it to coat. Let the fish marinate for at least 15 minutes. (In this case, more than 30 minutes isn't a great idea.)

Preheat your electric tabletop grill. Pour the marinade off of the fish and into a little saucepan, and put the fish in your grill. Set a timer for 2 minutes. When the 2 minutes are up, baste the fish with the marinade, turning it carefully so you can get both sides. Close the grill, and set the timer for another 2 minutes.

Put the saucepan with the marinade over medium-high heat, bring it to a boil, and boil it hard for at least a minute.

When the timer goes off, remove the fish to serving plates. Spoon a little of the boiled marinade over each steak, top each with 2 teaspoons of parsley and 1 teaspoon of red onion, and serve.

**Yield:** 4 servings

**Nutritional Analysis:** Each will have: 396 calories; 33 g fat; 24 g protein; 2 g carbohydrates; trace fiber; 2 g usable carbs.

| | | | | | |
|---|---|---|---|---|---|
| Potassium (mg): | 229 mg | Vitamin C (mg): | 4 mg | Thiamin/B1 (mg): | 0.1 mg |
| Calcium (mg): | 56 mg | Vitamin A (i.u.): | 395 i.u. | Riboflavin/B2 (mg): | 0.1 mg |
| Iron (mg): | 2 mg | Vitamin B6 (mg): | 0.5 mg | Folacin (mcg): | 8 mcg |
| Zinc (mg): | 1 mg | Vitamin B12 (mcg): | 1.7 mcg | Niacin/B3 (mg): | 3 mg |

## Citrus Poached Salmon

This is easy and elegant.

1/4 cup (60 ml) water

1/4 cup (60 ml) orange juice

1/4 cup (60 ml) lemon juice

1/4 cup (60 ml) white wine vinegar

1 teaspoon minced fresh tarragon, or 1/4 teaspoon dried tarragon

1 pinch ground allspice

1 pinch salt

12 ounces (340 g) salmon fillet, with skin

Combine the water, orange juice, lemon juice, vinegar, tarragon, allspice, and salt in a small, nonreactive skillet or other stovetop vessel. (Don't use iron or aluminum, although anodized aluminum with a nonstick surface is okay. Enamel or glass are best.) Simmer the mixture for 10 minutes.

Lay the salmon in the poaching mixture, skin side up. Simmer for about 6 minutes, flip carefully, and simmer for another 6 minutes, or until the fish is flakey. Serve with just 1 tablespoon (14 ml) of the poaching liquid spooned over each serving.

**Yield:** 2 servings

**Nutritional Analysis:** Each will have: 224 calories; 6 g fat; 34 g protein; 8 g carbohydrates; trace fiber; 8 g usable carbs.

| | | | | | |
|---|---|---|---|---|---|
| Potassium (mg): | 686 mg | Vitamin C (mg): | 30 mg | Thiamin/B1 (mg): | 0.4 mg |
| Calcium (mg): | 33 mg | Vitamin A (i.u.): | 278 i.u. | Riboflavin/B2 (mg): | 0.2 mg |
| Iron (mg): | 2 mg | Vitamin B6 (mg): | 0.4 mg | Folacin (mcg): | 28 mcg |
| Zinc (mg): | 1 mg | Vitamin B12 (mcg): | 5.1 mcg | Niacin/B3 (mg): | 9 mg |

**Note:** A garnish of fresh tarragon leaves would be nice with this, but it's not essential.

## Pecan and Tarragon–Crusted Salmon

This is impressive, considering how little work and time it takes.

Juice and zest of 2 oranges

1/4 cup (15 g) minced fresh tarragon

1 1/2 pounds (670 g) salmon fillet, with skin

4 teaspoons (20 g) Dijon mustard

4 teaspoons (20 g) light mayonnaise

4 tablespoons (24 g) chopped pecans

On a plate with a rim, mix together the orange juice, orange zest, and half of the tarragon. Place the salmon in this mixture, and let it marinate for at least 30 minutes, turning halfway through.

In a separate bowl, mix together the mustard, mayo, and the remaining tarragon.

When your marinating time is up, spray a shallow baking pan with nonstick cooking spray and put the salmon on it, skin side down. Discard the marinade. Spread the mustard-mayo mixture evenly over the meaty side of the fillets. Spread the chopped pecans evenly over that.

Set your broiler to low, and broil the salmon 4 to 5 inches from the heat for 4 to 5 minutes, or until it's opaque clear through.

**Yield:** 4 servings

**Nutritional Analysis:** Each will have: 295 calories; 12 g fat; 35 g protein; 10 g carbohydrates; 2 g fiber; 8 g usable carbs.

| | | | | | |
|---|---|---|---|---|---|
| Potassium (mg): | 721 mg | Vitamin C (mg): | 35 mg | Thiamin/B1 (mg): | 0.5 mg |
| Calcium (mg): | 62 mg | Vitamin A (i.u.): | 368 i.u. | Riboflavin/B2 (mg): | 0.3 mg |
| Iron (mg): | 2 mg | Vitamin B6 (mg): | 0.4 mg | Folacin (mcg): | 30 mcg |
| Zinc (mg): | 1 mg | Vitamin B12 (mcg): | 5.1 mcg | Niacin/B3 (mg): | 9 mg |

**Note:** Keep an eye on this while it broils; the line between toasted pecans and scorched pecans is pretty thin!

# Salmon Poached on Artichokes

There's nothing like artichokes to make a simple dish seem elegant.

12 ounces (340 g) salmon fillet, with skin
2 teaspoons (10 g) butter
2 cups (600 g) artichoke hearts, chopped
2 cups (260 g) chopped sweet red onion
2 tablespoons (28 ml) lemon juice
2 tablespoons (28 g) light sour cream
2 tablespoons (28 g) light mayonnaise
2 teaspoons (30 g) whole-grain Dijon mustard
1 tablespoon (14 ml) white wine vinegar
2 teaspoons chopped fresh tarragon
6 drops Tabasco sauce, or more to taste
Salt and pepper

Cut the salmon into 3 portions, and salt and pepper it lightly. Set aside.

Give a big, heavy skillet a shot of nonstick cooking spray. Melt the butter, and start sautéing the chopped artichoke hearts and onion. When the onion's just starting to soften, stir in the lemon juice, and arrange the vegetable mixture in an even layer in the skillet. Lay the salmon on top, skin-side down. Cover the pan, turn the burner to medium-low, and set a timer for 7 to 8 minutes.

While the salmon's poaching, stir together the lemon juice, sour cream, mayo, mustard, vinegar, tarragon, and Tabasco to make a sauce. Add salt and pepper to taste.

When the timer goes off, use your pancake turner to remove the salmon to a plate. Reserve 3 tablespoons (45 ml) of the sauce. Stir the rest of the sauce into the artichoke mixture, turn off the heat immediately, and spoon the vegetables onto serving plates. Top each plate of vegetables with a salmon fillet, top each with 1 tablespoon (15 ml) of the reserved sauce, and serve.

**Yield:** 3 servings

**Nutritional Analysis:** Each will have: 283 calories; 9 g fat; 28 g protein; 25 g carbohydrates; 8 g fiber; 17 g usable carbs.

| | | | | | |
|---|---|---|---|---|---|
| Potassium (mg): | 956 mg | Vitamin C (mg): | 23 mg | Thiamin/B1 (mg): | 0.3 mg |
| Calcium (mg): | 96 mg | Vitamin A (i.u.): | 435 i.u. | Riboflavin/B2 (mg): | 0.2 mg |
| Iron (mg): | 3 mg | Vitamin B6 (mg): | 0.5 mg | Folacin (mcg): | 84 mcg |
| Zinc (mg): | 1 mg | Vitamin B12 (mcg): | 3.4 mcg | Niacin/B3 (mg): | 7 mg |

# Sesame-Crusted Salmon with Orange-Soy Mayonnaise

This one had Julie doing her impression of Meg Ryan in the restaurant scene in *When Harry Met Sally*: "Yes! Yes! Yes!!"

1 cup (225 g) light mayonnaise

Juice and zest of 1 orange

1 tablespoon (14 ml) lemon juice

2 teaspoons (1 g) Splenda

2 teaspoons (10 ml) soy sauce

1 tablespoon (14 ml) dark sesame oil

1 teaspoon grated gingerroot

1/4 teaspoon orange extract

Salt and pepper

1 1/2 pounds (670 g) salmon fillets, with skin

1 tablespoon (14 ml) peanut oil

5 tablespoons (40 g) sesame seeds

Whisk together the mayo, orange juice and zest, lemon juice, Splenda, soy sauce, sesame oil, ginger, and orange extract until blended well. Add salt and pepper to taste. Cover and refrigerate until you start cooking your salmon. (This is best made at least several hours in advance, and the day before is brilliant.)

When it's getting to be near dinnertime, take the orange-soy mayonnaise out of the fridge and uncover it so it can come to room temperature.

Preheat the oven to 400°F (200°C, or gas mark 6).

Cut the salmon into 6 servings. Line a shallow baking pan with foil, and lay the salmon on it, skin side down. Brush the top with the peanut oil. Sprinkle with salt and pepper, then with the sesame seeds. Press the seeds gently into the surface of the fish.

Bake the fish until it's just cooked through—5 to 8 minutes. Transfer to serving plates. Put 3 tablespoons (45 ml) of orange-soy mayo on each plate for dipping, and serve.

**Yield:** 6 servings

**Nutritional Analysis:** Each will have: 320 calories; 20 g fat; 24 g protein; 11 g carbohydrates; 1 g fiber; 10 g usable carbs.

| | | | | | |
|---|---|---|---|---|---|
| Potassium (mg): | 453 mg | Vitamin C (mg): | 13 mg | Thiamin/B1 (mg): | 0.3 mg |
| Calcium (mg): | 97 mg | Vitamin A (i.u.): | 180 i.u. | Riboflavin/B2 (mg): | 0.2 mg |
| Iron (mg): | 2 mg | Vitamin B6 (mg): | 0.3 mg | Folacin (mcg): | 19 mcg |
| Zinc (mg): | 1 mg | Vitamin B12 (mcg): | 3.4 mcg | Niacin/B3 (mg): | 6 mg |

## Salmon with Pesto Mayonnaise

Made with jarred pesto, this couldn't be easier.

1 1/2 pounds (670 g) salmon fillet, with skin, cut into 4 portions

1/4 cup (55 g) light mayonnaise

4 teaspoons (20 g) pesto sauce

1/4 cup (20 g) shredded Parmesan cheese

Spray a shallow baking pan with nonstick cooking spray. Arrange the salmon fillets in it, skin side down.

Set the broiler for low heat, and broil the salmon about 4 inches (10 cm) from heat for 4 to 5 minutes.

Meanwhile, combine the mayonnaise and pesto sauce. When the initial broiling time is up, spread the pesto mayonnaise on the salmon. Top each serving with 1 tablespoon (5 g) of the Parmesan. Run it back under the broiler for 1 1/2 minutes, or until the cheese is lightly browned.

**Yield:** 4 servings

**Nutritional Analysis:** Each will have: 278 calories; 12 g fat; 37 g protein; 3 g carbohydrates; trace fiber; 3 g usable carbs.

| | | | | | |
|---|---|---|---|---|---|
| Potassium (mg): | 573 mg | Vitamin C (mg): | trace | Thiamin/B1 (mg): | 0.3 mg |
| Calcium (mg): | 119 mg | Vitamin A (i.u.): | 284 i.u. | Riboflavin/B2 (mg): | 0.2 mg |
| Iron (mg): | 2 mg | Vitamin B6 (mg): | 0.3 mg | Folacin (mcg): | 9 mcg |
| Zinc (mg): | 1 mg | Vitamin B12 (mcg): | 5.2 mcg | Niacin/B3 (mg): | 9 mg |

## Grilled Salmon with Peach Salsa

Julie tells us that when she has guests who eat fish, this is what she will serve. Anyone can make a professional-looking entrée with this recipe.

- 2 peaches, peeled and cut into 1/4-inch (6-mm) cubes
- 1 small jalapeño
- 1 tablespoon (4 g) minced cilantro
- 1 tablespoon (4 g) minced fresh mint leaves
- 1 tablespoon (14 ml) lime juice
- 1 teaspoon (.5 g) Splenda
- 1 1/2 pounds (670 g) fresh salmon fillets
- 1 tablespoon (14 ml) olive oil

Put the peach cubes in a small glass or china bowl. Seed the jalapeño, finely mince it, and add it to the peaches. Now wash your hands well! (If you don't, you'll be sorry the next time you touch your eyes or nose.)

Add the cilantro and mint to the bowl. Toss with the lime juice and Splenda, cover with plastic wrap, and refrigerate. (This will hold for at least a few hours.)

When dinnertime rolls around, either preheat your electric tabletop grill or get your barbecue grill going. Either way, cut your salmon into 4 portions, brush them all over with the oil, and then grill for 4 to 6 minutes in the electric grill or 4 to 5 minutes per side on your barbecue grill, or until they're opaque clear through. Thicker steaks will take a bit longer. Serve with the peach salsa.

**Yield:** 4 servings

**Nutritional Analysis:** Each will have: 251 calories; 9 g fat; 34 g protein; 6 g carbohydrates; 1 g fiber; 5 g usable carbs.

| | | | | | |
|---|---|---|---|---|---|
| Potassium (mg): | 666 mg | Vitamin C (mg): | 6 mg | Thiamin/B1 (mg): | 0.4 mg |
| Calcium (mg): | 28 mg | Vitamin A (i.u.): | 535 i.u. | Riboflavin/B2 (mg): | 0.3 mg |
| Iron (mg): | 2 mg | Vitamin B6 (mg): | 0.4 mg | Folacin (mcg): | 12 mcg |
| Zinc (mg): | 1 mg | Vitamin B12 (mcg): | 5.1 mcg | Niacin/B3 (mg): | 9 mg |

# Salmon with Spiced Cider Jus

Ray, who tested the Pork Tenderloin with Spiced Cider Jus (see page 423), suggested testing a similar sauce with salmon. Once he did, he raved, "Tastes great. Looks fabulous. Tastes great! Looks fabulous! Well, at any rate, it's a great way to impress a date or your boss."

2 pounds (905 g) salmon fillets, with skin
1/2 cup (120 ml) apple cider
1/2 cup (120 ml) cider vinegar
1 1/2 tablespoons (2.25 g) Splenda
3/4 cup (175 ml) chicken broth
1/2 cup (65 g) chopped onion
3 whole allspice berries
1/2 teaspoon anise seed
1 1/2 teaspoons dried thyme
2 cinnamon sticks
1 bay leaf
1 tablespoon (14 g) butter
1/2 teaspoon xanthan gum
3/8 ounce (about 15 g) chives
1 lemon
2 tablespoons (28 ml) olive oil
1/2 tablespoon black pepper

You should have about 3 salmon fillets. Cut them down the center (lengthwise) to make 6 portions.

Combine the apple cider, vinegar, Splenda, chicken broth, onion, allspice, anise, thyme, cinnamon, and bay leaf in a heavy, nonreactive saucepan. Put it over medium heat, and simmer till it's reduced by half.

Strain the mixture, put it back in the saucepan, and cook it down to 1/2 cup (120 ml). Whisk in the butter.

Use the xanthan to thicken the sauce. (You will probably need to use a shaker to do this, to prevent lumps.) You want it to reach the consistency of thin honey.

Chop the chives into pieces less than 1/2 inch (1.25 cm) long. Slice the lemon into slices about 1/4 inch (6 mm) thick. Leave about 1/2 inch (1.25 cm) of the ends.

While all that simmering is happening, rub the flesh side of your salmon fillets lightly with the oil, sprinkle the flesh side generously with pepper, and leave this side up. Sprinkle the chives over this, and then add a slice of lemon on top.

When the sauce is done, broil the salmon steaks flesh side up for about 8 minutes. Put the salmon on plates and cover it with the sauce to serve.

**Yield:** 6 servings

**Nutritional Analysis:** Each will have: 278 calories; 12 g fat; 31 g protein; 11 g carbohydrates; 4 g fiber; 7 g usable carbs.

| | | | | | |
|---|---|---|---|---|---|
| Potassium (mg): | 666 mg | Vitamin C (mg): | 10 mg | Thiamin/B1 (mg): | 0.3 mg |
| Calcium (mg): | 117 mg | Vitamin A (i.u.): | 375 i.u. | Riboflavin/B2 (mg): | 0.2 mg |
| Iron (mg): | 4 mg | Vitamin B6 (mg): | 0.4 mg | Folacin (mcg): | 16 mcg |
| Zinc (mg): | 1 mg | Vitamin B12 (mcg): | 4.6 mcg | Niacin/B3 (mg): | 8 mg |

**Note:** Your guests should be told to toss the lemons, but they sure make the dish look good!

## Smokey Lime-and-Rosemary Grilled Salmon

I came up with this smoky marinade to give that "charcoal grilled" flavor to salmon cooked in an electric tabletop grill—but it'll work fine outside, too.

- 1/4 cup (60 ml) lime juice
- 1 tablespoon (2 g) fresh rosemary, chopped, or 1/2 tablespoon dried ground rosemary
- 1/2 teaspoon prepared horseradish
- 1 1/2 teaspoons (7.5 ml) Liquid Smoke
- 12 ounces (340 g) salmon fillet, with skin

Mix together the lime juice, rosemary, horseradish, and Liquid Smoke. Heat this mixture in the microwave for 1 minute at 60 percent power, to blend the flavors.

Let it cool for a minute or two while you cut the salmon into 3 portions and put them in a zipper-lock bag.

Pour the cooled marinade in and seal the bag, pressing out the air as you go. Turn the bag a few times to coat. Toss the bag into your fridge, and let it sit for at least a few hours.

When dinnertime rolls around, pull the bag out of the fridge and preheat your electric tabletop grill or your outdoor barbecue grill. If your grill rack doesn't have a nonstick coating, brush it with oil just before cooking. Pour off the marinade into a small saucepan.

Grill the salmon for 5 minutes in your electric tabletop grill, or for about 4 minutes per side on your outdoor barbecue grill; you want the fish done through, but not dried out! Baste the fish with the reserved marinade halfway through cooking. When the fish is done, transfer it to serving plates.

Put the pan of marinade over high heat, and bring it to a boil. Boil it hard for a couple of minutes, to kill any raw fish germs. Now pour a little of the marinade over each serving of fish.

**Yield:** 3 servings

**Nutritional Analysis:** Each will have: 139 calories; 4 g fat; 23 g protein; 2 g carbohydrates; trace fiber; 2 g usable carbs.

| | | | | | |
|---|---|---|---|---|---|
| Potassium (mg): | 394 mg | Vitamin C (mg): | 7 mg | Thiamin/B1 (mg): | 0.2 mg |
| Calcium (mg): | 19 mg | Vitamin A (i.u.): | 153 i.u. | Riboflavin/B2 (mg): | 0.2 mg |
| Iron (mg): | 1 mg | Vitamin B6 (mg): | 0.2 mg | Folacin (mcg): | 7 mcg |
| Zinc (mg): | 1 mg | Vitamin B12 (mcg): | 34 mcg | Niacin/B3 (mg): | 6 mg |

## Deviled Pollock

Pollock is available frozen at my grocery year 'round, and it is invariably cheap. If you prefer, however, you can use cod. This recipe is very easy, and quite tasty.

- 6 pollock fillets
- 2 tablespoons (30 g) brown mustard
- 2 tablespoons (30 g) prepared horseradish
- 4 teaspoons (20 g) no-sugar-added ketchup
- 1/2 teaspoon chili garlic paste

Preheat the oven to 325°F (170°C, or gas mark 3).

Spray a shallow baking dish with nonstick cooking spray, and lay the fillets in it.

Mix together the mustard, horseradish, ketchup, and chili garlic paste. Spread this mixture over the fish, coating the top surface evenly.

Bake for 20 minutes, and serve.

**Yield:** 3 servings

**Nutritional Analysis:** Each will have: 142 calories; 2 g fat; 27 g protein; 2 g carbohydrates; trace fiber; 2 g usable carbs.

| | | | | | |
|---|---|---|---|---|---|
| Potassium (mg): | 540 mg | Vitamin C (mg): | 3 mg | Thiamin/B1 (mg): | 0.1 mg |
| Calcium (mg): | 26 mg | Vitamin A (i.u.): | 102 i.u. | Riboflavin/B2 (mg): | 0.1 mg |
| Iron (mg): | 1 mg | Vitamin B6 (mg): | 0.1 mg | Folacin (mcg): | 11 mcg |
| Zinc (mg): | 1 mg | Vitamin B12 (mcg): | 4.8 mcg | Niacin/B3 (mg): | 2 mg |

## Pollock Poached in Spicy Sauce

This has a sort of curried thing going on. A bed of cauli-rice would be nice with this, but it's hardly essential.

8 ounces (225 g) tomato sauce
1 clove garlic, peeled and crushed
1/2 teaspoon ground coriander
1/2 teaspoon ground cumin
1/2 teaspoon chili garlic paste
1 pound (455 g) pollock fillets
1/4 cup (15 g) chopped fresh cilantro

Give a big skillet a shot of nonstick cooking spray, and put it over medium-low heat. Pour in the tomato sauce. Add the garlic, coriander, cumin, and chili garlic paste, and stir it all up. Bring to a simmer, and let it cook for about 5 minutes, to blend the flavors.

While that's happening, cut the fish fillets into biggish chunks. Lay them in the tomato sauce and let the fish poach for 3 to 4 minutes, turn it, and give it another 3 minutes or so. Transfer it to serving plates, spooning the sauce over the fish. Scatter the chopped cilantro on top, and serve.

**Yield:** 3 servings

**Nutritional Analysis:** Each will have: 150 calories; 1 g fat; 27 g protein; 6 g carbohydrates; 1 g fiber; 5 g usable carbs.

| | | | | | |
|---|---|---|---|---|---|
| Potassium (mg): | 795 mg | Vitamin C (mg): | 5 mg | Thiamin/B1 (mg): | 0.1 mg |
| Calcium (mg): | 26 mg | Vitamin A (i.u.): | 931 i.u. | Riboflavin/B2 (mg): | 0.1 mg |
| Iron (mg): | 1 mg | Vitamin B6 (mg): | 0.2 mg | Folacin (mcg): | 13 mcg |
| Zinc (mg): | 1 mg | Vitamin B12 (mcg): | 4.7 mcg | Niacin/B3 (mg): | 3 mg |

## Mexican Baked Pollock

Quick, easy, tasty, and pretty to look at.

- 1 pound (455 g) pollock fillets
- 1/2 green bell pepper, chopped
- 1/2 cup (65 g) frozen corn kernels, thawed
- 1/2 cup (110 g) salsa

This is way easy! Preheat the oven to 450°F (230°C, or gas mark 8). Spray a glass baking dish with nonstick cooking spray.

If the fillets are too long to fit in your baking dish (mine were), cut 'em in half. Lay 'em in the baking dish. Scatter the pepper and corn over them, then top with the salsa. Cover with a lid or aluminum foil. Bake for 25 minutes, and serve.

**Yield:** 3 servings

**Nutritional Analysis:** Each will have: 164 calories; 2 g fat; 28 g protein; 10 g carbohydrates; 2 g fiber; 8 g usable carbs.

| | | | | | |
|---|---|---|---|---|---|
| Potassium (mg): | 678 mg | Vitamin C (mg): | 25 mg | Thiamin/B1 (mg): | 0.1 mg |
| Calcium (mg): | 23 mg | Vitamin A (i.u.): | 485 i.u. | Riboflavin/B2 (mg): | 0.1 mg |
| Iron (mg): | 1 mg | Vitamin B6 (mg): | 0.2 mg | Folacin (mcg): | 26 mcg |
| Zinc (mg): | 1 mg | Vitamin B12 (mcg): | 4.7 mcg | Niacin/B3 (mg): | 3 mg |

## Orange Perch

Fresh-tasting!

Zest and juice of 1 orange

2 tablespoons (30 g) brown mustard

2 teaspoons (1 g) Splenda

1 pound (455 g) perch fillets

Spray a big skillet with nonstick cooking spray, and put it over medium heat. Grate about 1 teaspoon of orange zest into it, then cut the orange in half and squeeze in all the juice. Stir in the mustard and Splenda. Bring this mixture to a simmer.

Lay the perch fillets in the sauce, turn the burner down to medium-low, cover the skillet, and let it simmer for 3 to 4 minutes. Turn the fillets over and let them simmer for another 2 minutes, or until they're opaque and flaky. Serve with the sauce poured over them.

**Yield:** 2 servings

**Nutritional Analysis:** Each will have: 254 calories; 3 g fat; 46 g protein; 9 g carbohydrates; 2 g fiber; 7 g usable carbs.

| | | | | | |
|---|---|---|---|---|---|
| Potassium (mg): | 749 mg | Vitamin C (mg): | 39 mg | Thiamin/B1 (mg): | 0.2 mg |
| Calcium (mg): | 227 mg | Vitamin A (i.u.): | 198 i.u. | Riboflavin/B2 (mg): | 0.3 mg |
| Iron (mg): | 2 mg | Vitamin B6 (mg): | 0.3 mg | Folacin (mcg): | 32 mcg |
| Zinc (mg): | 3 mg | Vitamin B12 (mcg): | 4.3 mcg | Niacin/B3 (mg): | 4 mg |

## Poached Trout with Dill

Classic.

2 tablespoons (28 ml) dry white wine

1 tablespoon (14 ml) lemon juice

1 tablespoon (2 g) snipped fresh dill weed, or 1 teaspoon dried dill weed

12 ounces (340 g) trout fillet

Salt and pepper

In a shallow, nonreactive pan with a lid, combine the wine and lemon juice. Put the pan over medium heat, and bring the wine and lemon juice to a simmer. Stir in the dill, and lay the trout fillets skin side up in the liquid. Turn the heat down to low, cover the pan, and set a timer for 8 minutes.

Carefully transfer the trout fillets to 2 serving plates, turning them skin side down in the process. Pour the pan liquid over them, salt and pepper lightly, and serve.

**Yield:** 2 servings

**Nutritional Analysis:** Each will have: 265 calories; 11 g fat; 35 g protein; 1 g carbohydrates; trace fiber; 1 g usable carbs.

| | | | | | |
|---|---|---|---|---|---|
| Potassium (mg): | 652 mg | Vitamin C (mg): | 5 mg | Thiamin/B1 (mg): | 0.6 mg |
| Calcium (mg): | 84 mg | Vitamin A (i.u.): | 130 i.u. | Riboflavin/B2 (mg): | 0.6 mg |
| Iron (mg): | 3 mg | Vitamin B6 (mg): | 0.3 mg | Folacin (mcg): | 24 mcg |
| Zinc (mg): | 1 mg | Vitamin B12 (mcg): | 13.2 mcg | Niacin/B3 (mg): | 8 mg |

# Teriyaki Grilled Trout

1/3 cup (80 ml) Teriyaki Sauce (see page 502)

20 ounces (560 g) trout fillets

2 scallions, sliced, including the crisp part of the green

Easy! Pour the teriyaki sauce into a glass pie plate or any other plate with a rim. Lay the trout fillets in it, skin side down, then flip them over right away. (You're just getting a little teriyaki on the skin, but you want most of the marinade on the meaty part.) Let it sit for 15 minutes.

Preheat your electric tabletop grill. When it's hot, grill the fish for just 3 minutes, basting about halfway through with the marinade. Remove to serving plates when done.

Scatter the scallions on top, and serve.

**Yield:** 4 servings

**Nutritional Analysis:** Each will have: 229 calories; 9 g fat; 30 g protein; 2 g carbohydrates; trace fiber; 2 g usable carbs.

| | | | | | |
|---|---|---|---|---|---|
| Potassium (mg): | 569 mg | Vitamin C (mg): | 2 mg | Thiamin/B1 (mg): | 0.5 mg |
| Calcium (mg): | 70 mg | Vitamin A (i.u.): | 111 i.u. | Riboflavin/B2 (mg): | 0.5 mg |
| Iron (mg): | 3 mg | Vitamin B6 (mg): | 0.3 mg | Folacin (mcg): | 26 mcg |
| Zinc (mg): | 1 mg | Vitamin B12 (mcg): | 11 mcg | Niacin/B3 (mg): | 7 mg |

## Teriyaki Tuna Steak with Wasabi Mayonnaise

This is an amazing flavor combination! Don't overcook your tuna steaks, or they'll get tough and dry.

8 ounces (225 g) tuna steak, cut 1-inch (2.5-cm) thick
2 tablespoons (28 ml) Teriyaki Sauce (see page 502)
2 tablespoons (28 g) Wasabi Mayonnaise (see page 490)
2 scallions, thinly sliced

Put the tuna on a plate, and coat both sides with the teriyaki sauce. Let it sit for 10 minutes.

Preheat your electric tabletop grill. When it's hot, put the tuna in the grill, and spoon any teriyaki sauce left on the plate over it. Grill for 4 minutes.

Top with the Wasabi Mayonnaise and scallions, and serve.

**Yield:** 2 servings

**Nutritional Analysis:** Each will have: 229 calories; 8 g fat; 27 g protein; 9 g carbohydrates; trace fiber; 9 g usable carbs.

| | | | | | |
|---|---|---|---|---|---|
| Potassium (mg): | 332 mg | Vitamin C (mg): | 3 mg | Thiamin/B1 (mg): | 0.3 mg |
| Calcium (mg): | 20 mg | Vitamin A (i.u.): | 2535 i.u. | Riboflavin/B2 (mg): | 0.3 mg |
| Iron (mg): | 1 mg | Vitamin B6 (mg): | 0.5 mg | Folacin (mcg): | 12 mcg |
| Zinc (mg): | 1 mg | Vitamin B12 (mcg): | 10.7 mcg | Niacin/B3 (mg): | 10 mg |

## Tuna Cakes

I confess to a seriously lowbrow love of canned tuna. I adore the stuff; I always have. This turns a can of tuna into a tasty supper for two—and it's easy to double.

4 teaspoons (20 g) butter
1/4 cup (30 g) finely diced celery
2 tablespoons (20 g) minced red onion
1/2 teaspoon curry powder
1/4 teaspoon grated gingerroot
1 can (6 ounces, or 170 g) tuna in water
1 tablespoon (14 g) light mayonnaise

1 egg yolk

1/2 teaspoon dry mustard

1 tablespoon (4 g) minced fresh parsley

1 tablespoon (4 g) minced fresh cilantro

1/4 teaspoon pepper

3 tablespoons (20 g) bread crumbs (from whole grain or low-carb bread, as you prefer)

2 tablespoons (28 g) Chili Cocktail Sauce (see page 479)

Spray a medium-size heavy skillet with nonstick cooking spray, and put it over medium-high heat. Add 1 teaspoon (5 g) of the butter. When it's melted, add the celery and onion, and sauté till they're just starting to soften.

Stir in the curry powder and ginger. Sauté for just another minute, then remove from the heat.

Drain the tuna and put it in a mixing bowl. Flake it up. Add the sautéed vegetables, mayonnaise, egg yolk, mustard, parsley, cilantro, and pepper. Mix it all up quite well.

Form the mixture into 2 patties, pressing together firmly.

Put the bread crumbs on a plate, and dip the patties in them, coating both sides lightly. At this point, you can refrigerate the patties for a while if you like, or you can go straight to cooking them.

When you want to cook them, spray a medium-size heavy skillet with nonstick cooking spray, and put it over medium-high heat. Add one-half of the remaining tablespoon of butter. When it's melted, slosh it around to cover the bottom of the skillet, then add the tuna cakes. Sauté until they're golden on the bottom. Add the remaining butter, turn the patties, and brown the other side. Serve with the Chili Cocktail Sauce.

**Yield:** 2 servings

**Nutritional Analysis:** Each will have: 272 calories; 13 g fat; 25 g protein; 12 g carbohydrates; 1 g fiber; 11 g usable carbs.

| | | | | | |
|---|---|---|---|---|---|
| Potassium (mg): | 335 mg | Vitamin C (mg): | 6 mg | Thiamin/B1 (mg): | 0.1 mg |
| Calcium (mg): | 64 mg | Vitamin A (i.u.): | 917 i.u. | Riboflavin/B2 (mg): | 0.2 mg |
| Iron (mg): | 3 mg | Vitamin B6 (mg): | 0.4 mg | Folacin (mcg): | 37 mcg |
| Zinc (mg): | 1 mg | Vitamin B12 (mcg): | 2.8 mcg | Niacin/B3 (mg): | 12 mg |

# Scallops with Stoplight Peppers and Creamy Lime Sauce

My grocery store sells packages of one green pepper, one yellow pepper, and one red pepper—they're labeled "Stoplight Peppers," and they are so pretty! That's what inspired this dish.

1 tablespoon (14 ml) lime juice
3 tablespoons (45 g) light mayonnaise
3 tablespoons (45 g) plain yogurt
1 tablespoon (14 g) butter
1 tablespoon (14 ml) olive oil
1 green bell pepper, seeded and sliced
1 red bell pepper, seeded and sliced
1 yellow bell pepper, seeded and sliced
1 1/2 pounds (670 g) bay scallops
1/2 teaspoon black pepper
Lime-Ginger Cream Sauce (see page 500)

Stir the lime juice, mayo, and yogurt together, and stash in the fridge.

Put a big skillet over medium-high heat, and add 1/2 tablespoon (7 g) of the butter and 1/2 tablespoon (7 ml) of the olive oil. Sauté the green, red, and yellow peppers until they're tender. Remove them from the heat and divide them up on 5 serving plates.

Drain the scallops well. Add the remaining butter and oil to the skillet, and add the scallops. Season with up to 1/2 teaspoon black pepper and sauté for just a few minutes, until they're opaque.

Pile the scallops on top of the peppers, and top with Creamy Lime Sauce.

**Yield:** 5 servings

**Nutritional Analysis:** Each will have: 211 calories; 8 g fat; 24 g protein; 10 g carbohydrates; 1 g fiber; 9 g usable carbs.

| | | | | | |
|---|---|---|---|---|---|
| Potassium (mg): | 595 mg | Vitamin C (mg): | 115 mg | Thiamin/B1 (mg): | trace |
| Calcium (mg): | 53 mg | Vitamin A (i.u.): | 1730 i.u. | Riboflavin/B2 (mg): | trace |
| Iron (mg): | 1 mg | Vitamin B6 (mg): | 0.3 mg | Folacin (mcg): | 39 mcg |
| Zinc (mg): | 1 mg | Vitamin B12 (mcg): | 2.0 mcg | Niacin/B3 (mg): | 2 mg |

## Scallops with Ginger

How much would you pay for this at a fancy restaurant?

- 1 pound (455 g) sea scallops
- 1 tablespoon (14 g) butter
- 1 tablespoon (8 g) grated gingerroot
- 8 scallions, sliced diagonally
- 1/4 cup (60 ml) dry vermouth
- 1 cup (230 g) light sour cream
- Salt and pepper
- 2 tablespoons (8 g) chopped fresh parsley

Split the scallops in half horizontally, making 2 thinner rounds of each. If the tough little muscle is still attached to one side, cut that off. Pat the scallops dry.

Spray a big, heavy skillet with nonstick cooking spray, and put it over medium-high heat. Melt the butter in it. Add the scallops, and sauté them for 2 to 3 minutes, or until they're turning golden—but do not overcook!

Remove the scallops with a slotted spoon and put them on 3 serving plates. Keep in a warm place.

Now add the ginger and scallions to the pan, and stir-fry for just a minute or two. Add the vermouth and let it cook down till it's almost all evaporated. Stir in the sour cream and heat through, but don't let it boil or your sauce will crack. Add salt and pepper to taste. Spoon the sauce over the scallops, sprinkle a bit of parsley on each plate, and serve.

**Yield:** 3 servings

**Nutritional Analysis:** Each will have: 232 calories; 6 g fat; 28 g protein; 11 g carbohydrates; 1 g fiber; 10 g usable carbs.

| | | | | | |
|---|---|---|---|---|---|
| Potassium (mg): | 629 mg | Vitamin C (mg): | 15 mg | Thiamin/B1 (mg): | trace |
| Calcium (mg): | 102 mg | Vitamin A (i.u.): | 504 i.u. | Riboflavin/B2 (mg): | trace |
| Iron (mg): | 1 mg | Vitamin B6 (mg): | 0.2 mg | Folacin (mcg): | 54 mcg |
| Zinc (mg): | 2 mg | Vitamin B12 (mcg): | 2.3 mcg | Niacin/B3 (mg): | 2 mg |

## Luigi Gonzalez Catfish

So-called because it combines Italian and Mexican flavors.

1 pound (455 g) catfish fillets

6 tablespoons (90 ml) bottled light Italian salad dressing

4 teaspoons (20 ml) lime juice

1 tablespoon (14 ml) tequila

Lay the fish in a glass pie plate. Mix the dressing, lime juice, and tequila together, and pour it over the fish. Let it marinate for 15 minutes.

Spray a big, heavy skillet with nonstick cooking spray, and put it over medium-high heat. When it's hot, lay the catfish in it. Let it cook for a couple of minutes, then turn it. Pour the marinade left in the dish over the fish. Let the whole thing cook together for another 2 to 3 minutes, or until the fish flakes easily. Serve.

**Yield:** 4 servings

**Nutritional Analysis:** Each will have: 141 calories; 5 g fat; 19 g protein; 2 g carbohydrates; trace fiber; 2 g usable carbs.

| | | | | | |
|---|---|---|---|---|---|
| Potassium (mg): | 415 mg | Vitamin C (mg): | 2 mg | Thiamin/B1 (mg): | 0.2 mg |
| Calcium (mg): | 17 mg | Vitamin A (i.u.): | 57 i.u. | Riboflavin/B2 (mg): | 0.1 mg |
| Iron (mg): | trace | Vitamin B6 (mg): | 0.1 mg | Folacin (mcg): | 12 mcg |
| Zinc (mg): | 1 mg | Vitamin B12 (mcg): | 2.5 mcg | Niacin/B3 (mg): | 2 mg |

# Pan-Fried Catfish

My husband's favorite! The cornmeal gives this a classic taste. Don't be afraid to use bacon grease if you want to—remember, it has more monounsaturated fat than saturated fat.

- 1/4 cup (70 g) whole grain cornmeal
- 1/4 cup (30 g) homemade almond meal
- 1 teaspoon Creole seasoning
- 1 pound (455 g) catfish fillets
- 1 1/2 tablespoons (21 g) butter or bacon grease

In a brown paper bag, combine the cornmeal, almond meal, and Creole seasoning. Hold the bag closed and shake it vigorously to mix. Now put the catfish fillets into the bag, one at a time, and shake to coat. Lay each fillet on a plate as it's coated.

Spray a big, heavy skillet with nonstick cooking spray and put it over medium-high heat. When it's hot, add the butter or bacon grease, and slosh it around as it melts.

Lay the fillets in the skillet, and sauté them for about 3 minutes per side, or until they're golden and cooked through.

**Yield:** 4 servings

**Nutritional Analysis:** Each will have: 237 calories; 12 g fat; 21 g protein; 12 g carbohydrates; 3 g fiber; 9 g usable carbs.

| | | | | | |
|---|---|---|---|---|---|
| Potassium (mg): | 456 mg | Vitamin C (mg): | 1 mg | Thiamin/B1 (mg): | 0.2 mg |
| Calcium (mg): | 39 mg | Vitamin A (i.u.): | 219 i.u. | Riboflavin/B2 (mg): | 0.1 mg |
| Iron (mg): | 1 mg | Vitamin B6 (mg): | 0.1 mg | Folacin (mcg): | 15 mcg |
| Zinc (mg): | 1 mg | Vitamin B12 (mcg): | 2.5 mcg | Niacin/B3 (mg): | 2 mg |

## Sun-Dried Tomato-Portobello Salmon Roast

Julie calls this "An 'I-can't-believe-this-could-be-diet-y' dish that you would order again and again in a restaurant!"

2 tablespoons (7 g) chopped sun-dried tomatoes

2 tablespoons (28 ml) boiling water

8 ounces (225 g) salmon fillet, cut into 2 pieces about the same shape

1 tablespoon (14 ml) olive oil

1/4 cup (25 g) sliced small Portobello mushrooms

1 ounce (28 g) provolone cheese, sliced

1 teaspoon minced parsley

Preheat the oven to 350°F (180°C, or gas mark 4).

Pour the boiling water over the sun-dried tomatoes. Let them sit while you use a sharp knife to remove the skin from the salmon, if the nice fish guy at the grocery store didn't do it for you.

Spray a small skillet with nonstick cooking spray, and add 2 teaspoons (10 ml) of the oil. Sauté the mushrooms until they soften and change color.

Spray a shallow baking tin with nonstick spray, and lay one slab of salmon fillet in it. Place the provolone on top of it. Drain the excess water off of the tomatoes, and make a layer of them, too. Add a layer of mushrooms, and finally lay the second piece of salmon on top. Pierce with a few toothpicks or skewers to keep the layers together.

Use a basting brush to brush your salmon roast with the remaining oil. Sprinkle on the parsley, and slide the whole thing into the oven for 20 to 30 minutes.

Slice in half through the layers to serve.

**Yield:** 2 servings

**Nutritional Analysis:** Each will have: 252 calories; 15 g fat; 27 g protein; 3 g carbohydrates; 1 g fiber; 2 g usable carbs.

| | | | | | |
|---|---|---|---|---|---|
| Potassium (mg): | 537 mg | Vitamin C (mg): | 2 mg | Thiamin/B1 (mg): | 0.3 mg |
| Calcium (mg): | 127 mg | Vitamin A (i.u.): | 311 i.u. | Riboflavin/B2 (mg): | 0.3 mg |
| Iron (mg): | 1 mg | Vitamin B6 (mg): | 0.3 mg | Folacin (mcg): | 11 mcg |
| Zinc (mg): | 1 mg | Vitamin B12 (mcg): | 3.6 mcg | Niacin/B3 (mg): | 6 mg |

# Poached Tuna Steaks in the Italian Manner

Great on presentation. A sure-fire recipe to impress guests.

- 2 large celery ribs
- 2 large carrots
- 1 medium onion
- 1 bay leaf
- 2 teaspoons (12 g) salt
- 1½ pounds (670 g) tuna steaks, cut into 4 pieces
- 2 cloves garlic
- ¼ cup (15 g) chopped parsley
- ¼ cup (60 ml) extra virgin olive oil
- 1 lemon, quartered
- Salt and pepper

Run the celery, carrots, and onion through the shredding blade of your food processor. Spray a big, heavy skillet with nonstick cooking spray, and add the shredded veggies, bay leaf, and salt. Cover with 2½ to 3 inches (6.25 to 7.5 cm) of water.

Turn the heat to medium-low, cover the skillet, and let the whole thing simmer for one-half hour. This will make a flavorful veggie broth to poach your tuna in.

When the broth is done simmering, slide the tuna steaks into the broth. Turn the whole thing to low, and let the fish poach for 15 to 25 minutes. (Don't overcook.) While that's happening, mince the garlic and parsley together.

Lift each tuna steak out with a slotted pancake turner, let it drain, and put it on a serving plate. Sprinkle with the parsley/garlic mixture, drizzle each serving with 1 tablespoon (14 ml) of olive oil, salt and pepper lightly, add a lemon quarter to each plate for squeezing over the fish, and serve.

**Yield:** 4 servings

**Nutritional Analysis:** Each will have: 400 calories; 22 g fat; 41 g protein; 9 g carbohydrates; 2 g fiber; 7 g usable carbs.

| | | | | | |
|---|---|---|---|---|---|
| Potassium (mg): | 694 mg | Vitamin C (mg): | 20 mg | Thiamin/B1 (mg): | 0.5 mg |
| Calcium (mg): | 56 mg | Vitamin A (i.u.): | 14072 i.u. | Riboflavin/B2 (mg): | 0.5 mg |
| Iron (mg): | 2 mg | Vitamin B6 (mg): | 0.9 mg | Folacin (mcg): | 26 mcg |
| Zinc (mg): | 1 mg | Vitamin B12 (mcg): | 16 mcg | Niacin/B3 (mg): | 15 mg |

## Salmon Steaks with Lime-Ginger Cream Sauce

2 tablespoons (28 ml) peanut oil or macadamia nut oil

2 tablespoons (28 ml) lime juice, or the juice of one lime

1 tablespoon (8 g) grated gingerroot

1/4 teaspoon pepper

2 pounds (905 g) salmon steaks

Lime-Ginger Cream Sauce (see page 500)

In a small bowl, combine the oil, lime juice, ginger, and pepper.

Place the steaks in a zipper-lock bag, and pour the marinade over the top. Seal, pressing out the air as you go. Turn the bag to coat the fish, then toss it in the fridge for at least 30 minutes.

When the marinating time is up, preheat your electric tabletop grill. Pull the fish out of the fridge, pour off the marinade, and reserve. Grill for 5 to 6 minutes, basting halfway through with the marinade. Serve with the Lime-Ginger Cream Sauce.

**Yield:** 4 servings

**Nutritional Analysis:** Each will have: 428 calories; 21 g fat; 52 g protein; 4 g carbohydrates; trace fiber; 4 g usable carbs.

| | | | | | |
|---|---|---|---|---|---|
| Potassium (mg): | 856 mg | Vitamin C (mg): | 4 mg | Thiamin/B1 (mg): | 0.5 mg |
| Calcium (mg): | 105 mg | Vitamin A (i.u.): | 568 i.u. | Riboflavin/B2 (mg): | 0.4 mg |
| Iron (mg): | 2 mg | Vitamin B6 (mg): | 0.5 mg | Folacin (mcg): | 19 mcg |
| Zinc (mg): | 2 mg | Vitamin B12 (mcg): | 7.2 mcg | Niacin/B3 (mg): | 11 mg |

**Note:** Use the time while your salmon marinades to make up your Lime-Ginger Cream Sauce.

# Halibut with Lemon Herb Sauce

6 tablespoons (90 ml) lemon juice

3 tablespoons (11 g) chopped fresh basil

3 tablespoons (11 g) chopped fresh parsley

5 tablespoons (75 ml) extra virgin olive oil

3 tablespoons (11 g) fresh chives chopped into 1-inch (2.5-cm) pieces

1 medium red bell pepper, sliced into rings

2$^{1}/_{4}$ pounds (1 kg) halibut fillets, cut into 6 servings

Salt and pepper

Put the lemon juice, basil, parsley, and 4 tablespoons (60 ml) of the oil in your food processor with the S-blade in place. Pulse until pureed. Add salt and pepper to taste.

Brush the fillets with the remaining oil, and salt and pepper them lightly. Broil them for about 5 minutes per side, or until just opaque through. Transfer to 6 serving plates. Sprinkle the chives over the fish, spoon the lemon herb sauce over that, arrange the pepper rings on top, and serve.

**Yield:** 6 servings

**Nutritional Analysis:** Each will have: 297 calories; 15 g fat; 36 g protein; 3 g carbohydrates; 1 g fiber; 2 g usable carbs.

| | | | | | |
|---|---|---|---|---|---|
| Potassium (mg): | 840 mg | Vitamin C (mg): | 52 mg | Thiamin/B1 (mg): | 0.1 mg |
| Calcium (mg): | 89 mg | Vitamin A (i.u.): | 1611 i.u. | Riboflavin/B2 (mg): | 0.1 mg |
| Iron (mg): | 2 mg | Vitamin B6 (mg): | 0.6 mg | Folacin (mcg): | 25 mcg |
| Zinc (mg): | 1 mg | Vitamin B12 (mcg): | 2.0 mcg | Niacin/B3 (mg): | 10 mg |

## Ginger-Wasabi Scallops

When my husband first tried this, his eyes got very big. Then he smiled and gave me a thumbs-up!

1/4 cup (60 ml) soy sauce
1/4 cup (60 ml) dry sherry
1/2 teaspoon wasabi paste
1 teaspoon (.5 g) Splenda
2 teaspoons (5 g) grated gingerroot
2 cloves garlic, peeled and very finely minced
1 tablespoon (14 ml) peanut oil
1 pound (455 g) sea scallops
3 scallions, minced

Mix together the soy sauce, sherry, wasabi paste, Splenda, ginger, and garlic. Have this in a cup or dish by the stove.

Spray a big, heavy skillet with nonstick cooking spray, and put it over medium heat. Add the peanut oil and let it get hot before you add the scallops. Sear them for a few minutes, until they're browned, then flip them over and sear the other side.

Add the sauce to the skillet. Let it simmer for a couple of minutes, then flip the scallops again, and let the whole thing cook for another couple of minutes. Let the sauce cook down until it's slightly syrupy.

Put the scallops on 3 plates, pour the sauce over them, and top each serving with a bit of minced scallion before serving.

**Yield:** 3 servings

**Nutritional Analysis:** Each will have: 218 calories; 6 g fat; 27 g protein; 8 g carbohydrates; 1 g fiber; 7 g usable carbs.

| | | | | | |
|---|---|---|---|---|---|
| Potassium (mg): | 597 mg | Vitamin C (mg): | 8 mg | Thiamin/B1 (mg): | trace |
| Calcium (mg): | 56 mg | Vitamin A (i.u.): | 133 i.u. | Riboflavin/B2 (mg): | trace |
| Iron (mg): | 1 mg | Vitamin B6 (mg): | 0.2 mg | Folacin (mcg): | 38 mcg |
| Zinc (mg): | 2 mg | Vitamin B12 (mcg): | 2.3 mcg | Niacin/B3 (mg): | 3 mg |

## Scallops with Orange-Sesame Dipping Sauce

2 tablespoons (15 g) sesame seeds

18 sea scallops

Salt and pepper

1 tablespoon (14 ml) peanut oil

1 tablespoon (14 ml) dark sesame oil

1 tablespoon (4 g) chopped fresh mint

1 tablespoon (4 g) chopped fresh cilantro

Orange-Sesame Dipping Sauce (see page 501)

Toast the sesame seeds by stirring them in a dry skillet over medium heat for a few minutes. Set them aside.

Spray a big, heavy skillet with nonstick cooking spray, and put it over high heat. While the skillet's heating up, sprinkle the scallops lightly with salt and pepper. When the skillet's hot, add the peanut and sesame oils, slosh to cover the bottom of the skillet, and then add the scallops. Sauté for 3 to 4 minutes per side, until they're just opaque in the center. Remove to 6 small plates.

Sprinkle each serving with mint and cilantro, then with 1 teaspoon of sesame seeds. Serve with the dipping sauce.

**Yield:** 6 servings

**Nutritional Analysis:** Each will have: 99 calories; 7 g fat; 6 g protein; 3 g carbohydrates; trace fiber; 3 g usable carbs.

| | | | | | |
|---|---|---|---|---|---|
| Potassium (mg): | 130 mg | Vitamin C (mg): | 2 mg | Thiamin/B1 (mg): | trace |
| Calcium (mg): | 40 mg | Vitamin A (i.u.): | 66 i.u. | Riboflavin/B2 (mg): | trace |
| Iron (mg): | 1 mg | Vitamin B6 (mg): | 0.1 mg | Folacin (mcg): | 9 mcg |
| Zinc (mg): | 1 mg | Vitamin B12 (mcg): | 0.5 mcg | Niacin/B3 (mg): | 1 mg |

## Ray's Salmon Patties

Here's a quick and simple supper from a can of salmon.

1 can (14 ounces, or 390 g) salmon
1 lemon
2 teaspoons (4 g) ground pepper
2 eggs
1/2 cup (50 g) wheat bran
1/2 cup (55 g) flax seed meal

Drain the salmon, put it in a mixing bowl, and flake it up. Grate the lemon rind into the bowl, then halve it and squeeze in the juice, too. Add the pepper, then the eggs. Mix everything together. Add the bran and flax meal and mix again, combining everything very well.

Let the mixture rest for 5 minutes, to give the dry ingredients a chance to absorb the excess moisture. Form the salmon mixture into 4 patties.

Spray a big, heavy skillet with nonstick cooking spray, and put it over medium heat. Fry the patties until they're browned and firm—about 5 minutes per side.

**Yield:** 4 servings

**Nutritional Analysis:** Each will have: 292 calories; 15 g fat; 28 g protein; 14 g carbohydrates; 9 g fiber; 5 g usable carbs.

| | | | | | |
|---|---|---|---|---|---|
| Potassium (mg): | 602 mg | Vitamin C (mg): | 8 mg | Thiamin/B1 (mg): | 0.1 mg |
| Calcium (mg): | 274 mg | Vitamin A (i.u.): | 201 i.u. | Riboflavin/B2 (mg): | 0.4 mg |
| Iron (mg): | 4 mg | Vitamin B6 (mg): | 0.6 mg | Folacin (mcg): | 87 mcg |
| Zinc (mg): | 3 mg | Vitamin B12 (mcg): | 4.6 mcg | Niacin/B3 (mg): | 8 mg |

**Note:** It's not a bad idea to squeeze the lemon into a little cup first, so you can easily remove the pits before adding the juice to the salmon.

## Chris's Salmon Bake

My pal Chris told me about a casserole like this. It sounded good but needed the carbs and calories reduced a bit. So I did that, and here's the result!

- 5 slices stale whole grain low-carb bread (or 100% whole wheat, if you can afford the carbs)
- 1 cup (235 ml) chicken broth
- 1 teaspoon chicken bouillon granules
- 1/4 teaspoon dry mustard
- 1 pound (455 g) canned salmon, flaked
- 2 eggs, beaten
- 1/2 teaspoon dried thyme
- 1 cup (120 g) grated reduced-fat cheddar cheese

Cut the bread into squares, like croutons. If you like, you can do this a day or two ahead and leave 'em out to get stale. If you don't think ahead, cut the bread into squares, put 'em on a cookie sheet, set your oven to its lowest setting, and slide 'em in for an hour or so.

Mix together the broth and bouillon concentrate until the bouillon is dissolved. Stir in the mustard. Mix this with the flaked salmon, dried bread squares, eggs, thyme, and 1/2 cup (60 g) of the cheese. Spray an 8 x 8-inch (20 x 20-cm) baking dish with nonstick cooking spray. Spread the salmon mixture in the dish and sprinkle the remaining cheese over the top.

Bake the whole thing at 325°F (170°C, or gas mark 3) for 20 to 25 minutes, or until it's set and lightly golden, then serve.

**Yield:** 4 servings

**Nutritional Analysis:** With low-carb bread, each will have: 202 calories; 10 g fat; 27 g protein; 1 g carbohydrates; trace fiber; 1 g usable carbs.

| | | | | | |
|---|---|---|---|---|---|
| Potassium (mg): | 452 mg | Vitamin C (mg): | trace | Thiamin/B1 (mg): | trace |
| Calcium (mg): | 259 mg | Vitamin A (i.u.): | 212 i.u. | Riboflavin/B2 (mg): | 0.3 mg |
| Iron (mg): | 2 mg | Vitamin B6 (mg): | 0.4 mg | Folacin (mcg): | 30 mcg |
| Zinc (mg): | 1 mg | Vitamin B12 (mcg): | 5.3 mcg | Niacin/B3 (mg): | 8 mg |

**Nutritional Analysis:** With whole wheat bread, each will have: 288 calories; 11 g fat; 30 g protein; 17 g carbohydrates; 2 fiber; 15 g usable carbs.

| | | | | | |
|---|---|---|---|---|---|
| Potassium (mg): | 540 mg | Vitamin C (mg): | trace | Thiamin/B1 (mg): | 0.1 mg |
| Calcium (mg): | 285 mg | Vitamin A (i.u.): | 212 i.u. | Riboflavin/B2 (mg): | 0.4 mg |
| Iron (mg): | 3 mg | Vitamin B6 (mg): | 0.4 mg | Folacin (mcg): | 47 mcg |
| Zinc (mg): | 2 mg | Vitamin B12 (mcg): | 5.3 mcg | Niacin/B3 (mg): | 10 mg |

## Tilapia in Oyster Sauce

Ray invented this Asian-inspired grilled tilapia. He recommends serving it on a bed of sautéed portobello mushrooms with parsley.

2 tablespoons (28 ml) oyster sauce

1 tablespoon (14 ml) soy sauce

1 tablespoon (14 ml) lemon juice

1 teaspoon chili garlic paste

1 clove garlic, minced

1 teaspoon (5 g) natural peanut butter

2 pounds (905 g) tilapia fillets, cut into 4 servings

In a bowl, whisk together the oyster sauce, soy sauce, lemon juice, chili garlic paste, garlic, and peanut butter. Lay your tilapia fillets on a plate, and coat both sides with the sauce. Let them sit for a few minutes while you preheat your electric tabletop grill.

Lay the fish in the grill, and cook for 2 minutes. Open the grill, baste the fish with the sauce left on the plate, turn, and baste the other side. Cook for another 3 minutes, then move the fillets to plates.

**Yield:** 4 servings

**Nutritional Analysis:** 4 servings, each with 200 calories; 2 g fat, 41 g protein; 2 g carbohydrate; trace fiber; 2 g usable carbs.

| | | | | | |
|---|---|---|---|---|---|
| Potassium (mg): | 963 mg | Vitamin C (mg): | 4 mg | Thiamin/B1 (mg): | 0.2 mg |
| Calcium (mg): | 40 mg | Vitamin A (i.u.): | 92 i.u. | Riboflavin/B2 (mg): | 0.2 mg |
| Iron (mg): | 1 mg | Vitamin B6 (mg): | 0.6 mg | Folacin (mcg): | 18 mcg |
| Zinc (mg): | 1 mg | Vitamin B12 (mcg): | 2.1 mcg | Niacin/B3 (mg): | 5 mg |

# Lemon-Lime Grilled Tilapia

Feel free to make this with any mild white fish.

2 teaspoons (4 g) pepper
2 pounds (905 g) tilapia fillets
1 lime
1 lemon
2 tablespoons (28 ml) red wine vinegar
3 tablespoons (45 ml) olive oil
1/3 ounce (9 g) fresh chives, chopped

Pepper the fillets, and put 'em in a big zipper-lock bag.

Pare away thin strips of lime rind with a vegetable peeler. Cut the strips of rind into skinny little threadlike strips.

Squeeze the lemon and lime juice into a bowl, and add the vinegar and oil. Whisk together, and add the strips of rind. Pour the whole thing into the bag with the chicken.

Seal the bag, leaving lots of air at the top. Turn and shake to spread the mix through the bag. Try and get the strips of rind distributed fairly evenly around the fillets. (Having air in the bag will help you manipulate the fillets to make this happen.) Once you have the mix distributed, open the top a bit and press out the air. Throw the bag in the fridge for at least several hours, and overnight would be great.

When dinnertime rolls around, preheat your electric tabletop grill. Pour the marinade off of the fillets and into a ceramic bowl or small saucepan.

Remove any strips of rind clinging to the fillets. Lay the fish in the grill, and sprinkle each fillet with chopped chives. Grill for 1 1/2 minutes, baste with the reserved marinade, and grill for another 1 1/2 minutes. Don't overcook the fish; you just want it opaque and starting to flake.

If your grill is small, you'll need to cook the fish in batches. Let the grill reheat for 2 to 3 minutes between each batch.

**Yield:** 4 servings

**Nutritional Analysis:** 4 servings each will have 288 calories; 12 g fat; 41g protein; 5 g carbohydrate; 1 g fiber; 4 g usable carbs.

| | | | | | |
|---|---|---|---|---|---|
| Potassium (mg): | 1004 mg | Vitamin C (mg): | 16 mg | Thiamin/B1 (mg): | 0.2 mg |
| Calcium (mg): | 53 mg | Vitamin A (i.u.): | 202 i.u. | Riboflavin/B2 (mg): | 0.2 mg |
| Iron (mg): | 1 mg | Vitamin B6 (mg): | 0.6 mg | Folacin (mcg): | 22 mcg |
| Zinc (mg): | 1 mg | Vitamin B12 (mcg): | 2.1 mcg | Niacin/B3 (mg): | 5 mg |

**Note:** A great way to pour off marinade from a zipper-lock bag is to snip a little bit off one corner of the bag and then pour the sauce out through the hole.

## Gingered Monkfish

This works equally well with lobster chunks, grouper, red snapper, or any other firm-fleshed fish. It looks very nice on the plate and can be served over a bed of cauli-rice to complete the meal.

1 pound (455 g) monkfish

1 tablespoon (8 g) grated gingerroot

1 tablespoon (15 g) no-sugar-added ketchup

2 teaspoons (10 g) chili garlic paste

6 ounces (170 g) thin spears asparagus

1 tablespoon (14 ml) peanut oil

3 scallions, sliced, including the crisp part of the green

1 teaspoon (5 ml) dark sesame oil

Use a sharp knife to remove any membrane from the monkfish, then cut it into thin, flat, round slices. Set them aside.

In a small dish, stir together the ginger, ketchup, and chili garlic paste. Brush this mixture over the monkfish slices and let it sit for 5 minutes.

Meanwhile, snap the ends off of the asparagus spears where they want to break naturally. Discard the ends and cut the spears into 1-inch (2.5-cm) pieces on the diagonal.

If you've got a wok, use it for this. If not, spray a big, heavy skillet with nonstick cooking spray. Put whatever pan you use over high heat, and add the peanut oil.

Add the monkfish, ginger sauce, asparagus, and scallions to the pan. Stir-fry very gently, so as not to break up the fish. Cook for about 5 minutes, or until the fish is done through and the vegetables are tender-crisp.

Drizzle in the sesame oil, toss gently to combine, and serve.

**Yield:** 4 servings

**Nutritional Analysis:** Each will have: 139 calories; 6 g fat; 17 g protein; 3 g carbohydrates; 1 g fiber; 2 g usable carbs.

| | | | | | |
|---|---|---|---|---|---|
| Potassium (mg): | 553 mg | Vitamin C (mg): | 6 mg | Thiamin/B1 (mg): | 0.1 mg |
| Calcium (mg): | 22 mg | Vitamin A (i.u.): | 285 i.u. | Riboflavin/B2 (mg): | 0.1 mg |
| Iron (mg): | 1 mg | Vitamin B6 (mg): | 0.3 mg | Folacin (mcg): | 44 mcg |
| Zinc (mg): | 1 mg | Vitamin B12 (mcg): | 1.0 mcg | Niacin/B3 (mg): | 3 mg |

chapter eleven

# Chicken and Turkey

What's not to like about poultry? Whether you're paying attention to calories, carbohydrates, or both, chicken and turkey are your friends. Chicken, in particular, is a world citizen, taking happily to a whole range of seasonings. You can serve the family poultry often and never hear, "This again?" That's especially true if you take advantage of the recipes in this chapter!

# Tasty Roasted Chicken

This recipe appeared in *500 Low-Carb Recipes*. I repeat it here because few things are simpler yet better than a plain roasted chicken—and it's inexpensive, too! Whole chickens frequently go on sale; I sometimes get them as low as 69 cents per pound. And now that most people buy their chicken cut up, there's something sort of festive about a whole roasted chicken.

1 whole chicken, about 5 pounds (2.3 kg)

1 heaping tablespoon (14 g) light mayonnaise

Salt

Pepper

Paprika

Onion powder

Preheat your oven to 375°F (190°C, or gas mark 5).

If your chicken was frozen, make sure it's completely thawed. If it's still a bit icy in the middle, run some hot water inside it until it's not icy anymore! Make sure you take out the giblets; if you've never cooked a whole chicken before, you'll find them in the body cavity.

Dry your chicken with paper towels and put it on a plate. Scoop your mayo out of the jar (and be sure that you don't get raw chicken germs in your mayonnaise jar!), and use it to give your chicken a nice massage. That's right, just rub that chicken all over with the mayonnaise, every inch of skin. Now sprinkle the chicken liberally with equal parts salt, pepper, paprika, and onion powder, on all sides. Put the chicken on a rack in a shallow roasting pan, and stick it in the oven. Leave it there for 1½ hours, or until the juices run clear when you stick a fork in where the thigh joins the body.

Remove the chicken from the oven, and let it sit for 10 to 15 minutes so the juices settle before carving.

**Yield:** 8 servings

**Nutritional Analysis:** Each will have 446 calories; 32 g fat; 35 g protein; a trace of carbohydrate; 0 g of fiber; trace usable carb

| | | | | | |
|---|---|---|---|---|---|
| Potassium (mg): | 406 mg | Vitamin C (mg): | 5 mg | Thiamin/B1 (mg): | 0.1 mg |
| Calcium (mg): | 21 mg | Vitamin A (i.u.): | 1746 i.u. | Riboflavin/B2 (mg): | 0.4 mg |
| Iron (mg): | 3 mg | Vitamin B6 (mg): | 0.7 mg | Folacin (mcg): | 54 mcg |
| Zinc (mg): | 3 mg | Vitamin B12 (mcg): | 2.0 mcg | Niacin/B3 (mg): | 13 mg |

## Chicken Paprikash with Faux-Po

Traditionally, Chicken Paprikash is served with noodles. If you can afford the extra carbs and calories and can get whole wheat egg noodles, go ahead. But the Faux-Po works extremely well here, and is luscious with the sour cream gravy. You can cut the calorie and carb counts still further by using Fauxtatoes instead.

- 1 pound (455 g) boneless, skinless chicken thighs
- 8 ounces (225 g) sliced mushrooms
- 1 medium onion
- 1 tablespoon (14 g) butter
- 1/2 cup (120 ml) chicken broth
- 1 tablespoon (7 g) paprika
- 1/2 cup (115 g) light sour cream
- Faux-Po (see page 123)
- Salt and pepper
- Guar or xanthan gum

Cut the chicken into bite-size chunks. Chop the mushrooms a bit more. Quarter the onion, then slice it.

Give a big, heavy skillet a shot of nonstick cooking spray, and put it over medium-high heat. Add the butter. When it melts, slosh it around and then throw in the chicken, mushrooms, and onion. Unless your skillet's bigger than mine, it'll be darned full! Sauté, turning everything over frequently, until the onions are turning translucent and the pink is gone from the chicken.

Add the chicken broth, and stir in the paprika. Turn the burner to low, cover the pan, and set a timer for 20 minutes. When the timer goes off, uncover the pan, and set the timer for another 10 minutes, to cook down the broth a bit.

While that's happening, make your Faux-Po, and have it standing ready.

When the timer goes off, turn off the burner and stir in the sour cream. Add salt and pepper to taste, and thicken the broth a tad with your guar or xanthan shaker.

Divide the Faux-Po between 3 serving plates, top with the Paprikash and all its lovely sour cream gravy, and serve.

**Yield:** 3 servings

**Nutritional Analysis:** Each will have: 336 calories; 17 g fat; 27 g protein; 21 g carbohydrates; 3 g fiber; 18 g usable carbs.

| | | | | | |
|---|---|---|---|---|---|
| Potassium (mg): | 974 mg | Vitamin C (mg): | 26 mg | Thiamin/B1 (mg): | 0.2 mg |
| Calcium (mg): | 54 mg | Vitamin A (i.u.): | 1744 i.u. | Riboflavin/B2 (mg): | 0.6 mg |
| Iron (mg): | 3 mg | Vitamin B6 (mg): | 0.6 mg | Folacin (mcg): | 49 mcg |
| Zinc (mg): | 3 mg | Vitamin B12 (mcg): | 0.3 mcg | Niacin/B3 (mg): | 10 mg |

# Coconut Curried Chicken

Using coconut milk in curries gives them an authentic touch and makes them unbelievably delicious! Plus, you get the benefits of coconut oil.

1 tablespoon (14 ml) coconut oil
4 pounds (1.8 kg) skinless, bone-in chicken thighs (ideally 6 thighs)
1 medium onion, thinly sliced
2 teaspoons (6 g) curry powder
1 tablespoon (14 ml) lemon juice
1 can (13½ ounces, or 380 g) coconut milk
1 teaspoon minced garlic
½ teaspoon salt
¼ cup (17 g) shredded coconut meat
1 head cauliflower

Put the coconut oil in a big, heavy skillet, and place it over medium-high heat. Brown the chicken in the oil—you want it golden on both sides. While that's happening, slice the onion.

Okay, the chicken's a pretty gold. Remove it from the skillet for a moment, and throw in the onion and curry powder. Sauté until the onion is limp.

Add the lemon juice, coconut milk, garlic, and salt. Stir it all up to make a sauce. Now put the chicken back in the skillet, turning it over once or twice to coat both sides with the sauce. Cover, turn the burner to the lowest setting, and let the whole thing simmer for 25 minutes.

While this is happening, put the coconut in a dry skillet, and stir it over medium heat until it's golden.

Time's almost up? Trim the leaves and bottom of the cauliflower stem, whack the cauliflower into big chunks, and run it through the shredding blade of your food processor. Put it in a microwaveable casserole with a lid, add a couple of tablespoons (30 ml or so) of water, cover, and nuke it on high for 7 minutes.

While the cauli-rice is cooking, uncover the chicken and let it cook for another 5 or 6 minutes, so the sauce cooks down just a tad. When the cauli-rice is done, drain it, make nice beds of it on 6 plates, and put a piece of chicken on each. Spoon the sauce over (don't miss a drop!), top with the toasted coconut, and serve.

**Yield:** 6 servings

**Nutritional Analysis:** Each will have: 370 calories; 27 g fat; 23 g protein; 11 g carbohydrates; 5 g fiber; 6 g usable carbs.

| | | | | | |
|---|---|---|---|---|---|
| Potassium (mg): | 692 mg | Vitamin C (mg): | 49 mg | Thiamin/B1 (mg): | 0.1 mg |
| Calcium (mg): | 50 mg | Vitamin A (i.u.): | 74 i.u. | Riboflavin/B2 (mg): | 0.2 mg |
| Iron (mg): | 3 mg | Vitamin B6 (mg): | 0.5 mg | Folacin (mcg): | 76 mcg |
| Zinc (mg): | 3 mg | Vitamin B12 (mcg): | 0.2 mcg | Niacin/B3 (mg): | 6 mg |

## Golden Triangle Grilled Chicken

The turmeric turns this Asian-inspired chicken a pretty color—and it tastes great, too. Did you know that turmeric has been studied for its tumor-fighting properties? Good stuff.

- 1 1/2 pounds (670 g) boneless, skinless chicken thighs
- 2 tablespoons (28 ml) lemon juice
- 1 tablespoon (14 ml) lime juice
- 1 shallot, minced
- 1 tablespoon minced garlic (about 8 or 9 cloves)
- 1 tablespoon (8 g) grated gingerroot
- 2 tablespoons (28 ml) soy sauce
- 1/2 teaspoon Splenda
- 1 teaspoon turmeric

Put the chicken in a zipper-lock bag. Stir together the lemon and lime juices, shallot, garlic, ginger, soy sauce, Splenda, and turmeric. Pour the mixture into the bag and seal it, pressing out the air as you go. Turn to coat the chicken. Stash the bag in the fridge for at least several hours, and 24 hours is brilliant.

When dinnertime rolls around, preheat your electric tabletop grill, or fire up your barbecue. Pull the bag of chicken out of the fridge, pour off the marinade into a small bowl, and reserve.

If you're using an electric grill, the chicken will take 5 to 6 minutes. (I set mine for 325°F/170°C/Gas mark 3, but if yours just has one setting, don't fret; you'll be fine.) Set a timer for 3 minutes and baste the chicken with the reserved marinade halfway through the cooking time, turning it to get both sides.

If you're using your outdoor barbecue grill, the chicken will take more like 5 to 6 minutes per side. Baste both sides when you flip it.

**Yield:** 4 servings

**Nutritional Analysis:** Each will have: 210 calories; 3 g fat; 40 g protein; 3 g carbohydrates; trace fiber; 3 g usable carbs.

| | | | | | |
|---|---|---|---|---|---|
| Potassium (mg): | 474 mg | Vitamin C (mg): | 8 mg | Thiamin/B1 (mg): | 0.1 mg |
| Calcium (mg): | 29 mg | Vitamin A (i.u.): | 362 i.u. | Riboflavin/B2 (mg): | 0.2 mg |
| Iron (mg): | 2 mg | Vitamin B6 (mg): | 1 mg | Folacin (mcg): | 11 mcg |
| Zinc (mg): | 2 mg | Vitamin B12 (mcg): | 0.6 mcg | Niacin/B3 (mg): | 18 mg |

## Grilled Chicken, Banana Peppers, and Vidalias

I came up with this when banana peppers were flooding into the local farmer's market. If you haven't tried them, they're wonderful cooking peppers. Don't confuse them with the similar-appearing Hungarian Waxed peppers—unless you like your food hot!

- 1 pound (455 g) boneless, skinless chicken breasts
- 2 tablespoons (28 ml) lime juice
- 1 clove garlic, peeled and minced
- 1/2 teaspoon cumin
- 1 medium Vidalia or other sweet onion
- 4 medium banana peppers
- Salt and pepper
- 3 tablespoons (45 g) Chipotle Mayonnaise (see page 486)

Put a chicken breast into a zipper-lock bag, and pound it until it's about 1/2 inch (1.25 cm) thick. Repeat with the remaining chicken breasts.

Mix together the lime juice, garlic, and cumin in a glass pie plate. Lay the chicken breasts in this mixture, turning to coat, and let them marinate for 20 to 30 minutes. Turn them once or twice during that time.

Meanwhile, cut the onion in half vertically, then into slices 1/4 inch (6 mm) thick. Split the peppers lengthwise, remove the seeds and ribs, and slice them into 1/4-inch (6-mm) lengthwise strips.

Heat your electric tabletop grill, and throw in the onion and peppers. Give them 6 to 7 minutes, or until they're softened and starting to brown. Remove and set them aside.

Throw the marinated chicken in the grill for about 5 minutes, or until done through. Move the chicken to 3 serving plates, divide the vegetables between the servings, and top each chicken breast with 1 tablespoon (15 g) of chipotle mayonnaise.

**Yield:** 3 servings

**Nutritional Analysis:** Each will have: 249 calories; 7 g fat; 35 g protein; 10 g carbohydrates; 3 g fiber; 7 g usable carbs.

| | | | | | |
|---|---|---|---|---|---|
| Potassium (mg): | 514 mg | Vitamin C (mg): | 56 mg | Thiamin/B1 (mg): | 0.1 mg |
| Calcium (mg): | 39 mg | Vitamin A (i.u.): | 236 i.u. | Riboflavin/B2 (mg): | 0.2 mg |
| Iron (mg): | 2 mg | Vitamin B6 (mg): | 0.9 mg | Folacin (mcg): | 29 mcg |
| Zinc (mg): | 1 mg | Vitamin B12 (mcg): | 0.4 mcg | Niacin/B3 (mg): | 16 mg |

## Chicken Puttanesca

"Puttanesca" means "whore's style!" The term has long been used in Italian cookery to denote a dish full of robust flavors like those of capers and olives.

1 tablespoon (14 ml) olive oil

1 1/2 pounds (670 g) boneless chicken thighs

4 cloves garlic, peeled and minced

1/4 cup (25 g) chopped kalamata olives

1 tablespoon (9 g) capers, drained

1 can (14 1/2 ounces, or 405 g) diced tomatoes

1/2 cup (30 g) chopped fresh parsley

1 can (14 1/2 ounces, or 405 g) quartered artichoke hearts, drained

Spray a big, heavy skillet with nonstick cooking spray. Put it over medium-high heat. When it's hot, add the olive oil, slosh it around to cover the bottom, and add the chicken thighs. You want to brown them a bit.

When the thighs are golden on both sides, remove them from the pan. Turn the heat down to medium-low. Add the garlic to the skillet, and sauté it for just a minute. Then add the olives, capers, canned tomatoes with their juice, parsley, and artichoke hearts. Stir it all together, put the chicken back in the skillet, cover the pan, and set a timer for 15 minutes.

When the time's up, serve each chicken thigh with the vegetables piled around and over it.

**Yield:** 4 servings

**Nutritional Analysis:** Each will have: 294 calories; 13 g fat; 28 g protein; 15 g carbohydrates; 1 g fiber; 14 g usable carbs.

| | | | | | |
|---|---|---|---|---|---|
| Potassium (mg): | 524 mg | Vitamin C (mg): | 26 mg | Thiamin/B1 (mg): | 0.1 mg |
| Calcium (mg): | 64 mg | Vitamin A (i.u.): | 1089 i.u. | Riboflavin/B2 (mg): | 0.2 mg |
| Iron (mg): | 2 mg | Vitamin B6 (mg): | 0.5 mg | Folacin (mcg): | 29 mcg |
| Zinc (mg): | 3 mg | Vitamin B12 (mcg): | 0.3 mcg | Niacin/B3 (mg): | 7 mg |

**Note:** Use the time while the chicken is browning to mince your garlic and pit and chop your olives. The easiest way to pit an olive is to press down on it with your thumb; you can then simply pick the pit out! Chop up your parsley, while you're at it.

## Crazy-Good Grilled Chicken

This is a clone of a clone of a popular restaurant's take-out chicken. The marinade points up the flavor of the chicken and helps keep it good and juicy.

2 cups (475 ml) water

4 teaspoons (24 g) salt or Vege-Sal

2 teaspoons (4 g) pepper

2 cloves garlic, peeled and minced

1 teaspoon turmeric

1/4 cup (50 g) crushed pineapple in juice

2 teaspoons (10 ml) lime juice

3 pounds (1.4 kg) chicken, cut up (legs from thighs, wings from breasts)

Put the water, salt, pepper, garlic, turmeric, pineapple, and lime juice in your blender, and run it for a minute or so.

Put the chicken in a big zipper-lock bag, and pour in the marinade. Seal the bag, pressing out the air as you go. Turn the bag to coat the chicken, and throw the whole thing in the fridge. Let the chicken marinate for 1 to 2 hours.

Remove the chicken from of the refrigerator, pour off the marinade and discard it. Get your grill going. (Charcoal really is best for this, but if you must use gas, you must!) You'll want to let your coals burn down till they're well covered with ash, or set your gas grill to medium or slightly lower and let it get thoroughly preheated.

Grill the chicken about 4 inches (10 cm) from the fire, if using charcoal. Put it on the grill boney-side down and close the lid, leaving the vent open just a bit. (You don't want your fire to go out!) Set a timer for 12 minutes. When it goes off, open the grill, turn the chicken with tongs, and close the lid again. Set the timer for 10 minutes. Then turn the chicken, and give it a final 10 minutes, at which point the juices should run clear when you pierce it to the bone.

**Yield:** 6 servings

**Nutritional Analysis:** Each will have: 364 calories; 26 g fat; 29 g protein; 3 g carbohydrates; trace fiber; 3 g usable carbs.

| | | | | | |
|---|---|---|---|---|---|
| Potassium (mg): | 362 mg | Vitamin C (mg): | 6 mg | Thiamin/B1 (mg): | 0.1 mg |
| Calcium (mg): | 35 mg | Vitamin A (i.u.): | 1402 i.u. | Riboflavin/B2 (mg): | 0.3 mg |
| Iron (mg): | 3 mg | Vitamin B6 (mg): | 0.6 mg | Folacin (mcg): | 44 mcg |
| Zinc (mg): | 2 mg | Vitamin B12 (mcg): | 1.6 mcg | Niacin/B3 (mg):: | 11 mg |

**Note:** If you can't grill your chicken, you could broil this 6 to 8 inches (15 to 20 cm) from the heat.

## Chicken Skewers Diavolo

These are Italian-style chicken kabobs.

- 2 pounds (905 g) boneless, skinless chicken thighs
- 1/4 cup (60 ml) olive oil
- 1/4 cup (60 ml) lemon juice
- 2 cloves garlic, peeled and minced
- 2 tablespoons (12 g) red pepper flakes
- Salt and pepper
- Fresh parsley to garnish (optional)
- 1 lemon, cut into 6 wedges

Cut the chicken into 1-inch (2.5-cm) cubes. Put the cubes in a big zipper-lock bag.

Combine the oil, lemon juice, garlic, and pepper flakes, and pour the mixture over the chicken. Seal the bag, pressing out the air as you go. Turn to coat, then throw the bag in the fridge, and let the chicken marinate for at least 4 to 5 hours. All day won't hurt a bit.

When cooking time comes, pour off the marinade into a dish and reserve. Thread the chicken chunks onto 6 skewers. Salt and pepper them lightly. Grill or broil them for about 8 minutes, or until done through (cut into a chunk to see), basting often with the reserved marinade. But stop basting with at least a couple of minutes of cooking time to go, to be sure all the raw chicken germs are killed!

Garnish each skewer with a little minced parsley and a lemon wedge to squeeze over it.

**Yield:** 6 servings

**Nutritional Analysis:** Each will have: 246 calories; 17 g fat; 22 g protein; 2 g carbohydrates; trace fiber; 2 g usable carbs.

| | | | | | |
|---|---|---|---|---|---|
| Potassium (mg): | 223 mg | Vitamin C (mg): | 13 mg | Thiamin/B1 (mg): | 0.1 mg |
| Calcium (mg): | 17 mg | Vitamin A (i.u.): | 165 i.u. | Riboflavin/B2 (mg): | 0.2 mg |
| Iron (mg): | 1 mg | Vitamin B6 (mg): | 0.3 mg | Folacin (mcg): | 9 mcg |
| Zinc (mg): | 2 mg | Vitamin B12 (mcg): | 0.3 mcg | Niacin/B3 (mg): | 5 mg |

## Glazed Drumsticks

A simple way to jazz up drumsticks. You could also use this sauce on wings, for a party.

- 2 pounds (905 g) chicken drumsticks
- 3 tablespoons (45 ml) soy sauce
- 2 tablespoons (40 g) low-sugar orange marmalade
- 1 tablespoon (14 ml) olive oil
- 2 tablespoons (30 g) no-sugar-added ketchup
- 1/4 teaspoon chili garlic paste
- 1 teaspoon grated gingerroot
- 1 clove garlic, peeled and minced

Preheat the oven to 350°F (180°C, or gas mark 4).

Arrange the drumsticks in a roasting pan, and put them in the oven. Set a timer for 15 minutes.

Mix together the soy sauce, marmalade, oil, ketchup, chili garlic paste, ginger, and garlic. When the 15 minutes are up, brush the drumsticks with this glaze. After another 15 minutes, brush them with the glaze again, use tongs to turn them, and brush the other side, too.

Roast the chicken for another 15 minutes, baste with the glaze one more time, give them 5 more minutes in the oven, and serve.

**Yield:** 4 servings

**Nutritional Analysis:** Each will have: 297 calories; 17 g fat; 30 g protein; 5 g carbohydrates; trace fiber; 5 g usable carbs.

| | | | | | |
|---|---|---|---|---|---|
| Potassium (mg): | 343 mg | Vitamin C (mg): | 4 mg | Thiamin/B1 (mg): | 0.2 mg |
| Calcium (mg): | 20 mg | Vitamin A (i.u.): | 275 i.u. | Riboflavin/B2 (mg): | 0.4 mg |
| Iron (mg): | 2 mg | Vitamin B6 (mg): | 0.5 mg | Folacin (mcg): | 16 mcg |
| Zinc (mg): | 3 mg | Vitamin B12 (mcg): | 0.5 mcg | Niacin/B3 (mg): | 9 mg |

## Lemon-Sage Chicken

Sage is a classic with poultry, and the lemon really complements its flavor.

- 4 chicken drumsticks
- 4 chicken thighs
- 1/2 cup (120 ml) lemon juice
- 2 tablespoons (4 g) ground sage
- 1/2 cup (80 g) minced onion
- 2 cloves garlic, peeled and finely minced
- 2 tablespoons (28 ml) dry sherry

Put the chicken in a zipper-lock bag.

In a small bowl, mix together the lemon juice, sage, onion, garlic, and sherry. Pour it over the chicken and seal the bag, pressing out the air as you go. Turn the bag to coat, and throw it in the fridge for a few hours.

When you're ready to cook, preheat your oven to 375°F (190°C, or gas mark 5). Pour the marinade off the chicken and reserve. Arrange the chicken in a roasting pan.

Roast the chicken for 30 minutes. Pull it out of the oven, pour the marinade over and around it, and put it back in for another 15 minutes. Baste the chicken with the liquid in the pan and let it roast for a final 15 minutes. Serve the chicken with the pan juices over it, on some brown rice or cauli-rice, if you like.

**Yield:** 4 servings

**Nutritional Analysis:** Each will have: 327 calories; 20 g fat; 29 g protein; 6 g carbohydrates; 1 g fiber; 5 g usable carbs.

| | | | | | |
|---|---|---|---|---|---|
| Potassium (mg): | 398 mg | Vitamin C (mg): | 20 mg | Thiamin/B1 (mg): | 0.2 mg |
| Calcium (mg): | 42 mg | Vitamin A (i.u.): | 260 i.u. | Riboflavin/B2 (mg): | 0.3 mg |
| Iron (mg): | 2 mg | Vitamin B6 (mg): | 0.5 mg | Folacin (mcg): | 23 mcg |
| Zinc (mg): | 3 mg | Vitamin B12 (mcg): | 0.5 mcg | Niacin/B3 (mg): | 8 mg |

## Orange-Pineapple Sweet-and-Sour Chicken

This easy chicken has a quasi-Polynesian thing going on.

1 teaspoon (5 ml) coconut oil

$1\frac{1}{2}$ pounds (670 g) boneless, skinless chicken thighs

2 tablespoons (19 g) canned pineapple chunks in juice

2 tablespoons (40 g) low-sugar orange marmalade

1 tablespoon (14 ml) rice vinegar

1 tablespoon (1.5 g) Splenda

1 tablespoon (14 ml) soy sauce

1 clove garlic, peeled and minced

1 teaspoon (5 g) brown mustard

Spray a big, heavy skillet with nonstick cooking spray, and put it over medium-high heat. When it's hot, add the coconut oil, and slosh it around as it melts. Add the chicken. You want to brown it just a touch, till it's golden all over.

Put the pineapple, marmalade, vinegar, Splenda, soy sauce, garlic, and brown mustard in your blender, and run it until the pineapple is pulverized. When the chicken is golden all over, pour the sauce over it. Cover the skillet, turn the burner to low, and let the whole thing cook for 20 minutes.

I like to serve this on a bed of cauli-rice, with the sauce spooned over it.

**Yield:** 4 servings

**Nutritional Analysis:** Each will have: 245 calories; 9 g fat; 35 g protein; 5 g carbohydrates; trace fiber; 5 g usable carbs.

| | | | | | |
|---|---|---|---|---|---|
| Potassium (mg): | 404 mg | Vitamin C (mg): | 6 mg | Thiamin/B1 (mg): | 0.1 mg |
| Calcium (mg): | 25 mg | Vitamin A (i.u.): | 126 i.u. | Riboflavin/B2 (mg): | 0.3 mg |
| Iron (mg): | 2 mg | Vitamin B6 (mg): | 0.6 mg | Folacin (mcg): | 18 mcg |
| Zinc (mg): | 3 mg | Vitamin B12 (mcg): | 0.6 mcg | Niacin/B3 (mg): | 11 mg |

# Red-Headed Stepchild Oven Barbecue

My idol Peg Bracken had a recipe in her classic The I Hate to Cook Book called "Bastard Barbecue." It was darned tasty, but had plenty of brown sugar in it. This is my attempt to come up with a similar flavor, without all that sugar.

- 3½ pounds (1.6 kg) chicken, cut up, with skin on
- 2 teaspoons (12 g) garlic salt
- 2 teaspoons (1 g) Splenda
- ½ teaspoon blackstrap molasses
- 2 tablespoons (28 ml) balsamic vinegar

Preheat the oven to 375°F (190°C, or gas mark 5).

Arrange the chicken in a roasting pan, skin side up. Mix together the garlic salt and Splenda, and sprinkle it evenly over the chicken.

When the oven is hot, put the chicken in. Let it roast for a good 20 minutes, during which time you need to measure your molasses and balsamic vinegar into a small dish and stir until the molasses is dissolved.

When the 20 minutes are up, baste the chicken with the balsamic mixture. Let it continue roasting for another 40 to 50 minutes, basting every 15 minutes or so with the rest of the vinegar mixture.

**Yield:** 6 servings

**Nutritional Analysis:** Each will have: 416 calories; 30 g fat; 33 g protein; 1 g carbohydrates; trace fiber; 1 g usable carbs.

| | | | | | |
|---|---|---|---|---|---|
| Potassium (mg): | 399 mg | Vitamin C (mg): | 5 mg | Thiamin/B1 (mg): | 0.1 mg |
| Calcium (mg): | 25 mg | Vitamin A (i.u.): | 1630 i.u. | Riboflavin/B2 (mg): | 0.3 mg |
| Iron (mg): | 3 mg | Vitamin B6 (mg): | 0.6 mg | Folacin (mcg): | 50 mcg |
| Zinc (mg): | 2 mg | Vitamin B12 (mcg): | 1.9 mcg | Niacin/B3 (mg): | 12 mg |

## Skillet Citrus Chicken

Orange, lemon, and lime—plus mustard—give a tangy snap to this chicken.

1 tablespoon (14 ml) olive oil

3 pounds (1.4 kg) chicken thighs without skin, but with the bone

2 tablespoons (40 g) low-sugar orange marmalade

2 tablespoons (28 ml) lemon juice

2 tablespoons (28 ml) lime juice

1 tablespoon (1.5 g) Splenda

2 teaspoons (10 g) brown mustard

2 cloves garlic, peeled and finely minced

1/2 cup (120 ml) chicken broth

Coat a big, heavy skillet with nonstick cooking spray, and put it over medium-high heat. When it's hot, add the olive oil, then the chicken, meaty side down. Sauté until the chicken is lightly golden, then turn it bone side down. Brown for another 5 minutes or so.

While the chicken's browning, stir together the marmalade, lemon juice, lime juice, Splenda, mustard, garlic, and broth. When the chicken is browned, pour this mixture into the skillet. Cover the skillet with a "tilted lid"; leave a crack of about 1/4 inch (6 mm) to let some steam out. Turn the burner to low, and let the chicken simmer for 20 minutes.

When time is up, uncover the chicken and remove it to a platter. Keep it in a warm place while you turn up the burner and boil down the sauce until it's a little syrupy. Pour the sauce over the chicken, and serve.

**Yield:** 5 servings

**Nutritional Analysis:** Each will have: 229 calories; 9 g fat; 31 g protein; 4 g carbohydrates; trace fiber; 4 g usable carbs.

| | | | | | |
|---|---|---|---|---|---|
| Potassium (mg): | 401 mg | Vitamin C (mg): | 10 mg | Thiamin/B1 (mg): | 0.1 mg |
| Calcium (mg): | 22 mg | Vitamin A (i.u.): | 103 i.u. | Riboflavin/B2 (mg): | 0.3 mg |
| Iron (mg): | 2 mg | Vitamin B6 (mg): | 0.5 mg | Folacin (mcg): | 17 mcg |
| Zinc (mg): | 3 mg | Vitamin B12 (mcg): | 0.6 mcg | Niacin/B3 (mg): | 10 mg |

# Tandoori Chicken

Okay, without an Indian tandoor oven it's not truly authentic—but oh my gosh, is this good. Feel free to use white meat chicken if you prefer, or just a cut-up chicken, but do use chicken on the bone.

5 pounds (2.3 kg) chicken thighs without skin, but with the bone
4 cloves garlic
2 tablespoons (16 g) grated gingerroot
2 bay leaves
2 teaspoons (6 g) chili powder
1 teaspoon salt or Vege-Sal
2 teaspoons (6 g) turmeric
1 teaspoon ground coriander
1/2 teaspoon cumin
1/2 teaspoon cinnamon
1/2 teaspoon ground cloves
1/4 cup (60 ml) olive oil
1 1/2 cups (370 g) plain yogurt
1 tablespoon (14 ml) lemon juice

Put the chicken in a nonreactive baking pan. Glass and enamel are ideal, but stainless steel will do. Don't use aluminum or iron.

Put the garlic, ginger, bay leaves, chili powder, salt, turmeric, coriander, cumin, cinnamon, cloves, oil, yogurt, and lemon juice in your blender. Run it until you have a smooth sauce.

Pour the sauce over the chicken, and use tongs to turn each piece to coat. Cover the baking pan with plastic wrap, slide it into the fridge, and let it sit for a minimum of 4 hours. (A whole day is ideal.)

When you're ready to cook, pull the chicken out of the fridge and let it come up to room temperature. Meanwhile, preheat the oven to 350°F (180°C, or gas mark 4).

When the oven's hot, put the chicken in. Roast for 45 minutes to an hour, turning the chicken occasionally with tongs.

Serve with a big salad and one of the rice dishes from Chapter 5; Peachy "Rice" would be ideal.

**Yield:** 6 servings

**Nutritional Analysis:** Each will have. 387 calories, 20 g fat, 45 g protein; 5 g carbohydrates; 1 g fiber; 4 g usable carbs.

| | | | | | |
|---|---|---|---|---|---|
| Potassium (mg): | 657 mg | Vitamin C (mg): | 10 mg | Thiamin/B1 (mg): | 0.2 mg |
| Calcium (mg): | 113 mg | Vitamin A (i.u.): | 513 i.u. | Riboflavin/B2 (mg): | 0.5 mg |
| Iron (mg): | 3 mg | Vitamin B6 (mg): | 0.8 mg | Folacin (mcg): | 28 mcg |
| Zinc (mg): | 5 mg | Vitamin B12 (mcg): | 1.0 mcg | Niacin/B3 (mg): | 14 mg |

## Tequila-Lime Chicken with Chipotle Sauce

Put the chicken into the marinade in the morning (or even the night before), and you'll be able to get dinner on the table 10 minutes after you get home. Add some bagged salad, and you're done!

- 1 1/2 pounds (670 g) boneless, skinless chicken breast
- 1/3 cup (80 ml) lime juice
- 2 tablespoons (28 ml) tequila
- 1 teaspoon (.5 g) Splenda
- 1 teaspoon ground cumin
- 2 cloves garlic, peeled and crushed
- 1/2 teaspoon soy sauce
- 1/2 cup (120 ml) Creamy Chipotle Dressing (see page 000)

Place the chicken breasts in a big zipper-lock bag. Stir together the lime juice, tequila, Splenda, cumin, garlic, and soy sauce, and pour it over the chicken. Seal the bag, pressing out the air as you go. Turn the bag to coat the chicken, and throw it in the fridge for several hours at least.

When dinnertime rolls around, preheat your electric tabletop grill. Pull out the bag of chicken and drain off the marinade into a little bowl. When the grill's hot, throw in the chicken. Set the timer for 3 minutes. When the timer beeps, baste the chicken with the reserved marinade, then give it another 2 to 3 minutes grilling time.

Remove the grilled chicken to plates, top each with 2 tablespoons (28 ml) of Creamy Chipotle Dressing, and serve.

**Yield:** 4 servings

**Nutritional Analysis:** Each will have: 272 calories; 8 g fat; 39 g protein; 6 g carbohydrates; trace fiber; 6 g usable carbs.

| | | | | | |
|---|---|---|---|---|---|
| Potassium (mg): | 378 mg | Vitamin C (mg): | 7 mg | Thiamin/B1 (mg): | 0.1 mg |
| Calcium (mg): | 47 mg | Vitamin A (i.u.): | 51 i.u. | Riboflavin/B2 (mg): | 0.2 mg |
| Iron (mg): | 2 mg | Vitamin B6 (mg): | 0.8 mg | Folacin (mcg): | 7 mcg |
| Zinc (mg): | 1 mg | Vitamin B12 (mcg): | 0.5 mcg | Niacin/B3 (mg): | 17 mg |

## Yucatan Chicken

In the Yucatan, they marinate chicken in the juice of bitter oranges. Well, I've got to tell you, those bitter oranges are mighty thin on the ground here in southern Indiana. So I've used lemon and lime juice with orange extract to get a similar flavor.

1 tablespoon (6 g) pepper
1 tablespoon (6 g) ground allspice
1 teaspoon dried oregano
1/2 teaspoon ground cumin
1 teaspoon (5 ml) lime juice
1 teaspoon (5 ml) lemon juice
3 drops orange extract
2 pounds (905 g) chicken thighs

Mix together the pepper, allspice, oregano, cumin, lime and lemon juice, and orange extract. Rub this mixture all over the chicken thighs, and even up under the skin. Refrigerate for several hours.

When it's time to cook, arrange the chicken on your broiler rack, skin side down, and broil about 6 inches (15 cm) from the heat for 15 minutes or so. Turn, and give it another 10 minutes. Turn again, and give it at least another 5 minutes. Now turn a piece skin side up, and pierce it to the bone. If the juice runs clear, it's done. If it runs red, you need to give it a little longer.

Serve with a big, green salad, preferably with orange sections and thinly sliced red onion in it!

**Yield:** 4 servings

**Nutritional Analysis:** Each will have: 389 calories; 28 g fat; 31 g protein; 3 g carbohydrates; 1 g fiber; 2 g usable carbs.

| | | | | | |
|---|---|---|---|---|---|
| Potassium (mg): | 394 mg | Vitamin C (mg): | 6 mg | Thiamin/B1 (mg): | 0.1 mg |
| Calcium (mg): | 43 mg | Vitamin A (i.u.): | 301 i.u. | Riboflavin/B2 (mg): | 0.3 mg |
| Iron (mg): | 3 mg | Vitamin B6 (mg): | 0.5 mg | Folacin (mcg): | 15 mcg |
| Zinc (mg): | 3 mg | Vitamin B12 (mcg): | 0.5 mcg | Niacin/B3 (mg): | 10 mg |

**Note:** You can also cook this on your barbecue grill, if you like. Indeed, if you want to take something along to the park or the beach to grill while you're there, do the flavoring step early in the day, and throw the chicken in a big zipper-lock bag. Then grab the bag of chicken, throw it in your cooler, and go. Cook it over a well-cooked-down charcoal fire for 10 minutes with the skin side down, then flip it, and give it another 10. Turn it again and give it another 5 to 6 minutes, or until the juice runs clear when it's pierced to the bone.

## Kim's Turmeric Chicken Kabobs

My sister Kim invented this recipe one day, using what she had on hand. She liked it so much that it became a party menu favorite.

1 cup (245 g) plain yogurt

1 tablespoon (9 g) turmeric

1/2 tablespoon (8 ml) lemon juice

2 teaspoons (1 g) Splenda

Salt and pepper

3 pounds (1.4 kg) boneless, skinless chicken breasts, cut into 1-inch (2.5-cm) cubes

4 small zucchini, sliced 1/2 inch (1.25 cm) thick

1 1/2 medium onions, chunked, layers separated

In a nonreactive bowl, mix together the yogurt, turmeric, lemon juice, and Splenda. Add salt and pepper to taste.

Throw the chicken into the yogurt mixture, stir to coat, and stick it in the fridge for a few hours. If you're going to use bamboo skewers, this would be a good time to put them in some water to soak, so they don't catch fire later on.

When it's time to cook, get your charcoal grill going—you'll want it cooked down to a bed of white-ashed coals before you cook. If you're using a gas grill, set it on medium to medium-low. You could also use your broiler, set on low.

Pull your bowl of chicken out of the fridge, and have the zucchini, onions, and skewers standing by.

Skewer a chicken cube, a zucchini round, and a piece of onion, repeating this order to fill the skewers.

Put your skewers on the grill or under the broiler. Grill or broil until the chicken and vegetables are getting little charred spots. (Kim says this is how you know they'll be done through.) Baste once or twice with the yogurt marinade, but stop a few minutes before you're done cooking, so the heat has time to kill the raw chicken germs!

**Yield:** 8 servings

**Nutritional Analysis:** Each will have: 245 calories; 6 g fat; 40 g protein; 7 g carbohydrates; 2 g fiber; 5 g usable carbs.

| | | | | | |
|---|---|---|---|---|---|
| Potassium (mg): | 657 mg | Vitamin C (mg): | 11 mg | Thiamin/B1 (mg): | 0.2 mg |
| Calcium (mg): | 76 mg | Vitamin A (i.u.): | 395 i.u. | Riboflavin/B2 (mg): | 0.2 mg |
| Iron (mg): | 2 mg | Vitamin B6 (mg): | 0.9 mg | Folacin (mcg): | 33 mcg |
| Zinc (mg): | 2 mg | Vitamin B12 (mcg): | 0.5 mcg | Niacin/B3 (mg): | 17 mg |

# Pollo con Limon y Ajo

Lemon and garlic—what could be simpler or better?

1 pound (455 g) boneless, skinless chicken breasts
2 tablespoons (28 ml) olive oil
2 shallots, minced
6 cloves garlic, peeled and minced
2 teaspoons (4 g) paprika
3 lemons
1/4 cup (15 g) chopped fresh parsley
Salt and pepper

Put a chicken breast in a heavy zipper-lock bag and seal it, pressing out the air as you go. Use the nearest blunt instrument to beat it till it's 1/4 inch (6 mm) thick all over. Repeat with the remaining breasts.

When you've beaten all your chicken into submission, cut it into 1/2-inch (1.25-cm) wide strips.

Spray a big, heavy skillet with nonstick cooking spray, put it over medium-high heat, and add the oil. Now throw in the chicken, shallots, and garlic. Stir them all together, then sprinkle the paprika over everything, and stir that in, too. Continue stir-frying until the chicken is cooked through and lightly browned.

Squeeze 2 of the lemons over the skillet, and stir in the parsley. Add salt and pepper to taste. Cut the third lemon into 4 wedges, and serve the chicken with the wedges to squeeze over it.

**Yield:** 4 servings

**Nutritional Analysis:** Each will have: 217 calories; 10 g fat; 26 g protein; 8 g carbohydrates; 1 g fiber; 7 g usable carbs.

| | | | | | |
|---|---|---|---|---|---|
| Potassium (mg): | 353 mg | Vitamin C (mg): | 31 mg | Thiamin/B1 (mg): | 0.1 mg |
| Calcium (mg): | 41 mg | Vitamin A (i.u.): | 1545 i.u. | Riboflavin/B2 (mg): | 0.1 mg |
| Iron (mg): | 2 mg | Vitamin B6 (mg): | 0.6 mg | Folacin (mcg): | 16 mcg |
| Zinc (mg): | 1 mg | Vitamin B12 (mcg): | 0.3 mcg | Niacin/B3 (mg): | 12 mg |

# Chicken Breasts Stuffed with Artichokes and Garlic Cheese

Delicious and filling, this is an impressive dish. It's great for dinner parties.

- 1 1/2 pounds (670 g) boneless, skinless chicken breasts
- 1 jar (6 ounces, or 170 g) marinated artichoke hearts, drained
- 3 ounces (85 g) light garlic-and-herb spreadable cheese
- 1/4 teaspoon pepper
- 1/2 tablespoon (21 g) butter

Preheat the oven to 375°F (190°C, or gas mark 5).

Place a chicken breast in a big, heavy zipper-lock bag and seal it, pressing out the air as you go. Use any heavy, blunt instrument available to beat that sucker till it's 1/4 inch (6 mm) thick all across. Repeat with all the chicken breasts.

Throw the artichoke hearts, cheese, and pepper into your food processor with the S-blade in place. Pulse until the artichokes are finely chopped, but not pureed.

Spread one-quarter of the cheese mixture on each breast. Roll each one up, jelly-roll fashion. Hold them closed with toothpicks.

Spray a big, heavy skillet with nonstick cooking spray, and put it over medium-high heat. When it's hot, add the butter and slosh it around to cover the bottom of the skillet. Add your chicken rolls, and sauté till they're lightly golden—about 3 minutes per side.

If your skillet's handle isn't oven-safe, wrap it in foil. Slide the whole thing into the oven and let it bake for 15 minutes, or until the rolls are done through. Serve.

**Yield:** 4 servings

**Nutritional Analysis:** Each will have: 298 calories; 12 g fat; 41 g protein; 4 g carbohydrates; 2 g fiber; 2 g usable carbs.

| | | | | | |
|---|---|---|---|---|---|
| Potassium (mg): | 314 mg | Vitamin C (mg): | trace | Thiamin/B1 (mg): | 0.1 mg |
| Calcium (mg): | 38 mg | Vitamin A (i.u.): | 171 i.u. | Riboflavin/B2 (mg): | 0.1 mg |
| Iron (mg): | 1 mg | Vitamin B6 (mg): | 0.7 mg | Folacin (mcg): | 4 mg |
| Zinc (mg): | 1 mg | Vitamin B12 (mcg): | 0.4 mcg | Niacin/B3 (mg): | 17 mg |

**Note:** I do mean any blunt implement can be used to pound your chicken flat—I use a 3-pound dumbbell!

# Lime Grilled Chicken over Portobellos

$1\frac{1}{2}$ pounds (670 g) boneless, skinless chicken breasts
Salt and pepper
2 whole limes
2 tablespoons (28 ml) white wine vinegar
4 tablespoons (60 ml) olive oil
Portobellos with Garlic and Parsley (see page 169)

Divide the chicken into 4 portions. Salt and pepper the pieces all over, and put 'em in a big zipper-lock bag.

Use a vegetable peeler to pare away thin strips of lime rind. Cut the strips of rind into skinny little threadlike strips. Then, in a small bowl, squeeze the juice from the limes and add it to the vinegar and 3 tablespoons (45 ml) of the oil. Add the strips of rind, and pour the whole thing into the bag with the chicken. Seal the bag, pressing out the air as you go. Turn the bag to coat the chicken, then throw the bag in the fridge for at least several hours, and overnight is great.

When dinnertime rolls around, either heat your electric tabletop grill or get your outdoor grill going.

Pour the marinade off of the chicken and into a small saucepan. Grill the chicken for about 6 minutes in your electric grill or 5 to 7 minutes per side on your outdoor grill, basting several times with the reserved marinade while it's cooking. Be sure to stop basting several minutes before the cooking is done, so all the raw chicken germs get killed by the heat!

When the chicken is done through, make beds of the portobellos on 4 plates, and arrange the chicken on top. Now bring the rest of the marinade to a boil over high heat, and boil it hard for at least 1 minute, to kill the raw chicken germs. Spoon over the chicken, and serve.

**Yield:** 4 servings

**Nutritional Analysis:** Each will have: 480 calories; 31 g fat; 41 g protein; 11 g carbohydrates; 2 g fiber; 9 g usable carbs.

| | | | | | |
|---|---|---|---|---|---|
| Potassium (mg): | 860 mg | Vitamin C (mg): | 35 mg | Thiamin/B1 (mg): | 0.2 mg |
| Calcium (mg): | 63 mg | Vitamin A (i.u.): | 1070 i.u. | Riboflavin/B2 (mg): | 0.7 mg |
| Iron (mg): | 4 mg | Vitamin B6 (mg): | 0.9 mg | Folacin (mcg): | 53 mcg |
| Zinc (mg): | 2 mg | Vitamin B12 (mcg): | 0.4 mcg | Niacin/B3 (mg): | 22 mg |

# Anaheim Chile Strata

Tasty and unique, this one is something all its own. Very hearty, but inexpensive—and a great way to use up after-Thanksgiving leftovers.

- 8 Anaheim chile peppers (poblanos may be substituted)
- 1 1/2 cups (175 g) shredded reduced-fat Monterey Jack cheese
- 1 1/2 cups (175 g) shredded reduced-fat cheddar cheese
- 1/4 cup (30 g) whole wheat flour (preferably pastry flour)
- 1 cup (235 ml) evaporated milk (Not condensed milk!)
- 1 cup (230 g) light sour cream
- 4 eggs
- 3 cups (330 g) diced cooked chicken or turkey
- 16 ounces (450 g) salsa, preferably chunky style

To begin, roast your peppers. Just put them on your broiler rack and broil, turning often, until all of the skin is blackened and blistered. Be patient and turn them often, so that they will peel more easily. (You can also do this on a gas burner, but for 8 peppers, that's a lot of trouble.)

Put the roasted peppers in a paper sack, and fold the top closed. Let them cool for 15 minutes, then take them out and peel the skin off of them. Cut them in half lengthwise, and seed them, discarding the seeds.

Preheat the oven to 350°F (180°C, or gas mark 4). Spray a 13 x 9-inch (32.5 x 22.5-cm) baking pan with nonstick cooking spray. Lay the chiles flat in the pan, cut side up. Toss together the Monterey Jack and cheddar cheeses, and sprinkle them evenly over the chiles.

Now whisk together the flour, milk, sour cream, eggs, and diced chicken. Pour this mixture over the chiles and cheese. Bake for 30 minutes.

Spread the salsa over the top, bake for another 15 minutes, and serve.

Yield: 8 servings

**Nutritional Analysis:** Each will have: 325 calories; 12 g fat; 37 g protein; 18 g carbohydrates; 2 g fiber; 16 g usable carbs.

| | | | | | |
|---|---|---|---|---|---|
| Potassium (mg): | 650 mg | Vitamin C (mg): | 154 mg | Thiamin/B1 (mg): | 0.2 mg |
| Calcium (mg): | 454 mg | Vitamin A (i.u.): | 1283 i.u. | Riboflavin/B2 (mg): | 0.5 mg |
| Iron (mg): | 2 mg | Vitamin B6 (mg): | 0.6 mg | Folacin (mcg): | 45 mcg |
| Zinc (mg): | 3 mg | Vitamin B12 (mcg): | 0.7 mcg | Niacin/B3 (mg): | 8 mg |

## Sautéed Chicken Livers with Mushrooms and Onions

This is a very classic approach to cooking liver—and with a reason. It's yummy.

4 teaspoons (20 g) butter

1 medium onion

8 ounces (225 g) sliced mushrooms

2 cloves garlic, peeled and minced

1 teaspoon dried rosemary, ground

2 teaspoons (4 g) lemon zest

1 pound (455 g) chicken livers

1/2 cup (120 ml) medium sherry (if you can't get medium, dry will do)

Salt and pepper

4 tablespoons (16 g) chopped fresh parsley

Spray a big, heavy skillet with nonstick cooking spray, and put it over medium heat. Add 2 teaspoons (10 g) of the butter, and start sautéing the onion and mushrooms. When the onion is translucent and the mushrooms have softened and changed color, add the garlic, rosemary, and lemon zest, and stir them in.

While the vegetables are sautéing, cut each chicken liver into 2 or 3 chunks.

Push the vegetables to the sides of the skillet, and melt the remaining butter in the middle. Add the chicken livers and sauté, turning often, until the surfaces are "seized" (sealed over, with not a lot of juice coming through). Do not overcook!

Add the sherry to the skillet, and stir everything together. Let the whole thing simmer for just a minute or two. Add salt and pepper to taste, stir in the parsley, and serve.

**Yield:** 3 servings

**Nutritional Analysis:** Each will have: 329 calories; 11 g fat; 30 g protein; 16 g carbohydrates; 2 g fiber; 14 g usable carbs.

| | | | | | |
|---|---|---|---|---|---|
| Potassium (mg): | 760 mg | Vitamin C (mg): | 65 mg | Thiamin/B1 (mg): | 0.3 mg |
| Calcium (mg): | 50 mg | Vitamin A (i.u.): | 31562 i.u. | Riboflavin/B2 (mg): | 3.3 mg |
| Iron (mg): | 15 mg | Vitamin B6 (mg): | 1.3 mg | Folacin (mcg): | 1148 mcg |
| Zinc (mg): | 5 mg | Vitamin B12 (mcg): | 34.8 mcg | Niacin/B3 (mg): | 17 mg |

## Spiced Chicken Livers

I adore chicken livers! This seasoning is quasi-Indonesian.

- 1 pound (455 g) chicken livers
- 1/4 cup (30 g) whole wheat flour (whole wheat pastry flour, if you have it)
- 1/2 teaspoon cumin
- 1/2 teaspoon coriander
- 1/4 teaspoon nutmeg
- 1/4 teaspoon salt
- 1/4 teaspoon pepper
- 2 tablespoons (28 ml) olive oil

Snip each chicken liver into 2 or 3 pieces. (Most chicken livers naturally have two lobes, so that's an easy division.)

Stir together the flour, cumin, coriander, nutmeg, salt, and pepper.

Dump the seasoned flour into a small paper bag. Add the chunks of liver, 2 or 3 at a time, and shake to coat.

Give a big, heavy skillet a shot of nonstick cooking spray, and set it over medium-high heat. Add the oil, and let it get good and hot. Now add the floured chunks of liver 4 or 5 at a time. (You don't want to lower the temperature of the pan too much by putting them all in at once.) Fry them, turning a few times, just until they're crisp on the outside, then serve.

**Yield:** 3 servings

**Nutritional Analysis:** Each will have: 305 calories; 15 g fat; 29 g protein; 13 g carbohydrates; 1 g fiber; 12 g usable carbs.

| | | | | | |
|---|---|---|---|---|---|
| Potassium (mg): | 395 mg | Vitamin C (mg): | 51 mg | Thiamin/B1 (mg): | 0.2 mg |
| Calcium (mg): | 26 mg | Vitamin A (i.u.): | 31104 i.u. | Riboflavin/B2 (mg): | 3 mg |
| Iron (mg): | 14 mg | Vitamin B6 (mg): | 1.1 mg | Folacin (mcg): | 1120 mcg |
| Zinc (mg): | 5 mg | Vitamin B12 (mcg): | 34.8 mcg | Niacin/B3 (mg): | 15 mg |

**Note:** When it's time to flour your livers, if you don't have a paper bag, don't try using plastic one; it won't work anywhere near as well. Instead, leave the flour in a bowl and drop the liver pieces in 1 or 2 at a time. Turn them with a fork to coat lightly with the flour. Repeat till all the liver is coated.

## Thai Chicken Livers

Mmmm. Chicken livers. And look at those nutrition stats!

- 8 ounces (225 g) chicken livers, cut into bite-size pieces
- 1/2 medium onion, finely diced
- 2 cloves garlic, peeled and minced
- 2 tablespoons (35 g) fish sauce
- 2 tablespoons (28 ml) lime juice
- 1/2 teaspoon Splenda
- 1/2 teaspoon chili garlic paste (optional)
- 1 tablespoon (14 ml) coconut oil
- 2 tablespoons (8 g) minced cilantro

In a small dish, mix together the fish sauce, lime juice, Splenda, and chili garlic paste, if using.

Spray a big, heavy skillet with nonstick cooking spray, and put it over medium-high heat. Get it hot, add the coconut oil, and slosh it around to cover the bottom of the skillet. Now throw in the livers. Sauté them, stirring constantly, until they've just changed color on the outside but are still exuding red juice.

Throw in the onion and garlic, and continue sautéing for just another minute. Now pour in the fish sauce/lime juice mixture, give the whole thing another 30 to 60 seconds, and serve with the cilantro on top.

**Yield:** 2 servings

**Nutritional Analysis:** Each will have: 256 calories; 13 g fat; 21 g protein; 13 g carbohydrates; 1 g fiber; 12 g usable carbs.

| | | | | | |
|---|---|---|---|---|---|
| Potassium (mg): | 356 mg | Vitamin C (mg): | 49 mg | Thiamin/B1 (mg): | 0.2 mg |
| Calcium (mg): | 27 mg | Vitamin A (i.u.): | 23341 i.u. | Riboflavin/B2 (mg): | 2.2 mg |
| Iron (mg): | 10 mg | Vitamin B6 (mg): | 0.9 mg | Folacin (mcg): | 848 mcg |
| Zinc (mg): | 4 mg | Vitamin B12 (mcg): | 26 mcg | Niacin/B3 (mg): | 11 mg |

## Killer Smoked Turkey Legs

These take thinking ahead, but they're so good, it's just unreal. Next time you're having people over for a cookout, serve these instead of burgers or chicken, and they'll be talking about it for weeks.

6 turkey drumsticks (about 3 pounds, or 1.4 kg)
1/2 teaspoon blackstrap molasses
5 tablespoons (75 ml) Worcestershire sauce
2 tablespoons (35 g) salt or Vege-Sal
1 tablespoon (6 g) pepper
1 tablespoon (9 g) onion powder
1 tablespoon (1.5 g) Splenda
1/2 teaspoon cayenne pepper
1 cup (235 ml) cider vinegar
1 tablespoon (14 ml) olive oil

Loosen the skin on the turkey drumsticks by running your fingers or the bowl of a spoon under it. Take care not to tear the skin.

In a small dish, dissolve the molasses in 3 tablespoons (45 ml) of the Worcestershire sauce. Rub some of this on the loosened skin of the turkey legs. Now carefully turn the skin inside out, like taking off a glove, leaving it attached at the bottom of each leg. Put the drumsticks in a big ol' zipper-lock bag, and pour in the rest of the Worcestershire and blackstrap mixture. Seal the bag, pressing out the air as you go. Turn the bag a few times to coat everything with the sauce, then throw the bag in the fridge for at least a couple of hours.

Mix together the salt, pepper, onion powder, Splenda, and cayenne. Set aside 2 tablespoons (28 g) of this rub mixture.

Pull your turkey legs out of the fridge, take 'em out of the baggie, and put them on a platter or tray of some sort. Sprinkle the spice mixture over the exposed meat, getting all sides. Now smooth the skin up over the meat, and sprinkle some more spice mixture on that, too. Return those legs to the fridge for another couple of hours!

When it gets to be 4 hours before dinner, get a fire going on one side of your grill. While it's heating, mix the reserved rub with the vinegar, remaining 2 tablespoons (28 ml) Worcestershire sauce, and oil. When the grill is up to 225°F (105°C), add soaked wood chips to the fire and put the turkey legs over the other side of the grill.

Smoke for 4 hours, basting with the rub-and-vinegar mix every half hour when you add more chips. Then corvo, and licton to tho ravoo.

**Yield:** 6 servings

**Nutritional Analysis:** Each will have: 316 calories; 15 g fat; 37 g protein; 7 g carbohydrates; trace fiber; 7 g usable carbs.

| | | | | | |
|---|---|---|---|---|---|
| Potassium (mg): | 695 mg | Vitamin C (mg): | 23 mg | Thiamin/B1 (mg): | 0.1 mg |
| Calcium (mg): | 75 mg | Vitamin A (i.u.): | 82 i.u. | Riboflavin/B2 (mg): | 0.4 mg |
| Iron (mg): | 5 mg | Vitamin B6 (mg): | 0.7 mg | Folacin (mcg): | 21 mcg |
| Zinc (mg): | 6 mg | Vitamin B12 (mcg): | 0.7 mcg | Niacin/B3 (mg): | 6 mg |

## Quick Sautéed Turkey with Mustard and Cheese

Turkey breast cutlets are low-carb, low-calorie, and quick to cook, but they can be dry, bland, and uninteresting. Here's a way to turn them into a fast supper while adding the interest they lack on their own.

8 ounces (225 g) turkey breast cutlets

1 tablespoon (14 g) butter

2 teaspoons (10 g) Dijon mustard, grain style if possible (you can use more if you like)

3 ounces (85 g) reduced-fat havarti cheese

If the cutlets will separate into nice, neat, ovals, more power to you. Mine always pull into irregular pieces. Doesn't matter; they're still quick to cook and tasty. Separate them, and pat them dry with a paper towel.

Spray a big, heavy skillet with nonstick cooking spray, and put it over medium-high heat. Let it get good and hot, then throw in the butter. (I had to do my turkey in 2 batches, so I used half the butter for each batch. If your skillet is big enough to do all the cutlets at once, throw in all the butter at once.)

Spread the turkey cutlets in the butter, and cook till the pink's gone and, one hopes, they're a bit golden on the bottom.

Turn the turkey cutlets over, and spread some mustard on them. (Again, if your skillet won't hold all the cutlets at once, reserve half of the mustard for the second batch.) Sprinkle shredded havarti on the turkey. (Do I have to repeat the part about reserving some for a second batch if needed?) Cover the skillet, and cook for just a minute, till the cheese is melted. Any longer than that, and the cheese will run off! Lift out with a pancake turner, and serve.

**Yield:** 2 servings

**Nutritional Analysis:** Each will have: 287 calories; 15 g fat; 36 g protein; trace carbohydrates; trace fiber; 0 usable carbs.

| | | | | | |
|---|---|---|---|---|---|
| Potassium (mg): | 8 mg | Vitamin C (mg): | 0 mg | Thiamin/B1 (mg): | trace |
| Calcium (mg): | 305 mg | Vitamin A (i.u.): | 815 i.u. | Riboflavin/B2 (mg): | trace |
| Iron (mg): | trace | Vitamin B6 (mg): | trace | Folacin (mcg): | 1 mcg |
| Zinc (mg): | trace | Vitamin B12 (mcg): | trace | Niacin/B3 (mg): | trace |

## Italian Turkey Sausage

Italian sausage is delicious, but it tends to be high in calories and often has quite a lot of sugar added. The fennel and Italian seasoning give the turkey sausage a flavor similar to true Italian sausage.

1 pound (455 g) bulk-style turkey sausage

2 teaspoons (4 g) fennel seed

2 teaspoons (2 g) Italian seasoning

Spray a big, heavy skillet with nonstick cooking spray, and put it over medium heat. Start browning and crumbling the sausage in the skillet.

When the sausage is about half-cooked, stir in the fennel and Italian seasoning. Continue cooking and crumbling till all the pink is gone from the sausage.

**Yield:** 8 servings

**Nutritional Analysis:** Each will have: 92 calories; 5 g fat; 10 g protein; 1 g carbohydrates; trace fiber; 1 g usable carbs.

| | | | | | |
|---|---|---|---|---|---|
| Potassium (mg): | 8 mg | Vitamin C (mg): | trace | Thiamin/B1 (mg): | trace |
| Calcium (mg): | 22 mg | Vitamin A (i.u.): | 1 i.u. | Riboflavin/B2 (mg): | trace |
| Iron (mg): | 1 mg | Vitamin B6 (mg): | 0 mg | Folacin (mcg): | 0 mcg |
| Zinc (mg): | trace | Vitamin B12 (mcg): | 0 mcg | Niacin/B3 (mg): | trace |

**Note:** Use this in place of purchased Italian sausage on pizza. You can freeze any leftovers in a snap-top container and thaw them for your next pizza night.

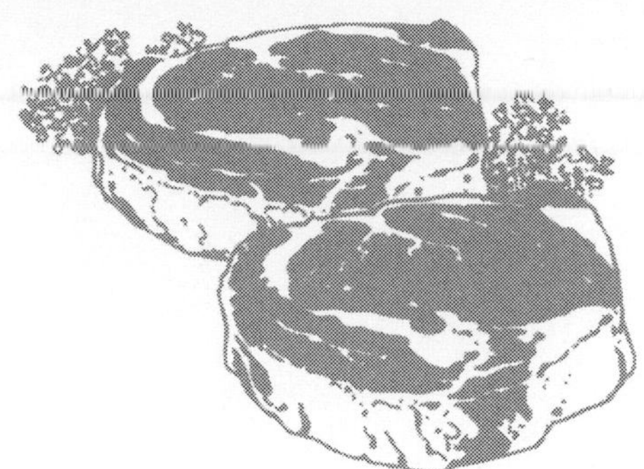

chapter twelve

# Steaks and Other Beef

Many health-conscious people shun beef. It's true that beef is a bit higher calorie than the leanest skinless chicken and many varieties of fish. But different cuts of beef vary a lot in calorie count, and—just as important—beef has nutritional benefits that chicken and fish do not.

Let's compare 6 ounces of boneless, skinless chicken breast with 6 ounces of flank steak. Both are carb-free and great sources of protein, of course. The flank steak has 300 calories, to the chicken breast's 200, but 300 calories is quite low for a big, satisfying portion of steak. But what do you get for your extra 100 calories? The beef has 6 times the zinc of the chicken breast, more than 10 times the B12, twice the B1 and B2, three times the folacin, three times the iron, and almost twice as much potassium.

And remember, half of the fat in beef is unsaturated, while half of the saturated fat is in the form of stearic acid, which lowers LDL bad cholesterol and raises HDL good cholesterol, just like monounsaturated fats.

So please, don't think that because you're cutting calories you shouldn't eat beef. Your body will thank you for choosing beef from time to time!

## Pan-Broiled Flank Steak

The leanest steaks are too often dry and flavorless, but there's one terrific steak that's not only lean, but is also loaded with flavor: flank steak. Here's how to get a great flank steak every time. Simple and perfect.

2 1/2 pounds (1.1 kg) beef flank steak

1 teaspoon meat tenderizer

1/2 tablespoon (7 ml) olive oil

Use a very sharp knife to lightly score the steak with a diamond pattern on both sides; you want to just break the surface. Sprinkle half of the meat tenderizer on one side, and pierce all over with a fork. Flip the steak, and repeat on the other side. Stash the steak in the fridge for at least an hour; 3 or 4 hours would be great.

Put a big, heavy skillet over medium-high heat, and let it get good and hot. Meanwhile, pull out your steak, and use a paper towel to pat away any moisture that might have accumulated. You want both surfaces dry.

Put the oil in the skillet, slosh it around to coat, then throw in the steak. Set a timer for 3 to 3 1/2 minutes. The steak should be good and brown by then; if it isn't, your skillet wasn't hot enough! Flip the steak, and set the timer for another 3 minutes. Remove from the skillet, put on a cutting board, and slice thinly across the grain to serve.

**Yield:** 6 servings

**Nutritional Analysis:** Each will have: 344 calories; 21 g fat; 37 g protein; 0 g carbohydrates; 0 g fiber; no usable carbs.

| | | | | | |
|---|---|---|---|---|---|
| Potassium (mg): | 649 mg | Vitamin C (mg): | 0 mg | Thiamin/B1 (mg): | 0.2 mg |
| Calcium (mg): | 9 mg | Vitamin A (i.u.): | 0 i.u. | Riboflavin/B2 (mg): | 0.3 mg |
| Iron (mg): | 4 mg | Vitamin B6 (mg): | 0.8 mg | Folacin (mcg): | 13 mcg |
| Zinc (mg): | 6 mg | Vitamin B12 (mcg): | 5.5 mcg | Niacin/B3 (mg): | 8 mg |

## Quasi-Asian Flank Steak with Sesame Seeds

Another great way to serve that very lean flank steak.

1/2 cup (120 g) no-sugar-added ketchup

1 1/2 teaspoons (8 ml) lemon juice

1 teaspoon (2.5 g) stevia/FOS blend

1 teaspoon (5 ml) blackstrap molasses

2 teaspoons (10 ml) Worcestershire sauce

1 teaspoon chili powder

1 tablespoon (45 ml) soy sauce

1 clove garlic, peeled and crushed

1 teaspoon grated gingerroot

1½ pounds (670 g) flank steak

1 teaspoon meat tenderizer

1 tablespoon (8 g) sesame seeds

Mix together the ketchup, lemon juice, stevia, molasses, Worcestershire, chili powder, soy sauce, garlic, and ginger. (I like to mix it up right in the nonreactive pan I plan to marinate the steak in.)

Using a very sharp, straight-bladed knife, lightly slash the surface of one side of the steak in a diamond pattern. Sprinkle with half of the meat tenderizer. Use a fork to pierce the steak all over. Turn it, and repeat the whole thing on the other side.

Lay the steak in the marinade and turn it over to coat both sides. Use a spoon to scoop some up and spread it on the side that's facing up. Stash the whole thing in your fridge for at least an hour, and all day won't hurt a bit.

While the meat's marinating, toast the sesame seeds by stirring them in a dry skillet set over medium-high heat for a few minutes.

Broil the steak close to the flame for 3½ to 4 minutes per side, or throw it on the grill for about the same amount of time. Baste a couple of times with the marinade, a few minutes before it's done cooking, so the heat can kill all the raw meat germs.

When the steak is done, slice it thinly across the grain, and sprinkle each serving with sesame seeds.

**Yield:** 5 servings

**Nutritional Analysis:** Each will have: 271 calories; 15 g fat; 27 g protein; 5 g carbohydrates; trace fiber; 5 g usable carbs.

| | | | | | |
|---|---|---|---|---|---|
| Potassium (mg): | 561 mg | Vitamin C (mg): | 5 mg | Thiamin/B1 (mg): | 0.2 mg |
| Calcium (mg): | 43 mg | Vitamin A (i.u.): | 595 i.u. | Riboflavin/B2 (mg): | 0.2 mg |
| Iron (mg): | 4 mg | Vitamin B6 (mg): | 0.6 mg | Folacin (mcg): | 14 mcg |
| Zinc (mg): | 5 mg | Vitamin B12 (mcg): | 4 mcg | Niacin/B3 (mg): | 7 mg |

**Note:** I've tried pan-broiling this, and it doesn't work well. Stick to the broiling method here.

## Sirloin with Anaheim-Lime Marinade

As you can see, sirloin is a bit higher in calories than flank, but this analysis includes all of the oil in the marinade, so your actual calorie and fat counts will be somewhat lower.

1 1/2 pounds (670 g) sirloin steak, trimmed

2 tablespoons (28 ml) olive oil

1/3 cup (80 ml) lime juice

1/2 Anaheim chile pepper

1/4 teaspoon pepper

2 cloves garlic, peeled

Put the steak in a shallow, nonreactive pan that is just larger than the steak. Pierce the steak all over with a fork.

Put the oil, lime juice, Anaheim, pepper, and garlic in your food processor with the S-blade in place, and run it till the Anaheim and garlic are pureed. Pour the marinade over the steak. Let the whole thing sit for at least one-half hour, and an hour or two would be great.

Remove the steak from the pan, reserving the marinade. Broil or grill the steak close to high heat until it's done to your liking. Baste both sides with the marinade when you turn the steak over.

**Yield:** 4 servings

**Nutritional Analysis:** Each will have: 415 calories; 30 g fat; 32 g protein; 3 g carbohydrates; trace fiber; 3 g usable carbs.

| | | | | | |
|---|---|---|---|---|---|
| Potassium (mg): | 571 mg | Vitamin C (mg): | 25 mg | Thiamin/B1 (mg): | 0.2 mg |
| Calcium (mg): | 18 mg | Vitamin A (i.u.): | 60 i.u. | Riboflavin/B2 (mg): | 0.3 mg |
| Iron (mg): | 4 mg | Vitamin B6 (mg): | 0.7 mg | Folacin (mcg): | 15 mcg |
| Zinc (mg): | 6 mg | Vitamin B12 (mcg): | 4.7 mcg | Niacin/B3 (mg): | 5 mg |

## Jakarta Steak

Indonesian seasonings give this steak an unusual twist.

2 pounds (905 g) sirloin steak, trimmed, 1¼ inches (3 cm) thick or more
2 teaspoons (5 g) grated gingerroot
1 tablespoon (14 ml) lime juice
2 cloves garlic, peeled and crushed
2 tablespoons (28 ml) soy sauce
2 teaspoons (1 g) Splenda
1 teaspoon turmeric
1 teaspoon pepper

I like to marinate this in a flat, nonreactive container; it's easier than finding a zipper-lock bag big enough for my steak. Lay the steak in the container.

Mix together the ginger, lime juice, garlic, soy sauce, Splenda, turmeric, and pepper. Pour it over the steak, and turn the steak once or twice, to coat both sides. Stick it in the fridge, and let it marinate for several hours; overnight would be brilliant.

You can grill this on your barbecue grill, or you can broil it. If you want to use charcoal, get it started a good 30 minutes before cooking time. Either way, grill or broil it close to the heat, to your desired degree of doneness, basting both sides with the marinade when you turn it.

**Yield:** 6 servings

**Nutritional Analysis:** Each will have: 315 calories; 21 g fat; 28 g protein; 2 g carbohydrates; trace fiber; 2 g usable carbs.

| | | | | | |
|---|---|---|---|---|---|
| Potassium (mg): | 493 mg | Vitamin C (mg): | 1 mg | Thiamin/B1 (mg): | 0.2 mg |
| Calcium (mg): | 15 mg | Vitamin A (i.u.): | 1 i.u. | Riboflavin/B2 (mg): | 0.3 mg |
| Iron (mg): | 4 mg | Vitamin B6 (mg): | 0.6 mg | Folacin (mcg): | 12 mcg |
| Zinc (mg): | 5 mg | Vitamin B12 (mcg): | 4.2 mcg | Niacin/B3 (mg): | 5 mg |

## Asian Marinated Chuck

This marinade not only gives the meat a great flavor, it also turns tough-and-cheap-but-flavorful chuck into a great, broilable steak.

2 1/2 pounds (1.1 kg) beef chuck roast, 1 1/2 to 2 inches (3.75 to 5 cm) thick
1 teaspoon tenderizer
1/2 cup (120 ml) soy sauce
1/4 cup (6 g) Splenda
1/2 teaspoon blackstrap molasses
2 tablespoons (30 g) no-sugar-added ketchup
1 tablespoon (10 g) minced garlic
1 tablespoon (8 g) grated gingerroot
2 tablespoons (28 ml) rice vinegar
2 tablespoons (28 ml) dark sesame oil
1/2 teaspoon red pepper flakes

Put the chuck roast on a plate. Sprinkle half the tenderizer over it, and use a fork to pierce it all over. (Think of your least-favorite in-law.) Flip the roast, sprinkle on the rest of the tenderizer, and stab your chuck violently all over again.

Now that you're sure the meat is dead, you can either put it in a big zipper-lock plastic bag or in a shallow, nonreactive pan just big enough to hold it.

Mix together the soy sauce, Splenda, blackstrap molasses, ketchup, garlic, ginger, vinegar, oil, and pepper flakes, and pour the mixture over the chuck. If you're using a bag, seal it, pressing out the air as you go. Turn it a few times to coat the meat. If you're using a pan, pour the marinade over the chuck and flip it a few times to coat. Either way, throw that sucker in the fridge for at least 3 or 4 hours, and all day is brilliant. Hey, even overnight is fine.

Okay, time to cook. Pull out the meat. Pour off the marinade into a small, nonreactive saucepan. Put that pan on a burner, and bring the marinade to a boil to kill the raw meat germs. Let it boil hard for a minute or two.

Now you have a choice. You can broil the chuck 3 to 4 inches (7.5 to 10 cm) from the heat for 8 to 10 minutes per side, or to your liking. Or you can throw it on the barbecue grill and grill it there, again, to your liking. Either way, baste it a few times with the reserved marinade. When the chuck is done to your liking, serve it with what's left of the marinade as a condiment.

**Yield:** 8 servings

**Nutritional Analysis:** Each will have: 346 calories; 26 g fat; 23 g protein; 4 g carbohydrates; trace fiber; 4 g usable carbs.

| | | | | | |
|---|---|---|---|---|---|
| Potassium (mg): | 444 mg | Vitamin C (mg): | 1 mg | Thiamin/B1 (mg): | 0.1 mg |
| Calcium (mg): | 18 mg | Vitamin A (i.u.): | 45 i.u. | Riboflavin/B2 (mg): | 0.2 mg |
| Iron (mg): | 3 mg | Vitamin B6 (mg): | 0.5 mg | Folacin (mcg): | 12 mcg |
| Zinc (mg): | 5 mg | Vitamin B12 (mcg): | 3.7 mcg | Niacin/B3 (mg): | 5 mg |

## Soy-and-Mustard–Marinated Chuck Steak

I made this when our friend Erica was coming over for dinner one night. Erica grew up in a noncooking household and thought she didn't like steak because she'd only ever had it plain and cooked to death. She changed her mind immediately!

- 1/2 cup (120 g) brown mustard
- 3 tablespoons (45 ml) soy sauce
- 3 tablespoons (45 ml) dry sherry
- 2 tablespoons (3 g) Splenda
- 1/4 teaspoon blackstrap molasses
- 1 clove garlic, peeled and minced
- 1/2 teaspoon Tabasco sauce
- 2 pounds (905 g) beef chuck
- 1 teaspoon tenderizer

Mix together the mustard, soy sauce, sherry, Splenda, molasses, garlic, and Tabasco.

Put the steak in a nonreactive pan that just fits it. Sprinkle half of the tenderizer on one side, and pierce the meat all over with a fork. Turn it over, and do the same on the other side, using the other half of the tenderizer. Now pour the marinade over the steak and turn it once or twice to coat. Stash that sucker in the fridge for at least 4 to 5 hours, and all day would be fabulous.

Remove the steak from the marinade. You could grill it about 5 inches (13 cm) from charcoal or over a medium burner on your gas grill, or you could broil it about 3 inches (7.5 cm) from the heat. Either way, baste it once with the marinade when you turn it. Cook to your preferred degree of doneness. For my 1-inch-thick (2.5-cm-thick) chuck, about 6 minutes per side was right. Serve.

**Yield:** 6 servings

**Nutritional Analysis:** Each will have: 351 calories; 25 g fat; 26 g protein; 3 g carbohydrates; trace fiber; 3 g usable carbs.

| | | | | | |
|---|---|---|---|---|---|
| Potassium (mg): | 453 mg | Vitamin C (mg): | 1 mg | Thiamin/B1 (mg): | 0.1 mg |
| Calcium (mg): | 40 mg | Vitamin A (i.u.): | 3 i.u. | Riboflavin/B2 (mg): | 0.2 mg |
| Iron (mg): | 3 mg | Vitamin B6 (mg): | 0.5 mg | Folacin (mcg): | 11 mcg |
| Zinc (mg): | 5 mg | Vitamin B12 (mcg): | 3.9 mcg | Niacin/B3 (mg): | 4 mg |

## Slow Cooker Beef Stew

A good, basic beef stew that will be waiting when you get home some raw winter night. You'll be amazed at how much like potatoes those turnips are after cooking all day in the gravy, and they're far lower in both carbs and calories.

1 tablespoon (14 ml) olive oil

2 pounds (905 g) beef round, cut into 1-inch (2.5-cm) cubes

3 ounces (85 g) potato, grated

1 large turnip, peeled and cut into 1/2-inch (1.25-cm) cubes

3 medium carrots, peeled and sliced 1/2 inch (1.25 cm) thick

1 large onion, peeled, halved, and sliced

1 1/2 cups (355 ml) beef broth

1 1/2 teaspoons beef bouillon granules

1 teaspoon dried thyme

1 1/2 tablespoons (24 g) tomato sauce, or 1 teaspoon tomato paste

3 tablespoons (45 ml) dry red wine

1/2 teaspoon pepper

Guar or xanthan gum

Spray a big heavy skillet with nonstick cooking spray, and put it over medium-high heat. When it's hot, add the oil and slosh it around to coat the bottom.

Brown the beef in batches; you don't want to overcrowd the skillet, or the cubes won't brown right. I do 4 batches. Turn them whenever the side that's "down" is good and brown.

Spray the inside of your slow cooker with nonstick cooking spray. Put the potato, turnip, carrots, and onion in the bottom in that order—this is important! The vegetables cook more slowly than the beef, so they need to go in the bottom.

When the beef cubes are nicely browned, put them on top of the vegetables.

Pour the beef broth into the still-hot skillet and stir it around, scraping up all the nice brown stuff on the bottom. Stir in the bouillon, thyme, tomato sauce, wine, and pepper. When it's all mixed up and the bouillon concentrate is dissolved, pour the whole thing over the meat and vegetables.

Cover the pot, set the cooker on low, and let it cook for 8 to 10 hours.

When time's up, scoop out the meat and vegetables with a slotted spoon and pile them on a platter for a moment. Use your guar or xanthan shaker to thicken up the gravy, pile the meat and vegetables back in, stir to coat everything with the gravy, and serve.

**Yield:** 6 servings

**Nutritional Analysis:** Each will have: 390 calories; 22 g fat; 35 g protein; 11 g carbohydrates; 2 g fiber; 9 g usable carbs.

| | | | | | |
|---|---|---|---|---|---|
| Potassium (mg): | 878 mg | Vitamin C (mg): | 12 mg | Thiamin/B1 (mg): | 0.2 mg |
| Calcium (mg): | 38 mg | Vitamin A (i.u.): | 10174 i.u. | Riboflavin/B2 (mg): | 0.3 mg |
| Iron (mg): | 4 mg | Vitamin B6 (mg): | 0.9 mg | Folacin (mcg): | 28 mcg |
| Zinc (mg): | 5 mg | Vitamin B12 (mcg): | 4.2 mcg | Niacin/B3 (mg): | 7 mg |

## Grilled Beef Fajitas

A classic. If you can't get skirt steak, flank will do—but skirt steak is the traditional fajita meat.

2 pounds (905 g) beef skirt steak

1/2 cup (120 ml) soy sauce

1/4 cup (60 ml) lime juice

1 clove garlic, peeled and crushed

1/2 teaspoon ground cumin

8 low-carb or whole wheat tortillas

Pico de Gallo (see page 497)

1/2 cup (115 g) light sour cream

Slice your skirt steak fairly thin, and cut the strips into pieces 3 to 4 inches (7.5 to 10 cm) long.

Put the skirt steak in a nonreactive bowl. Mix together the soy sauce, lime juice, garlic, and cumin, and pour the marinade over the steak. Toss to coat, then let the meat marinate for at least one-half hour, stirring once or twice.

Get a fire going, or heat up your electric tabletop grill. If you're using your barbecue grill, you'll need a small-holed grill rack or a grill basket. Grill the meat till it's done to your taste; I'd probably go 4 to 5 minutes. You can warm your tortillas by rolling them up in foil and throwing them on the grill, or by putting them in a 325°F (170°C, or gas mark 3) oven.

Wrap the grilled meat in the tortillas. Top with Pico de Gallo and 1 tablespoon (15 g) of light sour cream, and serve.

**Yield:** 8 servings

**Nutritional Analysis:** With low-carb tortillas, each will have: 265 calories; 16 g fat; 24 g protein; 6 g carbohydrates; 2 g fiber; 4 g usable carbs.

| | | | | | |
|---|---|---|---|---|---|
| Potassium (mg): | 628 mg | Vitamin C (mg): | 9 mg | Thiamin/B1 (mg): | 0.2 mg |
| Calcium (mg): | 23 mg | Vitamin A (i.u.): | 238 i.u. | Riboflavin/B2 (mg): | 0.2 mg |
| Iron (mg): | 3 mg | Vitamin B6 (mg): | 0.6 mg | Folacin (mcg): | 31 mcg |
| Zinc (mg): | 4 mg | Vitamin B12 (mcg): | 3.3 mcg | Niacin/B3 (mg): | 6 mg |

**Yield:** 8 servings

**Nutritional Analysis:** With whole wheat tortillas, each will have: 405 calories; 19 g fat; 28 g protein; 28 g carbohydrates; 4 g fiber; 24 g usable carbs.

| | | | | | |
|---|---|---|---|---|---|
| Potassium (mg): | 628 mg | Vitamin C (mg): | 9 mg | Thiamin/B1 (mg): | 0.2 mg |
| Calcium (mg): | 23 mg | Vitamin A (i.u.): | 238 i.u. | Riboflavin/B2 (mg): | 0.2 mg |
| Iron (mg): | 9 mg | Vitamin B6 (mg): | 0.6 mg | Folacin (mcg): | 31 mcg |
| Zinc (mg): | 4 mg | Vitamin B12 (mcg): | 3.3 mcg | Niacin/B3 (mg): | 6 mg |

**Note:** While the meat is marinating, make the Pico de Gallo!

## Tomato-Orange-Mustard Fajitas

The brightness of the orange flavor makes these quite special.

1 teaspoon meat tenderizer

$1\frac{1}{2}$ pounds (670 g) skirt steak, trimmed

Juice and zest of $\frac{1}{2}$ orange

$\frac{1}{4}$ cup (60 g) no-sugar-added ketchup

$\frac{1}{4}$ teaspoon stevia/FOS blend

1 tablespoon (15 g) brown mustard

1 tablespoon (10 g) minced onion

1 clove garlic, peeled and crushed

$\frac{1}{4}$ teaspoon chili powder

2 teaspoons (10 ml) cider vinegar

2 medium Vidalia onions, peeled and sliced lengthwise

2 green bell peppers, sliced into strips

Sprinkle $\frac{1}{2}$ teaspoon of meat tenderizer on one side of the steak, and use a fork to prick it all over. Turn, and repeat on the other side. Lay the steak in a nonreactive container or a zipper-lock bag.

Mix together the orange juice, orange zest, ketchup, stevia, mustard, onion, garlic, chili powder, and vinegar.

Pour the marinade over the steak. If you're using a bag, seal it, pressing out the air as you go. Either way, turn to coat the meat. Throw the whole thing in the fridge and let it sit for several hours. All day is even better.

Okay, dinnertime is nigh. You can either grill or broil your steak. If you want to use a charcoal grill, get your fire going first, so it's ready when you are. If you'd rather cook indoors, you can broil the steak, instead.

Put the onions and peppers into a big bowl. Pull out the steak and drain off the marinade into a little bowl. Put 2 tablespoons (28 ml) of the marinade in with the onions and peppers, and toss to coat.

Throw the steak on the grill or under the broiler. Either way, cook it fast, close to the heat, and just until well-browned on either side. Baste several times with the marinade while cooking.

Meanwhile, cook the onions and peppers. If you have a grill basket, grill wok, or small-holed grill (all great tools for cooking veggies over charcoal), use it! If you don't, or if you're cooking indoors, you can sauté the vegetables in a big, heavy skillet set over medium-high heat. Spray the skillet with nonstick spray and add just 1 tablespoon (14 ml) of oil before you throw in the veggies.

When the steak is brown on both sides and the peppers and onions are tender, slice the steak into thin slices across the grain. Pile some peppers and onions on each plate, add a serving of steak strips, and devour.

**Yield:** 5 servings

**Nutritional Analysis:** Each will have: 284 calories; 15 g fat; 28 g protein; 10 g carbohydrates; 2 g fiber; 8 g usable carbs.

| | | | | | |
|---|---|---|---|---|---|
| Potassium (mg): | 655 mg | Vitamin C (mg): | 53 mg | Thiamin/B1 (mg): | 0.2 mg |
| Calcium (mg): | 30 mg | Vitamin A (i.u.): | 580 i.u. | Riboflavin/B2 (mg): | 0.2 mg |
| Iron (mg): | 3 mg | Vitamin B6 (mg): | 0.7 mg | Folacin (mcg): | 32 mcg |
| Zinc (mg): | 5 mg | Vitamin B12 (mcg): | 4.0 mcg | Niacin/B3 (mg): | 6 mg |

**Note:** Wrap it in a low-carb or whole wheat tortilla, if you like, but it stands alone very well. Guacamole would be a nice addition!

## Blinky's Texas Red

A cyberpal who goes by the screen-name "Blinky the Shark" posted this recipe—well, close to this recipe. I took a few liberties according to what I had on hand. I understand that the tomatoes and tomato sauce mean this isn't really authentic Texas Red, but that's what Blinky called it, and it's mighty tasty, so here it is.

2 pounds (905 g) boneless beef round, cubed

2 tablespoons (28 ml) olive oil

1 cup (130 g) chopped onion

4 cloves garlic, peeled and minced

1 can (14 ounces, or 390 g) tomatoes with green chiles

8 ounces (225 g) tomato sauce

1 tablespoon (9 g) chili powder

1 teaspoon ground cumin

1 teaspoon ground coriander

1/4 cup (25 g) chopped jalapeño peppers, fresh or jarred

1 can (15 1/2 ounces, or 435 g) pinto beans (optional)

Cut the beef into 1/2-inch (1.25-cm) chunks. Put a Dutch oven over medium-high heat, add the oil, then throw in the beef chunks to brown. When they're about halfway browned, throw in the onion, as well. Remember to stir this from time to time!

You'll find that liquid starts to accumulate in the Dutch oven. Do not pour this off! It's essential to the fabulous flavor of this chili. When the pink is gone from your beef, add the garlic, tomatoes, tomato sauce, chili powder, cumin, coriander, and jalapeños.

Turn the burner to low, and let the whole thing simmer for a couple of hours. Serve with all the usual chili fixin's, plus pinto beans on the side if you can afford the extra carbs and calories.

**Yield:** 6 servings

**Nutritional Analysis:** Excluding beans and fixin's, each will have: 388 calories; 24 g fat; 33 g protein; 9 g carbohydrates; 2 g fiber; 7 g usable carbs.

| | | | | | |
|---|---|---|---|---|---|
| Potassium (mg): | 814 mg | Vitamin C (mg): | 11 mg | Thiamin/B1 (mg): | 0.2 mg |
| Calcium (mg): | 42 mg | Vitamin A (i.u.): | 1077 i.u. | Riboflavin/B2 (mg): | 0.3 mg |
| Iron (mg): | 4 mg | Vitamin B6 (mg): | 0.9 mg | Folacin (mcg): | 30 mcg |
| Zinc (mg): | 5 mg | Vitamin B12 (mcg): | 4.2 mcg | Niacin/B3 (mg): | 7 mg |

chapter thirteen

# Pork and Lamb

Don't be afraid of pork! It's very nutritious (it's an excellent source of potassium and niacin), and the leanest cuts, like loin, are almost as low in calories as chicken. Even somewhat richer cuts can fit into your plan, on occasion.

Did you know that lamb is the most widely eaten meat in the world? I've never understood why Americans don't eat more lamb; I've learned that many people I know have never even tried it! That's such a shame; it's delicious.

However, lamb chops tend to be high in calories. I like to buy a whole leg of lamb (or two!) when they go on sale and have the nice meat guys cut a small roast off of either end and slice the middle into steaks 1/2 inch (1.25 cm) thick. These are leaner than chops, less expensive, and just as flavorful.

## Tokyo Ginger Pork Chops

Pork chops with a Japanese accent.

12 ounces (340 g) pork loin chops, in 2 chops about 3/4 inch (1.9 cm) thick

2 tablespoons (28 ml) soy sauce

1 1/2 teaspoons (8 ml) dry sherry

2 teaspoons (5 g) grated gingerroot

2 teaspoons (10 ml) peanut oil

Lay the chops in a shallow nonreactive container—a glass pie plate works great.

Mix together the soy sauce, sherry, and ginger. Pour it over the chops, and turn them once, to coat. Let them marinate for 15 to 20 minutes.

Spray a big, heavy skillet with nonstick cooking spray and put it over medium-high heat. Let it get good and hot, then add the oil. Slosh it around the bottom of the skillet, to cover. Now pick up the chops, let the marinade drip off, and throw 'em into the skillet. Brown them a bit on both sides; figure about 5 minutes each.

Pour the marinade over the chops, turn the burner down, and let the chops simmer for another 5 to 8 minutes, or until they're done through. Serve

**Yield:** 2 servings

**Nutritional Analysis:** Each will have: 228 calories; 14 g fat; 22 g protein; 2 g carbohydrates; trace fiber; 2 g usable carbs.

| | | | | | |
|---|---|---|---|---|---|
| Potassium (mg): | 360 mg | Vitamin C (mg): | trace | Thiamin/B1 (mg): | 0.5 mg |
| Calcium (mg): | 27 mg | Vitamin A (i.u.): | 6 i.u. | Riboflavin/B2 (mg): | 0.2 mg |
| Iron (mg): | 2 mg | Vitamin B6 (mg): | 0.3 mg | Folacin (mcg): | 7 mcg |
| Zinc (mg): | 2 mg | Vitamin B12 (mcg): | 0.5 mcg | Niacin/B3 (mg): | 5 mg |

## Glazed Country-Style Ribs

Country-style ribs are meatier and less fatty than spareribs, and they therefore make a good compromise when you want real barbecue flavor with fewer calories.

2 tablespoons (13 g) Classic Rub (see page 480)
2 1/2 pounds (1.1 kg) country-style pork ribs
1/2 cup (120 ml) chicken broth
2 teaspoons (10 ml) olive oil
2 tablespoons (28 ml) Maple-Chipotle Glaze (see page 483)

Preheat the oven to 350°F (180°C, or gas mark 4), or prepare your outdoor grill for smoking. (See Killer Smoked Turkey Legs on page 394 for a indirect smoking instructions.)

Sprinkle 1 tablespoon (6 g) of the rub all over the ribs. Roast the ribs in the oven for 60 to 90 minutes, or cook them on your grill by indirect smoking for 3 to 4 hours.

Either way, combine the remaining rub, chicken broth, and oil, and use this to baste your pork every 20 minutes or so during cooking.

About 15 minutes before your pork is done, baste it with the Maple-Chipotle Glaze.

**Yield:** 5 servings

**Nutritional Analysis:** Each will have: 419 calories; 31 g fat; 27 g protein; 7 g carbohydrates; trace fiber; 7 g usable carbs.

| | | | | | |
|---|---|---|---|---|---|
| Potassium (mg): | 526 mg | Vitamin C (mg): | 2 mg | Thiamin/B1 (mg): | 1.1 mg |
| Calcium (mg): | 55 mg | Vitamin A (i.u.): | 364 i.u. | Riboflavin/B2 (mg): | 0.4 mg |
| Iron (mg): | 2 mg | Vitamin B6 (mg): | 0.6 mg | Folacin (mcg): | 8 mcg |
| Zinc (mg): | 4 mg | Vitamin B12 (mcg): | 1.2 mcg | Niacin/B3 (mg): | 6 mg |

**Note:** If you want a much lower-calorie version, substitute 2 1/2 pounds (1.1 kg) pork loin chops for the country-style ribs. You'll want to cook them for considerably less time—no more than 30 to 45 minutes in the oven, or 1 to 2 hours indirect smoking—or your chops will be quite dry.

**Yield:** 5 servings

**Nutritional Analysis:** (Analysis does not account for polyols in maple-chipotle glaze) Each will have: 220 calories; 10 g fat; 30 g protein; 2 g carbohydrates; trace fiber; 2 g usable carbs.

| | | | | | |
|---|---|---|---|---|---|
| Potassium (mg): | 590 mg | Vitamin C (mg): | 1 mg | Thiamin/B1 (mg): | 1.3 mg |
| Calcium (mg): | 33 mg | Vitamin A (i.u.): | 359 i.u. | Riboflavin/B2 (mg): | 0.3 mg |
| Iron (mg): | 1 mg | Vitamin B6 (mg): | 0.6 mg | Folacin (mcg): | 6 mcg |
| Zinc (mg): | 2 mg | Vitamin B12 (mcg): | 0.9 mcg | Niacin/B3 (mg): | 8 mg |

# Apple-Maple Glazed Pork

This is a great dish for an autumn evening.

1 1/2 pounds (670 g) boneless pork top loin, cut into 4 servings

1 tablespoon (14 ml) olive oil

1 medium onion, thinly sliced

1 Granny Smith apple, thinly sliced

2/3 cup (160 ml) chicken broth

1/2 teaspoon poultry seasoning

1 tablespoon (14 ml) sugar-free pancake syrup

1 clove garlic, peeled and crushed

Spray a big, heavy skillet with nonstick cooking spray, and put it over medium-high heat. When it's hot, saute the pork in 1 1/2 teaspoons of the olive oil until it's lightly golden on both sides. When the pork is browned, remove it to a plate and set it aside.

Add the rest of the olive oil to the skillet, and sauté the onion and apple slices together for a minute or two. Turn the burner to low, spread the apples and onions in an even layer in the skillet, and place the pork on top.

Stir together the broth, poultry seasoning, syrup, and garlic, and pour it over the pork. Cover the skillet and simmer for 10 to 12 minutes. Then uncover the skillet and simmer for another 10 minutes or so, or until the liquid is cooked down to a syrupy consistency. Serve the pork with the apples, onions, and pan liquid spooned over it.

**Yield:** 4 servings

**Nutritional Analysis:** (Analysis does not account for polyols in maple syrup) Each will have: 256 calories; 11 g fat; 31 g protein; 7 g carbohydrates; 1 g fiber; 6 g usable carbs.

| | | | | | |
|---|---|---|---|---|---|
| Potassium (mg): | 696 mg | Vitamin C (mg): | 4 mg | Thiamin/B1 (mg): | 1.2 mg |
| Calcium (mg): | 40 mg | Vitamin A (i.u.): | 27 i.u. | Riboflavin/B2 (mg): | 0.4 mg |
| Iron (mg): | 1 mg | Vitamin B6 (mg): | 0.7 mg | Folacin (mcg): | 16 mcg |
| Zinc (mg): | 2 mg | Vitamin B12 (mcg): | 0.8 mcg | Niacin/B3 (mg): | 7 mg |

# Bourbon-Maple Glazed Pork Chops

Quick!

- 1 teaspoon (5 ml) oil
- 12 ounces (340 g) thinly cut pork loin chops (2 chops)
- 1 clove garlic, peeled and crushed
- 1/4 cup (40 g) minced onion
- 1/4 cup (60 ml) chicken broth
- 1 tablespoon (14 ml) sugar-free pancake syrup
- 1 tablespoon (14 ml) bourbon

Spray a big, heavy skillet with nonstick cooking spray, and put it over medium-high heat. Add the oil, and slosh it around to coat the bottom of the skillet. When the oil and skillet are hot, throw in the chops, and brown them for about 5 minutes on each side.

Remove the chops from the skillet, and turn the heat down to medium-low. Add the garlic and onion, and sauté in the residual fat for a minute. Pour in the broth, syrup, and bourbon. Stir them around with a spatula, scraping up all the yummy brown bits stuck to the skillet.

Throw the chops back into the skillet. Turn the heat down to low, and set a timer for 3 minutes. When it goes off, flip the chops, and set the timer for another 3 minutes. By this time, the liquid in the skillet should have cooked down and become syrupy.

Put the chops on serving plates, and scrape the glaze and oniony, garlicky bits over them to serve.

**Yield:** 2 servings

**Nutritional Analysis:** (Analysis does not account for polyols in maple syrup) Each will have: 225 calories; 12 g fat; 22 g protein; 2 g carbohydrates; trace fiber; 2 g usable carbs.

| | | | | | |
|---|---|---|---|---|---|
| Potassium (mg): | 380 mg | Vitamin C (mg): | 2 mg | Thiamin/B1 (mg): | 0.5 mg |
| Calcium (mg): | 31 mg | Vitamin A (i.u.): | 6 i.u. | Riboflavin/B2 (mg): | 0.2 mg |
| Iron (mg): | 2 mg | Vitamin B6 (mg): | 0.3 mg | Folacin (mcg): | 9 mcg |
| Zinc (mg): | 2 mg | Vitamin B12 (mcg): | 0.5 mcg | Niacin/B3 (mg): | 4 mg |

# Memphis Baby Backs

I made these to impress my visiting father-in-law. It worked! Just watch your portions.

3 pounds (1.4 kg) pork backribs
2 tablespoons (14 g) paprika
2 teaspoons (12 g) pepper
2 teaspoons (1 g) Splenda
1 1/2 teaspoons salt
3/4 teaspoon celery salt
3/4 teaspoon garlic powder
3/4 teaspoon dry mustard
3/4 teaspoon ground cumin
1 cup (235 g) cider vinegar
1/2 cup (120 g) yellow mustard
2 teaspoons (10 ml) olive oil

Put the ribs on something long—I had to use my biggest roaster!

Mix together the paprika, pepper, Splenda, salt, celery salt, garlic powder, mustard, and cumin. Put 1 tablespoon (15 g) of this mixture in another bowl, then sprinkle the rest of it liberally all over the ribs. Let the ribs sit for a minimum of an hour before you start cooking, and 24 hours would be outstanding!

When the time comes to cook, set up your grill for slow smoking. (See Killer Smoked Turkey Legs on page 394 for a indirect smoking instructions.) Mix together the reserved rub, vinegar, yellow mustard, and oil; this is your mop.

Slow smoke your ribs for about 4 hours at 225°F (107°C). After the first half-hour of smoking, mop every time you add more chips to the fire.

If you don't want to slow-smoke your ribs, you can do them in the oven at the same temperature. They won't be as authentic, but they'll still taste good. If you do this, you might add 1 teaspoon of liquid smoke flavoring to your mop, to give a smokey taste to the ribs.

**Yield:** 6 servings

**Nutritional Analysis:** Each will have: 444 calories; 36 g fat; 24 g protein; 6 g carbohydrates; 1g fiber; 5 g usable carbs.

| | | | | | |
|---|---|---|---|---|---|
| Potassium (mg): | 560 mg | Vitamin C (mg): | 3 mg | Thiamin/B1 (mg): | 1.0 mg |
| Calcium (mg): | 94 mg | Vitamin A (i.u.): | 1694 i.u. | Riboflavin/B2 (mg): | 0.5 mg |
| Iron (mg): | 3 mg | Vitamin B6 (mg): | 0.7 mg | Folacin (mcg): | 12 mcg |
| Zinc (mg): | 4 mg | Vitamin B12 (mcg): | 1.4 mcg | Niacin/B3 (mg): | 8 mg |

# Pork with Camembert Sauce

This sauce is to die for.

1 pound (455 g) boneless pork loin, cut into 3 portions, each about 3/4 inch (1.9 cm) thick.

2 ounces (55 g) Camembert cheese

1 tablespoon (14 g) butter

3 tablespoons (45 ml) dry white wine—or better yet, hard cider

1 tablespoon (2 g) chopped fresh sage

1/3 cup (75 g) light sour cream

1 1/2 teaspoons (8 g) Dijon mustard

Pepper

One at a time, put the pieces of pork loin in a heavy zipper-lock bag, and pound them with any handy blunt object until they're 1/2 inch (1.25 cm) thick. (No, it's not better to just cut them that thick to begin with. All that pounding tenderizes the meat.)

Use a very sharp, thin-bladed knife to cut the rind off the Camembert. You want to cut as thin a slice off as possible, to leave as much of the actual cheese as possible! Cut the cheese into 1/2-inch (1.25-cm) chunks, and set it aside.

Spray a big, heavy skillet with nonstick cooking spray, and put it over medium-high heat. Add the butter. When the butter is melted and the pan is good and hot, slosh the butter around the bottom of the skillet, then lay the pork in it. Cook until lightly golden on both sides, but no more; it's easy to dry out boneless pork loin. Put the pork on a plate, and keep it warm.

Add the wine to the skillet and stir it around with a spatula, scraping up all the flavorful brown bits. Add the sage, and stir again. Turn the heat down to medium-low. Now throw in those chunks of Camembert. Use a spatula to stir it around and cut the chunks into smaller bits, until the cheese has completely melted.

Whisk in the sour cream and mustard and heat through without simmering again (or your sour cream will break). Add pepper to taste, and serve the pork with the sauce spooned over it.

**Yield:** 3 servings

**Nutritional Analysis:** Each will have: 287 calories; 16 g fat; 31 g protein; 1 g carbohydrates; trace fiber; 1 g usable carbs.

| | | | | | |
|---|---|---|---|---|---|
| Potassium (mg): | 576 mg | Vitamin C (mg): | trace | Thiamin/B1 (mg): | 1.1 mg |
| Calcium (mg): | 118 mg | Vitamin A (i.u.): | 339 i.u. | Riboflavin/B2 (mg): | 0.4 mg |
| Iron (mg): | 1 mg | Vitamin B6 (mg): | 0.6 mg | Folacin (mcg): | 21 mcg |
| Zinc (mg): | 3 mg | Vitamin B12 (mcg): | 0.9 mcg | Niacin/B3 (mg): | 6 mg |

## Island Pork Chops

A luau in your kitchen!

1 tablespoon (14 ml) olive oil

1 pound (455 g) pork loin chops

1/2 cup (100 g) crushed pineapple in juice

1/3 cup (80 g) no-sugar-added ketchup

1/2 teaspoon chili garlic paste

1 clove garlic, peeled

1/4 teaspoon cinnamon

1/4 teaspoon ground allspice

1/2 teaspoon ground ginger

1/4 cup (60 ml) chicken broth

1 medium onion, sliced

1 medium green bell pepper, cut into strips

Spray a big, heavy skillet with nonstick cooking spray, and put it over medium-high heat. Add the oil, and start browning your chops—you want them just golden on both sides.

While that's happening, put the pineapple, ketchup, chili garlic paste, garlic, cinnamon, allspice, ginger, and chicken broth in your blender. Run it to blend everything.

When the chops are browned on both sides, strew the onion and green pepper over them, and pour the sauce over everything. Turn the burner to low, cover, and simmer for 20 minutes. Uncover, and simmer for another 10 minutes or so to reduce the sauce. Serve the chops with the onions, peppers, and sauce on top.

**Yield:** 3 servings

**Nutritional Analysis:** Each will have: 233 calories; 10 g fat; 21 g protein; 15 g carbohydrates; 2 g fiber; 13 g usable carbs.

| | | | | | |
|---|---|---|---|---|---|
| Potassium (mg): | 570 mg | Vitamin C (mg): | 42 mg | Thiamin/B1 (mg): | 0.9 mg |
| Calcium (mg): | 41 mg | Vitamin A (i.u.): | 737 i.u. | Riboflavin/B2 (mg): | 0.2 mg |
| Iron (mg): | 1 mg | Vitamin B6 (mg): | 0.6 mg | Folacin (mcg): | 21 mcg |
| Zinc (mg): | 2 mg | Vitamin B12 (mcg): | 0.6 mcg | Niacin/B3 (mg): | 6 mg |

## Mustard Pork Loin with Balsamic Onions

The trick with this is to not overcook the pork. You want it done through, of course (no one likes rare pork!), but this is so lean that overcooking will dry it out.

18 ounces (505 g) boneless pork loin, 1 inch (2.5 cm) thick

2 tablespoons (30 g) brown mustard

2 teaspoons (10 ml) olive oil

1 large red onion, thinly sliced

1 tablespoon (14 ml) balsamic vinegar

Preheat your electric tabletop grill. Cut the pork into 4 servings. Spread 1/2 teaspoon of mustard on each side of each serving, for a total of 4 teaspoons mustard. Grill for 7 to 8 minutes.

While that's happening, put the oil in a big, heavy skillet placed over medium-high heat, and start sautéing the onions. Forget about tender-crisp—you want your onions to be soft and turning brown. When they're good and caramelized, stir in the balsamic vinegar. Set aside.

By now your pork is done. Spread an extra 1/2 teaspoon of mustard on each piece, top the pork with the onions, and serve.

**Yield:** 4 servings

**Nutritional Analysis:** Each will have: 255 calories; 15 g fat; 24 g protein; 4 g carbohydrates; 1 g fiber; 3 g usable carbs.

| | | | | | |
|---|---|---|---|---|---|
| Potassium (mg): | 529 mg | Vitamin C (mg): | 3 mg | Thiamin/B1 (mg): | 0.9 mg |
| Calcium (mg): | 41 mg | Vitamin A (i.u.): | 7 i.u. | Riboflavin/B2 (mg): | 0.3 mg |
| Iron (mg): | 1 mg | Vitamin B6 (mg): | 0.5 mg | Folacin (mcg): | 16 mcg |
| Zinc (mg): | 2 mg | Vitamin B12 (mcg): | 0.6 mcg | Niacin/B3 (mg): | 6 mg |

# Pork Loin with Red Wine and Walnuts

Elegantly understated.

- 4 teaspoons (20 g) butter
- 1 pound (455 g) boneless pork loin, cut into 4 servings
- 1 small onion, sliced
- 1 clove garlic, peeled and minced
- 1/2 teaspoon beef bouillon granules
- 1/2 cup (120 ml) dry red wine
- 1/4 cup (30 g) chopped walnuts
- 1/4 cup (15 g) chopped parsley

Spray a big, heavy skillet with nonstick cooking spray, and put it over medium-high heat. When it's hot, add 2 teaspoons (10 g) of the butter, slosh it around as it melts, then lay the pork in the skillet. Sauté the pork until it's just golden on both sides. Remove the pork from the skillet.

Add another teaspoon (5 g) of butter to the skillet, and let it melt. Add the onions and let them sauté until they're getting limp. Spread the onions in an even layer in the skillet, and lay the pork on top.

Mix together the garlic, beef bouillon, and wine. Pour it over the pork and onions, cover the pan with a tilted lid (leave a 1/4-inch or 6-mm gap for steam to escape), turn the burner to low, and let the whole thing simmer for 20 minutes.

Meanwhile, melt the last teaspoon (5 g) of butter in a small skillet over medium heat, and stir the walnuts in it for 5 minutes, until they smell a little toasty. Remove from the heat and reserve.

When the timer beeps, add the parsley to the pork. Let the whole thing simmer for another 5 minutes or so. Serve with the pan juices and 1 tablespoon (8 g) of walnuts on each serving.

**Yield:** 4 servings

**Nutritional Analysis:** Each will have: 305 calories; 19 g fat; 23 g protein; 4 g carbohydrates; 1 g fiber; 3 g usable carbs.

| | | | | | |
|---|---|---|---|---|---|
| Potassium (mg): | 546 mg | Vitamin C (mg): | 8 mg | Thiamin/B1 (mg): | 0.8 mg |
| Calcium (mg): | 41 mg | Vitamin A (i.u.): | 369 i.u. | Riboflavin/B2 (mg): | 0.3 mg |
| Iron (mg): | 1 mg | Vitamin B6 (mg): | 0.5 mg | Folacin (mcg): | 24 mcg |
| Zinc (mg): | 2 mg | Vitamin B12 (mcg): | 0.5 mcg | Niacin/B3 (mg): | 5 mg |

## Brined Rosemary-Mustard Pork

I originally tried this without the brining step, and the results tasted good, but were dry. Brining takes care of that problem nicely.

- 1 quart (945 ml) warm water
- 1 tablespoon (18 g) kosher salt
- 3 pork top loin chops totaling 1 pound (455 g), each about 3/4 inch (1.9 cm) thick
- 1/4 cup (60 g) brown mustard
- 2 teaspoons (1 g) Splenda
- 1/2 teaspoon ground rosemary, or 1 teaspoon fresh rosemary, chopped

In a flat, nonreactive container, mix together the water and kosher salt, stirring till the salt is dissolved. Lay the pork chops in this brine, and let them sit for 1 to 2 hours. Drain them and pat them dry.

Lay the chops on a plate. Mix together the mustard, Splenda, and rosemary. Spread half of the mixture on the chops, turn them over, and spread the other half on the other sides. Smear a little around the edges, too. Slide the plate into the fridge, and let the chops sit with the mustard on them for a couple of hours, at least.

When you're ready to eat, preheat your electric tabletop grill and grill your pork chops for about 6 minutes.

**Yield:** 3 servings

**Nutritional Analysis:** Each will have: 272 calories; 16 g fat; 29 g protein; 2 g carbohydrates; trace fiber; 2 g usable carbs.

| | | | | | |
|---|---|---|---|---|---|
| Potassium (mg): | 564 mg | Vitamin C (mg): | 1 mg | Thiamin/B1 (mg): | 1.1 mg |
| Calcium (mg): | 59 mg | Vitamin A (i.u.): | 8 i.u. | Riboflavin/B2 (mg): | 0.3 mg |
| Iron (mg): | 1 mg | Vitamin B6 (mg): | 0.6 mg | Folacin (mcg): | 10 mcg |
| Zinc (mg): | 2 mg | Vitamin B12 (mcg): | 0.7 mcg | Niacin/B3 (mg): | 6 mg |

## Pan-Fried Peach-and-Pepper Pork

Don't stand close to anyone when you say that!

2 tablespoons (28 ml) olive oil

4 pork loin chops, totaling 1 1/2 pounds (670 g)

1 1/2 teaspoons pepper

2 tablespoons (28 ml) dark rum

1 small onion, chopped

1 1/2 cups (375 g) frozen, no-sugar-added peach slices, thawed

1 tablespoon (14 ml) rice vinegar

1/4 cup (60 ml) chicken stock

Salt

Spray a big, heavy skillet with nonstick cooking spray, and put it over medium-high heat. Add 1 tablespoon (14 ml) of the oil, and let it heat while you sprinkle the pork chops with 1/2 teaspoon of the pepper. Put the chops in the pan, and brown on both sides. Transfer to a large plate.

Pour the rum into the skillet, stir it around while scraping up all the yummy brown bits, and then pour the rum over the chops. Let that sit.

Heat the remaining oil in the skillet. Add the onion and sauté it for a minute or two, till it just starts to soften. Add the peach slices, and sauté them with the onion until they start to soften, as well. Add the vinegar, chicken stock, and remaining pepper, and stir it all up.

Now put the pork and rum back in the pan. Turn the burner to low, cover the pan, and let the whole thing simmer for 5 minutes, then serve.

**Yield:** 4 servings

**Nutritional Analysis:** Each will have: 266 calories; 13 g fat; 23 g protein; 11 g carbohydrates; 2 g fiber; 9 g usable carbs.

| | | | | | |
|---|---|---|---|---|---|
| Potassium (mg): | 471 mg | Vitamin C (mg): | 109 mg | Thiamin/B1 (mg): | 1.0 mg |
| Calcium (mg): | 30 mg | Vitamin A (i.u.): | 324 i.u. | Riboflavin/B2 (mg): | 0.3 mg |
| Iron (mg): | 1 mg | Vitamin B6 (mg): | 0.5 mg | Folacin (mcg): | 8 mcg |
| Zinc (mg): | 2 mg | Vitamin B12 (mcg): | 0.6 mcg | Niacin/B3 (mg): | 6 mg |

## Pork Tenderloin with Spiced Cider Jus

What makes this special is the sauce. Our tester Ray liked it so much that he created a salmon recipe using it, too!

1/2 cup (120 ml) apple cider
1/2 cup (120 ml) cider vinegar
1 1/2 tablespoons (2.2 g) Splenda
3/4 cup (175 ml) chicken broth
1/2 cup (65 g) chopped onion
3 whole allspice berries
1/2 teaspoon anise seed, ground
1 1/2 teaspoons dried thyme
1 cinnamon stick
1 bay leaf
1 tablespoon (14 g) butter
2 pieces pork tenderloin, totaling 1 1/2 pounds (670 g)
2 tablespoons (28 ml) olive oil
Salt and pepper

Combine the cider, vinegar, Splenda, broth, onion, allspice, anise, thyme, cinnamon, and bay leaf in a heavy, nonreactive saucepan. Put the pan over medium heat, and bring the mixture to a simmer.

When the mixture has been reduced by one-half, strain it, put it back in the saucepan, and cook it down to 1/2 cup. Whisk in the butter.

While the cider mixture is reducing, rub the pork tenderloins with the oil and sprinkle them generously with salt and pepper. Grill or broil them, turning frequently, for about 20 minutes, or until an instant-read thermometer registers 145°F (65°C) when inserted into the middle of the pork. Remove them to a platter and let rest for 5 minutes.

Slice the pork thinly across the grain, divide among 6 serving plates, and spoon the sauce over the top.

**Yield:** 6 servings

**Nutritional Analysis:** Each will have: 239 calories; 11 g fat; 26 g protein; 10 g carbohydrates; 2 g fiber; 8 g usable carbs.

| | | | | | |
|---|---|---|---|---|---|
| Potassium (mg): | 606 mg | Vitamin C (mg): | 3 mg | Thiamin/B1 (mg): | 0.8 mg |
| Calcium (mg): | 71 mg | Vitamin A (i.u.): | 115 i.u. | Riboflavin/B2 (mg): | 0.4 mg |
| Iron (mg): | 3 mg | Vitamin B6 (mg): | 0.4 mg | Folacin (mcg): | 11 mcg |
| Zinc (mg): | 3 mg | Vitamin B12 (mcg): | 0.5 mcg | Niacin/B3 (mg): | 5 mg |

# Lamb Steaks with Lemon, Olives, and Capers

This is as good a fast dinner as I've ever made.

- 1 1/2 pounds (670 g) leg of lamb in steaks cut 3/4 inch (1.9 cm) thick
- 2 teaspoons (10 ml) olive oil
- 1 tablespoon (14 ml) lemon juice
- 1/4 cup (25 g) chopped kalamata olives
- 2 teaspoons (6 g) capers
- 1 clove garlic
- Salt and pepper

Spray a big, heavy skillet with nonstick cooking spray and put it over medium-high heat. While it's heating up, slash the edges of the lamb steaks, to keep them from curling.

When the skillet's hot, add the oil and steaks. You want to brown and sear them on both sides.

Add the lemon juice, olives, capers, and garlic around and over the steaks. Let the whole thing cook for another minute or two, but don't overcook. The lamb should still be pink in the middle. Salt and pepper the steaks, carve them into 4 portions, and serve with all the yummy lemon-caper-olive stuff from the skillet scraped over them.

**Yield:** 4 servings

**Nutritional Analysis:** Each will have: 343 calories; 26 g fat; 24 g protein; 1 g carbohydrates; trace fiber; 1 g usable carbs.

| | | | | | |
|---|---|---|---|---|---|
| Potassium (mg): | 344 mg | Vitamin C (mg): | 2 mg | Thiamin/B1 (mg): | 0.1 mg |
| Calcium (mg): | 22 mg | Vitamin A (i.u.): | 41 i.u. | Riboflavin/B2 (mg): | 0.3 mg |
| Iron (mg): | 3 mg | Vitamin B6 (mg): | 0.2 mg | Folacin (mcg): | 26 mcg |
| Zinc (mg): | 4 mg | Vitamin B12 (mcg): | 3.3 mcg | Niacin/B3 (mg): | 8 mg |

## Roman Lamb Steak

This marinade really complements the flavor of the lamb.

1 tablespoon (14 ml) olive oil

1 tablespoon (14 ml) lemon juice

1/2 cup (30 g) chopped parsley

2 anchovy fillets

1/4 teaspoon pepper

1/8 teaspoon salt

1 clove garlic, peeled and crushed

12 ounces (340 g) leg of lamb steak, 1/2 inch (1.25 cm) thick

Throw the oil, lemon juice, parsley, anchovies, pepper, salt, and garlic in your food processor with the S-blade in place, and pulse to finely chop everything.

Put the steak on a plate. Smear half of the chopped mixture on one side of the steak, turn it over, and smear the rest on the other side. Let the steak sit for at least one-half hour; a couple of hours would be great.

After marinating, broil the lamb close to the heat—with the parsley still all over it—for about 6 minutes per side. When it's done, it should still be pink in the middle. Serve.

**Yield:** 2 servings

**Nutritional Analysis:** Each will have: 387 calories; 30 g fat; 26 g protein; 2 g carbohydrates; 1 g fiber; 1 g usable carbs.

| | | | | | |
|---|---|---|---|---|---|
| Potassium (mg): | 458 mg | Vitamin C (mg): | 24 mg | Thiamin/B1 (mg): | 0.2 mg |
| Calcium (mg): | 47 mg | Vitamin A (i.u.): | 785 i.u. | Riboflavin/B2 (mg): | 0.3 mg |
| Iron (mg): | 3 mg | Vitamin B6 (mg): | 0.2 mg | Folacin (mcg): | 50 mcg |
| Zinc (mg): | 5 mg | Vitamin B12 (mcg): | 3.3 mcg | Niacin/B3 (mg): | 9 mg |

# Lamb Marinated in Yogurt

Marinating lamb in yogurt is common in India and the Middle East. Yogurt is a surprisingly good tenderizer! This seasoning is Indian.

1 pound (455 g) boneless leg of lamb, trimmed and cut into 1-inch (2.5-cm) cubes

1/2 cup (120 g) plain yogurt

2 cloves garlic, peeled and crushed

1 1/2 teaspoons grated gingerroot

3/4 teaspoon Garam Masala (see page 503)

Put the lamb cubes in a zipper-lock bag. Mix together the yogurt, garlic, ginger, and garam masala, and dump the mixture into the bag. Seal the bag, pressing out the air as you go. Now squish the bag around until the lamb is evenly coated with the yogurt mixture. Throw the bag in the fridge for at least several hours.

Now it's time to think about skewers. If you use metal, like I do, there's no prep to do. But if you're using bamboo skewers, you'll want to soak them in water for at least 30 minutes before you're ready to load 'em up, to prevent them from catching fire.

When the time comes to cook, you can either grill or broil the lamb. Either way, dump all the contents of the bag onto a plate, and thread the lamb onto skewers. You'll have some yogurt mixture left on the plate. Hang on to this.

Broil or grill the lamb skewers until they're done to your liking, basting once or twice with the remaining yogurt mixture. Stop basting at least a few minutes before you're done cooking, so the heat has time to kill the raw meat germs.

With a big salad, this is a heckuva meal!

**Yield:** 4 servings

**Nutritional Analysis:** Each will have: 228 calories; 16 g fat; 17 g protein; 2 g carbohydrates; trace fiber; 2 g usable carbs.

| | | | | | |
|---|---|---|---|---|---|
| Potassium (mg): | 280 mg | Vitamin C (mg): | 1 mg | Thiamin/B1 (mg): | 0.1 mg |
| Calcium (mg): | 48 mg | Vitamin A (i.u.): | 38 i.u. | Riboflavin/B2 (mg): | 0.2 mg |
| Iron (mg): | 2 mg | Vitamin B6 (mg): | 0.2 mg | Folacin (mcg): | 19 mcg |
| Zinc (mg): | 3 mg | Vitamin B12 (mcg): | 2.3 mcg | Niacin/B3 (mg): | 6 mg |

# Middle Eastern Marinated Lamb Kabobs

Call it shish kebab, or souvlakia—it's just good.

- 1 pound (455 g) boneless leg of lamb, cubed
- 1/4 cup (60 ml) olive oil
- 1/4 cup (60 ml) lemon juice
- 4 cloves garlic, peeled and finely minced
- 1 medium onion
- Salt and pepper

Put the lamb cubes in a big zipper-lock bag. Mix together the oil, lemon juice, and garlic. Pour this mixture over the lamb and seal the bag, pressing out the air as you go. Turn the bag once or twice to coat, and throw it in the fridge for several hours.

Okay, time to decide whether you're cooking these under the broiler or outside on your barbecue grill. If you want to cook them over charcoal—certainly a terrific way to go—get the fire going a good 30 minutes before you want to cook. You'll also need to think about soaking your skewers for at least 30 minutes before you're planning to cook, if you're planning on using bamboo. If you're using metal, you don't have to give your skewers another thought.

When dinnertime rolls around, cut the onion into hunks and separate them into individual layers. Pull out the lamb cubes, and pour off the marinade into a bowl.

Alternate threading the lamb cubes and onions onto 4 skewers. Keep it compact, with stuff touching, not strung out. When the skewers are full and all the lamb and onion is used up, sprinkle the whole thing with a little salt and pepper.

Now grill or broil, basting occasionally with the reserved marinade, for 8 or 10 minutes, or until done to your liking. (I prefer my lamb to still be a bit pink in the middle.) Serve 1 skewer per customer.

**Yield:** 4 servings

**Nutritional Analysis:** Each will have: 290 calories; 20 g fat; 24 g protein; 5 g carbohydrates; 1 g fiber; 4 g usable carbs.

| | | | | | |
|---|---|---|---|---|---|
| Potassium (mg): | 396 mg | Vitamin C (mg): | 10 mg | Thiamin/B1 (mg): | 0.2 mg |
| Calcium (mg): | 22 mg | Vitamin A (i.u.): | 3 i.u. | Riboflavin/B2 (mg): | 0.3 mg |
| Iron (mg): | 2 mg | Vitamin B6 (mg): | 0.2 mg | Folacin (mcg): | 33 mcg |
| Zinc (mg): | 5 mg | Vitamin B12 (mcg): | 3.1 mcg | Niacin/B3 (mg): | 7 mg |

chapter fourteen

# Soups

It is so sad that most people think of soup as something that comes out of a can—or worse, powdered in a little packet. You know how much better homemade bread is than store-bought bread? You know how much better mom's chocolate chip cookies are than Chips Ahoy? Homemade soup is at least that much better than canned—maybe even more so.

You can take a short-cut to homemade soup by buying canned or boxed broth, and if you're choosy, you'll do well. But if you want to know just how good soup can be—if you want a hint of what sort of soup the angels may be eating—nothing beats homemade broth. Which leads us to our first recipe.

## Bone Broth, or "Something For Nothing"

This is more of a rule than a recipe, but if you'll actually do this, I think you'll be astonished at how good the resulting broth is. It always gives me a little frugal thrill to get a pot of soup better than anything I could ever buy out of something most people would throw away.

Chicken bones

Water

Salt

Vinegar

Save all your chicken bones in a plastic grocery sack in your freezer. It doesn't matter how clean you've picked them—really. They can be completely naked and you will still be stunned at how much flavor they have. If you have turkey or duck bones, hey, throw them in, too. The only exception would be if you've cooked the poultry with some sort of strong seasoning and there's still a lot of seasoned meat clinging to the bones. You don't want to end up with conflicting seasonings.

When you've collected a bag full of bones, dump them, still frozen, into your biggest nonreactive pot; obviously, a stockpot is ideal. Add water to cover, throw in 2 to 3 teaspoons (12 to 18 g) of salt, and 1/4 cup (60 ml) of vinegar. (Don't worry that your broth will taste sour. The vinegar helps draw calcium out of the bones, making your broth very calcium-rich—and the calcium neutralizes the acidity.)

Set the whole thing over the lowest possible heat and just let it simmer all day long, uncovered. You want to cook it down by about half. Then strain your broth and discard the bones. You can use this in any recipe that calls for chicken broth, but I always make mine into soup. Soup made with this homemade bone broth is vastly better than soup made from packaged broth, both in flavor and in nutritional value. Don't be surprised when this broth jellies in the fridge, by the way; it's the natural gelatin from the bones.

If you're not going to use your broth up right away by making a pot of soup, it's a good idea to freeze it in ice cube trays, then pop out the broth cubes and store them in a zipper-lock bag. That way you can easily thaw just the amount you need.

It's impossible to give an exact nutritional count for this, but broth made this way will inevitably be higher in protein and minerals than store-bought broth, while still being very low in both calories and carbohydrates.

# African Peanut Soup

This is my attempt to clone a truly remarkable soup I tasted at the Ellicottville Brewing Company in Ellicottville, New York—and it's close. If you're ever in southwest New York, the EBC is worth a trip out of your way—honest food, perfectly prepared, in a casually elegant atmosphere. And no, they didn't pay me to say that.

2 teaspoons (28 g) butter

1/2 large onion, chopped

1/2 cup (60 g) diced celery

3 cans (14 ounces, or 390 g each) chicken broth

1/2 pound (225 g) boneless, skinless chicken thighs, cubed

1 can (14 ounces, or 390 g) tomatoes with green chiles

1 tablespoon (8 g) grated gingerroot

4 cloves garlic, peeled and minced

1 teaspoon paprika

1/2 teaspoon curry powder

3/4 cup (195 g) natural peanut butter (I like chunky, but creamy is fine.)

1/4 teaspoon cayenne pepper, or to taste

Set a big stockpot over medium-low heat. Add the butter to the pot, and when it's melted, sauté the onion and celery in it until soft.

Add the broth, chicken, tomatoes, ginger, garlic, paprika, and curry powder. Turn up the burner to bring the broth to a simmer, then turn the burner back down, and simmer for 30 to 45 minutes.

Whisk in the peanut butter, stirring till it melts in. Add the cayenne, check for spiciness, then add more if you like. Simmer for another 15 minutes or so, whisk again, then serve.

**Yield:** 6 servings

**Nutritional Analysis:** Each will have: 296 calories; 20 g fat; 18 g protein; 12 g carbohydrates; 3 g fiber; 9 g usable carbs.

| | | | | | |
|---|---|---|---|---|---|
| Potassium (mg): | 397 mg | Vitamin C (mg): | 7 mg | Thiamin/B1 (mg): | trace |
| Calcium (mg): | 38 mg | Vitamin A (i.u.): | 615 i.u. | Riboflavin/B2 (mg): | 0.1 mg |
| Iron (mg): | 2 mg | Vitamin B6 (mg): | 0.2 mg | Folacin (mcg): | 18 mcg |
| Zinc (mg): | 1 mg | Vitamin B12 (mcg): | 0.3 mcg | Niacin/B3 (mg): | 5 mg |

# Sopa Azteca

Readers of 500 Low-Carb Recipes will recognize this recipe. This Mexican chicken and vegetable soup is so delicious, so satisfying, and so incredibly full of a broad spectrum of nutrients that I reworked it for a slightly reduced calorie count to make it fit this book.

- 2 tablespoons (28 ml) olive oil
- 1 medium onion, chopped
- 2 large celery ribs, diced
- 1 green bell pepper, diced
- 1 carrot, shredded
- 1 small zucchini, diced
- 4 cloves garlic, peeled and finely minced
- 2 tablespoons (8 g) dried oregano
- 2 tablespoons (8 g) dried basil
- 2 teaspoons (4 g) pepper
- 3 quarts (2.8 l) chicken broth
- 2 cups (220 g) diced chicken, cooked
- 2 cans (14½ ounces, or 405 g each) tomatoes with green chiles, juice and all
- 10 ounces (280 g) frozen chopped spinach
- 8 ounces (225 g) shredded reduced-fat Monterey Jack cheese
- Chipotle chiles canned in adobo (optional)
- 3 ripe California avocados

Spray the bottom of a big soup kettle or a really big, heavy saucepan with nonstick cooking spray. Put it over medium heat, and add the oil. Throw in the onion, celery, green pepper, carrot, and zucchini, and sauté them together, stirring frequently, until they're soft. Stir in the garlic, oregano, basil, and pepper, and sauté for another minute or two.

Add the chicken broth, chicken, tomatoes, and spinach. Bring the whole thing to a simmer, turn the burner down to low, and let it cook for 30 minutes to an hour.

When you're ready to serve the soup, put a handful of shredded cheese in the bottom of each bowl. For those who like it hot, add a chipotle or two, then ladle the hot soup over the cheese and peppers.

Halve your avocados, and peel and seed them. Dice the flesh, and float a little avocado on each serving of soup.

**Yield:** 10 servings

**Nutritional Analysis:** Each will have: 352 calories; 23 g fat; 24 g protein; 13 g carbohydrates; 5 g fiber; 8 g usable carbs.

| | | | | | |
|---|---|---|---|---|---|
| Potassium (mg): | 1031 mg | Vitamin C (mg): | 30 mg | Thiamin/B1 (mg): | 0.2 mg |
| Calcium (mg): | 351 mg | Vitamin A (i.u.): | 5253 i.u. | Riboflavin/B2 (mg): | 0.4 mg |
| Iron (mg): | 3 mg | Vitamin B6 (mg): | 0.5 mg | Folacin (mcg): | 102 mcg |
| Zinc (mg): | 2 mg | Vitamin B12 (mcg): | 0.6 mcg | Niacin/B3 (mg): | 9 mg |

## Vegetable Beef Soup

A true classic. Eat it at the kitchen table, and you'll feel like mom is patting you on the back.

- 2 quarts (1.9 l) beef stock
- 1 medium turnip, peeled and cubed
- 1 medium onion, diced
- 1 large carrot, peeled and thinly sliced
- 1 large rib celery, thinly sliced
- 2 cans (14 ounces, or 390 g) diced tomatoes, juice and all
- 2 cups (300 g) frozen cross-cut green beans
- 3/4 pound (340 g) boneless beef chuck, in 1/2-inch (1.25-cm) cubes
- 1 teaspoon dried marjoram
- 1 teaspoon pepper
- 1 bay leaf

Put the stock in a big soup kettle, and put it over medium-high heat. While it's warming, do all your peeling and chopping and opening. Just throw everything into the pot as you get it cut up or measured.

Bring the whole thing to a simmer, cover, turn the burner down to low, and let it cook for at least an hour; two is better. That's it!

**Yield:** 6 servings

**Nutritional Analysis:** Each will have: 215 calories; 9 g fat; 12 g protein; 17 g carbohydrates; 2 g fiber; 15 g usable carbs.

| | | | | | |
|---|---|---|---|---|---|
| Potassium (mg): | 802 mg | Vitamin C (mg): | 32 mg | Thiamin/B1 (mg): | 1.5 mg |
| Calcium (mg): | 78 mg | Vitamin A (i.u.): | 4360 i.u. | Riboflavin/B2 (mg): | 0.4 mg |
| Iron (mg): | 4 mg | Vitamin B6 (mg): | 0.4 mg | Folacin (mcg): | 36 mcg |
| Zinc (mg): | 2 mg | Vitamin B12 (mcg): | 1.5 mcg | Niacin/B3 (mg): | 3 mg |

# Quick Hamburger Soup

Turns one-half pound of ground round into a satisfying soup for the family. If you can't have red wine, just add another 1/2 cup (120 ml) of broth.

1/2 pound (225 g) ground round

1/2 teaspoon salt

1/4 teaspoon pepper

8 ounces (235 ml) tomato sauce

2 medium carrots, sliced

1 can (6 1/2 ounces, or 185 g) mushrooms, undrained

1/2 medium onion, chopped

1/4 cup (25 g) pimiento-stuffed green olives, sliced

1 1/2 cups (355 ml) beef broth

1/2 cup (120 ml) dry red wine

4 tablespoons (20 g) shredded Parmesan cheese

In a big, heavy saucepan over medium-high heat, brown and crumble the ground round.

When it's browned, pour off any grease (though there shouldn't be much). Salt and pepper the beef.

Add the tomato sauce, carrots, mushrooms (water and all), onion, olives, broth, and wine. Cover and simmer till the carrots are tender, about 30 minutes. Spoon it into 4 bowls, and sprinkle 1 tablespoon (5 g) Parmesan on each serving.

**Yield:** 4 servings

**Nutritional Analysis:** Each will have: 252 calories; 12 g fat; 18 g protein; 13 g carbohydrates; 3 g fiber; 10 g usable carbs.

| | | | | | |
|---|---|---|---|---|---|
| Potassium (mg): | 702 mg | Vitamin C (mg): | 8 mg | Thiamin/B1 (mg): | 0.1 mg |
| Calcium (mg): | 109 mg | Vitamin A (i.u.): | 10748 i.u. | Riboflavin/B2 (mg): | 0.2 mg |
| Iron (mg): | 3 mg | Vitamin B6 (mg): | 0.3 mg | Folacin (mcg): | 24 mcg |
| Zinc (mg): | 3 mg | Vitamin B12 (mcg): | 1.2 mcg | Niacin/B3 (mg): | 5 mg |

## Taco Soup

Tacos in a bowl!

1 medium onion, chopped

1 tablespoon (14 ml) olive oil

2 cloves garlic, peeled and minced

1 pound (455 g) ground round

1 pound (455 g) ground turkey

1 tablespoon (9 g) chili powder

1/2 teaspoon ground cumin

Salt and pepper

1 can (15 ounces, or 420 g) tomato sauce, or two 8-ounce (225-g) cans, if you can't get a big one

1/2 head cauliflower, shredded

1 pound (455 g) reduced-fat cheddar cheese, shredded

1 can green chiles

1 can (15 ounces, or 420 g) black beans or black soy beans

3 tablespoons (20 g) canned jalapeño peppers

16 ounces (455 g) low-fat sour cream

In a soup kettle or a big, heavy-bottomed sauce pan, sauté the onion in the oil. When the onion's translucent, add the garlic and sauté briefly. Add the beef and turkey, and cook and crumble till completely browned.

Add the chili powder, cumin, salt and pepper to taste, and tomato sauce, and stir it all up. Add the cauliflower and let it cook for a few minutes.

Reduce the heat to low and stir constantly as you add the cheese a little bit at a time so that it melts nicely. Then add the green chiles, beans, and jalapeños, and let it get nice and hot. Add the sour cream, and stir again before serving.

**Yield:** 20 servings

**Nutritional Analysis:** With black beans, each will have: 192 calories; 9 g fat; 17 g protein; 9 g carbohydrates; 2 g fiber; 7 g usable carbs.

| | | | | | |
|---|---|---|---|---|---|
| Potassium (mg): | 340 mg | Vitamin C (mg): | 14 mg | Thiamin/B1 (mg): | 0.1 mg |
| Calcium (mg): | 135 mg | Vitamin A (i.u.): | 431 i.u. | Riboflavin/B2 (mg): | 0.2 mg |
| Iron (mg): | 1 mg | Vitamin B6 (mg): | 0.2 mg | Folacin (mcg): | 18 mcg |
| Zinc (mg): | 2 mg | Vitamin B12 (mcg): | 0.7 mcg | Niacin/B3 (mg): | 2 mg |

**Nutritional Analysis:** With black soy beans, each will have: 191 calories; 10 g fat; 17 g protein; 7 g carbohydrates; 2 g fiber; 5 g usable carbs.

| | | | | | |
|---|---|---|---|---|---|
| Potassium (mg): | 304 mg | Vitamin C (mg): | 9 mg | Thiamin/B1 (mg): | 0.1 mg |
| Calcium (mg): | 145 mg | Vitamin A (i.u.): | 510 i.u. | Riboflavin/B2 (mg): | 0.2 mg |
| Iron (mg): | 2 mg | Vitamin B6 (mg): | 0.2 mg | Folacin (mcg): | 15 mcg |
| Zinc (mg): | 2 mg | Vitamin B12 (mcg): | 0.7 mcg | Niacin/B3 (mg): | 2 mg |

## Pasta Fazool

Really this is called "Pasta e Fagioli"—pasta and bean soup. But everyone I know just calls it Pasta Fazool. You'll notice this doesn't have a second analysis for the Dreamfield's low-carb pasta. That's because blood sugar tests done by me and other folks in the field indicate that while Dreamfield's has a blood sugar impact less than "regular" pasta, it seems to be absorbed differently by different people—and even by the same people on different days. Still, I'd guess the usable carb count with Dreamfield's would be at least a few grams less per serving. (And if you haven't tried it, the taste and texture of Dreamfield's are indistinguishable from that of "regular" pasta.)

1 1/2 pounds (670 g) ground beef
1 medium onion, finely chopped
2 medium carrots, shredded
5 celery ribs, finely diced
4 cloves garlic, peeled and crushed
3 cans (14 ounces, or 390 g each) diced tomatoes, juice and all
1/2 can (7 1/2 ounces, or 210 g) kidney beans
1/2 can (7 1/2 ounces, or 210 g) great northern beans
1 can (15 ounces, or 420 g) soybeans, white ones
3 cans (8 ounces, or 225 g each) tomato sauce
12 ounces (340 g) V8 vegetable juice
1 1/2 tablespoons (21 ml) wine vinegar
2 teaspoons (35 g) salt
1 tablespoon (4 g) dried oregano
1 tablespoon (2.5 g) dried basil
1 teaspoon (2 g) pepper
1 quart (945 ml) beef broth

2 cups (475 ml) water

3/4 cup (115 g) uncooked whole wheat elbow macaroni or Dreamfield's low-carb elbows

Place a big, heavy soup pot over medium-high heat. Add the ground beef, and brown and crumble it. Drain the excess grease, and throw in the onion, carrots, and celery. Sauté until mostly softened, then throw in the garlic. Sauté for a few more minutes.

Add everything else but the pasta—do not drain the tomatoes or beans. Stir it up, and let it simmer over the lowest heat for an hour. About 10 minutes before serving time, stir in the pasta, and let it cook till it's al dente. Serve immediately!

**Yield:** 16 servings

**Nutritional Analysis:** Each will have: 292 calories; 14 g fat; 19 g protein; 25 g carbohydrates; 6 g fiber; 19 g usable carbs.

| Potassium (mg): | 1043 mg | Vitamin C (mg): | 24 mg | Thiamin/B1 (mg): | 0.3 mg |
|---|---|---|---|---|---|
| Calcium (mg): | 111 mg | Vitamin A (i.u.): | 3726 i.u. | Riboflavin/B2 (mg): | 0.3 mg |
| Iron (mg): | 4 mg | Vitamin B6 (mg): | 0.4 mg | Folacin (mcg): | 124 mcg |
| Zinc (mg): | 3 mg | Vitamin B12 (mcg): | 1.1 mcg | Niacin/B3 (mg): | 4 mg |

## Mexican Meatball Veggie Soup

This is a kind of a cross between the Pasta Fazool and Albondigas recipes, with some further creativity thrown in. Our tester, Ray, came up with this one.

2 quarts (1.9 l) water

1 can (14 ounces, or 425 ml) beef broth

3 cans (14 ounces, or 390 g each) diced tomatoes

1/2 can (7 1/2 ounces, or 210 g) kidney beans

1/2 can (7 1/2 ounces, or 210 g) great northern beans

1 can (15 ounces, or 420 g) soybeans, white ones

2 tablespoons (28 ml) cider vinegar

1 tablespoon (4 g) plus 1 teaspoon dried oregano

2 teaspoons (6 g) chili powder

3 teaspoons (9 g) cumin

1 pound (455 g) ground turkey

1 pound (455 g) ground round

1 medium onion, very finely chopped

1/4 cup (25 g) wheat bran

1/4 teaspoon cayenne pepper

1/2 teaspoon fresh ground black pepper

1 egg

1 tablespoon (14 ml) oil

2 chipotle chile canned in adobo sauce (fine diced)

2 medium carrots, shredded

2 1/2 cups (375 g) cauliflower, shredded

1 red pepper, cut into 1/4- to 1/2-inch (6-mm to 1.25-cm) pieces

6 cloves garlic, crushed

In a big soup kettle over medium heat combine the water and beef broth. Add the tomatoes, the kidney beans, Great Northern beans, soy beans, vinegar, 1 tablespoon (4 g) oregano, chili powder, and 2 teaspoons (6 g) cumin. Let this come to a simmer while you make your meatballs.

In a large mixing bowl, combine the ground turkey, ground round, onion, wheat bran, the remaining 1 teaspoon of oregano, the remaining 1 teaspoon of cumin, the cayenne, black pepper, and egg. Using clean hands, squish everything together until very well blended, then form into 1-inch (2.5-cm) balls.

Spray a big, heavy skillet with nonstick cooking spray, and put it over medium heat. Add the oil, and brown the meatballs in batches; this will take 4 or 5 batches, depending on the size of your skillet.

While your meatballs are browning, chop the chipotles, shred the carrots and cauliflower, and dice the red peppers. Throw 'em into the pot with the broth and the beans.

As your meatballs brown, drain them and add them to the soup. Once they're all in, turn the burner to the lowest heat, and let the whole thing simmer for at least an hour. Ray says 2 to 3 hours would be even better.

**Yield:** 20 servings

**Nutritional Analysis:** Each will have: 200 calories; 9 g fat; 16 g protein; 16 g carbohydrates; 4 g fiber; 12 g usable carbs.

| | | | | | |
|---|---|---|---|---|---|
| Potassium (mg): | 690 mg | Vitamin C (mg): | 29 mg | Thiamin/B1 (mg): | 0.2 mg |
| Calcium (mg): | 81 mg | Vitamin A (i.u.): | 2850 i.u. | Riboflavin/B2 (mg): | 0.2 mg |
| Iron (mg): | 3 mg | Vitamin B6 (mg): | 0.4 mg | Folacin (mcg): | 98 mcg |
| Zinc (mg): | 2 mg | Vitamin B12 (mcg): | 0.6 mcg | Niacin/B3 (mg): | 3 mg |

## Chicken Minestrone

Abbondanza!

4 quarts (3.8 l) chicken broth

1 pound (455 g) boneless, skinless chicken breast (or boneless, skinless thighs, if you prefer)

1 can (14 ounces, or 390 g) tomato wedges, diced

1 can (14 ounces, or 390 g) cannellini or Great Northern beans

2 medium onions, diced

2 medium zucchini, quartered lengthwise and sliced

1 large carrot, grated

1/2 head cabbage, shredded

8 ounces (225 g) mushrooms, sliced

3 cloves garlic, peeled and crushed

1 tablespoon (2.5 g) dried basil

1 tablespoon (4 g) dried oregano

Grated Parmesan cheese (optional)

Pour the chicken broth into a big saucepan or kettle, and put it over high heat.

While that's heating up, cut the chicken into 1/2-inch (1.25-cm) cubes; this is easiest if it's partly frozen.

When the broth is hot, stir in the chicken, and keep stirring for a minute or two , or your bits of chicken may cook themselves into a clump at the bottom of your pot! (The Voice of Experience is speaking, here. If this does happen, just use the edge of your spoon to break them apart.) Add the tomatoes and beans. Turn the burner to medium-low.

Add the onions, zucchini, carrot, cabbage, mushrooms, garlic, basil, and oregano to the pot. Let the whole thing simmer for at least 45 minutes to an hour before serving. Top with a sprinkle of grated Parmesan, if you like.

This soup is even better warmed up the next day!

**Yield:** 8 servings

**Nutritional Analysis:** Each will have: 229 calories; 5 g fat; 26 g protein; 19 g carbohydrates; 4 g fiber; 15 g usable carbs.

| | | | | | |
|---|---|---|---|---|---|
| Potassium (mg): | 1672 mg | Vitamin C (mg): | 21 mg | Thiamin/B1 (mg): | 0.4 mg |
| Calcium (mg): | 167 mg | Vitamin A (i.u.): | 3093 i.u. | Riboflavin/B2 (mg): | 0.4 mg |
| Iron (mg): | 6 mg | Vitamin B6 (mg): | 0.7 mg | Folacin (mcg): | 284 mcg |
| Zinc (mg): | 3 mg | Vitamin B12 (mcg): | 0.6 mcg | Niacin/B3 (mg): | 15 mg |

# Chicken Veggie Chowder

You could make this the night before and keep it warm in a slow cooker set on low, and serve it for a church or family event.

20 ounces (560 g) boneless chicken
28 ounces (780 ml) chicken broth
1 cup (225 ml) clam juice
2 medium carrots, sliced
1 small turnip, coarsely diced
1/2 medium onion, chopped
1 green pepper
4 cloves garlic, peeled and crushed
3 cups (670 ml) whole milk
1 cup (235 ml) heavy cream
2 teaspoons (9 g) hot sauce
2 teaspoons (1.5 g) dried basil
1 pound (455 g) reduced-fat cheddar cheese, shredded
1 teaspoon xanthan gum
Salt and pepper
3/4 cup (60 g) shredded Parmesan cheese

Grill and dice the chicken.

In a big, heavy saucepan, combine the chicken broth and clam juice. Bring to a boil. Add the carrots, turnip, onion, pepper, and garlic. Simmer covered for about 20 minutes, till the veggies are tender.

Add the milk and heavy cream. Put the pan over medium heat, and bring to a simmer. Add the chicken, hot sauce, and basil.

Whisk in the cheese a handful at a time, stirring each addition until it's melted before you add another handful.

Use your xanthan shaker to thicken the broth. In this case, this is not an optional step. At least 1 teaspoon is needed because the gum acts as a kind of emulsifying agent for the cheese and helps keep it mixed.

Spoon the soup into 4 bowls, add Parmesan cheese to the top of each bowl, and serve.

**Yield:** 12 servings

**Nutritional Analysis:** Each will have: 271 calories; 15 g fat; 26 g protein; 8 g carbohydrates; 1 g fiber; 7 g usable carbs.

| | | | | | |
|---|---|---|---|---|---|
| Potassium (mg): | 433 mg | Vitamin C (mg): | 15 mg | Thiamin/B1 (mg): | 0.1 mg |
| Calcium (mg): | 331 mg | Vitamin A (i.u.): | 3972 i.u. | Riboflavin/B2 (mg): | 0.3 mg |
| Iron (mg): | 1 mg | Vitamin B6 (mg): | 0.4 mg | Folacin (mcg): | 19 mcg |
| Zinc (mg): | 2 mg | Vitamin B12 (mcg): | 1.8 mcg | Niacin/B3 (mg): | 6 mg |

**Note:** Check the label to make sure that you buy unadulterated clam juice—it should have 1 gram of carbs or less. You do not want Clamato, and you'll majorly increase the number of carbs in this dish if that's what you use!

## Kale, Chorizo, and Turnip Soup

It's funny—I'm not fond of kale by itself, but I love it in soups. If you can't find chicken chorizo, smoked sausage would be good in this, too—different, but good.

- 3 quarts (2.8 l) chicken broth
- 10 ounces (280 g) kale
- 3 medium turnips
- 1 1/2 pounds (670 g) chicken chorizo
- 1 tablespoon (14 ml) olive oil
- 1/2 medium onion, diced
- 2 cloves garlic, peeled and crushed
- 1/2 teaspoon red pepper flakes
- 3 cups (670 ml) whole milk

Pour the broth into a big saucepan, and put it over high heat.

While the broth is heating, chop the kale, and peel and cut the turnips into 1/2-inch (1.25-cm) cubes. Add them to the broth.

Slice the chorizo 1/4 inch (6 mm) thick. Spray a big, heavy skillet with nonstick cooking spray, and put it over medium heat. Add the oil, then the slices of chorizo. Brown the slices on both sides, then add them to the broth.

Throw the onion and garlic into the skillet, sauté them for a few minutes, then add them to the broth, too. Use a ladle to dip out a little of the broth and pour it into the skillet. Stir the broth around to dissolve any brown, flavorful bits stuck to the skillet, then pour it all back into the saucepan. Stir in the pepper flakes.

When the soup is at a boil, turn it down to a bare simmer, and let it cook until the turnips are quite soft—at least 45 minutes.

Just before serving, stir in the milk, then bring your soup back up to a simmer. Serve!

**Yield:** 7 servings

**Nutritional Analysis:** With milk, each will have: 348 calories; 16 g fat; 32 g protein; 16 g carbohydrates; 2 g fiber; 14 g usable carbs.

| | | | | | |
|---|---|---|---|---|---|
| Potassium (mg): | 809 mg | Vitamin C (mg): | 66 mg | Thiamin/B1 (mg): | 0.1 mg |
| Calcium (mg): | 238 mg | Vitamin A (i.u.): | 4206 i.u. | Riboflavin/B2 (mg): | 0.3 mg |
| Iron (mg): | 3 mg | Vitamin B6 (mg): | 0.2 mg | Folacin (mcg): | 34 mcg |
| Zinc (mg): | 1 mg | Vitamin B12 (mcg): | 0.8 mcg | Niacin/B3 (mg): | 6 mg |

**Nutritional Analysis:** With Carb Countdown, each will have: 338 calories; 16 g fat; 34 g protein; 12 g carbohydrates; 2 g fiber; 10 g usable carbs.

| | | | | | |
|---|---|---|---|---|---|
| Potassium (mg): | 651 mg | Vitamin C (mg): | 65 mg | Thiamin/B1 (mg): | 0.1 mg |
| Calcium (mg): | 261 mg | Vitamin A (i.u.): | 4206 i.u. | Riboflavin/B2 (mg): | 0.2 mg |
| Iron (mg): | 3 mg | Vitamin B6 (mg): | 0.2 mg | Folacin (mcg): | 29 mcg |
| Zinc (mg): | 1 mg | Vitamin B12 (mcg): | 0.4 mcg | Niacin/B3 (mg): | 6 mg |

## Crab and Asparagus Soup

If you love egg drop soup, this is a fantastic twist on the original! Our tester Julie's son Austin calls it "the second best Dana Recipe I've ever had!" (His favorite is the broiled asparagus in 500 More Low-Carb Recipes!)

2 quarts (1.9 l) chicken broth

2 teaspoons (5 g) grated gingerroot

1 pound (455 g) asparagus

2 eggs

1½ tablespoons (21 ml) dry sherry

2 teaspoons (10 ml) dark sesame oil

1 tablespoon (14 ml) soy sauce

12 ounces (340 g) lump crabmeat, cooked

In a large, heavy saucepan, start the broth warming over medium heat. Stir in the ginger.

Snap the ends off of the asparagus spears where they want to break naturally. Discard the ends, and slice the asparagus on the diagonal into 1/2-inch (1.25-cm) pieces.

When the soup is simmering, add the asparagus to it. Let it simmer for about 3 minutes.

While that's happening, beat the eggs until blended in a glass measuring cup (or anything with a pouring lip). When the asparagus is just barely tender-crisp, take a fork in one hand and the cup of beaten egg in the other. Pour a stream of egg onto the surface of the soup, then stir with the fork. Repeat. It should take 3 or 4 additions to stir in all the egg. Now you have lovely egg drops!

Stir in the sherry, oil, and soy sauce. Add the crab, stir again, and cook for just 3 to 4 more minutes, then serve.

**Yield:** 4 servings

**Nutritional Analysis:** Each will have: 237 calories; 8 g fat; 31 g protein; 5 g carbohydrates; 1 g fiber; 4 g usable carbs.

| | | | | | |
|---|---|---|---|---|---|
| Potassium (mg): | 937 mg | Vitamin C (mg): | 10 mg | Thiamin/B1 (mg): | 0.2 mg |
| Calcium (mg): | 130 mg | Vitamin A (i.u.): | 495 i.u. | Riboflavin/B2 (mg): | 0.4 mg |
| Iron (mg): | 3 mg | Vitamin B6 (mg): | 0.3 mg | Folacin (mcg): | 134 mcg |
| Zinc (mg): | 4 mg | Vitamin B12 (mcg): | 1.1 mcg | Niacin/B3 (mg): | 9 mg |

## Curried Crab and Asparagus Bisque

Boy, is this fancy! But you can have it done in 20 minutes flat.

1 tablespoon (14 g) butter

1/2 medium onion, finely diced

1 tablespoon (9 g) curry powder

1 pound (455 g) crabmeat in bite-size chunks

2 ounces (60 ml) dry sherry

2 cups (475 ml) clam juice

1 pound (455 g) asparagus

6 cups (1.4 l) milk

2 cups (475 ml) half-and-half

Guar or xanthan gum

Salt and pepper

Spray the bottom of your biggest heavy saucepan or soup kettle with nonstick cooking spray, and put it over medium-low heat. Melt the butter, and add the onion. Sauté the onion until it's translucent. Now stir in the curry powder, and sauté for another minute or two, stirring constantly.

Add the crab, sherry, and clam juice. Leave that to come to a simmer.

Meanwhile, snap the ends off of the asparagus where they want to break naturally. Discard the ends and cut the asparagus into 1/2-inch (1.25-cm) pieces on the diagonal. When the asparagus is all cut up, throw it in the pot, as well. Let the soup simmer until the crab is cooked and the asparagus is tender-crisp.

Stir in the milk and half-and-half, and use your guar or xanthan shaker to thicken the soup to a heavy cream consistency. Add salt and pepper to taste.

**Yield:** 8 servings

**Nutritional Analysis:** Each will have: 275 calories; 15 g fat; 19 g protein; 14 g carbohydrates; 1 g fiber; 13 g usable carbs.

| | | | | | |
|---|---|---|---|---|---|
| Potassium (mg): | 741 mg | Vitamin C (mg): | 9 mg | Thiamin/B1 (mg): | 0.2 mg |
| Calcium (mg): | 353 mg | Vitamin A (i.u.): | 751 i.u. | Riboflavin/B2 (mg): | 0.5 mg |
| Iron (mg): | 1 mg | Vitamin B6 (mg): | 0.2 mg | Folacin (mcg): | 78 mcg |
| Zinc (mg): | 3 mg | Vitamin B12 (mcg): | 9 mcg | Niacin/B3 (mg): | 2 mg |

**Note:** Check the label to make sure that you buy unadulterated clam juice—it should have 1 gram of carbs or less. You do not want Clamato, and you'll majorly increase the number of carbs in this dish if that's what you use!

## Crab and Cabbage Soup

Ray called this "good and simple." (He also said his clam juice came in bottles that were a little bigger than 1 cup/235 ml. Don't sweat it; an extra quarter-cup of clam juice isn't going to hurt a thing. Soup's charmingly flexible like that.)

1 can (14 ounces, or 390 g) diced tomatoes, undrained

2 cups (475 ml) clam juice

2 cups (475 ml) chicken broth

1 medium onion, thinly sliced

2 cups (140 g) shredded cabbage (use bagged coleslaw mix, if you like)

1 small carrot, shredded

4 cloves garlic, peeled and finely minced

1 teaspoon chili garlic paste

1 cup (235 ml) water (optional)

8 ounces (225 g) lump crabmeat, picked over for shells and broken up

1 tablespoon (4 g) minced fresh oregano

1/3 cup (20 g) chopped fresh cilantro

Salt and pepper

1 lime, quartered

In a big, heavy saucepan, combine the undrained tomatoes, clam juice, chicken broth, onion, shredded cabbage, carrot, garlic, and chili garlic paste. Add up to 1 cup (235 ml) of water, depending on how thick you like your soup. Bring it to a boil, then turn down the heat, cover, and let the whole thing simmer for 20 minutes.

Stir in the crabmeat, oregano, and cilantro, and simmer for another 10 minutes.

Ladle the soup into bowls, add salt and pepper to taste, and serve with a wedge of lime to squeeze into it.

**Yield:** 4 servings

**Nutritional Analysis:** Each will have: 135 calories; 2 g fat; 15 g protein; 16 g carbohydrates; 2 g fiber; 14 g usable carbs.

| | | | | | |
|---|---|---|---|---|---|
| Potassium (mg): | 944 mg | Vitamin C (mg): | 39 mg | Thiamin/B1 (mg): | 0.2 mg |
| Calcium (mg): | 139 mg | Vitamin A (i.u.): | 5819 i.u. | Riboflavin/B2 (mg): | 0.1 mg |
| Iron (mg): | 2 mg | Vitamin B6 (mg): | 0.3 mg | Folacin (mcg): | 65 mcg |
| Zinc (mg): | 3 mg | Vitamin B12 (mcg): | 11.2 mcg | Niacin/B3 (mg): | 4 mg |

**Note:** Check the label to make sure that you buy unadulterated clam juice—it should have 1 gram of carbs or less. You do not want Clamato, and you'll majorly increase the number of carbs in this dish if that's what you use!

## Provençal Fish Soup

My sister Kim—a serious French food enthusiast—loved this. You could serve this unpureed, if you prefer.

1 tablespoon (14 ml) olive oil

2 onions, finely chopped

1 small carrot, peeled and shredded

1 medium celery rib, diced

1 small fennel bulb, finely chopped

3 cloves garlic, peeled and finely minced

1 cup (235 ml) dry white wine

1 can (14 ounces, or 390 g) diced tomatoes, undrained

1 bay leaf

1 teaspoon orange zest

1/4 teaspoon saffron threads

3 cups (670 ml) clam juice

2 cups (475 ml) water

1 pound (455 g) pollock or cod fillet, cut into chunks

Salt and pepper

Place a big, heavy pot or saucepan over medium heat, heat the olive oil in it, and start sautéing the onion. When the onion starts to soften, add the carrot, celery, fennel, and garlic. Continue sautéing for 5 minutes or so, stirring frequently.

Add the wine, undrained tomatoes, bay leaf, orange zest, saffron, clam juice, and water. Bring to a boil, turn the burner down till the soup's barely simmering, and simmer for 30 minutes, stirring occasionally.

When the 30 minutes are up, add the fish and cook for another 15 to 20 minutes, or until the fish flakes easily.

Remove the bay leaf, then transfer the soup to your blender or food processor. Puree it until smooth, working in batches if necessary.

Return the soup to the pan, add salt and pepper to taste, make sure it's hot through, and serve.

**Yield:** 4 servings

**Nutritional Analysis:** Each will have: 244 calories; 5 g fat; 23 g protein; 19 g carbohydrates; 4 g fiber; 15 g usable carbs.

| | | | | | |
|---|---|---|---|---|---|
| Potassium (mg): | 1361 mg | Vitamin C (mg): | 31 mg | Thiamin/B1 (mg): | 0.2 mg |
| Calcium (mg): | 116 mg | Vitamin A (i.u.): | 5861 i.u. | Riboflavin/B2 (mg): | 0.2 mg |
| Iron (mg): | 2 mg | Vitamin B6 (mg): | 0.3 mg | Folacin (mcg): | 49 mcg |
| Zinc (mg): | 1 mg | Vitamin B12 (mcg): | 12.5 mcg | Niacin/B3 (mg): | 3 mg |

**Note:** Check the label to make sure that you buy unadulterated clam juice—it should have 1 gram of carbs or less. You do not want Clamato, and you'll majorly increase the number of carbs in this dish if that's what you use!

## Clam and Cheddar Chowder

Now we can stop fighting over New England versus Manhattan Clam Chowder, and just eat this!

2 cups (475 ml) chicken broth
2 cups (475 ml) clam juice
2 cups (475 ml) whole milk
2 cups (475 ml) half-and-half
8 ounces (225 g) reduced-fat cheddar cheese, shredded
Guar or xanthan gum (optional)
20 ounces (560 g) canned clams, drained
4 cloves garlic, peeled and crushed
Salt and pepper
2 teaspoons Tabasco sauce, or to taste
1/2 cup (50 g) grated Parmesan cheese
1/2 cup (30 g) chopped fresh parsley

In a big, heavy saucepan, combine the broth, clam juice, milk, and half-and-half. Put the pan over medium heat, and bring to a simmer.

Once it's simmering, whisk in the cheese a handful at a time, stirring each addition until it's melted before you add another handful. Then use your guar or xanthan shaker to thicken it, if you like. Turn the burner to low.

Stir in the clams and garlic, and simmer for just a minute or two, to blend the flavors. Add salt and pepper to taste, and stir in the Tabasco.

Spoon the chowder into bowls and top each serving with 1 tablespoon (6 g) of Parmesan and a tablespoon (4 g) of parsley.

**Yield:** 8 servings

**Nutritional Analysis:** Each will have: 308 calories; 14 g fat; 33 g protein; 11 g carbohydrates; trace fiber; 11 g usable carbs.

| | | | | | |
|---|---|---|---|---|---|
| Potassium (mg): | 809 mg | Vitamin C (mg): | 24 mg | Thiamin/B1 (mg): | 0.2 mg |
| Calcium (mg): | 406 mg | Vitamin A (i.u.): | 1065 i.u. | Riboflavin/B2 (mg): | 0.6 mg |
| Iron (mg): | 21 mg | Vitamin B6 (mg): | 0.2 mg | Folacin (mcg): | 37 mcg |
| Zinc (mg): | 3 mg | Vitamin B12 (mcg): | 73.8 mcg | Niacin/B3 (mg): | 3 mg |

**Note:** Check the label to make sure that you buy unadulterated clam juice—it should have 1 gram of carbs or less. You do not want Clamato, and you'll majorly increase the number of carbs in this dish if that's what you use!

## Chinese-Style Tuna Soup

Quick, easy, and good.

- 1 quart (950 ml) chicken broth
- 1 teaspoon (2.5 g) grated gingerroot
- 2 teaspoons (10 ml) soy sauce
- 2 eggs
- 1½ cups (45 g) chopped fresh spinach
- 1 can (6 ounces, or 170 g) tuna in water
- 2 scallions, thinly sliced

In a big saucepan, combine the chicken broth, ginger, and soy sauce. Put it over medium-high heat and bring it to a boil, then turn the burner down till the broth is just simmering.

While the broth is heating up, break the eggs into a glass measuring cup or another container with a pouring lip. Beat 'em up with a fork. When the soup is simmering, pour about one-third of the egg into the soup, wait just 1 or 2 seconds, then stir with a fork, drawing out the egg into strands. Repeat with the rest of the egg, in 2 or 3 more additions.

Add the spinach and tuna, with the juice. Heat through and serve with scallions on top.

**Yield:** 3 servings

**Nutritional Analysis:** Each will have: 170 calories; 5 g fat; 25 g protein; 3 g carbohydrates; 1 g fiber; 2 g usable carbs.

| | | | | | |
|---|---|---|---|---|---|
| Potassium (mg): | 566 mg | Vitamin C (mg): | 6 mg | Thiamin/B1 (mg): | trace |
| Calcium (mg): | 56 mg | Vitamin A (i.u.): | 1264 i.u. | Riboflavin/B2 (mg): | 0.3 mg |
| Iron (mg): | 3 mg | Vitamin B6 (mg): | 0.3 mg | Folacin (mcg): | 59 mcg |
| Zinc (mg): | 1 mg | Vitamin B12 (mcg): | 2.3 mcg | Niacin/B3 (mg): | 12 mg |

## Cauli-Zucchini-Soise

This is an elegant starter and an updated version of an old favorite.

- 1 pound (455 g) leeks
- 1 tablespoon (14 g) butter
- 12 ounces (340 g) potatoes (Yukon Gold and Idaho baker are both good)
- 1 pound (455 g) cauliflower
- 1 pound (455 g) zucchini
- 8 cloves garlic, peeled and crushed
- 1 1/2 quarts (1.4 l) chicken broth
- 1 1/2 cups (355 ml) milk
- 1/2 cup (120 ml) cream
- Salt and pepper
- Guar or xanthan gum (optional)
- 2 tablespoons (8 g) chopped chives

Trim the roots off the leeks and thinly slice the tightly interleaved white and pale green part of each. Discard the green tops.

Spray a big, heavy pot with nonstick cooking spray, and put it over medium heat. Add the butter. When it's melted, throw in the leeks and sauté them until they're tender. (Don't overcook them, as they burn easily.) While that's happening, scrub and chop the potato, trim and cut up the cauliflower, and slice the zuke into 1/2-inch (1.25-cm) rounds. Remember to stir the leeks now and then!

Add the potatoes, cauliflower, zucchini, and garlic to the pot. Sauté for 5 minutes. Then add the chicken broth, and bring the whole thing to a boil. Turn it down to a simmer, and cook till all the vegetables are tender, about 20 minutes. Turn off the burner, cover, and let it cool for 20 minutes or so.

Scoop out the veggies with a slotted spoon and put them in your food processor or blender. (Add some of the liquid, if you use a blender.) Puree it smooth; you may have to do this in batches. Put the puree back in the pot, and whisk in the milk and cream. Season with salt and pepper to taste, and thicken a little with guar or xanthan, if you think it needs it.

Now you have a choice: The traditional way to serve a true vichyssoise is chilled, and you can certainly do that if you wish. But you can serve it hot, if you prefer. Either way, sprinkle a few chopped chives on top before you serve it.

**Yield:** 10 servings

**Nutritional Analysis:** Each will have: 145 calories; 6 g fat; 7 g protein; 16 g carbohydrates; 3 g fiber; 13 g usable carbs.

| | | | | | |
|---|---|---|---|---|---|
| Potassium (mg): | 670 mg | Vitamin C (mg): | 36 mg | Thiamin/B1 (mg): | 0.1 mg |
| Calcium (mg): | 96 mg | Vitamin A (i.u.): | 402 i.u. | Riboflavin/B2 (mg): | 0.2 mg |
| Iron (mg): | 1 mg | Vitamin B6 (mg): | 0.3 mg | Folacin (mcg): | 58 mcg |
| Zinc (mg): | 1 mg | Vitamin B12 (mcg): | 0.3 mcg | Niacin/B3 (mg): | 3 mg |

**Note:** If you have a hand blender, just puree your soup right there in the pot, rather than transferring the veggies out and then back in again.

## Cauliflower-Potato Soup

On a cold winter night? Heavenly. Just heavenly.

3 cups (450 g) cauliflower, cubed

1 cup (110 g) potato, peeled and cubed

3 cups (670 ml) plus 2 tablespoons (28 ml) water

1 tablespoon (14 g) butter

1 pound (455 g) turkey ham, cut into 1/2-inch (1.25-cm) cubes

3/4 cup (45 g) chopped onion

1/2 cup (60 g) shredded carrot

1 small green pepper, finely diced

1 teaspoon salt or Vege-Sal

1/2 teaspoon pepper

3 cups (670 ml) 2% milk or Carb Countdown Dairy Beverage

Guar or xanthan gum (optional)

In a soup kettle or large, heavy saucepan, combine the cauliflower, potato, and 3 cups (670 ml) of the water. Let the whole thing simmer until the vegetables are soft.

Meanwhile, spray a big, heavy skillet with nonstick cooking spray. Melt the butter, and sauté the turkey ham cubes until they're getting a few brown spots. Add the onion, carrot, and green pepper, and continue sautéing until the vegetables are soft.

Okay, back to the kettle. Use a slotted spoon to scoop out the cauliflower and potato, and put them in your blender or food processor. (You'll need to do this in batches.) Add a ladleful of broth, to help the vegetables process, and puree them smooth.

Put the puree back into the kettle, and add the ham cubes, onion, carrot, and pepper. Use the extra 2 tablespoons of water to rinse any tasty brown bits off the bottom of the skillet, and scrape that into the kettle, too.

Add the salt and pepper. Let everything simmer for another 15 to 20 minutes, to blend the flavors. Stir in the milk, and thicken the soup a bit with your guar or xanthan shaker, if you feel it needs it. Bring it back to a simmer, and serve.

**Yield:** 6 servings

**Nutritional Analysis:** With milk, each will have: 224 calories; 8 g fat; 20 g protein; 17 g carbohydrates; 3 g fiber; 14 g usable carbs.

| | | | | | |
|---|---|---|---|---|---|
| Potassium (mg): | 824 mg | Vitamin C (mg): | 49 mg | Thiamin/B1 (mg): | 0.1 mg |
| Calcium (mg): | 183 mg | Vitamin A (i.u.): | 3317 i.u. | Riboflavin/B2 (mg): | 0.4 mg |
| Iron (mg): | 3 mg | Vitamin B6 (mg): | 0.5 mg | Folacin (mcg): | 52 mcg |
| Zinc (mg): | 3 mg | Vitamin B12 (mcg): | 0.6 mcg | Niacin/B3 (mg): | 4 mg |

**Nutritional Analysis:** With Carb Countdown, each will have: 228 calories; 10 g fat; 22 g protein; 13 g carbohydrates; 3 g fiber; 10 g usable carbs.

| | | | | | |
|---|---|---|---|---|---|
| Potassium (mg): | 636 mg | Vitamin C (mg): | 48 mg | Thiamin/B1 (mg): | 0.1 mg |
| Calcium (mg): | 207 mg | Vitamin A (i.u.): | 3215 i.u. | Riboflavin/B2 (mg): | 0.2 mg |
| Iron (mg): | 3 mg | Vitamin B6 (mg): | 0.4 mg | Folacin (mcg): | 46 mcg |
| Zinc (mg): | 3 mg | Vitamin B12 (mcg): | 0.2 mcg | Niacin/B3 (mg): | 3 mg |

## Broccoli Soup with Almonds

Julie says, "Unique and healthy! You can't argue with a dish that gets a kid to eat broccoli!"

1/2 cup (65 g) ground almonds

1 1/2 pounds (670 g) frozen broccoli, thawed

1 quart (945 ml) chicken broth

1 1/2 cups (355 ml) whole milk

Salt and pepper

Preheat the oven to 350°F (180°C, or gas mark 4). Spread the ground almonds evenly in a shallow baking pan and toast in the oven until golden, about 10 minutes. Set aside 1/4 cup of the almonds.

While the almonds are toasting, combine the broccoli and chicken broth in a saucepan and bring to a simmer. Cook till the broccoli is just tender, but not turning gray—no more than 10 minutes.

If you have a hand-blender, use it to puree the broccoli right in the pan, and then blend in the 3/4 cup of ground almonds, plus the milk. If you don't have a hand-blender, transfer the broccoli and broth to your food processor with the S-blade in place, add the 1/4 cup ground almonds and milk, and puree until smooth. Transfer back to the pan.

Bring the soup back to a simmer, and add salt and pepper to taste. Ladle it into bowls, and serve with the reserved almonds sprinkled on top.

**Yield:** 6 servings

**Nutritional Analysis:** With milk, each will have: 197 calories; 13 g fat; 12 g protein; 13 g carbohydrates; 5 g fiber; 8 g usable carbs.

| | | | | | |
|---|---|---|---|---|---|
| Potassium (mg): | 601 mg | Vitamin C (mg): | 65 mg | Thiamin/B1 (mg): | 0.1 mg |
| Calcium (mg): | 190 mg | Vitamin A (i.u.): | 2422 i.u. | Riboflavin/B2 (mg): | 0.4 mg |
| Iron (mg): | 2 mg | Vitamin B6 (mg): | 0.2 mg | Folacin (mcg): | 93 mcg |
| Zinc (mg): | 1 mg | Vitamin B12 (mcg): | 0.4 mcg | Niacin/B3 (mg): | 3 mg |

## Cream of Broccoli Soup

A longtime favorite.

1 pound (455 g) frozen broccoli, thawed

1 quart (945 ml) chicken broth (or two 14-ounce or 390-ml cans)

1 tablespoon (14 g) butter

1 large onion, chopped

12 ounces (355 ml) evaporated milk

1 teaspoon dried basil

1/4 teaspoon pepper

1 teaspoon chicken bouillon granules

Guar or xanthan gum (optional)

Combine the broccoli and broth in a big saucepan over medium-high heat. Bring to a simmer, cover, and cook for 10 to 12 minutes, or until the broccoli is tender but stopping before it turns gray.

Meanwhile, melt the butter in a skillet and sauté the onion in it until it's translucent.

When the broccoli is tender, ladle it and the chicken broth into your blender. Add the onion, and puree the whole dang thing. Pour it back into your saucepan

Add the evaporated milk, basil, pepper, and bouillon, and whisk everything together. Bring it back to a simmer. Whisk in a little guar or xanthan, if you think it needs it, and serve.

**Yield:** 4 servings

**Nutritional Analysis:** Each will have: 221 calories; 11 g fat ; 14 g protein; 18 g carbohydrates; 4 g fiber; 14 g usable carbs.

| | | | | | |
|---|---|---|---|---|---|
| Potassium (mg): | 765 mg | Vitamin C (mg): | 68 mg | Thiamin/B1 (mg): | 0.1 mg |
| Calcium (mg): | 311 mg | Vitamin A (i.u.): | 2829 i.u. | Riboflavin/B2 (mg): | 0.4 mg |
| Iron (mg): | 2 mg | Vitamin B6 (mg): | 0.2 mg | Folacin (mcg): | 94 mcg |
| Zinc (mg): | 2 mg | Vitamin B12 (mcg): | 0.4 mcg | Niacin/B3 (mg): | 4 mg |

## Pumpkin-Leek Soup

A perfect first course for a fall gathering, such as Thanksgiving.

1 leek

2 tablespoons (28 g) butter

2 cups (475 ml) chicken broth

1 pound (455 g) canned pumpkin

1 can (12 ounces, or 355 ml) evaporated milk

1/4 teaspoon pepper

1/4 teaspoon dried thyme

1/4 cup (25 g) grated Parmesan cheese

Salt

Thinly slice the white part of the leek, and rinse off any grit. Melt the butter in a big, heavy skillet over medium heat, and sauté the leek until soft.

Put the sautéed leek and 1 cup (235 ml) of the chicken broth in your blender, and puree. Pour into a big, heavy saucepan and put over medium heat. Add the remaining chicken broth, pumpkin, and evaporated milk, and whisk together.

Whisk in the pepper and thyme. Heat to a simmer, and let it all cook for 5 minutes to blend the flavors. Add salt to taste.

Serve with 1 tablespoon of Parmesan sprinkled on each serving.

**Yield:** 4 servings

**Nutritional Analysis:** Each will have: 230 calories; 13 g fat; 10 g protein; 19 g carbohydrates; 4 g fiber; 15 g usable carbs.

| | | | | | |
|---|---|---|---|---|---|
| Potassium (mg): | 578 mg | Vitamin C (mg): | 9 mg | Thiamin/B1 (mg): | 0.1 mg |
| Calcium (mg): | 284 mg | Vitamin A (i.u.): | 25560 i.u. | Riboflavin/B2 (mg): | 0.3 mg |
| Iron (mg): | 3 mg | Vitamin B6 (mg): | 0.2 mg | Folacin (mcg): | 36 mcg |
| Zinc (mg): | 1 mg | Vitamin B12 (mcg): | 0.3 mcg | Niacin/B3 (mg): | 2 mg |

## Zucchini Stracciatella

Stracciatella is the Italian version of Egg Drop Soup. This version adds vegetables for flavor and texture.

1 tablespoon (14 g) butter

1 tablespoon (14 ml) olive oil

1/4 cup (35 g) chopped onion

1 1/2 pounds (670 g) zucchini, cut into 1/2-inch (1.25-cm) cubes

1 1/2 quarts (1.4 l) chicken broth

3 eggs

3 tablespoons (15 g) freshly grated Parmesan cheese

1/4 cup (15 g) chopped parsley (Italian flat-leaf is best)

1/4 teaspoon salt

1/8 teaspoon pepper

Give a big, heavy saucepan a shot of nonstick cooking spray, and put it over medium heat. Add the butter and oil, and swirl them together as the butter melts. Add the onion, and sauté for 5 minutes. Add the zucchini, and cook for another 5 minutes, stirring occasionally.

Add the broth to the pot, stir it all up, and turn the heat up to medium-high. Bring the soup to a simmer, turn the burner down to keep it just simmering, cover the pot, and let it cook for 30 minutes.

Whisk together the eggs, cheese, parsley, salt, and pepper.

Just before serving the soup, turn the heat up and bring it to a rolling boil. Stir the soup vigorously with a whisk or fork while you pour in the beaten egg mixture. As soon as the eggs are cooked—which will be almost instantly—remove the soup from the heat, and serve.

**Yield:** 4 servings

**Nutritional Analysis:** Each will have: 207 calories; 13 g fat; 15 g protein; 8 g carbohydrates; 2 g fiber; 6 g usable carbs.

| | | | | | |
|---|---|---|---|---|---|
| Potassium (mg): | 793 mg | Vitamin C (mg): | 20 mg | Thiamin/B1 (mg): | 0.1 mg |
| Calcium (mg): | 115 mg | Vitamin A (i.u.): | 1089 i.u. | Riboflavin/B2 (mg): | 0.3 mg |
| Iron (mg): | 2 mg | Vitamin B6 (mg): | 0.2 mg | Folacin (mcg): | 66 mcg |
| Zinc (mg): | 1 mg | Vitamin B12 (mcg): | 0.7 mcg | Niacin/B3 (mg): | 6 mg |

## Quick and Easy Sopa Tortilla (Con o Sin Tortilla)

Chicken-and-tomato broth with fried tortilla strips is a Mexican classic I fell in love with on a trip to the lovely city of Querétaro. I would routinely crack up the waiter at my hotel by ordering "Sopa tortilla sin tortilla, por favor"—"Tortilla Soup without the tortillas, please." Easy to cook, easy to clean up, and smells fabulous while it's cooking!

1 tablespoon (14 ml) oil (coconut is best, but peanut will do)

1 small onion, finely chopped

2 cloves garlic, peeled and crushed

1 can (14 ounces, or 390 g) tomatoes with green chiles, undrained

1 quart (945 ml) chicken broth

1 bunch cilantro

Salt and pepper

Tortilla chips (optional)

Heat up the oil in a large, heavy saucepan over medium-low heat. Add the onion and garlic and sauté until soft, but don't let the garlic burn or brown!

Add the undrained tomatoes and chicken broth. Add salt and pepper to taste. Bring to a simmer, cover, and let the whole thing simmer for 10 minutes before serving.

While the soup's simmering, chop up your cilantro.

If you can afford the extra carbs and calories, putting a few unsalted tortilla chips in each bowl before serving makes it more traditional. Top with the cilantro, and serve.

**Yield:** 4 servings

**Nutritional Analysis:** Each will have: 97 calories; 5 g fat; 6 g protein; 8 g carbohydrates; 1 g fiber; 7 g usable carbs.

| | | | | | |
|---|---|---|---|---|---|
| Potassium (mg): | 382 mg | Vitamin C (mg): | 11 mg | Thiamin/B1 (mg): | trace |
| Calcium (mg): | 43 mg | Vitamin A (i.u.): | 474 i.u. | Riboflavin/B2 (mg): | 0.1 mg |
| Iron (mg): | 1 mg | Vitamin B6 (mg): | 0.2 mg | Folacin (mcg): | 19 mcg |
| Zinc (mg): | trace | Vitamin B12 (mcg): | 0.2 mcg | Niacin/B3 (mg): | 4 mg |

## Quick Tomato Bisque

The pureed canned tomatoes give this a pleasant, slightly rough texture. If you'd like it smoother, use three 8-ounce cans of tomato sauce, instead—the carb and calorie count remain just about identical. These are cup-of-soup–size servings, by the way, since this isn't high enough in protein to make a meal.

- 1 small onion, chopped
- 1 medium celery rib, diced, including any leaves
- 2 teaspoons (10 ml) olive oil
- 2 cans (14 ounces, or 390 g each) diced tomatoes
- 2 cups (475 ml) whole milk or Carb Countdown Dairy Beverage

Spray a heavy-bottomed saucepan with nonstick cooking spray, put it over medium-low heat, and add the oil. Throw in the onion and celery, and sauté them without browning until they're softened. Transfer to your blender.

Now add both cans of tomatoes, cover the blender, and run it until everything is well pureed. Pour it all back into the saucepan, and stir in the milk.

Turn up the heat to medium-high, and bring the soup to a simmer before serving.

**Yield:** 5 servings

**Nutritional Analysis:** With milk, each will have: 127 calories; 5 g fat; 5 g protein; 17 g carbohydrates; 1 g fiber; 16 g usable carbs.

| | | | | | |
|---|---|---|---|---|---|
| Potassium (mg): | 604 mg | Vitamin C (mg): | 26 mg | Thiamin/B1 (mg): | 0.1 mg |
| Calcium (mg): | 165 mg | Vitamin A (i.u.): | 1051 i.u. | Riboflavin/B2 (mg): | 0.2 mg |
| Iron (mg): | 1 mg | Vitamin B6 (mg): | 0.3 mg | Folacin (mcg): | 27 mcg |
| Zinc (mg): | 1 mg | Vitamin B12 (mcg): | 0.3 mcg | Niacin/B3 (mg): | 1 mg |

**Nutritional Analysis:** With Carb Countdown, each will have: 118 calories; 5 g fat; 6 g protein, 13 g carbohydrates; 1 g fiber; 12 g usable carbs.

| | | | | | |
|---|---|---|---|---|---|
| Potassium (mg): | 456 mg | Vitamin C (mg): | 25 mg | Thiamin/B1 (mg): | 0.1 mg |
| Calcium (mg): | 187 mg | Vitamin A (i.u.): | 1047 i.u. | Riboflavin/B2 (mg): | trace |
| Iron (mg): | 1 mg | Vitamin B6 (mg): | 0.2 mg | Folacin (mcg): | 22 mcg |
| Zinc (mg): | trace | Vitamin B12 (mcg): | 0 mcg | Niacin/B3 (mg): | 1 mg |

## Tex-Mex Tomato Soup

Obviously, this is a variant of the tomato soup above—I just couldn't resist! Serve this with a handful of grated pepper-Jack cheese in it, if you like. Again, these are cup-size servings, not bowl-size servings.

1 small onion, chopped

2 cloves garlic, peeled and minced

2 teaspoons (28 ml) olive oil

28 ounces (785 g) canned tomatoes with green chiles

1 1/2 teaspoons ground cumin

1 teaspoon dried oregano

2 cups (475 ml) whole milk or Carb Countdown Dairy Beverage

Spray a heavy-bottomed saucepan with nonstick cooking spray, put it over medium-low heat, and add the oil. Throw in the onion and garlic, and sauté them without browning until they're softened. Transfer to your blender.

Now add the tomatoes with chiles, cover the blender, and run it until everything is well pureed. Pour it all back into the saucepan, and add the cumin and oregano. Bring to a simmer, and let it cook for 5 minutes to blend the flavors.

Stir in the milk, and bring back to a simmer before serving.

**Yield:** 5 servings

**Nutritional Analysis:** With milk, each will have: 113 calories; 5 g fat; 5 g protein; 13 g carbohydrates; 1 g fiber; 12 g usable carbs.

| | | | | | |
|---|---|---|---|---|---|
| Potassium (mg): | 373 mg | Vitamin C (mg): | 13 mg | Thiamin/B1 (mg): | 0.1 mg |
| Calcium (mg): | 165 mg | Vitamin A (i.u.): | 770 i.u. | Riboflavin/B2 (mg): | 0.2 mg |
| Iron (mg): | 1 mg | Vitamin B6 (mg): | 0.2 mg | Folacin (mcg): | 24 mcg |
| Zinc (mg): | 1 mg | Vitamin B12 (mcg): | 0.3 mcg | Niacin/B3 (mg): | 1 mg |

**Nutritional Analysis:** With Carb Countdown, each will have: 104 calories; 5 g fat; 6 g protein; 10 g carbohydrates; 1 g fiber; 9 g usable carbs.

| | | | | | |
|---|---|---|---|---|---|
| Potassium (mg): | 225 mg | Vitamin C (mg): | 12 mg | Thiamin/B1 (mg): | 0.1 mg |
| Calcium (mg): | 187 mg | Vitamin A (i.u.): | 766 i.u. | Riboflavin/B2 (mg): | trace |
| Iron (mg): | 1 mg | Vitamin B6 (mg): | 0.2 mg | Folacin (mcg): | 20 mcg |
| Zinc (mg): | trace | Vitamin B12 (mcg): | 0 mcg | Niacin/B3 (mg): | 1 mg |

## Fresh Tomato Soup

If you're worried about having leftover tomato paste, you can either freeze it in dabs on waxed paper, then store those in a zipper-lock bag, or you can just buy tomato paste in a tube, instead of a can, which is a whole heckuva lot easier. These servings are appetizer-size, since this soup isn't high in protein.

3 pounds (1.4 kg) ripe tomatoes

2 cups (475 ml) chicken broth

2 tablespoons (30 g) tomato paste

2 tablespoons (28 ml) balsamic vinegar

2 teaspoons (1 g) Splenda or 1/2 teaspoon stevia/FOS blend

2 tablespoons (8 g) minced fresh basil

Salt and pepper

6 tablespoons (90 g) light sour cream

6 tablespoons (30 g) shredded Parmesan cheese

Bring a pot of water to a boil, and have a big mixing bowl of ice water next to it. Dip your tomatoes in the boiling water for 30 seconds, then plunge them into the ice water. This will loosen the tomato skins so you can remove them easily. Skin and quarter each tomato.

Put the tomatoes in a big nonreactive saucepan, and add the broth. Bring just to a boil, then turn the burner to its lowest heat setting and simmer the tomatoes for 10 minutes.

If you have a hand-blender, use it to puree your cooked tomatoes right in the pan. If you don't have a hand-blender, transfer the tomatoes to your blender or food processor for pureeing, or use a potato masher and settle for chunkier soup (though you should mash it as fine as you can).

Anyway, you should now have your cooked and pureed tomatoes back in the pan. Stir in the tomato paste, vinegar, Splenda, basil, and salt and pepper to taste. Bring the soup back to a simmer if it has cooled a bit, then serve with a tablespoon (15 g) of sour cream in the middle of each serving and a tablespoon (5 g) of shredded Parmesan sprinkled on top.

**Yield:** 6 servings

**Nutritional Analysis:** Each will have: 88 calories; 3 g fat; 6 g protein; 12 g carbohydrates; 3 g fiber; 9 g usable carbs.

| | | | | | |
|---|---|---|---|---|---|
| Potassium (mg): | 593 mg | Vitamin C (mg): | 42 mg | Thiamin/B1 (mg): | 0.1 mg |
| Calcium (mg): | 86 mg | Vitamin A (i.u.): | 1486 i.u. | Riboflavin/B2 (mg): | 0.1 mg |
| Iron (mg): | 1 mg | Vitamin B6 (mg): | 0.2 mg | Folacin (mcg): | 35 mcg |
| Zinc (mg): | trace | Vitamin B12 (mcg): | 0.2 mcg | Niacin/B3 (mg): | 3 mg |

# Curried Zucchini-Cauliflower Soup

Mmm … curry.

1 tablespoon (14 ml) olive oil

1 medium onion, chopped

2 cloves garlic, peeled and finely minced

2 teaspoons (6 g) curry powder

3 medium zucchini, sliced

1/4 head cauliflower, cut into chunks

1 quart (945 ml) chicken broth

1/4 cup (30 g) slivered almonds, toasted

In a heavy-bottomed saucepan over medium heat, heat the olive oil and start sautéing the onion. When it's translucent, add the garlic and curry powder, and sauté for another minute or so.

Add the zucchini, cauliflower, and chicken broth. Bring to a boil, reduce the heat, and simmer for 15 to 20 minutes, or until the vegetables are soft.

Use a slotted spoon to fish out the vegetables and put them in your blender; you'll need to do this in batches, filling the blender about halfway each time. Add a ladle of broth to facilitate blending, and puree. Repeat until all the veggies are pureed, returning them to the pan as they're done.

Serve hot or cold, with a tablespoon of slivered almonds on each serving.

**Yield:** 4 servings

**Nutritional Analysis:** Each will have: 167 calories; 10 g fat; 10 g protein; 12 g carbohydrates; 4 g fiber; 8 g usable carbs.

| | | | | | |
|---|---|---|---|---|---|
| Potassium (mg): | 813 mg | Vitamin C (mg): | 32 mg | Thiamin/B1 (mg): | 0.1 mg |
| Calcium (mg): | 75 mg | Vitamin A (i.u.): | 517 i.u. | Riboflavin/B2 (mg): | 0.2 mg |
| Iron (mg): | 2 mg | Vitamin B6 (mg): | 0.3 mg | Folacin (mcg): | 68 mcg |
| Zinc (mg): | 1 mg | Vitamin B12 (mcg): | 0.2 mcg | Niacin/B3 (mg): | 4 mg |

# Garden Soup

"Ye Olde Englishe Soupe."

3 cups (390 g) frozen peas, thawed
1 small onion, finely chopped
2 cloves garlic, peeled and finely minced
1/4 cup (40 g) turkey ham, cut into 1/4-inch (6-mm) cubes
1 1/2 quarts (1.4 l) chicken broth, or three 14-ounce (390-ml) cans
1 tablespoon (14 ml) olive oil
2 cups (60 g) fresh spinach, chopped
1/2 cup (35 g) shredded cabbage (use bagged coleslaw mix, if you like)
1 cup (30 g) shredded lettuce (leaf lettuce is best)
1 small celery rib, finely diced
1/4 cup (15 g) chopped fresh parsley
1 tablespoon (4 g) chopped fresh oregano or mint
1 pinch ground nutmeg
Salt and pepper

In a big, heavy saucepan, combine the peas, onion, garlic, and turkey ham. Add the broth and bring to a simmer. Turn the burner to low and let it simmer for 20 minutes.

While that simmers, spray a big, heavy skillet with nonstick cooking spray. Put it over medium-low heat and add the oil. Throw in the spinach, cabbage, lettuce, celery, parsley, and oregano. Sauté the whole thing together till the greens are just soft.

When the pea mixture is done simmering, use a hand-blender, if you have one, to puree it in the pan until smooth. If you don't have a hand-blender, transfer the mixture to your blender or food processor for pureeing. Either way, puree it, then get it back in the pan.

Stir in the sautéed greens and nutmeg. Add salt and pepper to taste, then serve.

**Yield:** 6 servings

**Nutritional Analysis:** Each will have: 143 calories; 5 g fat; 11 g protein; 14 g carbohydrates; 5 g fiber; 9 g usable carbs.

| | | | | | |
|---|---|---|---|---|---|
| Potassium (mg): | 508 mg | Vitamin C (mg): | 25 mg | Thiamin/B1 (mg): | 0.2 mg |
| Calcium (mg): | 58 mg | Vitamin A (i.u.): | 1526 i.u. | Riboflavin/B2 (mg): | 0.2 mg |
| Iron (mg): | 3 mg | Vitamin B6 (mg): | 0.2 mg | Folacin (mcg): | 79 mcg |
| Zinc (mg): | 1 mg | Vitamin B12 (mcg): | 0.3 mcg | Niacin/B3 (mg): | 5 mg |

# Julie and Austin's Pea Soup

This is for my good friend and invaluable recipe tester, Julie, and her son Austin, a young man of considerable charm and impeccable manners. Julie needs to be quite careful about her carb intake, and she told me that she and Austin both missed split-pea soup very much. I came up with this version that combines split peas with the lower-carb-and-calorie green beans, and I dedicate it to them.

1 cup (225 g) split peas
3 cups (670 ml) water
3 ounces (85 g) turkey ham, diced small
1 small onion, diced small
2 large celery ribs, diced small, including any leaves
1 medium carrot, shredded
2 cans (14½ ounces, or 405 g each) green beans, undrained
1 clove garlic, peeled and finely minced
1 bay leaf
½ teaspoon dried thyme
Salt and pepper

Put the split peas in a mixing bowl, and cover them with the water. Let them sit for several hours.

After they've soaked, pour off the water into a measuring cup, and add enough water to it to make 5 cups. Put the split peas and the water into a pot, cover, and put it over your stove's lowest heat setting. Let it simmer for at least 1½ to 2 hours.

When it's done simmering, add the ham, onion, celery, and carrot to the split peas, and let it simmer some more.

Dump the canned beans into your blender, cover, and run the blender till the beans are pureed. Pour them into the soup, add the garlic, bay leaf, and thyme, and stir it all up. Let the whole thing simmer for another 30 to 45 minutes. Add salt and pepper to taste, and serve.

**Yield:** 8 servings

**Nutritional Analysis:** Each will have: 110 calories; 1 g fat; 8 g protein; 18 g carbohydrates; 7 g fiber; 11 g usable carbs.

| | | | | | |
|---|---|---|---|---|---|
| Potassium (mg): | 361 mg | Vitamin C (mg): | 3 mg | Thiamin/B1 (mg): | 0.2 mg |
| Calcium (mg): | 29 mg | Vitamin A (i.u.): | 2595 i.u. | Riboflavin/B2 (mg): | 0.1 mg |
| Iron (mg): | 2 mg | Vitamin B6 (mg): | 0.1 mg | Folacin (mcg): | 76 mcg |
| Zinc (mg): | 1 mg | Vitamin B12 (mcg): | trace | Niacin/B3 (mg): | 1 mg |

## Not Pea Soup

Before I came up with the hybrid version above, I came up with this. It's not exactly like split-pea soup, but it's remarkably similar, and it satisfied my craving. It's also quick and easy to make, requires no soaking time, and is far, far lower in carbs and calories than traditional split-pea soup.

2 teaspoons (10 g) butter
1/4 cup (35 g) chopped onion
1/4 cup (30 g) chopped celery
1/2 medium carrot, grated
2 ounces (55 g) turkey ham
2 cans (14.5 ounces, or 405 g each) green beans, undrained
1 clove garlic, peeled and finely minced
1 bay leaf
1/4 teaspoon dried thyme
1 pinch cayenne pepper
Salt and pepper

In a heavy saucepan, melt the butter and start sautéing the onion, celery, and carrot over medium heat.

While that's happening, put the turkey ham in your food processor with the S-blade in place, and pulse until it's chopped medium-fine. Scrape this out of the food processor and into the saucepan with the veggies. Give everything a stir while you're there.

Put the processor bowl back on its base with the S-blade in place. Dump in the green beans with their juice, and run the processor until the beans are pureed quite smooth.

Go back and look at the sautéing vegetables. When they're soft, add the garlic. Sauté it with the vegetables for just a minute.

Now dump in your green bean puree, and stir everything up. Add the bay leaf, thyme, and cayenne, and stir them in. Turn the burner to low, and bring the soup to a simmer. Let it cook for 15 minutes or so.

Add salt and pepper to taste, and serve.

**Yield:** 2 servings

**Nutritional Analysis:** Each will have: 93 calories; 5 g fat; 6 g protein; 5 g carbohydrates; 1 g fiber; 4 g usable carbs.

| Potassium (mg): | 246 mg | Vitamin C (mg): | 6 mg | Thiamin/B1 (mg): | trace |
|---|---|---|---|---|---|
| Calcium (mg): | 27 mg | Vitamin A (i.u.): | 5297 i.u. | Riboflavin/B2 (mg): | 0.1 mg |
| Iron (mg): | 1 mg | Vitamin B6 (mg): | 0.1 mg | Folacin (mcg): | 15 mcg |
| Zinc (mg): | 1 mg | Vitamin B12 (mcg): | 0.1 mcg | Niacin/B3 (mg): | 1 mg |

## Christ Church Bouillon

When I was growing up, this was served during the coffee hour after Sunday services at Christ Episcopal Church in Ridgewood, New Jersey. It's remarkably good for how simple it is. A cup of this will take the edge off of your appetite before supper—or anytime, really! Feel free to use low-sodium broth or salt-free juice to reduce the considerable sodium content of this one.

2 cups (475 ml) beef broth

2 cups (475 ml) tomato juice or 2 cups (475 ml) V8 vegetable juice

Just mix the two together, heat, and serve.

**Yield:** 4 servings

**Nutritional Analysis:** Each will have: 50 calories; trace fat; 6 g protein; 7 g carbohydrates; 1 g fiber; 6 g usable carbs.

| Potassium (mg): | 421 mg | Vitamin C (mg): | 23 mg | Thiamin/B1 (mg): | 0.1 mg |
|---|---|---|---|---|---|
| Calcium (mg): | 20 mg | Vitamin A (i.u.): | 676 i.u. | Riboflavin/B2 (mg): | 0.1 mg |
| Iron (mg): | 1 mg | Vitamin B6 (mg): | 0.1 mg | Folacin (mcg): | 27 mcg |
| Zinc (mg): | 1 mg | Vitamin B12 (mcg): | 0 mcg | Niacin/B3 (mg): | 2 mg |

# Strawberry Soup

Cold fruit soups as appetizers are a Scandinavian summer tradition. Try adding about 1/4 cup (60 ml) of sparkling water to this; it makes it into something more like a high-quality soda!

- 2 pints (700 g) strawberries, hulled
- 2 cups (490 g) plain yogurt
- 1/4 cup (60 ml) orange juice
- 1/4 cup (60 ml) lemon juice
- 1 teaspoon orange zest
- 2/3 cup (16 g) Splenda
- 1/2 cup (120 ml) water
- 1/8 teaspoon ground cardamom

Too easy! Throw everything into your blender or food processor, and run until it's smooth. Chill until you're ready to serve it.

**Yield:** 5 servings

**Nutritional Analysis:** Each will have: 118 calories; 4 g fat; 4 g protein; 16 g carbohydrates; 3 g fiber; 13 g usable carbs.

| | | | | | |
|---|---|---|---|---|---|
| Potassium (mg): | 389 mg | Vitamin C (mg): | 80 mg | Thiamin/B1 (mg): | trace |
| Calcium (mg): | 138 mg | Vitamin A (i.u.): | 181 i.u. | Riboflavin/B2 (mg): | 0.1 mg |
| Iron (mg): | trace | Vitamin B6 (mg): | trace | Folacin (mcg): | 37 mcg |
| Zinc (mg): | 1 mg | Vitamin B12 (mcg): | 0.4 mcg | Niacin/B3 (mg): | trace |

chapter fifteen

# Beverages

As a nation, we have developed a very nasty habit of swilling down vast amounts of sugar in the form of soft drinks and other sweetened beverages. Few things are so fattening and so bad for your health.

Certainly switching to sugar-free soda is an improvement—you lose the carbs and the calories. But it's still far from ideal because sugar-free soda has no nutritional value. Worse, it's high in phosphorus (as is sugar-sweetened soda), and since excessive phosphorus can interfere with your body's ability to use calcium, that makes diet soda rough on your bones.

Water is a great thing to drink, of course, but sometimes you want something with flavor. (And if you're like me, sometimes you want something with caffeine!) Here are a few recipes for beverages, all of which have at least some nutritional value—along with being tasty, of course!

## Tea

We start with a few tea recipes, both iced and hot. Tea is, to me, the one true addiction. My Great Aunt Grace treated my siblings and me to tea parties with real bone china cups and silver teaspoons when we were very small, and I've been hooked ever since. I drink pot after pot of hot tea in winter and glass after glass of iced tea in summer.

Back in the 1980s, when I was working as a massage therapist at a holistic health care center, my veggie-organic colleagues would scold me about my tea habit. "Tea is bad for you!" they'd say. "It has caffeine! It has tannic acid! You should drink herb tea!"

"No!" I would protest, "Tea is my friend! Tea would not hurt me! Aunt Grace wouldn't have given me tea if it were bad for me!" And I'd go brew another cup.

Well, during my tenure at the holistic health care center, the news came out: Tea is positively loaded with antioxidants. Green tea has the most, but black tea—from the same plant, only fermented—also has them. Tea prevents cancer, slows aging, and even helps keep your teeth from rotting.

I was pretty darned smug, I can tell you.

More recently, tea has been demonstrated to aid modestly in weight control. (No, it will not make you lose fantastic amounts of weight, or I would have vanished years ago.) And in September 2005, a medical study was published suggesting that tea may prevent or slow the progression of Alzheimer's disease.

In short, giving up soda for tea, hot or iced, is one of the healthiest changes you can make.

## Sweet Tea

I like my tea black, whether I'm drinking it hot or cold, but sweet tea is a Southern staple, so I had an Alabaman friend vet this for me. She doesn't promise it tastes exactly like your mama's or your auntie's sweet tea, but she says it tastes great. It also has a whole lot less sugar and nothing artificial in it.

The reason you use the blender to add the stevia/FOS blend is to prevent clumping. Who wants little lumps of ultra-sweetness floating in their tea?

6 cups (1.4 l) water

4 family-size tea bags

1 1/2 to 2 tablespoons (12 to 16 g) stevia/FOS blend

Water

Bring the 6 cups of water to a boil in a saucepan, then add the tea bags. Let it simmer for just a minute, then remove from the heat. Let it sit for 10 to 15 minutes.

Remove the tea bags, squeezing them out in the process.

Ladle 1 cup (235 ml) of the hot tea into your blender, and turn it on. Add the stevia/FOS blend, and let it blend for a few seconds. Pour into a 1-gallon (3.8-l) pitcher. Pour in the rest of the tea, then add water to fill.

Chill, and serve over ice!

**Yield:** 16 servings

**Nutritional Analysis:** Each will have: 1 calorie; 0 g fat; trace protein; trace carbohydrates; trace fiber; trace usable carbs.

| | | | | | |
|---|---|---|---|---|---|
| Potassium (mg): | 35 mg | Vitamin C (mg): | 0 mg | Thiamin/B1 (mg): | 0 mg |
| Calcium (mg): | 2 mg | Vitamin A (i.u.): | 0 i.u. | Riboflavin/B2 (mg): | trace |
| Iron (mg): | trace | Vitamin B6 (mg): | trace | Folacin (mcg): | 1 mcg |
| Zinc (mg): | trace | Vitamin B12 (mcg): | 0 mcg | Niacin/B3 (mg): | trace |

**Note:** Our tester liked it with 2 tablespoons of the stevia/FOS, but she admits she likes her sweet tea very sweet. Experiment and see what tastes best to you.

# Apricot Tea Punch

6 cups (1.4 l) boiling water

3 family-size tea bags

4 tablespoons (80 g) low-sugar apricot preserves

1 bottle (1 liter) diet ginger ale, chilled

Ice

In a heat-proof pitcher, pour the boiling water over the tea bags. Let them steep for 15 minutes, then remove the tea bags, squeezing them out as you do so.

Ladle 1 cup (235 ml) of the tea into your blender, and add the preserves. Run the blender until the two are completely combined and any chunks of fruit in the preserves are pureed. Pour back into the pitcher and stir. Now chill the tea for several hours.

To serve, fill tall glasses with ice, fill them three-quarters full with the tea, then fill the rest of the way with the chilled ginger ale.

**Yield:** 10 servings

**Nutritional Analysis:** Each will have: 9 calories; 0 g fat; 0 g protein; 2 g carbohydrates; 0 g fiber; 2 g usable carbs.

| | | | | | |
|---|---|---|---|---|---|
| Potassium (mg): | 2 mg | Vitamin C (mg): | 0 mg | Thiamin/B1 (mg): | 0 mg |
| Calcium (mg): | 7 mg | Vitamin A (i.u.): | 0 i.u. | Riboflavin/B2 (mg): | 0 mg |
| Iron (mg): | trace | Vitamin B6 (mg): | 0 mg | Folacin (mcg): | 0 mg |
| Zinc (mg): | trace | Vitamin B12 (mcg): | 0 mcg | Niacin/B3 (mg): | 0 mg |

## Iced Strawberry Tea

5 cups (1.1 l) boiling water

2 family-size tea bags

1/2 cup (120 ml) lemon juice

1/2 cup (12 g) Splenda, or 1 1/2 teaspoons (4 g) stevia/FOS blend

10 frozen strawberries, unsweetened

Ice cubes

In a heat-proof pitcher, pour the boiling water over the tea bags, and let them steep for 10 to 15 minutes. Fish out the teabags, squeezing them out in the process.

Stir in the lemon juice and Splenda. If you're using the stevia/FOS blend, just stir in the lemon juice now, and hang on to the stevia/FOS for a minute.

Put the strawberries in your blender, and ladle in 1 cup (235 ml) of the tea. If you're using stevia/FOS, add it now. Run the blender till the strawberries are pureed, then pour the whole thing back into the pitcher. Chill.

Fill glasses with ice, and pour the tea over them.

**Yield:** 4 servings

**Nutritional Analysis:** Each will have: 29 calories; trace fat; trace protein; 8 g carbohydrates; 1 g fiber; 7 g usable carbs.

| | | | | | |
|---|---|---|---|---|---|
| Potassium (mg): | 77 mg | Vitamin C (mg): | 25 mg | Thiamin/B1 (mg): | trace |
| Calcium (mg): | 12 mg | Vitamin A (i.u.): | 18 i.u. | Riboflavin/B2 (mg): | trace |
| Iron (mg): | trace | Vitamin B6 (mg): | trace | Folacin (mcg): | 8 mcg |
| Zinc (mg): | trace | Vitamin B12 (mcg): | 0 mcg | Niacin/B3 (mg): | trace |

## Hot Cranberry Tea

2 family-size tea bags

1 quart (945 ml) water

12 ounces (340 g) fresh cranberries

2 cups (50 g) Splenda, or 1 cup (25 g) Splenda plus 2 tablespoons (16 g) stevia/FOS blend

2 oranges

2 lemons

12 whole cloves

2 cinnamon sticks

Put the teabags in the bottom of a slow cooker. On the stovetop, bring the water to a boil, and pour it over the tea bags. Let them steep for 15 minutes, then remove the tea bags, squeezing them as you take them out.

Add the cranberries and Splenda, and stir them in. Plug in the slow cooker, and set it to low.

Slice the oranges and lemons as thinly as you possibly can, and add them to the slow cooker, along with the cloves and cinnamon.

Cover the cooker and let the whole thing brew for a couple of hours. Keep warm in the slow cooker while you're serving.

**Yield:** 14 servings

**Nutritional Analysis:** Each will have: 59 calories; 1 g fat; 1 g protein; 15 g carbohydrates; 5 g fiber; 10 g usable carbs.

| | | | | | |
|---|---|---|---|---|---|
| Potassium (mg): | 135 mg | Vitamin C (mg): | 23 mg | Thiamin/B1 (mg): | trace |
| Calcium (mg): | 73 mg | Vitamin A (i.u.): | 87 i.u. | Riboflavin/B2 (mg): | trace |
| Iron (mg): | 1 mg | Vitamin B6 (mg): | 0.1 mg | Folacin (mcg): | 13 mcg |
| Zinc (mg): | trace | Vitamin B12 (mcg): | 0 mcg | Niacin/B3 (mg): | trace |

## Sparkling Raspberry Tea

Light and refreshing!

4 tea bags

4 raspberry herbal tea bags

1 quart (945 ml) boiling water

1/4 cup (60 ml) lemon juice

1 1/2 teaspoons (4 g) stevia/FOS blend

1 quart (945 ml) raspberry-flavor sparkling water, unsweetened

Put all 8 tea bags in a heat-proof pitcher, and pour the boiling water over them. Let them steep until cool. Use clean hands to squeeze the tea bags dry, and discard.

Add the lemon juice. Start stirring the tea with a whisk before you start sprinkling the stevia/FOS blend on the surface. Whisk it all in gradually.

Fill a glass with ice. Add 1/2 cup (120 ml) of the tea and 1/2 cup (120 ml) chilled sparkling water, and serve.

**Yield:** 8 servings

**Nutritional Analysis:** Each will have: 5 calories; 0 g fat; trace protein; 1 g carbohydrates; trace fiber; 1 g usable carbs.

| | | | | | |
|---|---|---|---|---|---|
| Potassium (mg): | 79 mg | Vitamin C (mg): | 4 mg | Thiamin/B1 (mg): | trace |
| Calcium (mg): | 3 mg | Vitamin A (i.u.): | 2 i.u. | Riboflavin/B2 (mg): | trace |
| Iron (mg): | trace | Vitamin B6 (mg): | trace | Folacin (mcg): | 2 mcg |
| Zinc (mg): | trace | Vitamin B12 (mcg): | 0 mcg | Niacin/B3 (mg): | trace |

## Lemonade

You know—lemonade, but without the sugar. Since so many of you have expressed concern about artificial sweeteners, I wanted to give you a version with nothing artificial in it. If you like, you could use 1 cup (25 g) of Splenda instead of the stevia/FOS blend.

1 cup (235 ml) lemon juice

2 tablespoons (16 g) stevia/FOS blend

Water

This is quite simple. Put the lemon juice in your blender, turn it on, and add the stevia/FOS blend. Pour this mixture into a half-gallon pitcher. Fill with water, and stir again. Serve over ice.

**Yield:** 8 servings

**Nutritional Analysis:** Each will have: 8 calories; 0 g fat; trace protein; 3 g carbohydrates; trace fiber; 3 g usable carbs.

| | | | | | |
|---|---|---|---|---|---|
| Potassium (mg): | 38 mg | Vitamin C (mg): | 14 mg | Thiamin/B1 (mg): | trace |
| Calcium (mg): | 2 mg | Vitamin A (i.u.): | 6 i.u. | Riboflavin/B2 (mg): | trace |
| Iron (mg): | trace | Vitamin B6 (mg): | trace | Folacin (mcg): | 4 mcg |
| Zinc (mg): | trace | Vitamin B12 (mcg): | 0 mcg | Niacin/B3 (mg): | trace |

# Agua Fresca con Limon

This is a Latin American take on lemonade—in Spanish, limon applies to both limes and lemons. My pal Maria tested this and loved it as-is, but she said that some of you may want a little more sweetener.

- 2 quarts (1.9 l) water
- 1/3 cup (8 g) Splenda (or more or less, to taste)
- 10 limes, plus 1 lime for garnish (optional)
- Ice cubes

Put the water in a big pitcher, and stir in the Splenda. Stick it in the fridge to cool as you deal with the limes.

Grate the rinds of 10 limes, taking care to get only the green part. Now roll the skinned limes under your palm to loosen the juice.

Grab that pitcher out of the fridge. Stir in the lime rind. Now put a strainer over the pitcher (to catch the seeds) and squeeze the limes into the pitcher, too, extracting every drop of juice you can. Stir the whole thing up, and chill it some more.

Serve over ice, with lime slices to garnish, if using.

**Yield:** 6 servings

**Nutritional Analysis:** Each will have: 39 calories; trace fat; 1 g protein; 13 g carbohydrates; 1 g fiber; 12 g usable carbs.

| | | | | | |
|---|---|---|---|---|---|
| Potassium (mg): | 114 mg | Vitamin C (mg): | 32 mg | Thiamin/B1 (mg): | trace |
| Calcium (mg): | 43 mg | Vitamin A (i.u.): | 11 i.u. | Riboflavin/B2 (mg): | trace |
| Iron (mg): | 1 mg | Vitamin B6 (mg): | trace | Folacin (mcg): | 9 mcg |
| Zinc (mg): | trace | Vitamin B12 (mcg): | 0 mcg | Niacin/B3 (mg): | trace |

## Cider-Ade

You may think I'm nuts, but I'm very fond of this beverage. I invented it because I had read for years about the healthful qualities of apple cider vinegar. This drink has the same sort of sweet-and-sour quality you find in lemonade, but it's appley, instead. (And no, I haven't found that drinking vinegar makes me lose terrific amounts of weight.) I like to use organic apple cider vinegar for this.

2 cups (475 ml) apple cider vinegar (the best quality you can get)

4 teaspoons (11 g) stevia/FOS blend

Water

Put the vinegar in your blender, and turn on the blender. Add the stevia/FOS blend, and run for about 15 seconds. Pour this mixture into a clean, pint-size bottle.

To make Cider-Ade, put 2 tablespoons of the sweetened vinegar in a tall glass, add ice, and fill the rest of the way with water.

**Yield:** 16 servings

**Nutritional Analysis:** Each will have: 4 calories; 0 g fat; 0 g protein; 2 g carbohydrates; 0 g fiber; 2 g usable carbs.

| | | | | | |
|---|---|---|---|---|---|
| Potassium (mg): | 30 mg | Vitamin C (mg): | 0 mg | Thiamin/B1 (mg): | 0 mg |
| Calcium (mg): | 2 mg | Vitamin A (i.u.): | 0 i.u. | Riboflavin/B2 (mg): | 0 mg |
| Iron (mg): | trace | Vitamin B6 (mg): | 0 mg | Folacin (mcg): | 0 mcg |
| Zinc (mg): | 0 mg | Vitamin B12 (mcg): | 0 mcg | Niacin/B3 (mg): | 0 mg |

## Minted Orange-Lemon Fizz

Our tester, Ray, says you should be very careful to get unsweetened lemon-flavor sparkling water for this. He accidentally purchased a sweetened version first and didn't like the results, but thought it quite good when he tried it with unsweetened sparkling water. Always read the label!

1 1/4 cups (285 ml) water

3/4 cup (18 g) Splenda

1/2 cup (30 g) tightly packed fresh mint leaves, chopped

1 tablespoon (6 g) orange zest

1/2 cup (120 ml) orange juice

1 cup (235 ml) lemon juice

$2\frac{1}{2}$ cups (570 ml) lemon-flavor sparkling water, unsweetened

Combine the water, Splenda, mint leaves, orange zest, orange juice, and lemon juice. Refrigerate the mixture for several hours, to let the flavors marry.

Strain the mixture into a pitcher, discarding the mint and orange rind. Just before serving, add the sparkling water. Serve over ice and garnished with fresh mint, if you have any left.

**Yield:** 5 servings

**Nutritional Analysis:** Each will have: 43 calories; trace fat; 1 g protein; 11 g carbohydrates; 1 g fiber; 10 g usable carbs.

| | | | | | |
|---|---|---|---|---|---|
| Potassium (mg): | 154 mg | Vitamin C (mg): | 38 mg | Thiamin/B1 (mg): | trace |
| Calcium (mg): | 27 mg | Vitamin A (i.u.): | 432 i.u. | Riboflavin/B2 (mg): | trace |
| Iron (mg): | 1 mg | Vitamin B6 (mg): | trace | Folacin (mcg): | 30 mcg |
| Zinc (mg): | trace | Vitamin B12 (mcg): | 0 mcg | Niacin/B3 (mg): | trace |

## Raspberry Fizz

Maria liked this as is; her sugar-craving kids liked it better with diet lemon-lime soda.

1 pint (300 g) fresh or unsweetened frozen raspberries

2 tablespoons (3 g) Splenda or $1\frac{1}{2}$ teaspoons (4 g) stevia/FOS blend

1 liter carbonated water (club soda, unsweetened) chilled

Put the raspberries and the Splenda or stevia/FOS blend in your blender or food processor, and puree.

Divide the puree among 4 tall glasses, fill with ice, and top with carbonated water.

**Yield:** 4 servings

**Nutritional Analysis:** Each will have: 34 calories; trace fat; 1 g protein; 8 g carbohydrates; 4 g fiber; 4 g usable carbs.

| | | | | | |
|---|---|---|---|---|---|
| Potassium (mg): | 101 mg | Vitamin C (mg): | 16 mg | Thiamin/B1 (mg): | 0 mg |
| Calcium (mg): | 26 mg | Vitamin A (i.u.): | 82 i.u. | Riboflavin/B2 (mg): | trace |
| Iron (mg): | trace | Vitamin B6 (mg): | trace | Folacin (mcg): | 16 mcg |
| Zinc (mg): | trace | Vitamin B12 (mcg): | 0 mcg | Niacin/B3 (mg): | 1 mg |

**Note:** You can strain the seeds from the puree, if you like, but this involves putting it in your strainer and rubbing it through with the back of a spoon, which takes a bit of time. I wouldn't bother.

## Ginger-Melon Frappé

Our tester called this "very melony" and liked it very much. I think this would make a terrific dessert on a hot summer evening; sort of like a Slurpee, only a whole lot better and healthier.

- 1 medium cantaloupe
- 3 tablespoons (45 ml) lime juice
- 2 tablespoons (3 g) Splenda
- 36 ounces (1 l) diet ginger ale, chilled
- 1 lime, cut into rounds (optional)

This takes a little advance work. Whack the cantaloupe in half and scoop out the seeds. Now cut it into smaller wedges, cut off the rind, and chunk the melon flesh. Throw it in a container, and stash it in the freezer till it's frozen.

Pull that container out, throw the frozen melon chunks into your blender or food processor, and add the lime juice, Splenda, and 12 ounces of the ginger ale. Blend into a slush.

Pour this into 6 glasses, top with the rest of the ginger ale, stir, and serve with lime rounds, if using, to decorate.

**Yield:** 6 servings

**Nutritional Analysis:** Each will have: 40 calories; trace fat; 1 g protein; 10 g carbohydrates; 1 g fiber; 9 g usable carbs.

| | | | | | |
|---|---|---|---|---|---|
| Potassium (mg): | 307 mg | Vitamin C (mg): | 44 mg | Thiamin/B1 (mg): | trace |
| Calcium (mg): | 21 mg | Vitamin A (i.u.): | 2968 i.u. | Riboflavin/B2 (mg): | trace |
| Iron (mg): | trace | Vitamin B6 (mg): | 0.1 mg | Folacin (mcg): | 17 mcg |
| Zinc (mg): | trace | Vitamin B12 (mcg): | 0 mcg | Niacin/B3 (mg): | 1 mg |

## Hot Cocoa Mix

Keep this on hand for a quick winter warm up.

- 4 cups (520 g) instant dry milk
- 3/4 cup (65 g) unsweetened cocoa powder
- 1 1/4 cups (30 g) Splenda
- 1/8 teaspoon salt

Simply stir all the ingredients together well and store in a tightly lidded container. When you want a cup of cocoa, stir the mix up again, and put 1/4 cup (35 g) of it into a mug. Add 1 cup (235 ml) of boiling water, and stir till dissolved. Serve immediately!

**Yield:** 24 servings

**Nutritional Analysis:** Each will have: 84 calories; 1 g fat; 8 g protein; 13 g carbohydrates; 1 g fiber; 12 g usable carbs.

| | | | | | |
|---|---|---|---|---|---|
| Potassium (mg): | 400 mg | Vitamin C (mg): | 1 mg | Thiamin/B1 (mg): | 0.1 mg |
| Calcium (mg): | 255 mg | Vitamin A (i.u.): | 440 i.u. | Riboflavin/B2 (mg): | 0.3 mg |
| Iron (mg): | trace | Vitamin B6 (mg): | 0.1 mg | Folacin (mcg): | 11 mcg |
| Zinc (mg): | 1 mg | Vitamin B12 (mcg): | 0.8 mcg | Niacin/B3 (mg): | trace |

## Easy Iced Cappuccino

Do you have any idea how many carbs and calories those bottled coffee drinks have? Make this, instead—it's easy, quick, and tasty. Add a scoop of vanilla whey protein powder for a great take-along breakfast!

- 1 1/2 teaspoons instant coffee granules
- 1 cup (235 ml) skim milk, cold
- 1 teaspoon (.5 g) Splenda
- 2 ice cubes
- Dash nutmeg

Put the coffee, milk, Splenda, and ice cubes in your blender, and run it till it's smooth. Pour into a glass, sprinkle the nutmeg on top, and serve.

**Yield:** 1 serving

**Nutritional Analysis:** Each will have: 94 calories; trace fat; 9 g protein; 13 g carbohydrates; 0 g fiber; 13 g usable carbs.

| | | | | | |
|---|---|---|---|---|---|
| Potassium (mg): | 501 mg | Vitamin C (mg): | 2 mg | Thiamin/B1 (mg): | 0.1 mg |
| Calcium (mg): | 307 mg | Vitamin A (i.u.): | 500 i.u. | Riboflavin/B2 (mg): | 0.3 mg |
| Iron (mg): | trace | Vitamin B6 (mg): | 0.1 mg | Folacin (mcg): | 13 mcg |
| Zinc (mg): | 1 mg | Vitamin B12 (mcg): | 0.9 mcg | Niacin/B3 (mg): | 1 mg |

chapter sixteen

# Condiments, Sauces, and Seasonings

We all know about keeping an eye on the big stuff, but have you ever read the labels on condiments? Two tablespoons (30 g) of standard ketchup has 31 calories and 8 grams of carbohydrate—and many people don't stop at 2 tablespoons. Barbecue sauces, glazes, and the like often have far more sugar than that. You'd never pour pancake syrup over your meat, but nutritionally speaking, it's not far-off.

Other sauces, such as the newly popular flavored mayonnaises, tend to be high in calories even when they're not full of sugar.

With that in mind, here is a selection of recipes for sauces, condiments, glazes, and such that will keep your meals savory and varied without undermining your good intentions!

## Dana's No-Sugar Ketchup

This is the recipe I have repeated more than any other; it's appeared in every cookbook I've written. Why? Because ketchup isn't just a condiment, it's used as an ingredient in myriad other recipes. If you can get no-sugar-added ketchup in your grocery store (Heinz One Carb Ketchup is quite good), go ahead and use it. If you can't, this is very simple to make and tastes, well, like ketchup. The one difference here from previous books is that I've worked out the quantity of stevia/FOS to use in place of Splenda, if you prefer not to use artificial sweeteners.

6 ounces (170 g) tomato paste
2/3 cup (160 ml) cider vinegar
1/2 cup (120 ml) water
2 teaspoons (5 g) stevia/FOS or 1/3 cup (8 g) Splenda
2 tablespoons (20 g) minced onion
2 cloves garlic
1 teaspoon salt
1/8 teaspoon ground allspice
1/8 teaspoon ground cloves
1/8 teaspoon pepper

Just combine everything in your blender, and run it until the onion and garlic disappear. Store it in a snap-top container in the fridge, and use it the way you would any ketchup.

**Yield:** 1 2/3 cups (400 g), or 14 servings

**Nutritional Analysis:** Each will have: 13 calories; trace fat; trace protein; 3 g carbohydrates; 1 g fiber; 3 g usable carbs.

| | | | | | |
|---|---|---|---|---|---|
| Potassium (mg): | 130 mg | Vitamin C (mg): | 5 mg | Thiamin/B1 (mg): | trace |
| Calcium (mg): | 7 mg | Vitamin A (i.u.): | 297 i.u. | Riboflavin/B2 (mg): | trace |
| Iron (mg): | trace | Vitamin B6 (mg): | 0.1 mg | Folacin (mcg): | 3 mcg |
| Zinc (mg): | trace | Vitamin B12 (mcg): | 0 mcg | Niacin/B3 (mg): | trace |

## Chili Cocktail Sauce

Easy.

1 tablespoon (15 g) no-sugar-added ketchup

1/4 teaspoon chili garlic paste

1/2 teaspoon lemon juice

1/2 teaspoon horseradish

Just mix everything together. Use as a dip for shrimp, or with any seafood.

**Yield:** 1 serving

**Nutritional Analysis:** Each will have: 7 calories; trace fat; trace protein; 2 g carbohydrates; trace fiber; 2 g usable carbs.

| | | | | | |
|---|---|---|---|---|---|
| Potassium (mg): | 12 mg | Vitamin C (mg): | 2 mg | Thiamin/B1 (mg): | trace |
| Calcium (mg): | 2 mg | Vitamin A (i.u.): | 261 i.u. | Riboflavin/B2 (mg): | trace |
| Iron (mg): | trace | Vitamin B6 (mg): | trace | Folacin (mcg): | trace |
| Zinc (mg): | trace | Vitamin B12 (mcg): | 0 mcg | Niacin/B3 (mg): | trace |

## Kansas City Barbecue Sauce Redux

This is a reworking of a sauce from The Low-Carb Barbecue Book, and it's what most of us think of when we think of barbecue sauce: tomatoey, spicy, and sweet. Unbelievably close to a top-flight commercial barbecue sauce—and my Kansas City–raised husband agrees!

1 tablespoon (14 g) butter

1 clove garlic, peeled and minced

1/4 cup (40 g) chopped onion

1 tablespoon (14 ml) lemon juice

1 cup (240 g) no-sugar-added ketchup

1/3 cup (8 g) Splenda

1 tablespoon (14 ml) blackstrap molasses

2 tablespoons (28 ml) Worcestershire sauce

1 tablespoon (9 g) chili powder

1 tablespoon (14 ml) white vinegar

1 teaspoon pepper

1/4 teaspoon salt

Just combine everything in a saucepan over low heat. Heat until the butter melts, stir the whole thing up, and let it simmer for 5 minutes or so. That's it!

**Yield:** About 1 3/4 cups (440 g), or 14 servings

**Nutritional Analysis:** Each will have: 24 calories; 1 g fat; trace protein; 4 g carbohydrates; trace fiber; 4 g usable carbs.

| | | | | | |
|---|---|---|---|---|---|
| Potassium (mg): | 74 mg | Vitamin C (mg): | 5 mg | Thiamin/B1 (mg): | trace |
| Calcium (mg): | 19 mg | Vitamin A (i.u.): | 519 i.u. | Riboflavin/B2 (mg): | trace |
| Iron (mg): | 1 mg | Vitamin B6 (mg): | trace | Folacin (mcg): | 1 mcg |
| Zinc (mg): | trace | Vitamin B12 (mcg): | trace | Niacin/B3 (mg): | trace |

**Note:** If you like a smoky note in your barbecue sauce, add 1 teaspoon (5 ml) of liquid smoke flavoring to this.

## Classic Rub

Sprinkle on pork or chicken before slow smoking, for a true barbecue flavor. Good as a sprinkle-on seasoning at the table, too.

1/4 cup (6 g) Splenda

1 tablespoon (18 g) seasoned salt

1 tablespoon (9 g) garlic powder

1 tablespoon (18 g) celery salt

1 tablespoon (9 g) onion powder

2 tablespoons (7 g) paprika

1 tablespoon (9 g) chili powder

2 teaspoons (4 g) pepper

1 teaspoon lemon pepper

1 teaspoon sage

1 teaspoon mustard

1/2 teaspoon thyme

1/2 teaspoon cayenne pepper

Just stir everything together. It's nice to store this in a shaker-top jar with a lid, such as one from a purchased seasoning blend that you've used up.

**Yield:** 13 servings

**Nutritional Analysis:** Each will have: 15 calories; trace fat; 1 g protein; 3 g carbohydrates; 1 g fiber; 2 g usable carbs.

| | | | | | |
|---|---|---|---|---|---|
| Potassium (mg): | 55 mg | Vitamin C (mg): | 1 mg | Thiamin/B1 (mg): | trace |
| Calcium (mg): | 10 mg | Vitamin A (i.u.): | 879 i.u. | Riboflavin/B2 (mg): | trace |
| Iron (mg): | 1 mg | Vitamin B6 (mg): | 0.1 mg | Folacin (mcg): | 3 mcg |
| Zinc (mg): | trace | Vitamin B12 (mcg): | 0 mcg | Niacin/B3 (mg): | trace |

# Apricot-Chipotle Mopping Sauce

Great for basting poultry or pork during slow smoking, grilling, or just roasting.

1/3 cup (80 g) chicken broth

1/4 cup (80 g) low-sugar apricot preserves

1 tablespoon (14 ml) lime juice

1 clove garlic, peeled and crushed

1 chipotle chile canned in adobo

1 tablespoon (10 g) onion

2 teaspoons (10 ml) olive oil

Just throw everything in your blender, and run it until the chipotle is pureed.

**Nutritional Analysis:** Per batch: 193 calories; 10 g fat; 3 g protein; 25 g carbohydrates; 1 g fiber; 24 g usable carbs.

| | | | | | |
|---|---|---|---|---|---|
| Potassium (mg): | 113 mg | Vitamin C (mg): | 6 mg | Thiamin/B1 (mg): | trace |
| Calcium (mg): | 12 mg | Vitamin A (i.u.): | 2 i.u. | Riboflavin/B2 (mg): | trace |
| Iron (mg): | trace | Vitamin B6 (mg): | 0.1 mg | Folacin (mcg): | 5 mcg |
| Zinc (mg): | trace | Vitamin B12 (mcg): | 0.1 mcg | Niacin/B3 (mg): | 1 mg |

## Balsamic Mustard Basting Sauce

Glorious!

- 1/3 cup (80 ml) apple cider vinegar
- 1/3 cup (8 g) Splenda
- 2 tablespoons (28 ml) balsamic vinegar
- 1 tablespoon (14 ml) lemon juice
- 1/4 cup (60 g) brown mustard
- 1/4 cup (80 g) tomato sauce
- 1/2 teaspoon salt or Vege-Sal
- 1 clove garlic, peeled and minced
- 1/4 teaspoon pepper

Just whisk everything together in a nonreactive bowl. Use to baste chicken or pork.

**Yield:** 6 servings

**Nutritional Analysis:** Each will have: 22 calories; 1 g fat; 1 g protein; 4 g carbohydrates; trace fiber; 4 g usable carbs.

| | | | | | |
|---|---|---|---|---|---|
| Potassium (mg): | 77 mg | Vitamin C (mg): | 2 mg | Thiamin/B1 (mg): | trace |
| Calcium (mg): | 18 mg | Vitamin A (i.u.): | 101 i.u. | Riboflavin/B2 (mg): | trace |
| Iron (mg): | trace | Vitamin B6 (mg): | trace | Folacin (mcg): | 2 mcg |
| Zinc (mg): | trace | Vitamin B12 (mcg): | 0 mcg | Niacin/B3 (mg): | trace |

## Maple-Chipotle Glaze

This is good for basting chicken or pork, but even better for basting salmon steaks!

- 1/4 cup (60 ml) sugar-free pancake syrup
- 1 chipotle chile canned in adobo
- 1 clove garlic, peeled and crushed

Put everything in your food processor, and run it till the chipotle is finely minced.

**Yield:** 5 servings

**Nutritional Analysis:** Each will have: 1 calorie; trace fat; trace protein; trace carbohydrate; trace fiber; no usable carbs. (Analysis does not include polyols in the pancake syrup.)

| | | | | | |
|---|---|---|---|---|---|
| Potassium (mg): | 2 mg | Vitamin C (mg): | trace | Thiamin/B1 (mg): | 0 mg |
| Calcium (mg): | 1 mg | Vitamin A (i.u.): | 0 i.u. | Riboflavin/B2 (mg): | 0 mg |
| Iron (mg): | trace | Vitamin B6 (mg): | trace | Folacin (mcg): | trace |
| Zinc (mg): | trace | Vitamin B12 (mcg): | 0 mcg | Niacin/B3 (mg): | trace |

## Sweet-and-Sour Orange Glaze

Would this be cooler if we called it "Sauce Bigerade"?

- 6 tablespoons (120 g) low-sugar orange marmalade preserves
- 2 tablespoons (28 ml) soy sauce
- 1 tablespoon (14 ml) rice vinegar
- 1 1/2 teaspoons chili garlic paste
- 1 tablespoon (3 g) Splenda

Just mix everything together. Great for basting pork, chicken, salmon, or tuna.

**Yield:** 6 servings

**Nutritional Analysis:** Each will have: 27 calories; trace fat; trace protein; 6 g carbohydrates; trace fiber; 6 g usable carbs.

| | | | | | |
|---|---|---|---|---|---|
| Potassium (mg): | 13 mg | Vitamin C (mg): | 0 mg | Thiamin/B1 (mg): | trace |
| Calcium (mg): | 1 mg | Vitamin A (i.u.): | 0 i.u. | Riboflavin/B2 (mg): | trace |
| Iron (mg): | trace | Vitamin B6 (mg): | trace | Folacin (mcg): | 1 mcg |
| Zinc (mg): | trace | Vitamin B12 (mcg): | 0 mcg | Niacin/B3 (mg): | trace |

## "Honey" Mustard Dipping Sauce

You know what that "honey" on the label means, right? The stuff is sugary. Not this one, and it's great.

- 2 tablespoons (30 g) Country-style Dijon mustard (the grainy kind)
- 2 tablespoons (3 g) Splenda
- 1 tablespoon (14 ml) water
- 1 tablespoon (10 g) minced onion
- 1/2 clove garlic, peeled and finely minced
- 1/4 teaspoon dried thyme
- 1/8 teaspoon salt or Vege-Sal
- 1/8 teaspoon pepper

Just mix everything together! This is a terrific dip for cold shrimp or hot chicken wings.

**Yield:** 1 serving

**Nutritional Analysis:** Each will have: 42 calories; 1 g fat; 2 g protein; 7 g carbohydrates; 1 g fiber; 6 g usable carbs.

| | | | | | |
|---|---|---|---|---|---|
| Potassium (mg): | 67 mg | Vitamin C (mg): | 1 mg | Thiamin/B1 (mg): | trace |
| Calcium (mg): | 40 mg | Vitamin A (i.u.): | 14 i.u. | Riboflavin/B2 (mg): | trace |
| Iron (mg): | 1 mg | Vitamin B6 (mg): | 0.1 mg | Folacin (mcg): | 5 mcg |
| Zinc (mg): | trace | Vitamin B12 (mcg): | 0 mcg | Niacin/B3 (mg): | trace |

**Note:** Leave out the water, and this makes a good spread for wraps, too.

## Blackberry Jam

This is remarkably good and should take you no more than 20 minutes, start to finish.

- 1 3/4 teaspoons gelatin powder
- 1 1/2 tablespoons (21 ml) water
- 1 pound (455 g) frozen blackberries, unsweetened, thawed
- 2/3 cup (16 g) Splenda
- 1/2 teaspoon lemon juice

Put the gelatin in the water to soften.

While that sits, put the blackberries and Splenda in a nonreactive saucepan over medium heat. Stir in the gelatin. Heat, stirring often, until the berries soften and break down. Stir in the lemon juice, pour into a clean pint jar, cap, and chill. Use like you'd use any jam.

**Yield:** 2 cups (640 g), or 32 servings

**Nutritional Analysis:** Each will have: 9 calories; 0 g fat; trace protein; 2 g carbohydrates; trace fiber; 2 g usable carbs.

| | | | | | |
|---|---|---|---|---|---|
| Potassium (mg): | trace | Vitamin C (mg): | trace | Thiamin/B1 (mg): | trace |
| Calcium (mg): | 4 mg | Vitamin A (i.u.): | 10 i.u. | Riboflavin/B2 (mg): | trace |
| Iron (mg): | trace | Vitamin B6 (mg): | trace | Folacin (mcg): | trace |
| Zinc (mg): | trace | Vitamin B12 (mcg): | 0 mcg | Niacin/B3 (mg): | trace |

## Every Calorie Counts Mayonnaise

I'm of two minds about this mayonnaise. It's nutritionally excellent; it has far better quality oil in it than commercial light mayonnaise, as well as more vitamins, minerals, and protein. It tastes good, too. I think it's just as good as commercial light mayonnaise as a spread. But in dishes like UnPotato salads, chicken salads, or that sort of thing, it lacks the very creamy texture of the stuff you can get in a jar. So I offer it for those of you who want to avoid all cheap oils and want everything to be as nutritionally beneficial as it can possibly be—and you may substitute it in any recipe calling for "light mayonnaise" with little change in carb or calorie count.

1 egg

2 tablespoons (28 ml) vinegar

2 tablespoons (28 ml) lemon juice

1 teaspoon dry mustard

1 teaspoon salt

3/4 cup (355 ml) peanut or macadamia oil

Fromage Blanc (see page 494)

Guar or xanthan gum (optional)

Put the egg, vinegar, lemon juice, mustard, and salt in your blender. Measure the oil and have it standing by in a glass measuring cup with a pouring lip. Turn on the blender, and slowly pour in the oil; the stream should be no bigger than the diameter of a pencil lead. The mayonnaise will start to thicken and turn white, but won't get quite as thick as "regular" mayonnaise.

When all the oil is in, add the Fromage Blanc and continue to blend, scraping down the sides of the blender, until everything is well combined. If the mayo is still a little thin, add a touch of guar or xanthan, starting with just 1/4 teaspoon.

Store in a snap-top container in the fridge, and use like regular mayonnaise.

**Yield:** 3 cups (675 g), or 48 servings

**Nutritional Analysis:** Each will have: 45 calories; 4 g fat; 1 g protein; 1 g carbohydrates; trace fiber; 1 g usable carbs.

| | | | | | |
|---|---|---|---|---|---|
| Potassium (mg): | 17 mg | Vitamin C (mg): | trace | Thiamin/B1 (mg): | trace |
| Calcium (mg): | 27 mg | Vitamin A (i.u.): | 44 i.u. | Riboflavin/B2 (mg): | trace |
| Iron (mg): | trace | Vitamin B6 (mg): | trace | Folacin (mcg): | 2 mcg |
| Zinc (mg): | trace | Vitamin B12 (mcg): | trace | Niacin/B3 (mg): | trace |

## Chipotle Mayonnaise

Good for dipping chicken or shrimp, or as a spread for wrap sandwiches.

1 cup (225 g) light mayonnaise

1 chipotle chile canned in adobo

1/2 teaspoon ground cumin

1 clove garlic, peeled and minced

Just throw everything in your food processor with the S-blade in place, and process till the chipotle and garlic are pulverized.

**Yield:** 1 cup (225 g), or 16 servings

**Nutritional Analysis:** Each will have: 35 calories; 3 g fat; trace protein; 3 g carbohydrates; trace fiber; 3 g usable carbs.

| | | | | | |
|---|---|---|---|---|---|
| Potassium (mg): | 3 mg | Vitamin C (mg): | trace | Thiamin/B1 (mg): | trace |
| Calcium (mg): | 1 mg | Vitamin A (i.u.): | 1 i.u. | Riboflavin/B2 (mg): | trace |
| Iron (mg): | trace | Vitamin B6 (mg): | trace | Folacin (mcg): | trace |
| Zinc (mg): | trace | Vitamin B12 (mcg): | 0 mcg | Niacin/B3 (mg): | trace |

## Mustard-Caper Sauce

Great with salmon or as a dip for cooked, chilled shrimp.

2 tablespoons (30 g) plain yogurt

1 tablespoon (14 g) light mayonnaise

1 tablespoon (15 g) country-style Dijon mustard (the grainy kind)

1 teaspoon (9 g) capers, drained and chopped

Just mix it all up!

**Yield:** 3/4 cup (170 g), or 2 servings

**Nutritional Analysis:** Each will have: 65 calories; 5 g fat; 2 g protein; 5 g carbohydrates; trace fiber; 5 g usable carbs.

| | | | | | |
|---|---|---|---|---|---|
| Potassium (mg): | 69 mg | Vitamin C (mg): | trace | Thiamin/B1 (mg): | trace |
| Calcium (mg): | 50 mg | Vitamin A (i.u.): | 38 i.u. | Riboflavin/B2 (mg): | trace |
| Iron (mg): | trace | Vitamin B6 (mg): | trace | Folacin (mcg): | 3 mcg |
| Zinc (mg): | trace | Vitamin B12 (mcg): | 0.1 mcg | Niacin/B3 (mg): | trace |

## Quick and Easy Blue Cheese Dip

For all your blue cheese dip needs! Great with cut-up vegetables, or as a dip for hot wings or Buffalo Shrimp (see page 328).

1/4 cup (55 g) light mayonnaise

6 tablespoons (90 g) plain yogurt

1/4 cup (30 g) crumbled blue cheese

1/4 teaspoon Worcestershire sauce

1 clove garlic, peeled and crushed

Just stir everything together!

**Yield:** 7 fluid ounces (200 ml), or 3 servings

**Nutritional Analysis:** Each will have: 107 calories; 8 g fat; 4 g protein; 5 g carbohydrates; trace fiber; 5 g usable carbs.

| | | | | | |
|---|---|---|---|---|---|
| Potassium (mg): | 86 mg | Vitamin C (mg): | 1 mg | Thiamin/B1 (mg): | trace |
| Calcium (mg): | 99 mg | Vitamin A (i.u.): | 119 i.u. | Riboflavin/B2 (mg): | 0.1 mg |
| Iron (mg): | trace | Vitamin B6 (mg): | trace | Folacin (mcg): | 6 mcg |
| Zinc (mg): | 1 mg | Vitamin B12 (mcg): | 0.3 mcg | Niacin/B3 (mg): | trace |

## Red Pepper Mayonnaise

This is easy, and it improves all sorts of things—especially roast beef wraps.

12 ounces (340 g) roasted red peppers, jarred in water

1/2 cup (110 g) light mayonnaise

Easy! Drain the peppers and pat them dry with a paper towel. Put them in your food processor with the S-blade in place. Add the mayonnaise and run the processor, scraping down the sides as needed, until the mixture is very smooth. You're done!

**Yield:** 1 cup (225 g), or 16 servings

**Nutritional Analysis:** Each will have: 23 calories; 1 g fat; trace protein; 3 g carbohydrates; trace fiber; 3 g usable carbs.

| | | | | | |
|---|---|---|---|---|---|
| Potassium (mg): | 38 mg | Vitamin C (mg): | 40 mg | Thiamin/B1 (mg): | trace |
| Calcium (mg): | 2 mg | Vitamin A (i.u.): | 1212 i.u. | Riboflavin/B2 (mg): | trace |
| Iron (mg): | trace | Vitamin B6 (mg): | 0.1 mg | Folacin (mcg): | 5 mcg |
| Zinc (mg): | trace | Vitamin B12 (mcg): | 0 mcg | Niacin/B3 (mg): | trace |

## Roasted Garlic-Lemon Mayonnaise

This is good with artichokes, asparagus, fish, or chicken.

8 cloves garlic, unpeeled

1 lemon

1/3 cup (75 g) light mayonnaise

Preheat the oven to 400°F (200°C, or gas mark 6).

Put the unpeeled garlic cloves on a shallow baking tin, and roast 'em for 30 to 40 minutes, or until they're good and soft. Take 'em out, put 'em on a plate or cutting board, and use the back of a fork to press out the pulp. Put that pulp in a bowl, and use the fork to mash it up as fine as you can.

Grate the zest of the lemon into the bowl, then whack the lemon in half. Flick the pits out with the tip of a knife, then squeeze the juice into the garlic pulp. (Fish out any stray seeds!)

Add the mayonnaise, and mix until everything is very well combined.

**Yield:** 4 servings

**Nutritional Analysis:** Each will have: 58 calories; 4 g fat; 1 g protein; 7 g carbohydrates; trace fiber; 7 g usable carbs.

| | | | | | |
|---|---|---|---|---|---|
| Potassium (mg): | 47 mg | Vitamin C (mg): | 10 mg | Thiamin/B1 (mg): | trace |
| Calcium (mg): | 15 mg | Vitamin A (i.u.): | 4 i.u. | Riboflavin/B2 (mg): | trace |
| Iron (mg): | trace | Vitamin B6 (mg): | 0.1 mg | Folacin (mcg): | 2 mcg |
| Zinc (mg): | trace | Vitamin B12 (mcg): | 0 mcg | Niacin/B3 (mg): | trace |

## Sun-Dried Tomato and Basil Mayonnaise

Intense sun-dried tomato flavor.

2 packed tablespoons (7 g) chopped sun-dried tomatoes

2 packed tablespoons (8 g) chopped fresh basil

1 clove garlic, peeled and minced

1/2 cup (110 g) light mayonnaise

1 tablespoon (14 ml) lemon juice

1 teaspoon (5 ml) water

Put everything in your food processor with the S-blade in place. Run the processor, stopping it every now and then to scrape down the sides and get things back into the path of the blade. You want the basil and tomatoes pretty finely chopped, and you want the mayonnaise to have taken on a slightly pinky-brown color.

**Yield:** 3/4 cup (170 g), or 12 servings

**Nutritional Analysis:** Each will have: 25 calories; 2 g fat; trace protein; 2 g carbohydrates; trace fiber; 2 g usable carbs.

| | | | | | |
|---|---|---|---|---|---|
| Potassium (mg): | 25 mg | Vitamin C (mg): | 1 mg | Thiamin/B1 (mg): | trace |
| Calcium (mg): | 2 mg | Vitamin A (i.u.): | 22 i.u. | Riboflavin/B2 (mg): | trace |
| Iron (mg): | trace | Vitamin B6 (mg): | trace | Folacin (mcg): | 1 mcg |
| Zinc (mg): | trace | Vitamin B12 (mcg): | 0 mcg | Niacin/B3 (mg): | trace |

## Wasabi Mayonnaise

Oh, my gosh, is this fabulous! Fabulous, fabulous, fabulous. On asparagus. On shrimp. On artichokes. On fingers. Just fabulous.

- 1/2 cup (110 g) light mayonnaise
- 2 teaspoons (10 ml) soy sauce
- 1/2 teaspoon Splenda
- 1 teaspoon (5 ml) lemon juice
- 1 teaspoon (3 g) wasabi paste

Just combine everything in a bowl, and whisk together well. Unbelievably good.

**Yield:** 1/2 cup (110 g), or 8 servings

**Nutritional Analysis:** Each will have: 36 calories; 3 g fat; trace protein; 3 g carbohydrates; trace fiber; 3 g usable carbs.

| | | | | | |
|---|---|---|---|---|---|
| Potassium (mg): | 5 mg | Vitamin C (mg): | trace | Thiamin/B1 (mg): | trace |
| Calcium (mg): | trace | Vitamin A (i.u.): | trace | Riboflavin/B2 (mg): | trace |
| Iron (mg): | trace | Vitamin B6 (mg): | trace | Folacin (mcg): | trace |
| Zinc (mg): | trace | Vitamin B12 (mcg): | 0 mcg | Niacin/B3 (mg): | trace |

## Lemon-Basil Mayonnaise

Good on fish, chicken, vegetables, tuna salad—all sorts of things.

- 1/2 cup (110 g) light mayonnaise
- 2 tablespoons (28 ml) lemon juice
- 2 tablespoons (8 g) minced fresh basil
- 1 clove garlic, peeled and finely minced

Simply stir everything together. Heck, make a double batch!

**Yield:** 2/3 cup (150 g), or 8 servings

**Nutritional Analysis:** Each will have: 36 calories; 3 g fat; trace protein; 3 g carbohydrates; trace fiber; 3 g usable carbs.

| | | | | | |
|---|---|---|---|---|---|
| Potassium (mg): | 11 mg | Vitamin C (mg): | 2 mg | Thiamin/B1 (mg): | trace |
| Calcium (mg): | 2 mg | Vitamin A (i.u.): | 26 i.u. | Riboflavin/B2 (mg): | trace |
| Iron (mg): | trace | Vitamin B6 (mg): | trace | Folacin (mcg): | 1 mcg |
| Zinc (mg): | trace | Vitamin B12 (mcg): | 0 mcg | Niacin/B3 (mg): | trace |

## Seriously Inauthentic Reduced-Calorie Shortcut Aioli

Aioli is just very garlicky mayonnaise, and it's good with lots of things. This version is inauthentic, but really good—not to mention easy.

1 cup (225 g) light mayonnaise

4 cloves garlic, peeled

2 teaspoons (10 ml) lemon juice

This couldn't be easier: Just put everything in your food processor with the S-blade in place, and run it until the garlic is pulverized. Serve with asparagus, artichokes, fish—just about anything!

**Yield:** 1 cup (225 g), or 16 servings

**Nutritional Analysis:** Each will have: 36 calories; 3 g fat; trace protein; 3 g carbohydrates; trace fiber; 3 g usable carbs.

| | | | | | |
|---|---|---|---|---|---|
| Potassium (mg): | 5 mg | Vitamin C (mg): | 1 mg | Thiamin/B1 (mg): | trace |
| Calcium (mg): | 1 mg | Vitamin A (i.u.): | trace | Riboflavin/B2 (mg): | trace |
| Iron (mg): | trace | Vitamin B6 (mg): | trace | Folacin (mcg): | trace |
| Zinc (mg): | trace | Vitamin B12 (mcg): | 0 mcg | Niacin/B3 (mg): | trace |

## Tzatziki

You know that great sauce that comes with gyros? This is it.

1 pound (455 g) plain yogurt

2 large cucumbers

4 cloves garlic, peeled and crushed

2 tablespoons (28 ml) extra virgin olive oil

2 tablespoons (28 ml) red wine vinegar

Salt and pepper

Line a colander with a clean coffee filter, and set them both in a bowl. Dump the yogurt into the filter. Let it sit for several hours to drain; overnight isn't too long. (Though you might want to refrigerate it if you'll be draining it for more than a few hours.)

When the yogurt has drained for at least an hour or two, run the cukes through the shredding blade of your food processor, or grate them. (If necessary, you can get the pieces even smaller by running them through the processor a second time, but with the S-blade in place.) Sprinkle them with a little salt, and leave them in a bowl for at least an hour.

When the time's up, pour off the water that has gathered in the bowl. Use clean hands to squeeze out all the moisture that you can.

Stir together the yogurt, cucumbers, garlic, oil, and vinegar. Add salt and pepper to taste. Chill for at least an hour before serving. This is great with grilled lamb or a gyros salad. If you can afford the carbs, you can serve it as a dip with whole wheat pita.

**Yield:** 8 servings

**Nutritional Analysis:** Each will have: 77 calories; 5 g fat; 3 g protein; 4 g carbohydrates; 1 g fiber; 3 g usable carbs.

| | | | | | |
|---|---|---|---|---|---|
| Potassium (mg): | 206 mg | Vitamin C (mg): | 5 mg | Thiamin/B1 (mg): | trace |
| Calcium (mg): | 82 mg | Vitamin A (i.u.): | 232 i.u. | Riboflavin/B2 (mg): | 0.1 mg |
| Iron (mg): | trace | Vitamin B6 (mg): | 0.1 mg | Folacin (mcg): | 14 mcg |
| Zinc (mg): | 1 mg | Vitamin B12 (mcg): | 0.2 mcg | Niacin/B3 (mg): | trace |

**Note:** If you have the time, shred the cukes and drain both the cukes and yogurt overnight.

## Hollandaise for Sissies Redux

This is as easy and low-carb as the version in 500 Low-Carb Recipes, and it's lower in calories, too. This mock-hollandaise won't win any prizes for authenticity, but it's super with asparagus, artichokes, vegetables, omelets, "Antoine Wept" Eggs Sardou (see page 101)—anywhere you might use hollandaise, really.

4 egg yolks

1 cup (230 g) light sour cream

1 tablespoon (14 ml) lemon juice

3/4 teaspoon dry mustard

1/2 teaspoon salt or Vege-Sal

1 dash Tabasco sauce

1/4 teaspoon paprika

1/2 tablespoon (7 ml) white wine vinegar

**Important:** This needs very gentle heat, so use a double-boiler or a heat diffuser. If you're using a double boiler, you want the water in the bottom to be hot, but not boiling. If you're using a heat diffuser, use the lowest possible heat under it.

Put all of the ingredients in a heavy-bottomed saucepan or the top of your double boiler. Whisk everything together, heat through, and serve it over whatever you like.

**Yield:** 8 servings

**Nutritional Analysis:** Each will have: 41 calories; 3 g fat; 2 g protein; 2 g carbohydrates; trace fiber; 2 g usable carbs.

| | | | | | |
|---|---|---|---|---|---|
| Potassium (mg): | 14 mg | Vitamin C (mg): | 1 mg | Thiamin/B1 (mg): | trace |
| Calcium (mg): | 24 mg | Vitamin A (i.u.): | 206 i.u. | Riboflavin/B2 (mg): | 0.1 mg |
| Iron (mg): | trace | Vitamin B6 (mg): | trace | Folacin (mcg): | 12 mcg |
| Zinc (mg): | trace | Vitamin B12 (mcg): | 0.3 mcg | Niacin/B3 (mg): | trace |

## Creole Sauce

I first made this for the Creole Eggs on page 95 and was stunned to discover how good this simple sauce was. I've made it many times since and have found it good for poaching shrimp, simmering chicken—you name it.

2 teaspoons (10 ml) olive oil

1 clove garlic, peeled and minced

1 teaspoon dried basil

8 ounces (225 g) tomato sauce

1 teaspoon Creole seasoning

1/4 teaspoon black pepper

Hot sauce (Louisiana Hot Sauce is best)

Give a medium-size, heavy skillet a squirt of nonstick cooking spray, and put it over medium-low heat. Add the oil and garlic and sauté, not letting the garlic brown, for just a couple of minutes. Add the basil, tomato sauce, Creole seasoning, pepper, and hot sauce to taste. Stir it all up, and let it come to a simmer. Let it cook for a couple of minutes to blend the flavors.

**Yield:** 2 servings

**Nutritional Analysis:** Each will have: 83 calories; 5 g fat; 2 g protein; 10 g carbohydrates; 2 g fiber; 8 g usable carbs.

| | | | | | |
|---|---|---|---|---|---|
| Potassium (mg): | 456 mg | Vitamin C (mg): | 8 mg | Thiamin/B1 (mg): | 0.1 mg |
| Calcium (mg): | 36 mg | Vitamin A (i.u.): | 1181 i.u. | Riboflavin/B2 (mg): | 0.1 mg |
| Iron (mg): | 1 mg | Vitamin B6 (mg): | 0.2 mg | Folacin (mcg): | 13 mcg |
| Zinc (mg): | trace | Vitamin B12 (mcg): | 0 mcg | Niacin/B3 (mg): | 1 mg |

## Fromage Blanc

This is a simple, soft, white cheese that lends itself to flavoring with herbs, garlic, or even fruit. Should you use cottage cheese, be careful about what brand you use; some are far saltier than others, and excessive saltiness doesn't work here.

15 ounces (420 g) skim milk ricotta or cottage cheese

1/4 cup (60 g) plain nonfat yogurt

1 pinch salt

Simply put everything in your food processor with the S-blade in place, and process for 3 to 5 minutes, until it's silky smooth. Put in a snap-top container and refrigerate for at least 12 hours before using.

**Yield:** 2 cups (300 g)

**Nutritional Analysis:** Per batch: 619 calories; 34 g fat; 52 g protein; 23 g carbohydrates; 0 g fiber; 23 g usable carbs.

| | | | | | |
|---|---|---|---|---|---|
| Potassium (mg): | 676 mg | Vitamin C (mg): | trace | Thiamin/B1 (mg): | 0.1 mg |
| Calcium (mg): | 1271 mg | Vitamin A (i.u.): | 1841 i.u. | Riboflavin/B2 (mg): | 0.9 mg |
| Iron (mg): | 2 mg | Vitamin B6 (mg): | 0.1 mg | Folacin (mcg): | 63 mcg |
| Zinc (mg): | 6 mg | Vitamin B12 (mcg): | 1.6 mcg | Niacin/B3 (mg): | trace |

## Grande Mere Mignonnette Sauce

This easy relishlike sauce is a fabulous accompaniment to meat, fish, poultry, or just about anything.

1 Granny Smith apple

1 cup (235 ml) lime juice

3 cloves garlic, peeled and crushed

3 tablespoons (4.5 g) Splenda

3 tablespoons (28 g) diced fresh tomato

3 anchovy fillets

1½ teaspoons red pepper flakes

Whack the apple in half, and remove the core and stem. Cut the apple into eighths, and throw it in your food processor with the S-blade in place. Add everything else, then pulse till the apple's chopped medium fine. That's it!

**Yield:** Makes 2½ cups (615 g), or 12 servings

**Nutritional Analysis:** Each will have: 15 calories; trace fat; trace protein; 4 g carbohydrates; trace fiber; 4 g usable carbs.

| | | | | | |
|---|---|---|---|---|---|
| Potassium (mg): | 51 mg | Vitamin C (mg): | 8 mg | Thiamin/B1 (mg): | trace |
| Calcium (mg): | 6 mg | Vitamin A (i.u.): | 38 i.u. | Riboflavin/B2 (mg): | trace |
| Iron (mg): | trace | Vitamin B6 (mg): | trace | Folacin (mcg): | 2 mcg |
| Zinc (mg): | trace | Vitamin B12 (mcg): | trace | Niacin/B3 (mg): | trace |

## Quick-and-Easy Pineapple Chutney

Good with anything curried. Remember, though, that pineapple has a high glycemic index for a fruit, and watch your portions.

1 cup (150 g) canned pineapple chunks in juice

2 cloves garlic, peeled and crushed

1 teaspoon dry mustard

1 teaspoon cinnamon

2 tablespoons (28 ml) cider vinegar

1 tablespoon (1.5 g) Splenda

1 tablespoon (8 g) grated gingerroot

Chop the chunks of pineapple a bit finer. Put them and their juice into a small, non-reactive saucepan. Add everything else, and simmer for 10 minutes. That's it! Serve with anything curried—or not curried, for that matter.

**Yield:** 8 servings

**Nutritional Analysis:** Each will have: 23 calories; trace fat; trace protein; 6 g carbohydrates; trace fiber; 6 g usable carbs.

| | | | | | |
|---|---|---|---|---|---|
| Potassium (mg): | 51 mg | Vitamin C (mg): | 3 mg | Thiamin/B1 (mg): | trace |
| Calcium (mg): | 10 mg | Vitamin A (i.u.): | 13 i.u. | Riboflavin/B2 (mg): | trace |
| Iron (mg): | trace | Vitamin B6 (mg): | trace | Folacin (mcg): | 2 mcg |
| Zinc (mg): | trace | Vitamin B12 (mcg): | 0 mcg | Niacin/B3 (mg): | trace |

# East India Sauce

This is good as a dip, as well as a sauce on fish or chicken.

- 1/2 cup (160 g) low-sugar apricot preserves
- 1 tablespoon (14 ml) cider vinegar
- 1 tablespoon (1.5 g) Splenda
- 1/2 teaspoon blackstrap molasses
- 1/2 teaspoon curry powder
- 1 teaspoon grated gingerroot
- 2 teaspoons (10 ml) Worcestershire sauce
- 2/3 cup (155 g) light sour cream

In a small, nonreactive saucepan, combine the preserves, vinegar, Splenda, molasses, curry powder, gingerroot, and Worcestershire sauce. Stir them over low heat until the preserves melt and everything is a nice, homogenous mass (except for any little chunks of apricot in the preserves, which I like to chop up smaller with the edge of my spoon). Scrape this mixture into a bowl, and let it cool.

When it's cool, stir in the sour cream. Serve with chicken or pork satay, cold shrimp, as a sauce over fish, or with anything curried.

**Yield:** 1 1/3 cups (325 g), or 10 servings

**Nutritional Analysis:** Each will have: 27 calories; trace fat; trace protein; 6 g carbohydrates; trace fiber; 6 g usable carbs.

| | | | | | |
|---|---|---|---|---|---|
| Potassium (mg): | 20 mg | Vitamin C (mg): | 2 mg | Thiamin/B1 (mg): | trace |
| Calcium (mg): | 11 mg | Vitamin A (i.u.): | 2 i.u. | Riboflavin/B2 (mg): | trace |
| Iron (mg): | trace | Vitamin B6 (mg): | trace | Folacin (mcg): | trace |
| Zinc (mg): | trace | Vitamin B12 (mcg): | 0 mcg | Niacin/B3 (mg): | trace |

## Pico de Gallo

You know, you can never have too much pico! This easily accompanies 8 yummy fajitas, with some left for chip dippin'. (Low-carb chips, for me!)

1 California avocado

1½ tablespoons (21 ml) lime juice

1 medium tomato

½ cup (80 g) minced red onion

1 medium jalapeño (or more, to taste)

1 tablespoon (4 g) minced cilantro

Salt

Seed and peel the avocado, cut it into chunks, and put it in a mixing bowl. Sprinkle it with the lime juice and toss, to prevent browning. Finely dice the tomato, and add it to the avocado. Throw the onion in, too.

Seed the jalapeño, and cut out as much of the pithy inner ribs as you can. Finely dice it, and add it to the mixing bowl. Now wash your hands with plenty of soap immediately, or you'll be sorry the next time you touch your nose or eyes!

Finally, stir in the minced cilantro, salt the whole thing to taste, and serve.

**Yield:** 8 servings

**Nutritional Analysis:** Each will have: 47 calories; 4 g fat; 1 g protein; 3 g carbohydrates; 1 g fiber; 2 g usable carbs.

| | | | | | |
|---|---|---|---|---|---|
| Potassium (mg): | 195 mg | Vitamin C (mg): | 7 mg | Thiamin/B1 (mg): | trace |
| Calcium (mg): | 6 mg | Vitamin A (i.u.): | 236 i.u. | Riboflavin/B2 (mg): | trace |
| Iron (mg): | trace | Vitamin B6 (mg): | 0.1 mg | Folacin (mcg): | 19 mcg |
| Zinc (mg): | trace | Vitamin B12 (mcg): | 0 mcg | Niacin/B3 (mg): | 1 mg |

## Gorgonzola Sauce

This sauce tastes far richer than it is, and it turns a simple chicken breast into a gourmet meal. It's also good tossed with cooked spaghetti squash or over whole wheat pasta, if you can afford the carbs and calories. Gorgonzola's mild blue cheese flavor is especially good here, but you could use any soft domestic blue cheese, as well.

1 tablespoon (14 g) butter

1 shallot, minced

3/4 cup (175 ml) whole milk or Carb Countdown Dairy Beverage

1 cup (120 g) crumbled Gorgonzola cheese

In a heavy saucepan, melt the butter over medium-high heat and start sautéing the shallot. When it's soft, add the milk and Gorgonzola. Turn the burner down to medium-low and cook, stirring often, until the Gorgonzola is melted.

**Yield:** 4 servings

**Nutritional Analysis:** With milk, each will have: 155 calories; 12 g fat; 8 g protein; 3 g carbohydrates; 1 g fiber; 2 g usable carbs.

| | | | | | |
|---|---|---|---|---|---|
| Potassium (mg): | 79 mg | Vitamin C (mg): | 1 mg | Thiamin/B1 (mg): | trace |
| Calcium (mg): | 56 mg | Vitamin A (i.u.): | 478 i.u. | Riboflavin/B2 (mg): | 0.1 mg |
| Iron (mg): | trace | Vitamin B6 (mg): | trace | Folacin (mcg): | 3 mcg |
| Zinc (mg): | trace | Vitamin B12 (mcg): | 0.2 mcg | Niacin/B3 (mg): | trace |

**Nutritional Analysis:** With Carb Countdown, each will have: 151 calories; 12 g fat; 8 g protein; 2 g carbohydrates; 1 g fiber; 1 g usable carbs.

| | | | | | |
|---|---|---|---|---|---|
| Potassium (mg): | 9 mg | Vitamin C (mg): | trace | Thiamin/B1 (mg): | 0 mg |
| Calcium (mg): | 66 mg | Vitamin A (i.u.): | 476 i.u. | Riboflavin/B2 (mg): | trace |
| Iron (mg): | trace | Vitamin B6 (mg): | trace | Folacin (mcg): | 1 mcg |
| Zinc (mg): | trace | Vitamin B12 (mcg): | trace | Niacin/B3 (mg): | trace |

# Alfredo Sauce

If he didn't know what it would do to his waistline, my husband would live on Fettuccine Alfredo. This sauce cuts the calorie count of the traditional Alfredo quite radically, without adding carbs. Serve it over chicken, stirred into skillet suppers, or tossed with broccoli or spaghetti squash. Or, of course, with whole wheat fettuccine. This is enough for 4 cups of fettuccine or cooked spaghetti squash.

2 teaspoons (10 g) butter

2 cloves garlic, peeled and finely minced

1 1/3 cups (315 ml) skim milk or Carb Countdown Dairy Beverage

1 ounce (28 g) Neufchâtel cheese or light cream cheese

1 cup (100 g) freshly grated Parmesan cheese

Guar or xanthan gum

Melt the butter in a heavy-bottomed saucepan over medium-low heat. Sauté the garlic in the butter for a minute before adding the milk. Let it warm for 7 to 8 minutes, stirring often.

When the milk is hot, add the Neufchâtel, whisking until it's melted.

Now whisk in the Parmesan a little at a time, stirring till it's melted. Use your guar or xanthan shaker to thicken it a little more, if you think it needs it. This will keep for a few days in a snap-top container in the fridge.

**Yield:** 2 cups (520 g), or 6 servings

**Nutritional Analysis:** With milk, each will have: 105 calories; 6 g fat; 8 g protein; 4 g carbohydrates; trace fiber; 4 g usable carbs.

| | | | | | |
|---|---|---|---|---|---|
| Potassium (mg): | 114 mg | Vitamin C (mg): | 1 mg | Thiamin/B1 (mg): | trace |
| Calcium (mg): | 256 mg | Vitamin A (i.u.): | 306 i.u. | Riboflavin/B2 (mg): | 0.1 mg |
| Iron (mg): | trace | Vitamin B6 (mg): | trace | Folacin (mcg): | 5 mcg |
| Zinc (mg): | 1 mg | Vitamin B12 (mcg): | 0.4 mcg | Niacin/B3 (mg): | trace |

**Nutritional Analysis:** With Carb Countdown, each will have: 114 calories; 8 g fat; 9 g protein; 2 g carbohydrates; trace fiber; 2 g usable carbs.

| | | | | | |
|---|---|---|---|---|---|
| Potassium (mg): | 24 mg | Vitamin C (mg): | trace | Thiamin/B1 (mg): | trace |
| Calcium (mg): | 266 mg | Vitamin A (i.u.): | 261 i.u. | Riboflavin/B2 (mg): | trace |
| Iron (mg): | trace | Vitamin B6 (mg): | trace | Folacin (mcg): | 2 mcg |
| Zinc (mg): | trace | Vitamin B12 (mcg): | 0.2 mcg | Niacin/B3 (mg): | trace |

## Lime-Ginger Cream Sauce

You'd think a sauce this creamy would be very high in calories—but it's not!

3 ounces (85 g) Neufchâtel cheese or light cream cheese

1/2 cup (110 g) cottage cheese

1/2 cup (125 g) plain yogurt

1 tablespoon (8 g) grated gingerroot

1 1/2 teaspoons Splenda

Zest of 1/2 lime

Just put everything in your food processor, and run it until the sauce is very smooth.

**Yield:** 4 servings

**Nutritional Analysis:** Each will have: 102 calories; 7 g fat; 7 g protein; 3 g carbohydrates; trace fiber; 3 g usable carbs.

| | | | | | |
|---|---|---|---|---|---|
| Potassium (mg): | 107 mg | Vitamin C (mg): | 2 mg | Thiamin/B1 (mg): | trace |
| Calcium (mg): | 74 mg | Vitamin A (i.u.): | 299 i.u. | Riboflavin/B2 (mg): | 0.1 mg |
| Iron (mg): | trace | Vitamin B6 (mg): | trace | Folacin (mcg): | 9 mcg |
| Zinc (mg): | trace | Vitamin B12 (mcg): | 0.4 mcg | Niacin/B3 (mg): | trace |

## Orange-Sesame Dipping Sauce

Seafood and poultry both benefit from this dipping sauce.

1/4 cup (6 g) Splenda

1/4 cup (60 ml) rice vinegar

2 teaspoons (10 ml) soy sauce

2 teaspoons (10 g) chili garlic paste

1 teaspoon (5 ml) dark sesame oil

1 teaspoon (2 g) orange zest

Just stir everything together! It's great to make this ahead so the flavors can "marry," but it's not essential.

**Yield:** 6 servings

**Nutritional Analysis:** Each will have: 15 calories; 1 g fat; trace protein; 2 g carbohydrates; trace fiber; 2 g usable carbs.

| | | | | | |
|---|---|---|---|---|---|
| Potassium (mg): | 14 mg | Vitamin C (mg): | trace | Thiamin/B1 (mg): | trace |
| Calcium (mg): | 1 mg | Vitamin A (i.u.): | 1 i.u. | Riboflavin/B2 (mg): | trace |
| Iron (mg): | trace | Vitamin B6 (mg): | trace | Folacin (mcg): | trace |
| Zinc (mg): | trace | Vitamin B12 (mcg): | 0 mcg | Niacin/B3 (mg): | trace |

## Hoisin Sauce

Hoisin sauce is a Chinese barbecue sauce, and it's useful in Asian recipes. However, commercial Hoisin, like American barbecue sauce, is quite sugary. The peanut butter is not traditional, but it works very well, here.

- 4 tablespoons (60 ml) soy sauce
- 2 tablespoons (35 g) natural peanut butter
- 2 tablespoons (3 g) Splenda
- 2 teaspoons (10 ml) white vinegar
- 1 clove garlic minced
- 2 teaspoons (10 ml) dark sesame oil
- 1/8 teaspoon five-spice powder

Put all of the ingredients in your blender and run until everything is smooth and well combined. Store in a snap-top container in the refrigerator.

**Yield:** Just under 1/3 cup (75 g), or 6 servings

**Nutritional Analysis:** Each will have: 54 calories; 4 g fat; 2 g protein; 3 g carbohydrates; trace fiber; 3 g usable carbs.

| | | | | | |
|---|---|---|---|---|---|
| Potassium (mg): | 25 mg | Vitamin C (mg): | trace | Thiamin/B1 (mg): | trace |
| Calcium (mg): | 3 mg | Vitamin A (i.u.): | 0 i.u. | Riboflavin/B2 (mg): | trace |
| Iron (mg): | trace | Vitamin B6 (mg): | trace | Folacin (mcg): | 2 mcg |
| Zinc (mg): | trace | Vitamin B12 (mcg): | 0 mcg | Niacin/B3 (mg): | trace |

## Teriyaki Sauce

This recipe has appeared in several of my other cookbooks, but it's so easy and useful that I figured I'd include it here, too.

- 1/2 cup (120 ml) soy sauce
- 1/4 cup (60 ml) dry sherry
- 2 tablespoons (3 g) Splenda
- 1 clove garlic, crushed
- 1 tablespoon (8 g) grated gingerroot

Simply combine everything. Keep it in a snap-top container in the fridge.

**Yield:** 12 servings

**Nutritional Analysis:** Each will have: 14 calories; trace fat; 1 g protein; 1 g carbohydrates; trace fiber; 1 g usable carbs.

| | | | | | |
|---|---|---|---|---|---|
| Potassium (mg): | 27 mg | Vitamin C (mg): | trace | Thiamin/B1 (mg): | trace |
| Calcium (mg): | 3 mg | Vitamin A (i.u.): | 0 i.u. | Riboflavin/B2 (mg): | trace |
| Iron (mg): | trace | Vitamin B6 (mg): | trace | Folacin (mcg): | 2 mcg |
| Zinc (mg): | trace | Vitamin B12 (mcg): | 0 mcg | Niacin/B3 (mg): | trace |

## Garam Masala

This traditional Indian spice blend can be hard to find in regular grocery stores, but it's easy to make your own.

- 2 tablespoons (14 g) ground cumin
- 2 tablespoons (14 g) ground coriander
- 2 tablespoons (14 g) ground cardamom
- 1 1/2 tablespoons (9 g) black pepper
- 4 teaspoons (9 g) ground cinnamon
- 1/2 teaspoon ground cloves
- 1 teaspoon ground nutmeg

Just stir everything together and store in a tightly lidded container.

**Yield:** 9 servings

**Nutritional Analysis:** Each will have: 19 calories; 1 g fat; 1 g protein; 4 g carbohydrates; 1g fiber; 3 grams usable carbs.

| | | | | | |
|---|---|---|---|---|---|
| Potassium (mg): | 73 mg | Vitamin C (mg): | 1 mg | Thiamin/B1 (mg): | 0 mg |
| Calcium (mg): | 214 mg | Vitamin A (i.u.): | 22 i.u. | Riboflavin/B2 (mg): | trace |
| Iron (mg): | 2 mg | Vitamin B6 (mg): | trace | Folacin (mcg): | 1 mcg |
| Zinc (mg): | trace | Vitamin B12 (mcg): | 0 mcg | Niacin/B3 (mg): | trace |

## Peanut Sauce

Oh, man, I love peanut sauce!

1/2 cup (120 ml) chicken broth

1/4 cup (60 ml) soy sauce

3 tablespoons (45 ml) rice vinegar

3 tablespoons (45 ml) dry sherry

1/4 cup (65 g) natural peanut butter, creamy

2 cloves garlic, peeled and crushed

1 1/2 tablespoons (3.25 g) Splenda

1 tablespoon (8 g) grated gingerroot

1 teaspoon (5 ml) dark sesame oil

1/2 teaspoon red pepper flakes

1/4 cup (60 g) soft tofu

Toss it all in the blender and mix it up good. That's it!

**Yield:** 1 1/2 cups (325 g), or 12 servings

**Nutritional Analysis:** Each will have: 50 calories; 3 g fat; 2 g protein; 2 g carbohydrates; trace fiber; 2 g usable carbs.

| | | | | | |
|---|---|---|---|---|---|
| Potassium (mg): | 36 mg | Vitamin C (mg): | trace | Thiamin/B1 (mg): | trace |
| Calcium (mg): | 8 mg | Vitamin A (i.u.): | 9 i.u. | Riboflavin/B2 (mg): | trace |
| Iron (mg): | 1 mg | Vitamin B6 (mg): | trace | Folacin (mcg): | 2 mcg |
| Zinc (mg): | trace | Vitamin B12 (mcg): | trace | Niacin/B3 (mg): | trace |

chapter seventeen

# Desserts

Personally, I feel the best approach to dessert is to generally ignore it. We'd all do well to get over the feeling that dinner isn't over until we've had something sweet and save desserts for special occasions. Still, we're all going to want a dessert now and then, and it is in that spirit of "something special now and then" that this chapter is offered.

Now, for my previous books I've developed recipes primarily with the carbohydrate count in mind. For this book, I've tried to offer sugar-free desserts that also go easy on the calories and offer some serious nutrition. It's a fairly tall order, I can tell you. I've tried to achieve a balance between the three.

We'll start with a harvest of fruit-based desserts. Since fruit contains naturally occurring sugars, these are not the lowest-carbohydrate recipes of all time. But since most fruit has a low glycemic index, these desserts should still be fine for all but the most carb-intolerant—and they're certainly some of the most nutritious of desserts.

## Blueberries with Lime and Mint

3 tablespoons (4.5 g) Splenda

1/4 cup (60 ml) lime juice

1 1/2 pints (600 g) blueberries

1 1/2 teaspoons chopped fresh mint

1 teaspoon lime zest

1/2 cup (120 g) Creamy Dessert Topping (see page 538)

In a large, nonreactive bowl, combine the Splenda and lime juice, and stir to dissolve. Add the blueberries and toss, coating the berries. Add the mint and lime zest, and toss again. Divide the berries among 5 bowls and serve topped with the Creamy Dessert Topping.

**Yield:** 5 servings

**Nutritional Analysis:** Each will have: 90 calories; 3 g fat; 1 g protein; 15 g carbohydrates; 2 g fiber; 13 g usable carbs.

| | | | | | |
|---|---|---|---|---|---|
| Potassium (mg): | 127 mg | Vitamin C (mg): | 16 mg | Thiamin/B1 (mg): | trace |
| Calcium (mg): | 34 mg | Vitamin A (i.u.): | 222 i.u. | Riboflavin/B2 (mg): | 0.1 mg |
| Iron (mg): | trace | Vitamin B6 (mg): | trace | Folacin (mcg): | 9 mcg |
| Zinc (mg): | trace | Vitamin B12 (mcg): | 0.1 mcg | Niacin/B3 (mg): | trace |

## Peach Mousse with Raspberry Coulis

A light and refreshing dessert for a warm summer night. Since this calls for raw egg whites, make very sure your eggs are uncracked and have been properly refrigerated.

1 tablespoon (7 g) unflavored gelatin

2 tablespoons (28 ml) cold water

4 cups (1 kg) frozen peach slices, no sugar added, thawed

1 tablespoon (14 ml) lemon juice

1/3 cup (8 g) Splenda

3 egg whites

1/4 teaspoon cream of tartar

1/2 cup (120 ml) heavy cream, chilled

1 cup (245 g) plain yogurt

1 batch Raspberry Coulis (see page 538)

In a small cup, sprinkle the gelatin on the water, and let it sit for 10 minutes to soften.

Chop the peach slices a bit. Put the peaches, lemon juice, gelatin, and Splenda in a nonreactive saucepan over medium heat. Bring to a simmer and cook, stirring frequently, until the peaches are soft (5 to 6 minutes).

Put the cooked peaches in your blender or food processor, and puree them. Let the mixture cool to room temperature.

While that's cooling, whip your egg whites. Beat the whites till they're frothy, add the cream of tarter, and whip until they're stiff.

In another bowl, whip the heavy cream until it's stiff, too.

When the peach puree is room temperature, beat in the yogurt. Gently fold in the beaten egg whites and then the heavy cream. Pour into 6 pretty dessert cups and chill for 4 to 6 hours, or until set. Top with Raspberry Coulis before serving.

**Yield:** 6 servings

**Nutritional Analysis:** Each will have: 197 calories; 9 g fat; 5 g protein; 25 g carbohydrates; 5 g fiber; 20 g usable carbs.

| | | | | | |
|---|---|---|---|---|---|
| Potassium (mg): | 193 mg | Vitamin C (mg): | 202 mg | Thiamin/B1 (mg): | trace |
| Calcium (mg): | 73 mg | Vitamin A (i.u.): | 961 i.u. | Riboflavin/B2 (mg): | 0.2 mg |
| Iron (mg): | 1 mg | Vitamin B6 (mg): | trace | Folacin (mcg): | 16 mcg |
| Zinc (mg): | trace | Vitamin B12 (mcg): | 0.2 mcg | Niacin/B3 (mg): | trace |

**Note:** When you're whipping egg whites, make sure that your bowl and beaters are grease-free and that there's not even a speck of yolk in your whites. Otherwise, they will stubbornly refuse to whip.

# Avocado-Fruit Mold

It can be hard deciding which category a food fits into, you know? Is this a dessert? Or is it a molded salad? Darned if I know. So I threw up my hands and put it here. Use it as you will. Our tester, Kelly, compared the flavor to key lime pie.

2 tablespoons (14 g) unflavored gelatin
1/3 cup (80 ml) lemon juice
1/3 cup (80 ml) lime juice
1/4 cup (6 g) Splenda
1 teaspoon lemon zest
1 teaspoon lime zest
1 1/2 cups (355 ml) boiling water
12 apricots, pitted
3 avocado, pitted and peeled
Green food coloring
1/2 cup (115 g) light sour cream
1/2 cup (120 g) plain yogurt

In a big mixing bowl, sprinkle the gelatin over the lemon and lime juice, and let it sit for 10 minutes to soften.

When the gelatin's soft, stir in the Splenda, lemon zest, and lime zest. Add the boiling water, and stir until the gelatin is completely dissolved. Set the bowl aside.

Put the apricots and avocado flesh in your food processor with the S-blade in place. Puree the two together. Scrape this mixture into the gelatin mixture, and stir to combine everything very well. Add a touch of green food coloring, if you feel it needs it.

Let it all sit until the mixture thickens a bit. While you're waiting, whisk together the sour cream and yogurt. Fold them into the thickened mixture.

Pour the whole thing into a 6-cup (1.4-l) mold you've sprayed very well with nonstick cooking spray. Chill until firm—at least several hours, and overnight is better. (Don't expect this to be ready in a couple of hours; it won't be.) Unmold on a platter lined with greenery, and cut into slices to serve. You can garnish this with melon balls or strawberries, if you wish, but it's not essential.

**Yield:** 6 servings

**Nutritional Analysis:** Each will have: 245 calories; 17 g fat; 5 g protein; 24 g carbohydrates; 4 g fiber; 20 g usable carbs.

| | | | | | |
|---|---|---|---|---|---|
| Potassium (mg): | 874 mg | Vitamin C (mg): | 26 mg | Thiamin/B1 (mg): | 0.1 mg |
| Calcium (mg): | 58 mg | Vitamin A (i.u.): | 2473 i.u. | Riboflavin/B2 (mg): | 0.2 mg |
| Iron (mg): | 1 mg | Vitamin B6 (mg): | 0.3 mg | Folacin (mcg): | 73 mcg |
| Zinc (mg): | 1 mg | Vitamin B12 (mcg): | 0.1 mcg | Niacin/B3 (mg): | 2 mg |

## Dulce de Naranja y Frutillas

This simple Mexican dessert is delightfully refreshing. My husband rated it a perfect 10.

8 ounces (225 g) fresh strawberries

2 navel oranges

1 lime

1 tablespoon (1.5 g) Splenda

Hull the strawberries (remove the green bit) and quarter them. Put 'em in a nonreactive bowl—glass is good, and it'll show off the pretty colors of this dessert.

Peel the oranges. After peeling, hold each orange over the bowl with the berries (to catch any juice) and use a paring knife to cut off the membrane as thinly as possible, leaving the sections intact. You want to expose the juicy flesh of the orange without cutting too much of it away. Now cut down on both sides of each section to release the sections. You'll be left with a handful of joined membranes, with the orange sections in the bowl. Squeeze all the residual juice into the bowl, then discard the membranes. When both oranges have been cut up, cut each section in half to make 2 shorter sections.

Roll the lime under your palm fairly hard, to loosen up the juice (you'll get more out of it if you do this). Before you cut it, grate 1 teaspoon of zest and set it aside. Now halve the lime and squeeze the juice into the fruit in the bowl. Stir it in, sprinkle the Splenda over the top, and stir again. Sprinkle the zest over the top and refrigerate till dessert time. Divide among 4 dessert plates, and serve.

**Yield:** 4 servings

**Nutritional Analysis:** Each will have: 55 calories; trace fat; 1 g protein; 14 g carbohydrates; 2 g fiber; 12 g usable carbs.

| | | | | | |
|---|---|---|---|---|---|
| Potassium (mg): | 230 mg | Vitamin C (mg): | 75 mg | Thiamin/B1 (mg): | 0.1 mg |
| Calcium (mg): | 41 mg | Vitamin A (i.u.): | 144 i.u. | Riboflavin/B2 (mg): | trace |
| Iron (mg): | trace | Vitamin B6 (mg): | 0.1 mg | Folacin (mcg): | 34 mcg |
| Zinc (mg): | trace | Vitamin B12 (mcg): | 0 mcg | Niacin/B3 (mg): | trace |

## Fragole al Limone

This is a classic Italian dessert. And you thought it was all cannoli and tiramisu!

1 lemon

2 tablespoons (3 g) Splenda (or more, to taste)

1 quart (700 g) strawberries

Grate 1 teaspoon of zest from the lemon and set it aside. Roll the lemon hard under your palm for a few moments, to make it easier to juice, then cut it in half and squeeze the juice into a glass or ceramic serving dish. Lift out any wayward pits with a fork, and add the zest to the juice.

Stir in the Splenda till dissolved.

Wash, drain, hull, and cut up your strawberries, then add them to the bowl with the lemon juice. Toss well, and serve.

**Yield:** 4 servings

**Nutritional Analysis:** Each will have: 50 calories; 1 g fat; 1 g protein; 13 g carbohydrates; 3 g fiber; 10 g usable carbs.

| | | | | | |
|---|---|---|---|---|---|
| Potassium (mg): | 266 mg | Vitamin C (mg): | 91 mg | Thiamin/B1 (mg): | trace |
| Calcium (mg): | 24 mg | Vitamin A (i.u.): | 44 i.u. | Riboflavin/B2 (mg): | trace |
| Iron (mg): | 1 mg | Vitamin B6 (mg): | trace | Folacin (mcg): | 28 mcg |
| Zinc (mg): | trace | Vitamin B12 (mcg): | 0 mcg | Niacin/B3 (mg): | trace |

## Strawberry, Pineapple, and Nectarine Compote with Rum

This is a very versatile recipe. Substitute other fruits and give it a try. You can even toss it in your blender to make a smoothie!

1½ pints (525 g) fresh strawberries, hulled and quartered

2 cups (300 g) fresh pineapple chunks, cut into ½-inch (1.25-cm) cubes

3 nectarines, cut into 1-inch (2.5-cm) cubes (peeled or not, as you prefer)

3 tablespoons (45 ml) dark rum

2 teaspoons (1 g) Splenda

1 cup (230 g) light sour cream

Assemble the strawberries, pineapple, and nectarines in a big bowl—preferably glass, to show off the pretty colors.

Mix together the rum and Splenda, pour over the fruit, and toss. Let the fruit marinate, stirring now and then, for at least 30 minutes.

Serve with 2 tablespoons (about 28 g) of sour cream on each serving.

**Yield:** 8 servings

**Nutritional Analysis:** Each will have: 83 calories; 1 g fat; 2 g protein; 16 g carbohydrates; 3 g fiber; 14 g usable carbs.

| | | | | | |
|---|---|---|---|---|---|
| Potassium (mg): | 244 mg | Vitamin C (mg): | 40 mg | Thiamin/B1 (mg): | trace |
| Calcium (mg): | 25 mg | Vitamin A (i.u.): | 399 i.u. | Riboflavin/B2 (mg): | trace |
| Iron (mg): | trace | Vitamin B6 (mg): | trace | Folacin (mcg): | 16 mcg |
| Zinc (mg): | trace | Vitamin B12 (mcg): | 0 mcg | Niacin/B3 (mg): | 1 mg |

**Note:** Feel free to buy precut pineapple chunks at the grocery, so long as they're fresh. Just cut them up a bit smaller, and you're good to go.

# Pineapple and Mango with Tequila and Mint

Not for kids, but what a great end to a grown-up barbecue!

- 1/2 fresh pineapple
- 2 mangos
- 1 lemon
- 1/4 cup (6 g) Splenda
- 3 tablespoons (45 ml) tequila
- 1/4 cup (15 g) fresh mint

Cut the skin off of the pineapple, and remove the core. Cut the remaining flesh into chunks, and put it in a pretty bowl.

Peel the mangos, remove the seeds, and cut them into chunks, too. Add the mango chunks to the pineapple chunks.

Roll the lemon under your palm to loosen up the juice, then cut it in half and squeeze the juice into a small cup or dish. Pick out the seeds, and pour the juice over the pineapple and mango chunks. Toss well.

Now sprinkle on the Splenda and tequila, and toss again. Chill until serving time.

Just before you're ready to serve this, roll the mint leaves into little bundles and slice across them to make thin strips. Sprinkle over the fruit, toss, and serve.

**Yield:** 8 servings

**Nutritional Analysis:** Each will have: 66 calories; trace fat; 1 g protein; 14 g carbohydrates; 2 g fiber; 12 g usable carbs.

| | | | | | |
|---|---|---|---|---|---|
| Potassium (mg): | 138 mg | Vitamin C (mg): | 23 mg | Thiamin/B1 (mg): | 0.1 mg |
| Calcium (mg): | 15 mg | Vitamin A (i.u.): | 2140 i.u. | Riboflavin/B2 (mg): | trace |
| Iron (mg): | 1 mg | Vitamin B6 (mg): | 0.1 mg | Folacin (mcg): | 14 mcg |
| Zinc (mg): | trace | Vitamin B12 (mcg): | 0 mcg | Niacin/B3 (mg): | trace |

# Broiled Peaches with Rum

Keep in mind that most of the alcohol will cook off of these; you won't get swacked, and there's no reason the kids shouldn't try them.

- 6 peaches
- 1/4 cup (60 ml) lime juice
- 1/3 cup (8 g) Splenda
- 1/4 cup (60 ml) rum
- 1/4 teaspoon ground nutmeg
- 6 tablespoons (85 g) light sour cream

Halve your peaches, stone them, and peel them.

Mix together the lime juice, Splenda, and rum.

Dip the peaches in the lime juice mixture, and arrange them in a shallow baking pan with the flat side up. Spoon the lime mixture over them, making sure to fill the hollows. Sprinkle with nutmeg.

Broil for 3 to 4 minutes, or until lightly browned. Serve with the sour cream.

**Yield:** 6 servings

**Nutritional Analysis:** Each will have: 77 calories; trace fat; 1 g protein; 14 g carbohydrates; 2 g fiber; 12 g usable carbs.

| | | | | | |
|---|---|---|---|---|---|
| Potassium (mg): | 205 mg | Vitamin C (mg): | 9 mg | Thiamin/B1 (mg): | trace |
| Calcium (mg): | 12 mg | Vitamin A (i.u.): | 525 i.u. | Riboflavin/B2 (mg): | trace |
| Iron (mg): | trace | Vitamin B6 (mg): | trace | Folacin (mcg): | 4 mcg |
| Zinc (mg): | trace | Vitamin B12 (mcg): | 0 mcg | Niacin/B3 (mg): | 1 mg |

# Fried Peaches

A good dessert for a winter night.

2 tablespoons (28 g) butter

1 pound (455 g) frozen peach slices, no sugar added, thawed

1/2 cup (12 g) Splenda

1/2 teaspoon blackstrap molasses

1/3 cup (80 ml) heavy cream

1/4 teaspoon ground nutmeg

Give a big, heavy skillet a shot of nonstick cooking spray and put it over medium heat. Melt the butter, and add the peach slices, Splenda, and molasses. Sauté, turning frequently, for 15 minutes or until soft. Stir in the cream and serve, sprinkled with nutmeg.

**Yield:** 6 servings

**Nutritional Analysis:** Each will have: 116 calories; 9 g fat; 1 g protein; 10 g carbohydrates; 1 g fiber; 9 g usable carbs.

| | | | | | |
|---|---|---|---|---|---|
| Potassium (mg): | 26 mg | Vitamin C (mg): | 91 mg | Thiamin/B1 (mg): | trace |
| Calcium (mg): | 15 mg | Vitamin A (i.u.): | 609 i.u. | Riboflavin/B2 (mg): | trace |
| Iron (mg): | trace | Vitamin B6 (mg): | trace | Folacin (mcg): | 1 mcg |
| Zinc (mg): | trace | Vitamin B12 (mcg): | trace | Niacin/B3 (mg): | trace |

## Cherry Burritos

These seem pretty fancy, considering how easy they are! Don't let the need to make the cherry pie filling deter you—it takes roughly a minute and a half to throw together.

No-Sugar-Added Cherry Pie Filling (see page 537)

6 low-carb or whole wheat tortillas

1/2 teaspoon cinnamon

2 tablespoons (3 g) Splenda

3 tablespoons (45 g) butter, melted

Preheat the oven to 375°F (190°C, or gas mark 5).

Place 3 tablespoons (45 g) of cherry filling in the center of each tortilla. Fold 1 edge over the filling, and roll tightly to the opposite side. Place each burrito seam side down on a baking sheet or in a shallow pan.

Mix together the cinnamon and Splenda. Brush each burrito with the butter, and sprinkle with the cinnamon and Splenda mixture.

Bake for 15 to 18 minutes.

**Yield:** 6 servings

**Nutritional Analysis:** With low-carb tortillas, each will have: 139 calories; 8 g fat; 6 g protein; 20 g carbohydrates; 9 g fiber; 11 g usable carbs.

| | | | | | |
|---|---|---|---|---|---|
| Potassium (mg): | 3 mg | Vitamin C (mg): | 2 mg | Thiamin/B1 (mg): | 0 mg |
| Calcium (mg): | 75 mg | Vitamin A (i.u.): | 496 i.u. | Riboflavin/B2 (mg): | trace |
| Iron (mg): | 1 mg | Vitamin B6 (mg): | trace | Folacin (mcg): | trace |
| Zinc (mg): | trace | Vitamin B12 (mcg): | trace | Niacin/B3 (mg): | trace |

**Nutritional Analysis:** With whole wheat tortillas, each will have: 229 calories; 9 g fat; 5 g protein; 31 g carbohydrates; 3 g fiber; 28 g usable carbs.

| | | | | | |
|---|---|---|---|---|---|
| Potassium (mg): | 3 mg | Vitamin C (mg): | 2 mg | Thiamin/B1 (mg): | 0 mg |
| Calcium (mg): | 15 mg | Vitamin A (i.u.): | 496 i.u. | Riboflavin/B2 (mg): | trace |
| Iron (mg): | 6 mg | Vitamin B6 (mg): | trace | Folacin (mcg): | trace |
| Zinc (mg): | trace | Vitamin B12 (mcg): | trace | Niacin/B3 (mg): | trace |

## Peach and Cheesecake Burritos

4 ounces (115 g) Neufchâtel or light cream cheese, softened

1 egg

1 teaspoon vanilla

1 tablespoon (7 g) cinnamon

6 tablespoons (9 g) Splenda

1½ cups (375 g) frozen sliced unsweetened peaches

6 large low-carb or whole wheat tortillas

2 tablespoons (3 g) Splenda

Preheat the oven to 350°F (180°C, or gas mark 4). Spray a 9 x 13-inch (22.5 x 32.5-cm) pan with nonstick cooking spray.

Use an electric mixer or food processor to combine the Neufchâtel or light cream cheese, egg, vanilla, 1 teaspoon of the cinnamon, and 4 tablespoons (6 g) of the Splenda. Chop the peaches into ½-inch (1.25-cm) chunks, and fold them into the cheese mixture.

Spoon this mixture onto the tortillas, and wrap them up. Place each burrito seam side down in the prepared pan.

Combine the remaining 2 tablespoons (3 g) Splenda with the remaining 2 teaspoons of cinnamon, plus 1½ tablespoons (21 ml) of water. Brush this on top of the burritos as a glaze.

Bake for 25 minutes, and allow to cool a little before serving.

**Yield:** 6 servings

**Nutritional Analysis:** With low-carb tortillas, each will have: 142 calories; 7 g fat; 8 g protein; 20 g carbohydrates; 9 g fiber; 11 g usable carbs.

| | | | | | |
|---|---|---|---|---|---|
| Potassium (mg): | 36 mg | Vitamin C (mg): | 71 mg | Thiamin/B1 (mg): | trace |
| Calcium (mg): | 92 mg | Vitamin A (i.u.): | 475 i.u. | Riboflavin/B2 (mg): | 0.1 mg |
| Iron (mg): | 1 mg | Vitamin B6 (mg): | trace | Folacin (mcg): | 6 mcg |
| Zinc (mg): | trace | Vitamin B12 (mcg): | 0.1 mcg | Niacin/B3 (mg): | trace |

**Nutritional Analysis:** With whole wheat tortillas, each will have: 232 calories; 8 g fat; 7 g protein; 31 g carbohydrates; 3 g fiber; 28 g usable carbs.

| | | | | | |
|---|---|---|---|---|---|
| Potassium (mg): | 36 mg | Vitamin C (mg): | 71 mg | Thiamin/B1 (mg): | trace |
| Calcium (mg): | 32 mg | Vitamin A (i.u.): | 475 i.u. | Riboflavin/B2 (mg): | 0.1 mg |
| Iron (mg): | 7 mg | Vitamin B6 (mg): | trace | Folacin (mcg): | 6 mcg |
| Zinc (mg): | trace | Vitamin B12 (mcg): | 0.1 mcg | Niacin/B3 (mg): | trace |

## Maple-Cinnamon Baked Apples

An old-fashioned autumn dessert.

- 4 medium apples (Rome Beauties preferred)
- 2 tablespoons (16 g) chopped walnuts
- 4 whole cinnamon sticks
- 1/2 cup (120 ml) sugar-free pancake syrup
- 4 teaspoons (20 g) butter

Preheat the oven to 375°F (190°C, or gas mark 5). Spray an 8 x 8-inch (20 x 20-cm) glass baking dish with nonstick cooking spray.

Cut the top off each apple, then cut out the cores and seeds, leaving the bottom skin intact. Put the apples in the prepared dish.

Put 1 cinnamon stick and 1 1/2 teaspoons of walnuts in the center of each apple. Drizzle 2 tablespoons (30 ml) of the syrup on each, putting most of it in the hole in the center and a bit on the outside.

Put 1 teaspoon of butter on top of the filling of each apple.

Bake the apples for 15 to 25 minutes or until soft, basting once or twice with any liquid that cooks out.

**Yield:** 4 servings

**Nutritional Analysis:** (Analysis does not account for polyols in maple syrup.) Each will have: 175 calories; 7 g fat; 2 g protein; 32 g carbohydrates; 11 g fiber; 21 g usable carbs.

| | | | | | |
|---|---|---|---|---|---|
| Potassium (mg): | 248 mg | Vitamin C (mg): | 12 mg | Thiamin/B1 (mg): | trace |
| Calcium (mg): | 180 mg | Vitamin A (i.u.): | 265 i.u. | Riboflavin/B2 (mg): | trace |
| Iron (mg): | 6 mg | Vitamin B6 (mg): | 0.1 mg | Folacin (mcg): | 10 mcg |
| Zinc (mg): | trace | Vitamin B12 (mcg): | trace | Niacin/B3 (mg): | trace |

## Maple-Cinnamon Grilled Pears

Here's another recipe, courtesy of Ray, that lets you make a quick hot fruit dessert in your electric tabletop grill.

- 2 medium pears
- 1/4 cup (60 ml) sugar-free pancake syrup
- 4 whole cinnamon sticks
- 1/4 cup (60 ml) dark rum
- 1/2 teaspoon nutmeg

Slice the pears into 1/4-inch (6-mm) slices, and remove the cores.

Mix the syrup, cinnamon sticks, rum, and nutmeg together.

Dip each pear slice into the mix and lay it on a plate to dry a bit. After 5 minutes, redip each slice.

Cook the pear slices in a tabletop grill for about 20 minutes, basting with the syrup mix every 5 minutes. Turn off or unplug the grill and let the pears sit in the cooling grill for 5 minutes before serving.

**Yield:** 4 servings

**Nutritional Analysis:** (Analysis does not account for polyols in maple syrup.) Each will have: 118 calories; 1 g fat; 1 g protein; 24 g carbohydrates; 9 g fiber; 15 g usable carbs.

| | | | | | |
|---|---|---|---|---|---|
| Potassium (mg): | 173 mg | Vitamin C (mg): | 7 mg | Thiamin/B1 (mg): | trace |
| Calcium (mg): | 177 mg | Vitamin A (i.u.): | 52 i.u. | Riboflavin/B2 (mg): | trace |
| Iron (mg): | 5 mg | Vitamin B6 (mg): | trace | Folacin (mcg): | 10 mcg |
| Zinc (mg): | trace | Vitamin B12 (mcg): | 0 mcg | Niacin/B3 (mg): | trace |

## Lime-Ginger Yogurt Dip for Fruit

This is a great casual dessert for a picnic or cookout: Just put out the dip and the fruit, and let everyone serve themselves.

1 1/2 cups (365 g) plain yogurt

5 tablespoons (75 ml) lime juice

2 tablespoons (3 g) Splenda or 1 1/2 teaspoons (4 g) stevia/FOS blend

1 teaspoon grated gingerroot

Just stir everything together and chill! Good with strawberries, or chunks of honeydew and cantaloupe. You could switch things around and use this as a topping, if you prefer.

**Yield:** 6 servings

**Nutritional Analysis:** With Splenda, each will have: 43 calories; 2 g fat; 2 g protein; 3 g carbohydrates; trace fiber; 3 g usable carbs.

| | | | | | |
|---|---|---|---|---|---|
| Potassium (mg): | 110 mg | Vitamin C (mg): | 4 mg | Thiamin/B1 (mg): | trace |
| Calcium (mg): | 75 mg | Vitamin A (i.u.): | 77 i.u. | Riboflavin/B2 (mg): | 0.1 mg |
| Iron (mg): | trace | Vitamin B6 (mg): | trace | Folacin (mcg): | 6 mcg |
| Zinc (mg): | trace | Vitamin B12 (mcg): | 0.2 mcg | Niacin/B3 (mg): | trace |

## Strawberry Yogurt Cups

Easy and pretty.

2 tablespoons (28 ml) lemon juice

1/3 cup (80 ml) boiling water

1 tablespoon (7 g) unflavored gelatin

2 cups (600 g) frozen unsweetened strawberries, thawed

2 tablespoons (3 g) Splenda

1/2 cup (120 g) plain yogurt

Put the lemon juice, boiling water, and gelatin in your blender. Run for a second or two to dissolve the gelatin, then add the strawberries, Splenda , and yogurt. Run till blended, though you might want to stop while there are still a few bits of strawberry. Pour into 4 dessert dishes, and chill for at least a few hours before serving.

**Yield:** 4 servings

**Nutritional Analysis:** Each will have: 65 calories; 1 g fat; 2 g protein; 12 g carbohydrates; 2 g fiber; 10 g usable carbs.

| | | | | | |
|---|---|---|---|---|---|
| Potassium (mg): | 171 mg | Vitamin C (mg): | 35 mg | Thiamin/B1 (mg): | trace |
| Calcium (mg): | 50 mg | Vitamin A (i.u.): | 74 i.u. | Riboflavin/B2 (mg): | trace |
| Iron (mg): | 1 mg | Vitamin B6 (mg): | trace | Folacin (mcg): | 16 mcg |
| Zinc (mg): | trace | Vitamin B12 (mcg): | 0.1 mcg | Niacin/B3 (mg): | trace |

# Lemon-Vanilla Custard

I think this would make a nice breakfast, too.

2 cups (475 ml) skim milk

5 eggs

1/3 cup (8 g) Splenda

1 teaspoon lemon zest

1 teaspoon lemon extract

1/2 teaspoon vanilla extract

1 pinch salt

Preheat the oven to 300°F (150°C, or gas mark 2). Spray a 1-quart (1.1-l) casserole with nonstick cooking spray.

Put all of the ingredients in your blender, and blend 'em up. Pour the mixture into the prepared casserole.

Place the casserole in a larger pan filled with hot water, and place the entire thing in the oven. Bake for 2 hours. Cool, and chill well.

**Yield:** 4 servings

**Nutritional Analysis:** Each will have: 136 calories; 6 g fat; 11 g protein; 9 g carbohydrates; trace fiber; 9 g usable carbs.

| | | | | | |
|---|---|---|---|---|---|
| Potassium (mg): | 270 mg | Vitamin C (mg): | 2 mg | Thiamin/B1 (mg): | 0.1 mg |
| Calcium (mg): | 179 mg | Vitamin A (i.u.): | 599 i.u. | Riboflavin/B2 (mg): | 0.4 mg |
| Iron (mg): | 1 mg | Vitamin B6 (mg): | 0.1 mg | Folacin (mcg): | 32 mcg |
| Zinc (mg): | 1 mg | Vitamin B12 (mcg): | 1 mcg | Niacin/B3 (mg): | trace |

## Pot-de-Pumpkin

I came up with this for Julie, who adores pumpkin in every form. She says that if you want to go all-out on presentation, you should mold this in little hollowed-out pumpkins! Mighty good just the way it's written, though—like a lighter version of pumpkin pie.

15 ounces (420 g) canned pumpkin
1/4 cup (6 g) Splenda
2 tablespoons (28 ml) sugar-free pancake syrup or genuine maple syrup
3/4 cup (175 ml) water
1/2 teaspoon blackstrap molasses
1 teaspoon cinnamon
1/2 teaspoon ground nutmeg
1 teaspoon ground ginger
1 1/2 tablespoons (11 g) unflavored gelatin
3/4 cup (175 ml) evaporated milk
1 1/2 teaspoons lemon juice
Creamy Dessert Topping (see page 538)

In a large, heavy saucepan, combine the pumpkin, Splenda, maple syrup, 1/2 cup (120 ml) of the water, molasses, cinnamon, nutmeg, and ginger. Stir together well, and set over medium heat.

Meanwhile, sprinkle the gelatin over the remaining 1/4 cup (60 ml) of water, to soften. Then go back to stirring the pumpkin! When it boils, let it cook for just a minute more to combine the flavors, then remove it from the heat.

Whisk in the gelatin, stirring till it's completely dissolved. Set the pumpkin mixture aside to cool and thicken a bit.

Pour the evaporated milk into a mixing bowl, and put it in your freezer. Throw the beaters to your electric mixer in there, too. Spray a 6-cup (1.4-l) mold with nonstick cooking spray. Put it in the refrigerator.

When the pumpkin mixture has cooled enough to thicken a bit, take the evaporated milk and chilled beaters out of the freezer. Start whipping the milk at high speed, and add the lemon juice as you whip. Keep whipping till the evaporated milk has thickened and just about tripled in volume. Spoon about one-third of the whipped milk into the pumpkin mixture, and stir it in well. Now gently fold the rest of the whipped milk into the pumpkin. Pull the mold out of the fridge, and spoon the whole thing into it. Chill until set, at least 5 to 6 hours.

Unmold to serve, and serve with the Dessert Topping.

**Yield:** 8 servings

**Nutritional Analysis:** With real syrup, each will have: 80 calories; 2 g fat; 2 g protein; 14 g carbohydrates; 2 g fiber; 12 g usable carbs.

| | | | | | |
|---|---|---|---|---|---|
| Potassium (mg): | 208 mg | Vitamin C (mg): | 3 mg | Thiamin/B1 (mg): | trace |
| Calcium (mg): | 89 mg | Vitamin A (i.u.): | 11819 i.u. | Riboflavin/B2 (mg): | 0.1 mg |
| Iron (mg): | 1 mg | Vitamin B6 (mg): | trace | Folacin (mcg): | 9 mcg |
| Zinc (mg): | trace | Vitamin B12 (mcg): | trace | Niacin/B3 (mg): | trace |

**Nutritional Analysis:** With sugar-free syrup, each will have: 67 calories; 2 g fat; 2 g protein; 11 g carbohydrates; 2 g fiber; 9 g usable carbs.

| | | | | | |
|---|---|---|---|---|---|
| Potassium (mg): | 198 mg | Vitamin C (mg): | 3 mg | Thiamin/B1 (mg): | trace |
| Calcium (mg): | 84 mg | Vitamin A (i.u.): | 11819 i.u. | Riboflavin/B2 (mg): | 0.1 mg |
| Iron (mg): | 1 mg | Vitamin B6 (mg): | trace | Folacin (mcg): | 9 mcg |
| Zinc (mg): | trace | Vitamin B12 (mcg): | trace | Niacin/B3 (mg): | trace |

## Lemon Cheese Mousse

Like a light-and-fluffy cheesecake in a cup.

2 tablespoons (28 ml) cold water

1 tablespoon (7 g) unflavored gelatin

1/4 cup (60 ml) lemon juice

4 egg whites

1/4 teaspoon cream of tartar

8 ounces (225 g) part-skim ricotta cheese

1 egg

1/4 cup (6 g) Splenda

1/4 cup (120 g) plain yogurt

2 tablespoons (12 g) lemon zest

Put the water in a small cup, and sprinkle the gelatin on top to soften. Let that sit for 10 minutes.

Put the lemon juice in a small, nonreactive saucepan. Put it over low heat, and warm it up. When the gelatin is softened, add it to the lemon juice, and stir until the gelatin is completely dissolved.

Beat the egg whites until they're frothy, add the cream of tartar, and beat until stiff peaks form. Set them aside.

In a mixing bowl, use your electric mixer (don't bother to wash the beaters) to beat the ricotta with the egg and Splenda until the mixture's light and fluffy. Now beat in the yogurt, lemon zest, and gelatin mixture.

Gently fold this ricotta mixture into the egg whites. Pour the mousse into 6 pretty dessert dishes, and chill for at least 4 to 6 hours before serving.

**Yield:** 6 servings

**Nutritional Analysis:** Each will have: 104 calories; 4 g fat; 9 g protein; 7 g carbohydrates; trace fiber; 7 g usable carbs.

| | | | | | |
|---|---|---|---|---|---|
| Potassium (mg): | 156 mg | Vitamin C (mg): | 7 mg | Thiamin/B1 (mg): | trace |
| Calcium (mg): | 136 mg | Vitamin A (i.u.): | 238 i.u. | Riboflavin/B2 (mg): | 0.2 mg |
| Iron (mg): | trace mg | Vitamin B6 (mg): | trace | Folacin (mcg): | 12 mcg |
| Zinc (mg): | 1 mg | Vitamin B12 (mcg): | 0.3 mcg | Niacin/B3 (mg): | trace |

**Note:** Make sure the bowl and beaters are completely grease free and that there's not even a tiny speck of yolk in the egg whites, or they won't whip!

## Chocolate Gelatin

Sounds odd, I know. But my sister, who tested this recipe, pronounced it delicious.

1 1/2 cups (355 ml) water

2 1/2 teaspoons (6 g) unflavored gelatin

1/2 cup (120 ml) heavy cream

1/3 cup (8 g) Splenda

1/4 cup (22 g) cocoa powder

1 1/3 cups (315 g) Creamy Dessert Topping (see page 538)

Put 1/2 cup (120 ml) of the water in a small bowl, and sprinkle the gelatin on top, to soften.

In a big, heavy saucepan, whisk together the remaining 1 cup (235 ml) water, cream, Splenda, and cocoa powder. Put over medium heat and bring to a boil, stirring gently. When it's boiling, add the gelatin, and stir till it's thoroughly dissolved.

Cool to room temperature, and divide into 4 little dessert dishes. Chill for at least several hours, and overnight isn't a bad idea. Serve with Creamy Dessert Topping.

**Yield:** 4 servings

**Nutritional Analysis:** Including topping, each will have: 246 calories; 21 g fat; 4 g protein; 11 g carbohydrates; 2 g fiber; 9 g usable carbs.

| | | | | | |
|---|---|---|---|---|---|
| Potassium (mg): | 214 mg | Vitamin C (mg): | 1 mg | Thiamin/B1 (mg): | trace |
| Calcium (mg): | 115 mg | Vitamin A (i.u.): | 805 i.u. | Riboflavin/B2 (mg): | 0.2 mg |
| Iron (mg): | 1 mg | Vitamin B6 (mg): | trace | Folacin (mcg): | 8 mcg |
| Zinc (mg): | 1 mg | Vitamin B12 (mcg): | 0.3 mcg | Niacin/B3 (mg): | trace |

## Cafe-au-Lait Parfait

Mocha goodness.

3/4 cup (175 ml) evaporated milk

2 tablespoons (14 g) unflavored gelatin

1 1/2 cups (355 ml) brewed coffee, hot

3/4 cup (18 g) Splenda

1/4 cup (22 g) cocoa powder

1 1/2 teaspoons vanilla extract

1 1/4 cups (285 ml) ice cubes

Creamy Dessert Topping (see page 538)

Pour the evaporated milk into your blender, and sprinkle the gelatin on top. Let this sit for a minute or two, so the gelatin can soften.

When the gelatin has had a chance to soften, add the coffee, and cover the blender. Blend for a minute or two, till the gelatin is completely dissolved.

Add the Splenda, cocoa powder, and vanilla extract, and blend for about a minute. Add the ice cubes, one at a time, running the blender till one is melted before adding the next.

Pour the coffee mixture into 6 pretty dessert glasses, and chill for at least 3 or 4 hours, or until set, before serving.

Meanwhile, make the Creamy Dessert Topping. Top each parfait with a dollop of topping just before serving.

**Yield:** 6 servings

**Nutritional Analysis:** Each will have: 197 calories; 12 g fat; 6 g protein; 15 g carbohydrates; 1 g fiber; 14 g usable carbs.

| | | | | | |
|---|---|---|---|---|---|
| Potassium (mg): | 202 mg | Vitamin C (mg): | 1 mg | Thiamin/B1 (mg): | trace |
| Calcium (mg): | 176 mg | Vitamin A (i.u.): | 493 i.u. | Riboflavin/B2 (mg): | 0.2 mg |
| Iron (mg): | 1 mg | Vitamin B6 (mg): | trace | Folacin (mcg): | 9 mcg |
| Zinc (mg): | 1 mg | Vitamin B12 (mcg): | 0.3 mcg | Niacin/B3 (mg): | trace |

## Soft and Chewy Chocolate Chip Cookies

Just as the name says, these are soft and chewy cookies, not dissimilar to Mrs. Field's—only these are more nutritious and a whole lot easier on your blood sugar.

1 cup (125 g) homemade almond meal

1/2 cup (55 g) vanilla whey protein powder

1/4 cup (30 g) whole wheat flour (whole wheat pastry flour is best)

1/2 teaspoon salt

1 teaspoon (4.6 g) baking soda

3/4 cup (170 g) butter, softened

1 cup (25 g) Splenda

1/2 cup (75 g) polyol (Use the same amount of Sucanat and omit the molasses; this will dramatically increase the blood-sugar impact.)

1 1/2 teaspoons blackstrap molasses

2 eggs

2 teaspoons (10 ml) vanilla extract

1 tablespoon (14 ml) milk

1/2 cup (40 g) rolled oats

3/4 cup (95 g) chopped walnuts or pecans

12 ounces (340 g) sugar-free dark chocolate

Preheat the oven to 325°F (170°C, or gas mark 3). Spray a cookie sheet with nonstick cooking spray.

In a mixing bowl, stir together the almond meal, protein powder, flour, salt, and baking soda. Keep this standing by.

Use your electric mixer to beat the butter, Splenda, polyol, and molasses together until light and fluffy.

Beat in the eggs, one at a time, then add the vanilla and milk. Now beat in the dry mixture, adding about one-third of it at a time.

Beat in the rolled oats, then the chopped walnuts and chocolate.

I use a 2-tablespoon cookie scoop to scoop these onto my cookie sheet. This makes nice big cookies. However you may scoop them with a tablespoon to make more, smaller cookies, if you like.

Bake for about 15 minutes (a little less, if you make those smaller cookies). The cookies will be quite soft when they come out. Carefully use a spatula to transfer the cookies to wire racks to cool.

These cookies will remain soft when cool. This means that if you stack them in a can, they'll stick together a bit. Try putting a sheet of waxed paper between the layers of cookies.

**Yield:** 30 servings

**Nutritional Analysis:** Each will have: 164 calories; 10 g fat; 5 g protein; 6 g carbohydrates; 3 g fiber; 3 g usable carbs. (Analysis does not include the polyol or Sucanat.)

| | | | | | |
|---|---|---|---|---|---|
| Potassium (mg): | 65 mg | Vitamin C (mg): | trace | Thiamin/B1 (mg): | 0.2 mg |
| Calcium (mg): | 35 mg | Vitamin A (i.u.): | 203 i.u. | Riboflavin/B2 (mg): | 0.3 mg |
| Iron (mg): | trace | Vitamin B6 (mg): | 0.3 mg | Folacin (mcg): | 6 mcg |
| Zinc (mg): | 1 mg | Vitamin B12 (mcg): | 0.8 mcg | Niacin/B3 (mg): | trace |

**Note:** If you can't find sugar-free chocolate chips, use your food processor to chop up sugar-free dark chocolate bars into chip-size bits.

# Peanut Butter Cookies

1/2 cup (112 g) butter, softened

1/4 cup (6 g) Splenda

1/4 cup (40 g) Sucanat or 1/4 cup (40 g) polyol sweetener plus 1/2 teaspoon blackstrap molasses

1 egg

1 cup (260 g) natural peanut butter

1/2 teaspoon salt

1/2 teaspoon baking soda

1/2 teaspoon vanilla extract

1/2 cup (55 g) almond meal

1/4 cup (30 g) vanilla whey protein powder

1/4 cup (30 g) whole wheat pastry flour

2 tablespoons (13 g) oat bran

1 tablespoon (8 g) stevia/FOS blend

Preheat the oven to 375°F (190°C, or gas mark 5). Spray a cookie sheet with nonstick cooking spray.

Use an electric mixer to beat the butter till it's creamy. Add the Splenda and Sucanat and beat until well combined.

Beat in the egg, peanut butter, salt, baking soda, and vanilla. Finally, beat in the almond meal, protein powder, flour, and oat bran.

Roll the dough into 1-inch (2.5-cm) balls, and place them on the prepared cookie sheet. Use the back of a fork to press the balls of dough flat, leaving those traditional peanut butter cookie crisscross marks. Bake for 10 to 12 minutes, and cool on wire racks.

**Yield:** 36 servings

**Nutritional Analysis:** With Sucanat, each will have: 91 calories; 7 g fat; 3 g protein; 4 g carbohydrates; 1 g fiber; 3 g usable carbs.

| | | | | | |
|---|---|---|---|---|---|
| Potassium (mg): | 31 mg | Vitamin C (mg): | trace | Thiamin/B1 (mg): | 0.1 mg |
| Calcium (mg): | 17 mg | Vitamin A (i.u.): | 122 i.u. | Riboflavin/B2 (mg): | 0.1 mg |
| Iron (mg): | trace | Vitamin B6 (mg): | 0.1 mg | Folacin (mcg): | 2 mcg |
| Zinc (mg): | trace | Vitamin B12 (mcg): | 0.3 mcg | Niacin/B3 (mg): | trace |

**Nutritional Analysis:** With polyol and blackstrap (analysis does not include the polyol), each will have: 85 calories; 7 g fat; 3 g protein; 3 g carbohydrates; 1 g fiber; 2 g usable carbs.

| | | | | | |
|---|---|---|---|---|---|
| Potassium (mg): | 21 mg | Vitamin C (mg): | trace | Thiamin/B1 (mg): | 0.1 mg |
| Calcium (mg): | 17 mg | Vitamin A (i.u.): | 104 i.u. | Riboflavin/B2 (mg): | 0.1 mg |
| Iron (mg): | trace | Vitamin B6 (mg): | 0.1 mg | Folacin (mcg): | 2 mcg |
| Zinc (mg): | trace | Vitamin B12 (mcg): | 0.3 mcg | Niacin/B3 (mg): | trace |

## Chocolate Velvet

This elegant company dessert is not the lowest-calorie recipe. However, it is spectacularly delicious and incredibly easy to make. It is also easy on your blood sugar, and because it's rich in texture and flavor, a small serving is plenty—so the calorie count is still under 300. I wouldn't recommend this for everyday consumption, but for a special occasion? It's the bomb.

10 ounces (280 g) sugar-free dark chocolate

1 1/4 cups (285 ml) half-and-half

2 egg yolks

1/2 teaspoon rum extract

Break up the chocolate into small chunks about the size of chocolate chips.

Pour the half-and-half into a glass measuring cup, and microwave it at 70 percent power for 1 to 2 minutes or until hot through, but not boiling.

While that's happening, separate the eggs. Do what you want with the whites (I give them to my dogs), and keep the yolks.

Put the chocolate and egg yolks in your blender, then pour in the hot half-and-half. Turn on the blender, and let it blend until the rattling stops. Add the rum extract, and blend for just a few seconds longer.

Now pour into 6 pretty little cups; this is rich, so servings should be small. Chill for at least 5 to 6 hours before serving.

**Yield:** 6 servings

**Nutritional Analysis:** Each will have: 298 calories; 22 g fat; 5 g protein; 9 g carbohydrates; 7 g fiber; 2 g usable carbs. (Analysis does not include polyol sweeteners in the sugar-free chocolate.)

| | | | | | |
|---|---|---|---|---|---|
| Potassium (mg): | 168 mg | Vitamin C (mg): | trace | Thiamin/B1 (mg): | trace |
| Calcium (mg): | 66 mg | Vitamin A (i.u.): | 332 i.u. | Riboflavin/B2 (mg): | 0.2 mg |
| Iron (mg): | 1 mg | Vitamin B6 (mg): | 0.1 mg | Folacin (mcg): | 10 mcg |
| Zinc (mg): | 1 mg | Vitamin B12 (mcg): | 0.3 mcg | Niacin/B3 (mg): | trace |

**Note:** Let me mention something that doesn't show up in this analysis: Chocolate, especially dark chocolate, is loaded with antioxidants. Studies suggest that eating a little dark chocolate regularly is good for your heart!

## Plum Sorbet

Of all the dessert recipes I came up with for this book, this is the one that I love the most. It's unbelievably good. If you like plums, it would be worth your while to go buy an ice cream freezer just so you can make this sorbet. It has a true, intense plum flavor.

$1\frac{1}{2}$ pounds (670 g) plums—red ones, good and ripe

1 cup (235 ml) water

$\frac{1}{2}$ cup (12 g) Splenda (or a little more, if needed)

1 tablespoon (7 g) unflavored gelatin

Put the plums in a saucepan, add the water, and place them over medium heat. Bring to a simmer, turn the burner down to a level that keeps it just barely simmering, and cover the pan. Set a timer for 20 minutes.

The plums should be soft and their skin peeling when time is up. If not, give them a few more minutes. When they're ready, turn off the burner, uncover, and let them cool just enough so you can handle them without scalding your hands. (If you let them get really cool, you'll have to warm them up again for the processing stage, because you need their warmth to dissolve the gelatin.)

With clean hands, peel off the skin—this will be very easy—and discard it. Break the plums open and remove the pits, too, discarding as little flesh as possible.

Now put the plum flesh and the liquid from the pan into a blender or food processor, and start blending or processing. Add the Splenda and gelatin, and puree until quite smooth. Pour the mixture back into the pan, and put it back over medium heat. Bring it back to a simmer, stirring often. Turn off the burner and let the mixture cool to room temperature.

Once it's cool, pour the mixture into your ice cream freezer, and freeze according to the directions that came with your unit. Serve. If you have leftovers, they'll keep nicely in a snap-top container in your freezer, but they will get very hard. Just remove the sorbet from the freezer at the beginning of supper, and it should have softened enough to serve by dessert time.

**Yield:** 6 servings

**Nutritional Analysis:** Each will have: 76 calories; 1 g fat; 1 g protein; 18 g carbohydrates; 2 g fiber; 16 g usable carbs.

| | | | | | |
|---|---|---|---|---|---|
| Potassium (mg): | 184 mg | Vitamin C (mg): | 10 mg | Thiamin/B1 (mg): | trace |
| Calcium (mg): | 5 mg | Vitamin A (i.u.): | 345 i.u. | Riboflavin/B2 (mg): | 0.1 mg |
| Iron (mg): | trace | Vitamin B6 (mg): | 0.1 mg | Folacin (mcg): | 2 mcg |
| Zinc (mg): | trace | Vitamin B12 (mcg): | 0 mcg | Niacin/B3 (mg): | 1 mg |

# Peach Frozen Yogurt

Ray says that this recipe makes enough for an ice cream social or other hungry crew!

- 1 tablespoon (7 g) unflavored gelatin
- 1/2 cup (120 ml) water
- 1 pound (455 g) sliced, unsweetened frozen peaches, thawed
- 1/3 cup (8 g) Splenda
- 1 tablespoon (14 ml) lemon juice
- 1 cup (245 g) plain yogurt, chilled

First sprinkle the gelatin on the water, and let it sit for 10 minutes to soften.

When the time's up, combine the peach slices, water and gelatin, Splenda, and lemon juice in a nonreactive saucepan over medium heat. Bring to a simmer and let cook gently until the peaches are softened (about 10 minutes).

Transfer the peach mixture to your food processor, and puree. Now let it cool to room temperature in the processor bowl or blender container.

When the peach mixture has cooled, add the yogurt and run the processor or blender to combine.

Pour the whole thing into your ice cream freezer, and freeze according to the directions for your unit.

**Yield:** 5 servings

**Nutritional Analysis:** Each will have: 81 calories; 2 g fat; 3 g protein; 14 g carbohydrates; 1 g fiber; 13 g usable carbs.

| | | | | | |
|---|---|---|---|---|---|
| Potassium (mg): | 80 mg | Vitamin C (mg): | 111 mg | Thiamin/B1 (mg): | trace |
| Calcium (mg): | 60 mg | Vitamin A (i.u.): | 385 i.u. | Riboflavin/B2 (mg): | 0.1 mg |
| Iron (mg): | trace | Vitamin B6 (mg): | trace | Folacin (mcg): | 4 mcg |
| Zinc (mg): | trace | Vitamin B12 (mcg): | 0.2 mcg | Niacin/B3 (mg): | trace |

## Blackberry Ice

Rich blackberry flavor, and that gorgeous purple-red color!

1 tablespoon (7 g) unflavored gelatin

2 cups (475 ml) water

1 pound (455 g) unsweetened frozen blackberries, thawed

3 tablespoons (45 ml) lemon juice

1/2 cup (12 g) Splenda

Sprinkle the gelatin on 1 cup (235 ml) of the water to soften.

Put the remaining cup (235 ml) of water in a saucepan with the berries. Place over medium heat, bring to a simmer, and cook until the berries mush.

If you wish, you can remove the seeds by pressing the pulp through a sieve with the back of a spoon, but it is fine with the seeds left in, too.

Add the water with gelatin, lemon juice, and Splenda. Whisk until the gelatin is completely dissolved.

Let the whole thing cool until it's about the texture of egg white. Pour it into your ice cream freezer, and process it according to the instructions that came with your unit.

**Yield:** 5 servings

**Nutritional Analysis:** Each will have: 75 calories; 0 g fat; trace protein; 17 g carbohydrates; 3 g fiber; 14 g usable carbs.

| | | | | | |
|---|---|---|---|---|---|
| Potassium (mg): | 12 mg | Vitamin C (mg): | 6 mg | Thiamin/B1 (mg): | trace |
| Calcium (mg): | 29 mg | Vitamin A (i.u.): | 67 i.u. | Riboflavin/B2 (mg): | trace |
| Iron (mg): | 1 mg | Vitamin B6 (mg): | trace | Folacin (mcg): | 1 mcg |
| Zinc (mg): | trace | Vitamin B12 (mcg): | 0 mcg | Niacin/B3 (mg): | trace |

# Lemon Sherbet

Sunny, lemony taste—and just look at the carb and calorie counts!

3 lemons

1 tablespoon (7 g) unflavored gelatin

2 cups (475 ml) boiling water

2 cups (490 g) plain yogurt

1/2 cup (12 g) Splenda

Grate the rind (zest) of the lemons, then halve them and squeeze out the juice. Put the juice and lemon zest into your blender, and sprinkle the gelatin on top. Let it sit for 10 minutes, so the gelatin can soften a bit.

When the 10 minutes are up, add the boiling water and run the blender until the gelatin is dissolved.

Put the blender container in the fridge, and let it chill for 15 minutes. Pull it out, put it back on the blender base, and add the yogurt and Splenda. Blend again until everything is well combined.

Put the blender back in the fridge until the mixture is cool to the touch and starting to thicken. Then pour it into your ice cream freezer and freeze according to the instructions that came with your unit.

**Yield:** 8 servings

**Nutritional Analysis:** Each will have: 55 calories; 2 g fat; 3 g protein; 6 g carbohydrates; trace fiber; 6 g usable carbs.

| | | | | | |
|---|---|---|---|---|---|
| Potassium (mg): | 126 mg | Vitamin C (mg): | 12 mg | Thiamin/B1 (mg): | trace |
| Calcium (mg): | 81 mg | Vitamin A (i.u.): | 82 i.u. | Riboflavin/B2 (mg): | 0.1 mg |
| Iron (mg): | trace | Vitamin B6 (mg): | trace | Folacin (mcg): | 7 mcg |
| Zinc (mg): | trace | Vitamin B12 (mcg): | 0.2 mcg | Niacin/B3 (mg): | trace |

## Pineapple Pops

Easy! However, pineapple is one of those rare fruits with a fairly high glycemic index, so if you're seriously carb intolerant, these are not for you.

14 1/2 ounces (405 g) crushed pineapple in juice

1/4 cup (6 g) Splenda

1/2 cup (125 g) plain yogurt

Just mix everything together well, and pour the mixture into popsicle molds. Freeze for at least 4 to 5 hours before eating. If you want, you can unmold these, wrap them in plastic wrap, and return them to the freezer.

**Yield:** 8 servings

**Nutritional Analysis:** Each will have: 43 calories; 1 g fat; 1 g protein; 9 g carbohydrates; trace fiber; 9 g usable carbs.

| | | | | | |
|---|---|---|---|---|---|
| Potassium (mg): | 86 mg | Vitamin C (mg): | 5 mg | Thiamin/B1 (mg): | 0.1 mg |
| Calcium (mg): | 26 mg | Vitamin A (i.u.): | 38 i.u. | Riboflavin/B2 (mg): | trace |
| Iron (mg): | trace | Vitamin B6 (mg): | trace | Folacin (mcg): | 4 mcg |
| Zinc (mg): | trace | Vitamin B12 (mcg): | 0.1 mcg | Niacin/B3 (mg): | trace |

## Strawberry Pops

Yummy—and just look at those carb and calorie counts!

1 pound (455 g) strawberries, crushed

1/4 cup (6 g) Splenda

1/2 cup (125 g) plain yogurt

Just mix everything together well, and pour it into popsicle molds. Freeze for at least 4 to 5 hours before eating. If you want, you can unmold these, wrap them in plastic wrap, and return them to the freezer.

**Yield:** 8 servings

**Nutritional Analysis:** Each will have: 28 calories; 1 g fat; 1 g protein; 5 g carbohydrates; 1 g fiber; 4 g usable carbs.

| | | | | | |
|---|---|---|---|---|---|
| Potassium (mg): | 112 mg | Vitamin C (mg): | 30 mg | Thiamin/B1 (mg): | trace |
| Calcium (mg): | 26 mg | Vitamin A (i.u.): | 33 i.u. | Riboflavin/B2 (mg): | trace |
| Iron (mg): | trace | Vitamin B6 (mg): | trace | Folacin (mcg): | 11 mcg |
| Zinc (mg): | trace | Vitamin B12 (mcg): | 0.1 mcg | Niacin/B3 (mg): | trace |

# Gingerbread

1/2 cup (55 g) whole wheat flour (preferably pastry flour)

1/2 cup (55 g) homemade almond meal

1/2 cup (55 g) vanilla whey protein powder

1 teaspoon (1.5 g) baking soda

1/2 teaspoon salt

2 1/2 teaspoons (13 g) ground gingerroot

1/2 teaspoon ground cinnamon

1/4 cup (6 g) Splenda

1/4 cup (40 g) polyol

1/2 cup (125 g) plain yogurt

1/4 cup (60 ml) oil

1 teaspoon (5 ml) blackstrap molasses

1 egg

2 tablespoons (28 ml) water

1/2 cup (50 g) shredded zucchini

Preheat the oven to 350°F (180°C, or gas mark 4). Spray an 8 x 8-inch (20 x 20-cm) baking pan with nonstick cooking spray.

In a mixing bowl, combine the flour, almond meal, protein powder, baking soda, salt, ginger, cinnamon, Splenda, and polyol. Mix them together well.

In a separate bowl or measuring cup, whisk together the yogurt, oil, molasses, egg, and water. (If you have one, a power whisk would be handy for this step.) Pour this mixture into the dry ingredients, and whisk until everything is well combined and there are no dry spots. Add the zucchini, and whisk briefly to distribute it evenly.

Pour the batter into the prepared pan and bake for 30 minutes, or until a toothpick inserted in the middle comes out clean.

**Yield:** 9 servings

**Nutritional Analysis:** Each will have: 183 calories; 11 g fat; 13 g protein; 9 g carbohydrates; 2 g fiber; 7 g usable carbs. (Analysis does not include the polyol.)

| | | | | | |
|---|---|---|---|---|---|
| Potassium (mg): | 141 mg | Vitamin C (mg): | 1 mg | Thiamin/B1 (mg): | 0.7 mg |
| Calcium (mg): | 102 mg | Vitamin A (i.u.): | 72 i.u. | Riboflavin/B2 (mg): | 0.8 mg |
| Iron (mg): | 1 mg | Vitamin B6 (mg): | 1.0 mg | Folacin (mcg): | 10 mcg |
| Zinc (mg): | 3 mg | Vitamin B12 (mcg): | 2.6 mcg | Niacin/B3 (mg): | 1 mg |

## Apple Walnut Cake

This makes a fruit-and-nut filled loaf cake that's just the thing with a cup of tea or coffee.

1/2 cup (75 g) polyol
1/2 cup (12 g) Splenda
1 teaspoon cinnamon
1/4 teaspoon nutmeg
1 teaspoon baking soda
1/2 teaspoon salt
2/3 cup (80 g) whole wheat pastry flour
2/3 cup (80 g) almond meal
2/3 cup (80 g) vanilla whey protein powder
1/2 cup (120 ml) coconut oil, melted
2 eggs
1/2 cup (125 g) plain yogurt
1 cup (125 g) walnuts, coarsely chopped
1 apple, coarsely chopped (don't bother peeling it)

Spray 2 loaf pans well with nonstick cooking spray.

In a mixing bowl, combine the polyol, Splenda, cinnamon, nutmeg, baking soda, salt, flour, almond meal, and protein powder. Stir them together so everything is evenly distributed.

In a separate bowl, whisk together the oil, eggs, and yogurt. Dump this into the dry ingredients, and whisk everything together until all the dry ingredients are moistened.

Stir in the walnuts, then the apple.

Pour the batter into the prepared loaf pans. Put them in a cold oven, set it for 350°F (180°C, or gas mark 4), and bake for 45 to 50 minutes, or until a toothpick inserted in the middle comes out clean (except for the possible bit of apple).

**Yield:** 24 servings

**Nutritional Analysis:** Each will have: 138 calories; 10 g fat; 8 g protein; 6 g carbohydrates; 1 g fiber; 5 g usable carbs. (Analysis does not include the polyol.)

| | | | | | |
|---|---|---|---|---|---|
| Potassium (mg): | 82 mg | Vitamin C (mg): | 1 mg | Thiamin/B1 (mg): | 0.3 mg |
| Calcium (mg): | 49 mg | Vitamin A (i.u.): | 48 i.u. | Riboflavin/B2 (mg): | 0.4 mg |
| Iron (mg): | 1 mg | Vitamin B6 (mg): | 0.5 mg | Folacin (mcg): | 8 mcg |
| Zinc (mg): | 2 mg | Vitamin B12 (mcg): | 1.3 mcg | Niacin/B3 (mg): | trace |

# Pineapple Cake

Having tested the Apple Walnut Cake (page 535), Ray came up with this variation. Remember, because pineapple is a high glycemic index fruit and this cake has no chopped walnuts, its blood sugar impact is likely to be greater than that of the Apple Walnut Cake.

1/2 cup (75 g) polyol
1/2 cup (12 g) Splenda
2 teaspoons (6 g) cinnamon
1 1/2 teaspoons baking soda
1/2 teaspoon salt
2/3 cup (80 g) whole wheat pastry flour
2/3 cup (80 g) homemade almond meal
2/3 cup (80 g) vanilla whey protein powder
1/2 cup (120 ml) coconut oil, melted
2 eggs
1/2 cup (125 g) plain yogurt
1 can (14 1/2 ounces, or 405 g) crushed pineapple in juice

Preheat the oven to 350°F (180°C, or gas mark 4). Spray 2 loaf pans or 8 x 8-inch (20 x 20-cm) baking pans well with cooking spray.

In a mixing bowl, combine the polyol, Splenda, cinnamon, baking soda, salt, flour, almond meal, and protein powder. Stir them together so everything is evenly distributed.

In a separate bowl, whisk together the oil, eggs, and yogurt. Dump the wet ingredients into the dry ingredients, and whisk everything together until all of the dry ingredients are moistened. Stir in the crushed pineapple and juice.

Place half of the batter into each prepared pan.

If you're using loaf pans, bake for 1 hour, or until a toothpick inserted in the middle comes out clean. If you're using square baking pans, 45 minutes should be enough.

Allow the cake to cool, and then loosen the edges from the pan. Turn it upside down on a serving tray, and tap it on the counter to remove the cake. Serve.

For a change of pace, you could put pineapple rings in the bottom of the pan before adding the batter.

**Yield:** 24 servings

**Nutritional Analysis:** Each will have: 110 calories; 7 g fat; 7 g protein; 6 g carbohydrates; 1 g fiber; 5 g usable carbs. (Analysis does not include the polyol.)

| | | | | | |
|---|---|---|---|---|---|
| Potassium (mg): | 61 mg | Vitamin C (mg): | 1 mg | Thiamin/B1 (mg): | 0.3 mg |
| Calcium (mg): | 48 mg | Vitamin A (i.u.): | 34 i.u. | Riboflavin/B2 (mg): | 0.4 mg |
| Iron (mg): | trace | Vitamin B6 (mg): | 0.5 mg | Folacin (mcg): | 5 mcg |
| Zinc (mg): | 2 mg | Vitamin B12 (mcg): | 1.3 mcg | Niacin/B3 (mg): | trace |

## No-Sugar-Added Cherry Pie Filling

Very, very simple.

- 1 can (14½ ounces, or 405 g) sour cherries packed in water
- ½ cup (12 g) Splenda
- 2 teaspoons guar or xanthan gum
- Red food coloring (optional)

Open the can of cherries and dump the whole thing, water and all, into a bowl. Stir in the Splenda and guar, plus 4 to 6 drops of red food coloring, if you want a pretty color. Let stand for 5 minutes before using.

**Yield:** 8 servings

**Nutritional Analysis:** Each will have: 27 calories; 0 g fat; 1 g protein; 6 g carbohydrates; 1 g fiber; 5 g usable carbs.

| | | | | | |
|---|---|---|---|---|---|
| Potassium (mg): | 0 mg | Vitamin C (mg): | 2 mg | Thiamin/B1 (mg): | 0 mg |
| Calcium (mg): | 8 mg | Vitamin A (i.u.): | 209 i.u. | Riboflavin/B2 (mg): | 0 mg |
| Iron (mg): | trace | Vitamin B6 (mg): | 0 mg | Folacin (mcg): | 0 mcg |
| Zinc (mg): | 0 mg | Vitamin B12 (mcg): | 0 mcg | Niacin/B3 (mg): | 0 mg |

## Creamy Dessert Topping

- 1/2 cup (120 ml) heavy cream, chilled
- 1 1/2 cups (370 g) plain yogurt
- 1 tablespoon (1.5 g) Splenda
- 2 teaspoons (10 ml) vanilla extract

Use an electric mixer to whip the cream, incorporating as much air as possible, until it's stiff.

Beat the yogurt with the Splenda and vanilla extract until it's very creamy.

Gently fold the two together, and chill. Serve over fruit or as a topping for any dessert.

**Yield:** 12 servings

**Nutritional Analysis:** Each will have: 56 calories; 5 g fat; 1 g protein; 1 g carbohydrates; 0 g fiber; 1 g usable carbs.

| | | | | | |
|---|---|---|---|---|---|
| Potassium (mg): | 55 mg | Vitamin C (mg): | trace | Thiamin/B1 (mg): | trace |
| Calcium (mg): | 43 mg | Vitamin A (i.u.): | 183 i.u. | Riboflavin/B2 (mg): | 0.1 mg |
| Iron (mg): | trace | Vitamin B6 (mg): | trace | Folacin (mcg): | 3 mcg |
| Zinc (mg): | trace | Vitamin B12 (mcg): | 0.1 mcg | Niacin/B3 (mg): | trace |

## Raspberry Coulis

Serve as a sauce over vanilla yogurt, sugar-free ice cream, or anything that could use a beautiful and tasty fruit sauce!

- 1 pint (300 g) raspberries, fresh, or unsweetened frozen, thawed
- 1 tablespoon (14 ml) lemon juice
- 2 tablespoons (3 g) Splenda

This is a cinch. Put everything in your blender or food processor, and puree. Pass the puree through a sieve to remove the seeds, if you like. (It's not essential, though—the seeds are actually nutritious.) That's it!

**Yield:** 10 servings

**Nutritional Analysis:** Each will have: 14 calories; trace fat; trace protein; 3 g carbohydrates; 2 g fiber; 1 g usable carbs.

| | | | | | |
|---|---|---|---|---|---|
| Potassium (mg): | 40 mg | Vitamin C (mg): | 7 mg | Thiamin/B1 (mg): | trace |
| Calcium (mg): | 6 mg | Vitamin A (i.u.): | 33 i.u. | Riboflavin/B2 (mg): | trace |
| Iron (mg): | trace | Vitamin B6 (mg): | trace | Folacin (mcg): | 7 mcg |
| Zinc (mg): | trace | Vitamin B12 (mcg): | 0 mcg | Niacin/B3 (mg): | trace |

# Lemon-Vanilla Cheesecake

Almond Crust (see page 540; optional)

2 cups (450 g) 2% cottage cheese

1/2 cup (115 g) light sour cream

2 eggs

Juice and zest of 1 lemon

5 tablespoons (8 g) Splenda

2 teaspoons (10 ml) vanilla extract

Preheat the oven to 325°F (170°C, or gas mark 3). If you'll be using the almond crust, make that now. If not, spray a 9-inch (22.5-cm) pie plate well with nonstick cooking spray.

Put the cottage cheese, sour cream, eggs, lemon juice and zest, Splenda, and vanilla in your food processor with the S-blade in place, and run till it's very smooth, scraping down the sides of the processor bowl as necessary.

Pour this mixture into the prepared crust (if using), or pie plate. Put your cake on a rack in the middle of the oven. Partially fill another pie plate or other pan with water, and place it on the rack below your cake; this will make steam, keeping your cheesecake moist.

Bake for 40 to 45 minutes. Remove from the oven, cool, and chill before serving.

**Yield:** 8 servings

**Nutritional Analysis:** Excluding the crust, each will have: 80 calories; 2 g fat; 10 g protein; 5 g carbohydrates; trace fiber; 5 g usable carbs.

| | | | | | |
|---|---|---|---|---|---|
| Potassium (mg): | 78 mg | Vitamin C (mg): | 4 mg | Thiamin/B1 (mg): | trace |
| Calcium (mg): | 52 mg | Vitamin A (iu): | 112 i.u. | Riboflavin/B2 (mg): | 0.2 mg |
| Iron (mg): | trace | Vitamin B6 (mg:) | 0.1 mg | Folacin (mcg): | 13 mcg |
| Zinc (mg): | trace | Vitamin B12 (mcg): | 0.5 mcg | Niacin/B3 (mg): | trace |

# Almond Crust

This is one of those recipes where keeping calories down took a back seat to maintaining nutritional standards. Graham cracker crumbs are lower in calories, but they're full of sugar and refined flour. Almonds, on the other hand, are good food.

1 cup (150 g) almonds

2 tablespoons (28 g) butter, melted

2 tablespoons (28 ml) water

2 tablespoons (16 g) vanilla whey protein powder

2 tablespoons (3 g) Splenda

Preheat the oven to 325°F (170°C, or gas mark 3). Coat a 9-inch (22.5-cm) pie plate with nonstick cooking spray.

Put the almonds in your food processor with the S-blade in place. Run the processor until the almonds are the consistency of cornmeal.

Add the butter, water, protein powder, and Splenda, and pulse till you have a dough.

Turn the dough out into your prepared pie plate. Using clean hands, press the dough evenly across the bottom and up the sides of the pie plate. Bake for 10 to 12 minutes, or until it's just starting to turn golden.

**Yield:** 8 servings

**Nutritional Analysis:** Each will have: 145 calories; 12 g fat; 6 g protein; 4 g carbohydrates; 2 g fiber; 2 g usable carbs.

| | | | | | |
|---|---|---|---|---|---|
| Potassium (mg): | 131 mg | Vitamin C (mg): | trace | Thiamin/B1 (mg): | 0.2 mg |
| Calcium (mg): | 64 mg | Vitamin A (iu): | 108 i.u. | Riboflavin/B2 (mg): | 0.3 mg |
| Iron (mg): | 1 mg | Vitamin B6 (mg:) | 0.3 mg | Folacin (mcg): | 11 mcg |
| Zinc (mg): | 1 mg | Vitamin B12 (mcg): | 0.7 mcg | Niacin/B3 (mg): | 1 mg |

# Resources

## Where to Find Polyols, aka Sugar Alcohols

At this writing, the Web sites listed below have these sweeteners available. However, a quick Web search using whichever sweetener you're looking for as your keyword should turn up other sources, as well.

Maltitol:
www.carbsmart.com
www.lowcarbgrocery.com
www.lowcarbnexus.com

Erythritol:
www.netrition.com
www.lowcarbgrocery.com
www.lowcarbnexus.com

Xylitol:
www.carbsmart.com
www.netrition.com
www.locarbdiner.com
www.lowcarbnexus.com

Diabetisweet (Isomalt with acesulfame potassium):
www.drugstore.com
www.low-carb.com

# Index

## A

## B

## C

## D



## E

**H**



**I**



**J**



**K**



**L**



**M**

## N



## O



## P

## R



## S

## T

# Acknowledgments

My thanks to my recipe testers, without whom this book would have been a good 200 recipes shorter: Julie McIntosh, Ray Todd Stevens, Kimberly Carpender, Kelly Rauch, Maria Vander Vloedt, Doris Courtney, Leslie Small, Kim Pulley, and Barbara Bennett. Guys, you rock.

And once more, my undying thanks to my husband, Eric Schmitz. With every book he takes on new tasks. For this one, he not only coordinated all the recipe testers, he also inserted all of the information regarding vitamins and minerals—no small task. Not to mention all of the computer geek stuff he's always done, as well as uncomplainingly eating my less-successful culinary experiments. Sweetheart, it is no small comfort to know that you always have my back.

# About the Author

**Dana Carpender** is the author of six cookbooks, including the national best-seller *500 Low-Carb Recipes*. She is also the author of *How I Gave Up My Low-Fat Diet and Lost 40 Pounds*. Her books have sold over a million copies worldwide. Dana writes a weekly newspaper column called "Low-Carb for Life" that is syndicated in over 50 markets, and is the publisher of an online newsletter called *Lowcarbezine!* that has well over 20,000 subscribers.

## Also available from Dana Carpender:

15-Minute Low-Carb Recipes
ISBN: 1-59233-041-X
$17.95

200 Low-Carb Slow Cooker Recipes
ISBN:1-59233-076-2
$17.95

500 Low-Carb Recipes
ISBN: 1-931412-06-5
$19.95

500 More Low-Carb Recipes
ISBN: 1-59233-089-4
$19.95

Dana Carpender's Carb Gram Counter
ISBN: 1-59233-144-0
$4.99

Dana Carpender's Weight-Loss Tracker
ISBN: 1-59233-151-3
$6.95

How I Gave Up My Low-Fat Diet and Lost 40 Pounds
ISBN: 1-59233-040-1
$14.95

The Low-Carb Barbecue Book
ISBN: 1-59233-055-X
$17.95

Low-Carb Smoothies
ISBN: 1-59233-122-X
$12.95